**McGraw Hill/Irwin/MarketspaceU "Series in e-Commerce" Website** – Visit the joint-imprint site to find out more about these titles and package components available for students and instructors. *http://www.mhhe.com/marketspace*

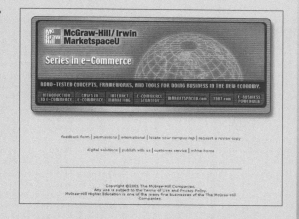

*Introduction to e-Commerce Website* – For students, online materials include a chapter overview and quizzes for each chapter help them master essential concepts and competencies. For instructors, online materials include sample syllabi, lecture outlines and teaching notes, suggested test/discussion questions for each chapter, new articles, additional case study suggestions, and PPT presentation slides for each chapter. *http://www.mhhe.com/marketspace* : Select Introduction to e-Commerce.

**MarketspaceU.com** – Instructors in the area of e-Commerce continually confront the problem of staying current in the field. Securing fresh material and cases for the classroom and staying on the cutting edge of theory and practice are among the most important - and time-consuming - instructor duties. MarketspaceU solves these problems by offering outstanding instructor support: 1) Case Dashboards updated every 30 days with case-specific news feeds, PPT case timelines, video snippets, and additional lecture notes for in-class use, 2) Pre-made lectures for each chapter including teaching notes and PPT slides, 3) Sample syllabi for text and case-based courses, and 4) Multimedia materials for use in the classroom. *http://www.marketspaceu.com*

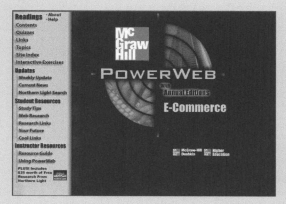

D1317779

**e-business PowerWeb** – Online access to current full-text articles, quizzing and assessment, validated links to relevant material, interactive glossaries, weekly updates, and interactive web exercises. *http://www.dushkin.com/powerweb*

# Introduction to e-Commerce

**Jeffrey F. Rayport**
*Marketspace, a Monitor Group company*

**Bernard J. Jaworski**
*Marketspace, a Monitor Group company*

**McGraw-Hill/Irwin**
**marketspaceU**

Boston   Burr Ridge, IL   Dubuque, IA   Madison, WI   New York   San Francisco   St. Louis
Bangkok   Bogotá   Caracas   Kuala Lumpur   Lisbon   London   Madrid   Mexico City
Milan   Montreal   New Delhi   Santiago   Seoul   Singapore   Sydney   Taipei   Toronto

# McGraw-Hill Higher Education

*A Division of The McGraw-Hill Companies*

INTRODUCTION TO E-COMMERCE
Published by McGraw-Hill, an imprint of The McGraw-Hill Companies, Inc. 1221
Avenue of the Americas, New York, NY 10020. Copyright © 2002 by Rayport and
Jaworski. All rights reserved. No part of this publication may be reproduced
or distributed in any form or by any means, or stored in a data base or retrieval system,
without the prior written consent of The McGraw-Hill Companies, Inc., including, but
not limited to, in any network or other electronic storage or transmission, or broadcast for
distance learning. Some ancillaries, including electronic and print components, may not be
available to customers outside the United States.

This book is printed on acid-free paper.

1 2 3 4 5 6 7 8 9 0 CCW/CCW 0 9 8 7 6 5 4 3 2 1

ISBN 0-07-251024-2

Publisher:   *John E. Biernat*
Executive editor:   *Gary L. Bauer*
Developmental editor:   *Tracy L. Jensen*
Marketing manager:   *Kim Kanakes Szum*
Project manager:   *Natalie J. Ruffatto*
Production associate:   *Gina Hangos*
Producer, media technology:   *Todd Labak*
Coordinator freelance design:   *Artemio Ortiz Jr.*
Supplement producer:   *Erin Sauder*
Cover design:   *Corey McPherson Nash*
Typeface:   *10/12 Minion*
Compositor:   *Proof Positive/Farrowlyne Associates, Inc.*
Printer:   *Courier Westford*

Library of Congress Cataloging-in-Publication Data

Rayport, Jeffrey F.
    Introduction to e-commerce/Jeffrey F. Rayport, Bernard J. Jaworski.
        p. cm.
    Includes bibliographical references and index.
    ISBN 0-07-251024-2
        1. Electronic commerce. I. Jaworski, Bernard J. II. Title.

HF5548.32 .R393 2001
658.8'4—dc21

                                                                2001045284

www.mhhe.com

# MCGRAW-HILL/MARKETSPACEU "MISSION STATEMENT"

McGraw-Hill/marketspaceU was created to develop exceptional higher-education teaching materials on the latest business practices and theories by leading thinkers in the field of e-commerce. McGraw-Hill/marketspaceU is committed to providing the business instructor with a comprehensive set of pedagogical tools with the most current materials in an easy-to-use learning system, which includes textbooks, casebooks, video interviews, and Web support for teaching the state-of-the-art in e-commerce business practice and theory. We aim to equip present and future executives, managers, and strategists in becoming successful creators of value in the networked economy.

To accomplish this task, we offer a suite of cutting-edge tools to help you navigate the networked economy:

- *e-Commerce* text
- *Cases in e-Commerce*
- *Introduction to e-Commerce*
- *Internet Marketing: Building Advantage in a Networked Economy*
- marketspaceU.com
- *Introduction to e-Commerce* website

For more information about these tools, see Supporting Materials, page xv.

# ACKNOWLEDGEMENTS

We are grateful to the team of outstanding colleagues who made the preparation of this book possible. We acknowledge specific contributions chapter by chapter throughout the book, but we want to thank heartily, and with great enthusiasm, our fearless group project leader JoAnn Kienzle. This book would not have been possible without her combination of project management, writing (all public policy chapters as well as contributions to several other sections), and team management skills. Thank you, JoAnn!

We also wish to acknowledge the valuable contributions to portions of the manuscript from Colin Gounden, Joe Hartzell, Ellie Kyung, Dickson Louie, Dorsey McGlone, and Eugene Wang, as well as the two technology chapters written by Vijay Manwani and Andy Macaleer at Breakaway Solutions. We thank Leo Griffin for his contribution to the strategy chapters; Yannis Dosios for writing the Marketwatch.com case studies at the end of each of the strategy chapters; and Mike Yip for his overall "first-mate" skills including writing, contract negotiation, assistance in project management, and other Jack-of-all-trades contributions. And we also thank Jenny Johnston and Jennifer Sturak for their excellent copy editing work. We are also truly grateful to Allison Reese for her editorial and administrative work on the project. We also thank Britin Prust and Kathy Ivanciw for their coordination efforts.

This book also draws from the video production work of Lori Cohen and the content of tnbt.com under the direction of Josh Clark. We would like to acknowledge the people who, under the fearless direction of Steve Szaraz, are responsible for the marketspaceU website: Craig Thompson and Katarina Gizzi have worked very hard to provide excellent content, while Pete Giorgio, Blair Hotchkies, Ryan Jones, Brian Barkley, and Dan Carroll have all done an outstanding job of creating the website.

In managing the project, we are indebted to Rafe Sagalyn, our literary agent, and Alan M. Kantrow, our local knowledge-management czar.

We also gratefully acknowledge the editorial support at Irwin/McGraw-Hill of Rob Zwettler, Gary Bauer, and Tracy Jensen.

Finally, none of this would have been possible without the generous support and enthusiasm of Mark Fuller, Joe Fuller, and Mark Thomas, cofounders and leaders of Monitor Group, a strategy consulting company and merchant bank based in Cambridge, Massachusetts.

# ABOUT THE AUTHORS

## Jeffrey F. Rayport

Jeffrey F. Rayport, founder of Marketspace, is regarded as one of the most influential thinkers in the field of e-commerce. Nearly six years ago he launched the first e-commerce strategy course at Harvard Business School, and to date has written nearly 100 case studies on e-commerce. His second-year elective course on this subject consistently enrolled nearly half of the Harvard Business School class of 800 students. For the past three years, he was voted "best professor" at Harvard Business School by the student body, the first Harvard Business School professor to receive this award three years in a row.

Dr. Rayport's research has focused on the impact of information technologies on service management and marketing strategies for business and has involved a wide array of high-tech and service firms, industry associations, and professional practices. In addition to his HBS case studies, he has written numerous articles that have appeared in industry and popular business publications.

Dr. Rayport earned an A.B. from Harvard College, an M.Phil. in international relations at the University of Cambridge (U.K.), an A.M. in the history of American civilization, and a Ph.D. in business history at Harvard University. His doctoral research examined diversification strategies among the regional Bell operating companies after the breakup of AT&T, with a focus on the transformation of high-tech companies from technology-driven to marketing-oriented firms.

## Bernard J. Jaworski

Bernard J. Jaworski is a cofounder and senior advisor at Marketspace and holds the Markets Chair within Monitor University. He has been the Jeanne and David Tappan Marketing Fellow and a tenured full professor of marketing at the University of Southern California. He previously served on the faculty of the University of Arizona and was a visiting professor at the Harvard Business School. In 1997, he received a Golden Apple Award as the MBA teacher of the year at USC. Dr. Jaworski is one of a few two-time winners of the prestigious Alpha Kappa Psi award for best marketing-practice article published in the *Journal of Marketing*. He currently serves on the review board of the *Journal of Marketing*, the *Journal of Marketing Research*, the *Journal of Business-to-Business Marketing*, the *Asian Journal of Marketing*, and other journals.

## About Marketspace and Contributing Authors

MarketspaceU is a community of award-winning academics and talented business practitioners dedicated to developing managers for the networked economy. We are part of Marketspace, a Monitor Group company, founded in 1998 as a multimedia enterprise to provide advice on, research about, and analysis of the impact of new media and technology on businesses. Marketspace activities include consulting to freshly minted dot-coms, as well as to Global 1000 companies, and providing new-economy insights to the public through a variety of media, which include the Web, television, and print.

Drawing upon the resources at Marketspace and other Monitor Group companies, as well as a network of academic institutional partners and CEO visionaries, marketspaceU brings together the diverse talents of practitioners, management consultants, academic experts, and writers.

# PREFACE

We are in the midst of a social, business, and cultural revolution. This revolution was enabled and accelerated by technology change. At the center of this change is the Internet, and, more specifically, e-commerce. Our purpose in writing this comprehensive textbook was to take a point of view about the scope of activities that fall within the responsibilities of business practitioners who must cope with this change.

Narrowly conceived, it is possible to write a book about the technology that underlies the Internet. More broadly, one can address how firms compete and win in this arena, which is the heart of business strategy. Alternatively, one can address the culture of capital formation and investments that have paved the way for the revolution. We believe that each of these views provides only one piece of the more general understanding that is necessary. The successful practitioner must know all of the above—and more—for he must also know how to deal with the fundamental changes in laws, public policy, and regulation. Moreover, the Internet is a media vehicle at its core. Therefore, the manager must also know the economics and design considerations of media businesses.

So, how can all of this be accomplished? We believe that this textbook captures all of these issues in a simple "four-infrastructures-plus-strategy" framework. Strategy will always be center stage in the board room. However, a deep understanding of the four infrastructures—technology, media, policy, and capital—is also a requirement for the senior executive.

## Approach

This book is written for present and future practitioners who desire to know more about all aspects—strategy, technology, policy, and financing—of the networked economy. As such, it provides a deep exploration of core concepts of online strategy and associated enablers, and it is enriched by a wide variety of examples, case studies, and explanations culled directly from practice.

We take this approach for a variety of reasons:

Management and strategy are being invented in real time as we go to press. Every marketspace business we have studied—and our work is based on nearly 100 case studies completed at Harvard Business School over the last six years—has been engaged in the creation of "new science" for doing business. The true insights will be generated at this stage by deep observation of both new and established businesses wrestling with new challenges. Thus, we take a militantly field-based and practitioner-focused perspective on this work. This is not to say that management theory is irrelevant. Existing concepts and theories such as network effects and increasing returns to scale do apply. However, in general, that practice is far ahead of theory at this time in history.

The result presented in this book is a collection of rigorous concepts, frameworks, and approaches that represent an entire applications suite of tools for doing business in the networked economy. Observation of business practices, while often fascinating and instructive, is not enough. We have taken our knowledge of practice as developed through case studies and followed through with conceptualization. Our tools represent a critical source of competitive advantage for companies and their managers, and we have tested them with our own students in MBA and executive education programs and with our consulting clients in the context of their own businesses. In other words, these are "road-tested" approaches to business, developed out of rigorous observation from the inside of such businesses and then tested in real firms.

Because today's businesses operate in rich-media or new-media environments, we have endeavored to make this book reflect that environment. We provide deeper exploration of topics that appear in the text through Drill-Down sidebars. Point-Counterpoints highlight the two sides to some of the unresolved contemporary debates in businesses. POVs are sidebar commentary from leading practitioners. We transcribe excerpts from our videotaped conversations with thought leaders into Sound Byte sidebars. And at the end of every chapter in the strategy module, MarketWatch.com serves as a living case study to which we apply the ideas and concepts presented in each chapter. We show exactly how these ideas apply, and how they have created real and substantial value for a company doing business in the real world.

## Content and Organization

This book serves as a comprehensive introduction to the field of e-commerce. At the core of e-commerce activities is the strategy of the enterprise. Wrapped around this strategy process are four critical infrastructures: technology, capital, public policy, and media. These four infrastructures provide the context—both the opportunities and the constraints—within which the strategy operates.

**The Strategy Process.** We begin with a discussion of the strategy process. There are six interrelated, sequential decisions to this strategy—market opportunity analysis, business model, customer interface, market communications and branding, implementation, and evaluation. In order to fully understand how these six decisions interrelate, we apply them to the well-known MarketWatch.com website. This includes our secondary analysis of the MarketWatch.com strategy, as well as our interviews with its senior management team.

**Technology Infrastructure.** In this four-chapter sequence, we take the reader through two basic chapters on how the Internet and the World Wide Web work—the core software, applications, and hardware. After discussing strategy formulation, we turn our attention to the B2B marketplace to discuss the more complex technology associated with the B2B marketplace and collaborative commerce more generally. We conclude with a discussion of the evolution of these critical technologies.

**Capital Infrastructure.** Where does the money come from to launch these new businesses? How does the process work—from finding the right managers to building the business plan and seeking funding sources? This chapter provides a primer on what we term the capital infrastructure of the networked economy.

**Media Infrastructure.** Just as we observe the convergence of multiple technologies, we have also observed the convergence of digitized content—radio, TV, magazines, books, and other print media. Here we discuss the evolution of each of these media and the convergence of these media on the Internet. We also discuss the evolution of rich-media interfaces—and project several interesting developments in this cross-industry evolution.

**Public Policy Infrastructure.** All of the previous decisions—related to the strategy, technology, capital, and media—are based on public policy decisions. In this two-chapter sequence, we introduce and discuss some of the most important regulatory issues that confront firms today.

The sequence and topics of chapters reflect the intellectual architecture of our approach to managing in this field. Our chapters are organized to reflect the framework sequence of the strategy process and associated infrastructures.

## Overview of the Book

**Chapter 1—Overview.** Many of our students and clients have asked us what is different about managing in the networked economy. In this chapter, we set forth those differences in detail, attempting to frame the unique attributes of the networked economy and the implications for managers and strategists. In doing this, we present a working definition and framework for the study and practice of electronic commerce, discussing both the strategy involved in running an e-commerce company and the four infrastructures—technical, capital, media, and public policy—that can influence that strategy.

## The Basic Technology of the Internet and Web

**Chapter 2—Introduction to the Web and Internet.** In this chapter we give a basic history of the Internet and the underlying technology involved to provide a framework for the proceeding chapters. This chapter explains basic technology concepts, including webpages, hyperlinks, and protocols. Webpages are documents whose content (which can include text, images, and multimedia) is most often described with a text-based language called HTML. Using hyperlinks, webpages can connect to other related webpages to form a website and can also be connected to any other page in the world automatically. Web browsers are programs that interpret the HTML on the webpage and display it in a form that is most suitable for the device on which the browser is running. Worldwide acceptance of standards such as HTML and TCP/IP have helped fuel the explosive growth of the Internet by making the process of creating and consuming content on the Net inexpensive and easy.

**Chapter 3—The Basics of Selling on the Internet.** Selling on the Internet requires several abilities above and beyond page-creation skills. Web merchants need to be able to drive traffic to their site through the use of search engines, affiliate and viral marketing programs, online and offline media buys, the ability to build customer loyalty, and other means. Once an e-commerce storefront is up and the buyers have arrived, the site needs to be able to provide secure transactions over fast and reliable connections. Finally, Web marketers must be able to contend with the logistics of inventory management and order fulfillment to keep customers satisfied and coming back.

## Strategy Formulation for Online Firms

**Chapter 4—Framing the Market Opportunity.** In this chapter, we revisit the basics of any business to construct an original approach to formulating business strategy. In so doing, we focus on the players who make up the dynamics of any business—customers, competitors, and strategic partners. The goal here is to understand what market analysis becomes in this new world and to introduce a process not only to understand the market, but also to identify those portions of the market that are unserved or underserved. This chapter identifies five conditions that must be carefully analyzed to determine if there is a market opportunity for the firm.

**Chapter 5—Business Models.** While many believe that Internet businesses in many cases do not have business models, we strongly disagree. There may be poorly articulated models out there, but the business-model definition is essential to competition in this new space. Here we introduce the four components of the Marketspace business model. These are (1) the value proposition or "cluster," (2) the product offering, which we call a "marketspace" offering, (3) the resource system that the firm selects to deliver the offering, and (4) a financial model that enables the business to generate revenues, cash flows, and, ultimately, profit margins or valuation potential. These four choices constitute the foundation of the strategy decisions that we explore throughout the book.

**Chapter 6—The Customer Interface.** The visible presence of most e-commerce businesses is a digital or rich-media interface. While online businesses may make substantial use of traditional offline interfaces—such as retail points of sale, printed catalogs, stand-alone kiosks, and call centers—they rely primarily on a virtual storefront connected to the Internet. In this chapter, we fully develop the set of design tools and elements that we refer to as the 7Cs of the customer interface. These elements include: content, context, community, commerce, customization, communications, and connection. In particular, we focus on the levers management can use to create competitive advantage and generate customer value through these essential elements of interface design.

**Chapter 7—Communications and Branding.** In the demand-oriented business world, there is nothing more valuable than mind share, or the ability to attract and hold the attention of markets and customers. The traditional tools of attention management are marketing communications. In this chapter, we explore the variety of traditional and new-media communications approaches that provide competitive advantage to businesses, and delve into the extraordinary power of brands in this new information-enabled world. Many believed that the Web would create a world of downward price pressures and rapid commoditization of goods and services of all kinds. As we explain, the opposite has occurred. Brands are more important than ever—and some would argue that, at least in business-to-consumer ventures, they are essential to success.

**Chapter 8—Implementation.** If strategy is about "what to do," implementation is about "how to do it." Most management texts focus on strategy, and implementation is often left to the last chapters. Indeed, in the management literature, it has constituted a "poor cousin" of fashion-forward fields such as strategy, marketing, and finance. Doing business in the networked economy demands a different approach. Because such businesses operate in constant dynamic dialogue with their markets, it is difficult—and unproductive—to approach strategy and implementation in a linear, sequential fashion. Rather, they are two elements in a real-time cycle, wherein each set of decisions pertaining to strategy and implementation must constantly be reevaluated based on new data one from the other. In this chapter, we consider both the delivery system and innovation components of strategy implementation.

**Chapter 9—Metrics.** The dynamic relationship between strategy and market feedback demands new approaches to measurement and evaluation of business results. We know that e-commerce businesses offer unprecedented opportunities for capturing information on how markets operate and how customers engage in search and shopping behavior. Because this kind of data is available in rich granular forms and, as importantly, in real-time, we introduce a new management tool called the Performance Dashboard. It is a set of metrics that reflect both the early-warning indicators of the progress of an e-commerce strategy and outcome measures such as customer satisfaction and financial performance.

# Technology Infrastructure

## Chapter 10—The Emergence and Growth of B2B Marketplaces.
This chapter covers the key technologies that provide the foundation for B2B marketplaces. The chapter is organized into two broad sections: MRO procurement and net marketplaces. With respect to MRO procurement, the chapter covers the technology components, including multi-supplier catalog management, approval workflow, and supplier integration. In the domain of Net marketplaces, we cover alternative types of marketplaces, including vertical versus horizontal, focus of value creation (i.e., buyer, seller, neutral), and public versus private marketplaces. Four alternative technology approaches are considered, including building from scratch, all-encompassing solutions, point solutions, and outsourced marketplaces. Regardless of approach, four technology areas need to be addressed: commerce, content, community, and third-party service suppliers.

## Chapter 11—Collaborative Commerce.
This chapter discusses how collaborative commerce unfolds in the marketplace—with a particular emphasis on supply-chain and demand-chain management. All organizations must engage in several basic activities, including product design, planning, sourcing materials, selling, making, fulfilling, and service functions. In order to run an effective online organization, software and applications related to each of these functions need to be designed and implemented. Consider, for example, the design phase: An organization needs to make choices related to engineering and product development (new product introductions, engineering change management) and project management (engineer-to-order, collaborative planning, and execution). For each of these seven key functions, we discuss the relative software and applications that the collaborative enterprise must consider in the design of its technology infrastructure.

# Capital Infrastructure

## Chapter 12—Early-Stage Business Development: Human and Financial Capital.
While a business may have the best idea or new technology, getting capital—both human and financial—is critical. Choosing the right management team and writing an effective business plan are often the most important—and overlooked—elements in getting a company off the ground. In this chapter, we explore the relationship between human and financial capital, namely, the elements of a business plan, the roles and responsibilities of an entrepreneur, articulating the idea, and forming the management team. In this chapter we also discuss different sources of financing.

**Chapter 13—Working with Funders: From Seed Stage to Liquidity.** Once a startup has its business plan and management team together, it is ready to look for financing. This chapter goes into greater depth on the sources of funding and how to choose the right mix for a startup. It describes the various stages of funding, with emphasis on the beginning and liquidity stages (including explanations of the IPO process and mergers and acquisitions). We will also discuss various methods of valuation and how the negotiation process works. The chapter ends with a discussion of where the capital market is heading.

## Media Infrastructure

**Chapter 14—Media Transformation.** This chapter discusses the transformation of media. It covers the past three decades, from analog to digital platforms. Among the key issues are the increased fragmentation of media usage among consumers and the resulting megamergers of the past decade, such as the AOL-Time Warner, Viacom-CBS, and Disney-ABC/Capital Cities deals, where the goal is to maximize the use of similar content across multiple media platforms. Case examples of media convergence—ABCNews.com, Sony PlayStation 2, MSNBC, and Time-CNN-Netscape—will be discussed, along with the economics of various media, including newspapers, television, and radio.

**Chapter 15—The Future of Media Usage.** In this chapter, we preview the future of media usage. With continued media fragmentation expected—especially with the increased usage of new applications such as broadband, video-game players, and personal digital assistants (PDAs)—several possible scenarios emerge. What will the world be like with the increased usage of smart phones and PDAs? Will video-game players replace home computers as the primary way for consumers to access media? How will increased use of broadband impact consumer demand for content-based products? The scenarios are endless, but this chapter provides a beginning point for a lively discussion about the future of media.

## Public Policy Infrastructure

In this two-chapter section, we introduce and discuss some of the most important regulatory and societal issues confronting firms in this space.

**Chapter 16—Regulation.** In this chapter, we explore how government is currently regulating the Internet and what it may regulate in the future. We discuss self-regulation versus government regulation, and how the Internet's new technology and lack of boundaries have created regulatory challenges. We explore issues such as privacy, free speech, intellectual property, and gambling—and determine how the laws and regulations currently governing these issues will affect e-commerce and Internet businesses.

**Chapter 17—Internet and Society.** We explore how the Internet is changing society, and how society is changing the Internet. With issues such as community, education, e-government, and the digital divide, the Internet is changing how people communicate, seek information, and shop, and even how they interact with the government. These changes have implications for society, but also for the e-commerce businesses working within this new society.

# USER'S GUIDE

## Textbook Navigation

Because new-economy businesses operate in rich media or new-media environments, we have endeavored to make this book a rich information environment. You will see that every chapter has a variety of standard features that augment the text. You can count on these to enrich your understanding of the material covered, to introduce new and often controversial perspectives, and to provide greater detail on topics of current and future salience. Look for these features as you read:

• **Drill-Downs:** These sidebars provide deeper explorations of topics that appear in the text. Not every reader will want to explore the intricacies of collaborative filtering or viral marketing, but many will find these additional materials useful. Think of Drill-Downs as hypertext—there when you need them, out of your way when you do not.

• **Point-Counterpoints:** These segments acknowledge the reality that many debate in current business—such as whether profits matter or whether Internet-company valuations are rational—remain unresolved. Rather than take an artificial approach to these issues and present the "right" answers, we make the case for and against. Of course, we do have our points of view, and you will find these clearly indicated.

• **POVs (Points of View):** Throughout the chapters, we have included sidebar commentary from leading practitioners in the networked economy—people who have invented new business approaches, developed new network architectures, created major Web brands, and influenced policy in the field. These comments are excerpted from articles published in leading periodicals, such as *The Industry Standard, Upside,* and *Business 2.0.*

• **Sound Bytes:** These are transcribed excerpts from our ongoing videotaped conversations with contemporary business thought leaders, such as Netscape cofounder Marc Andreessen; Ethernet inventor Bob Metcalfe; and the creators of ICQ instant messaging, Yair Goldfinger and Sefi Vigiser. These interviews represent fresh, up-to-date, and exclusive perspectives on the state of play in our field. Longer streaming-video excerpts are available on our website at *www.marketspaceu.com,* and full interviews are available on videotape for purchase.

• **MarketWatch.com Case Study:** At the end of every strategy chapter, we visit one company, the financial-news site MarketWatch.com (*www.market-watch.com*). MarketWatch.com serves as a living case study to which we apply the ideas and concepts presented in each chapter. We show exactly how these ideas apply, and we help you see the ideas in action in ways that have created substantial value for a company doing business in the real world. Furthermore, we provide relevant interviews with key executives within MarketWatch.com to obtain a richer, "inside" view of its strategy.

## Supporting Materials

To facilitate the teaching of the book content, we realize that instructors need teaching support materials. In an effort to assist instructors, we have developed a comprehensive support package that includes materials available in print and on the Web.

- **Online Instructor's Manual.** Our instructor's manual is designed and written to help faculty using our textbook to teach an e-commerce course or module. Our online manual offers a concise summary of each chapter's key themes, classroom questions (and answers) that highlight those themes and spur lively classroom debates, and relevant student project assignments (and answers) designed to reinforce key learning points in each chapter. The *Introduction to e-Commerce Instructor's Manual* provides teaching tips and suggestions for presenting each chapter, PowerPoint slides for each of the chapters (10–15 slides per chapter), suggested test/discussion questions for each chapter, and suggested exercises and associated websites that illustrate the chapter content.

- **Marketspace Multimedia Materials.** We draw upon the extensive professional media capabilities of the Marketspace media group and of our partners to let the networked economy speak for itself.

- The Marketspace media archives contain over 100 broadcast-quality interviews with leading CEOs, investors, inventors, and implementers, conducted at leading business conferences around the world. Streaming-video excerpts are available on our website at *www.marketspaceu.com*, and full interviews are available on videotape for purchase.

- We have captured Professors Rayport and Jaworski in a series of "Dot-Com Debates" on lively issues in the networked economy. Does profit matter? Do the valuations make sense? Who has it better, dot-com startups or dot-coms backed by bricks-and-mortar giants? Does segmentation matter on the Web? Tune in by visiting us at *www.marketspaceu.com* as Dr. Rayport and Dr. Jaworski provide an educational—and entertaining—Point-Counterpoint discussion.

- **Our Teaching Notes.** We offer teaching notes to assist instructors who are using our cases in an e-commerce course or module. Our concise teaching notes help instructors understand the case and teaching themes and provide several helpful resources. Each teaching note offers a case synopsis, case teaching objectives, several case-analysis questions (and answers), potential problems with teaching the case, an end note that provides a general update on what has happened to the company since the case was written, and several board plans that offer suggestions on how the classroom boards should be organized when teaching a case.

- **Case Dashboards at MarketspaceU.com.** For each case, we offer an enhanced multimedia teaching note to keep instructors informed on the cases and in control in the classroom. Each dashboard provides a quick summary of the case—since the date it was written, as well as a list of key articles, teaching aids (e.g., a timeline of company developments), discussion questions, Point-Counterpoint debates, and real-time company news updates powered by our sister site, tnbt.com.

- **Lecture Dashboards at MarketspaceU.com.** For each textbook chapter, we offer enhanced PowerPoint slide decks designed to capture key chapter themes and insights. These slide decks offer visual aids to assist instructors who are using our textbook to teach an e-commerce course or module presentations on various networked–economy topics. Similar to the case dashboards, we provide 24/7 news feeds on themes related to the lectures as well as streaming videos with various business leaders.

- **Syllabus.** For instructors using our textbook to teach an e-commerce course or module, we offer a course syllabus that outlines a 13-week course structure that specifies suggested course timing, class-session summaries, and class preparation questions.

- **Our Cases.** Our library includes cases written for top business schools and our own cases written by our team of scholars and practitioners. Case studies—

long used in clinical psychology, medical, and business school programs—are designed to facilitate a dialogue, or more appropriately, a healthy debate on the alternative solutions to a particular problem.

Today, there are precious few case studies that illustrate "what works" in the networked economy. Our casebook provides a unique and comprehensive selection of cases that are both timely and relevant. The interesting challenge in crafting cases on evolving firms is that the solution seems to be changing as rapidly as the practitioner is able to diagnose the problem. We use the term *seems* because there are some basic strategy principles that do last the test of time. Our intent in providing these case studies is to challenge your thinking—and debate with your classmates, colleagues, or friends—about the lasting principles that will emerge in the networked economy.

- **Irwin/McGraw-Hill Website.** Instructors using our textbook to teach an e-commerce course or module are able to access the Irwin/McGraw-Hill website at *www.mhhe.com/marketspace* for sample syllabi for different approaches to teaching the material; descriptions of how to use the various pedagogical features, such as the POVs, Point-Counterpoints, and videos; suggested test/discussion questions for each chapter; guidelines for different types of projects; and PowerPoint slides for each of the chapters—these vary from 10 to 15 slides per chapter.

# For Faculty

The changes taking place in real time in the networked economy have both energized the classroom and brought a new set of challenges to faculty teaching in this space. Students have unprecedented access to sources of information and data, and they have had a greater range of experiences—from investments in dot-coms to their own startup battle scars—so support for teachers in the classroom has advanced from a blackboard or two to a multimedia tool kit to make lessons more immediate.

These developments make the job of staying on top of the new businesses and effectively conveying their lessons more difficult. Given the speed of change, how can we prevent being blindsided by late-breaking developments? Since the "old war horse" cases often no longer work, what *can* we repurpose, and where do we turn for new frameworks?

- Our *Introduction to e-Commerce* textbook, along with our *e-Commerce* and *Internet Marketing* textbooks, provides a strong knowledge foundation to help chart your course through these challenges.

- Our casebook and stand-alone cases raise the key issues to show how new knowledge is applied in the business world and to drive productive discussions.

- Our teaching-support materials give you unequalled confidence in the classroom: our teaching notes outline the issues and chart the questions; our case updates give you real-time intelligence on the case, timelines of case developments, key articles, and focused Point-Counterpoint questions.

- Our articles and forums provide in-depth insights on what academic and business leaders are thinking and doing.

- Our extensive media library of interviews provides the first—and the last—word on networked-economy issues from the men and women who are driving them.

- And every day, our sister site tnbt.com provides fresh news updates—knowledge to keep you on the cutting edge of the networked economy.

## For Students

You are riding the wave of a technological revolution that is changing the way the economy operates. Businesses, entrepreneurs, governments, academic institutions, nonprofit organizations—they all are scrambling to hire students that understand, can operate in, and can lead in this economy.

- Our *Introduction to e-Commerce* textbook, along with our *e-Commerce* and *Internet Marketing* textbooks, provides a strong business knowledge foundation.

- Our case studies show how this knowledge is applied in the business world.

- Our articles and forums provide in-depth insight on what academic and business leaders are thinking and doing.

- And every day, our sister site tnbt.com provides fresh news updates—knowledge to keep you on the cutting edge of the networked economy.

**Jeffrey F. Rayport**
**Cambridge, Massachusetts**

**Bernard J. Jaworski**
**Los Angeles, California**

March 15, 2001

# BRIEF CONTENTS

# CONTENTS

# Part II Strategy Formulation for New-Economy Firms

## 4 Framing Market Opportunity — 95

# A Framework for E-Commerce

Many of our students and clients have asked us to explain what is different about being a manager in the new economy. In this chapter we set forth those differences in detail while attempting to frame the unique attributes of the "new" or "networked" economy and the implications for managers and strategists. In doing so we present a working definition and framework for the study and practice of electronic commerce, discussing both the strategy involved in running an e-commerce company and the four infrastructures—technical, capital, media, and public policy—that can influence that strategy. We conclude the chapter with an overview of each of the remaining chapters in the book.

## QUESTIONS

*Please consider the following questions as you read this chapter:*

1. What are the categories of e-commerce?

2. What are the new views of strategy in the new—or networked—economy?

3. What is the framework for the field of e-commerce?

4. Why does a manager need to know all four infrastructures?

5. What are the roles and responsibilities of senior e-commerce managers?

6. What are the key challenges of senior leaders today?

# INTRODUCTION

In spite of the recent market fluctuations of Internet stocks, it is difficult to ignore the depth and breadth of the impact of e-commerce in daily life. As we each read the morning papers, we observe interesting stories on companies helping the growth of the Internet. These articles cover companies that engage in e-commerce (such as Amazon.com or eBay), provide access to the Internet (America Online), create software for the Internet (Ariba and Commerce One), or supply the hardware that builds the Internet (IBM, Cisco, and Nortel). Morning television programs carry 30-second ads for pure dot-coms as well as the dot-coms of well-known bricks-and-mortar stores. As we drive to work, we observe many billboards pointing us to websites for entertainment, commerce, information, or community. We pass buildings that display the corporate signage of dot-coms. As we climb out of cars in the public parking lot, we overhear conversations about friends or family members who became rich (or took a beating) on new-economy firms. And so the day goes—with constant stimuli related to the Internet, e-commerce, and the new economy—as we work, shop, dine, or drive through our communities.

So how is this a "revolution" in both business and society? The best way of understanding it is to realize that we are operating today in what some call the "new" or "networked" economy. While there are many definitions of this term, new-economy businesses have several key traits in common. They

- create value largely or exclusively through the gathering, synthesizing, and distribution of information. Their success is predicated on creating value by tapping the power of electronic information networks and new-media interfaces.
- formulate strategy in ways that make management of the enterprise and management of technology convergent.
- compete in real time rather than in "cycle time" and operate in constantly responsive dialogue with their customers and markets.
- operate in a world characterized by low barriers to entry, near-zero variable costs of operation, and—as a result—intense, constantly shifting competition.
- organize resources around the demand side (e.g., customers, markets, trends, and needs) rather than the supply side, as business has done in the past.
- manage relationships with customers and markets often through "screen-to-face" channels and interfaces, which means that technology, rather than people, manages these relationships.
- use technology-mediated channels, and have ongoing operations that are subject to measurement and tracking in unprecedented and granular ways.

Taking these themes together does more than furnish a rigorous understanding of what business managers and pundits alike mean when they talk about doing business in the networked economy. Every one of these statements implies significant changes in how practitioners determine strategy, deploy resources, operate firms, manage relationships with their markets, and measure results. This does not mean that everything we know about business up to this point becomes irrelevant and obsolete, but it does mean that significant changes in the environment of business justify—indeed, demand—new approaches to thinking about strategy and management.

The purpose of this book is to provide an overview of the entire field of e-commerce. Hence, the book is written for present and future practitioners who desire to know more about all aspects—strategy, technology, capital, media, and public policy—of the networked economy. Our intent is to provide a deep exploration of core concepts of networked-economy strategy and associated enablers, and it is enriched by a wide variety of examples, case studies, and explanations culled directly from practice.

In the next section, we turn to a discussion of the various forms of e-commerce activities, including traditional, retail-like companies such as Amazon, Yahoo, and Gap.com, as well as business-to-business players such as Dell, Cisco, and General Electric.

# DEFINITION AND SCOPE OF E-COMMERCE

## Definition

Digital technology has transformed the economy. Value creation for consumers has shifted from the physical goods to an economy that favors service, information, and intelligence as the primary sources of value creation. In essence **e-commerce** is characterized by several attributes:

- *It Is About the Exchange of Digitized Information Between Parties.* This information exchange can represent communications between two parties, coordination of the flows of goods and services, or transmission of electronic orders. These exchanges can be between organizations or individuals.

- *It Is Technology-Enabled.* E-commerce is about technology-enabled transactions. The use of Internet browsers in the World Wide Web is perhaps the best known of these technology-enabled customer interfaces. However, other interfaces—including ATMs, electronic data interchange (EDI) between business-to-business partners, and electronic banking by phone—also fall in the general category of e-commerce. Businesses once managed transactions with customers and markets strictly through human interaction; in e-commerce, such transactions can be managed using technology.

- *It Is Technology-Mediated.* Furthermore, the focus is moving away from the simply technology-enabled transaction to a technology-mediated relationship. Purchases in the marketplace at Wal-Mart are technology-enabled in that we have human contact along with a cash register that does PC-based order processing. What is different now is that the transaction is mediated not so much through human contact but largely by technology—and, in that sense, so is the relationship with the customer. The place where buyers and sellers meet to transact is moving from the physical-world "marketplace" to the virtual-world "marketspace." Hence, the success of the business rests on screens and machines in managing customers and their expectations. Coming from a past of transactions with human-human contact, that is a big difference.

- *It Includes Intra- and Interorganizational Activities That Support the Exchange.* The scope of electronic commerce includes *all electronically based* intra- and interorganizational activities that directly or indirectly support marketplace exchanges.[1] In this sense, we are talking about a phenomenon that affects both how business organizations relate to external parties—customers, suppliers, partners, competitors, and markets—and how they operate internally in managing activities, processes, and systems.

# A Contemporary Definition

In summary, electronic commerce can be formally defined as . . .

> . . . *technology-mediated exchanges between parties (individuals or organizations) as well as the electronically based intra- or interorganizational activities that facilitate such exchanges.*

# Distinct Categories

**Business-to-Business.** **Business-to-business (B2B)** activity refers to the full spectrum of e-commerce that can occur between two organizations (see Table 1-1). Among other activities, this includes purchasing and procurement, supplier management, inventory management, channel management, sales activities, payment management, and service and support. While we may be familiar with major players such as FreeMarkets, Dell, and General Electric, there are some exciting emerging consortia that combine the purchasing power of heretofore competitors, such as GM, Ford, and Daimler Chrysler, which joined together to create Covisint. Similar initiatives are under way with industry groups, including pharmaceuticals, commercial real estate development, and electronic subcomponents.

**Business-to-Consumer.** **Business-to-consumer (B2C)** e-commerce refers to exchanges between businesses and consumers, such as those managed by Amazon, Yahoo, and Charles Schwab & Co. Often, transactions take place that are

**Table 1-1**

## FOUR CATEGORIES OF E-COMMERCE

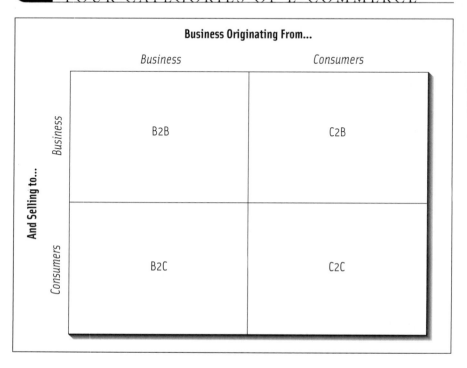

similar to those in the B2B context. For instance, as with smaller B2B interactions, transactions that relate to the "back office" of the customer (e.g., inventory management at the home) are often not tracked electronically. However, all customer-facing, or front-office, activities are typically tracked. These include sales activities, consumer search, frequently asked questions, and service and support.

### Consumer-to-Consumer.
**Consumer-to-consumer (C2C)** exchanges involve transactions between and among consumers. These exchanges can include third-party involvement, as in the case of the auction website eBay. Other activities include classified ads (*www. numberoneclassifieds.com*), games (*www.heat.net*), jobs (*www. monster.com*), Web-based communications (*www.icq.com*), and personal services (*www.webpersonals.com*). C2C is also often referred to as peer-to-peer (P2P).

### Consumer-to-Business.
Consumers can band together to present themselves as a buyer group in a **consumer-to-business (C2B)** relationship. These groups may be economically motivated, as with demand aggregators, or socially oriented, as with cause-related advocacy groups at SpeakOut.com.

## Emergent Categories of E-Commerce

Some authors argue that ultimately a single chain of e-commerce will emerge. This chain will be a superset of the categories noted above. Therefore, it is increasingly important to think of a single demand-and-supply chain that can be most accurately characterized as initiating with end-customers and rippling backward through a supply chain to the eventual raw-materials producers. Moreover, the chain can ripple through the C2C to C2B exchanges as well.

Consider, for example, the purchase of a Harry Potter book at Amazon.com. Exhibit 1-1 illustrates how the sale of Harry Potter books can ripple throughout the four e-commerce quadrants. At time period one, thousands of consumers buy the most recent Harry Potter book through Amazon. This purchase triggers an electronic exchange between Amazon and the publisher to request more books. This ordering forces the publisher to print new copies. The new copies trigger a reordering of new paper products, shipping materials (from cardboard suppliers), and ink. Meanwhile, consumers may be able to "demand aggregate" through public sites or through corporate bulk-purchase rates. Finally, after the books are consumed, they may be saved or sold on eBay. Thus, it could be argued that the categories of e-commerce are not distinct, but rather, they are intimately linked in a broader network of supply and demand.

## STRATEGY-MAKING IN A RAPIDLY CHANGING ENVIRONMENT

The online environment is changing so quickly that it is difficult for a company to select a strategy and stay the course. Indeed, a hallmark of online companies is the quick shifting of resources, revenue models, and content. How can a company faced with these changes set a strategy? In this section we begin with a discussion of a classical approach to strategic analysis and planning. Next, we discuss how recent authors have challenged this perspective and how the Internet may force a reconsideration of central tenets of this approach. We conclude with a discussion of emergent strategy.

## Exhibit 1-1 CONVERGENCE OF E-COMMERCE CATEGORIES

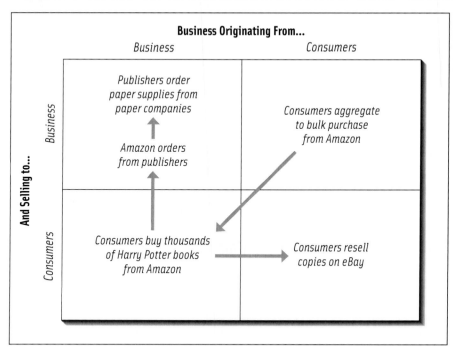

## Classical Strategic Planning

Exhibit 1-2 provides a simple, classical framework that outlines the strategic management process. This process begins with the identification of the mission, or vision, of the firm. A mission specifies why the organization exists, with a particular focus on the benefits it provides to chosen customers. Once the mission is spelled out, the firm can begin to address its specific goals; these goals may be financial, customer-oriented, internally focused, or shareholder-based. Given the broad company goals, the firm is in a position to carefully analyze its core strengths and competencies, as well as the forces that operate outside its official boundaries. This includes competitive forces as well as broader developments related to economic, political, and social conditions.

The careful balance of internal and external analysis leads to a choice of strategy for the company as a whole, called "corporate strategy." Strategies that relate to specific divisions within a company are termed "business-unit strategies." Once the strategies have been agreed upon by the senior managers, the firm can implement the strategies in the marketplace through a series of specific policies, programs, procedures, and budgets. Once implemented, the senior management team can monitor marketplace success and take corrective action as needed.

## What Are the New Views of E-Commerce Strategy?

The speed of change and adaptation must be figured into the classical strategic-management equation. While the basic tools of strategy remain the same—external and internal analysis, strategy choice, and implementation—the speed of change in

Exhibit
1-2

## CLASSICAL FRAMEWORK FOR STRATEGIC MANAGEMENT

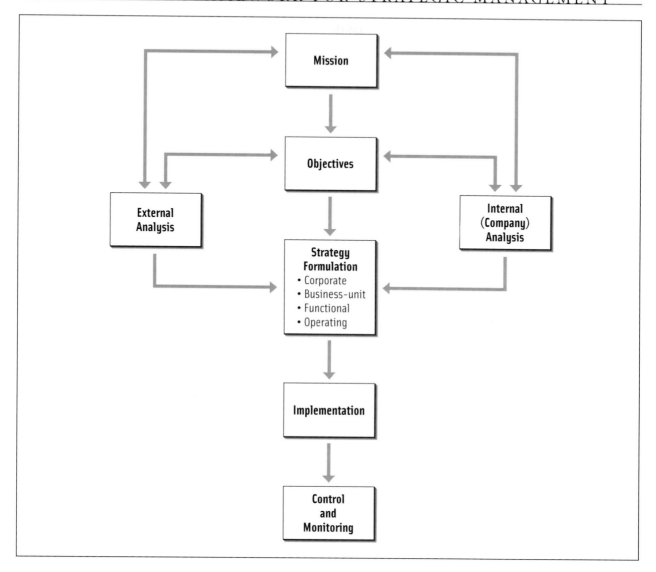

the online environment has forced companies to act and react more quickly. In this section, we discuss two new perspectives on strategy. The first perspective, termed "sense and respond," focuses on the agility of the firm in the face of rapid change. The second, termed "strategy as rules," points to the need for simple decision rules—as opposed to massive strategy analysis—that can guide managers in spotting and acting on market opportunities. Finally, we conclude with a focus on two key consumer-based aspects of Internet commerce: individualization (i.e., customization) and interactivity.

**Sense and Respond.** In 1998, Professors Stephen Bradley and Richard Nolan of Harvard Business School noticed a shift had taken place from what they called the "make and sell" approach that characterized traditional business to more of a **sense**

**and respond** approach.[2] Faced with so much experimentation and unexpected change, the sense and respond paradigm was important from two perspectives:

- *It provided an approach to strategic thinking that was intuitive, actionable, and easy to implement.* Executives were no longer paralyzed in attempts to over-analyze the unknown challenges and problems that they were facing; they could start working on experimenting with solutions instead.

- *It made companies focus on **listening in a new manner to customers** to reduce the high levels of uncertainty.* The make and sell paradigm made most companies "very good at responding, but not very good at sensing [the customer]."[3] By proactively soliciting feedback from the customers, companies could get a better sense of what was—and was not—going to be hot in the market. It had become increasingly difficult to predict what was going to be successful in the first Internet age.

The sense and respond approach has two shortcomings, though. First, it is a reactive approach that appears most appropriate for incremental competitive moves. The starting point is always the customer. By sensing what the customer likes and dislikes, the company can figure out how to best respond. At no point is there an attempt to proactively change or influence the likes and dislikes of the customer. This is not very apt for strategies that require significant customer education (because breakthrough innovations are at the core of the strategy/value proposition) or in industrial markets.

Second, this approach is more appropriate for traditional offline companies defending themselves against new Internet entrants in their markets. And even then, no sensing in the world would have predicted the rise of Napster, or provided companies in the field with a means to react to it.

**Strategy as Rules.** A second perspective on strategy has recently emerged that stresses the need to focus the organization on **simple rules** rather than complex strategic planning exercises.[4] The basic idea is that environments are both rapidly changing and unpredictable. Thus, it is impossible to anticipate all of the possible market conditions that may unfold. In light of these situations, organizations should follow very simple decision rules (e.g., Cisco's early acquisition rule that companies that it acquired should have less than 75 employees, 75 percent of whom should be engineers). Much like the United States Marine Corps' rules of engagements, these simple decision rules are doctrines that guide choices in the heat of battle. Just as all future military battlefields cannot be anticipated, all future business environments cannot be predicted. Hence, simple rules help senior e-commerce managers recognize positive (or negative) situations and react accordingly. Psychologists—or more specifically, decision scientists—term these cognitive approaches "pattern recognition." For example, expert chess players intuitively recognize various board patterns as they emerge and can anticipate the reactions of competitors and perhaps even the winning moves as the battle unfolds.

Table 1-2 illustrates the recent ideas of Kathleen Eisenhardt and Donald Sull on the strategy of simple rules. They highlight the differences among three strategy approaches: the "position" approach typically taught in marketing or strategy courses, the resource-based view of the firm (which emerged in the past decade), and the simple-rules approach. Perhaps the most interesting aspect of this chart is the key strategic question. The positioning approach asks, "Where should we be?" versus the competition. The resources approach asks, "What resources should we possess?" And the simple-rules approach asks, "What process should we follow?"

Within the context of the classical strategic-management framework (Exhibit 1-2), the positioning approach emphasizes the external environment, the resource approach emphasizes the internal environment, and the simple-rules approach focuses on the organization process within the internal environment. Hence, all focus is on one part of the framework. While we agree that firms need to move very quickly—much like the battlefield commander in the "fog of the battlefield"—it also makes sense that the commander is able to bring resources to bear on the field and his position versus the competition. Hence, it may be that all three approaches have important contributions to the strategy formulation and execution process for new-economy firms.

## Factors of Consumer Behavior in the Online Environment

The notions of sense and respond as well as strategy as simple rules have evolved in response to increasingly unpredictable and rapidly changing business environments. We now turn to two factors that, having increased in importance with the rise of the Internet, are now the consumer-behavior constants of the new economy: customization and interactivity.

**Customization.** **Customization**, or individualization, refers to the personalization of communications between users and a website. This customization can be initiated by the firm (i.e., the firm customizes its site for the user) or by the user (i.e., user builds a custom version of the site, such as MyYahoo). This ability to create a

**Table 1-2**

### THREE APPROACHES TO STRATEGY

|  | Position | Resources | Simple Rules |
|---|---|---|---|
| *Strategic Logic* | • Establish position | • Leverage resources | • Pursue opportunities |
| *Strategic Steps* | • Identify an attractive market<br>• Locate a defensible position<br>• Fortify and defend | • Establish a vision<br>• Build resources<br>• Leverage across markets | • Jump into the confusion<br>• Keep moving<br>• Seize opportunities<br>• Finish strong |
| *Strategic Question* | • Where should we be? | • What should we be? | • How should we proceed? |
| *Source of Advantage* | • Unique, valuable position with tightly integrated activity system | • Unique, valuable, inimitable resources | • Key processes and unique simple rules |
| *Works best in . . .* | • Slowly changing, well-structured markets | • Moderately changing, well-structured markets | • Rapidly changing, ambiguous markets |
| *Duration of Advantage* | • Sustained | • Sustained | • Unpredictable |
| *Risk* | • It will be too difficult to alter position as conditions change | • Company will be too slow to build new resources as conditions change | • Managers will be too tentative in executing on promising opportunities |
| *Performance Goal* | • Profitability | • Long-term dominance | • Growth |

Source: Kathleen M. Eisenhardt and Donald Sull (2001), "Strategy As Simple Rules," *Harvard Business Review*. (January) p. 109

custom experience through the use of technology is one of the profound changes that is affecting the evolution of consumer behavior.

**Interactivity.** The second force that affects consumer behavior is the real-time (or delayed) two-way communication between users and the site. **Interactivity** is defined as the users' ability to conduct two-way communication. This includes user-to-user and firm-to-user communication. Typically, strategy execution—or, more narrowly, market communications—has focused on mass-market programs that involve large sums of money allocated for one-way communication (e.g., television, radio, magazines). With the advent of direct mail and telemarketing, we have witnessed the emergence of so-called one-to-one marketing. However, it should be stressed that the dialogue in these situations is typically one-way and often "one-time." In sharp contrast the Internet affords the opportunity for a dialogue, which may be in real time or asynchronous (over hours or days). This ability to converse is at the heart of the revolution. It puts the customer in control of the interaction and, hence, increases the probability of a positive outcome for both parties.

## The Process of Emergent Strategy

Consider a final note on strategic change. Much has been written about how the new economy has forced companies to react more quickly—perhaps even with limited forethought. There is evidence in prior strategic-management literature of a phenomenon that closely parallels this view. Henry Mintzberg, one of the foremost contributors to the field of strategic management, has observed what he terms "emergent strategy."[5] A firm first sets out its intended strategy. This strategy is what the firm hopes to achieve in, say, the course of the new fiscal year. However, a series of developments unfolds in the marketplace—or within the firm itself—that give rise to unplanned, or emergent, strategies. According to Mintzberg, these emergent strategies are the unplanned responses to unseen changes. They are not the classical top-down analyses of the formal planning process; rather, they are the real-time changes in strategy that are often felt and initiated by the troops within the company.

Thus, emergent strategy is not unlike the sense and respond approach discussed earlier. The major difference is that the sense and respond approach is typically directed by senior managers, while emergent strategy often comes from the line executives who are at the frontlines executing the strategy. Regardless of approach, it is clear that firms often modify their intended strategy as the forces of the four infrastructures change.

## THE FRAMEWORK FOR THE FIELD OF E-COMMERCE

Now that we have explored e-commerce and the new challenges it brings to strategy development, we will set up a framework that best illustrates how to learn and think about the new economy. Exhibit 1-3 shows how we view the dynamics of the field and, consequently, how this book is structured.

At the core of e-commerce activities is the strategy of the enterprise. Wrapped around this strategy process are four critical infrastructures: technology, capital, media, and public policy. These four infrastructures provide the context—both the opportunities and the constraints—in which the strategy operates.

**Exhibit 1-3** A COMPREHENSIVE FRAMEWORK

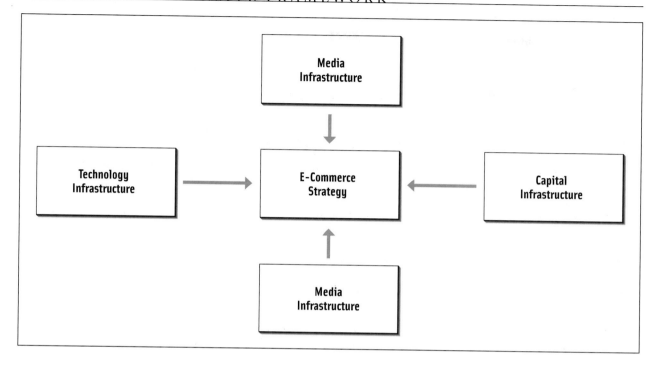

## The Strategy Formulation Process

There are six interrelated, sequential decisions to this strategy: market-opportunity analysis, business models, customer interface, market communications and branding, implementation, and evaluation (see Exhibit 1-4). In order to fully understand how these six decisions interrelate, we apply them to MarketWatch.com at the end of each strategy chapter, using both our secondary analysis of the MarketWatch.com strategy and interviews with the company's senior leadership team.

## The Context of Strategy Formulation: The Four Infrastructures

Successful strategies emerge from a deep understanding of where the market—and, hence, the cash flow—will be in both the short-term and long-term future. The important word in this sentence is *market*. While the market certainly involves the customer—indeed, the customer is at the center—a market also includes the buyers and sellers as well as the broader contextual forces that shape the nature of the marketplace exchange. We argue that there are four critical forces that the e-commerce manager must know and manage if the online firm is to be successful. These four forces are technology, capital, media, and public policy. We review each of these forces and provide a simple illustration.

**Exhibit 1-4** E-COMMERCE STRATEGY

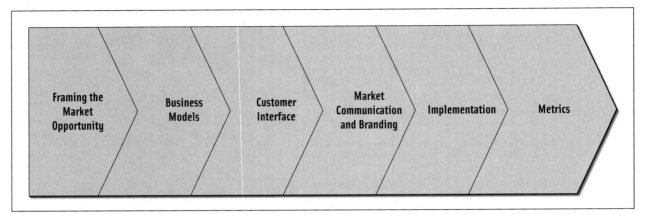

**Technology Infrastructure.** The **technology infrastructure** of the Internet is both an enabler and a driver of change. An infrastructure is defined as "the foundation of a system." In this case, the technological foundation of the Internet, simply put, enables the running of the e-commerce enterprises. The hardware backbone of computers, routers, servers, fiber optics, cables, modems, and other network technologies provides half of the technology equation. The other half includes the software and communications standards that run on top of the hardware, including the core protocols for the Web. Understanding technology infrastructure—and therefore understanding what is and is not achievable—is essential to formulating a company's vision and strategy.

**Capital Infrastructure.** Where does the money to launch these new businesses come from? How does the process work, from finding the right managers to building the business plan and seeking funding sources? Does the process vary depending on whether the proposed venture is a stand-alone dot-com or an internal venture of a larger company like Wal-Mart? Finally, how should this venture be valued? Any successful senior e-commerce manager must understand the **capital infrastructure** and know how to secure funding for a venture (whether independently or in a global 2000 company) and subsequently value that business.

**Media Infrastructure.** Why is the **media infrastructure** an important issue for all e-commerce managers, whether they run GE Medical Systems, USAToday.com, Gamesville.com, or Enron? The answer is that the Internet is a mass communication platform. Just as technology evolution sets the context for technology choices and the capital markets set the context for funding, media convergence provides both opportunities and constraints for the practicing manager. Managers who run e-commerce enterprises must learn to manage a staff responsible for design interface, stylistic choices, editorial policies, and, most important, content choices associated with this new communication venue. Thus, in addition to all other tasks, the e-commerce manager is now a publisher of digital content on the Web.

As a publisher of digital content, the e-commerce manager must make choices about the types of media employed (e.g., print, audio, video), the nature of the media, and editorial policy (including style, content, and look-and-feel). Just as we observe the convergence of multiple technologies (e.g., the fight between DSL, cable, and satellite companies), we have also observed the convergence of digitized content—radio, TV, magazines, books, and other print media.

**Public Policy Infrastructure.** All of the decisions related to strategy, technology, capital, and media are influenced by laws and regulation—in short, public policy decisions. The **public policy infrastructure** affects not only the specific business but also direct and indirect competitors. Senior managers must understand both the current laws and how the laws may change to hurt or help their businesses and those around them. Also, understanding how the Internet is affecting society and how society is affecting the Internet can help the manager see the potential market instead of just the current one.

## Why Does a Senior Manager Need to Know All Four Infrastructures?

Consider the case of Bertelsmann and, in particular, its Bertelsmann Music Group (BMG). Bertelsmann is a major player in the music industry. Recent statistics place it as one of the largest music companies in the world. Music companies are organized around several functions, including (1) artist and repertoire (i.e., signing new artists), (2) recording, (3) manufacturing, (4) distribution, (5) marketing, and (6) music sales. At the core of the revenue stream is the CD recorded by the artist. The lion's share of the revenue in the music industry is garnered by the record companies (e.g., BMG or Sony) and the retail store outlets. The artist typically receives approximately 10 percent of the revenue from each CD sale.

Historically, the most significant challenge for BMG was the discovery of new talent. Once the talent was discovered, BMG invested significant sums of money in marketing the talent through radio play on local FM stations, concert tours, publicity tours, and so on. The cash cow for BMG was CD sales. Because BMG was vertically integrated—it owned, or controlled, the production and manufacturing of each group's CDs—it was able to reap healthy sales margins.

Enter the Internet. With the digitization of music files, it is now possible to copy and exchange files through popular software programs that allow downloads (e.g., MP3) or streaming audio. This certainly poses a significant problem for the music companies, because consumers can download music files and cut out the record companies. In 1999, another problem arose: file-swapping software such as Napster, Gnutella, and Aimster. These programs allow users to swap music files with other users without the intervention of a third party such as a music company. Hence, a student in a dorm at the University of Southern California could swap music with a student at the University of New Hampshire. The problem is significant; recent data suggests that Napster has more than 50 million registered users.

In this new file-swapping era, music companies such as BMG could disappear altogether. So what could BMG do? One move was to create a partnership with Naspter. However, as of mid-February 2001, a court ruled that Napster was in violation of copyright laws. This will certainly not stop file swapping; indeed, the industry evolution has just begun. In light of these developments, BMG senior executives need to ask key questions related to their strategic online choices, but BMG will be successful only if those executives also consider the impact of the four infrastructures on their strategic choices.

We highlight the types of questions that BMG executives should have been asking at the time this book went to press in the spring of 2001. Consider the following set of sample questions in each domain:

### E-Commerce Strategy

- Can BMG find a sustainable revenue model on the Internet?
- With an operating agreement with Napster in place, how does BMG monetize the 56 million users?
- How will talent be discovered? Will BMG be able to retain its big-name artists?
- What is the impact of NTT DoCoMo Inc.'s service and Sony's delivery of music over wireless networks in Japan?

### Technology Infrastructure

- How effective are streaming versus downloadable files? Which do customers want?
- How can BMG leverage Napster's software for its own benefit? What other technologies will emerge?
- Should BMG wait for other major music firms to solve the problem, or should it acquire or partner with other emerging technology players?
- What devices does BMG need to support (portables, PCs, wireless)?

### Capital Infrastructure

- What is the business plan for BMG in the file-swapping era?
- How does BMG continue to secure funding inside of Bertelsmann?
- What is the new pitch to the office of the chairman?
- How does Bertelsmann invest in online, digital music? What portfolio does it support?
- How should BMG be valued?

### Media Infrastructure

- Bertelsmann is a media empire. What media integration is necessary to support its music websites—is it print, audio, video? Does it integrate only its media, or does it access competitor media?
- What are the implications of media convergence for BMG?
- Do customers want rich media or simple music files?

### Public Policy Infrastructure

- How does the recent emergence of digital rights management (DRM) technology impact music distribution?
- What is the impact of recent legislation on patents, copyright infringement, and taxation on BMG?
- Who uses the Internet? Is that the customer base that BMG wants to capture?

The above questions highlight the most central point of our framework (Exhibit 1-2), namely, that strategic online choices cannot be made in the isolation of these four infrastructures, which provide the context for BMG 's online strategy. Most notably, the legal outcome of the copyright infringement suit of the major record companies (excluding BMG, which cut a deal with Napster in winter 2001) may (or may not) influence the evolution of the recording industry. Moreover, the emergence of new software such as Aimster—which allows users to control access to their own PCs—is on the horizon. This new software is interesting in that it is now exceptionally difficult to track who is swapping with whom. Finally, the biggest play for BMG is likely to be related to media convergence—how it brings its vast magazine, music, TV, and Web properties together in a single bundled offering.

# WHAT ARE THE ROLES AND RESPONSIBILITIES OF A SENIOR E-COMMERCE MANAGER?

Given the evolving online environment, what is the role of the senior e-commerce manager? The previous section focused on the strategic questions and choices that confront the senior management team at BMG. However, we can shift our focus to ask, "What are the roles and responsibilities of all senior e-commerce managers? Do these managers need the same skill set as senior executives of leading bricks-and-mortar companies, or does the skill set of e-commerce managers need to vary?" The answer is, naturally, both. Senior managers need to have the basic business skill set of traditional managers and must also incorporate new knowledge, skills, and capabilities. In this section, we overview the roles and responsibilities of the senior manager.

## Cross-Discipline, Integrative Position

Exhibit 1-5 provides one perspective on the evolving skills, knowledge, and capabilities that are expected of senior leaders in the e-commerce arena. The exhibit highlights a few observations about the role. First, entrepreneurship is at the heart of any online business. Keep in mind that the Internet became a significant commercial entity only since the 1990s. By definition, therefore, almost all businesses are new. The e-commerce manager must be able to act quickly and with authority to make strategic decisions—much like the classical entrepreneur for offline businesses. Second, the executive must be trained in a variety of traditional disciplines, including marketing, logistics, accounting, and finance. Assuming the role of general manager, the individual must be well schooled in the basic business disciplines. Third, the senior manager must add two new disciplines to the mix: technology sophistication and media knowledge. The senior executive must be comfortable with the hardware and software that make the business run. Finally, because we noted earlier that an Internet business is a media business at its core, the manager must understand the role of mass communication and what works in terms of media choices and media integration.

## Responsibilities of the Position

While Exhibit 1-5 provides an overview of the areas of responsibilities, in the next section we take a deeper look at the day-to-day responsibilities of the senior e-commerce manager.

**Provide a Vision.** One of the most important tasks of the senior manager is to establish the vision for the online business. As Patricia Seybold notes in *Customers.com*, this is a tricky exercise, because focusing too narrowly means you are probably describing the world as it exists today, while looking too far into the future does not provide concrete direction for employees—or revenue for the business.

**Exhibit 1-5** RELEVANT DISCIPLINES FOR A SENIOR E-COMMERCE EXECUTIVE

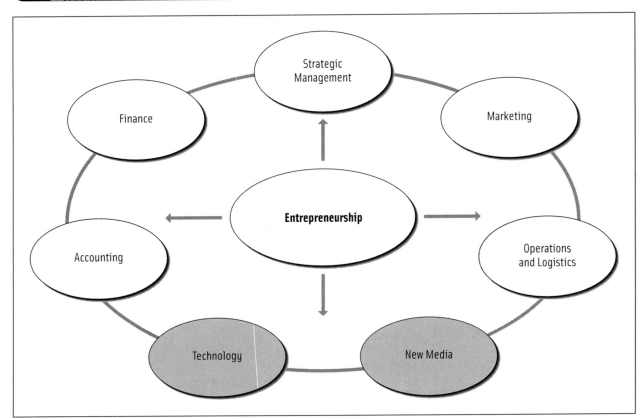

So, how does one balance the need to be concrete while providing a vision that gives direction to the troops? In *Built to Last*, James Collins and Jerry Porras note that superior visions often reflect something more than simple revenue or business goals. They point to visions that stress higher-order impacts on society. Hence, a vision that says, "We want to be the largest online supplier of ethical, over-the-counter drugs" is not as exciting as saying, "We want to help people recover from illness to improve their social, medical, and family welfare."

Strong visions provide direction for employees to rally around, motivate investors to "bet" on the company, and send a signal to the market that the firm is able to provide leadership in the evolution of industries. This last point is particularly critical for networked economy firms.

**Set Process and Outcome Goals.** The second major task for the senior leader is to set the strategic direction of the company by specifying clear performance targets. As will be discussed in Chapter 9, the metrics for success vary depending upon the stage of the business life cycle. For the past few years, it may have been appropriate to specify objectives related to customer acquisition and growth. However, as Wall Street has reversed course and exerted increasing pressure, firms that have focused on customer acquisition now have a clear need to specify the "path to profitability." This does not mean the firm needs to be profitable next month, but senior management must show how the firm will be profitable in the future. This may involve concrete case studies on the monetization of customers or may show financial projections that illustrate a trajectory to profitability.

As we discuss in Chapter 9, we believe that the successful e-commerce executive must track both "process" measures of success and "outcome" measures of success. In this context, outcome measures reflect the concrete financial measures that appeal to investors, while process measures illustrate the firm's performance in variables such as customer satisfaction, employee recruitment, new product development, and access to new markets. These process measures provide the triggers for financial success.

**Formulate Strategic Direction and Choices.** After communicating the vision and target goals of the firm, the senior manager must specify its strategy. This involves making concrete choices—and associated tradeoffs—related to each phase of the e-commerce strategy process, including market-opportunity choice, business-model specification, the design of the customer interface, and other aspects.

This process is typically managed by the most senior executive. Much of the groundwork comes from careful analysis of the market and the firm's capabilities, and while it is not one person's job, the most senior manager leads and directs the process. It is that manager's responsibility to build consensus, make the tough calls, and be accountable for the strategic direction.

| **Exhibit 1-6** | A FLOW DIAGRAM OF THE STRATEGIC RESPONSIBILITIES |

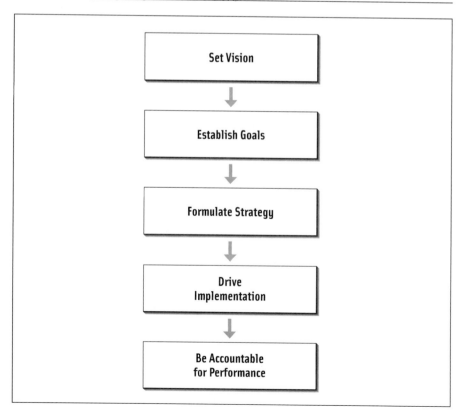

**Drive Implementation.** Strategy implementation is about making the right choices related to the people, structure, systems, and processes to execute the strategy. The most senior manager must make these choices related to all of the executional elements of the strategy. As noted earlier, this involves a deep understanding of technology implementation as well as new-media integration.

**Accountable for Performance.** The senior manager is responsible for the performance of the organization. While the organization as a whole produces (or does not produce) the desired results, it is the senior leader who is accountable to the board or other relevant stakeholders.

## Location in the Organization

Senior e-commerce managers are found in many parts of a conventional bricks-and-mortar company. In Table 1-3 we provide a framework for understanding the organizational location of e-commerce businesses and, hence, senior e-commerce managers within traditional companies. The framework is composed of a cross between the responsibilities (e.g., line versus. staff role) and location within the organizational hierarchy (e.g., corporate, business unit, stand-alone).

**Line Executive.** The senior manager may be a line executive who is responsible for the profit and loss of an online initiative. Think of a general manager who is responsible for all aspects of the business: setting strategy, hiring, supervising technology choices, and taking responsibility for success or failure. This is particularly true when the firm shifts its focus to become demand-centric and attempts to aggregate products or services across the business units of the corporation, or the senior manager may be responsible for a business within a particular business unit of a corporation. Here it is likely that the firm has a digital equivalent of its traditional business. Finally, the company could have a stand-alone e-commerce business, perhaps with its own brand name.

**Staff Executive.** A staff executive does not have formal profit-and-loss responsibility for a business. His role is to support the efforts of the line executives in the execution of their strategy. The senior e-commerce executive may be a staff function at the corporate or business unit level (see Table 1-3).

**Table 1-3** WHERE TO FIND SENIOR E-COMMERCE MANAGERS WITHIN EXISTING BRICKS-AND-MORTAR COMPANIES

|  | Corporate | Business Unit | Stand-Alone |
|---|---|---|---|
| *Line Executive* | • Corporate site management<br>• Cross business unit integration site | • Reports to GM of business unit | • Separate business from corporate parent |
| *Staff Executive* | • Supports corporate-wide initiatives | • Supports and advises SBU e-Commerce initiatives | – |

Note: Line executives are accountable for profit and loss of the business; staff personnel provide support services to line personnel.

# KEY CHALLENGES FOR SENIOR LEADERSHIP IN TODAY'S ENVIRONMENT

As the Internet's "post-bubble" era begins, several challenges must be confronted by the firm's most senior e-commerce executives. These challenges represent forces related to factors inside the firm, such as the integration of online and offline operations, as well as forces outside the firm, such as changing customer dynamics and the evolution of technology. Below we briefly review the five major challenges.

## Understanding Customer Evolution

Customer behavior evolves. Winning firms anticipate the features and functions that matter most to target customers. Currently, Amazon and Barnes & Noble.com compete on a set of benefits—convenience, price, variety of offerings, trustworthiness, and security—that matters most to the various segments of their customers. However, as these benefits that once differentiated the firm are taken for granted—or perceived as simply the cost of doing business—the firm must continually innovate to stay abreast of changes in consumer tastes, desires, and needs. The firm must invest ahead of the customer tastes to produce a product or service that matches the evolution of the market.

Amazon's well-regarded 1-Click shopping service is one such innovation. When people started shopping on the Web, speed of checkout was not an important variable. Customers were most concerned about reliability, correct invoices, and receiving the order. Once these benefits became expected, speed became important. To address this concern, Amazon invested ahead of consumer tastes to develop its 1-Click service, which automatically stores customers' shipping and billing information. Amazon's introduction of the service was timed exactly with the evolution of consumer desires and, hence, was a great success.

The challenge for senior executives is to invest heavily in understanding the evolution of customer needs—and to invest ahead of these needs, so that the launch of the innovation coincides exactly with customer desires.

## Charting Changing Technology

It is almost impossible to stay on top of changing technology. By the time this book is printed, technologies discussed in later chapters may be replaced by next-generation products and services. Much like the evolution of consumer tastes, the evolution of technology—and the firm's investment in it—must coincide with the development of the market. Consumer tastes and technology choices need to match to ensure competitive advantage.

It is perhaps obvious to state that what matters most is not the technology itself, but the evolution of consumer needs—and how the technology supports and reinforces those needs. The senior executive must be well schooled in basic and emergent technologies. Hence the role of chief technology officer is critical to online firms. New technologies are constantly emerging and disappearing. Picking the right ones, and investing ahead of the curve, is a constant, high-stakes gamble for the senior management team.

## Balancing Irrational Exuberance and Irrational Doom

In spring 2001, when this book went to print, we witnessed a large number of layoffs in the dot-com sector. Recently eToys closed its doors, buy.com was feeling considerable financial pressure, and Amazon laid off 1,300 workers. So is the e-commerce sector dead? Hardly. Many pundits who have followed the evolution of technology-intensive innovations argue that this is part of a normal pattern. The impact of new technologies in the first two to three years is typically overestimated, but the impact over 10 years is severely underestimated. Thus the market had expectations that were too high for the year 2000, but perhaps too low for the year 2010.

What is the senior executive's role in this investment environment? To some degree, it is a question of riding out the storm. That is, the executive must continually reassure the workforce that the company will weather the current environment, reassure investors that the business model makes sense, spell out the path to profitability (as relevant), and paint a vision that can rally all relevant stakeholders, including partners, customers, and employees.

## Integration of Offline and Online Activities

Certainly one of the most important unfolding trends is the increasing pressure on offline firms to integrate their online activities. This is particularly true of "customer-facing" activities such as advertising, branding, retail and online store design, service, warranties, and returns. Depending on the executive's position within the firm (see Table 1-4), the importance and degree of influence on this integration will vary. However, regardless of their location in the hierarchy, we anticipate the senior executives will be under increasing pressure to be closely aligned—in terms of systems, structure, processes, compensation, and employee welfare—with the traditional offline business.

## Identifying the Key Levers of Competitive Advantage

Consistent with the idea that the senior leader needs to anticipate changing consumer and technology trends, the executive must also realign the resource system of the firm in advance of these trends. Stated differently, the key levers of competitive advantage are also likely to evolve as the market evolves. The best senior leaders are able to reallocate their resources and capabilities in anticipation of an evolving competitive landscape.

## OVERVIEW OF THE BOOK

As noted before, this book reflects our framework for understanding e-commerce. We will now discuss each chapter as a reflection of the overall "five box" framework of the book—strategy decisions at the core, with the four infrastructures influencing those decisions. We begin with a discussion of basic Internet technology. With this foundation in mind, we turn to an overview of the strategy formulation and execution process. This process is applied to MarketWatch.com throughout the strategy section. In addition to our secondary research, we interviewed key executives of MarketWatch.com. We then turn to the four key infrastructures: technology, capital, media, and public policy. Below are brief previews of each chapter.

# The Basic Technology of the Internet and Web

In order to provide both the novice and expert reader with an understanding of technology infrastructure, we divide this section into two parts. The first part focuses on the basics of Internet hardware and software—specifically, how the Internet and the Web work.

### Chapter 2—Introduction to the Web and Internet.
We give a basic history of the Internet and its underlying technology to provide a framework for the later chapters on technology. This chapter explains basic technological concepts, including webpages, hyperlinks, and protocols. Webpages are documents whose content (which can include text, images, and multimedia) is most often written in a text-based language called Hypertext Markup Language (HTML). Using hyperlinks, webpages connect to other related webpages to form a website and can also be connected to any other page in the world. Web browsers are programs that interpret the HTML on the webpage and display it in a form that is most suitable for the device on which the browser is running. Worldwide acceptance of standards such as HTML and Transmission Control Protocol/Internet Protocol (TCP/IP) have helped fuel the explosive growth of the Internet by making the creation and consumption of Internet content inexpensive and easy.

### Chapter 3—The Basics of Doing Business on the Internet.
Selling on the Internet requires several capabilities above and beyond page-creation skills. To succeed, Web merchants must manage the same issues that traditional bricks-and-mortar businesses have dealt with for decades. They need to know how to handle the inflow and outflow of products, how to choose the proper site for their store, and how to manage the security of their businesses. In addition, they must manage payment processing, selection of products, communications and branding, and the development of effective storefront designs to maximize sales. Finally, Web merchants, like their competitors in the bricks-and-mortar world, need to service their customers before, during, and after the sale to ensure customer satisfaction and loyalty. All of these offline business issues, along with issues specific to online commerce, must be dealt with effectively for an e-commerce store to succeed.

# Strategy Formulation for Online Firms

### Chapter 4—Framing the Market Opportunity.
In this chapter, we revisit the business basics to construct an original new-economy approach to formulating business strategy. In doing so, we focus on the players. Who makes up the dynamics of any business—customers, competitors, and strategic partners? The goal is to understand what market analysis becomes in this new world and to introduce a process not only to understand the market but also to identify those unserved or underserved portions of the market. This chapter identifies five conditions that must be carefully analyzed to determine if there is a market opportunity.

### Chapter 5—Business Models.
While some believe that many Internet businesses do not need business models, we strongly disagree. There may be poorly articulated models out there, but business-model definition is essential to competition in this new space. We introduce the four components of the Marketspace Business Model. They are: (1) the value proposition or cluster, (2) the product offering, which we call a "marketspace" offering, (3) the resource system that the firm selects to deliver

the offering, and (4) a financial model that enables the business to generate revenues, cash flows, and ultimately, profit margins or valuation potential. These four choices constitute the foundation of the strategy decisions that we explore throughout the book.

### Chapter 6—The Customer Interface.

The visible presence of most e-commerce businesses is a digital- or rich-media interface. While networked-economy businesses may make substantial use of traditional offline interfaces—retail points of sale, printed catalogs, stand-alone kiosks, or call centers—they rely primarily on a virtual storefront connected to the Internet. In this chapter, we develop the set of design tools and elements that we refer to as the 7Cs of the customer interface: content, context, community, commerce, customization, communications, and connection. In particular, we focus on the levers management can use to create a competitive advantage and generate customer value through these essential elements of interface design.

### Chapter 7—Communications and Branding.

In the demand-oriented world of the new economy, there is nothing more valuable than "mind share," or the ability to attract and hold the attention of markets and customers. The traditional tools of attention management are marketing communications. In this chapter, we explore the variety of traditional and new-media communications approaches that provide competitive advantages to networked-economy businesses, and we delve into the extraordinary power of brands in this new information-enabled world. Many believed that the Web would create a world of downward price pressures and rapid commoditization of goods and services of all kinds. As we will explain, the opposite has occurred. Brands are more important than ever—and some would argue that, at least in business-to-consumer ventures, they are essential to success.

### Chapter 8—Implementation.

If strategy is about "what to do," implementation is about "how to do it." In most management texts focused on strategy, implementation is left to the last chapters. Indeed, in management literature, implementation has become a poor cousin to fashion-forward fields such as strategy, marketing, and finance. Doing business in the networked economy demands a different approach. Because such businesses operate in constant dynamic dialogue with their markets, it is difficult—and unproductive—to approach strategy and implementation in a linear, sequential fashion. Rather, they are two elements in a real-time cycle, wherein each set of decisions pertaining to strategy and implementation must constantly be reevaluated based on new data from the other. In this chapter we consider both the "delivery system" and innovation components of strategy implementation.

### Chapter 9—Metrics.

The dynamic relationship between strategy and market feedback demands new approaches to measurement and evaluation of business results. We know that e-commerce businesses offer unprecedented opportunities for capturing information on how markets operate and how customers engage in search and shopping behavior. Because this kind of data is available in rich granular forms and, as importantly, in real time, we introduce a new management tool called the Performance Dashboard. It is a set of metrics that reflect both the early warning indicators of the progress of an e-commerce strategy, as well as outcome measures such as customer satisfaction and financial performance.

# Technology Infrastructure

In the second part of our technology infrastructure discussion, we turn to the B2B marketplaces to discuss the more complex technology-associated collaborative commerce. We conclude with a discussion of the evolution of these critical technologies.

### Chapter 10—The Emergence and Growth of B2B Marketplaces.
This chapter covers the key technologies that provide the foundation for B2B marketplaces. The chapter is organized in two broad sections: MRO procurement and Net marketplaces. With respect to MRO procurement, the chapter covers the technology components, including multi-supplier catalog management, approval workflow, and supplier integration. In the domain of Net marketplaces, we cover alternative types of marketplaces, including vertical versus horizontal, focus of value creation (buyer, seller, neutral), and public versus private marketplaces. Four alternative technology approaches are considered, including building from scratch, all-encompassing solutions, point solutions, and outsourced marketplaces. Regardless of approach, four technology areas need to be addressed: commerce, content, community, and third-party service suppliers.

### Chapter 11—Collaborative Commerce.
This chapter discusses how collaborative commerce unfolds in the marketplace, with a particular emphasis on supply-chain and demand-chain management. All organizations must engage in several basic activities, including product designing, planning, sourcing materials, selling, making, fulfilling, and servicing functions. In order to run an effective online organization, software and applications related to each of these functions need to be designed and implemented. Consider, for example, the design phase: An organization needs to make choices related to engineering and product development (new product introductions, engineering change management) and project management (engineer-to-order, collaborative planning and execution). For each of these seven key functions, we discuss the relative software and applications that the collaborative enterprise must consider in the design of its technology infrastructure.

# Capital Infrastructure

This two-chapter section is a primer on what we term the capital infrastructure of the networked economy. It is designed to give the student an understanding of how a startup can obtain capital, focusing primarily on the types of capital most online companies pursue—venture capital and angel financing.

### Chapter 12—Early Stage Business Development: Human and Financial Capital.
While a business may have the best idea or new technology, getting capital—both human and financial—is critical. Choosing the right management team and writing an effective business plan are often the most important—and overlooked—elements in getting a company off the ground. In this chapter, we explore the relationship between human and financial capital, namely, the elements of a business plan, the roles and responsibilities of an entrepreneur, articulating the idea, and forming the management team. We also discuss different sources of financing.

### Chapter 13—Working with Funders: From Seed Stage to Liquidity.
Once a startup has its business plan and management team together, it is ready to look for financing. This chapter goes into greater depth on the sources of funding and how to choose

the right mix for a startup. It describes the various stages of funding, with emphasis on the beginning and liquidity stages (including explanations of the IPO process and mergers and acquisitions). Also discussed are the various methods of valuation and how the negotiation process works. The chapter ends with a discussion of where the capital market is heading.

## Media Infrastructure

In this section we discuss the evolution of each media and the convergence of media on the Internet (Chapter 14). We also discuss the evolution of rich-media interfaces—and project several interesting developments in this cross-industry evolution (Chapter 15).

**Chapter 14—Media Transformation.** This chapter discusses the transformation of media over the past three decades, from analog to digital platforms. Among the key issues are the increased fragmentation of media usage among consumers and the resulting megamergers of the past decade, such as the AOL-Time Warner, Viacom-CBS, and Disney-ABC/Capital Cities deals, in which the ultimate goal was to maximize the use of similar content across multiple media platforms. Case examples of media convergence—ABCNews.com, Sony PlayStation 2, MSNBC, and Time-CNN-Netscape—will be discussed, along with the economics of various media, including newspapers, television, and radio.

**Chapter 15—The Future of Media Usage.** In this chapter, we preview the future of media usage. With continued media fragmentation expected—especially with the increased usage of new applications such as broadband, video-game players, and handheld computers—several possible scenarios emerge. What will the world be like with the increased usage of smart phones and handhelds? Will video-game players replace home computers as the primary way for consumers to access media? How will increased use of broadband impact consumer demand for content-based products? The scenarios are endless, but this chapter provides a beginning point for a lively discussion about the future of the media.

## Public Policy Infrastructure

In this two-chapter section, we introduce and discuss some of the most important regulatory and societal issues confronting firms in this space.

**Chapter 16—Regulation.** In this chapter, we explore how the government is currently regulating the Internet and what it may regulate in the future. We discuss self-regulation versus government regulation and how the Internet's new technology and lack of boundaries have created regulatory challenges. We explore issues such as privacy, free speech, intellectual property, and gambling and determine how the laws and regulations currently governing these issues will affect e-commerce and Internet businesses.

**Chapter 17—Internet and Society.** We explore how the Internet is changing society, and how society is changing the Internet. With issues such as community, education, e-government, and the "digital divide," the Internet is changing how people communicate, seek information, shop, and even how they interact with the government. These changes have implications for society, but also for the e-commerce businesses working within this new society.

# SUMMARY

**1. What are the categories of e-commerce?**

Four distinct categories of electronic commerce can be identified: business-to-business, business-to-consumer, consumer-to-consumer (peer-to-peer), and consumer-to-business.

Business-to-business refers to the full spectrum of e-commerce that can occur between two organizations. Many of the same activities that occur in business-to-business also occur in the business-to-consumer context, except transactions that relate to the "back office" of the customer are often not tracked electronically. Consumer-to-consumer activities include auction-exchanges, classified ads, games, bulletin boards, instant-messaging services, and personal services. In a consumer-to-business relationship, consumers can band together to form buyer groups.

**2. What are the new views of strategy in the new—or networked—economy?**

Several new views have emerged, changing the classical strategic planning process. Sense and respond offers an approach that is intuitive, actionable, and easy to implement. It also makes companies listen in a new manner to customers. The sense and respond approach makes companies reactive to consumer opinion, though, instead of proactive in trying to change the market.

The simple-rules approach stresses that an organization should focus on simple rules instead of complex strategy planning. It creates a battlefield mentality that causes the company to recognize pattern behavior and respond quickly, instead of developing grand strategies that are pushed into the marketplace.

**3. What is the framework for the field of e-commerce?**

E-commerce does not consist only of the businesses themselves. While business strategy (market opportunity, business models, customer interface, market communications and branding, implementation, and metrics) is at the core of e-commerce, technology, capital, media, and public policy infrastructures all affect it. Technology consists of the hardware and software upon which the Internet is built; finding the right source and amount of capital—both human and financial—affects whether or not the business can become, or stay, a business; media affects opportunities and constraints placed on a company; and government regulations affect what a company can and cannot do. Exhibit 1-3 illustrates how, in the field of e-commerce, strategy is influenced by the infrastructures.

**4. Why does a senior manager need to know all four infrastructures?**

A senior manager needs to know all four infrastructures because they will affect the strategy he chooses for his firm. Bertelsmann is a good example of a company whose managers would greatly benefit from understanding all four infrastructures. Knowledge of the technology infrastructure is important in understanding issues such as streaming versus downloadable files and how BMG can leverage Napster's software to its own benefit. A manager must understand the capital infrastructure in order to make decisions about BMG's business plan in the file-swapping era and how the music group should be valued. He must also understand the media infrastructure in order to figure out how best to leverage Bertelsmann's media empire on the Internet. Finally, he must understand public policy issues in order to understand issues such as the regulation of copyright, patents, and trademarks on the Internet.

### 5. What are the roles and responsibilities of senior e-commerce managers?

Senior e-commerce managers have many roles and responsibilities. They must act quickly and with authority to make strategic decisions; they must understand the traditional disciplines associated with offline managing such as marketing, finance, logistics, and accounting. Senior managers must also have an understanding of technology and media. Finally, they must understand the role of mass communications to be able to make the best choices in terms of media integration.

### 6. What are the key challenges of senior leaders today?

The key challenges include understanding customer evolution, charting changing technology, balancing irrational exuberance and irrational doom, integrating offline and online activities, and identifying the key levers of competitive advantage.

## KEY TERMS

| | |
|---|---|
| e-commerce | customization |
| business-to-business | interactivity |
| business-to-consumer | technology infrastructure |
| consumer-to-consumer | capital infrastructure |
| consumer-to-business | media infrastructure |
| sense and respond | public policy infrastructure |
| simple rules | |

## Endnotes

[1]Kosiur, David. *Understanding Electronic Commerce* (Washington: Microsoft Press,1997).

[2]Bradley, Stephen, and Richard Nolan. *Sense and Respond* (Cambridge, MA: Harvard Business School Press, 1998).

[3]Ibid.

[4]Eisenhardt, Kathleen, and Donald N. Sull. "Strategy as Simple Rules," *Harvard Business Review* January 2001, 107–116.

[5]Mintzberg, Henry, "Patterns in Strategy Formulation," *Management Science* (24), 1978, 934–948.

# Introduction to the Web and Internet

This chapter provides a basic history of the Internet and the underlying technology that enables it. The discussion begins with a brief section about why the so-called new economy that we are currently experiencing may not be so new after all. We continue with a history of the development of network technology, then dive into a discussion of the basic technology that powers the Internet, including TCP/IP, routing, and packet switching. The remaining sections focus on the World Wide Web: How Web documents are created, what webpages can contain, and the importance of hypertext documents. Finally, we examine some of the key drivers of the Web's explosive growth over the last few years.

## QUESTIONS

*Please consider the following questions as you read this chapter:*

1. What is the Internet?

2. What are the characteristics of the Internet that make it work?

3. What are the content types on the Web?

4. How are websites created?

5. What is behind the growth of the Web and Internet?

This chapter was coauthored by Bernie Jaworski, Jeffrey Rayport, Eugene Wang, Joseph Hartzell, and Colin Gounden.

# THE *NEW* NEW ECONOMY

Welcome to the *new* new economy. Every so often, a communications medium emerges that captures the public's imagination and inspires widespread excitement. Soon to follow is speculation that this new technology might signal the birth of new revenue models, new ways of life—even a new economy. The telegraph, radio, television, and, most recently, the Internet are all examples of technologies that have changed the ways in which people communicate and have gained the attention of investors and businesspeople around the globe.

## The Original WWW[1]

Before diving into today's Internet fervor, let us examine the original WWW: "World Wide Wireless," RCA's[2] early descriptor for radio technology. The development of radio technology and radio applications is particularly instructive in understanding the development of the Internet. Like the Internet, radio began as a communications medium; it generated an onslaught of excitement during the 1920s, as entrepreneurs and investors scrambled to find feasible ways to build businesses and generate revenue around this new technology. However, it took years for a viable revenue model to emerge. In addition, many of the revenue models that

**Exhibit 2-1** INTERNET ADOPTION RATES VERSUS OTHER MEDIA

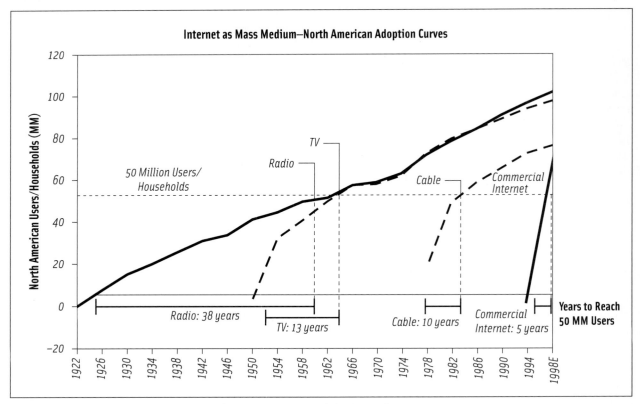

*Launch of HBO in 1976 used to estimate the beginning of cable as an entertainment/advertising medium

prevailed were powered by applications of the technology unanticipated by the inventors. Such uncertainty played a large role in the excitement that surrounded radio. The same excitement surrounds the Internet today.

Radio began as a point-to-point communications medium. It was originally viewed by the public as a wireless alternative to the popular mediums of the time—namely, the telegraph and telephone. The major difference between those mediums and the radio was the issue of ownership. The public was clear on who controlled or owned telephone and telegraph lines; the question of who owned the less-tangible radio airwaves was less apparent. At the time, it was not at all clear how, or even if, corporations could own or manage radio. Many hoped the radio would prove itself a decentralized communications technology that was truly democratic, a technology that individuals could control and use whenever they pleased, without corporate fees or tolls; many hold the same hope for the Internet.[3]

## Rise of Regulation and Corporations

Radio remained largely unregulated in the United States until the 1910s, when the *Titanic* disaster caused the government to think about the implications of uncontrolled airwaves. The sinking of the *Titanic* in the North Atlantic the morning of April 15, 1912, caused a public backlash against the way radio communications were handled at sea. At the time of the disaster, round-the-clock radio operation aboard ships was not required. Though there was a ship close enough to the *Titanic* to rescue its passengers, no one aboard the *Californian* was manning the radio when the *Titanic* issued its distress calls. In addition, radio signals sent to the mainland reporting the status of the *Titanic* were for the most part either inaccurate or undecipherable. There were no regulations restricting any radio operators, valid or not, from transmitting signals about the status of the *Titanic*; as a result, a large number of transmissions were issued simultaneously, leaving many of them jumbled. When the U.S. and British press discovered that many of the messages sent to the mainland were false, public opinion turned quickly against unregulated radio.

During World War I the U.S. Navy commandeered the sole rights to virtually all airwaves, with little room left for private or corporate use. However, after the war, the issue of radio ownership remained unresolved. A government-regulated monopoly did not appeal to the public, nor did foreign ownership of radio, given the recent war. In 1919, RCA was incorporated to become the sole legitimate provider of radio reception equipment, taking over the British-owned American Marconi radio company, among others. Radio had gone corporate.

## Early Revenue Models

Radio's original revenue model was reflective of radio's early use. Known originally as wireless telegraphy or wireless telephony, radio's early market was primarily point-to-point wireless messaging. Wireless soon became a profitable and growing market for RCA. This success was based on a well-understood business model—the pay-for-service model—that allowed radio to compete directly with competing communications mediums (namely, the telegraph). Radio's competitive advantage was well understood; high-powered radio facilities were an inexpensive means of global communications. As a result, RCA was able to undercut the price of wire-based telegraph messages by approximately 30 percent, thereby securing a profitable position in the wireless messaging market. By 1921, transoceanic communication revenues had reached $2.1 million. However, this represented only the tip of the iceberg for the radio market that was about to emerge.

## Enormous Demand and Revenue Uncertainty

A fundamental change in the radio market occurred in 1922, when radio shifted from a point-to-point communications tool to a widespread broadcast medium. (The early 1990s witnessed a similar change in the Internet with the emergence of the World Wide Web.) Demand for radio broadcasting surged; the mere presence of a radio broadcasting station in a town caused a rush to buy radio sets. However, despite this demand, broadcasting stations and companies could not figure out how to generate revenue from their broadcast content.

At first, broadcast revenue did not matter. Revenue generated from radio unit sales dwarfed all other radio-related revenues during the 1920s as radio broadcast stations were set up all across the country, and consumers flocked to buy radio sets. By the end of 1922, the first real year of broadcasting, there were 576 broadcasting stations in the United States. From 1922 through 1926, anyone who wanted to enter the radio broadcasting market could do so. Consumers were enchanted by broadcast radio, and corporations and entrepreneurs were delighted by the radio-driven new economy.

## Revenue Matters

Even when radio-set sales began to slow down, the number of market players continued to increase; shakeouts and a reevaluation of revenue models soon followed. During the early 1920s, all 48 states in the U.S. had at least one radio station. Of the 48 radio stations that were first to broadcast in their respective states, 27 were out of business by 1925 (see Exhibit 2-2).

RADIO STATIONS OPENED AND CLOSED, 1921-24

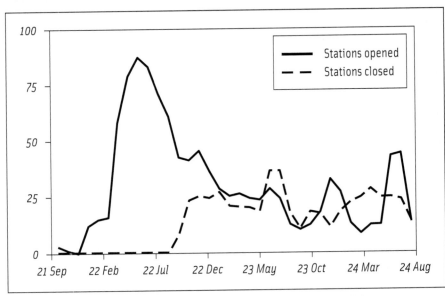

Source: Hanson, Ward. "The Original WWW: Web Lessons from the Early Days of Radio." 7/15/96.

In this new environment, entrepreneurs were faced with the task of devising ways to profit directly from radio broadcasts (excluding radio-set sales). As radio shifted from a point-to-point communications medium to a broadcast medium, pay-per-use service agreements became impractical. Consumers were simply not willing to pay for broadcast content, and so radio corporations had to figure out how to profit indirectly from the content they provided. Revenue models and ideas popped up everywhere—programming subsidies from radio-set sales, generalized goodwill from corporate sponsors, radio taxes, and advertising were popular revenue sources under consideration. The last one, advertising, proved to be the prevailing business model.

If the story of the emergence of a radio-driven new economy sounds familiar, it should. We are currently experiencing a similar revolution, only this time it is driven by the emergence and development of the Internet. We are experiencing the creation of another new economy. Once again investors and entrepreneurs are ardently searching for the next big thing, and young companies are fighting to prove new revenue models, even while many of their competitors are failing.

The remaining sections of this chapter will help you understand how the Internet works. Such knowledge will allow you to formulate ideas and create business plans that might enable you to help define the Internet's rendition of a new economy.

# WHAT IS THE INTERNET?[4]

## Early Networks

The Internet's beginnings can be traced back to a series of memos written in 1962 by MIT's Joseph Carl Robnett Licklider outlining what he called the "Galactic Network" concept. Licklider envisioned a global network through which everyone could share and access data and programs. Shortly after writing the memos, he became the head of computer research at the Defense Advanced Research Projects Agency, later referred to as ARPA. ARPA would play a large role in spearheading and funding the Internet's early development.

Over the next decade, great advances were made in network technology, specifically in packet switching and the beginnings of what would eventually become TCP/IP, the basic protocol that defines how information is exchanged over the Internet. By the late 1970s, network computing began to flourish. Several computer manufacturers introduced minicomputers with enough computational power to support multiple users. As these minicomputers became less expensive, they began to populate businesses and organizations to a point where most departments in a large organization had at least one. To connect these computers together and permit the transfer of information between them, many organizations began installing **local area networks (LAN)**. Also by the late 1970s, ARPA had several operational computer networks and had begun to introduce the technology to the military. However, LAN technology was limited by geographical distance: It could only connect computers and networks that spanned a few square kilometers or less. To allow computers and networks separated by larger geographical distances to communicate, ARPA developed a **wide area network (WAN)** called the ARPANET. WAN technology allowed engineers to build networks to connect computers and LANs separated by large geographical distances. Unlike LAN technology, a WAN contains an additional set of special-purpose computers that keep communication independent of the computers that use that WAN.

**Exhibit 2-3**    WIDE AREA NETWORKS AND LOCAL AREA NETWORKS

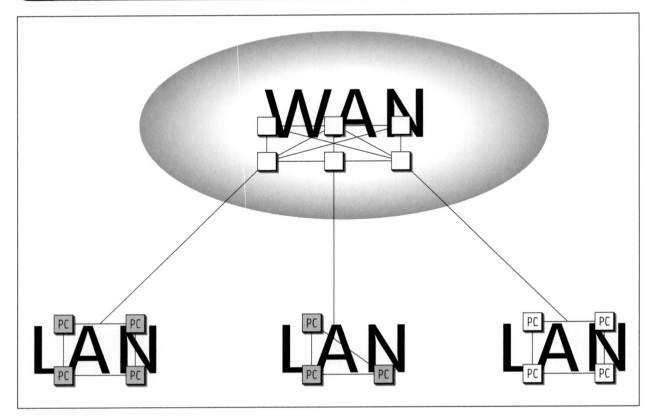

With the rapid proliferation of computer networks, LANs, and WANs, ARPA realized that the military and organizations that employed multiple networks would soon face a problem: Each network connected a set of computers, but the individual networks had no way of communicating with one another; each computer manufacturer built hardware that would read a certain type of software or that could only communicate with hardware from the same manufacturer—computers built by different manufacturers could not connect with one another. As a result, computer networks of that time formed isolated islands, with no paths existing between them.

## Compatibility

With that in mind, ARPA researched how to interconnect all computers in a large organization regardless of who the manufacturer was or what type of software the LAN connecting the computers was running. The technology that resulted was a new approach to connecting computer networks known as internetworking. The Internet that we know today is named after this technology.

Computer software forms an important part of the technology that enables internetworking. Many pieces of software enable internetworking; however, the two most well-known pieces of internetworking software are the **Internet Protocol (IP)**

and the **Transmission Control Protocol (TCP).** The IP software sets the rules for data transfer over a network, while the TCP software ensures the safe and reliable transfer of the data. Together these components are referred to as TCP/IP. Because these two components are the best known internetworking software, the abbreviation TCP/IP is commonly used to represent the whole suite of internetworking software.

## Open System

To encourage the adoption of a standard network communications protocol, ARPA decided to publish its research results and make public the internetworking technology it developed. Such a decision was shocking at the time because most corporations carefully guarded their internetworking technologies; they believed that by keeping their technologies proprietary, they could achieve maximum profitability. They also reasoned that keeping their technologies private ensured that no technologies or hardware of competing firms would be able to integrate with their hardware and infiltrate their customer base.

Despite efforts to sell closed systems, customers persisted in purchasing several brands of computers. As a result, not all software worked on all computers, and large organizations typically needed to purchase different brands of computers to serve a variety of purposes. Additionally, incompatible network technologies often made it very difficult for departments within a large organization to communicate with each other.

However, with the open system nature of TCP/IP development, software developers and computer companies could more easily build TCP/IP-compliant software and hardware. TCP/IP soon became the standard network protocol. This standard would enable compatibility between different computers with different software packages. The TCP/IP standard laid the groundwork that enabled the deep internetworking that makes the Internet possible.

## HOW THE INTERNET WORKS

Several characteristics of Licklider's original vision of a Galactic Network were important in creating such a network of shared access and data. These pieces include:

- Unique identification of each computer on the network
- Human-friendly addressing
- Packet switching
- Routing
- Reliability
- Standardization

## Identification

Although the Internet seems like a single, giant network to which many computers attach, it is not. The Internet is a consortium of networks; it is a network of millions of computers and thousands of networks intertwined together. Wide area networks allow the Internet to overcome physical boundaries by providing efficient long-distance technology that can connect many sites. Often the term **backbone network** is used to describe a major WAN to which other networks attach. The backbone reaches some, but not all, sites; these locations are called **backbone sites**. In fact the building blocks of the Internet are often described as a collection of WAN backbones connected to LANs that, in turn, connect to individual computers.

With so many computers on the Internet, it is important that each computer be uniquely identified. Each computer connected to the Internet is assigned an Internet Protocol address. An IP address, when represented in an application, is expressed by four groups of numbers separated by decimal points. For example: 198.108.95.145.

IP addresses function just like the Internet addresses we are accustomed to seeing. For example, the IP address for *http://www.philanthropy.com* is 198.108.95.145.

## Addressing and Domain Name System (DNS)

However, early network engineers soon realized that it was difficult to remember numeric addresses when they wanted to get in touch with someone or with a certain computer. Additionally, numeric IP addresses sometimes change, so even if one were able to remember the numbers, it would be nearly impossible to keep up with every change to that numeric IP address.

To remedy this situation, Sun Microsystems developed the Domain Name System (DNS) in the early 1980s as an easier way to keep track of addresses. The DNS gives each computer on the Internet an address comprised of easily recognizable letters and words, instead of a numeric IP address. For example, the DNS address *http://www.philanthropy.com* is much easier to remember than the IP address *http://198.108.95.145*, and the same site appears if either the DNS address or the IP address are used.

The rightmost portion of the DNS address is known as the **top-level domain**. The top-level domain characters refer to the nature of the organization that uses that particular address. Common top-level domains include: .com for commercial, .org for organization, .edu for education, .mil for military, .gov for government, and .net for network. Other top-level domain standards pending at the time of this writing include: .biz, .aero, .coop, .info, .museum, .pro, and .name.

For computers located outside of the United States, there exists an additional country domain that appears to the right of the top-level domain. Countries are identified with two letters; for example, .uk represents the United Kingdom, .au represents Australia, and .cn represents China. The address *http://www.amazon.co.uk* points to Amazon's U.K. site.

## Packet Switching

Licklider's Galactic Network would also require an efficient way to transfer large amounts of data across a large and complicated network. Engineers realized early on that smaller pieces of data would be far easier to transfer. As a result, early engineers developed what is called the Internet Protocol. Every computer connected to the Internet must run IP software and follow the rules of the IP, which specify exactly how a computer is to communicate with other computers—including how large data files are to be broken up into smaller, more manageable data files, or **packets**. The IP defines exactly how a packet must be formed.

In addition to breaking down large files into smaller packets, the Galactic Network notion would require a system for sharing the limited resources of a network. Before the development of network technology, computer engineers realized that if only one data transfer can occur on a given wire at a given time, then multiple devices that share the same wire must take turns using the wire.

Early telephone networks exemplify this point. Like early computer networks, these networks were **circuit-switched networks**—networks in which only one data transfer can occur at a given time. In early telephone networks all the subscribers in a given neighborhood shared the same telephone line. If two neighbors were having a telephone conversation with one another, a third neighbor would be unable to use the telephone. The third neighbor would have to wait until the conversation was over before placing a call, as the shared telephone line would only accommodate one conversation at a time. The same applies for computers connected to a circuit-switched network.

This problem is compounded when the data being transferred is of varying size. Exhibit 2-4 presents a network of 10 computers that all share the same transmission line. Computer 1 wants to transfer a large amount of data to 7, while 4 wants to transfer a very small amount of data to 6. Although the data transfer from 4 to 6 is much smaller than the transfer from 1 to 7, 6 must wait until 1 has transferred all of its data to 7 before 6 can begin receiving data from 4.

To remedy the delays associated with unequally sized data transfers, computer engineers developed **packet switching**, which has become the fundamental technique that computer networks use to ensure fair access to shared network resources. Instead of transferring files in their entirety, whole files are broken up into data packets before being transferred over a network. In this way the simultaneous transfer of a large file does not delay the transfer of a smaller file.

For example, similar to Exhibit 2-4, Exhibit 2-5 presents a network of 10 computers that all share the same transmission line. Computer 1 still wants to transfer a large amount of data to 7, and 4 still wants to transfer a small amount of data to 6. In Exhibit 2-4, 6 was forced to wait until the transfer from 1 to 7 was complete before it could receive any data. However, the network in Exhibit 2-5 employs packet switching. Internet Protocol defines how computers are to divide data into

## Exhibit 2-4 CIRCUIT-SWITCHED NETWORK

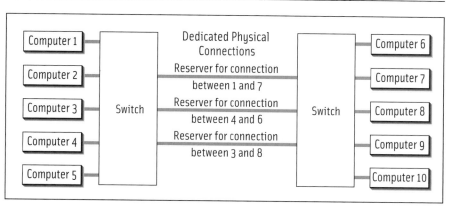

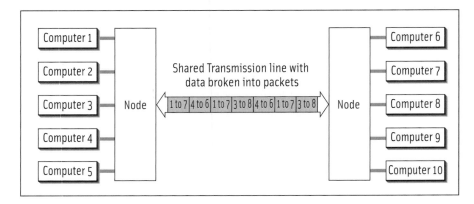

**Exhibit 2-5** PACKET-SWITCHING NETWORK

smaller packets. Because 1 wants to send a large amount of data to 7, IP mandates that computer 1 divide its data into many smaller packets. Since 4 wants to transfer a smaller amount of data, 4 can send its data in a single packet or divide it into a small number of packets. Computers 1 and 4 then take turns sending the respective data packets. Packet switching is a more equitable method of transferring data, since it allows 4 to complete its smaller data transfer without having to wait for 1 to complete its large data transfer.

Like most computer networks, the Internet is a packet-switching system. All data transferred across the Internet is done so in packets. Packet switching allows many communications to occur simultaneously, without requiring an application to wait for all other communications to finish.

# Routing

Another key piece to bringing the Galactic Network notion to fruition was figuring out how to efficiently route the Internet packets to the appropriate destinations within an environment comprised of many different networks. A key piece to inter-networking technology is the **router**. The thousands of computer networks that make up the Internet are interconnected by dedicated, special-purpose computers called routers. Routers serve as intermediaries between networks; that is, routers direct traffic and translate messages so that different network technologies can communicate with one another. It is for this reason that routers are often referred to as the building blocks of the Internet.

# Reliability and Transmission Control Protocol (TCP)

Another important technology that enabled the Internet is Transmission Control Protocol (TCP). In addition to IP software, most computers also run TCP software. While IP software handles packet deliveries, TCP software ensures safe delivery of

**Exhibit 2-6** ROUTERS

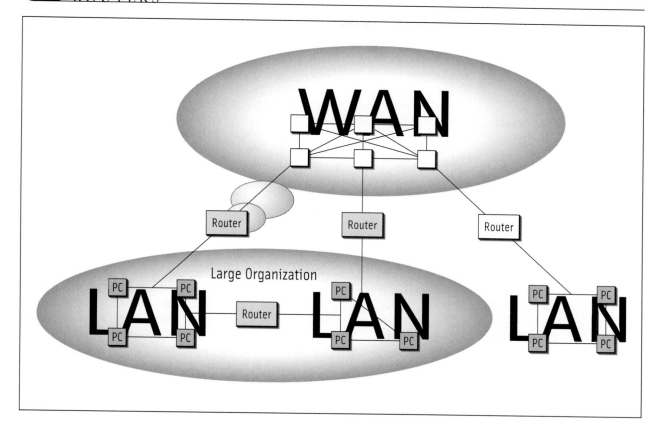

the packets. Realizing that networks are not always fully functional 100 percent of the time or 100 percent error free, network engineers developed a system of checks and balances. TCP is software that enables reliable, error-free communication over the Internet.

Often, routers will route too many packets to a network, so that the network is unable to accommodate and process all of the data. When this occurs the network is forced to discard some of the packets. Without TCP these discarded packets would be lost and would never reach their intended destination.

For example, TCP prevents the loss of packets by requiring that the destination for each packet send a confirmation message once the packet is received. If this message is not received, then the TCP retransmits the packet. In addition, the TCP puts incoming packets in the correct order. Different packets from the same original message may take many different paths to their final destination. Some paths may be shorter, some may be longer; as a result, packets do not always arrive at their final destination in the order they were sent. TCP automatically checks the packets upon arrival and puts them in the correct order. Finally, because network hardware failure sometimes results in duplicate packets, TCP automatically checks for duplicate packets and accepts only the first copy that arrives.

## TCP Retransmission Is Dynamic

To ensure the safe delivery of packets, TCP requests that the destination computer send a confirmation message for every packet received. If the TCP does not receive the message within a certain amount of time, then the TCP automatically resends the packet. One could imagine, however, that if this TCP timer were static, the Internet would slow down or be prone to constant data transmission error.

For example, packets do not always travel the same route or distance to their final destination. As a result, the delivery times for packets vary greatly. If the TCP timer were static, the packets that take a longer time to deliver may cause the timer to expire, triggering the retransmission of duplicate packets. In addition, with a static timer, lost packets whose destinations are close by would experience a delay in retransmission.

TCP does not encounter these problems because it adapts to maximize its efficiency everywhere on the Internet. For example, if the destination computer resides near the sender, TCP will allow only a short delay for receiving a confirmation message before resending the data packet. However, if the destination computer resides far away from the sender, TCP will allow a longer delay for receiving confirmation that the data packet has been received.

In addition, if the Internet is trafficking a lot of data and slows down as a result, TCP automatically lengthens the retransmission timer; if conditions change and packets begin traveling across the Internet more quickly, TCP automatically shortens the timer. TCP's ability to automatically adjust time-out values has contributed greatly to the success of the Internet. Without TCP's ability to adapt to changing Internet conditions, the Internet could not support the diverse network hardware and applications that it does today.

## Standardization

None of the technologies previously described would help enable the Internet if they were incompatible with one another. For this reason, standardization of network technology and communications protocols is a crucial aspect of making the Internet work.

Network technologies are not inherently compatible. Before the development of internetworking technology, an organization with networks had two options. One option was to choose and mandate one set of network technologies that would satisfy the entire organization. While this alternative would enable communication

## UDP (User Datagram Protocol)

UDP is an alternative to TCP that sacrifices quality for speed. UDP provides non-guaranteed packet delivery; that is, unlike TCP, UDP does not check for lost packets. As a result, UDP transmissions, though less reliable, are generally faster than TCP transmissions.

Many streaming media types, such as RealPlayer, use UDP because it is fast (important for video) and does not need to guarantee quality (small gaps are less noticeable in full-motion video).

between all networks and computers within the organization, it also brought with it many negative trade-offs, such as inflexibility and increased functional and switching costs.

The other option was to allow groups within the organization to choose the network technology that best suited them, without regard to compatibility issues. While this option did give organizations more flexibility in negotiating and purchasing network hardware and applications, there was a downside: More often than not, computer networks within the same organization would be unable to communicate with one another. The development of internetworking technology eliminated this negative trade-off.

The open-system development of TCP/IP not only helped to establish TCP/IP as the Internet standard, but also played a key role in the rapid development and success of the Internet. The global acceptance of TCP/IP helped to ensure compatible communication between diverse hardware. This universal compatibility allows the Internet to function like one single network, even though the Internet is actually a collage of many networks. Without the TCP/IP standard, the Internet could not function as it does today.

# INTRODUCTION TO THE WEB[5]

Every day the World Wide Web (aka WWW, W3, or simply "the Web") is used by millions of people connected to thousands of computers all over the world. The explosive growth in the popularity of the Web has much to do with the fact that it is made up of very simple standardized components that are accepted by content creators and consumers worldwide. The entire Web is built upon just three primary concepts: **webpages**, which are the documents that a user sees when he opens up his browser (Netscape Navigator or Microsoft Internet Explorer, for example); **links** that connect these webpages to one another; and **servers** that store and transmit the information to the browsers for display. A website consists of a series of linked webpages that can be found under the same **Web address** or **URL**, such as *www.yahoo.com* (for more information on URLs, see the "Behind the Scenes" section later in this chapter).

## Hypertext Documents Vs. Paper

This ability to link pages together makes webpages fundamentally different from standard paper-based documents. Unlike paper documents, hypertext documents do not have to conform to a rigid serial structure. For example, if a reader consults a paper-based encyclopedia for information about lions, she is confined by the author's knowledge and document structure when researching this subject. Hypertext, on the other hand, puts the reader in control of her interaction with the document. The reader may be able to click on various words in the document to get definitions, click on a photo of a lion to hear it roar, or click on the lion's habitat and be taken to a website about Africa. In addition, hypertext lets users jump around inside of a document with no regard for page order, which can make documents more confusing as well. Hypertext documents have changed the way people think about how to create and share information because they allow content authors and readers to interact with one another in entirely new ways. This flexibility can also be a source of frustration for site creators, since it is hard to anticipate how users will navigate through the site they are constructing.

# What Is the Difference Between the Web and the Internet?

A common misnomer is that the Internet and World Wide Web are the same thing. The terms Internet, World Wide Web, "Net," and "Web" are often used interchangeably. However, from a technical perspective, the Internet and World Wide Web are not one in the same.

The Internet is a collection of wires, protocols, and hardware that allows the electronic transmission of data over TCP/IP. Any data can be transferred over this collection of hardware and software components. Examples might include e-mail, faxes, video, voice, and webpages. The Internet is the hardware and software infrastructure that allows for this data transfer and global networking.

The World Wide Web exists on the Internet. The Web is comprised of hypertext pages viewed by a browser, which are served from a Web server over TCP/IP. Webpages always begin with http:// or https:// signifying that the content being viewed is hypertext and transferred using the Hypertext Transfer Protocol. Examples of the Web are webpages that we come across everyday, including, *http://www.yahoo.com, http://www.amazon.com,* and *http://www.ebay.com.*

So while the Internet is the infrastructure, the Web can be thought of as an application for the Internet. It is important to note that there are other types of applications that use the Internet but are not part of the Web. For example, e-mail, file transfer protocol (FTP), and peer-to-peer applications such as Napster use the Internet, but not the Web.

## What Webpages Are Made Of

Like the Web itself, a webpage is made of relatively simple components. In fact, all webpages are constructed of text, just like the sentences on this page. No special software is required to create a webpage. All that a potential Web author needs to get started is a simple text editing program (Notepad in Microsoft Windows, for example) and an understanding of HyperText Markup Language (HTML), the language Web browsers interpret to display. This simplicity is one of the reasons the Web has become so popular. Since the vast majority of computers are capable of creating text documents and the syntax of HTML is so simple, almost anyone with access to a computer has the ability to author webpages. The ease with which one can create webpages is evidenced by the enormous growth in the number of webpages over the last several years.

## HTML as a Standard Description Language

The vast majority of pages on the Web were created using HyperText Markup Language ("hypertext" because of their ability to link to other pages and "markup" to describe the way content is displayed). HTML is a text-based language that is used to describe how to display content on a webpage. This content can include, but is not limited to, text, links, images, sound, buttons, and forms. Text is the only content contained within the HTML file—and is used to describe the appearance of the content on the page. Other languages exist that not only describe how to display the content but also describe the content itself (Extensible Markup Language, or **XML**). Others are designed for specific devices (Wireless Markup Language, or **WML**, used for cellphone browsers). Much of the content referenced by the HTML is stored outside of the webpage that displays the content. This is why it is common for the size of content files, such as images, to be larger than the HTML file that describes the page on which the image is displayed.

## Web Content Types

Although the Web does not limit the number of content types available, most content found on the Web falls into a few broad categories:

**Links.** As mentioned earlier, hypertext "links" (aka "hyperlinks") are used to connect webpages together into websites. Links are typically text or graphics that a user clicks on to jump to another place in a document or elsewhere on the Web. Links can be categorized into three general types: internal anchors, page links, and mail to.

*Internal Anchors.* Internal anchors are hyperlinks that connect with other locations within the same document. Internal anchors are often found in long documents that contain a lot of text. For example, a long, multichapter text document might contain a table of contents with hyperlinks for each chapter. Users who want to skip to a particular chapter in that document could simply click on a hyperlink in the table of contents to instantly jump to the chapter they want to read.

*Page Links.* The same technology that allows users to link within a webpage also allows users to link to other webpages. A page link is simply a hyperlink that connects with another webpage. This webpage can be another page within the website or can be located on a site thousands of miles away.

*Mail To.* When a user clicks an e-mail link, the browser automatically starts up the user's e-mail program, opens up a new e-mail message, and inserts an e-mail address (dictated by the HTML code on the webpage) in the "To" field of the e-mail message. E-mail links are a convenient way for webpage authors to let users send feedback and questions to them directly.

**Forms.** Another way a webpage can solicit information from users is by providing fields on a page where users can enter information either by typing in text or selecting from a list of options. Users enter their information into the form, then click a submit button that transmits the information to a computer program that processes that form (i.e., e-mails it, stores it in a database, responds to it programmatically). Forms are useful for getting highly structured feedback and user information such as shipping addresses and phone numbers.

**Images.** Images are one of the most popular content types on the Web. Before the advent of Tim Berners-Lee's WorldWideWeb browser in late 1990, the Internet was largely accessed with text prompts and text commands through browsers such as Lynx (a Web browser for text-based terminals). Rich-media webpages did not exist. Instead, the Web consisted primarily of file directories and text. However, with the introduction of graphical browsers such as Mosaic and Netscape in the mid-1990s, the way users viewed and interacted with the Web transformed completely.

## Exhibit 2-7   WORLDWIDEWEB—THE FIRST GRAPHICAL WEB BROWSER

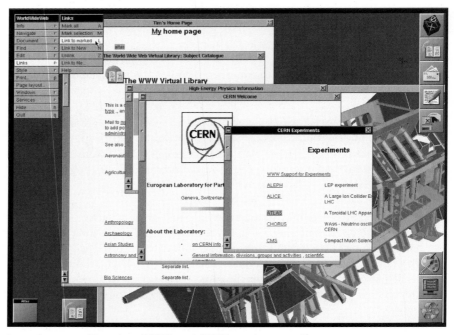

Source: (www.w3.org/History/1994/WWW/Journals/CACM/screensnap2_24c.gif)    © 1994-2001 W3C

The most widely supported image formats on the Web are Graphics Image Format (GIF) and Joint Picture Encoding Group (JPEG). One reason these are so widely supported is because both are native MIME types to most browsers. This means that users will be able to see these images easily, without having to change any settings within their browser, because all popular browsers support these file types. Clearly, getting a file format recognized as a MIME type by browser vendors or the W3C (World Wide Web Consortium) heavily dictates the viability of a file type.

*GIF.* The GIF format was designed specifically for online delivery, and was originally developed for CompuServe in the late 1980s. It is an 8-bit file format, which means that it can support up to 256 colors. However, GIF files can do many things

## DRILL-DOWN

# MIME

MIME stands for Multipurpose Internet Mail Extensions. Initially, this protocol was developed for sending attachments in e-mail. Now browsers honor predefined MIME types as well, meaning that the browser recognizes certain file formats by their extensions. For example, the file format and file name extension ".gif" is a known file format to all browsers. Whenever a GIF file is included in an HTML document, it appears in the browser window without the need for an external "player" application.

that other file types cannot, such as animation, transparency, and interlacing. In this regard, there are two different types of GIF files: GIF87a and GIF89a. GIF87a supports transparency (which allows images to have transparent sections) and interlacing (which allows images to be viewed as they are downloaded). GIF89a supports transparency, interlacing, and animation.

**JPEG.** The JPEG file format is a 24-bit alternative to the 8-bit GIF format; it can support millions of colors rather than just 256. As such, the JPEG format was developed specifically for photographic-style images.

JPEG files use "lossy" compression, which removes information from images and causes a loss in quality. However, the visual difference in information data is often not visible or objectionable. Unlike the GIF file format, the JPEG file format requires both compression and decompression. This means that JPEG files have to be decompressed before being viewed. Although a GIF and JPEG might be identical in size, or sometimes even when the JPEG is smaller, the JPEG will take longer to render in a Web browser because of the added decompression time.

## Multimedia.
In addition to these content types, the Web also supports multimedia file types such as images, audio, and video. The ability to support multimedia formats plays a large role in the Web's current popularity. Images and multimedia files, such as video (e.g., AVI and MPEG) and audio (e.g., WAV), can be easily embedded into webpages. If the browser does not support the file type in the link natively, a **plug-in** can be used to display the multimedia content. Plug-ins are software programs that extend the capabilities of browsers in a specific way, giving you, for example, the ability to listen to audio samples or view video.

## Capturing Content

It is becoming much easier to capture content from the real world, compress it, and save it. Printed images can be captured with low-cost scanners, photos can now be directly downloaded to a PC with digital cameras, and digital video cameras now make it easy for anyone to capture their video content and save it to a hard disk for use on the Web. PC software is then used to compress the content to make it more Web-friendly.

## Capturing Images.
The two most popular tools for converting images into electronic files that can be used and viewed on a website are digital cameras and digital scanners. Unlike regular cameras that use film, digital cameras store the pictures electronically in the camera's memory. The images stored in memory can then be sent to a computer and stored on the computer's hard drive. Digital scanners, on the other hand, are more like copy machines. They scan pictures and then convert the scanned images into files. In the same manner as a digital camera, the image file is transferred to a computer, where it is stored on the computer's hard drive and can then be compressed, stored, and used on a webpage.

## Capturing Audio.
Like images, sounds can also be captured, compressed, and stored for use on the Web. A simple way to record sounds from the real world is to use the microphone port on the sound card of a computer. To record a voice, for example, a person can simply plug a microphone into the microphone port (assuming it has sound capability) and record his or her voice using the recorder program included with the operating system. To capture sounds from recordings, a device such as a

DVD player, CD player, cassette deck, or MiniDisc player can be connected to the microphone jack of the computer, and the recordings can be captured using the same method as a microphone. For a cleaner recording of CDs, however, the computer's own CD-ROM or DVD-ROM drive can be used to capture the audio digitally. Most media-player software has an ability to redirect CD output from the speakers to a file on the computer's hard drive. This is a fast and easy way to create high-quality recordings of CD audio.

Uncompressed audio files (e.g., those in WAV format) tend to be very large. An uncompressed three-minute song, recorded in CD-quality stereo on a hard drive, consumes about 25 megabytes of hard-drive space. The enormous size of these files has made compression technologies like MP3 and RealAudio popular formats for downloading and streaming audio off the Web. Many vendors now offer **ripping** software that allows users to convert their CDs into highly-compressed MP3 and RealAudio files. These files can then be played back on a user's computer (and in the case of MP3, on portable players/recorders such as the Diamond Rio and Sony Network Walkman) without the inconvenience and power drain of playing CDs on that computer. Currently, issues relating to the legality of distributing copyrighted music over the Internet remain unresolved. Although it may be possible for Internet users to access copyrighted music and video on the Internet, it may not always be legal.

**Capturing Video.** As more manufacturers recognize the opportunity the Web is creating for video, capturing video is becoming easier and less expensive. Video capture cards allow users to capture the analog video output of camcorders, VCRs, and DVD players and record the content onto a PC's hard drive. Some digital video (DV) cameras interface directly with PCs (e.g., Sony Vaio PCs and some Sony DV camcorders support the IEEE1394 "i-Link/firewire" standard) over a digital connection so that no quality is sacrificed in the capture process. This uncompressed video can then be converted to a compressed format, such as MPEG, to save storage space and reduce download times.

## How Is HTML Converted into a Webpage?

All webpages are viewed through programs called Web browsers. Web browsers are specifically designed to display content in a standard file type (such as HTML, WML, or XML) in the form of a webpage. Depending on the hardware that is running the browser, some or all of the content described by such a standard file will be displayed. For example, a webpage that contains text, photos, and sounds will display differently on a PC, PalmPilot, and cellphone. On a PC, the Web-browsing software will most likely display all three of these content types to the user. On a personal digital assistant (PDA), such as the PalmPilot, the browser will most likely display the text and possibly the photos but will not play the audio, since most PDAs do not have the ability to play anything other than simple sounds, such as beeps. A cellphone's browsing software will most likely only display the text elements on the page, since most cellphones today are not able to display more than that (also, all WAP phone browsers interpret pages that have been converted from HTML into WML by the cellular service provider). Regardless of what type of content is included on a webpage, it is the browser's job to know what it is capable of effectively communicating to the user. The browser's capabilities are defined by both the hardware it relies upon as well as the capabilities programmed into it at the time it was designed.

# Compression

 All computers and networks have a finite amount of critical resources that are required to do the job. Limitations on processor speed, RAM, hard-drive space, and network bandwidth all create limits on how much Web content can be stored on servers and how quickly that content can be downloaded and displayed on users' computers. These resource limitations have been an issue for computer users and programmers since the inception of the computer. In fact, this resource scarcity was the key driver behind the "Y2K bug" issues of the late 1990s. In the 1960s and 1970s, some programmers discovered that they could save precious memory space on computers by using a two-digit number to represent a calendar year instead of a four-digit number (68 instead of 1968, for example). Thirty years later, this shortcut had to be undone to prevent millions of computers worldwide from thinking that "00" meant the year 1900 instead of the year 2000.

## Smaller Is Better

These hardware limitations, particularly limitations in network bandwidth, have made compression an important technology on the Web. Compression was critical in the evolution of graphical Web browsing, since the ability to compress graphics files made image-rich pages load fast enough to be usable over relatively slow Internet connections. Standard compression types vary for different multimedia content types. For example, JPEG and GIF are often used for images; MP3 and RealAudio (RA) are commonly used for music; and MPEG, QuickTime, and RA are often used for video. These file formats are used to compress otherwise enormous media files into smaller, more manageable units that require less Web-server space and consume less network bandwidth.

## Lossy vs. Lossless Compression

Web-based image file formats have to implement impressive schemes to compress large images to small file sizes. Unfortunately, there is a trade-off. At times compression results in a loss of quality. There are two main terms used to describe compression: lossless and lossy. Lossless compression means that even though the file is compressed, it will not lose any quality; a lossless image will contain identical data regardless of whether it is compressed or uncompressed. The GIF file format uses lossless compression.

Lossy compression is the opposite of lossless compression: Data is removed from the image file in order to achieve compression. Often this loss of data is not terribly significant, as the compression procedure was designed to reduce data that is not essential. The JPEG file format uses lossy compression.

# How Are Websites Created?

As mentioned before, a webpage is simply a text file. Although there are hundreds of Web authoring programs available, they are not required to create a well-designed site. With a text editing program, anyone can create a website. Using text-based codes called HTML "tags," text, images, multimedia, and links can easily be added to webpages. Although more time-consuming than other methods, using a text editor to create webpages allows the author more flexibility and control over the layout and design of the page. A sample of what HTML code looks like is included in Exhibit 2-8.

Although it is possible to create great-looking websites by handcrafting each page with a text editor, most website authors rely on other tools once their sites exceed more than a few pages. There are a wide variety of tools available for this task. They fall into two main categories: content conversion tools and Web authoring tools.

**Exhibit 2-8** BROWSER VIEW AND SOURCE VIEW OF A WEBPAGE

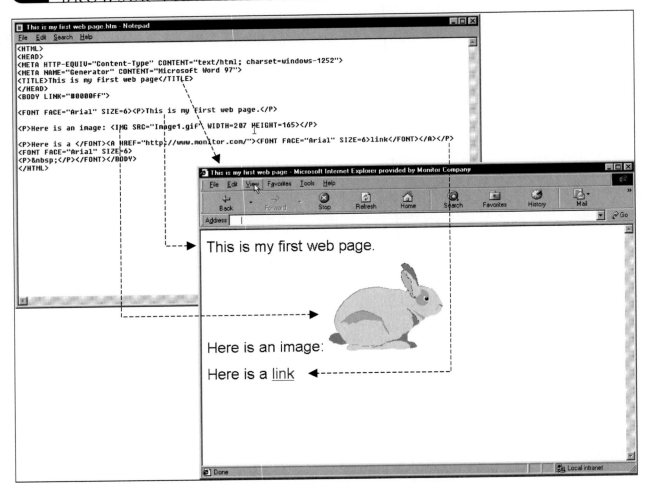

**Content Conversion Tools.** Document conversion tools allow someone who has created a document in another application, such as a word processor or desktop publishing program, to convert that file into a standard markup language, such as HTML or XML. Although most word processing and desktop publishing programs have some features that are not currently supported by webpages, good-looking documents can still be created using these tools. For example, someone who has created a document in Microsoft Word can convert it into a webpage by simply using the "Save As" command to save the document as a webpage. Most word processors and desktop publishing programs support the creation of hyperlinks and other Web-enabled functions straight out of the box. Document conversion tools enable both existing documents and new documents to be created and posted on the Web with a minimal investment in learning a markup language. It should be noted, however, that use of these simple tools significantly limits one's ability to control the look-and-feel of the pages created. To build pages that are more interactive and visually interesting, one must use specific Web authoring tools and/or modify these documents with native HTML or XML code.

Although these tools are easy to use, there are limits to what they can do. Some documents in a desktop publishing program may not convert easily to HTML. In this case, the document may look very different on the Web than it does coming out of the printer. Also, these programs offer minimal, if any, site management capabilities. This means that although they may be able to convert individual pages, they will not be able to, for example, automatically update the links on 50 pages that point to a URL that has changed.

In addition to converting text documents to HTML, it is possible to convert multimedia content from one format to another. For example, Apple's iMovie will convert MPEG video into QuickTime video. Also, ripping programs from companies like RealNetworks and Xing allow users to convert CDs to compressed audio formats (such as MP3) in one step.

**Web Authoring Tools.** Since it can be time-consuming to create pages that take advantage of the interactive capabilities of the Web, more advanced tools can be used to speed up the process. Several packages are available to expedite both page generation and site maintenance. Popular authoring software such as Microsoft FrontPage not only allows users to easily integrate text and images into their pages, but also allows users to add multimedia objects, such as sound and animation, to their webpages. In addition to content creation features, these programs usually offer site generation and management features. For example, if a page is moved or renamed, the program will automatically update all links to that page on the site, saving hours of work on large sites. Other popular features include collaboration tools such as comments, to-do lists, and discussion groups, as well as other convenient tools such as search-form generators and counters.

High-end Web authoring tools, such as Macromedia Dreamweaver and Adobe GoLive, offer more powerful site creation and management features, and allow expanded features, such as database integration, to be built into a website. These capabilities come at a price, however. These products tend to be more expensive and have steeper learning curves than less powerful competitors.

As we have seen, the Web eases the creation and display of rich-media content on a variety of devices. The real power of the Web, though, is the ability to combine one's own content with the content of others around the world. Going back to the lion book example, we can create a site about lions without having to own all of the content. The dictionary definitions could come from an encyclopedia website and information about Africa can come from a variety of sources in Africa itself. Unlike paper documents, hypertext documents on the Web make it easy to integrate others' knowledge with our own quickly and inexpensively.

# Behind the Scenes

The Internet provides access to an enormous quantity of content spread out over many computers using many services. Today's Web browsers attempt to allow users to access this content without having to think about which computer is actually storing the data, where that computer is, and what service is being used to access the data. In other words, browsers make the process of retrieving information on much of the Internet as **transparent** to users as possible.

As mentioned before, webpages use links to connect users to other content that may or may not be located on the same server as the page from which it links. The address used to identify the location of this content is called a Uniform Resource Locator (URL). The URL tells the browser several things about how to access the desired content:

# Dynamic Web Functionality

 When the Web was first emerging, virtually all websites consisted solely of static pages of text and images. As the Web has evolved, the manner in which content is generated, as well as the way users interact with this content, has changed. Most of the sites run by large corporations, particularly corporations engaged in e-commerce, include pages that generate content in a dynamic manner instead of just static webpages connected by HTML links. This is because users are expecting more interesting and interactive sites, and because as sites get larger, it becomes much easier to manage the thousands of pages on a site by modifying a few page templates instead of thousands of individual pages. Templates allow Web authors to format a single template page and then have copies of the template populated with information from a dynamic source, such as a database.

The type of information a company posts on the Web, as well as the anticipated level of usage of the site, will determine the way in which the back end of the system will be set up. There are essentially two options when creating a dynamic back end:

1. *Set up a database that periodically generates new static HTML pages at regular intervals.* This type of system might make sense for a site that is reporting weather forecasts and wants to update them every 30 minutes by plugging new data from a weather service into HTML page templates. Since the pages that the browser is viewing are actually static, they can be served easily and quickly by Web servers. This allows the site to manage a lot of traffic without investing enormous amounts of computing horsepower in its servers. However, one drawback of this type of system is that the information is not real time. The pages are generated on a periodic basis; the data on them does not automatically update, nor can calculations be done on the fly.

2. *Create a Web-based user interface to a computer program running on the server.* Allowing users to directly interact with a computer program over the Web allows far more flexibility and power when designing a site. For example, a person might use this type of system to get real-time stock quotes from her stock broker's site. When the user submits a request for the current value of her portfolio, the program could contact the stock exchange and provide an immediate update of the prices of each of her stocks. The program could then calculate the sum values of each holding and the percentage value change from the previous day's closing prices. This type of real-time calculation is a major benefit to this server-side program approach to creating a website. One drawback, however, is the fact that such systems require much more processing power to serve many users in a timely manner.

• *The transmission protocol to access the content.* Several protocols are supported by browsers, including HyperText Transfer Protocol (HTTP) for webpages, File Transfer Protocol (FTP) for transmission of files, and the extended S-HTTP for a higher degree of security. One reason that browsers are so powerful is that they need to have the ability to integrate access to several Internet services with one easy-to-use user interface. Because the type of transmission protocol required to access these services is defined in the URL, the browser can automatically let a user access that service without requiring the user to run another program.

- *The name of the computer where the content can be found.* All servers on the Internet are assigned a numerical address for the purposes of identifying that computer on the Net on a worldwide basis. These numbers, known as IP addresses, function very similarly to telephone numbers, making it easy for computers to uniquely identify other computers on the Internet; in fact, you can use IP addresses to get access to a server through your browser. As discussed before, to prevent people from having to memorize long strings of numbers, **domain names** were introduced. Domain name servers basically function like electronic phone books that look up numerical IP addresses when they are given a server's name. You can see how transparently domain name servers do their job by first entering a server's IP address into a browser and then typing in its corresponding domain name.

- *The directory on the computer where the content is stored and the name of the file containing the content.* Each file on a server is stored in a directory. The browser needs to know both the name of the file and the directory in which it is stored.

---

## DRILL-DOWN

### IP Address Sharing

Although routers see each IP address on the Internet as identifying a unique computer, it is quite common for one IP address to be used for multiple computers and for one computer to use several IP addresses. For example, the vast majority of dial-up modem connections to the Internet are made using dynamic IP addressing. Dynamic IP addressing allows a *dial-up* to actually own fewer IP addresses than it has customers. Since most of the dial-up subscribers to an ISP are not on the Internet 24 hours a day, ISPs share a limited set of IP addresses among all dial-up customers. When a user dials in to his ISP, his computer sends a **discovery packet** that requests an IP address along with other connection information from a **Dynamic Host Configuration Protocol (DHCP)** server. The DHCP server responds to the computer with an assigned IP address that the computer can use while connected to the Internet for that session.

Dynamic IP addressing can be used to let several computers on a LAN share the same Internet connection as well. For example, if you have three computers networked together at your home office and want to connect them all to the same **cable modem** or **DSL** modem, all three of these computers could simultaneously access the Internet on one account. Software such as Microsoft's Internet Connection Sharing program can be installed on the computer that is physically connected to the modem (this computer would be called a **host** computer). The host would connect to the ISP through this modem and be assigned a dynamic IP address by the ISP's DHCP server. The Internet Connection Sharing software would then take packets from the other computers on the LAN (called **client** computers) and send them out to the Internet as if they were from the host. When the information (such as a webpage) came back from the Internet to the host, the host would forward the information to the client that had requested the information in the first place. In this scenario, all of the routers on the Internet think only one computer (the host) is associated with the IP address making the request. The client computers are only visible to other clients on the LAN and to the host computer.

Exhibit
2-9

## SHARING A CABLE OR DSL MODEM

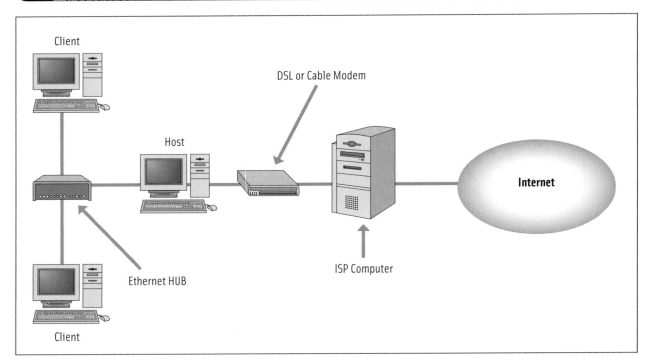

Exhibit
2-10

## COMPONENTS OF A URL

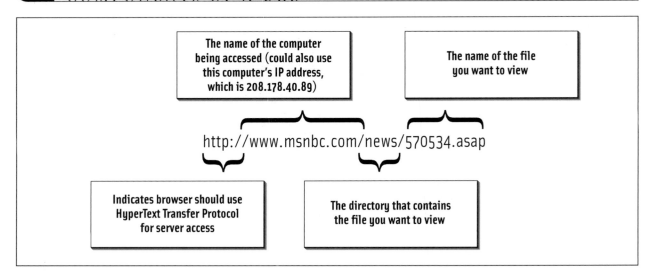

**Functions Browsers Support.** Most popular PC-based browsers actually consist of a bundle of client programs that enable them to support multiple Internet services in addition to HTTP for Web access. For example, both Netscape Navigator and Microsoft Internet Explorer allow users to transfer files using the FTP protocol and also include powerful e-mail programs. As mentioned before, the protocol information at the beginning of a URL (http://) makes it possible for browsers to seamlessly integrate all of these services for the user. Many users surfing the Web end up accessing these services without realizing they have switched to a completely different transmission protocol.

**Differences in Appearance.** Although most webpages can be read by most browsers on the market today, the same page might look a little (or a lot) different depending on the system on which it is viewed.

**Different Devices.** Obvious differences exist among browsers run on different types of devices. For example, PC browsers tend to support myriad functions such as high-quality graphics, multiple fonts, and multimedia, while a cellphone browser will support a much simpler subset of these features—typically 3 to 10 lines of text. As a result, the same website might look significantly different when viewed on these two devices.

**Different Operating Systems.** Though less significant, there are still substantial differences in the way different types of computers and operating systems treat the display of visual content. For example, the display of the font named Helvetica renders slightly differently on a Macintosh computer than on a Windows-based PC. A Macintosh also tends to display Web fonts as if they were approximately two points smaller than on a Windows-based PC, even when both computers are running the same browser.

**Different Browsers.** In addition to device and operating-system differences, there are also differences in the way browser manufacturers choose to display the content described on a page. For example, tables look somewhat different in Internet Explorer than they do in Netscape Navigator.

# WHAT IS BEHIND THE GROWTH OF THE WEB AND INTERNET?

Four key drivers, all related to ease of use and low cost, contributed to the rapid growth of the Web and Internet in the mid-1990s:

## Ease of Content Consumption

One of the reasons for the Web's rapid growth is that no one company "owns" the right to create content for the Web. Since HTML is simply text, almost anyone with access to a computer can publish content on the Web. In addition, because all browsers are set up to read the same file type (HTML), anyone with a Web browser can read the content that is created. This is different than, say, a program like Microsoft Word, where someone needs to buy a copy of the program to be able to create a Word document, and then someone else needs to buy a copy of Word to read that document.

**Exhibit 2-11**    DRIVERS OF INTERNET GROWTH

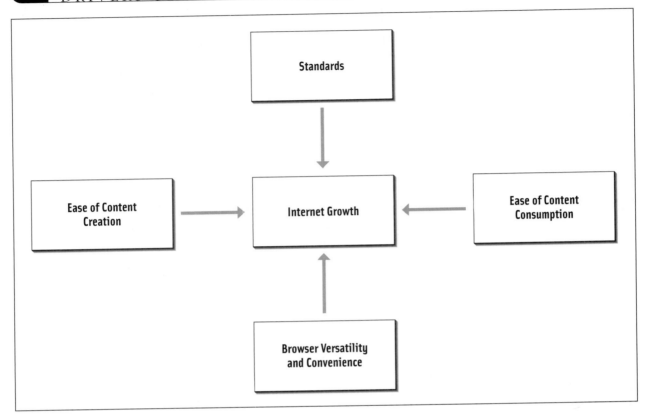

## Browsers' Lower Barriers to Adoption

**Browsers Are Versatile and Convenient.** While a word-processing program can cost hundreds of dollars, browsers are freely accessible (the user may, however, have to pay to connect to the Internet). This means that anyone with a device connected to the Internet can view most of the content on the Web free of charge.

Compared to other programs, browsers are designed to do a small set of tasks. Since browsers do not have thousands of features and functions embedded in them (for example, browsers do not have "helpful" animated paper clips offering you unsolicited assistance), they tend to be small in size and simple. Their simplicity has contributed to their widespread adoption.

**Speed.** Browsers tend to do their job quickly, even when they are run on relatively slow computers.

**Easy to Download.** Since early browsers tended to be small programs, they could be downloaded and updated rather quickly even over slow **analog modem** connections. This would be next to impossible with most productivity programs, such as Microsoft Word, which require hundreds of **megabytes** of space.

**Platform Independence.** Historically, a browser's small size has made it a lot easier to put on devices that are less powerful than PCs (although PC-based browsers are becoming large very quickly). Browsers are either currently or expected soon to be built into myriad devices such as phones, TVs, cars, PDAs, and retail kiosks. Putting a full-featured word-processing program on devices such as these would be prohibitively expensive since the memory and processing power requirements of these devices would have to be increased substantially in order for them to operate.

## Ease of Content Creation

### New Content Types Can Always Be Added.
The flexibility of browsers allows new types of functions to be added constantly. For example, multimedia animation was not available on early browsers until a company named Macromedia created a new content type called Shockwave to support animation on the Web. Now, by downloading a Shockwave plug-in for a browser, support for Shockwave animation can be added to any computer with Internet Explorer or Netscape Navigator in minutes. The openness of browsers allows anyone with the initiative, ability, and a little bit of computer hardware to develop new content capabilities for the Web. These entrepreneurs can add functionality to the Web that can be accessed by millions of users worldwide without the prior approval of any person or company. This is completely different than the previous paradigm, in which the only people who were allowed to add functionality to a program were the engineers employed by the company who developed that program in the first place.

## Standards Drive the Process

Because everyone publishing and consuming Web documents agrees on a set of **standards**, the Web is open to everyone and no one person or company can control it. Standards are rules that companies agree to adhere to so that their products can interact. For example, there is a standard in the United States that everyone drive on the right side of the road; if everyone failed to adhere to this standard, traveling on U.S. roads would be both slower and more dangerous. The TCP/IP standard has ensured universal access to the Internet by preventing any one company from controlling access to it. The common language of HTML has made publishing a website as easy as creating a text document. This standardization of HTML has also made it possible for anyone with a free browser to read almost everything on the Web. The combination of everyone agreeing to speak the same language on the Web and no single entity being able to control access to the Web has resulted in its explosive growth.

# CONCLUSION

In this chapter, we have reviewed the basics of how the Internet and the World Wide Web work. We have also explored the Internet and Web in a historical context, and examined some of the key drivers of the Internet and Web's rapid growth. This chapter should provide a foundation of basic knowledge for you to build upon as you proceed through the chapters that follow.

# SUMMARY

## 1. What is the Internet?

The Internet is a collection of wires, protocols, and hardware that allows the electronic transmission of data over TCP/IP. The Internet forms a global network through which connected computers share and access data and programs. The computers are connected through a series of local area networks (LAN) and wide area networks (WAN) and transfer data through the communication rules set forth by the Transmission Control Protocol (TCP) and Internet Protocol (IP).

## 2. What are the characteristics of the Internet that make it work?

The six characteristics of the Internet are unique identification, human-friendly addressing, packet switching, lack of traffic jams, reliability, and standardization. Each computer connected to the Internet must be uniquely identified with an Internet Protocol (IP) address. The Domain Name System (DNS) gives each computer on the Internet an address comprised of easily recognizable letters and words that provide human-friendly addressing. Packet switching is used by computer networks to ensure fair access to shared network resources and to remedy the delays associated with unequally-sized data transfers. Routing directs traffic and translates messages so that different network technologies can communicate easily and efficiently with one another. Transmission Control Protocol (TCP) is software that enables reliable, error-free communication over the Internet. Standardization ensures compatible communication between diverse hardware with the use of TCP/IP.

## 3. What are the content types on the Web?

The four Web content types are links, forms, images, and multimedia. Links can be categorized into three general types: internal anchors, page links, or mail-to links. Internal anchors are hyperlinks that connect with other locations within the same document. Page links allow users to link to other webpages. The mail-to link allows the browser to automatically start up the user's e-mail program, open up a new e-mail message, and insert the e-mail address in the "To" field for the user. Forms allow the user to enter information in fields on the page by typing in text or selecting from a list of options. Image formats, such as Graphics Image Format (GIF) and Joint Picture Encoding Group (JPEG), allow users to see images easily, without having to change any settings within their browser, because all popular browsers support these file types. Multimedia files contain images, audio, and video that are embedded into webpages.

## 4. How are websites created?

A webpage is simply a text file that contains a text-based code called HTML. Web content, such as text, images, multimedia, and links, can easily be added to webpages through the use of HTML "tags," which describe Web content. Web authoring tools help to expedite both page generation and site maintenance. Users can also use content conversion tools to create a document in another application and convert that file into a standard markup language, such as HTML or XML.

## 5. What is behind the growth of the Web and Internet?

The main reason for the growth of the Web and Internet is the fact that no one company "owns" the right to create content for the Web. Anyone with access to a computer can publish content on the Web. In addition, anyone with a Web browser can read the content that is created.

# KEY TERMS

| | |
|---|---|
| local area network (LAN) | XML |
| wide area network (WAN) | WML |
| Internet Protocol (IP) | plug-in |
| Transmission Control Protocol (TCP) | ripping |
| | transparent |
| backbone network | domain names |
| backbone sites | discovery packet |
| top-level domain | Dynamic Host Configuration Protocol (DHCP) |
| packets | |
| circuit-switched networks | cable modem |
| packet switching | DSL |
| router | host |
| webpages | client |
| links | analog modem |
| servers | megabytes |
| Web address | standards |
| URL | |

# Endnotes

[1] Information for this section came from the following sources:

Douglas, Susan. *Inventing American Broadcasting 1899–1922* (Baltimore: Johns Hopkins University Press, 1987).

Hanson, Ward. "The Original WWW: Web Lessons from the Early Days of Radio." Stanford University, Graduate School of Business. 1996.

Hargittai, Eszter. "Radio's Lessons for the Internet." Communications of the ACM. January 2000, 43/1.

White, Thomas H. "Early US Radio History," United States Early Radio History. URL: *www.ipass.net/~whitetho/part1.htm#companies.*

Continelli, Bill. "The Wayback Machine." URL: *www.charlotte.u104.k12.me.us/roff/titanic.htm/.*

[2] RCA stands for the Radio Corporation of America, which was created in 1919 to be the sole provider of radio reception equipment. RCA was actually an alliance between several companies, GE, Westinghouse, AT&T, United Fruit, among others.

[3] Douglas, Susan. *Inventing American Broadcasting 1899–1922.* (Baltimore: Johns Hopkins University Press, 1987).

[4] Information for this section came from the following sources:

Comer, Douglas. *The Internet Book, 3rd ed.* (New Jersey: Prentice Hall, 2000).

Gralla, Preston. *How the Internet Works* (Indiana: Que, 1999).

Hedrick, Charles. "Introduction to the Internet Protocols." Center for Computers and

Information Services, Rutgers University July,1987. URL: *www.stud.ifi.uio.no/~od/tcp-ip-intro/tcp-ip-intro.html.*

Rheingold, Howard. *Tools for Thought,* Rheingold.com, 1985. URL: *www.rheingold.com/texts/tft/.*

[5]Information for this section came from the following sources:

Comer, Douglas. *The Internet Book, 3rd ed.* (New Jersey: Prentice Hall, Inc., 2000).

Gralla, Preston. *How the Internet Works* (Indiana: Que, 1999).

Turban, Efraim, Jae Lee, David King, and H. Michael Chung. *Electronic Commerce, A Managerial Perspective* (Englewood Cliffs, NJ: Prentice Hall, Inc., 2000).

Levine-Young, Margaret. *Internet: The Complete Reference, Millennium Edition* (California: Osborne/McGraw-Hill, 1999).

Mohler, James L., and Jon M. Duff. *Designing Interactive Web Sites* (New York: Delmar Thomson Learning, 2000).

Meeker, Mary. *The Internet Marketing Report.* (Morgan Stanley, U.S. Investment Research, *Technology: Internet/New Media* (December, 1996):1–5.

Berners-Lee, Tim. "The WorldWideWeb browser," URL: *www.w3.org/people/Berner-Lee/WorldWideWeb.html 2000.*

# The Basics of Doing Business on the Internet

This chapter provides an introduction to the fundamental concepts behind e-commerce. We begin by creating a framework for understanding the basic tenets of traditional commerce and then apply those tenets to e-commerce. In the process, we uncover key similarities and differences between conducting business across the two different mediums/channels.

In addition to identifying and exploring these fundamental concepts, we provide brief overviews, where appropriate, of the technologies that support these basic business concepts on the Web, including Web hosting, encryption software, and firewalls. The chapter concludes with a discussion of the particular challenges of e-commerce fulfillment.

## QUESTIONS

*Please consider the following questions as you read this chapter:*

1. What are the key similarities and differences between e-commerce and bricks-and-mortar selling in regard to location?

2. What are popular methods for marketing an e-commerce store?

3. How does e-commerce payment differ from bricks-and-mortar payment?

4. What roles does security play in e-commerce?

5. What challenges exist in e-commerce fulfillment?

---

This chapter was coauthored by Bernie Jaworski, Jeffrey Rayport, Joseph Hartzell, Eugene Wang, and Colin Gounden.

# INTRODUCTION

E-commerce is playing an increasingly prevalent role in the lives of consumers. The United States Department of Commerce reports a 67 percent growth in e-commerce retail sales between the fourth quarter of 2000 and the fourth quarter of 1999, when the agency first began tracking e-commerce data.[1]

However, despite this robust growth, not all e-commerce stores have been successful. In fact, a recent study shows that less than one quarter of pure-play e-commerce retailers are profitable.[2] However, that same study shows considerable improvement in profitability of online ventures backed by traditional bricks-and-mortar merchants.

Selling on the Web requires many of the same activities and components needed to conduct business in the offline world. In this chapter, we examine the similarities and differences between bricks-and-mortar and e-commerce selling as they relate to the five key components of running an e-commerce store:

- location and hosting
- marketing and presentation
- payment
- security
- fulfillment

# LOCATION AND HOSTING

## Bricks-and-Mortar

Location is an important component of creating an offline store. When thinking about location, merchants consider a variety of issues, including traffic, competition, convenience, image, and size.

**Traffic.** A store's physical and geographic location has a large effect on determining what type and how much traffic will flow to and from the store. For example, a store located in a busy mall will likely have more traffic than a store that resides alone. Also, a store located near a freeway is more convenient for customers to get to; this location allows customers who live farther away to easily get to the store. If the store were accessible only by local roads, customers who lived farther away would not have such easy access.

**Image.** In addition, location helps determine the quality of traffic that a store will receive and, therefore, helps to determine its image. For example, a jewelry store located on Rodeo Drive in Beverly Hills will attract a very different type of customer, and be perceived as more exclusive, than a jewelry store located in a suburban shopping center.

**Competition.** However, when choosing a location, merchants also consider competition. Generally, merchants prefer to set up stores in locations where there is little competition for customers. For example, a coffee-shop owner would be hesitant to open next door to a Starbucks. Instead, she might prefer to set up shop in a location where there is less competition.

**Convenience.** In addition to considering convenience for the customer, merchants also consider how convenient a location is for themselves. For instance, a merchant, such as Wal-Mart, that chooses to locate a store on a self-enclosed lot must also consider issues such as security, parking, and cleaning. On the other hand, in a mall, issues such as security, parking, cleaning, and even some advertising are often pooled together and outsourced for all the stores. As such, individual merchants within the mall do not have to worry about these additional responsibilities.

**Size.** After a manager has evaluated the amount of traffic the store should expect, she must consider how large the store needs to be to accommodate its products and customers. For example, some types of products require a larger store than others; a store selling furniture would probably need a larger showroom floor than a jewelry store. Also, stores that expect heavy traffic flow will need to choose a location with adequate parking and entrances and walkways large enough to accommodate such traffic.

# E-Commerce

Location is also an important piece in setting up an e-commerce store. Just as bricks-and-mortar managers must think about location in the context of traffic, image, and size, so must e-commerce managers.

**Traffic.** While geographic location is an important determinant of traffic for a bricks-and-mortar store, virtual location is an important determinant of traffic for an e-commerce store. For example, as a bricks-and-mortar store locates itself in a mall to gain access to all of the traffic that flows through the mall, an e-commerce store would choose to locate itself in a virtual mall, such as Yahoo Shopping, for the same reason. Yahoo attracts traffic from all across the Internet. An e-commerce store on Yahoo Shopping would gain access to Yahoo's traffic, expecting that some of that traffic would find its way to that particular e-commerce store.

**Image.** Just as in the bricks-and-mortar world, an e-commerce store's location also lends itself to influence how the store is perceived. For instance, a store located on a low-traffic virtual mall, such as Valley Center Virtual Mall (*www.vcvmall.com*), may be perceived very differently than a store listed in a larger mall, such as Amazon zShops (*www.zshops.com*) or Yahoo Shopping (*www.shopping.yahoo.com*). Both Yahoo and Amazon have gone to extensive lengths to build brand and establish trust with Web consumers. Thus, e-commerce stores listed on these types of virtual malls can benefit from this brand and trust, while an e-commerce store located on a smaller mall may not.

In addition, the actual domain name or virtual location of an e-commerce store can heavily influence the perceived positioning of the store. For example, the travel store *www.cheaptickets.com* connotes discounted travel; the domain name *www.drugstore.com* communicates an online pharmacy; a domain name such as *www.buy.com* connotes a broader shopping experience.

Another important detail in choosing a domain name is name recognition. Intuitive and memorable domain names are generally preferable. For example, if a potential customer is looking for Sony products, rather than searching with a Web browser she might just type in *www.sony.com*. If a merchant's domain name is *www.ilmhwiamn.com*, customers will have a hard time remembering it, in contrast to a domain name such as *www.business.com*.

**Competition.** Like the bricks-and-mortar example of a coffee shop opening near a Starbucks, competition is also an issue when considering e-commerce location. An online merchant selling books and CDs would not want to choose Amazon zShops as a store location, since Amazon is one of the largest sellers of books and CDs on the Internet; a smaller merchant would certainly have trouble competing.

**Convenience.** Some e-commerce locations offer more convenience to the merchant than others. We have already discussed the convenience outsourced services in a mall provides merchants. The e-commerce equivalent is that large online malls, such as Amazon zShops and Yahoo, can also take care of many of the mundane aspects of running an online business, such as payment processing, hosting, and maintenance, allowing the merchant to focus solely on running the core business.

**Size.** Just as a bricks-and-mortar manager must evaluate how large a store must be to accommodate its customers and products, so must an e-commerce store manager. Stores that expect a lot of traffic need to be designed to handle that traffic. Just as bricks-and-mortar stores must consider accommodating parking and having wide enough aisles and entranceways, e-commerce stores need enough **bandwidth, processing power**, and **data storage capacity** to provide the proper service to their customers.

*Bandwidth.* Bandwidth is the amount of data than can be sent through a connection at once. Imagine a supermarket checkout. During a business day a supermarket will experience peaks and valleys in the number of customers shopping. Since the supermarket checkout area must be large enough to accommodate all of its customers all of the time, the manager of it must make sure that the supermarket is large enough to accommodate all of its customers during peak hours. This is the reason most supermarkets always seem to have a few empty checkout stands; the additional checkout stands exist so that the supermarket can accommodate all of its customers during peak hours.

The same applies online. The merchant must plan to have enough bandwidth to accommodate customers during peak times. A general rule of thumb is that the average bandwidth utilization should not exceed 30 percent of the total bandwidth available, and during peak times, bandwidth should not exceed 70 percent of the total available.[3] Beyond these levels, performance of an e-commerce store will begin to deteriorate. As such, sites such as Amazon and Yahoo must have very large stores in terms of bandwidth to adequately serve their customers.

Another factor that merchants consider when thinking about bandwidth is the type of products or content offered on the store. For example, are the products being sold best displayed with graphics or streaming multimedia? If so, these types of stores need more bandwidth than those stores that sell products best sold with simple descriptions.

Sites where customers download files also require a lot of bandwidth. For example, CNET's Download.com is a site dedicated to providing its customers with the latest software and applications for their computers. Since downloads require the transfer of a lot of data, Download.com requires a lot of bandwidth to serve its customers.

*Processing Power.* Processing power, as we refer of it, is the amount of data that can be processed by a website at a given time. Different e-commerce merchants have varied needs for processing power. In general, the larger the e-commerce site is in

Table
3-1

## BANDWIDTH TYPES

| Quick Circuit Reference | |
|---|---|
| **Circuit Type** | **Capacity** |
| DS0 | 64Kbps |
| T1, DS-1 | 1.544Mbps |
| E1, DS-1 | 2.048Mbps |
| T2, DS-2 | 6.312Mbps |
| E2 | 8.448Mbps |
| E3 | 34.368Mbps |
| T3 or DS3 | 44.736Mbps |
| OC-1, STS1 | 51.840Mbps |
| Fast Ethernet | 100.00Mbps |
| OC-3, STS3 | 155.520Mbps |
| OC-3c | 155.520Mbps |
| OC-12, STS12 | 622.080Mbps |
| OC-48 | 2.488Gbps |
| OC-96 | 4.976Gbps |
| OC-192 | 10Gbps |
| OC-255 | 13.21Gbps |

Source: About.com

terms of product breadth, number of transactions, and level of interactivity, the greater the need is for processing power.

- *Product breadth.* Imagine an e-commerce store that is dedicated to selling only one book. Because the merchant has only one *stock-keeping unit*, or *SKU*, this business is fairly simple. Inventory and orders are easy to track and maintain, and the store requires little processing power.

  Now imagine the online book-selling behemoth, Amazon. Amazon claims to have over 1 million SKUs available to its customers. As a result, managing and organizing these SKUs is a significant and complicated task. Amazon must be able to collect, organize, and display an enormous amount of data. For example, Amazon must provide its customers with a search engine capable of finding over 1 million titles, authors, publishers, keywords, and topics. In addition, Amazon must be able to accurately track inventory levels, and process (potentially) over 1 million different types of orders. The complexity that Amazon's product breadth adds to its e-commerce store requires a significant amount of processing power.

- *Number of transactions.* Let us revisit the one-book store we mentioned earlier. Since this store sells only one item, it probably does not conduct very many transactions per day, perhaps even per month. Given this low number of transactions, the e-commerce store does not require much processing power.

  In contrast, Amazon.com may process thousands of orders per day. Many of these transactions occur simultaneously. Amazon must be able to simultaneously process orders from a customer in Memphis, Tennessee, who orders *The Works of Alfred Lord Tennyson*, a customer in Manila, Philippines, who orders John Grisham's *The Chamber*, and a customer in Palo Alto, California, who orders the Richard Wright novel, *Black Boy*. Amazon's ability to process large numbers of transactions involving different SKUs requires copious amounts of processing power.

  To drive this point home, consider another example: the Nasdaq Stock Market. Nasdaq operates three websites—*www.nasdaq.com, www.amex.com,* and *www.americanstocks.com*—which receive over 20 million hits and conduct roughly 2 million transactions per day.[4] Because Nasdaq must be responsive, providing instant and accurate market data to traders, investors, and others, powerful servers are needed to quickly and reliably process enormous amounts of data.

- *Level of interactivity.* In addition to product breadth and number of transactions, the level of interactivity on an e-commerce website also helps to determine the amount of processing power required. Continuing with the Nasdaq example, Nasdaq interacts with a variety of parties and data sources to serve its customers. For instance, Nasdaq interacts with the markets, traders, investors, and others to collect and display accurate market data. In addition, Nasdaq provides its customers with news, research, and financial analysis; it even allows users to customize their own content and track the performance of their individual portfolio. These levels of interactivity and customization require that Nasdaq employ some of the most powerful servers available.

***Data Storage Capacity.*** Our previous examples have focused on the power needed to process different types of data. We have also hinted at the enormous amounts of data involved in e-commerce and e-commerce transactions. Online businesses collect huge amounts of customer data such as demographics, purchase patterns, billing histories, and *click stream* (the sequence of pages visited). A relatively large B2C (business-to-consumer) website that receives about 100 million hits per day will log about 200 bytes of data per hit.[5] This amounts to about 20 *gigabytes* (1,024 bytes equals one kilobyte; 1,024 kilobytes equals one megabyte; 1,024 megabytes equals one gigabyte) of stored data per day. While 20 gigabytes of data does not seem overwhelming, given that large online merchants tend to keep this data for about three years, those 20 gigabytes can quickly add up to dozens of *terabytes* (1,024 gigabytes), more information than is contained in the entire printed collection of the U.S. Library of Congress![6]

# Implementation

Having addressed some of the location issues that managers consider, we will now discuss implementation. There are a variety of technology components necessary for creating an effective e-commerce store location.

**Table 3-2**

DATA POWERS OF TEN

| Term | Definition |
|------|------------|
| Byte | 8 Bits |
| Kilobyte | 1,000 Bytes |
| Megabyte | 1,000,000 Bytes |
| Gigabyte | 1,000,000,000 Bytes |
| Terabyte | 1,000,000,000,000 Bytes |
| Petabyte | 1,000,000,000,000,000 Bytes |
| Exabyte | 1,000,000,000,000,000,000 Bytes |
| Zettabyte | 1,000,000,000,000,000,000,000 Bytes |
| Yottabyte | 1,000,000,000,000,000,000,000,000 Bytes |

Note: These numbers are approximate and are simplified for illustrative purposes. A kilobyte is actually 1,024 bytes, a megabyte 1,024 kilobytes, a gigabyte 1,024 megabytes, and the remaining terms scaled accordingly.
Source: Williams, Roy. Center for Advanced Computing Research, California Institute of Technology. "Data Powers of Ten." URL: *http://www.cacr.caltech.edu/~roy/dataquan/*.

**Domain Name Registration.** The first step to creating an e-commerce location is to register a suitable **domain name**. The domain name serves as the e-commerce store's virtual location on the Web. Just as a bricks-and-mortar store has a physical location, an e-commerce store has a Web-based location. For example, when someone asks for directions to the nearest electronics store, he may be directed to the corner of Fifth Street and Main Street. However, if he were to ask how to get to an electronics store on the Web, he might be directed to the domain name, *www. bestbuy.com.*

However, before anyone gets too excited about a particular domain name, they need to see if the domain is available. Given the enormous number of websites and webpages currently on the Internet, many domain names have already been

---

D R I L L - D O W N

# An Information Society

We are hearing more and more about the influence of information on our lives. Electronic information has permeated everything from credit histories to marketable securities to driving and birth records. In 1999, the world created 1.5 exabytes of unique information, which equates to about 250 megabytes of information for every person on the planet. According to Forbes Magazine, this amount of data is expected to double every year for the foreseeable future.

While the number of webpages on the Internet is growing rapidly, e-mail represents the bulk of new data produced. Over 600 billion e-mails are sent each year in the United States alone; worldwide, e-mail creates up to 500 times more data than webpages.[7]

registered. If a suitable domain name is not available for registration, then a "used" domain name can be considered. Many of the domain names that are currently registered are for sale. For example, in November 1999, the domain name *www.business.com* sold for $7.5 million! This case, however, is not representative of the current market for domain names—most domain names can be purchased for a few hundred dollars to a few thousand dollars.

After an aspiring Web merchant finds an available domain name, registering it is a relatively easy process. Domain names that end in .com, .org, and .net can be registered through a multitude of domain-name brokers, called registrars. Only registrars accredited by the Internet Corporation for Assigned Names and Numbers (ICANN) are authorized to register .com, .org, and .net domain names. A list of all accredited registrars can be found at *www.icann.org/registrars/accredited-list.html.*

Once a registrar is found, it will ask the user to provide various contact and technical information that makes up the registration. The registrar then sends this information to a central directory called the *registry.* This registry provides to other computers on the Internet the information necessary to communicate with and find the website. The user will also enter into a contract with the registrar to set the terms under which the registration is accepted and will be maintained. This process of registration is very similar to the process of getting the licenses and registration necessary to conduct a business at a bricks-and-mortar location.

**Selecting a Host.** In addition to registering a domain, an e-commerce store will also need to select a suitable hosting alternative.

***What Is a Web Host?*** Generally, a **Web host** serves as a website's secure, high-bandwidth, professionally-maintained connection to the Internet. Professional Web hosting works in a variety of ways depending on the entity's need. Most Web hosts have a high-bandwidth, dedicated connection to the Internet that they lease out to customers. All of a customer's website content actually resides at the Web host's location, and the customer manages her content from a remote location. Any changes made to the website are uploaded to the host's servers by the customer. In essence, the Web host

- provides the website owner a high-bandwidth connection to the Internet
- stores all of the website content on its servers, which process all of the information trafficked to and from the website

***Hosting Alternatives.*** There are a variety of Web hosting alternatives available, including free, shared server, dedicated server, colocated server, and in-house hosting.

- *Free hosting.* For very simple websites, such as personal homepages, free hosting is often a reasonable alternative. There are a variety of hosts that offer free service such as *www.geocities.com* (Yahoo), *www.homestead.com,* and *www.tripod.com* (Lycos). While these hosts can provide you a space on the Web, they are limited in the amount of data you can store with them, the amount of bandwidth that you receive, and the kind of content you are allowed to host.

- *Shared server hosting.* For companies that want to do business on the Web, *shared server hosting*—where many websites are placed on the same Web server—is often a better alternative than free hosting. Shared server hosting is the cheapest alternative for small businesses looking for options such as increased bandwidth, more storage space, increased security, electronic payment software, and database software. While a sufficient alternative for small businesses that do not need a large amount of bandwidth or processing power, this is not a reasonable choice for larger sites.

- *Dedicated server hosting.* For larger websites, *dedicated server hosting*—where a website is allocated its own dedicated server—is often a suitable alternative. Dedicated servers are the next step up from shared servers and provide additional bandwidth and processing power. In addition, the servers are often monitored 24 × 7, and most simple problems with the server can be dealt with by the hosting facility.

- *Colocated server hosting.* Finally, *colocated server hosting* offers the most control for an outsourced hosting alternative. With colocation, the customer actually owns the server, and all the customer is paying for is bandwidth and a physical space for the server. The customer makes all hardware decisions and has complete control over the configuration of the server. While this alternative provides the customer with an increased level of control, a disadvantage for resource-constrained organizations is that the customer is responsible for most maintenance, including hardware and software maintenance.

- *In-house hosting.* The previous alternatives are all examples of outsourced hosting solutions. For those companies with adequate resources, another alternative is *in-house hosting.* Typically, only large firms (e.g., Global 1000) are successfully able to host their websites themselves, given the demanding resource needs. These needs include 24-hour dedicated personnel, power backup, security, maintenance, and *redundancy* (redundant systems such as multiple servers, server locations, Internet connections, and power supplies). For example, the hosting provider NaviSite boasts of services and resources that include a full-time security team, biometric locks (locks that recognize a person based upon unique physiological identifiers such as retina patterns, fingerprints, or the density of the bones in one's hand), redundant network architecture, multiple connections to the Internet backbone in physically different locations, seismic bracing, and backup power supplies including 50,000-gallon diesel fuel tanks.

***A Typical Example of Hosting.*** Given the extreme resource needs for in-house hosting for a large website, most merchants choose an outsourced solution that provides these resources, while also allowing the merchant to maintain an

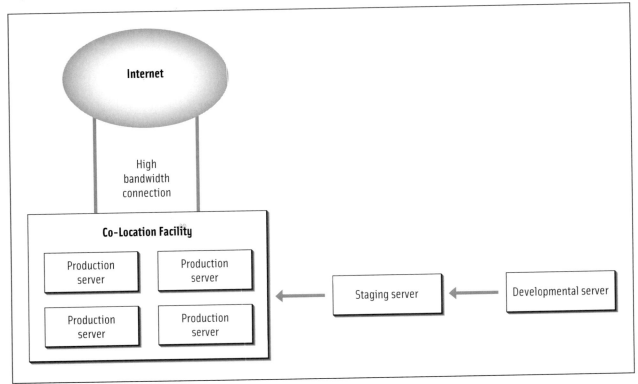

acceptable level of control over the website. Outsourcing allows the merchant to ensure a secure and reliable website without having to assume the entire responsibility for the resources necessary.

Typically, large websites are maintained with a set of servers, as described in Exhibit 3-1. Notice that there are actually three sets of servers involved: development, staging, and production.

- *Development server.* The *development server* is used primarily for the design and development of the website and Web applications. This server is not available to the general public, as its content is often largely in development mode, but it is available to the entire development team.

- *Staging server.* The *staging server* is the server that prepares the content on the development server for the Web. This is where the website and Web applications under development are tested under more realistic conditions. The work done on the staging server also ensures that newly developed content will function correctly with content already on the website.

- *Production server.* Once the content on the staging server has been thoroughly tested and perfected, the content goes to the *production server*. The production server mirrors the finalized content on the staging server. It is the only server available to customers.

# MARKETING AND PRESENTATION

## Bricks-and-Mortar

Once a bricks-and-mortar merchant has opened her store, the next task is to attract customers to shop there. Traditionally, merchants have achieved this through a variety of awareness-building and promotional activities. Just as important as initiating these activities is measuring their effectiveness.

**Advertising.** Traditional advertising takes a variety of forms. Advertising can be a listing in the yellow pages, a classified ad in the Sunday paper, a billboard on a busy street, or even a television spot during the Super Bowl. These types of advertising are typically priced and evaluated in relation to the number and type of people who will see them. For example, a Super Bowl television ad will be more expensive than a television ad run during the local high-school football game.

**Targeting.** Also, ads are priced in relation to the type of audience that will view them, a strategy commonly referred to as **targeting**. When deciding on which advertising avenues to pursue, marketing professionals often consider how targeted they wish their advertisement to be. For example, Ford Motor Company probably would not choose to run a print advertisement in *Highlights*, a leading children's magazine. Instead, a more effective advertisement might be placed in *Motor Trend* or *Automobile Magazine*. Effective targeting requires marketers to understand their audience.

**Guerrilla Marketing.** Another effective, yet less obvious, form of advertising is called **guerrilla marketing**. This type of marketing is often used by companies with limited budgets. As a result, guerrilla marketing typically does not include overt media buys, but less expensive, grassroots types of advertising. Examples of guerrilla marketing might include passing out flyers on college campuses or giving away free samples on a well-trafficked street. Often, guerrilla marketing relies heavily on word of mouth to spread its message. Many cash-strapped musicians have made a name for themselves through guerrilla marketing. The rock band *Korn* and rap group *Wu-Tang Clan* both gained enormous popularity through guerrilla marketing efforts.

**Direct Marketing.** **Direct marketing** is a marketing method that involves direct contact between the company selling a product or service and the intended consumer. For example, most people have experienced phone solicitation before. Some people will hang up immediately, or some people will listen politely to the message from the telemarketer before hanging up. However, occasionally a call recipient will find real value in the long-distance rates (or other product) the telemarketer is selling and will actually make a purchase. This is what the phone companies and other companies that use telephone direct marketing are hoping for. Nonetheless, many customers may find this type of marketing intrusive and annoying; companies that employ it must be careful not to alienate potential customers. As a result, most companies that do use telemarketing are firms that have little to lose by alienating customers of competitors—namely, credit-card companies and long-distance carriers.

Other types of direct marketing might include door-to-door sales (e.g., Girl Scout cookies) or direct mail, often referred to as "junk mail."

**Presentation.** Presentation includes the variety of components implemented at the store that serve to add or detract from the product's appeal to customers. These components include store layout and customer service.

*Store layout.* Store layout often speaks volumes about the image a store wishes to project and the type of customers it wishes to retain. As a result, marketers and merchants often pay great attention to how their stores should be presented to customers. Good examples of the importance of store layout include upscale restaurants and department stores, which are often able to charge a premium, not because of the quality of their products but because of the elaborate presentation.

*Customer service.* Customer service is another important aspect of presentation. Customer service is a necessity for a successful merchant; and as such, it has become a staple in U.S. retailing. Virtually every large U.S. retailer employs personnel dedicated to customer service. Customer service often defines a customer's experience and is a leading driver of customer retention. Similar to store layout, great customer service also often enables merchants to charge premiums for their products. Examples include the luxury hotel chain Ritz-Carlton and upscale department stores, such as Nordstrom.

**Measuring Effectiveness.** Finally, measuring the effectiveness of advertising and presentation efforts is an essential key to successful marketing. Marketing professionals are constantly trying to evaluate the effectiveness of their campaigns, specifically the impact of marketing on traffic and revenue. In addition, marketers try to better understand their customers' wants and needs and appeal to these wants and needs through more targeted advertising. Methods by which marketers gather data about their customers include feedback forms and customer surveys.

## E-Commerce

Similar to bricks-and-mortar merchants, e-commerce merchants also must drive and retain traffic to their stores.

**Advertising.** Offline and e-commerce merchants can advertise in many of the same ways that offline merchants advertise. In addition, e-commerce merchants can utilize a variety of Web-based marketing efforts, including search engine and directory listings, classified listings, banner ads, and viral and affiliate programs.

*Search Engine and Directory Listings.* Search engine and directory listings are the most popular method people employ when searching for information or stores on the Web. What the yellow pages does offline, search engines and directories do online, serving as the default source for finding information about stores and products. As a result, Web merchants have to take the appropriate steps necessary to get their websites listed in search results and directory listings, mainly through the use of **meta tags** or by paying for placement.

- *Meta tags.* Meta tags are HTML tags that most search engines read when indexing the Web. These tags allow website developers to get their websites listed or indexed properly within a search engine. There are a variety of meta tags, but two of them stand out in importance for search engine indexing: keyword and description tags. Keyword tags provide keywords for search engines to associate with a developer's website, and description tags allow the website developer to substitute his or her own description for the website in place of the description that the search engine would normally generate.[8]

Meta tags are useful tools for getting a website noticed, but they certainly are not an end-all solution. With the rapid growth of the Web, search engines are having a hard time keeping up. A recent study found that from December 1997 to February 1999, the Web grew from 320 million pages to 800 million pages. During that time, the top-ranking search engine's coverage of those pages dropped from approximately 34 percent to just 16 percent.[9]

- *Paid placements.* To differentiate their websites from the hoards of websites out there, many e-commerce merchants turn to paid placements in addition to meta tags. In the yellow pages, the bigger and more noticeable the placement, the more that particular placement costs. With directories and search engines, the same applies. By paying for placement, Web merchants can gain increased visibility with potential customers. Web merchants might pay to have their websites listed as more relevant or higher on the list of results, or they can buy highly-targeted keywords that serve up their listing when a potential customer performs a search on a particular keyword. As you might have guessed, the pricing and evaluation criteria for these types of advertisements mirror those of the offline world. The more targeted the advertisement and the greater its reach, the more expensive and effective it is.

**Banner Ads.** **Banner ads** represent the most common advertising product on the Web. Banner ads can be found on virtually every commercial webpage in existence, along with many non-commercial webpages. Banner ads, like paid placements on search engines and Web directories, can also be highly targeted. For example, when browsing the automobiles section of *The New York Times* on the Web, a banner ad advertising automobiles appears on the page. When browsing the travel section, a travel advertisement appears.

Banner ads can be purchased for display on large websites by contacting their respective ad sales departments. For banner advertising on smaller sites, many companies aggregate ad products and sell them in blocks. For example, if you were looking to purchase banner advertising for your travel store, you might contact DoubleClick to arrange to buy advertising impressions on a variety of travel-related websites that DoubleClick serves.

**Guerrilla Marketing.** In addition to offline guerrilla marketing techniques, the Web gives Web merchants additional methods for marketing websites. Two of the most popular guerrilla marketing techniques used on the Web are affiliate programs and viral marketing.

- *Affiliate programs.* Affiliate programs are marketing programs designed to enable merchants to mobilize other websites, or affiliates, to help them sell products, procure traffic, or build brand. These affiliates, in essence, serve as new distribution channels for merchants. An example is Amazon's affiliate program, the Amazon.com Associates Program. Amazon has approximately 500,000 associates signed to the program, who agree to put Amazon links on their websites. In return for this placement, Amazon pays referral fees (usually between 5 and 15 percent of the purchase price) to the associates for every sale generated through their respective links.

- *Viral marketing.* Viral marketing can be defined as company-developed products, services, or information that is passed from user to user, the way a virus is passed between two people. The idea here is for companies to get their customers to market their products for them. A common example is the "e-mail this page to a friend" functionality employed by many websites, such as CNET's News.com. This functionality allows the reader to share his or her experience on that particular webpage with a friend. The website operator provides this functionality in the hopes of adding that friend to its customer base. Viral marketing is often considered effective because marketing messages are sent between friends—consumers are often more receptive to these subtle marketing messages than they are to more overt methods of advertising.

**Direct Marketing.** The most popular forms of direct marketing on the Internet are direct e-mail and newsgroup postings. These often unsolicited messages are referred to as *spam*. The Internet term spam does not refer to Hormel's Spam meat product; instead the term gathers its roots from a Monty Python sketch that takes place in a cafeteria. During the sketch, the word spam replaces every item on the menu until the entire dialogue becomes, "spam, spam, spam, spam, spam, spam, and spam." This sketch so closely resembles what can happen on the Internet that the term spam has come to represent the mass unsolicited e-mails and messages that can often take over an e-mail inbox or newsgroup discussion board.

Like offline direct marketing, online direct marketing is often considered intrusive. Just as most people do not appreciate a telephone solicitation to their homes during dinner time, most people do not appreciate mass, unsolicited e-mail flooding their inboxes. As a result, spam is typically not well received in the Internet community. Many organizations have even developed applications designed to filter out and delete spam.

**Presentation.** As in the bricks-and-mortar medium, presentation is an important component of e-commerce selling that can help draw and retain customers. Online presentation encompasses all aspects of the store that face the customer. Two important pieces of online presentation are user interface and customer service.

**User Interface.** The online concept of *user interface*, or *UI*, is similar to the offline concept of store layout. A well thought-out user interface is crucial to successful Web selling. An appropriate user interface should reflect the theme of the store represented, be easy to navigate, and be pleasing and viewable to the store's customers.

- *Ensure your customers see what you want them to.* With bricks-and-mortar stores, a merchant can be certain that the store layout he or she designs and implements will be accurately viewed by customers. However, this is not always the case online. Despite an online merchant's efforts, not all of a store's customers will see what the merchant intends for them to see. On the Web what customers can see is often limited by the hardware, software, and bandwidth available to them. For example, websites that employ heavy java application within their webpages will be difficult for customers to view if they have older, less powerful hardware. Websites that employ flash animation can only be viewed by customers with the Macromedia Flash plug-in installed on their browser. Websites that are multimedia intensive can be appropriately viewed only by customers with high-bandwidth connections.
- *Know your customer, technically speaking.* Before Web merchants design and decide upon a user interface, they must make an effort to get to know their

customers. Specifically, the merchants must be aware of how technically savvy their customers are from a hardware, software, and bandwidth point of view.

A great example of the importance of this last point can be garnered when we compare eBay's website (*www.ebay.com*) to Gartner's website (*www.gartner.com*). Gartner's audience is technologically savvy; one would expect a typical Gartner customer to have the latest browser technology and plug-ins. As a result, Gartner can employ all of the latest features and functions on its website without worrying about whether or not their customers can view or use them. On the other hand, eBay has a much broader audience and its user interface must be viewable to all customers, from technologically savvy Gartner-like users to the least technologically savvy Web users with older hardware, older software, and low-bandwidth connections. As a result, eBay must sacrifice "cool" features for simplicity.

***Databases.*** It is important that websites are not only easily viewable but fast and easy to navigate. For most sites with many pages of information, databases are used to help facilitate this. Although the pages on these sites may look like static HTML, they are, in fact, generated by databases. For example, eBay's site has thousands of customers buying and selling thousands of products every day. For users to easily navigate the eBay site, the pages of the site should have a consistent look-and-feel. Databases make this possible by laying out the various products for sale in templates. Templates make it possible for sellers on eBay to upload photos and write up descriptions of their products without having to worry about formatting. The templates automatically layout the seller's information in a consistent format with all of the other products on the site. Buyers are presented with product pages that have a consistent look-and-feel so that navigating the site and comparing products on eBay is easier. Without databases using templates to generate the product webpages

**Exhibit 3-2** EBAY'S SIMPLE USER INTERFACE

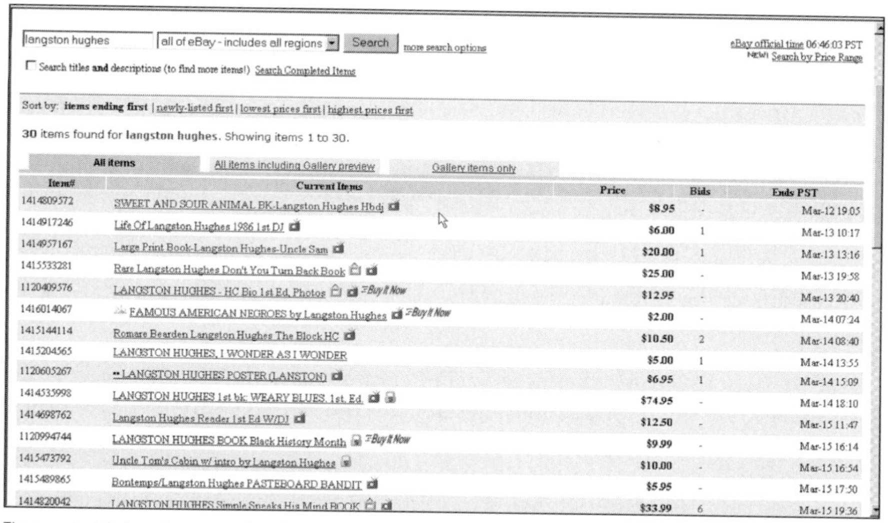
langston hughes | all of eBay - includes all regions | Search | more search options

eBay official time 06:46:03 PST
NEW! Search by Price Range

Search titles **and** descriptions (to find more items!) Search Completed Items

Sort by: **items ending first** | newly-listed first | lowest prices first | highest prices first

**30** items found for **langston hughes**. Showing items 1 to 30.

**All items** | All items including Gallery preview | Gallery items only

| Item# | Current Items | Price | Bids | Ends PST |
|---|---|---|---|---|
| 1414809572 | SWEET AND SOUR ANIMAL BK-Langston Hughes Hbdj | **$8.95** | - | Mar-12 19:05 |
| 1414917246 | Life Of Langston Hughes 1986 1st DJ | **$6.00** | 1 | Mar-13 10:17 |
| 1414957167 | Large Print Book-Langston Hughes-Uncle Sam | **$20.00** | 1 | Mar-13 13:16 |
| 1415533281 | Rare Langston Hughes Don't You Turn Back Book | **$25.00** | - | Mar-13 19:58 |
| 1120409576 | LANGSTON HUGHES - HC Bio 1st Ed, Photos Buy It Now | **$12.95** | - | Mar-13 20:40 |
| 1416014067 | FAMOUS AMERICAN NEGROES by Langston Hughes Buy It Now | **$2.00** | - | Mar-14 07:24 |
| 1415144114 | Romare Bearden Langston Hughes The Block HC | **$10.50** | 2 | Mar-14 08:40 |
| 1415204565 | LANGSTON HUGHES, I WONDER AS I WONDER | **$5.00** | 1 | Mar-14 13:55 |
| 1120605267 | ** LANGSTON HUGHES POSTER (LANSTON) | **$6.95** | 1 | Mar-14 15:09 |
| 1414535998 | LANGSTON HUGHES 1st bk: WEARY BLUES, 1st. Ed. | **$74.95** | - | Mar-14 18:10 |
| 1414698762 | Langston Hughes Reader 1st Ed W/DJ | **$12.50** | - | Mar-15 11:47 |
| 1120994744 | LANGSTON HUGHES BOOK Black History Month Buy It Now | **$9.99** | - | Mar-15 16:14 |
| 1415473792 | Uncle Tom's Cabin w/ intro by Langston Hughes | **$10.00** | - | Mar-15 16:54 |
| 1415489865 | Bontemps/Langston Hughes PASTEBOARD BANDIT | **$5.95** | - | Mar-15 17:50 |
| 1414820042 | LANGSTON HUGHES Simple Speaks His Mind BOOK | **$33.99** | 6 | Mar-15 19:36 |

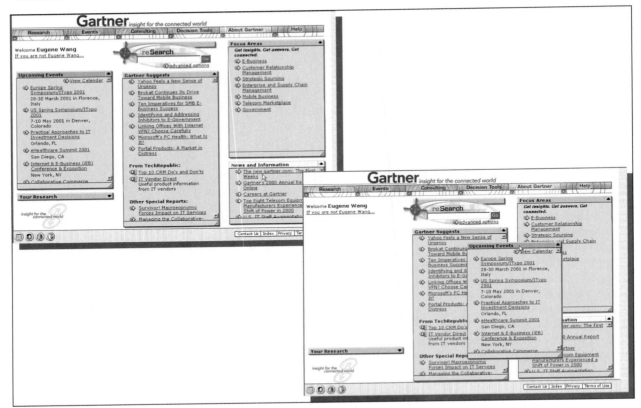

Source: Gartner Inc.

in a consistent format, it would be very difficult for buyers to find what they are looking for and compare products (for more information, see the Drill-Down on Dynamic Web Functionality in Chapter 2).

***Online Customer Service.*** The biggest difference between the customer service experience in a bricks-and-mortar store versus an e-commerce store is the lack of direct interaction between the customer and the purchasing environment. For example, e-commerce does not allow for real person-to-person live interaction, whereas in a bricks-and-mortar environment, customer service can often be conducted in person. On the Web, however, customer service needs are most often addressed over the Internet or with Internet applications such as e-mail, chat, or discussion groups.

- *The Web.* If organized effectively and comprehensively, a website can be an excellent method for distributing static information to customers. Web-based customer service can take the form of static information pages or informational webpages that anticipate customer questions, often referred to as *FAQs* (frequently asked questions). The Web can provide a lower-cost customer service alternative for Web-based merchants and faster access to information

**Exhibit 3-4**

MY YAHOO USES TEMPLATES TO LET USERS CUSTOMIZE
THE LOOK AND FEEL OF THEIR PAGES.

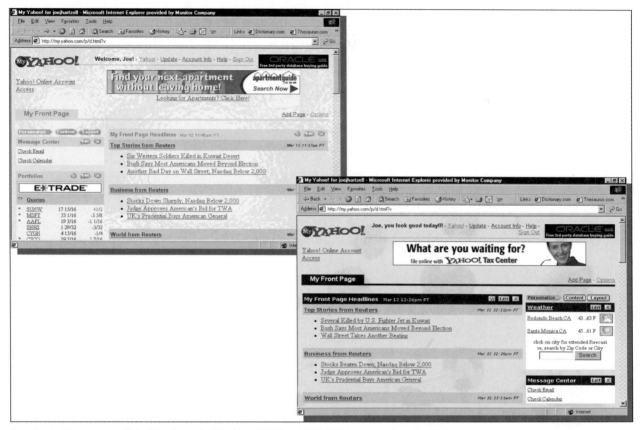

for consumers than the phone-based solutions of many bricks-and-mortar retailers. Once the site is set up, the cost of providing information is minimal, as no personnel need to be directly involved in the information distribution. Though webpages can be an effective means of customer service, it is important to note that the information contained on them is rarely entirely comprehensive and not suitable for customers requiring specific information. This is often used by bricks-and-mortar stores for common questions such as nearest store location, hours, directions, and return policy.

- *E-Mail.* One way to help customers get information that has not been provided on the website is to allow for e-mail inquiries to be sent directly to customer service representatives (CSRs). It is easy to provide e-mail links to the CSRs on the site's webpages, and in most cases (especially when the questions asked by customers can be answered in a concise manner), e-mail is more cost effective for companies than having a phone-based customer service call center. Although the company does have to pay for customer service staff to respond to the e-mail inquiries, there are no phone bills to pay, and usually more customers can be served per CSR via e-mail than over the phone. The primary disadvantage of e-mail support for customers, as compared to phone or live support, is that e-mail is not real time. Customers are required to wait for a response and trust that the company will respond in a timely manner.

- *Chat.* A potential solution to the lack of real-time interactivity of webpages and e-mail is chat-based support. Online chat rooms allow a customer to directly interact with a CSR over a text-based interface. Chat support lets companies provide real-time support with immediate answers to customer questions without incurring the cost of a phone call. In addition, chat support allows CSRs to handle multiple customers at once, which reduces the cost per customer interaction significantly. This low cost per customer makes chat support attractive to sites where revenue per customer is very low (e.g., advertising-supported sites).

- *Discussion groups.* Although e-mail support tends to be much less expensive than phone support, it still requires the use of relatively expensive CSRs. Discussion groups are another low-cost alternative to customer service. A discussion group helps customers to interact in a way that allows them to help themselves. A discussion group is essentially an electronic bulletin board where customers can post questions and other customers can post responses. The company sets up the discussion group and assigns

## Exhibit 3-5   LANDS' END USES CHAT ROOMS TO PROVIDE QUICK AND INEXPENSIVE CUSTOMER SUPPORT

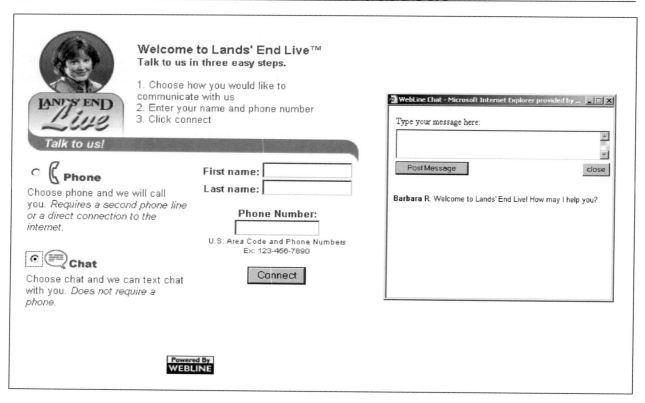

very few people to manage it. The result is essentially a user-generated list of frequently asked questions to which customers can refer. For example, Hewlett-Packard uses discussion groups to enable users of its printers to help each other with technical questions.

Another advantage to discussion groups is that the information on the discussion boards can be referenced by the company so that it can see where customers are frequently having problems. This information can help in the redesign of product information, the website, and other company operations.

However, a major drawback of discussion groups is that the quality of the information posted on them is difficult for the company to control. Angry customers or competitors may use them to spread disinformation, or customers may just post information that is not entirely accurate. Also, like e-mail support, discussion-group support is not real time. If a customer has a new question that has not already been answered by the group, she will have to wait to see if another customer posts a reply that answers her question. Depending on the interest, activity level, and knowledge base of the customers in the discussion group, questions might get answered quickly or not at all.

**Measuring Effectiveness.** As in marketing offline, tracking the effectiveness of online marketing is critical to maximizing the return on investment. Online marketing can generate enormous volumes of user activity data. The large amount of data collected can be difficult to work with, but when it is collected and sorted effectively, it can provide insight into the behavior of users to a degree not possible with traditional advertising and direct marketing programs.

One of the benefits of online marketing is that, in comparison to offline methods, companies can usually get feedback on effectiveness much more quickly. For example, credit-card companies that market through direct mail generally have to wait six weeks or more to get a reliable measure of how effective their direct mail was at attracting new customers. In contrast, NextCard, a company that uses banner ads to market its credit cards, gets effectiveness data on its ads within two weeks.[10]

Although effectiveness can be measured quickly on the Web, there are limits to what types of data can be collected. Most marketers can easily get *click-through* data for their banner ads, which reveals how many people clicked on their ad. What is more difficult to measure is how many click-throughs result in an order being placed. This is changing, however. With sophisticated tools, some companies can quickly measure the profitability of their advertising. For example, NextCard can tell how much each dollar of a customer balance costs in advertising.

Web-based marketers still face challenges in tracking effectiveness and user behavior. Because so many people use ISPs or connect to sites using dynamic IP addressing, it is often difficult to identify individual user behavior. Since IP addresses are oftentimes shared by most of an ISP's customers, it may only be possible to track behavior at the ISP level, instead of the individual user level. Another issue is that although the Web is increasingly good at measuring *what* users who click through do, no new tools exist to help understand *why* they do the things they do. Understanding the drivers behind user behavior is key to developing marketing messages that create click-throughs and purchases.

# PAYMENT

A key component to conducting business is accepting payment. At a high level, payment seems very simple: A buyer receives some type of value from the product or service purchased, and in return, the seller receives some form of payment. Here we examine some aspects of payment, uncovering different issues in the bricks-and-mortar and e-commerce mediums.

## Bricks-and-Mortar

In the bricks-and-mortar world, customers pay in a variety of methods, including cash, personal check, traveler's check, debit card, credit card, coupon, and gift certificate. Each one of these payment types carries with it distinct characteristics, and as such, a manager must carefully determine which types of payment to accept. Here we will briefly examine some of the issues a manager thinks about when accepting the two most popular payment forms: cash and credit cards.

**Cash.** Cash is the most popular form of payment in the bricks-and-mortar world. Virtually all offline stores accept cash, from the largest department stores to the corner hot-dog stands. Cash is the simplest type of payment to accept; as a result, many smaller businesses, such as restaurants, will only accept payment in the form of cash. These businesses are typically referred to as *cash businesses*.

*Theft.* The most pressing issue for managers whose businesses accept cash as payment is theft. Not only are cash businesses more susceptible to robbery, but employee theft is also a major concern. As an example, consider cash register theft. Beyond the simple scenario where the clerk reaches into the cash register, the register provides employees many indirect and less obvious opportunities to steal. For example, a customer could pay for an item with exact change and not ask for a receipt. With no record of sale, the clerk could very easily pocket the customer's money. In another scenario, a clerk could enter discounted prices into the cash register for friends shopping at the store. These indirect methods of theft can be discouraged through standardized cash-handling procedures such as giving a receipt to every customer or having separate cash drawers for each employee.

*Cash Fees.* Another issue that managers must consider is cash fees. Though one would imagine that a cash-intensive business allows the manager to keep all revenue and eliminate bank fees associated with credit-card or personal-check transactions, this is not always the case. Banks often charge businesses a cash deposit fee. For example, banks often charge supermarkets a cash fee up to 1 percent of their cash deposit.

**Credit Cards.** Credit cards are another popular form of payment at bricks-and-mortar stores. Credit cards, in addition to the convenience of not having to handle cash, allow consumers to extend their purchasing power. As a result, these cards are often used for larger purchases, where the consumer may not have enough cash on hand to complete the transaction.

*Fraud.* Theft is also an issue with credit-card payments. For example, fraud occurs when someone purchases something with a card that does not belong to him. This can occur when the merchant does not request picture identification to validate the card holder or when the merchant does not check for a signature match on the back of the card.

However, in the bricks-and-mortar world, credit card and cash theft differ as to which party assumes liability for the theft. With cash theft, the merchant typically assumes the liability for the theft; however, with credit-card purchases, as long as the merchant has a complete and legitimate record of sale (usually a receipt signed by the cardholder), the fraud is committed against the card company, not the merchant. In this case, the merchant still receives payment, and the card company assumes liability.

It is important to note that in some instances, the merchant may be held liable for the loss. For example, if a consumer contacts her credit-card company to dispute a sale, a merchant's primary protection is a complete and valid record of sale, such as a signed receipt. Without such information, a consumer's claim may be deemed legitimate, in which case the merchant would have to pay the money back to the card company and consumer. This is called a *chargeback*.

*Fees.* In return for their services, credit-card companies charge transaction fees to participating merchants. Fees typically are charged per transaction along with a small percentage of the purchase price.

In addition to transaction fees, merchants often have to spend money to lease or buy the equipment necessary to accept credit-card payments. This equipment might include a terminal that reads the magnetic strip on the back of a card, dials into an acquiring bank for validation, and prints credit-card receipts.

# E-Commerce

The main difference between e-commerce and bricks-and-mortar payment methods can be uncovered when evaluating the natures of the two media. Bricks-and-mortar implies the physical, whereas e-commerce implies the virtual. As such, an electronic medium prohibits the use of cash and encourages transactions, such as credit-card transactions, that do not require the physical transfer of payment but involve only data transfer.

## Cashless Society.
Given the security risks involved with mailing in cash payments, few, if any, e-commerce stores accept cash as a method of payment. Many do, however, accept personal checks, cashier checks, or money orders. Because these forms of payment are traceable, they are generally considered much safer from theft than cash. To pay by check or money order, customers usually mail in their payment, and the merchant will ship the purchased items once payment is received. Because of the delays involved with mailing payments, this form of payment is not especially popular on the Web.

## Credit Cards.
Despite the willingness of online merchants to accept checks and money orders, credit cards are still the dominant form of payment on the Web. Their electronic nature allows customers and e-commerce stores to pay and receive payment immediately. While check and money-order payments might take days to complete, credit-card payment takes only seconds. As a result, credit cards account for a large majority of online transactions.

*Card-Not-Present Transactions.* A major difference between offline and online credit-card transactions is that in an offline transaction, the credit card is physically present, while in an online transaction, the card is not physically present. Credit-card companies often refer to online credit-card transactions as *card-not-present transactions.* When fraud occurs online, e-commerce merchants are often helpless to protect themselves. Since the card was not physically present during the transaction, an e-commerce merchant is typically unable to produce a valid record of sale, such as a signed receipt. This is an important distinction to make between offline and online merchants because it shifts the onus of fraud away from the credit-card companies and onto the merchants. In the online medium, merchants are forced to absorb all of the costs of their chargebacks.

*Higher Fraud Rates.* Given the virtual nature of e-commerce transactions, credit-card fraud is much more prevalent online than offline. All a potential thief needs to commit a crime online is to produce a valid credit-card number and its corresponding expiration date. No signature and no identification are required. The thief does not even need to physically have the card; the number and expiration date are all that are necessary. As a result, credit-card fraud occurs in more than 1 percent of all online transactions. This rate is at least 10 times greater than the credit-card fraud rate in the offline world.[11]

*Higher Fees.* In addition to absorbing chargebacks and dealing with higher fraud rates, online merchants must also cope with higher credit-card fees than the fees charged to bricks-and-mortar merchants. Because credit-card fees vary according to a merchant's risk category, on average, e-commerce merchants pay credit-card companies fees that are 66 percent higher than the fees paid by less risky bricks-and-mortar merchants. Offline retailers typically pay rates around 1.5 percent of the purchase price, plus an additional per transaction fee of 10 to 30 cents. However Web-based retailers pay credit-card companies an average of 2.5 percent of the purchase price plus an additional 20 to 30 cents per transaction.

However, the costs of accepting credit-card payments online do not stop there. Many e-commerce merchants also have to absorb the costs associated with connecting their stores to credit-card processing networks and fraud protection services, which can add up to another 50 cents to the cost of each transaction.

Despite these higher fees, online merchants have no choice but to accept credit cards, as they are the customer-preferred and dominant form of payment on the Web.

*Security.* Given the increased opportunity for credit-card theft and fraud on the Web, security is an important component of enabling credit-card transactions. Most credit-card transactions are completed by submitting electronic information over the Internet. Data routed through the Internet can be easily monitored or intercepted if not secured. To enable safe and secure electronic payment, merchants must take steps to ensure the security of their transactions.

There are three primary concerns that merchants must address when thinking about credit-card security: the transfer of data from the customer's computer to the merchant's e-commerce store, the transfer of data from the merchant to the payment processors, and the protection of customer data stored in the merchant's database.

The first two issues concern data transfer on the Internet and are addressed with the use of secure protocols. The most popular security protocol in the United States is **Secure Sockets Layer**, more commonly referred to as **SSL**. SSL is used to encrypt either data sent between the customer's computer and the merchant's Web server or data sent between the merchant and payment processor. The two most popular Web browsers, Netscape Navigator and Microsoft Internet Explorer, are both SSL-capable. A customer using these applications can check to see if his or her connection is secure by checking for a closed lock or key icon at the bottom of the browser window or checking to see if the URL begins with "https://" as opposed to "http://."

The third issue concerns data, such as credit-card numbers, stored by the merchant. To protect this data, merchants usually store it in a secure database that cannot be accessed over the Internet. In addition, such data are often left in the database in encrypted form to protect the merchant from internal theft.

## Implementation

To enable credit-card transactions, an e-commerce merchant must establish connections with two parties. First he or she must create a merchant account with a financial institution called an **acquiring bank**, and second, he or she must establish a **payment gateway** connection from the store to the credit-card processing networks. The acquiring bank processes the credit-card transaction through the card networks and then deposits the funds into the merchant's bank account. The payment gateway connection to the credit-card networks allows the merchant to gain real-time authorizations of customers' credit cards.

There are two key components of implementing credit-card payment on the Web. The first is integrating the orders coming to an e-commerce site with an existing credit-card payment infrastructure that was originally designed for the bricks-and-mortar world. The second component is security. Not only must e-commerce sites be able to provide confidential transmission of payment information for customers when they place an order, but they also must be able to provide secure storage of customer payment information once it is received. Integrating these systems and providing customers a secure transaction environment requires significant technical expertise and technological investment.

## SECURITY[12]

Keeping assets (including products, cash, and employees) secure has been an issue for merchants for as long as commerce has existed. As the technology of commerce has progressed, so have the threats to commerce. The worldwide economies of scale enjoyed by merchants on the Internet are also enjoyed by hackers who have an unprecedented ability to steal from literally millions of e-commerce customers in an instant. Keeping a store safe has been and always will be a constant battle. As electronic commerce becomes a part of our daily lives, this battle will increasingly be fought on a front defined by technology.

## Bricks-and-Mortar

Until recently, managing security for a bricks-and-mortar store had more to do with physical security than anything else. Physical security of inventory, cash, and customer records is still and always will be important in the bricks-and-mortar world. Security technologies employed in the offline world include overt and covert cameras, alarms and security tags, and security guards.

### Overt and Covert Cameras. To monitor both shoplifting activity and *shrink* (employee theft of inventory), store management may install cameras in areas where theft is likely. In locations where aesthetics are not an issue (such as in a ware-

house or discount store) or in situations (such as at a bank) where preventing a robbery attempt is important, easily recognized overt cameras are used. In situations where management is concerned about aesthetics, difficult-to-detect covert cameras are used that allow store managers to minimize their visual impact on the store while monitoring employee and customer activity.

**Alarms and Security Tags.** Stores can use alarms to monitor entry and exit activity during off hours to reduce the threat of burglary and robbery. In addition, some stores with high-value items, such as designer clothing, place security tags on expensive items so that an alarm will sound if the items are taken from the store without being paid for.

**Security Guards.** Security personnel do both in-store activity monitoring and off-hours monitoring. These guards can be uniformed or they can perform an undercover surveillance function to monitor store activity.

# E-Commerce

Physical security issues still exist with most e-commerce companies. For example, Web merchants who sell physical products (as opposed to downloadable products) still need to be concerned with shrink and burglary. But e-commerce security is complicated by several factors that are less prevalent or nonexistent in offline commerce.

**Technologically Complex.** Since selling products on the Web is so technology-dependent, significant technological expertise is required to secure an e-commerce site.

**Many More Potential Attackers.** Other issues exist due to the worldwide scale of e-commerce enterprises. Since the Internet allows a site to be accessed by a worldwide base of customers, it also allows it to be accessed by a worldwide base of hackers and criminals. This means that the number of potential attackers on a site at any given time is significantly greater than the number of people who could physically attack a store. It also means that an attack can originate from a foreign location, which makes law enforcement on the Internet much more difficult than local enforcement due to the differences in laws of various countries.

**Much More Potential Damage.** Because an e-commerce site is functionally the equivalent of a large single store, the scale of crimes that can be committed against an online store is far larger than it is for any single outlet of a chain of physical stores. For example, if a hacker gets access to the customer database of an e-commerce site, he probably has access to every customer credit card the company has worldwide, whereas someone rifling through records at a physical store would most likely only have access to data for credit cards used at that location.

# E-Commerce Security Technology

The unique nature of the threats to e-commerce companies requires new technologies and systems to provide a secure transaction environment. Due to the openness of many of the networks that comprise the Internet, it is relatively easy to have your privacy invaded (e.g., it is relatively easy for cable-modem users to view the e-mail of neighboring cable-modem users on the same system by downloading free software to their computers). Although no site on the Internet is ever 100 percent secure, several technologies can be employed to help reduce the risk to companies and their customers when conducting e-commerce transactions.

**Passwords.** Password protection may be the most common security measure found in computing today. *Logins* and passwords are used to identify who is trying to access a site or part of a site. When attempting to access a secure area, customers are presented with a screen that requests a user ID or login and a password (the password protects secure accounts). Upon supplying the appropriate password for that user ID, the customer is allowed to access confidential information pertaining to his or her account (e.g., order status, shipping address, and payment information). By setting up and using an account, customers are prevented from having to reenter their name, address, and payment information every time they place an order. As you can see from Exhibit 3-6, buy.com uses the e-mail address of the customer as a login to aid memorization. There are two primary drawbacks that tend to make passwords less secure than other security methods mentioned later in this chapter. First, people are not always diligent about keeping passwords secret. Users can share their passwords with "friends," write down their passwords in places where they can be found, or choose passwords that are easy to guess. Second, many websites allow for login information to be sent in an unencrypted manner. Because of this, a hacker with *sniffing software* (software that allows a hacker to read packets moving between a site and its users) could inspect packets going to the server and steal user passwords.

**Exhibit 3-6**

## BUY.COM CUSTOMER LOGIN SCREEN

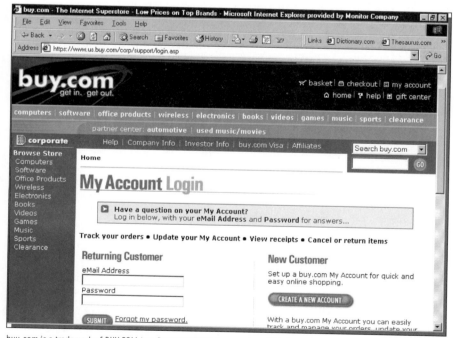

**Encryption.** Since so much personal information (e.g., names, addresses, and credit-card information) is sent across the Internet during e-commerce transactions, there is a need to ensure that this information is kept private while it is being communicated between the customer and the site. **Encryption** technology encodes and decodes information transmitted over the Internet so that only the sender and intended recipient can read the information. This is accomplished through the use of complex mathematical formulas. Well-designed encryption software uses formulas so complex that it would take most powerful computers years to figure out how to decode the messages (although with processor power increasing exponentially, there is a need to keep improving and upgrading encryption standards). This is why encryption is not used for every transaction on the Internet. The processing load of making the calculations to encrypt all data sent to a server would make those servers run too slowly for practical use. Instead, encryption use is reserved for the transmission of sensitive data, such as credit-card numbers.

*How to Use Encryption.* Use of encryption requires that software be installed on both the sending and receiving computers that will be communicating. For example, if somebody wants to send a secure e-mail to a friend, she would write her message, use her encryption software to encrypt the message, and then send the message. The friend would receive the message in encrypted form, use her software to decrypt the message, and read it. If other people somehow get a copy of the message in transit or by other means, they would not be able to read it since the message is encrypted.

Most people who have placed orders online have probably already used encryption technology. The Secure Sockets Layer (SSL) discussed earlier in the payment section is a type of encryption software that automatically sets up an encrypted "pipe" through which the browser and server can communicate. This happens whenever the browser hits a secure section of a website. On most browsers the lock or key icon will be shown as closed if a user is on a secure connection and will appear as open (or not appear at all) if the user is not on a secure connection.

**Public Key Infrastructure (PKI).** You might be wondering if a third party who steals encrypted information could just use any piece of encryption software to decrypt the stolen information. This cannot happen. Encryption software uses pieces of additional software called **keys** to ensure that only the creators and intended recipients of encrypted information are able to access it.

For encrypted data to be transmitted from one computer to another, a set of two keys is required. One of the keys is called a *public key* and the other is called a *private key*. The public key is used for encrypting data that will be sent to a computer that has the corresponding private key. This private key is used for decryption of data sent to it from a computer that has encrypted the data with its corresponding public key. Any user who wants to be able to receive encrypted data from other users can use a set of these keys to accomplish the task.

For example, if you wanted all of your friends to send you e-mail in encrypted format, you would simply get a set of keys (one private key and one public key) and distribute a copy of the public key to each of the friends you want to have send you encrypted e-mail. Your friends would then use their encryption software with your public key to encrypt their e-mail to you, and e-mail the message to you. You would use your private key (which only you possess) to decrypt your friends' messages and read them. However, if you wanted to be able to send one of these friends encrypted replies to her messages, then your friend would have to get a set of keys for herself and send you a copy of her public key. Only then could you encrypt messages to send to her. Therefore, for two parties to carry on encrypted communication back and forth each has to have a set of two keys (one public and one private) for a total of four keys altogether.

**Public-Key Infrastructure in E-Commerce.** Public-key encryption is commonly used on e-commerce websites as a way to ensure that sensitive data from customers (e.g., credit-card numbers) is kept private while being transmitted across the Internet. Most e-commerce Web servers contain a private key for decryption. This private key along with its corresponding public key are oftentimes created and distributed by trusted third-party companies (such as VeriSign). When an e-commerce Web server is first set up, it will have a private key and public key installed on it. Once running, the Web server will automatically send a copy of the public key to any customer's browser who logs on to a secure page on the site for the first time. This public-key (also known as a **digital certificate**) is stored in the customer's browser and used for that session and all future sessions with that Web server until the private-key changes (e.g., some users might update their digital certificate as even more secure encryption methods become available). The transmission of keys from server to browser is automatic. The only involvement the user has in the process is in agreeing that she trusts the Web server she is connecting to (see "Authentication" later in this chapter). Once the user agrees to trust the site, an encrypted "tunnel" for communication is established between the browser and the server that allows secure transmission of data between the two. This secure tunnel is known as *Secure Sockets Layer (SSL)* and is created automatically when a user attempts to connect to a page that requires secure data transmission (i.e., any page whose URL begins with "https://"). Once an SSL session has begun, the user can confidently send encrypted information to the Web server that only the server can decrypt.

**Public-Key Infrastructure for Authentication.** How can a customer know whether or not the site he is communicating with is the "real" site he thinks he is connecting to? The process of ensuring that the website that customers are using is really the one they think is called *authentication*. Although in e-commerce transactions customers use public keys to encrypt the data they transmit and servers use their private keys to decrypt this information, the process can work in reverse as well. To prove that they are who they say they are, Web servers can encrypt a special document called a *digital signature* and send it to a customer's browser. The customer's browser with the public key can then decrypt the digital signature file to see if it is legitimate. Because private keys are held only by the company that owns them, if the corresponding public key for that company (acquired from a third party such as VeriSign) successfully decrypts the digital signature, then the customer knows it has come from the company he expects. Authentication is important since it is possible for someone to make a fake website that looks like the real thing, and then use that website to illegally collect credit-card numbers from unsuspecting customers.

**Managing Secure Transactions.** Although SSL makes the process of sending order information in a secure manner easy for customers, there are many things that have to happen behind the scenes when an order is placed on the Web. To process the payment, the credit-card number for the order must be authorized by the cardholder's bank. **Secure Electronic Transaction (SET)** is a protocol that facilitates the secure authentication of credit-card transactions on the Web as well as other

Exhibit
3-7 DIGITAL CERTIFICATE TRANSMISSION IN E-COMMERCE

**Trusted Third Party Certificate Provider**

**Customer's PC**

1. Digital certificate/public key and private key are sent to server (when server is initially set-up).

2. A copy of public key is sent to customer's PC. The customer accepts this certificate to create SSL "pipe" between user's PC and server.

3. An encrypted "tunnel" is created.

Credit card information
VISA

4. Certificate is used to encrypt data.

Encrypted credit card information

5. Encrypted data is sent to the server via internet.

**Web Server with Private Key**

7. Server stores and processes credit card data.

Credit card information
VISA

6. Private key is used to decrypt data.

Encrypted credit card information

**Internet**

**Note:** Step 3 indicates the creation of an SSL encrypted "tunnel" for data to pass through. Steps 4 through 7 show what happens behind the scenes in SSL.

= non-SSL transmission

= SSL transmission

Exhibit
3-8  DIGITAL SIGNATURE TRANSMISSION

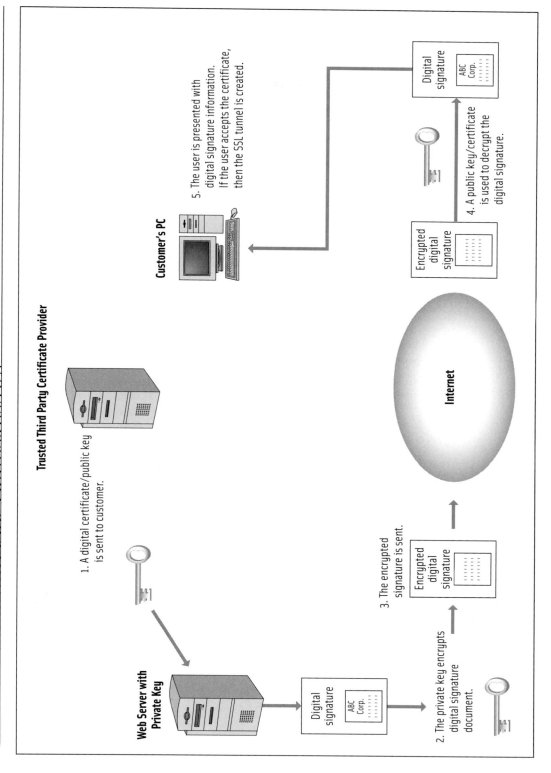

**Trusted Third Party Certificate Provider**

1. A digital certificate/public key is sent to customer.

**Web Server with Private Key**

2. The private key encrypts digital signature document.

Digital signature
ABC Corp.

3. The encrypted signature is sent.

Encrypted digital signature

Internet

**Customer's PC**

5. The user is presented with digital signature information. If the user accepts the certificate, then the SSL tunnel is created.

Encrypted digital signature

4. A public key/certificate is used to decrypt the digital signature.

Digital signature
ABC Corp.

payment processing issues such as debit-card transactions and credits back to credit cards.

### Securing Companies from External Attack.
Consumers are not the only ones who need to be protected from unscrupulous interests on the Internet. Companies need to protect themselves against the threat of a worldwide base of hackers who can damage a company's reputation and profitability. These attacks can range from virus attacks to stealing customer credit-card information from internal company databases.

*Screening Routers.* Most routers today can do more than just identify the best path for a packet and pass it on. Routers can also be set up to screen packets as well. Routers set up for this purpose are known as "screening routers." The primary difference in their function is that they not only look at whether they can forward a packet, but also check to see whether they *should* forward a packet. This determination is made based on rules that the network administrator sets according to the company's security policy. For example, if users inside of a company need Web access but do not need FTP access, a screening router can be configured to prevent all FTP traffic from traveling between the Internet and the company's internal network. This setup would prevent any employees from accidentally downloading a virus via FTP. It would also prevent an employee from setting up an Internet-accessible FTP server on her PC that could allow hackers to see sensitive files.

*Proxy Servers.* The primary purpose of a **proxy server** (also called a *gateway*) is to forward packets on behalf of PCs on a company's internal network to the Internet. When using a proxy, if a computer on the company's network wants to request something from the Internet (e.g., a webpage), instead of directly contacting the server it wants to access, it requests the information from the proxy server. The proxy server then contacts the site on the Internet and makes the request for the information as if it were requesting the information for itself. After receiving the information, the proxy-server forwards it on to the appropriate computer on the internal network. The true identity of the computer requesting the information is never transmitted across the Internet. To computers on the Internet, all requests for information from proxy-server users appear to be coming from the proxy server itself. This has an important security benefit because it prevents the identities (IP addresses) of individual computers inside a company's network from being "published" to the Internet whenever a computer on the internal network accesses the Internet. This anonymity makes it more difficult for hackers to access computers on the internal network, keeping the network more secure.

Proxy servers provide other benefits beyond security. Many proxy servers support *caching* (temporary local storage) of recently requested information. This means that if several people in a company use the same website often, the proxy server will automatically store a copy of the viewed pages for that site on its local hard disk. When a user makes a request for a page that is cached, the proxy server will send a copy of the page from its local hard disk over the company's fast local network instead of going out onto the Internet and pulling the page down again. This saves users time, since obtaining the document is faster over the local network, and it also preserves Internet bandwidth, since the most frequently used pages will not require frequent redownloading from the Internet. Another benefit of using proxies is that they increase scalability. Because individual computers on the company's local network are not directly accessing the Internet, they do not need to have globally unique IP addresses. Only the proxy server needs to have such an address, because (according to other computers on the Internet) only the proxy server is making requests. This simplifies adding new users to the internal network, since addresses for computers on the local network need to be unique only to the local network, not worldwide.

*Firewalls.* A key piece of infrastructure used to keep hackers out of a company's internal network is the *firewall*. A firewall is essentially a computer (or specialized appliance) that sits between the Internet and anything a company wants to protect (such as a Web server or the company's internal network). A firewall functions similarly to antivirus software for PCs, except that instead of looking on a hard disk for malicious content, it looks at packets coming over a network connection, while they are in transit. Firewalls perform what is known as *stateful inspection*. This means that rather than just looking at source and destination information, or the type of service the packet is used for (such as FTP or HTTP), the firewall actually looks more closely inside the packet to determine whether or not it could be harmful. If a packet looks dangerous, the firewall will prevent it from passing into the company from the Internet. Firewalls can be actual computers with specialized software running on them, or they can be specialized pieces of hardware (like some routers) that are designed to perform firewall functions very quickly.

# FULFILLMENT

Fulfillment is often considered the least glamorous component of e-commerce. Many early e-commerce startups spent millions on customer acquisition and brand building, while paying little to no attention on fulfillment. As a result, many early customers complained of late or erroneous orders, which lead those customers to look elsewhere for their future purchases.

Fulfillment is, in fact, a crucial component of online selling. Fulfillment encompasses all activities that enable merchants to adequately complete customer orders. These activities include taking orders on the front end, processing these orders, picking and packing, delivery, and processing customer returns.

## Bricks-and-Mortar

Fulfillment has long been a component of bricks-and-mortar selling. Fulfillment in the offline world can take many forms, depending on the type of business. For example, a chain of national discount stores, such as Wal-Mart, would have very different fulfillment needs than a cataloger, such as Fingerhut.

Fulfillment for Wal-Mart includes all the steps necessary to distribute products to individual Wal-Mart stores, where customers can conveniently purchase and take home the products of their choice. These steps might be ensuring that there are enough Wal-Mart stores to adequately serve customers, build relationships with suppliers, create a distribution network of warehouses and trucks to maintain inventory levels at individual stores, and provide customer-service counters at individual stores to process customer returns.

Fingerhut has different fulfillment needs than Wal-Mart. Fingerhut must still build relationships with suppliers, but as a company that specializes in catalog sales, Fingerhut does not need to create a distribution network of regional warehouses, trucks, and retail stores. Instead, Fingerhut must deal with a different set of issues surrounding filling individual orders and delivering these orders to individual customers. Instead of building retail stores that customers can access to pick up their desired items, Fingerhut must take the extra step of delivering those items to their customers. In addition, customer returns must also be handled through delivery instead of through face-to-face interaction at a physical store.

## E-Commerce

If you are beginning to think that catalog-fulfillment issues look a lot like the fulfillment issues that e-commerce merchants must confront, you are probably right. With both types of businesses, the burden of delivery is placed squarely on the shoulders of the merchant. Instead of bulk-shipping items to distribution channels, individual items must be picked and packed and delivered to individuals. This scenario creates a significant fulfillment challenge for both catalogers and e-commerce merchants, particularly when considering the challenge of managing the logistics of thousands of individual orders and unique deliveries and controlling the costs of shipping.

A recent study reports that approximately 44 percent of online retailers lose money on shipping and handling, while 37 percent cite the cost of shipping as their primary fulfillment challenge.[13] The fact that many e-commerce merchants (particularly online retailers who must fulfill individual orders) are not profitable is well publicized. The online retailing graveyard is a large and illustrious one, filled with billions of lost dollars, and former household names such as Pets.com and eToys. In fact, a recent study found that of established e-commerce pure-plays, only 24 percent were profitable.[14]

However, despite these grim numbers, hope is not lost. The same study found that of catalog-based e-commerce plays nearly 80 percent were profitable. Catalogers are experienced in fulfilling remote orders, and this experience filters down to the bottom line. Fulfillment is a significant factor in determining the profitability of an e-commerce venture. Major issues facing merchants as they consider e-commerce fulfillment are discussed in the following sections.

### Customer Demand for Transparency.
The Web provides customers with an easy interface to collect and track information. Web customers often demand increased information about their purchases, such as order status and delivery tracking. In contrast, most bricks-and-mortar mail-order businesses do not offer this level of transparency. With bricks-and-mortar merchants, after the order is placed either through mail-in forms or telephone, the customer typically has very little information about the status of their order. Usually the only data the customer has is a range of dates within which her order is likely to arrive. On the Web, however, customers demand much more. Most established e-commerce merchants try to please their customers by providing as much information as possible. This information might include product availability, order status, and shipping status. After an order is placed over the Web, the customer often has the ability to check the status of the order at any time. Most major e-commerce delivery services, such as Federal Express, UPS, and the United States Postal Service, even offer package tracking to precise geographic detail; the customer always knows where her package is and how much time is necessary for the package to complete its route. Web customers' demand for transparency creates significant challenges for e-commerce merchants because providing this information often requires the coordination of many different systems and information sources into a seamless Web-based information experience for the customer.

## Many Activities and Parties.

A key challenge for e-commerce fulfillment is handling the logistics of accommodating many activities and parties simultaneously. E-commerce merchants have to coordinate the many activities involved in fulfillment, but to complicate things further, these activities are often handled by different parties. For shipping alone, an e-commerce merchant could use a variety of providers (UPS, FedEx, U.S. Postal Service, Airborne Express, etc.) simultaneously, depending on customer-preferred variables, such as cost or delivery time. On top of that, an e-commerce merchant could use different providers to address customer service needs, electronic order processing, product sourcing, and warehouse logistics.

## Multiple Systems.

In addition to keeping track of these multiple parties, an e-commerce merchant must also be able to coordinate between different platforms and multiple computer systems. For example, many catalog companies rely on older mainframe and minicomputer systems to handle their inventory and may rely on completely different computer platforms to handle payment. We have already discussed some of the challenges to setting up a website capable of displaying the company's products and taking order information securely. In addition to these challenges, companies wishing to add e-commerce capabilities to existing fulfillment systems need to find ways to integrate all of their systems such that they can automatically process orders taken over the Web. Many times these *legacy systems* are not compatible with each other (e.g., they may run on different operating systems) and were set up before the advent of the Web. Making all of these disparate technologies work together seamlessly requires significant planning, equipment, and technical expertise.

## Capacity Utilization.

Another issue that e-commerce merchants often cite as a major challenge is capacity utilization. According to a recent survey, online merchants struggle with adequately accommodating order volatility.[15] About 60 percent of online merchants report the number of orders during peak days to be at least four times the number of orders for an average day. About one quarter report peak days of over eight times the number of orders on an average day.

Reluctant to turn away orders, early e-commerce merchants were forced to build the distribution and fulfillment resources necessary to adequately fulfill orders during peak times. A specific example is Webvan, a $1.2 billion bet on revolutionizing the grocery business. Webvan designed its state-of-the-art San Francisco fulfillment warehouse to handle about 8,000 orders per day. However, in reality, Webvan fulfills just over 2,100 orders per day, leaving three quarters of the facility unutilized.[16] Webvan is not alone in its utilization troubles. Often running fulfillment facilities at a mere fraction of capacity, many e-commerce merchants are beginning to feel the ramifications of their inefficiencies. Other early e-commerce players such as Amazon.com built elaborate fulfillment facilities, equipped with the latest technology designed to fulfill massive numbers of orders per day. However, with these facilities sitting idle or operating at low capacity, these merchants decided to scale back and sell these facilities, in many cases, at a deep discount.[17]

As a result, most e-commerce merchants are migrating towards more flexible fulfillment solutions that can efficiently accommodate their fulfillment peaks and valleys. These fulfillment solutions often include the use of third-party outsourced fulfillment providers, often referred to as *e-commerce service providers (ESP)*, who, while serving a multitude of customers, can reach the economies of scale associated with effective capacity utilization.

**Exhibit 3-9** FULFILLMENT—INTEGRATING MULTIPLE PARTNERS, TECHNOLOGIES, AND SYSTEMS IS A MAJOR CHALLENGE.

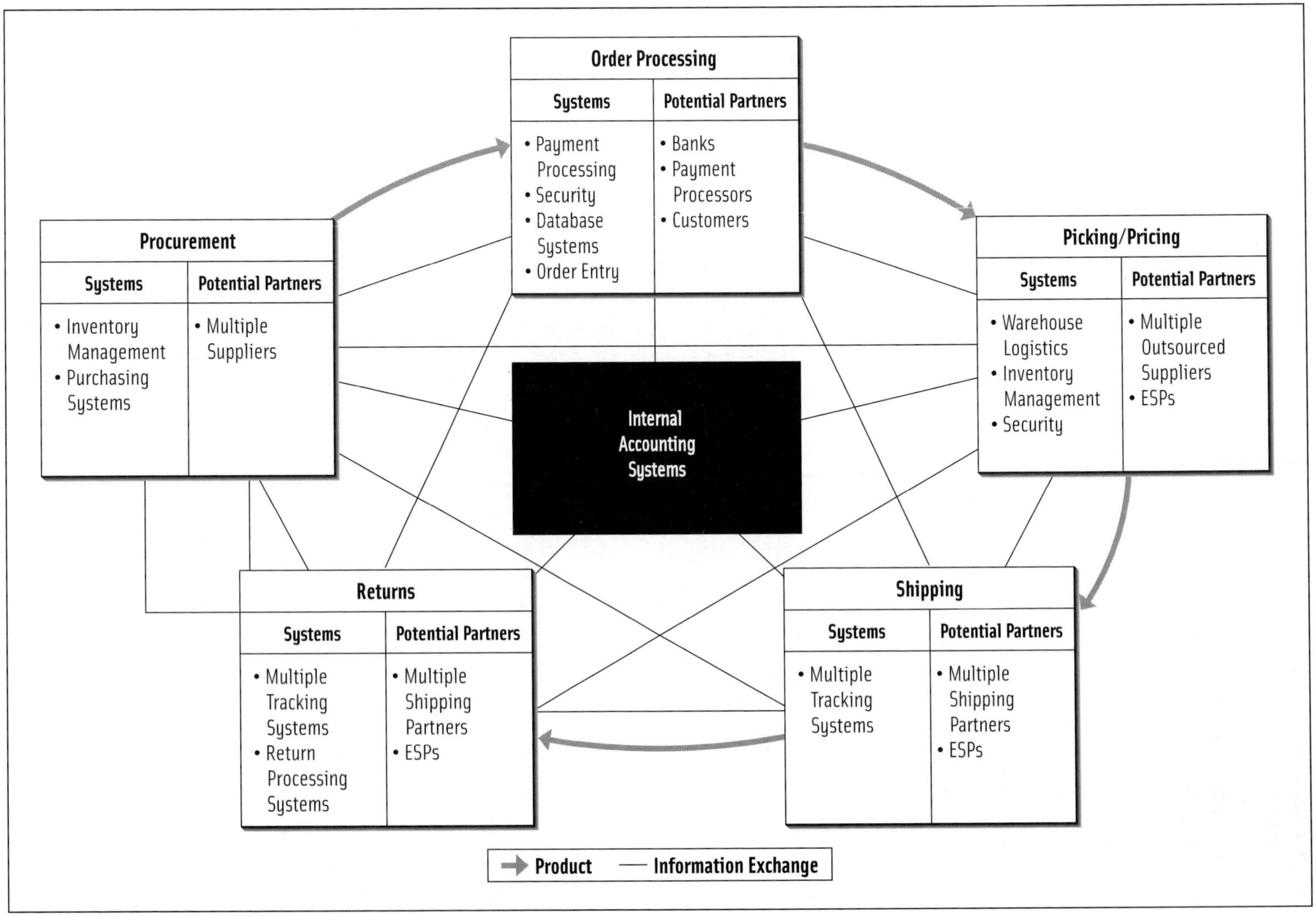

**Procurement**

| Systems | Potential Partners |
|---|---|
| • Inventory Management • Purchasing Systems | • Multiple Suppliers |

**Order Processing**

| Systems | Potential Partners |
|---|---|
| • Payment Processing • Security • Database Systems • Order Entry | • Banks • Payment Processors • Customers |

**Picking/Pricing**

| Systems | Potential Partners |
|---|---|
| • Warehouse Logistics • Inventory Management • Security | • Multiple Outsourced Suppliers • ESPs |

**Shipping**

| Systems | Potential Partners |
|---|---|
| • Multiple Tracking Systems | • Multiple Shipping Partners • ESPs |

**Returns**

| Systems | Potential Partners |
|---|---|
| • Multiple Tracking Systems • Return Processing Systems | • Multiple Shipping Partners • ESPs |

**Internal Accounting Systems**

→ Product — Information Exchange

# SUMMARY

### 1. What are the key similarities and differences between e-commerce and bricks-and-mortar selling in regard to location?

The "location" and naming of an online or bricks-and-mortar store are important to driving traffic to it. Having an easy-to-remember and logical domain name for a virtual store increases brand awareness and makes locating the store easier for customers. Physical stores can locate on popular streets or in malls to maximize foot traffic, while online stores can "locate" their stores in virtual malls to generate traffic. In addition, making sure that the location has enough capacity to handle the number of customers it will attract is critical. In a bricks-and-mortar store, having enough capacity involves making sure there is enough physical space to handle the foot traffic generated by the store. Online, having enough capacity involves maintaining enough server bandwidth and processing power to allow fast and reliable access to the store during peak hours of use.

### 2. What are popular methods for marketing an e-commerce store?

The vehicles used for marketing many bricks-and-mortar stores (e.g., advertising, public relations, and guerrilla marketing) are also available to online storefronts. In addition, the online medium provides new marketing options such as banner advertising, spam, and viral marketing.

### 3. How does e-commerce payment differ from bricks-and-mortar payment?

A variety of popular payment forms exists in the offline world. In the online world, however, credit card is king. When a credit card is used in a physical store, the clerk can check the buyer's identification, and the store has a signed receipt for the purchase to keep in its records. Online purchases, however, do not have this paper trail and are therefore referred to as card-not-present transactions. Because of this difference, the financial responsibility for credit-card fraud is placed on the credit-card company for bricks-and-mortar purchases and on the merchant for online card-not-present transactions.

### 4. What roles does security play in e-commerce?

The key components of online security are privacy and authentication. SSL is the most popular encryption technology used to ensure privacy during online purchases. Encryption utilizes public key infrastructure to encrypt and decrypt sensitive information. Digital signatures are used to authenticate the identity of websites so that consumers can be sure they are giving their payment information to the company they intend to. Firewalls are used to decrease the risk of Internet hackers gaining access to a company's private networks and sensitive information.

### 5. What challenges exist in e-commerce fulfillment?

Along with the complexities associated with warehousing, picking, packing, shipping, and handling returns, e-commerce companies must also contend with issues specific to Web businesses. E-commerce customers are increasingly expecting better information on the status of their orders. E-commerce businesses have to integrate the activities of many different parties to ensure proper delivery, as well as contend with the difficulties of integrating Web order-taking capabilities with multiple systems for procurement, payment, inventory management, and delivery. Finally, online retailers have to ensure that they maintain high-capacity utilization while having adequate capacity to handle customers' fulfillment needs during peak order cycles.

## KEY TERMS

| | |
|---|---|
| bandwidth | Secure Sockets Layer (SSL) |
| processing power | acquiring bank |
| data storage capacity | payment gateway |
| domain name | encryption |
| Web host | keys |
| guerrilla marketing | Secure Electronic Transaction (SET) |
| direct marketing | proxy servers |
| meta tags | |
| banner ads | |

## Endnotes

[1]U.S. Department of Commerce. 16 February, 2001. URL: *www.census.gov/mrts/www/current.html*.

[2]Lawrence, Stacy. "Catalogers wise to the Net," *The Industry Standard*, 22 May, 2000. URL: *www.thestandard.com/research/metrics/display/0,2799,15270,00.html*.

[3]"E-commerce 101: Common problems in hosting an online store," Top Hats.com. URL: *www.tophosts.com/pages/articles/ecom10101.htm*.

[4]Intel e-business center "Nasdaq Snapshot" Intel Corporation 2001. URL: *www.intel.com/eBusiness/casestudies/snapshots/nasdaq.htm*.

[5]Medford, Cassimir. "Analytics," *PC Magazine*, 4 January, 2001. URL: *www.zdnet.com/pcmag/stories/reviews/0,6755,2668446,00.html*.

[6]Clickery, Roy Williams. "Data powers of ten," California Institute of Technology, 1995. URL: *www.cacr.caltech.edu/~roy/dataquan/*.

[7]Bowles, Jerry. "E-storage: Managing your data in a networked world," *Forbes*. URL: *www.forbes.com/specialsections/estorage/intro.htm*.

[8]Sullivan, Danny. "How to use HTML meta tags," SearchEngineWatch.com, 15 December, 2000. URL: *searchenginewatch.com/webmasters/meta.html*.

[9]Thompson, Maryann Jones. "Search engines can't keep up with web," *The Industry Standard*, 7 July, 1999. URL: *www.thestandard.com/article/display/0,1151,5423,00.html*.

[10]Beckett, Paul. "Online ads don't work? They do for this dot-com," *The Wall Street Journal*, 29 January, 2001. URL: *startup.wsj.com/n/SB98086768058091553-main.html*.

[11]Gartner Group. "E-tailers squeezed by higher credit card fraud and rates," July 28, 2000.

[12]Information for this section came from the following sources:
Comer, Douglas. *The Internet Book, 3rd Ed*. (Englewood Cliffs, NJ: Prentice Hall, Inc., 2000).
Turban, Efraim, Jae Lee, David King, and H. Michael Chung. *Electronic Commerce, A Managerial Perspective* (Englewood Cliffs, NJ: Prentice Hall, 2000).
Gralla, Preston. *How the Internet Works* (Indianapolis: Que, 1999).
Korper, Steffano, and Juanita Ellis. *The E-Commerce Book, Building the E-Empire, 2nd Ed*. (California: Academic Press, 2001).

[13]Wolf, Jason. *Internet Commerce and the Last Mile* (Jupiter Research, 2001).

[14]Lawrence, Stacy. "Catalogers wise to the Net," *The Industry Standard*, 22 May, 2000. URL: *www.thestandard.com/research/metrics/display/0,2799,15270,00.html*.

[15]Schatsky, David. "Fulfillment Nets," Jupiter Communications, 2000.

[16]Hansell, Saul. "Some hard lessons for online grocer," *The New York Times,* 19 February, 2001.

[17]Helft, Miguel. "Wanna buy a warehouse?" *The Industry Standard,* 12 March, 2001. URL: *www.thestandard.com/article/display/0,1151,22759,00.html.*

# 4

# Framing Market Opportunity

In Chapter 1, we examined the impact of e-commerce and some of its distinguishing features. We also briefly reviewed the decision-making process that companies must go through in order to develop an e-commerce strategy. In this chapter, we answer the first question a company must address when formulating its strategy: "Where will the business compete?" Ideally, a company would like to compete in an arena in which the financial opportunity is considerable and the competitors are scarce, and in which it can position itself well to fulfill unmet customer needs either on its own or through partnerships. Obviously, this is very difficult

to accomplish. Hence, a firm needs to follow a rigorous approach—such as the one outlined below—to isolate market opportunities.

In this chapter, we introduce a five-step process that a company can use to address this first question: (1) seeding an opportunity in an existing or new value system, (2) uncovering an opportunity nucleus, (3) identifying target segments, (4) declaring a company's resource-based opportunity, and (5) assessing the opportunity attractiveness. By following these five steps, a company can make an educated "go/no-go" decision about pursuing the opportunity.

## QUESTIONS

*Please consider the following questions as you read this chapter:*

1. What is the market-opportunity analysis framework?

2. Is market-opportunity analysis different in the networked economy?

This chapter was coauthored by Toby Thomas and Mark Pocharski. Substantive input was also provided by Robert Lurie, Leo Griffin, Yannis Dosios, Bernie Jaworski, and Scott Daniels.

3. What are two generic "value types"?

4. How do we identify unmet and/or underserved needs?

5. What determines the customer segment a company will pursue?

6. Who provides the resources to deliver the benefits of the offering?

7. How do we assess the attractiveness of the opportunity?

8. How do we prepare a "go/no-go" assessment?

# INTRODUCTON

In the last three years, we have seen an unprecedented launch (and failure) rate of Internet startups. For some, enduring the risks associated with starting a new business will prove rewarding. But most will watch their businesses crash and burn—the historical failure rate of startup companies is over 80 percent.

Market-opportunity analysis is an essential tool for both entrepreneurs and senior managers who plan to launch new businesses. While good opportunity analysis will not guarantee a startup's success, thinking through the conditions that define opportunity attractiveness increases the likelihood of pursuing an attractive idea. Poor or no opportunity analysis increases the chance that a new venture will fail.

This chapter examines the key question, "Where will the business compete?" and will also touch on the question of how the business will succeed. Regardless of the reasons a firm seeks online business opportunities, the successful company defines its marketspace early in the business development process. The term **marketspace** refers to the digital equivalent of a physical-world marketplace. By defining the intended marketspace, the company identifies the customers it will serve and the competitors it will face. Over time, a company's defined marketspace may change as both the company and the market evolve, but a clear, initial definition is necessary to develop the business model.

In this chapter, we propose a framework for **market-opportunity analysis** and review some of the tools that can be used to "frame" the market opportunity. A lot of this spadework will be deepened and refined as the company moves toward developing and launching a market offering. This is discussed in subsequent chapters.

# WHAT IS THE MARKET-OPPORTUNITY ANALYSIS FRAMEWORK?

The framework for our market-opportunity analysis consists of five main investigative stages and a final go/no-go decision. Exhibit 4-1 illustrates the five conditions that firms should satisfy in order to frame market opportunity. Taken together, these five conditions comprise the scope of a sound market-opportunity analysis:

**Seed Opportunity.** Opportunity identification and analysis is anchored within an existing or new value system, or the "playing field." The **value system** can be thought of as the entire chain of suppliers, distributors, competitors, buyers, and intermediaries that brings an existing offering to market. In the networked economy, the starting point for opportunity identification is often someone with a belief

**Exhibit 4-1**

# FRAMEWORK FOR MARKET OPPORTUNITY

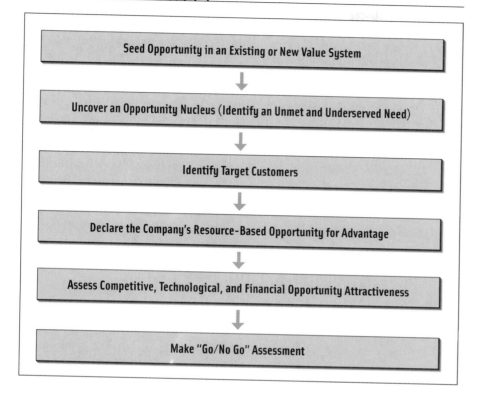

Seed Opportunity in an Existing or New Value System

↓

Uncover an Opportunity Nucleus (Identify an Unmet and Underserved Need)

↓

Identify Target Customers

↓

Declare the Company's Resource-Based Opportunity for Advantage

↓

Assess Competitive, Technological, and Financial Opportunity Attractiveness

↓

Make "Go/No Go" Assessment

about a value system that can be reinvented or transformed. This value system becomes the anchor for framing the opportunity. Then, economic activities can be identified to be harnessed, redirected, or created, and customers and current market players can be identified.

**Uncover Opportunity Nucleus.** Once a rough definition of the playing field is set, the company can define the opportunity to increase customer satisfaction or create a new, highly valued customer experience. What experiences frustrate customers today? What are companies missing, consciously or unconsciously, while foregoing benefits? What can be fixed, even if customers do not know it is broken?

A key activity at this stage is uncovering either unmet needs (needs not currently being served) or underserved needs (needs being served but in an improvable manner).

**Identify Target Customers.** Identifying and choosing priority customers leads to a preliminary understanding of the potential audience the company could seek to serve. Who are they and what makes them attractive to pursue? What experiences do these customers seek? What would the company need to offer them? What barriers would the company need to overcome to get these customers to participate in an offering? In identifying and selecting target segments, the company should develop an initial sketch of these customers to both shape the business concept and to estimate the size of the opportunity. This knowledge is essential as the company begins to determine the nature of its offering.

**Declare the Company's Resource-Based Opportunity.** The fourth step is to examine the distinct capabilities and activities the company would bring to the offering to achieve advantage, either through its own resources or those of potential partner companies. In Chapter 5, we will examine the concept of a company's "resource system" in depth. In the meantime, we will simply state that the firm must have a reason to believe it will be able to bring a set of distinct resources to win in the market. Without these resources, the company will not have the advantages it needs to build or sustain a highly profitable business and will fail to generate cash flow.

**Assess Opportunity Attractiveness.** Finally, to assess opportunity attractiveness, the company must assess the market's financial, technological, and competitive situations. Financial attractiveness focuses on segment size, growth rates, profitability, and other company-specific performance criteria. Technological assessment and a reality check ensure that available technology does or will enable the business' dream to be realized without being needlessly constrained by rapidly changing technologies. Checks on both underserved customer needs and the strength of prospective competition must also be made to satisfy this opportunity assessment condition. What competition would the firm face? Does the firm see ways to surpass this competition?

## IS MARKET-OPPORTUNITY ANALYSIS DIFFERENT IN THE NETWORKED ECONOMY?

Before exploring market-opportunity analysis in greater depth, we should consider whether this type of analysis should be any different from an analysis of opportunities in more traditional sectors of the economy. Some authors and analysts believe that opportunity analysis in the marketspace is unique and requires a different approach. We summarize this reasoning in the following paragraphs.

**Competition Occurs *Across* Industry Boundaries Rather Than *Within* Industry Boundaries.** Web-enabled business models can operate across traditional industry boundaries because they lack the constraints of physical product manufacturing or service delivery. Consequently, these businesses can more accurately match value creation from the customer's perspective. For example, Cars.com (*www.cars.com*) allows customers to research and purchase new and used vehicles; finance them; insure them; and purchase parts, accessories, and even extended warranties through the website and its partners. Limiting opportunity assessment to traditional definitions of industry or value system could result in missed market opportunities.

**Competitive Developments and Response Are Occurring at an Unprecedented Speed.** Advances in technology and the adoption of creative business models are occurring at a rapid pace. During the "browser wars" between Microsoft and Netscape, each firm introduced a new version of its product approximately every six months. Any market-opportunity assessment must be continually refreshed by keeping abreast of important trends or events that could redefine opportunity attractiveness.

**Competition Occurs Between Alliances of Companies Rather Than Between Individual Companies.** Many technology-based products have a high degree of reliance on other related, complementary products; for example, Web businesses are reliant on browser technology, and browsers are dependent on operating systems, PCs, and modem technologies. Furthermore, the networked nature of the Web means that several companies can easily ally to create a seamless offer. Companies can often find themselves in "**co-opetition**"[1] with each other; in other words, they find themselves as both competitors and collaborators at the same time. BizBuyer.com and Staples.com, for example, compete as suppliers of products such as computers and photocopiers to small- and medium-size businesses, yet they are also partners. Staples customers can use BizBuyer to source business services such as Web design and consulting from an extensive supplier network. In assessing the resources necessary to succeed, managers must examine both internal and external possibilities, rather than assume the company must perform all alone.

### Consumer Behavior Is Still in the Early Stages of Being Defined, Thus It Is Easier to Influence and Change Consumer Behavior. 

Most modern marketing textbooks emphasize the importance of being customer-focused. This means that businesses must analyze customer needs, define products that meet those needs, and implement defendable strategies. In the old economy, competitive battles were frequently fought over a well-defined set of consumer behavior patterns (e.g., consumers shopping in grocery stores). However, in the networked economy, new software and hardware tilt the landscape of consumer behavior. Companies introduce products leading to new behavior and new customer requirements. The challenge is to listen closely enough to today's customers to develop insights about opportunities without being lulled into simply meeting customers' stated needs. To state the obvious: "Customers don't know what they don't know." The company's task is to define new experiences that customers will recognize and seek, based on insights into how customers are acting today and why.

Take, for example, the emergence of file-sharing service Napster, which enables users to search, share, and copy MP3 song files across a global distributed network. Introduced in the fall of 1999, Napster revolutionized consumer behavior in the recorded music industry. Then, in the spring of 2000, a new use of Napster emerged—the "swapping" of not just MP3 files but files of any format, including games, movies, software, and spreadsheets. Again, this new version could have a major impact on incumbent players.[2] Napster's future is uncertain—it has attracted venture-capital investment as well as a partnership with German media giant Bertelsmann, which is intent on transforming the company into a subscription service. Yet Napster continues to fight a legal battle aimed at shutting the service down. On February 12, 2001, an appellate court ruled that Napster is responsible for its users' copyright infringements. This may force the company to close down. Whether or not Napster survives, there is no doubt that consumers' attitudes and behaviors toward digital recordings of music have been permanently changed.

### Industry Value Chains, or Systems, Are Rapidly Being Reconfigured. 

The Internet allows businesses to reconfigure their interactions with customers by increasing the level of information throughout the value chain, enabling contact between customers and businesses 24/7, and eradicating or significantly reducing the cost of stages in the value chain. Examples of this online reengineering are easy to find. FreeMarkets.com (*www.freemarkets.com*) constructed a reverse auction for B2B markets and, in doing so, eliminated many of the costly process steps for businesses to find product price quotes.

Obviously, many existing companies and startups begin opportunity framing from a base of experience about a market or a technology. This experience base may enable a management team to accelerate through meeting one or more of the five conditions. Regardless of where a company enters the opportunity-framing process, satisfying all five conditions should create a sufficient base of knowledge and perspective needed to frame a winning business model. In this chapter, we will move sequentially through the five opportunity-framing conditions. We will start by defining the opportunity space within a specific value system or a collection of linked activities.

Whether you choose to spend one day, one month, or one year examining a market opportunity, the framework laid out in this chapter provides a useful way to discuss whether and how to pursue an opportunity in the marketspace.

---

## DRILL-DOWN

# Fashionably Late

### by Sarah Milstein, contributor to tnbt.com

Amazon.com launched in July 1995—the Cretaceous period of Internet time—and was the first national bookseller on the Web. Barnes & Noble, the nation's largest bricks-and-mortar book retailer, did not open its virtual doors until 1997. By then, Amazon was Tyrannosaurus Rex, king of the online booksellers, and it dominated the terrain. Three years later, Barnes & Noble has yet to catch up. Does being second—or late—to the Web mean a company will have to lag behind its competitors in sales and performance? Not necessarily. For some companies, being late to the online market can be an advantage. Virgin Megastores Online launched its e-commerce platform in May 1999, well after sites like CDNOW and Amazon had gained broad recognition for selling music and videos via the Web. "We didn't want to replicate existing entertainment online sites, and we had the advantage of watching our competitors, particularly in terms of marketing," says Dave Alder, Virgin Megastores Online's general manager and senior vice president. "We didn't want to spend $200 per head on customer acquisition."

Virgin leveraged the brand it had developed over 30 years in dozens of stores worldwide and tapped a loyal customer base through cross-marketing. Alder cites webcasts of exclusive in-store artist appearances as a particularly successful element of the company's clicks-and-bricks strategy. "We're very determined to utilize the marketing tools we've already got in the business. We can use online events to liven up the stores and vice versa." Alder says the website has

already paid off, since it was used to create a system that tracks whether store revenues are affected by the online research of customers. But what strategies can startups use to gain an edge? Underselling your competitors to attract a large customer base is one possibility. PC Data Inc., a firm that tracks Internet usage, began offering its online services in February 1999—more than three years after the industry leader, Media Metrix, and well after NetRatings, which has a strategic alliance with the television-ratings giant, Nielsen Media Research. Despite the uneven playing field, PC Data has become a contender by pricing its reports at fractions of its competitors' fees.

Latecomers can also employ new, attention-grabbing strategies to draw customers. When Hotmail introduced its free e-mail service in July 1996, several similar services were already on the market. But Hotmail managed to sign up 10 million subscribers in its first 18 months, surpassing competitors while spending far less on marketing, by turning its users into salespeople. Every message sent from a Hotmail account included the simple tagline, "Get your private, free e-mail from *http://www.hotmail.com.*" Viral marketing was born, and Hotmail became a household name. "Latecomers," says Michele Pelino, program manager of the Yankee Group's Internet marketing strategies team, "can really learn from what early entrants have done in the past." A common mistake is not planning for spikes in usage when driving traffic to a site. This can be as simple as not having appropriate hosting in place (remember that overloaded Victoria's Secret webcast?), or as complex as

*(continued on page 101)*

*(continued from page 100)*

not having ramped-up customer service and support. "You can also learn from what is working," notes Pelino. She cites user-friendly design and easy-to-use navigation tools, when they exist, as successful elements that can be gleaned from predecessors.

Finally, careful examination of prototype businesses can help inform a late-mover's decisions. Contentville.com, launched in July 2000, sells books, magazines, speeches, dissertations, and other print media. Although the company does not officially consider itself in direct competition with established online booksellers, it has observed its forerunners and created a notably different business model. Where

Amazon has built a network of warehouses, does its own fulfillment and has an in-house customer service unit, Contentville has pulled together partners—such as powerhouse book distributor Ingram Book Group and national magazine distributor EBSCO—who will each handle separate aspects of the site's business.

"Sometimes when you come to market later, you can benefit from watching what has gone on," notes Matthew Sappern, Contentville's vice president for marketing. "It's great Monday morning quarterbacking."

*Read more articles about The Next Big Thing at www.tnbt.com.*

# WHAT ARE THE TWO GENERIC VALUE TYPES?

The first step in framing the business opportunity is to broadly identify the business arena in which the new business will participate. The purpose is to declare both what is "in" and what is "out" of the business-model consideration set. For our purposes, the business arena is typically defined within or across an industry value chain or value system. Businesses are made up of discrete collections of individual and organizational activities that work together to create and deliver customer benefits via products or services. These integrated activities describe a value chain. Value chains are linked within an industry or, in the new-economy environment, across industries to create a value system. A value system is an interconnection of processes and activities within and among firms that creates benefits for intermediaries and end consumers.[3] Value is created from the first inputs through customer purchase, usage, and disposal activities.

Exhibit 4-2 shows a simplified value system for the automobile industry. The value system encompasses the value chains of multiple companies, each of which plays a part in the automobile industry; for example, this value system includes steel manufacturers, component manufacturers, auto manufacturers, dealerships, maintenance shops, and used-car dealers. Each of these industry members has its own value chain. The value chain of auto manufacturers includes primary activities (such as designing autos, building and testing prototypes, sourcing components and parts, and assembling the autos) as well as key support activities (such as marketing and finance).

A number of Internet businesses have chosen to compete in the automotive marketspace, in part because the value system is extremely complicated and presents many opportunities for value creation. Autobytel.com is one such company. Autobytel.com was launched in 1995 to create an entirely new channel for the sale of cars. This site allows car buyers to research vehicles—the site offers specifications, reviews, and even 360-degree panoramic photos of vehicle interiors—and then e-mail a purchase inquiry to a local dealer, asking for a quote on a particular car.

# Which Is Better?
## Analysis ("Ready, Aim, Fire")
## Vs. No Analysis ("Fire, Ready, Aim")

An interesting debate has been raging in the new economy concerning whether market-opportunity assessment is helpful, valueless, or, worse still, harmful. Many argue that speed, not precision, is critical. A basic economic force referred to as "network economics" is at work in many marketspace businesses. Businesses with network economics capitalize on "first-mover momentum"—rapidly connecting with and locking in large numbers of customers. In situations such as these, it is extremely difficult for the competition to "catch up" with the first mover. A cycle is created in which the large customer base provides lower costs. This allows the first mover to win customers at a faster rate than its competitors.

Another argument supporting the "Fire, Ready, Aim" approach states that companies must take advantage of the high stock-market multiples. This argument often points out that the new economy is nascent, a place where the old rules no longer apply and no one really understands the forces that drive the market. As a consequence, companies are better off learning by doing.

Finally, some argue even more vociferously that market analysis is a waste of time. In the end, they argue a company will be further behind having passed up major market opportunities during the time that it

took to perform the analysis.

However, an alternate point of view is beginning to emerge that the "Fire, Ready, Aim" approach outlined earlier actually limits a company's potential. While speed is important, the real goal is to reach critical mass with key customer segments in as short a time as is practical. The sheer number of potential-channel blind alleys, time-intensive partner negotiations, and customer-complaint black holes inevitably bogs companies down if they do not sort out a clear opportunity path from the start. Although a company may feel it is moving fast without assessing its opportunity, it is in fact "generating more heat than light." Furthermore, in some cases second and third movers actually survive and perform better than first pioneers. They can capitalize on the mistakes and on the groundwork done by others and capture more mind and market share for less effort. At the time of this writing, there were still no clear winners or losers. Peapod, the first entrant into the online grocery market, was saved from bankruptcy by Ahold, a Dutch conglomerate and seemed to be recovering. Webvan and HomeGrocer.com, although much later entrants to the game, merged and appeared to be succeeding where Peapod failed, partly because they learned from their rival's mistakes, but have now begun to falter.

Having found a price that they like, customers can settle the terms of the purchase, arrange financing, and schedule the delivery of the vehicle—all without leaving the keyboard. Once the purchase is complete, Autobytel.com users can comparison shop for insurance and set up a schedule to manage their car's maintenance. Autobytel.com also offers used-car classifieds, so that customers can sell their old cars through the site when the time comes to buy a newer model. Exhibit 4-2 on page 104 shows a simplified value chain for Autobytel.com. As the exhibit illustrates, the company's value chain is relatively complex and spans more than one area of the automobile industry's value system.

In order to explore the notion of value creation, we must first look for a set of activities ripe for positive transformation, either within a firm or across activities conducted by multiple firms. A firm is made up of a series of connected activities—from purchasing inputs to manufacturing to marketing and sales to product deliv-

# Network Economics

Network economics[4] (an aspect of the networked economy) is a fundamental driving force in the new economy. This law of economics states that users of "network" products tend to value those products more highly (because they get more utility from them) when there are a large number of users. In fact, the value of a product to each of its users increases with the addition of each new user. Telephones are an example of a product subject to network economics. The first purchaser of a telephone had no use for it—it was impossible to call anyone. The second purchaser made the telephone valuable for the first purchaser (they could now call each other), and the third purchaser increased the utility of the telephones purchased by the other two (it was now possible to make conference calls).

Named after Bob Metcalfe, the inventor of the network technology known as Ethernet, **Metcalfe's Law** states that the value of a network to each of its members is proportional to the number of other users (which can be expressed as $(n^2 - n)/2$). The near-universal adoption of Windows as an operating system for PCs is a good example of network economics. The more users adopted Windows, the more software companies wrote Windows-compatible products, making Windows more and more valuable to its users.

In many cases, however, computers with Windows are not connected to a network, so why does this product benefit from network economics? Windows users may or may not be physically networked together, but they do operate in a form of "community." They use software written for the Windows operating system, and they share files with each other. These activities make Windows subject to network economics.

Network economics has a profound impact on the equilibrium states of the markets in which it operates. Because users tend to prefer products that already have many users, strong companies tend to get stronger (this is known as "positive reinforcement") and weak companies weaker ("negative reinforcement"). As a result, markets with many competing technologies tend to converge on one product standard.

ery to after-sales support—that result in the creation of an end product or the delivery of a service. In addition, there are supporting activities necessary to ensure a company's viability, from financial planning and control to employee recruiting and training to research and development. Just as many of these activities are interconnected within one company, there are also connections with other companies or consumers. Both the activities within a firm (the value chain) and those connecting firms with other firms and customers (the value system) are potential candidates for new-economy value creation. Furthermore, if we look across several related industries in the same manner as customers, we may find cross-value chain opportunities. Autobytel.com created value both within the value chain (for example, by providing panoramic interior photos) and across the value system (by allowing users to check car inventories at dealers across the country).

Firms should look at the value system with a lens that yields ideas about new business possibilities. Specifically, a firm looks for either **trapped value** to be liberated, or **new-to-the-world value** to be introduced.

## Trapped Value

New-economy companies have unlocked trapped value by creating more efficient markets or more efficient value systems, by enabling easier access, or by disrupting current pricing power.

**Exhibit 4-2** CAR MANUFACTURE AND SALES VALUE SYSTEM

**Raw Material Manufacture**
- Sourcing
- Processing
- Sales
- Etc.

**Component Manufacture**
- Sourcing
- Design
- Manufacture
- Etc.

**Assembly**
- Design
- Marketing
- Manufacture
- Etc.

**Distribution**
- Marketing
- Inventory
- Sales
- Etc.

**Maintenance**
- Parts Inventory
- Training
- Servicing
- Etc.

**Used Resale**
- Purchasing
- Inventory
- Sales
- Etc.

**Autobytel.com**

| Collect Research | Request Dealer Quote | Finance | Make Sale | Source Warranty, Insurance Quotes | Track Vehicle Service | Publish Classified Ads |

- New and used car purchasing
- Financing comparison and purchase
- Real time insurance quotes
- Wholesale anchors
- Service tracking

**Creating More Efficient Markets.** By lowering search and transaction costs, the market is more efficient—customers can buy what they want at a lower net cost. BizBuyer.com, for example, brings together suppliers and buyers of products and services for small- and medium-size businesses. Customers submit a request for proposal, and qualified suppliers can provide their quotes. The entire transaction can be arranged over the Web.

**Creating More Efficient Value Systems.** Compressing or eliminating steps in the current value system can result in greater efficiencies in time or cost. For example, Federal Express has been moving its customer interactions into the marketspace since 1982, when the firm first started equipping its major customers with dedicated terminals. Enabling customers to request pick-ups, find drop-off points, and track shipments over the Internet was a natural development. Today, the company estimates that it would need an additional 20,000 employees to handle the tasks that customers handle themselves. By connecting directly with its customers, FedEx removed the duplication of tasks such as the reentry of shipping data.

**Enabling Ease of Access.** Enabling ease of access entails enhancing the access points and the degree of communication between relevant exchange partners. Guru.com expedites access to hard-to-find professional experts across a wide range of fields. Another way in which ease of access increases is through the use of the Internet as a channel. J. Crew used to sell clothes only through offline stores and catalogs, but then the company added jcrew.com as a new sales channel. The website offers the same products as its offline channels, but it also provides the added convenience associated with shopping online.

**Disrupting Current Pricing Power.** Beyond making markets more efficient, this value-unlocking activity changes current pricing-power relationships. Customers can gain more influence over pricing and capture a portion of the vendor's margin when they have more information about relative vendor performance, a deeper understanding of vendor economics, or insight into the vendor's current supply-demand situation. By providing customers with greater access to these types of information and demystifying vendor economics, a new-economy company can give customers greater negotiating power. For example, R S Sure (*www.rusure.com*) informs its users when they are about to buy something that is priced lower elsewhere.

## New-to-the-World Value

In addition to reconfiguring existing value chains to release trapped value, new-economy companies can create new-to-the-world benefits. These new benefits can enhance an existing offering or be the basis for creating a new offering. There are at least five generic ways companies can create new value: customize the offerings, radically extend reach and access, build community, enable collaboration among multiple people across locations and time, and introduce new-to-the-world functionality or experience.

**Customize Offerings.** The Internet allows companies to tailor their offerings more flexibly than they ever could in the offline environment. For example, companies can allow their customers to customize the specific products or services they receive, as well as make their products more attractive to customers by removing features that customers do not value. Yahoo exemplifies both dimensions. By adding personalization to news and stock quotes through its "My Yahoo" function, Yahoo created value for customers who previously had to navigate through "one size fits all" news and information services over the Web. A My Yahoo page contains just a small subset of all available information, but it is information that is relevant to the user.

**Radically Extend Reach and Access.** Companies may extend the boundaries of an existing market or create a new market by delivering a cost-effective reach. Keen.com created an entirely new market by building a virtual marketplace for advice. Anyone can advertise their services as an advisor on such subjects as "managing your love life" or "choosing a career." Customers log on to the site, choose an advisor, and are connected to the advisor for a per-minute fee. Keen.com and the advisor share these revenues.

**Build Community.** The Internet enables efficient community building, as demonstrated by the explosion of chat rooms addressing myriad topics. Beyond chat rooms, companies also foster the building of public and private communities. MyFamily.com seeks to bring together the far-flung modern family by enabling conversation, picture sharing, and recipe exchange, among other things. Natural communities can be leveraged in many ways, including enhancement of the effectiveness and impact of viral marketing.

**Enable Collaboration Among Multiple People Across Locations and Time.** In the networked world, people are working together more efficiently and more effectively than ever before. Construction portal Buzzsaw.com offers its users a place to buy or sell materials, create a shared project workspace, and review building plans—regardless of the physical location of the buyers, sellers, and colleagues.

**Introduce New-to-the-World Functionality or Experience.** The convergence of communications, computing, and entertainment, and the ever-changing form and functionality of access devices, are making new experiences possible. The Internet fosters broad access and participation in these new experiences. Owners of Apple's iMac can use their computers to create and edit digital "iMovies," which can then be uploaded (for free) to an Apple Web server and shared with friends around the world.

An interesting question to consider is whether companies can both unlock trapped value and create new benefits at the same time. Companies such as Amazon.com appear to do both; not only has the company eliminated steps from and reduced the hassle of book shopping, but it has also introduced extra services and functionality to enhance the experience. Through "collaborative filtering" technology from Net Perceptions, readers can browse while simultaneously getting reader recommendations or recommendations based on previous orders. Amazon has changed how people think about shopping and purchasing in product categories such as books, music, and toys.

To define where in a value system or value chain a company should focus its development activities, there are two simple dimensions to first consider—*horizontal* versus *vertical* plays. In the business world, horizontal plays improve functional operations that are common to multiple industries and types of value systems. In the software world, horizontal play typically tackle improving functional areas such as accounting and control, customer service, inventory management, and standard CAD/CAM applications. In the consumer world, horizontal plays reflect common activities in which most consumers broadly engage (e.g., paying taxes).

Vertical plays, on the other hand, focus on creating value within or among activities that are central to a particular business (e.g., Creative Planet in the entertainment industry). These vertical plays can often be thought of as industry-specific plays—steel industry, chemical industry, automotive industry. There are, of course, niches within each industry (e.g., specialty steel), so there may be vertical niches, such as an automotive parts distributor site versus a supply-chain site in the automotive industry.

At its most extreme, a "white sheet" exercise—a thorough analysis beginning from a blank slate—could systematically look for and evaluate the trapped and new-to-the-world value potential across all functions and activities pursued by businesses and individual consumers. More typically, a group of managers will have some familiarity with or interest in a particular horizontal function or vertical activity. The challenge for this group is to map out the major sets of activities related to that horizontal function or vertical business at a high level. After mapping out the activities, the group should consider a series of questions designed to guide the knowledgeable manager to uncover trapped value or recognize the opportunity for new value creation.

The guiding questions the group should consider include the following:

- Is there a high degree of asymmetric information between buyers and sellers or colleagues at any step in the value system that traps value?
- Are significant amounts of time and resources consumed in bringing people together to make a transaction or complete a task?
- Do customers view activities as more collapsed than do industry participants?
- Are key participants in an activity able to collaborate effectively and efficiently at critical stages in a process?
- Do people have access to necessary advice and information to maximize their effectiveness or the ability to extract maximum benefits from a given activity?
- Are people foregoing opportunities to participate in an activity due to privacy or other concerns?

While identification of hot spots in a business or consumer value system is a necessary starting point, the process is not sufficiently developed to make the leap from identification to creation of the value proposition or the business model. At this point, the manager has a sense of where the opportunity may lie in terms of business and customer activities. The next step is to specify the nature of that opportunity from a customer's perspective. As the manager begins to specify the opportunity, the potential associated with the opportunity should become more apparent.

# HOW DO WE IDENTIFY UNMET AND/OR UNDERSERVED NEEDS?

New value creation is based on doing a better job of meeting customer needs. What customer needs will the new business serve? Are these needs currently being met by other companies in the market, and if so, why will customers choose your business over the competition? Customers will choose to switch from their old supplier only if the new company does a better job of meeting some set of needs. This condition of our opportunity-analysis framework describes the uncovering of an **opportunity nucleus**—a set of unmet or underserved needs.

# Customer Decision Process

The **customer decision process** is an organizing framework that looks systematically for unmet or underserved needs. The customer decision process maps the activities and choices customers make in accessing a specific experience within a value system. Then the process lays out the series of steps: awareness of the experience, the purchase experience, and the use experience. The process of generating a map of the customer decision process may help generate new ideas about unmet or underserved needs. For example, an examination of the process people go through to buy books might identify the fact that people rely on recommendations from others. Jeff Bezos of Amazon.com successfully identified this need and created a website where customers can read reviews and comments about a book being considered for purchase while they are in the store—an activity that customers in a bricks-and-mortar bookstore can almost never do.

In order to discover unmet or underserved needs, senior management should map out the customer decision process. When properly answered, the following questions will help structure that process (see Exhibit 4-3):

- What are the steps that the typical customer goes through?
- Who gets involved and what role does he or she play?
- Are there any distinct and significant activities and paths that different customers go through?
- Where does the process take place?
- How much time does the overall process take? How much time is associated with individual steps? Does the customer move through the entire process at once or does he or she take breaks?
- What product category and competitors does the customer consider and choose along the way?
- What choices do customers not consider? What choices are they unaware of?
- Which customers are not participating in this customer decision process for a specific value system? Why not?

Of course, not all businesses involve purchases just by users. Access to CNN's website is free to users but is paid for by advertisers, so the business has two sets of customers. In this case it is worthwhile developing a customer decision process cycle for both visitors (who use the site, but do not purchase from it) and for advertisers (who purchase advertisement space on the site).

Exhibit 4-3 illustrates the customer decision process for document shipping in a consulting company. The illustration shows how consultants and their administrative assistants interact to make choices about shipping providers. Some decision processes are highly linear while others may have multiple pathways or loop-backs. Each process is organized into three broad categories: prepurchase, purchase, and postpurchase.

# Revealing Unmet or Underserved Needs

Having identified the steps in the customer decision process, the management team can look to uncover unmet or underserved needs. The following questions can help identify these needs:

**Exhibit 4-3**

CONSUMER BUYING PROCESS TREE
FOR SHIPMENT SERVICES

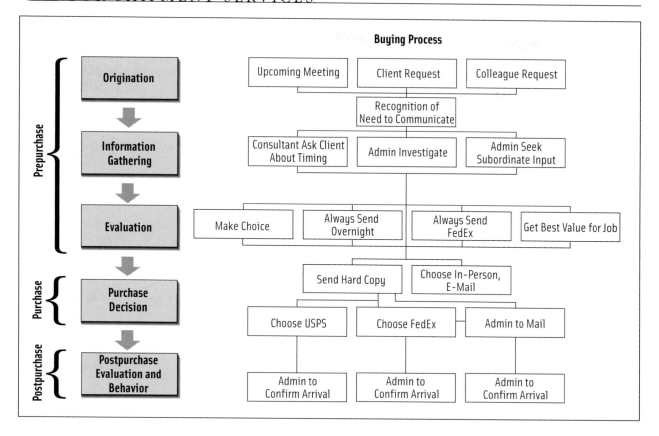

- What are the series of activities or steps of the customer decision process in which a customer participates to receive an experience?

- What is the nature of the ideal experience the customer wishes to receive both functionally and emotionally? How does it vary step-by-step in the activity?

- How closely does the actual experience compare to the customer's view of the ideal? What are the key frustration points? What compensating behaviors do we observe (i.e., what actions does the customer engage in to overcome these frustrations)? How successful has the customer been and why? What underserved needs do you observe, regardless of whether or not the customer is conscious of them?

- Does the experience customers seek vary according to their environment (e.g., how often they participate in the activity, with whom they are working, where they are using the product or service, or their role in an organization)?

- What are customer beliefs and associations about carrying out this activity? How do they view their relative competence and role? How positively or negatively do they view the current set of company offerings?

- What barriers block some or all participation by potential customers? What would potentially block adoption of an online activity?

- What are the online opportunities to enhance or transform the customers' experience? What will be the most important drivers for getting customers to adopt an online activity in this value system?

- How do the customers define value for critical steps in the process? Would they be willing to pay for certain elements of that value?

Uncovering these needs may be as straightforward as having a conversation with a number of customers, or may be as complex as creating observation opportunities to watch customers in action and identify behaviors of which they may be unaware. Immersion in the customer decision process is the most effective way to reveal opportunities for a better way of doing things.

# WHAT DETERMINES THE SPECIFIC CUSTOMERS A COMPANY WILL PURSUE?

So far we have talked about where a company is likely to play in the value system, how customers go through their decision-making process, and where potential areas for value creation might be found. Now we will discuss the specific customer segment that the company plans to pursue. Companies need to develop a sense for the type(s) of customers they ultimately seek to serve. This understanding allows a company to assess opportunity attractiveness at a high level and to focus on crafting an offering that will best appeal to the target customer.

In analyzing the outcome of the customer decision process, companies are likely to identify subsets of customers with very different patterns of behavior, underlying needs, and drivers of behavior. **Segmentation** is the process of grouping customers based on their similarities. Once the different segments have been identified, the company must determine the segments (or customers) it will target in order to further refine the type of opportunity the company will seek to capture. Of course, the digital play that a company has in mind may radically change how customers act in this value system. Hence, a company would look both for segments that disproportionately benefit from some change in the status quo and those more predisposed to adopt an entirely new product or service.

## Approaches to Market Segmentation

There are many approaches to segmentation, and the best way to segment a market is an often debated topic. The best segmentation for the opportunity depends on the value system that the opportunity is centered upon, how the customer can and will make decisions within that value system, and what action your company is likely to take. Before we describe a practical approach to segmentation for the networked economy, it is important to briefly review the different ways a market (and customers) can be segmented. Academic literature and textbooks often cite the following segmentation approaches:[5]

- *Demographics (or Firmographics).* For individuals, the demographic approach includes grouping by age, gender, occupation, ethnicity, income, family status, life stage, Internet connectivity, and browser type. In a firmographic approach, companies are segmented based on number of employees, online or offline status, company size, job function, and purchasing process.

## Empathic Design[6]

 All companies, particularly technology companies, rely on innovation to survive. A natural choice is to rely on customers to tell you their needs and ways to better serve them. The problem is that customers are particularly bad at doing that. They rarely are able to imagine or describe innovations.

One solution is to use "empathic design," a set of techniques described by Dorothy Leonard and Jeffrey Rayport in the *Harvard Business Review* article, "Spark Innovation Through Empathic Design." Two things distinguish empathic design research techniques from those used in traditional market research: (1) they are based on *observation* (watching consumers) rather than *inquiry* (asking consumers), and (2) unlike traditional lab-based usability testing (which typically involves observing consumers using a product in a laboratory), empathic design research is conducted in the environment where the consumers would commonly use the product.

Empathic design is not a substitute for traditional research, but it can yield the following five types of information that are not ordinarily revealed by traditional techniques:

- Triggers of use: What circumstances cause people to use a product?

- Interactions with the users' environment: How does the product fit with users' idiosyncratic environments and habits?
- User customization: Do users redesign the product to fit their needs? If so, how?
- Intangible product attributes: Intangible attributes may be important in creating an emotional franchise with the consumer.
- Unarticulated user needs: Observation can discover unarticulated user needs that can be easily fulfilled.

Different people notice different things, and the use of a small team with a diverse set of skills (e.g., interface design, product management, etc.) may observe otherwise unnoticed subtleties. The team should observe and record a subject's normal behavior. The team should also take detailed notes of observations and minimize interruptions or interference with the subject. Photographs, videos, and sketches can all help the team record what it finds.

A common criticism of the innovative ideas that can emerge from empathic design is, "But users didn't ask for that. . . ." This is precisely the point of the exercise. By the time customers ask you for an innovation, they will be asking your competitors, too.

- *Geographics.* Country, region, city, city size, density (urban, suburban, rural), ISP domain, etc.

- *Behavioral.* Online shopping behavior, offline shopping behavior, Web usage, website loyalty, prior purchases, etc.

- *Occasion (or Situational).* Routine occasion, special occasion, time (time of day, day of week, holidays), location (from home, while on the road), event (while writing a business plan, when shopping), trigger (out of supply), etc.

- *Pyschographics.* Lifestyle (thrill-seekers, fun-lovers, recluses), personality (laidback, type A, risk-takers), affinity (community builders, participants, outcasts), etc.

- *Benefits.* Convenience, economy, quality, ease of use, speed, information, selection, etc.

- *Beliefs and attitudes.* Brand beliefs (new economy, old-fashioned), attitude toward the category, channel-effectiveness beliefs, beliefs about themselves (technically savvy), etc.

# Zaltman Metaphoric Elicitation Technique

"Most of what influences what we say and do occurs below the level of awareness. That's why we need new techniques: to get at hidden knowledge—to get at what people don't know they know," says Harvard Business School professor Jerry Zaltman.[7] His revolutionary market-research technique, the Zaltman Metaphoric Elicitation Technique (ZMET), tries to get to that hidden knowledge. The technique uses consumer metaphors to shed light into the consumer's subconscious—into the way he or she thinks.

In his book *Strategic Brand Management: Building, Measuring, and Managing Brand Equity,* Kevin Lane Keller identifies the following seven basic premises on which ZMET is based:[8]

1. Most human communication is nonverbal.
2. Thoughts often occur as nonverbal images.
3. Metaphors are essential units of thought and are the key mechanism for viewing consumer thoughts and feelings and understanding consumer behavior.
4. Sensory images provide important metaphors.
5. Consumers have mental models—interrelated ideas about a market experience—that represent their knowledge and behavior.
6. Hidden or deep structures of thought can be accessed.
7. Emotion and reason are forces that commingle in the minds of consumers.

So how does ZMET work? ZMET participants are asked the question: "What are your thoughts and feelings about this experience or that product?" They are then asked to collect pictures that capture these thoughts and feelings or display the exact opposite of these thoughts and feelings. Each participant returns 7 to 10 days later to discuss the pictures with a specially trained ZMET interviewer over a two-hour period. During that interview, the participant describes each picture as well as any pictures that he or she was looking for but was unable to obtain. Next, the participant organizes the pictures and describes the pictures that portray the opposite of his or her thoughts and feelings. The participant then explains his or her reaction in sensory terms, such as color, sound, smell, taste, and touch. Finally, with the help of a graphic artist, the participant and the interviewer build a collage with the selected images. A careful examination of this collage can shed light into the participant's mind, thoughts, and associations.

To illustrate the output of ZMET, let us consider the results of ZMET in the panty hose industry.[9] Twenty panty hose–wearing women were selected to participate in a study. They were asked, "What are your thoughts and feelings about buying and wearing panty hose?" The pictures they selected included fence posts encased in plastic wrap, twisted telephone cords, and steel bands strangling trees. These images are relatively easy to interpret: Panty hose are tight and inconvenient. However, other images were selected that shed a different light on the story. For example, one selected image showed flowers resting peacefully in a vase. The discussion with the ZMET interviewer eventually revealed that the flowers in a vase referred to the fact that wearing the product made a woman feel thin and tall. Further discussion revealed that panty hose made women feel they had longer legs and that this was important because men think long legs are sexy. Hence, a desired experience from wearing panty hose is to feel sexy around men. A traditional research method would have great difficulty revealing this type of finding.

Zaltman is currently working on expanding ZMET to new frontiers. Using brain scans, interviewers can see how people think and where thoughts take place inside the brain. Messages with a negative effect on respondents lead to activity in an area of the brain associated with negative feelings. In contrast, messages that lead to positive feelings stimulate activity in a different part of the brain. By massaging their marketing messages, companies may at some point be able to create messages that activate only areas of the brain associated with positive feelings. This technique is still in development but has great potential to further revolutionize the way market research is conducted.

# Which Is Better?
# Online Consumer Tracking Vs. Holistic View

In the online world, there is no lack of data. Click-stream information reveals purchase patterns, online habits, basic demographics, and potentially a host of other consumer information. Is this information sufficient to define new business opportunities?

Many argue that studying past and real-time behavior will yield enough sufficient information about customers to make choices about the services they need at that time. The Web enables companies to watch customers interacting in real time with their product with a high degree of precision and allows them to intervene while the customer is still in the buying process—the marketing Holy Grail. Procedures like collaborative filtering allow real-time suggestive selling. An example of this is Amazon.com's success at cross-selling customers.

An alternative view is that click-through-based data provides an insufficient picture of the reasons customers behave the way they do. In other words, click-stream analysis explains what customers do but not why they do it. A total customer view brings together consumer behavior and insights about motivations for that behavior; this view considers the behavior plus the customer context and environment, the functional and emotional desires of the customer, and the customer's beliefs and associations about the product, service, and current purveyors of the offering. Without a total customer view, managers are unlikely to generate real insight into key customer groups. Companies such as DoubleClick are responding to this concern by trying to merge their online data sets with behavioral data that has been gathered offline.

Table 4-1 provides a more comprehensive listing of variables, with illustrations. Over time, segmentation has evolved from the use of observable and customer-external variables (age, income, geography) in the 1960s and 1970s to more meaningful customer-internal variables (needs, attitudes) in the 1980s and 1990s. The fact remains that neither is sufficient on its own to fully define a segment. The difficulty comes with selecting the segmentation approach and the variables that most effectively describe and reflect the nature of the networked-economy opportunity being analyzed.

## Actionable and Meaningful Segmentation

Unfortunately, most segmentation efforts fail to deliver on the intended objective—to be both useful and insightful. The segments are often either easy to recognize but do not provide much insight into customer motivations (actionable, but not meaningful), or they generate real insight about customers but are difficult to address (meaningful, but not actionable). The goal of market segmentation is to identify the intersection or combination of marketplace variables that will generate **actionable segmentation** and **meaningful segmentation** of customers.

**Actionable Segmentation.** To be actionable, segmentation must be consistent with how a company can go to market, and it must be able to be sized and described. A segmentation is actionable if it fulfills the following criteria:

Table
4-1 SEGMENTATION APPROACHES

| Segmentation Type | Description | Examples—Variables |
|---|---|---|
| *Geographics* | Divides market into different geographical units | Country, region, city |
| *Demographics* | Divides market on the basis of demographic variables | Age, gender, income |
| *Firmographics* | Divides market on the basis of company-specific variables | Number of employees, company size |
| *Behavioral* | Divides market based on how customers actually buy and use the product | Website loyalty, prior purchases |
| *Occasion (Situational)* | Divides market based on the situation that leads to a product need, purchase, or use | Routine occasion, special occasion |
| *Psychographics* | Divides market based on lifestyle and/or personality | Personality (laid-back, type A), lifestyle |
| *Benefits* | Divides market based on benefits or qualities sought from the product | Convenience, economy, quality |

- The segments are easy to identify.
- The segments can be readily reached.
- The segments can be described in terms of their growth, size, profile, and attractiveness.

**Meaningful Segmentation.** To be meaningful, segmentation must help describe and begin to explain why customers currently behave—or are likely to behave—in a specific way. A segmentation is meaningful if it fulfills the following criteria:

- Customers within a segment behave similarly while customers across segments behave in different ways.
- It provides some insight into customers' motivations.
- It corresponds to the set of barriers customers face when they buy or use a product or service.
- It corresponds with how customers currently (or could) buy or use the product or service.
- It correlates to differences in profitability or cost to serve.
- The segments and/or their differences are large enough to warrant a different set of actions by a company.

Webvan, an online grocery service, provides a good illustration of the value of segmentation and how it can be both actionable and meaningful. The company looked at the market and determined that the core users of its service were likely to be affluent families who regularly use the Internet from their homes. In addition, the economics of delivering goods to customers is heavily dependent on how close they are to one another. Webvan used income (affluent), family status (families), Internet connectivity (Internet from home), and density (close to one another) as categories to segment the market—variables readily found through available geo-targeting software. As a consequence, Webvan selected the San Francisco Bay Area and metropolitan Atlanta as the locations in which to launch its grocery-delivery service. Both areas contain a large number of busy, high-income families with Internet access—characteristics that meaningfully influence customers' likelihood of using Webvan.

## The Right Blend of Segmentation Variables

Finding the right blend of segmentation variables that are both actionable and meaningful is difficult to do in practice; a company is often forced to trade off one variable for another. In the online world, this trade-off can be made more easily than in the offline world because firms can quickly collect data that is both actionable and meaningful. Online companies have access to a rich source of segmentation data through a registration form that asks customers for basic demographic information (such as income, gender, age, and zip codes) or through real-time tracking of customer click streams on both search data and final purchase behavior.

"Clickographics," the demonstrated behavior of an online customer using click-stream data, is an interesting example of a behavioral variable that tends to be highly meaningful and actionable. Website server logs can capture every step a customer takes while surfing a company's site. Using clickographics, a company can easily identify and communicate with its target customers. For example, Launch.com is an online radio station that plays songs for users and asks them to rate each song they hear. Based on user response, the site builds a musical taste profile unique to each user and selects songs the user will like. The customer's song ratings are meaningful variables because the site is responding to the customer's musical tastes. The segment is also actionable because the site can communicate with customers at any given moment and offer them new albums by their favorite artists.

Often, an intersection—or combination—of demographic, geographic, situational, and behavioral variables will create a market segmentation that is both actionable and meaningful. Typical variables to consider include intersections of user demographics, life stage, purchase occasion, and online behavior. The end result is a segmentation scheme that tends to favor one factor or another; for example, online holiday purchasers (more occasion-based), first-time users (more behavior-based), or graduating high-school seniors from affluent neighborhoods (demographics and geography). Pyschographic or attitudinal variables in isolation are rarely recommended as a basis for a segmentation; these approaches often maximize meaningful dimensions but are rarely actionable, and therefore are often rejected by managers. It would be difficult for Ashford.com to identify a customer as a high achiever before—or as—he or she interacts with the website. Rather, a company may need to look at prior purchase data (other luxury brands purchased on sale) and the path taken into the site (click-through from mySimon.com) to determine the likelihood that this customer would shop for a Rolex watch at a bargain price. The point is to use the more observable information to generate insight on the motivation, not the other way around.

**Segmentation Variables About the Customers.** To gain some insight into what variables to use, ask yourself the following questions about the customers:

- Who are they? Where do they live? What do they do for a living? How busy are they? What else do they do? What do they like to do in their spare time? How much spare time do they have?
- What is their purchase process?
- When and where do they shop? What else do they buy? How much did they pay for the product? How often do they buy? What channels do they have ready access to?
- Where do they get their information? Is there anyone else who influences the purchase or use of the product? If so, who?
- What is their usage process? What external factors affect their product use? When do they use the product? How often do they use the product? For which occasions are the products purchased or used? Are these occasions frequent or episodic?
- Where do they use the product? What is the setting they are in? How often are they in this setting?
- Is the purchase or usage planned? What happens to them if they do not purchase the product?

**Segmentation Variables About the Microeconomics.** To gain some insight into what variables to use, ask yourself the following questions about the microeconomics:

- What are the major cost drivers? Are they related to physical proximity? Are they affected by time?
- Are there major learning-curve effects? Are they scale sensitive? Are they scope sensitive?

Priceline.com offers a good illustration of effective market segmentation. Priceline.com saw the opportunity to use its reverse-auction technology to enable a buyer-driven model in the purchase of airline tickets. The company wanted to make the average air traveler a "price-setter," not a "price-taker." Under this model, customers name their price for a roundtrip flight between two cities on a certain date. This price request is then submitted to a group of airline partners that considers the offer and, the consumer hopes, accepts the bid.

Priceline.com saw the conventional airline ticket-buying process as cumbersome and frustrating for the consumer. The tiered-seat pricing structure is complex and confusing, and the process the consumer has to go through to check across airlines for schedules, availability, and pricing is convoluted. Moreover, discount ticket hunters are given little consideration by the airlines. In short, the budget airline ticket buyer had no power over the carriers. Priceline.com set out to change that.

However, Priceline.com's service does not appeal to all travelers. The service has many constraints; for example, customers' bids may or may not be accepted, customers do not receive frequent-flier miles, and they cannot specify the flight times, the routing, or the carrier.

If you were Priceline.com and suspected there was an opportunity, how would you make it concrete? How would you segment the market? Which consumer segments are most likely to be interested in the concept? How much opportunity is there likely to be?

Start by looking at the broad list of segmentation variables. Identify the ones that, when combined with other variables, correlate to customer motivations, barriers, use habits, and profitability. Look for combinations of variables that generate insight. For Priceline.com, these variables would include the following:

- *Occasion (or Situation).* The reason for the trip (business or personal) corresponds to a customer's willingness to be flexible on schedule and price-sensitivity. Furthermore, lead time for a trip (schedulable weeks in advance, last minute) corresponds to the ability of customers to coordinate other elements of the trip around specific flight times.

- *Demographics.* The life stage of a consumer (student, retiree, parent) corresponds to his or her price sensitivity, schedule flexibility, and tolerance for a less-than-efficient itinerary. Income/occupation (low to moderate income with an occupation that is not travel-intensive, moderate to high income with a travel-intensive occupation) corresponds to the customer's price sensitivity and his or her tolerance for a less-than-efficient itinerary.

- *Behavior.* The number of flights that the customer takes during the year (frequent flier or infrequent flier) will correlate to the customer's ability to use frequent-flier miles to secure a ticket, his or her airline brand loyalty, and his or her tolerance of inconvenience or of a less-than-efficient itinerary.

Combining these variables yields distinct, actionable, and meaningful market segments for Priceline.com to target. Exhibit 4-4 illustrates the segmentation that emerges from this analysis. The vertical axis divides the population into different demographic groups (for example, students and families with children); the vertical axis also categorizes some groups by their behavior—whether or not they fly

**Exhibit 4-4** PRICELINE.COM SEGMENTATION

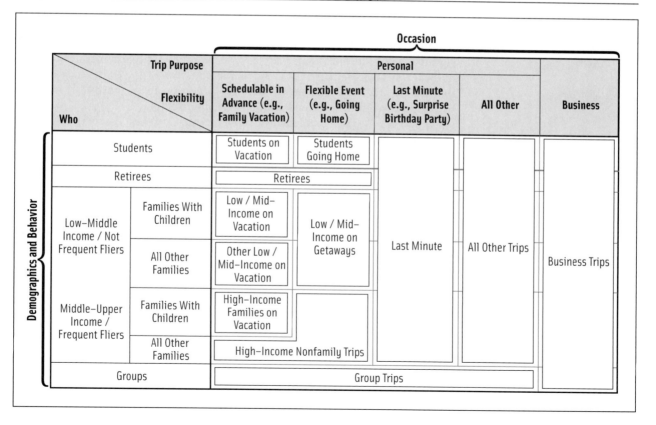

frequently. The horizontal axis shows occasions, or reasons, for flying. These include business trips, family vacations, and last-minute trips. Cross-tabulating the two axes and blocking some of the subsegments together creates a matrix of behaviorally distinct segments.

The Priceline.com example illustrates the value of going beyond simply using "price conscious" as a market-segmentation variable. First, the characteristic does not provide any clue about who the consumer is or why he or she may be price conscious. Is the consumer price conscious because he or she has no discretionary income? Or is the itinerary so flexible that the consumer feels no need to pay a premium for a specific time? Second, as companies extend their business concepts into new arenas, a price-conscious customer in one arena may not be a price-conscious customer in another. For example, Priceline.com also offers "name your price" mortgages. The target consumer in this arena is the middle/upper-income individual who has a high degree of comfort with sophisticated financial instruments—not the cash-starved student or retiree, who is the target in the airline-ticket arena.

## Market Mapping and Target Customers

With the set of actionable and meaningful dimensions identified, management can construct a basic marketing map to show the segment's size, growth rate, and financial attractiveness. For Priceline.com, several of the travel segments noted in Exhibit 4-4 are small. For example, several segments represent about 5 percent of the market (students on vacation, last-minute travelers), a few represent about 10 percent of the market (groups), while business trips represents about 40 percent of the market. Exhibit 4-5 is shaded to show the size of each segment.

These simple maps are important for several reasons. First, the maps identify the location of the money and the relative opportunities in the market. Second, a clear representation of the business opportunity makes it easier to select initial target segments and to lay out a game plan for sequencing the approach to other segments in the future. Third, a map provides structure for synthesizing additional information and insight. Finally, the segmentation shown in a map is a touchstone for identifying future shifts in market definition and opportunity.

Look at each segment, and identify those most likely to find the service valuable. For Priceline.com, the high-priority segments are students on vacation, retirees, low/middle-income families on vacation, low/middle-income families on getaways, others of low/middle-income on vacation, and last-minute travelers. Each of these segments are likely to find the Priceline.com buying constraints acceptable in order to get a lower price. Together these segments constitute 45 percent to 55 percent of the total number of trips taken—a very large opportunity.

As stated at the beginning of the chapter, it is often as important to identify the segments of the market unlikely to find a business idea attractive as it is to identify those who are likely to find it attractive—in other words, to identify who is "out" as well as who is "in." It is also important to communicate who is in/out to potential collaborators to minimize the negative response that could otherwise ensue. The Priceline.com example also illustrates this concept well. For the name-your-price concept to work you need to have willing buyers and sellers. We just discussed the buyers' perspective; now look at the opportunity from the airline's perspective.

It is well known that airlines make most of their money on customers traveling for business, customers who are brand loyal (top-tier frequent fliers), and customers who cannot plan ahead. Airlines look to other customer segments to contribute to the fixed cost of their highly "perishable" product—once the door of a

Exhibit
4-5

PRICELINE.COM NUMBER OF AIRLINE TRIPS

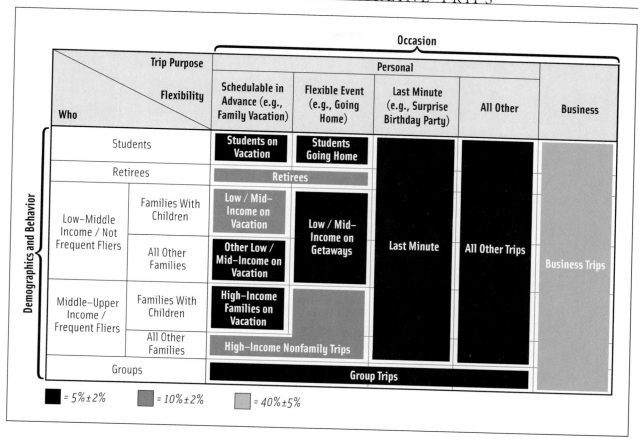

| Occasion | | | | | |
|---|---|---|---|---|---|
| Trip Purpose | **Personal** | | | | |
| Who / Flexibility | Schedulable in Advance (e.g., Family Vacation) | Flexible Event (e.g., Going Home) | Last Minute (e.g., Surprise Birthday Party) | All Other | **Business** |
| **Students** | Students on Vacation | Students Going Home | | | |
| **Retirees** | Retirees | | | | |
| Low–Middle Income / Not Frequent Fliers — Families With Children | Low / Mid–Income on Vacation | Low / Mid–Income on Getaways | Last Minute | All Other Trips | Business Trips |
| Low–Middle Income / Not Frequent Fliers — All Other Families | Other Low / Mid–Income on Vacation | | | | |
| Middle–Upper Income / Frequent Fliers — Families With Children | High–Income Families on Vacation | | | | |
| Middle–Upper Income / Frequent Fliers — All Other Families | High–Income Nonfamily Trips | | | | |
| **Groups** | Group Trips | | | | |

■ = 5%±2%   ▦ = 10%±2%   ▢ = 40%±5%

plane closes, the carrier has forever lost the opportunity to sell an empty seat. Not only is Priceline.com not undercutting the airlines' bread-and-butter business, but it is also providing airlines with a way to offload their unsold capacity quickly and cheaply. In other words, Priceline.com targets customers who are precisely the customers most airlines ignore because they are not attractive.

A final note on market demographics. Some analysts and faculty have argued that online businesses no longer need to focus on demographics or other traditional criteria because the online world enables the firm to track consumer behavior in real time; hence, this behavior by itself combines both actionability and meaningfulness. To some degree, this argument is correct, because behavior data (and an e-mail address) is sufficient information to interact with current customers. However, standard demographic data is highly relevant in the online world for three reasons. First, the online firm can collect demographic data on its consumer set, then more effectively sell advertising to potential advertisers. Second, with the demographic data, the firm will, in turn, know where to place offline advertising to attract customers to its site. Third, for companies with both bricks-and-mortar and online operations, this picture of the customer will foster more effective activation of channels, product-mix decisions, and other marketing-mix decisions.

**Exhibit 4-6**

PRICELINE.COM SEGMENT PRIORITIZATION

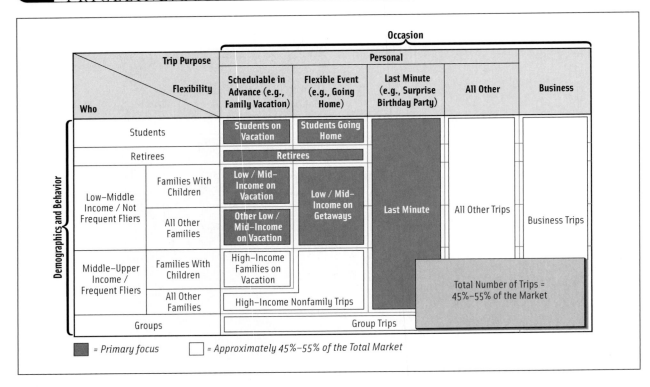

| Who \ Trip Purpose \ Flexibility | | Occasion — Personal | | | | Business |
|---|---|---|---|---|---|---|
| | | Schedulable in Advance (e.g., Family Vacation) | Flexible Event (e.g., Going Home) | Last Minute (e.g., Surprise Birthday Party) | All Other | |
| Students | | Students on Vacation | Students Going Home | Last Minute | All Other Trips | Business Trips |
| Retirees | | Retirees | | | | |
| Low–Middle Income / Not Frequent Fliers | Families With Children | Low / Mid–Income on Vacation | Low / Mid–Income on Getaways | | | |
| | All Other Families | Other Low / Mid–Income on Vacation | | | | |
| Middle–Upper Income / Frequent Fliers | Families With Children | High–Income Families on Vacation | | | | |
| | All Other Families | High–Income Nonfamily Trips | | | | |
| Groups | | Group Trips | | | | |

Total Number of Trips = 45%–55% of the Market

■ = Primary focus     □ = Approximately 45%–55% of the Total Market

# WHO PROVIDES THE RESOURCES TO DELIVER THE BENEFITS OF THE OFFERING?

Having determined the initial customer focus of the business, we are ready to make a first attempt at describing the business concept. At this stage, the company should stake out what experience and benefits **the offering** will provide and what capabilities and technology will be needed to deliver the benefits of the offering. While the offering and the means to deliver its benefits will be revisited and refined many times, these details will play a vital part in influencing and determining the company's rationale for success in this endeavor.

## Company Resources

Before spending a great deal of time crafting a specific business model to support a concept, the management team should assess whether or not it can identify at least three or four resources or assets that it can leverage successfully into the selected online space. These resources should be central to delivering new benefits or unlocking trapped value—the core of the company's value story. These resources should also hold the promise for advantage, considering the current and prospective players in the targeted space. With three or four such resources, the management team will have the beginnings of a robust business.

# Does Segmentation Matter?

An interesting debate has surfaced in the online world. Namely, there are people who have begun to question whether the segmentation concept applies in the online world. Because the online world enables consumers to customize products, services, and information specifically to their needs, the segmentation concept has been reduced to "segments of one."

Proponents of this approach have labeled the direct approach variously with terms such as "1:1," "segment-of-one," or "one-to-one-marketing." Furthermore, they argue that Web businesses such as eBay often attract an exceptionally wide variety of customers who weigh buying criteria (e.g., low price, most convenient buying method, best online information and reviews, or broadest selection) quite differently. Hence, it is foolish to attempt to cluster these widely divergent groups. Rather, customization enables firms to uniquely meet the needs of each customer. Additionally, they argue that the back-office supply systems and infrastructure can easily accommodate every type of customer. Finally, multiple storefronts—even 1:1 storefronts—can be constructed in a real-time basis. (Amazon's homepage is an excellent example of this, since it is tailored to each customer who comes to the store. Exhibit 4-7 shows the Amazon.com homepage for two different customers who visited the site at exactly the same time.)

Conversely, the proponents of segmentation argue that all Web storefronts are, by definition, already segmenting the market. That is, if a given Web storefront simultaneously attracts selected customers and repels certain customers, it is segmenting the market. By disregarding these segments and focusing exclusively on 1:1 marketing, the company would miss the fundamental economics of which particular class of customer is most profitable or least profitable. For example, Buy.com offers some of the lowest prices on a wide variety of products. It is not clear that the store explicitly targets a particular customer segment; however, the store's focus on prices is likely to attract the most price-sensitive customers.

In this step, the team will already have a strong understanding of the following:

- The selected value system in which the company will be participating
- The key stages of the target's customer decision process and the benefits sought/value trapped at each stage
- The target customer segments

Looking across these insights, the management team should identify which winning resources it can create or provide through business partnerships. In Chapter 5, we will introduce an analytical tool that we call the **resource system**; this is a useful framework for assessing the new business's resources. A resource system is a discrete collection of individual and organizational activities and assets that, when taken together, create organizational capabilities that allow the company to serve customer needs. Resources that a company can bring to bear can be classified into the following three groupings:

- *Customer-Facing.* Customer-facing resources include brand name, a well-trained sales force, and multiple distribution channels.
- *Internal.* These resources are associated with the company's internal operations. Examples include technology, product development, economies of scale, and experienced staff.

Exhibit
4-7

# AMAZON.COM HOMEPAGE FOR
# TWO DIFFERENT CUSTOMERS

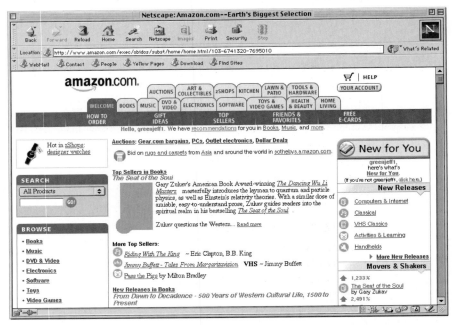

- *Upstream.* These resources are associated with a company's relationship to its suppliers. Examples include partnerships with suppliers and the degree of operational seamlessness between the company and its suppliers.

# Partners

On its own, a company may not be able to bring to bear all of the resources necessary to deliver value to its target segments. In opportunity assessment, a company must be realistic about any capability gaps. If a gap is insurmountable, the company should not proceed; if the gaps can somehow be closed, then a company must find a way to do so. Partnering may be an effective alternative to building or acquiring the capability. New-economy companies find partnerships particularly relevant because their offerings span traditional value-system boundaries. In fact, effective partnering can be an important source of advantage—Barnes & Noble.com's exclusive marketing deal with AOL and Amazon.com's use of Net Perceptions for collaborative filtering are two examples. The potential partners for a company can be grouped into two categories: complementor partners and traditional, or capability, partners.

**Complementor Partners.** These partners provide offerings that are complementary to those of another company. For example, Intel is a complementor to PC manufacturers. Also, an increase in the sales of a complementor offering is likely to lead to an increase in the partner company's sales (e.g., a boost in the sale of Intel's Pentium processor is likely to lead to an increase in PC sales).

**Capability Partners.** Capability partners are companies that give and receive value from partnering with the company. For example, Merrill Lynch is a traditional partner for Works.com, a website that automates purchasing for small- and medium-size businesses and gives them volume-purchasing power. Merrill Lynch provides financial assistance, management, and advice to Works.com customers. By doing so, it is adding a financing resource to Works.com's capabilities. In return, Works.com offers additional volume by sending business to the Merrill Lynch site.

In Chapter 5, we will consider in greater detail how the company can determine what capabilities it needs to develop and how to develop them.

Combining the benefits to be delivered with the way in which the company will deliver them fills in the business concept. With this high-level business concept in mind, we can assess the attractiveness of the opportunity from financial, technical, and competitive points of view.

# HOW DO WE ASSESS THE ATTRACTIVENESS OF THE OPPORTUNITY?

There is little point in targeting a new business concept in general, or a meaningful and easy-to-reach segment specifically, if the opportunity is not attractive. The following four areas can help you determine the character and magnitude of the opportunity:

- *Competitive intensity.* Factors that relate to overall competitive intensity can be expressed in a competitors map that includes (a) the number and identity of competitors and (b) their respective strengths and weaknesses at delivering benefits.
- *Customer dynamics.* Elements that frame the overall customer dynamics of the market are (a) the level of unmet need and the magnitude of unconstrained opportunity, (b) the level of interaction between major customer segments, and (c) the likely rate of growth.

- *Technology vulnerability.* Technology vulnerability includes (a) the impact of the penetration of enabling technologies and (b) the impact of new technologies on the value proposition.
- *Microeconomics.* The microeconomics of the opportunity include (a) the size/volume of the market and (b) the level of profitability.

Later, we discuss how to look across these factors to assess the overall attractiveness of the opportunity and quantify the financial benefits.

## Competitive Intensity

**Identify Competitors.** To measure competitive intensity, a company obviously needs to identify the competitors it will face. In the discussion of value systems, a company's key competitors would have been identified, and white-space opportunities (those in which there is no apparent competition) would have been isolated. At this stage, the task is to develop a better understanding of the threats and opportunities associated with various participants.

Identifying online competitors is both easier and more difficult than identifying offline competitors. On the one hand, the firm can simply use search engines to begin identifying competitors (although generic searches may deliver thousands of relevant pages), then visit the websites of these potential competitors to gain an understanding of their offerings. On the other hand, competition in the marketspace typically occurs across traditional industry boundaries. No matter what online business you are in, there is a good chance that either Microsoft or AOL Time Warner (or both) are your competitors.

In the online world, companies that one would not consider **direct competitors** (a company offering a similar or competing product) can become **indirect competitors** because they are reaching and attracting the same customers, or because they are developing a technology, platform, or offering that might compete with your offering.

In other words, direct competitors are rivals in the same industry. In his book *Competitive Strategy*, Michael Porter defines these firms as offering products or services that are "close substitutes" for each other.[10] For example, PetSmart.com and Petco.com are direct competitors; both sell pet supplies. Direct competitors reach and compete for the same customers. However, Webvan and HomeRuns.com are not (at the time of writing) direct competitors, even though both allow customers to order groceries online, and both deliver to the customer's door. This is because Webvan serves San Francisco, Chicago, and Atlanta customers, while HomeRuns.com serves Boston and Washington, D.C. customers.

Indirect competitors include two categories of companies:

- *Substitute producers.* Porter defines substitute producers as companies that, though they reside in different industries, produce products and services that "perform the same function."[11] Keen.com and Britannica.com are substitute producers. Keen.com is a switchboard that connects people with questions to individuals who can answer them knowledgeably. Britannica.com offers answers to a wide range of questions through its online encyclopedia.
- *Adjacent competitors.* Adjacent competitors do not currently offer products and services that are direct substitutes, but they have the potential to quickly do so. For example, adjacent competitors may have a relationship with a company's current customers. The free ISP NetZero had relationships with many

customers who used Yahoo or Excite frequently, but until recently it did not compete directly with those companies. Then NetZero partnered with the search engine LookSmart to create My NetZero, a personalized portal that directly competes with the personalized portal offers of Yahoo and Excite. NetZero automatically routes all users to its My NetZero page when signing on, transforming the company into a powerful direct competitor to other portals. Adjacent competitors might also use a similar technology or platform or have similar activity systems.

A useful tool for identifying direct and indirect competitors is the profiling approach in Exhibit 4-8, which illustrates the "radar screen" for Kodak. The screen consists of three concentric circles. The innermost circle contains the set of customer activities that are central to the industry being examined (we will explore this concept more fully in Chapter 5). In Kodak's case, these include purchasing a camera, purchasing film, taking pictures, digitally manipulating pictures, downloading and choosing pictures to print, printing and receiving pictures, sharing pictures, storing them on a CD, and purchasing accessories. Kodak faces competition in each of these areas. The middle circle contains Kodak's direct competitors. For example, in the purchase-camera step, Kodak competes with a number of companies that include Fuji, Sony, Nikon, and Olympus. In the downloading and choosing pictures to print stage, Kodak faces both offline and online players that include Ofoto, Photo Access, Seattle Filmworks, Shutterfly, and Snapfish. Finally, the outermost circle contains Kodak's indirect competitors. In the purchase-camera stage, HP and Intel

## Exhibit 4-8
### COMPETITOR PROFILING—EASTMAN KODAK

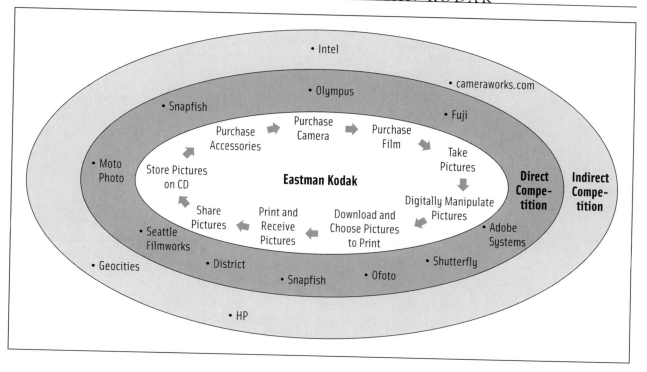

do not offer cameras, but they do provide accessory hardware products that are targeted to the same customer groups; the hardware products conceivably could be leveraged toward offering cameras in the future.

**Competitor Maps.** Current and prospective competitors can significantly shape the nature of a company's online opportunity. In previous steps, we identified the customer segments that the company wants to target and the competitors (direct and indirect) that a company may face. To assess competitive intensity, we need to map the competitors to the target segments. In other words, we need to map out where current competitor companies are participating and determine their effectiveness in delivering benefits to our target customers. This analysis will help the company do the following:

- Demarcate any white space, or underserved areas, in the market and, conversely, the most competitive areas.
- Identify the companies it will compete against and gain preliminary understanding of their strengths.
- Spot companies that could be potential collaborators—in other words, companies that might offer a critical capability or unique access to customers at a specific stage of the customer decision process.

The competitor mapping of segments can also be used to record the relative strengths and weaknesses of current competitors and their offerings at each relevant cell in the map. Ultimately, the customer seeks specific benefits. Assessing the current player performance in meeting the customer standard will provide an indication of the potential for a company to move in and win. Understanding current competitor capabilities will also give a sense of the height of competitive hurdles a company may face in its selected space.

Exhibit 4-9 illustrates a mapping of Priceline.com's competitors to two of its target segments. The competitors considered are Travelocity and American Airlines E-Fares (the weekly discount fares offered by American). A closer study of the low-to-middle-income families with children segment reveals that Priceline.com performs moderately. It offers low prices; however, the flight schedules can be inconvenient for families, and the quality of service on the Priceline.com site is low. In contrast, Travelocity seems to serve this segment well. It offers vacation planning tools and a large selection of destinations, and allows customers to select their schedules. Finally, American Airlines E-Fares performs very poorly for this segment. The airline often does not give enough notice of its special fares, has a poor selection of destinations, and offers a limited number of seats—all of which make it potentially difficult for a family to book tickets for all its members.

## Customer Dynamics

Once we have identified competitor vulnerabilities, we next need to turn our attention to the customer dynamics of the market and how they create, accelerate, and sustain unit demand. When analyzing customer dynamics, three central factors must be considered:

**Unconstrained Opportunity.** This is the amount of white space that is still apparent in the marketplace. Markets with a high degree of trapped or relatively untapped new-to-the-world value are particularly prized. Note the explosive growth of eBay in the online auction space. The number of goods that individuals wanted to buy and sell,

**Exhibit 4-9** COMPETITOR MAPPING TO SELECTED SEGMENTS FOR PRICELINE

| Target Segments | Priceline | Travelocity | AA E-Fares |
|---|---|---|---|
| *Students — Flexible Events* | ◔ • Low prices<br>• Only 24% of bids get matched | ◔ • Special deals<br>• Fare watch | ◑ • Often not enough notice<br>• Poor selection |
| *Low/Middle-Income Families With Children* | ◑ • Low prices<br>• Inconvenient flight schedules | ● • Vacation planning tools<br>• Large selection | ◔ • Often not enough notice<br>• Limited seats |
| *Last-Minute Travelers* | ◕ • Last-minute prices<br>• Considerably cheaper than consolidators | ◔ • Typically very high last-minute prices<br>• Large selections | ◕ • Very low prices |

● High Performance Level     ◑ Medium Performance Level     ○ Low Performance Level

combined with the relatively arcane auction system in which they found themselves trading, signaled a massive opportunity.

**Segment Interaction.** This level of reinforcing activity generates more purchase and usage. Companies that have member-influencing-member dynamics—in other words, viral dynamics—can quickly capture much of the opportunity. For example, through its self-serve customer feedback offering Zoomerang.com, MarketTools created a geometric viral effect. Each member can send a customer-feedback survey to 30 customers, who then experience the Zoomerang offering and decide whether to write their own survey and send it to 30 of their customers, and so on.

**Growth.** Growth usually refers to the percentage of annual growth of the underlying customer market. Markets with high expected growth represent significant opportunities for players. For example, Onvia.com, which is a general-services portal to small businesses, can benefit from the high rate of growth in the small-business sector—the fastest growing sector of the economy. Onvia benefits from a growth "three-fer": a growing number of small businesses, penetration of existing small businesses, and a growing number of services that small businesses require.

# Technology Vulnerability

Beyond the competitive arena, the company must make a high-level judgment on the concept's vulnerability to technology trends, both in the penetration of enabling technologies and in the impact of new technologies on the value proposition.

**Technology Adoption.** Is there sufficient penetration of the technologies (e.g., cable modems, scanners) that enable the customer to take advantage of or participate in the offering? What penetration is necessary to make the offering financially viable? When is the minimum penetration likely to be met? Is there an introductory version that could be upgraded as technology penetration increases?

**Impact of New Technologies.** What new technologies could radically alter the economics of delivering an offering or require adjustment of the actual features and functionality of an offering? How likely is it that your target population or competitors will use these technologies?

The pace and discontinuity of technological change make forecasting the future particularly challenging, and it is not our intent to provide an exhaustive treatment of the subject here.[12] Fortunately, several rules of thumb about technological development can guide entrepreneurs. One of them is that computers will continue to increase in power. Moore's Law, which we examine in greater depth elsewhere in the book, forecasts the pace at which processing power increases. Our definition of what a computer is will also probably change. Andy Grove of Intel predicts that by 2002 there will be 500 million computers in the world, and already there are over 6 billion computer chips embedded in devices such as phones and cars.[13] Soon every device will be a computer. Many believe these devices will all be connected by a vastly larger Internet. George Gilder, a technology forecaster who has given his name to Gilder's Law, predicts that total bandwidth of communications systems will triple every 12 months for the foreseeable future. The challenge for entrepreneurs is to understand what these macro-trends will mean for their proposed businesses.

## Microeconomics

So far in this section, we have assessed the magnitude of the opportunity from a competitive perspective (how easy it is to enter the space and to differentiate the company from competitor offerings), from the perspective of customer dynamics (how unit demand is created, accelerated, and sustained), and from a technology standpoint. We now need to assess the level of financial opportunity. In doing so, the following two factors are of critical importance:

**Market Size.** This is the dollar value of all of the sales generated in a particular market. Opportunities with a large market size are very attractive, since winning even a small piece of the pie may correspond to a significant revenue flow. For example, a large number of competitors in the online pet-products industry emerged in response to the huge size of the pet food and supplies market, estimated at $23 billion.[14] Despite this large market, many of the entrants (for example, Petopia.com and Pets.com) were unable to create successful businesses.

**Profitability.** This is the profit margin that can be realized in the market. Markets with high profit margins are highly attractive because they can generate high levels of profit with moderate sales volume. For example, eBay's auction market provides a highly attractive opportunity in part because it generates profit margins in excess of 80 percent.[15]

An important aspect of the assessment of market size and profitability is determining how the company will generate revenue. What are the opportunities for monetizing the value creation? Consider typical sources of revenue in the new economy—advertising revenue, referrals, affiliate-program fees,[16] customer subscriptions, and the purchase of products and services.

To assess the overall opportunity attractiveness, managers must not only rate each factor separately but also rate them together as a whole. Whether a particular factor helps, is neutral, or hinders the overall market opportunity, the manager must try to gauge the magnitude of its impact. It is important to look across all factors to see the overall effect, because these effects may be multiplicative and not additive (see Exhibit 4-10).

# HOW DO WE PREPARE A GO/NO-GO ASSESSMENT?

At this point, the management team should have a clear picture of the market opportunity. Its members should be able to describe the value system for the industry, and have a strong sense for how intervention into this value system and the customer decision process could either create new benefits, enhance existing ones, or unlock value trapped in the current system. The team should be able to clearly identify the customer segments that it will be targeting, and support its determination with data or strong hypotheses about the underserved or unmet needs of one or more of these customer segments. This understanding provides the basis for creating a high-level value proposition and determining capabilities that the team can bring to bear to participate successfully in the business. The examination of potential competitors enhances the team's thinking about where to participate in the identified market and what to bring to the opportunity.

The management team should then craft an **opportunity story**—in essence, the first rough outline of the business plan. The opportunity story should

- Briefly describe the target segment(s) within the selected value system.
- Articulate the high-level value proposition.
- Spell out the expected elements of customer benefits (we largely focused on functional benefits in this chapter; however, needs can be emotional or self-expressive).
- Identify the critical capabilities and resources needed to deliver the customer benefits.
- Lay out the critical "reasons to believe" that the identified capabilities and resources will be a source of advantage over the competition.
- Categorize the critical capabilities (and supporting resources) as in-house, build, buy, or collaborate.
- Describe how the company will monetize the opportunity (i.e., how it will capture some portion of the value that it creates for its customers).
- Provide an initial sense for the magnitude of the financial opportunity for the company.

The team now must decide whether or not it is ready to define the specific value proposition and design a business model. This should be the first of several go/no-go decision gates. If it has not already done so, the team should define the criteria to be met before members will feel comfortable about proceeding to the next step of the business development process.

If uncertainty remains about one or more of the gating questions, the management team must judge whether additional analysis would remove uncertainty or if there are ways to proceed while revisiting the areas of greatest concern. The team should not proceed too far down the path toward business-model development if members cannot reach a consensus on passing these initial gates.

**Exhibit 4-10** PRICELINE.COM OVERALL OPPORTUNITY ASSESSMENT

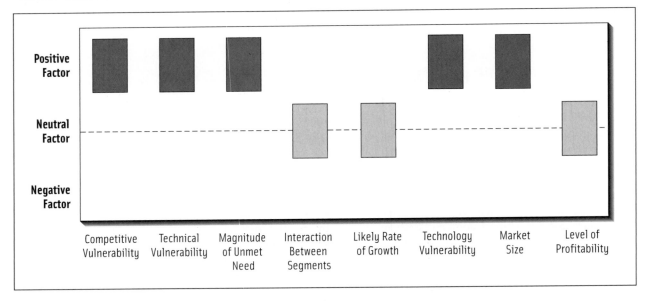

## MARKETWATCH.COM MARKET OPPORTUNITY

On October 30, 1997, MarketWatch.com was launched as a joint partnership between CBS News and Data Broadcasting Corporation (DBC). At the end of 2000, after three successful years of growth, MarketWatch.com faced an interesting dilemma. There were new markets it could enter and new services it could introduce; at the same time, there were an increasing number of competitors entering the market and building their capabilities. Let us now apply the market-opportunity framework to MarketWatch.com as it stood at the end of 2000.

The first step is to identify the business arena in which MarketWatch.com was participating. More specifically, in what areas could MarketWatch.com release trapped value or create new value? Exhibit 4-11 illustrates some of the areas of potential value release or generation. One way that MarketWatch.com had been able (and was continuing) to release value was by delivering its financial content across a number of different media platforms. In addition to having content on its website, MarketWatch.com contributed content to CBS NewsPath (a CBS news service to affiliate stations) as well as to popular CBS TV shows (such as the *CBS Early Show* and *CBS Evening News*). It also introduced its own television program, *CBS MarketWatch Weekend*. The program became widely popular; by year-end 2000 the show was airing on 131 stations, and reaching more than 80 percent of the U.S. viewing audience. MarketWatch.com also made its content available through radio, with its content airing on 154 stations, including the top-10 U.S. markets, and reaching 11.5 million unduplicated listeners each week. Furthermore, the site's content was increasingly becoming available through wireless devices.

MarketWatch.com could also create new value for its users. Since its inception, it had provided CBS News with a reliable financial news capability, and it had increasingly offered personal finance tools to its users. MarketWatch.com could create more value by further personalizing the experience of its users, allowing them to fully cus-

**Exhibit 4-11** MARKETWATCH.COM: DEFINING EXISTING OR NEW VALUE SYSTEM

|  | How? |
|---|---|
| *Release Trapped Value* | • Up-to-the minute financial information<br>• Multiple media access points:<br>　—Website<br>　—PDAs/Wireless<br>　—Television<br>　—Radio |
| *Create New Value* | • Extend reach<br>• Personalize experience<br>• Provide CBS News with financial news capability<br>• Develop easy to use personal finance tools |

tomize their site layout, content, and tools. It could further extend its reach and offer its existing (or new) products to new markets. It could develop even more easy-to-use personal finance tools to help its users make and save money. As we will see in later chapters, MarketWatch.com acted on many of these opportunities.

In order to effectively compete in the personal-finance market, MarketWatch.com had to continuously identify its competitors' unmet or underserved needs (see Exhibit 4-12). The purchase process is broken into three main areas: prepurchase (including steps such as viewing news, reading analysis, learning about investing, and planning the investment strategy), purchase (the order-placement step), and post-purchase (including the portfolio performance tracking and tax-reporting steps). An examination of the purchase process reveals that a number of customer needs were insufficiently addressed by competitors. For example, competitors did not offer comprehensive and elegant charting tools for displaying financial information; there was not a single reliable source for in-depth commentary and analysis by a staff of journalists with combined financial and editorial experience. Furthermore, even though many sites did offer investment tools (Schwab's Stock Analyzer, for example), there was still room for improving these tools' capabilities. For example, more sophisticated forecasting tools could be created or existing tools could be further personalized to investor needs. MarketWatch.com sought to address many of these needs by providing original, in-depth financial content and by continuously developing tools to assist investors with the planning and tracking of their investments.

Consider the user groups that MarketWatch.com was targeting in late 2000. We can analyze this by breaking down the market into meaningful and actionable segments and then identifying the segments of highest priority. We have selected the following variables to help segment the personal-finance market:

**Demographics.** The age of the user (under 25, 25 to 54, and over 54 years of age) and the sex of the user correspond to their level of comfort with using the Internet for information searches and transactions. The income level (under $75,000, over $75,000) corresponds to the degree of interest in and knowledge of financial

# Exhibit 4-12  MARKETWATCH.COM: UNMET AND UNDERSERVED NEEDS

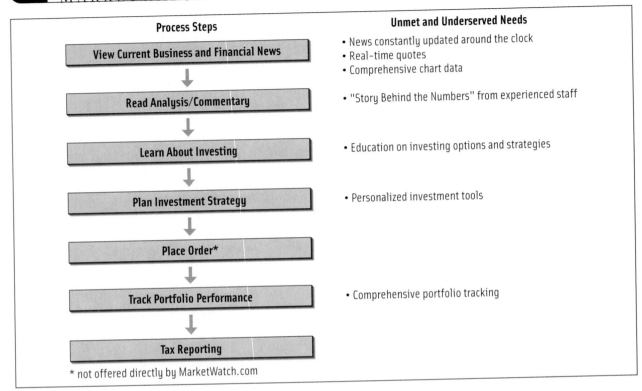

**Process Steps**

- View Current Business and Financial News
- Read Analysis/Commentary
- Learn About Investing
- Plan Investment Strategy
- Place Order*
- Track Portfolio Performance
- Tax Reporting

**Unmet and Underserved Needs**

- News constantly updated around the clock
- Real-time quotes
- Comprehensive chart data

- "Story Behind the Numbers" from experienced staff

- Education on investing options and strategies

- Personalized investment tools

- Comprehensive portfolio tracking

\* not offered directly by MarketWatch.com

---

concepts and information. Users making more than $75,000 are more likely to invest funds, making it more likely for them to need in-depth financial news and analysis.

**Behavior.** The frequency of accessing financial information (less than once a day, more than once a day) correlates to the degree of the user's need for in-depth and real-time financial information. Furthermore, the medium used to retrieve financial information (online, offline) relates to the user's comfort with the Internet and his or her need for up-to-the-minute news updates.

Combining these variables can yield a meaningful and actionable segmentation of the market. Exhibit 4-13 illustrates this segmentation and indicates the primary, secondary, and low-priority target segments for MarketWatch.com. The segment that MarketWatch.com primarily targeted during its first year of existence was the "savvy investor" (segment A). This segment required in-depth analysis and up-to-the-minute updates on financial information. Savvy investors are generally long-term online users, primarily male, 25 to 54 years old, have income over $75,000, and access online financial news very frequently (more than once a day). Once MarketWatch.com felt that it had a strong grasp on that segment (around the beginning of 1999), it shifted its focus to a broader audience of users who were either actively seeking financial information or were "newbies" to personal finance and needed to be educated and introduced to financial concepts. The new target segments became the "seekers" (segments B and C) and the "dabblers" (segments D and E), with savvy investors moving to a secondary priority.

Exhibit 4-13   MARKETWATCH.COM ACTION SEGMENTATION

**Legend:**
- ■ Primary target segments — (A) Savvy Investors
- ■ Secondary target segments — (B) and (C) Seekers
- □ Low Priority — (D) and (E) Dabblers

So-called seekers need current financial information and analysis, but are not as interested in real-time updates or really sophisticated analysis. This segment generally consists of online users, 25 to 54 years old, who are primarily male. They can be further classified into two subgroups. Some have a high income (over $75,000) but do not access financial information often (indicating a moderate interest in financial news and analysis), while others have a lower income (under $75,000) but frequently access financial information. Dabblers indicate a need for education on financial concepts and general financial information without deep analysis or up-to-the-minute updates. They cover all age groups, are both male and female, and can also be classified into two subgroups. Some are online users who make less than $75,000 a year and infrequently access financial information. Others primarily access financial information offline.

Having identified MarketWatch.com's target segments as well as its prioritization, we can now look at the factors that determine the attractiveness of each segment. An important component of measuring the magnitude of the opportunity is the degree of competitive intensity—namely, how well these segments were being served by competitors. Exhibit 4-14 compares how well MarketWatch.com was serving its target segments by the end of 2000 to how well the target segments were being served by three of MarketWatch.com's key competitors: CNNfn.com, The Motley Fool, and MSN MoneyCentral. MarketWatch.com was serving the seekers very well by offering a mix of news, tools, and analysis. It served the dabblers moderately well, providing some guidance through financial news and some educational tools, but not as much as its competitors' sites. MarketWatch.com's offer was also attractive to savvy investors, providing them with useful tools and real-time analysis.

However, CNNfn.com better-served savvy investors by providing up-to-the-minute news and analysis, paying little attention to aesthetics. This made the CNNfn.com offering less appealing to seekers and even less attractive (possibly

**Exhibit 4-14**  MARKETWATCH.COM COMPETITION: MAPPED TARGET SEGMENTS

| Segments | CBS MarketWatch | CNNfn.com | Money Central | Motley Fool |
|---|---|---|---|---|
| A. Savvy Investors | ● | ● | ◑ | ◑ |
| B. Seekers | ● | ◑ | ◕ | ◕ |
| C. Dabblers | ◑ | ◔ | ◑ | ◕ |

● High Performance Level
◑ Medium Performance Level
○ Low Performance Level

even somewhat intimidating) to dabblers. MSN MoneyCentral offered financial news with limited site-generated analysis, limited insight on spending and saving for family needs, and very limited educational tools for people new to personal finance. This made the site more appealing to seekers and less appealing to savvy investors or dabblers. The Motley Fool's brand message—"Educate, Amuse, Enrich"—clearly demonstrated its intent to educate users and to enrich them with information. Consequently, the site appealed more to dabblers and seekers than to savvy investors.

Competitive intensity is just one of the seven factors to consider when determining how attractive the opportunity was for MarketWatch.com at the end of 2000. Exhibit 4-15 demonstrates these factors and their effect on the opportunity attractiveness. As discussed earlier, competitive vulnerability was a negative factor, given the intensity of the competition. The magnitude of unmet needs was a neutral factor, since many of the basic user needs were addressed, though there was room for more effective tools and more insightful analysis. The likely growth rate of the MarketWatch.com target segments and the potential size of the market (both in terms of advertising and content licensing) were very high—both positive factors in assessing the opportunity. The combination of these factors led to an attractive opportunity for MarketWatch.com, while at the same time signaling the need to closely monitor competitor moves.

 **Exhibit 4-15**

## MARKETWATCH.COM OPPORTUNITY ASSESSMENT

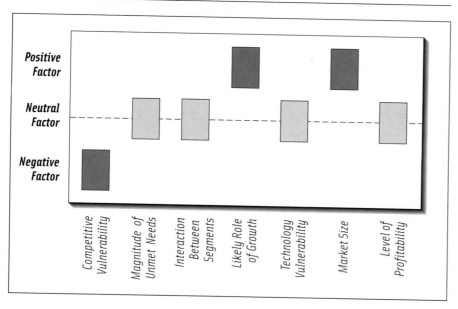

# SUMMARY

### 1. What is the market-opportunity analysis framework?

The market-opportunity analysis framework consists of five main investigative stages, a final assessment of the opportunity, and a final go/no-go decision. The five stages are read: stages are (1) seed opportunities in the existing or new value system, (2) uncover the opportunity nucleus, (3) identify the target customers, (4) declare the company's resource-based opportunity for advantage, and (5) assess competitive, technological, and financial attractiveness.

### 2. Is market-opportunity analysis different in the networked economy?

The networked economy has affected market-opportunity analysis in five main ways: (1) networked-economy competition occurs across industry boundaries rather than within industry boundaries, (2) competitive developments and responses are occurring at an unprecedented speed, (3) competition occurs between alliances of companies rather than between individual companies, (4) consumer behavior is still in the early stages of being defined, making it easier to influence and change consumer behavior, and (5) industry value chains or systems are rapidly being reconfigured.

### 3. What are the two generic "value types"?

Firms should look at the value system as a lens that yields ideas about new business possibilities. Specifically, a firm is looking for trapped value to be liberated, or new-to-the-world value to be introduced.

### 4. How do we identify unmet and/or underserved needs?

New value creation comes with doing a better job of meeting customer needs. Customers will switch from their old supplier only if the new company does a better job of meeting customers' requirements. The customer decision process is an organizing framework that helps a company look systematically for unmet or underserved needs. The process maps the activities and the choices customers make in accessing a specific experience within a value system. The customer decision process lays out a series of steps, from awareness of the experience to the purchase experience and finally the use experience. The process of generating a map of the customer decision process may help in generating new ideas about unmet or underserved needs.

### 5. What determines the specific customers the company will pursue?

To be effective and efficient, it is essential for the company to know which customer groups are most attractive, which groups the company should pursue, which groups the company should de-emphasize, and what offerings to present to which target segment. Customer segmentation, or the grouping of similar customers in order to better serve their needs, must be both actionable (consistent with how the company can take action in the market) and also meaningful (correlating to differences in how customers will behave). Simple market maps profiling the segments will identify where the money is, how well competitors serve the segments, and where underserved customers reside.

## 6. Who provides the resources to deliver the benefits of the offering?

After the initial customer focus of the business is determined, the company should stake out the capabilities and technology needed to deliver the benefits of the offering. The management team should identify at least three or four assets of a winning resource system that it can create or provide through business partnerships. This resource system is central to delivering new benefits or unlocking trapped value—the core of the company's value story—and should hold the promise for an advantage when compared with the current and prospective players in the targeted marketspace. A resource system is a discrete collection of individual and company activities and assets that, when combined, create organizational capabilities. These capabilities allow the company to serve customer needs.

On its own, a company may not be able to offer all the necessary resources to deliver value to its target segments. In opportunity assessment, a company must be realistic about any capability gaps. Partnering may be an effective alternative to building or acquiring the capability. The potential partners for a company can be grouped into two categories—complementors and capability partners.

## 7. How do we assess the attractiveness of the opportunity?

There are eight factors to consider when assessing the character and magnitude of the opportunity:

- Competitive intensity with a (1) map of direct and indirect competitors
- Customer dynamics with levels of (2) unconstrained opportunity, (3) segment interaction, and (4) the likely rate of growth
- Technology vulnerability with the impact of (5) the penetration of enabling technologies and (6) new technologies on the value proposition
- Microeconomics with an estimate of the (7) size/volume of the market and (8) level of profitability

## 8. How do we prepare a "go/no-go" assessment?

An opportunity story may be thought of as the first draft of a business plan. The story should articulate the value proposition and the target customers. It should demonstrate the benefits to these customers and the way in which the company will monetize the opportunity. It should estimate the financial magnitude of the opportunity, identify the key capabilities and resources, and then, finally, discuss the reasons to believe. In other words, the story should tell why the company's capabilities will create a competitive advantage for the new business in serving its target customers.

The management team must decide whether or not to proceed to defining the specific value proposition and designing the business model. This should be the first of several go/no-go decision gates. The team should define the criteria to be met in order for each member to feel comfortable in proceeding to the next step of the business development process. If uncertainty remains about one or more of the gating questions, the management team must judge whether or not additional analysis would remove uncertainty, or if there are ways to proceed while revisiting the areas of greatest concern. The team should not proceed too far down a path toward business-model development if its members cannot reach a consensus on passing these initial gates.

# KEY TERMS

marketspace

market-opportunity analysis

value system

"co-opetition"

Metcalfe's Law

trapped value

new-to-the-world value

opportunity nucleus

customer decision process

segmentation

actionable segmentation

meaningful segmentation

the offering

resource system

direct competitors

indirect competitors

opportunity story

# Endnotes

[1]Brandenburger, Adam M. and Barry J. Nalebuff. 1996. *Co-opetition.* New York: Currency Doubleday.

[2]Web: Napster's program, which raised copyright issues, has been adapted to search and copy other types of files without a firm's OK. Hufstutter, P. J. and Greg Miller. 2000. Hackers find new uses for song-swap software. *Los Angeles Times,* 24 March, Home edition, Business section.

[3]Interested readers could learn more about value chains and value systems in the following cited reference: Porter, Michael E. 1985. *Competitive advantage: Creating and sustaining superior performance.* New York: The Free Press; London: Collier Macmillan.

[4]Shapiro, Carl and Hal R. Varian. 1999. *Information rules.* Boston: Harvard Business School Press. This book contains an excellent and detailed examination of network economics.

[5]Kotler, Philip. 2000. Chapter 9 in *Marketing management.* 10th ed. Upper Saddle River, NJ: Prentice Hall.

[6]This sidebar is summarized from the following article: Leonard, Dorothy, and Jeffrey F. Rayport. 1997. Spark innovation through empathic design. *Harvard Business Review* 75, no. 6 (Nov–Dec): 102–13.

[7]This sidebar is partly drawn from an article authored by the following individual. Pink, Daniel H. 1998. Metaphor marketing. *Fast Company,* issue no. 14 (April): 214.

[8]Keller, Kevin Lane. 1998. *Strategic brand management: Building, measuring and managing brand equity.* Upper Saddle River, NJ: Prentice Hall, Inc., pp. 317–8.

[9]Pink, Daniel H. 1998. Metaphor marketing. *Fast Company,* issue no. 14 (April): 214.

[10]Porter, Michael E. 1980. *Competitive strategy.* New York: The Free Press, p. 5.

[11]*ibid.,* p. 23.

[12]Interested persons should refer to these references for further reading: Foster, Richard N. 1986. *Innovation: The attacker's advantage.* New York: Summit Books. Christensen, Clayton M. 1997. *The innovator's dilemma: When new techniques cause great firms to fail.* Boston: Harvard Business School Press.

[13]Kelly, Kevin. 1998. *10 new rules for the new economy.* New York: Viking, p. 11.

[14]Stone, Brad. 1999. Amazon's pet projects: Start-Ups jump when the online giant comes calling. *Newsweek,* 21 June.

[15]Simons, David. 1999. What's the deal: The true cost of marketing. *Industry Standard,* 2 December.

Zacks Investment Research, Inc. 2000. EBAY INC annual income statement, 14 May. URL: *http://www1.zacks.com/cgi-bin/JMFR/Free Report?ref=DEF&ticker=EBAY&hist=1.*

[16]For more information on affiliate programs see Chapter 6.

# Business Models

The previous chapter on market-opportunity analysis answered the question, "Where will the business compete?" In this chapter we turn our attention to the question, "How will the business win?" Certainly, winning is relative to the goals of the business. A business may choose to define victory in terms of revenue targets, gross margin, number of unique visitors, or other criteria.

Regardless of the goals of the enterprise, the business must first specify its business model. In this chapter, we introduce the concept of a business model for the new economy. A networked-economy business model requires four choices on the part of senior management. These include the specification of (1) a value proposition or a value cluster for targeted customers; (2) a marketspace offering—which could be a product, a service, information, or all three; (3) a unique, defendable resource system; and (4) a financial model.

## QUESTIONS

*Please consider the following questions as you read this chapter:*

1. What is a business model?

2. Do firms compete on value propositions or value clusters?

3. How does a firm develop an online offering—whether it consists of a product, a service, or information?

4. What is a successful, unique resource system? What are characteristics of good resource systems?

This chapter was coauthored by Bernie Jaworski, Jeffrey Rayport, Leo Griffin, and Yannis Dosios. Substantive input was also provided by Yankir Siegal, Sharon Grady, and Lisa Ferri.

5. What are the financial models available to firms?

6. What business classification schemes seem most appropriate for the new economy?

# INTRODUCTION

In order to understand the four components of a business model, we will apply the framework to the highly competitive, rapidly changing flower industry. The domestic retail-flower business is a $15 billion industry. The industry is highly fragmented, with no national brand, multiple layers of distribution, and uneven product quality. Given the complexity of the supply chain, flowers are typically sold 10 to 12 days after they are harvested. On the customer side, approximately 60 percent of all flower purchases are made by walk-in customers. When flowers are delivered, 80 percent are local—that is, they are ordered and delivered in the same area.

The market for online flower sales was approximately $350 million in 1999. Industry experts predict that it will be a $2.5 billion market by the year 2004. However, at the current time, there is no clear standout that will win this space. The value propositions of the major online retailers are quite similar, so some consolidation and industry fallout are expected.

In April 2000, a *Los Angeles Times* article noted that FTD.com had lost 75 percent of its value since going public in the fall of 1999.[1] Equally important, FTD.com and other major flower websites were experiencing a significant cash drain. In particular, the article made the following observations and forecasts:

- FTD.com was spending $6.1 million per month to stay in business but was taking in only $2.2 million in gross revenues, for a $3.9 million monthly deficit. Because FTD.com had $37.9 million in cash and current assets, the *Los Angeles Times* calculated that without a significant improvement in performance, the business would run out of cash by the end of 2000.

- 1-800-Flowers was running a monthly deficit of $22.4 million and could hold out for 8.4 months.

- Gerald Stevens was losing $17.7 million a month and would last less than 2 months.

- PC Flowers & Gifts was losing $326,000 a month and could hold on for 13 months with its current cash and assets.

Therefore, the prediction was that the number of online flower retailers would "shrink dramatically." Indeed, FTD.com's CEO predicted that by year-end 2000 there would be only two remaining players, FTD.com and 1-800-Flowers. In fact, all of these companies were still operating in early 2001, and FTD.com had actually achieved profitability. Nonetheless, it is likely that the industry will consolidate and quite possible that 1-800-Flowers will be one of the victims of this shakeout.

In this chapter, we will consider components of the business models of key players in this industry (see Exhibit 5-1). Significant cross-industry competition is emerging in this product category. Flowers are sold online by conventional bricks-and-mortar flower merchants (e.g., FTD.com connects approximately 21,000 North American retail florists to exchange orders for out-of-town deliveries), new online flower merchants (e.g., proflowers.com), and cross-industry players in the

## Exhibit 5-1  COMPONENTS OF A BUSINESS MODEL

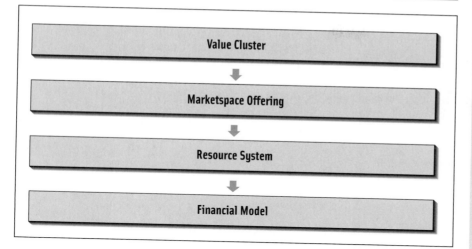

- Value Cluster
- Marketspace Offering
- Resource System
- Financial Model

gift, card, and crafts markets and in other categories (e.g., Hallmark.com). With this backdrop, firms must make critical decisions concerning how to win in the online world.

## WHAT IS A BUSINESS MODEL?

The new-economy **business model** requires four choices on the part of senior management, which include specifying (1) a value proposition or a value cluster for targeted customers; (2) a marketspace offering—which could be a product, service, information, or all three; (3) a unique, defendable resource system; and (4) a financial model.

In this chapter, we consider each of the components of the business model. While each component is considered sequentially, it is likely that the senior management team will reexamine the various steps as it considers these critical decisions. Our most important message in this chapter is the need to base all of these decisions on the forces that are unfolding in the marketplace. In other words, each step in the proposed process is based on the benefits that matter most to customers. All else being equal, firms that are able to understand both current and future customer needs are likely to be the long-term winners in their respective industries.

## Do Firms Compete on Value Propositions or Value Clusters?

The first step in the articulation of the business model is to clearly specify the **value proposition** for the business. Construction of a value proposition requires management to specify the following three items: (1) target segment, (2) focal customer benefits, and (3) the rationale for why the firm can deliver the benefit package in a significantly better way than its competitors.

A value proposition can be considered a basic or baseline case. However, a recent alternative view, which we term a "value-cluster approach," argues that because of the customization capabilities available to online businesses, they can address multiple customer segments and offer a variety of benefits. The value proposition is no longer singular but is a **value cluster** composed of three parts: (1) the choice of target customer segments, (2) a particular focal combination of customer-driven benefits that are offered, and (3) the rationale for why this firm and its partners can deliver the value cluster in a significantly better way than competitors.

**Choice of Segments.** The first decision in the construction of a value cluster (or proposition) is the selection of target segments. A careful market-opportunity analysis, as reviewed in Chapter 4, should reveal the segments in which a particular firm can be competitive. While a number of classical frameworks exist to assess the segment-choice decision, most reduce the analysis to two basic dimensions: the attractiveness of the market and the firm's ability to compete in the market. Market attractiveness is a function of many variables,[2] but the key decision variables are frequently reduced to the following:

- *Market Size and Growth Rates.* The overall dollar size of the market and percentage growth rates of the market segments should be significant.
- *Unmet or Insufficiently Met Customer Needs.* Customers are either not being served or not being served well by existing players.
- *Weak or Nonexistent Competitors.* Obviously, it is best to enter markets where competition is either not evident, performing poorly, or does not have sufficient resources to win the market.

The firm's ability to compete in a particular segment can be assessed by examining how well its business strengths (relative to competitors) match the customer benefits sought in a segment. For example, if a particular online flower retailer has unique strengths (such as exclusive sourcing of fresh flowers) and the target segment highly desires that strength (in this example, fresh flowers), then there would be a strong match between the relative business strength and the desires of this segment.

Another important factor strongly enters into the online segment-choice decision—degree of fit (or conflict) with existing channels. The offline businesses of 1-800-Flowers.com and proflowers.com are very compatible—indeed synergistic—with the new online businesses because they share order fulfillment processes, payment services, and supply chains.

In Chapter 4, we discussed alternative ways that a given firm can segment the online market. In the flower industry, this can translate into demographic segments, benefit segments, or some combination of the two. Thus, firms such as 1-800-Flowers.com must decide which market segment they will attempt to dominate. Segmentation-approach options are many, including such demographic approaches as (1) the under-30 segment or (2) the upper-income segment. Benefit-segment options include selecting those who are looking for the (1) freshest flowers, (2) most convenient buying method, or (3) lowest-priced flowers. As shown in Chapter 4, it is critical to select a segmentation approach that maximizes both actionability and meaningfulness.

**Choice of Focal Customer Benefits.** The second step in the articulation of a value proposition or cluster is to specify the key benefits that will be delivered to the target segment. Conventional offline marketing and business textbooks recommend that firms focus on one or two critical benefits. The examples often cited include Volvo (known for safety), Southwest Airlines (known for convenience and low prices), and the Four Seasons (known for outstanding service). However, some authors argue that firms that attempt to compete on more than one benefit create two basic problems. The first, on the demand side, is that multiple messages will confuse customers. The second, on the supply side, is that systems must be uniquely constructed to deliver certain benefits. Choosing two highly conflicting benefits (e.g., fast delivery and low prices) will lead to compromises in strategy development—the classic "stuck in the middle"—and average performance on two benefits, while other firms focus on delivering high performance on only one of the benefits.

Now let us turn to the online world. The question, as we begin to examine various online businesses, is whether they focus on one, two, or multiple benefits. Most of the well-respected flower sites seem to focus on providing the freshest flowers. However, after providing this core benefit, they differ somewhat in their other benefit offerings. Some focus on complementary gifts, some on fast delivery, and others on low prices. For example, FTD.com emphasizes both fresh flowers and complementary gift offerings.

## POINT-COUNTERPOINT

# Should the Firm Deliver a Single Benefit or a Cluster of Benefits?

Should online firms focus exclusively on delivering a single benefit exceptionally well (e.g., either lowest prices or freshest flowers) or should they attempt to deliver all the benefits that online customers are seeking?

The argument in favor of delivering a single benefit centers largely on the alignment of the organization and its ability to easily communicate with target customers. Proponents of the single-benefit view note that this does not imply they will only deliver one benefit, but rather the organization's focal communication primarily emphasizes one critical benefit. Thus, while Buy.com is clearly focused on low price, it simultaneously must deliver breadth of inventory, ease of use, and order fulfillment. This strong adherence to a single critical benefit and message aligns the back-office systems of the organization and makes a clear statement to the market. Here we define the market broadly to include targeted customers, potential partner firms, and potential employees.

Proponents of the multiple-benefit approach note that this emphasis on a single benefit is a legacy of the offline world. The online world enables firms to provide multiple "storefronts" to multiple segments within the context of a single URL. Moreover, it is much more customer-focused in the long run because customers do desire multiple benefits. For example, Yahoo.com provides a wide variety of benefits (e.g., single access point, fresh information, easy-to-use navigation tools) through its information and service offerings (e.g., information services, travel services, search, news, weather, stock quotes, and other services).

Thus, in sharp contrast to offline business models, firms in the online world are often able to compete on multiple benefits that are delivered by a single, tightly conceived, and implemented set of activities. But because of the multiple-benefits approach, it is difficult to evaluate any key benefit of these companies. For example, what is the key benefit of Amazon.com's position in the marketplace? Is it price? Customer intimacy? Depth of the product line? Product leadership and service innovation? All of the above? Traditional business strategies would argue that the firm needs to select one critical benefit. This would miss the emergence of hybrid-benefit models, such as Amazon.com.

Some authors argue that the Internet will lead to the commodization of products, whereby all products are viewed equally and the customer selects vendors based solely on price. For example, these proponents argue that products—for example, the Palm VII—can be comparatively shopped across the Internet using "bots" such as mySimon.com. Once the product is located, these authors argue, customers select the lowest price, and no other criteria matter.

However, we would argue that while this search process results in more customer information, it does not necessarily lead to the choice of the lowest-priced site. New research suggests that price sensitivity can actually decrease when usability of quality information increases. Moreover, even when consumers have access to competitive price information, the quality of information on the site can actually increase customer retention.[3] The success of Amazon.com illustrates this point well. A quick search on mySimon.com shows that Amazon rarely offers the lowest prices in any product category, yet it has become the largest e-retailer.

In Exhibit 5-2, we provide the results of a study included in a J.P. Morgan report on retailing.[4] This study illustrated that price is indeed an important decision point for customers (19 percent reported caring about that attribute). However, a host of other services that imply different benefits were significantly more likely to influence the purchase decision. These included such attributes as customer support, on-time delivery, shipping and handling, and privacy protection.

Thus, a strong argument could be made that the Internet will lead to much more differentiation than the bricks-and-mortar business world. Firms that are better able to offer services—and the associated benefits—will continue to compete and win on attributes other than price. Thus, to return to our Palm VII example, customers who use shop bots such as mySimon.com may find the lowest price on a

**Exhibit 5-2** SHATTERING THE MYTH THAT CONSUMERS CARE ONLY ABOUT PRICES ONLINE

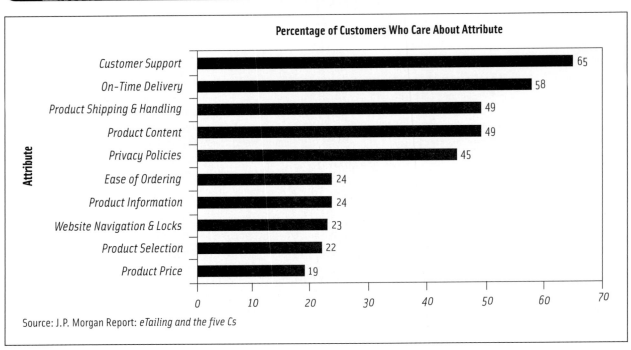

Percentage of Customers Who Care About Attribute

Source: J.P. Morgan Report: *eTailing and the five Cs*

largely unknown site and the next-lowest price on Palm.com, the website owned by the same company that designed and manufactured the Palm VII. Will customers choose the lowest-priced Palm VII on the unknown site or use other criteria? Our view is that some customers will buy the product from the unknown site, but that the vast majority of customers will use other criteria and buy from dealers that they think will deliver other attributes such as customer support and on-time delivery. That is, customers will choose to buy from direct dealers such as Palm.com.

### Choice of Unique and Differentiating Capabilities.
The third component of the value proposition is the compelling rationale for why a particular online firm can provide a single benefit (or multiple benefits) significantly better than its competitors. Thus, in contrast to segment choice and benefits, this component focuses on factors inside the firm (or with partners) that lead to the superior delivery of a targeted benefit or benefits. These factors have been called core competencies, business strengths, strategic control points, unique resources, and unique capabilities.[5]

The key issue is whether these unique capabilities can be linked directly to the core benefit or benefits that form the value proposition. Here, we broadly define capabilities to include tangible assets (e.g., location), intangible assets (e.g., brand name), and capabilities or skills of the organization (e.g., supply-chain management).[6] In other words, firms can have superior performance of selected capabilities, but these capabilities can be unrelated to the delivery of the critical benefit. A litmus test for the unique capability is whether it can be directly tied to the customer benefits that matter most. We more fully elaborate on the capability concept in the resource-system portion later in the chapter.

### Value Propositions or Clusters.
We now have a good understanding of the three concepts needed to construct a value proposition or cluster. Following are sample value propositions for four of the major dot-com flower retailers.[7] Keep in mind that these are not necessarily defendable value propositions. Rather, the intent is to illustrate how a proposition can be constructed.

- PC Flowers & Gifts serves the special-occasions segment (the target segment) with "fresh flowers, complementary gifts, and lower prices" (the three key benefits) because of its accumulated online experience and knowledge since 1989 and its broad product line of complementary gifts (the two key differentiating capabilities).

- Proflowers.com serves the price-sensitive and convenience-oriented customers with the "freshest cut flowers at a competitive price" because of its unusual sourcing and FedEx shipping arrangements.

- FTD.com serves the mid- to high-end market by providing the "easiest way to send flowers and gifts" because of its strong brand name, market communications, and supplier network.

- 1-800-Flowers.com serves the mid- to high-end market with a broad gift assortment, fresh flowers, reasonable prices, and easy access because of its strong brand name, product and media partnerships, and bricks-and-mortar network of franchises.

The question at this point is how differentiated are these value propositions? Consider not simply the desired position, but the firm's ability to "own" this position in the minds of customers. Three specific classes of criteria should be used to assess the quality of the value proposition or cluster:

- *Customer criteria.* Do target customers understand the proposition or cluster? Is it relevant to their needs? Is it believable? Is it perceived as unique, or as "me too," or indistinguishable from other propositions or clusters? Will it provoke action on the part of the target customer?

- *Company criteria.* Will the organization rally around the proposition or cluster? Does the company have the resources or capabilities to own this cluster? Will it block or facilitate the eventual move to additional vertical markets?

- *Competitive criteria.* Are other competitors attempting to hold a similar proposition or cluster? Will competitors allow the focal company to own the stated cluster in the market? Can current competitors match this cluster? How easy is it for future competitors to match this cluster?

A casual review of many of the principal flower sites reveals that several competitors are attempting to own similar segments with similar benefits. Equally significant is that few of the sites have unique capabilities that cannot be replicated by others. Collectively, this suggests that the markets are likely to be intensely competitive, with no clear indication of who has the unique capabilities or activities needed to win this segment.

## How Does a Firm Develop an Online Offering?

Once the value proposition has been articulated, the next step is to fully articulate the online product, service, and information offering. Keep in mind that at this stage, we are not designing the content and "look-and-feel" of the website (this will be the focus of Chapter 6, Customer Interface). Rather, we are providing a broad description of the actual product or service that will be provided online.

In particular, the senior management team must complete three sequential tasks: (1) identify the scope of the offering, (2) identify the customer decision process, and (3) map the offering to the customer decision process.

**Scope of Offering.** The scope refers to the number of categories of products and services that are offered on the site. There is a continuum of scope that exists from a firm focusing on one product category (termed a "category killer") as compared to a firm focusing on a large number of categories. The websites SecondSpin.com, Reel.com, and DealTime illustrate the various levels of scope. SecondSpin.com, at one end of the spectrum, focuses on selling used CDs. DealTime, at the other end of the spectrum, sells a wide variety of electronics and other goods. Reel.com, somewhere in the middle, focuses on multiple video products, including DVDs and VHS videotapes. The following describe two specific types of scope:

- *Category-specific dominance.* Category-specific dominance refers to companies that focus exclusively on one product category, such as flowers, candy, or gifts. However, from observation, it is increasingly difficult to isolate firms that are focusing on only one category. Within the online flowers category, firms seem to be focusing on a combination of flowers, gifts, and other complementary goods, such as candy.

- *Cross-category dominance.* One of the most interesting developments in the online world is the extension of product offerings from a single category to additional product categories in an attempt to achieve cross-category dominance. The most well-known example, of course, is Amazon's initial domination of the book market and subsequent extension to CDs, videos, toys, home improvement, and auctions. Amazon is an interesting example of supply-side cross-category dominance because it offers products that naturally group together from a logistics and distribution point of view. Amazon's products (1) are physical goods, (2) can be stored in inventory, (3) cannot be digitized, and (4) are consumer-focused, as opposed to being business-to-business focused. However, the products do not naturally cluster around specific themes. In short, in contrast to websites such as BabyCenter.com, these particular product combinations do not necessarily make sense from the customer's point of view.

Recently, the term "metamarkets" has been used to refer to sites that group naturally clustering categories of goods and services. According to Northwestern University marketing professor Mohanbir Sawhney, this new breed of "metamediaries" is significant because it is based on a simple insight—products and services are grouped based on how customers engage in activities, rather than being based on a categorization of products and services from the physical world. Sawhney notes:

> Customers think in terms of activities, while firms think in terms of products. Activities that are logically related in "cognitive space" may be spread across very diverse providers in the marketplace. Metamarkets, then, are clusters of markets in the minds of customers. Their boundaries are derived from activities that are closely related in the minds of customers, and not from the fact that they are created or marketed by related firms in related industries.[8]

Interestingly, this observation by Sawhney has a parallel in academic literature. Consumers naturally group together products or services based upon the goals that the products help the consumers achieve.[9] For example, consumers may classify a wide variety of disparate products under an entertainment category. Do consumers categorize entertainment in terms of favorite sports, clubs/organizations, food, shows, art, or dining out? Or do they categorize based on things to do with the family or things to do when the weather is problematic? The answer is that consumers categorize products and services in a variety of ways. By implication, therefore, online businesses can be organized in a variety of goal-derived ways.

If you consider Citysearch.com, you will see that consumer classification can provide significant challenges. Its homepage has two broad categories of search—complete city guides and less extensive movies-and-entertainment guides for smaller cities. Once you search for a destination, you can choose from a broad selection of activities. For Los Angeles, you arrive at the calendarlive.com site that is supported by the *Los Angeles Times*. You can navigate this site by searching events by date or by choosing a category such as arts, bars and nightlife, movies, restaurants, shopping, or traffic reports.

In effect, one can first select an activity for the evening (by viewing events for that date), then purchase the tickets (Dodgers baseball tickets, for example), read a review of the players, read a review of a nearby restaurant, book reservations (offline, by calling the restaurant), check the various traffic reports, choose a route, and take the directions with you. These activities cross a wide range of industries—entertainment, automotive, travel, literature, and so on.

A good example of another goal-derived metamarket is BabyCenter.com. BabyCenter.com involves a wide variety of products and information, and it features a support community that is based on one overarching goal—raising a healthy baby. The site is packed with reference information, links to other online destinations, helpful hints and checklists, and ways to connect with other parents. It also provides a search engine to research by topic, or the user can personalize the site to get information on a specific pregnancy or parenting stage. The site provides high-quality, medically reviewed information, a community of supportive fellow parents, and a store that sells baby and maternity items and offers advice on products best suited for particular lifestyles and needs.

**Identify Customer Decision Process.** The second step in the construction of an online offering is articulating the consumer decision process for the various product categories. Table 5-1 provides a simplified version of the customer decision process, which can be divided into three stages: prepurchase, purchase, and postpurchase. In the prepurchase stage, consumers go through a number of steps, including recognizing a problem or need, searching for ideas and offerings, and evaluating the alternatives. In the purchase stage, the consumer decides to purchase and goes through the process of purchasing. The postpurchase stage involves the evaluation of levels of satisfaction and, eventually, the consideration of becoming a loyal customer. Finally, when the consumer is done with the product, he or she may or may not choose to dispose of the goods.

Table 5-1 provides an overview of actions that a consumer in the flower category might take. The recognition of a need for flowers may be triggered by a holiday (for example, Valentine's Day), a personal life event (an anniversary), or an everyday event (a first date). The consumer searches for ideas and offerings among online or offline flower vendors. After gathering gift ideas, recommendations, and advice, the consumer evaluates the options using a number of criteria, including price, appeal, availability, and convenience. At this point, the consumer may decide to make a purchase and enclose an appropriate note or message along with the flowers. After the purchase, the consumer may gain satisfaction if he or she learns that the flower order has been successfully delivered. After the transaction has been completed, the consumer may want to learn more about flowers and arrangements, and the vendor may give some kind of incentive to gain customer loyalty.

**Table 5-1** CUSTOMER DECISION PROCESS— FLOWER PURCHASE EXAMPLE

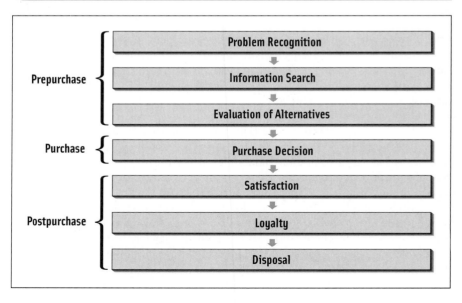

The third step in the construction of the offering involves mapping products and services onto the customer decision process. The idea is that the website should walk the consumer through the entire purchase-decision cycle and encourage the consumer to continually revisit the cycle. This decision cycle should be repeated for each of the product categories on the site. Thus, for 1-800-Flowers.com, the cycle should be completed for flowers, specialty foods, garden hardware, and other gift categories.

Exhibit 5-3 illustrates the mapping exercise. We refer to this process as the mapping of an **egg diagram**. We have enhanced Mohanbir Sawhney's metamarkets work by adding the consideration of the purchase and by mapping the product and service offering to this decision process. Creation of this diagram begins by articulating the steps of the customer decision process that the consumer passes through for a particular product category. Next, one identifies the products, services, and information that will aid the consumer in moving through these various stages.

Returning to the flower example, we can identify site activities that assist the consumer through each step of the decision process. To match need recognition, there might be a gift reminder service or holiday specials, for example. To aid in the information search, a site could provide ideas in various categories, a store locator, recommendations by budget, a gift guru, lists of favorite gifts, or lists of bestsellers. During the evaluation of alternatives, a site could provide product price, description, availability, and special delivery information. To support the purchase decision, the site could accept credit cards over the phone or online, provide a shopping basket, and show an assortment of cards and notes with appropriate messages to be delivered with the flowers. For customer satisfaction and loyalty, it could provide exceptional customer support, various free benefits or incentives, and special flower events and workshops to induce customers to return to its stores.

## What Is a Successful, Unique Resource System?

**The Resource System.** The value proposition and offering specification are critical steps in forming a business model because they dictate the resource system of the company.[10] The resource system shows how a company must align its internal systems (and partners) to deliver the benefits of the value proposition or cluster. Conventional wisdom suggests that the factor that sets highly successful companies apart from lesser companies is not simply the value proposition but the choice of actions and assets that are used to deliver the value proposition. These actions include the selection of capabilities and activities that uniquely deliver the value proposition.[11]

We agree with the logic that unique activities, tied to the value proposition, lead to a competitive advantage. However, we make four important modifications to the activity-system logic in order to make it applicable to the online marketplace. The actions to take now not only include the selection of capabilities and activities to deliver the value proposition uniquely; they also involve the supply of all the resources needed to make the capabilities and activities a reality. Briefly, the four modifications are as follows:

- *Shift from physical world to virtual and physical world.*[12] The first key modification is to shift from activities and capabilities in the physical world to a combination of marketplace and marketspace capabilities. Resource systems, for many companies, are a combination of the physical and virtual asset bases.

- *Shift from a supply-side focus to a demand-side focus.* Many activity systems focus heavily on the internal capabilities of the firm. Although this may seem

**Exhibit 5-3**  EGG DIAGRAM FOR 1-800-FLOWERS.COM

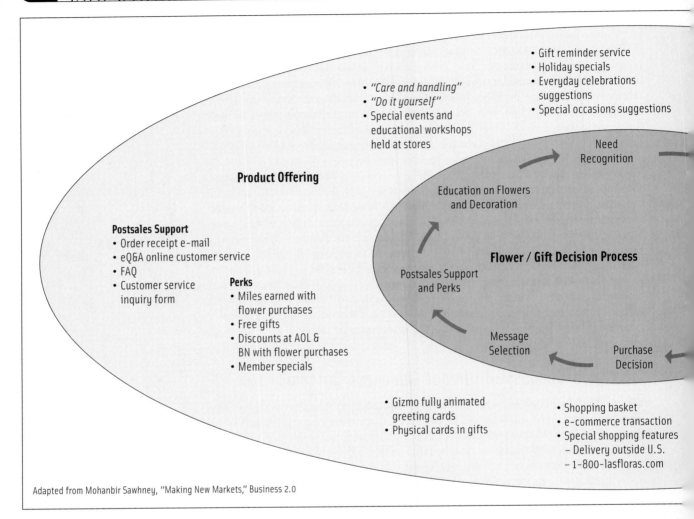

- Gift reminder service
- Holiday specials
- Everyday celebrations suggestions
- Special occasions suggestions

- "Care and handling"
- "Do it yourself"
- Special events and educational workshops held at stores

**Product Offering**

**Need Recognition**

Education on Flowers and Decoration

**Flower / Gift Decision Process**

**Postsales Support**
- Order receipt e-mail
- eQ&A online customer service
- FAQ
- Customer service inquiry form

Postsales Support and Perks

**Perks**
- Miles earned with flower purchases
- Free gifts
- Discounts at AOL & BN with flower purchases
- Member specials

Message Selection

Purchase Decision

- Gizmo fully animated greeting cards
- Physical cards in gifts

- Shopping basket
- e-commerce transaction
- Special shopping features
  – Delivery outside U.S.
  – 1-800-lasfloras.com

Adapted from Mohanbir Sawhney, "Making New Markets," Business 2.0

reasonable, it is more appropriate to initially focus on the benefits desired by targeted customers. The desired benefits should largely dictate the choice of capabilities.

- *Shift from activities to capabilities.* Capabilities are the higher-order skills and assets of the company. Capabilities are typically supported by a cluster of resources that helps to build and differentiate one or more of a company's capabilities. Resources[13] may take various forms. They might be physical assets (such as warehouses or server farms) or intangible assets (such as Yahoo's brand name or Priceline's patents on its business model). Activities might also be considered resources. For example, the incubator Idealab would argue that it is better at launching new companies than a competitor.

- *Shift from single to multifirm systems.* A key aspect of the online environment is the need for partnerships. Resource systems require capabilities that must

**Ideas and Information**
- Floral ideas
- Garden ideas
- Home ideas
- Gift ideas
- Gourmet ideas
- Store locator
- Recommendations by budget
- Best-sellers

**Gift Recommendations**
- Gift guru
- Favorite gifts
- Gift frequency
- Gift impossible
- Gift baskets
- Corporate gift services

Search for Ideas and Offerings

Evaluation of Alternatives

- Product price
- Product picture
- Product description
- Delivery information
- Delivery availability

be in place and ready to use in order to win various markets. These capabili-ties may be resident in the firm, developed in-house, acquired in the open market, or accessed through strategic partnerships and alliances.

## Specifying a Resource System.
With these four modifications in mind, we turn to the construction of a resource system.

***Step One: Identify Core Benefits in the Value Cluster.*** The core benefits have been identified in the construction of a value proposition or cluster. For 1-800-Flowers the value proposition is as follows:

*1-800-Flowers.com serves the mid- to high-end market with a broad gift assort-ment, fresh flowers, reasonable prices, and easy access because of its strong brand name, product and media partnerships, and bricks-and-mortar network of fran-chises.*

Thus, its cluster of benefits includes fresh flowers, broad assortment, reasonable prices, and easy access. Aspects of the cluster of benefits are shown in Exhibit 5-4.

**Step Two: Identify Capabilities That Relate to Each Benefit.** The second step is to link the capabilities that are required to deliver a particular customer benefit. At this stage, we are not concerned about whether the company can deliver the capability. We are simply concerned about the link between the capability and the benefit.

Exhibit 5-4 identifies the capabilities that deliver each of the four benefits. For example, widespread, easy access is linked to four capabilities: popularity of website, wide reach to customers, multiple contact points, and brand name.

**Step Three: Link Resources to Each Capability.** After the capabilities are identified, the firm can identify the resources that deliver each capability. These are the key assets, activities, actions, and partnerships or alliances that create the firm's capability. For example, Snap.com, AOL, MSN, and StarMedia provide media partnerships that, in turn, provide widespread points of access. The capability of multiple contact points is driven by the choice to use as many contact points as possible, including telephone representatives, online store, retail stores, and affiliate programs.

**Step Four: Identify to What Degree the Firm Can Deliver Each Capability.** The fourth step entails a close internal look at the company. Does this particular company, 1-800-Flowers, contain all the necessary capabilities, or must the company outsource or partner with others to gain missing capabilities? It is clear from the resource system chart that this firm does not hold all of the needed capabilities on its own. In particular, both product and media partnerships are required in order to make the system operate effectively.

**Step Five: Identify Partners Who Can Complete Capabilities.** The final step is to identify key players who can complete the resource system. For 1-800-Flowers, this would principally include product partnerships, such as those with Plow & Hearth and Greatfood.com, and media partnerships with some of the major online sites. Exhibit 5-4 represents our best approximation of the complete resource system of 1-800-Flowers.com.[14]

To continue our 1-800-Flowers example, we have crafted an egg diagram that reflects both online and offline components. Exhibit 5-5 provides an overview of the types of offline and online products and services that are offered by 1-800-Flowers. You will notice that many of the offline products and services integrate both telephone representatives and in-store personnel.

We would also need to adjust our resource-system model to integrate online and offline activities and assets in various combinations. For example, the capability of "wide reach to customers" might need to be supported by four online partnerships. The capability of "multiple contact points" may need to be supported by three offline (telephone representatives, franchise stores, catalog) and two online (affiliates, online store) assets.

## Criteria to Assess the Quality of a Resource System.
A number of criteria can be used to assess the quality of the resource system.

**Uniqueness of the System.** Uniqueness refers to the extent to which the organization provides benefits, capabilities, and activities that differ from competitors. Are there capabilities unique to the 1-800-Flowers.com activity system? Which themes have not been copied by FTD.com, PCFlowers.com, and proflowers.com? One

**Exhibit 5-4** 1-800-FLOWERS.COM RESOURCE SYSTEM

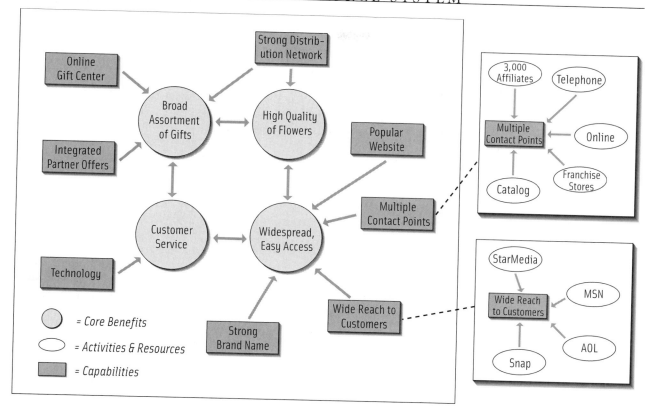

could argue that the PC Flowers & Gifts model is similar to the 1-800-Flowers model at the benefit level, but a counter argument could show that these competitors differ at the activity level. In particular, only 1-800-Flowers.com partners with AOL. Moreover, and perhaps more troubling to competitors in this industry, is that most of the competitors look very similar—nationwide florist network, combined offline and online presence, clear fit between offline and online systems, strong brand names, excellent order fulfillment, and integrated technologies.

***Links Between Capabilities and Benefits.*** Does each of the capabilities support the delivery of a customer benefit? Is the support strong or weak?

***Links Among Capabilities in the System.*** How well do the capabilities and activities complement and support one another? Are there tight linkages between the capabilities and activities? Are they consistent with the overall value cluster?

***Links Among Resources.*** Are the specific resources mutually reinforcing? Are they complementary? Are they consistent with the various benefits?

***Links Between Virtual-World and Physical-World Business Systems.*** Does the online resource system support or conflict with the offline system?

**Exhibit 5-5** ONLINE/OFFLINE EGG DIAGRAM FOR 1-800-FLOWERS.COM

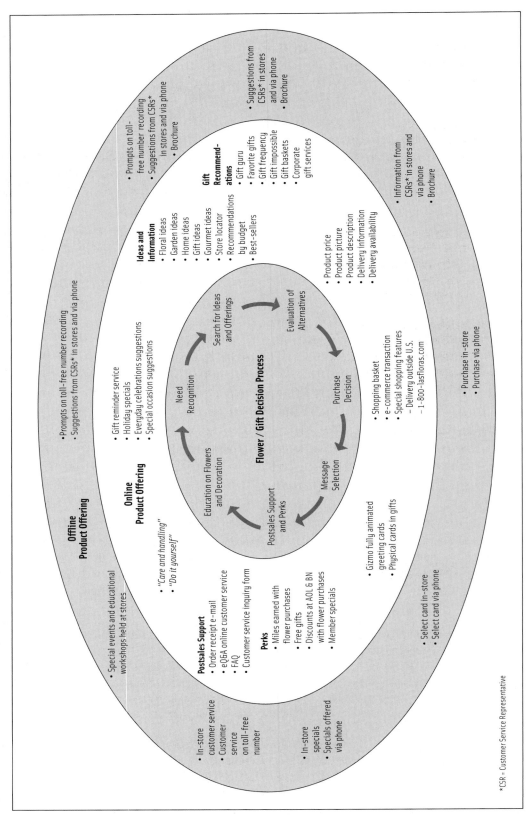

**Offline Product Offering**

- *"Care and handling"*
- *"Do it yourself"*

• Special events and educational workshops held at stores

**Online Product Offering**

**Postsales Support**
- Order receipt e-mail
- eQ&A online customer service
- FAQ
- Customer service inquiry form

**Perks**
- Miles earned with flower purchases
- Free gifts
- Discounts at AOL & BN with flower purchases
- Member specials

• Prompts on toll-free number recording
• Suggestions from CSRs* in stores and via phone

• Gift reminder service
• Holiday specials
• Everyday celebrations suggestions
• Special occasion suggestions

• Prompts on toll-free number recording
• Suggestions from CSRs* in stores and via phone
• Brochure

**Ideas and Information**
- Floral ideas
- Garden ideas
- Home ideas
- Gift ideas
- Gourmet ideas
- Store locator
- Recommendations by budget
- Best-sellers

**Gift Recommendations**
- Gift guru
- Favorite gifts
- Gift frequency
- Gift impossible
- Gift baskets
- Corporate gift services

• Suggestions from CSRs* in stores and via phone
• Brochure

**Flower / Gift Decision Process**

- Need Recognition
- Search for Ideas and Offerings
- Evaluation of Alternatives
- Purchase Decision
- Message Selection
- Postsales Support and Perks
- Education on Flowers and Decoration

• Product price
• Product picture
• Product description
• Delivery information
• Delivery availability

• Information from CSRs* in stores and via phone
• Brochure

• Shopping basket
• e-commerce transaction
• Special shopping features
  – Delivery outside U.S.
  – 1-800-lasfloras.com

• Purchase in-store
• Purchase via phone

• Gizmo fully animated greeting cards
• Physical cards in gifts

• Select card in-store
• Select card via phone

• In-store specials
• Specials offered via phone

• In-store customer service
• Customer service on toll-free number

*CSR = Customer Service Representative

## An Integrated Online and Offline Business Model

 One of the decisions firms must confront is whether to provide both an online and offline interface to customers. The benefits of using a hybrid strategy include a persistent connection with customers, new value for customers, access to new customers, and scalability. The challenges of hybridization include cannibalization, channel conflict, customer confusion, and investor confusion.

The potential benefits for a company that uses both an online and offline strategy—such as the Gap, Williams-Sonoma, or Wal-Mart—are many. First, there is a constant connection with customers, 24 × 7. Also, there are new value possibilities for customers because the firm is now able to provide new-to-the-world offerings that would not be possible if they pursued only an online or an offline strategy. For example, it is now possible to place an online order any time of day but return the merchandise to the bricks-and-mortar store. Third, it is also possible to increase the size of the customer base. Wal-Mart can now reach customers that are hundreds of miles from the nearest bricks-and-mortar store. Finally, the approach is scalable in the sense that the new integrated strategy can be replicated across regions of the world.

There are, however, potential drawbacks for the firm that does not carefully manage the integration.

Many writers are concerned that the opening of an online store will cannibalize, or draw down sales revenues, from the bricks-and-mortar stores. Here they frequently cite a study conducted in fall 1999 that purportedly showed that online ventures did not provide significant new revenue increases. Rather, some 94 percent of sales were simply transfers of sales that normally would have occurred offline.[15] On the other hand, in the year 2000, we witnessed a number of players who went online and saw a sales rise in offline products. A good example is the well-known Zagat restaurant guide. Zagat placed the entire contents of the book online and discovered that offline sales actually increased by 35 percent.[16]

One potential drawback of going online includes channel conflicts. For example, at one point in its online strategy, Compaq was forced by the dealer network to shut down its online store due to potential offline sales decreases expected by the dealers. There is also the potential for customer confusion. If the online and offline interfaces are not tightly linked, customers can become confused and frustrated. For example, if customers purchase products online but cannot return them to the bricks-and-mortar stores, the customers may decide not to frequent either the online or offline store. Finally, investors may not understand how to value the online/offline integrated enterprise.

*Sustainable Advantage.* Is the resource system difficult to replicate? Possessing a unique but easily copied resource system will deliver only a fleeting advantage to a firm. Sustained high profits will come only from a sustainable competitive advantage. The ease with which a resource system can be imitated may depend on a number of factors.[17]

## The Role of Partnerships.

One of the most important features of the online world is the use of partnerships. While partnerships are important in the offline world, they take on added significance in the online world as firms compete with partners to lock-in customer relationships. Often firms will look for exclusive partnerships to prevent competitors from accessing a customer base, critical technology, or key competencies that are necessary to gain competitive advantage in a particular sector. The types of partnerships that 1-800-Flowers.com has pursued include the following:

**Portal Agreements.** Portals such as AOL, Yahoo, and MSN provide significant brand exposure for 1-800-Flowers. The AOL agreement is particularly significant given that it is an exclusive agreement through 2003.

*America Online:* First agreement signed in 1994; exclusive marketer of fresh-cut flowers across key AOL brands until 2003; one-year exclusive agreement to market gardening products commencing November 1999.

*MSN:* Premier floral partner and anchor in the MSN Home and Garden Department; products, advertising, and links featured on MSN Shopping Channel.

*Yahoo Inc.:* Will run banner advertisements throughout the Yahoo network, with additional presence in shopping area.

*Excite@Home:* Markets flowers and other gifts through Excite.com and WebCrawler websites; products, advertisements, and links featured in the Excite Shopping Channel; entered second year of marketing relationship in October 1999.

*StarMedia Network:* Developing Spanish and Portuguese language versions of 1-800-Flowers.com website.

**Anchor-Tenant Agreements.** Similar to other flower sites, 1-800-Flowers arranged to be the exclusive provider of flowers for retail sites such as Snap.com and Sears, Roebuck and Co.

*Snap.com* (now NBCi.com): 1-800-Flowers was one of the 45 premier merchants in Snap shopping service (online e-superstore); was an anchor tenant in Snap.com Flower Shop; was spotlighted in select Snap.com on-air promotions, scheduled to run on the NBC Television Network during the Valentine's Day and Mother's Day time periods.

*Sears, Roebuck and Co.:* Licensing relationship that enables Sears' customers to use their store charge cards when shopping with 1-800-Flowers.com.

**Promotion Agreements.** Agreements have also been signed with various airlines (American Airlines, Delta) and MCI WorldCom.

*American Airlines® Advantage®, Delta Airlines SkyMiles®, United Airlines Mileage Plus®:* Earn frequent-flier miles with 1-800-Flowers.com purchases.

*MCI WorldCom:* Receive 1-800-Flowers.com gift certificates with long distance sign-up; receive 10 percent off every 1-800-Flowers.com purchase with MCI WorldCom membership.

*PeoplePC:* Signed one-year agreement to become key floral and gift provider for 1-800-Flowers.com starting in October 1999.

*Zapa.com* (now gizmoz.com): Offered selection of online greeting cards on 1-800-Flowers.com website; users could personalize greetings with their own photos, clip art, or other multimedia creations.

# What Are the Financial Models Available to Firms?

In this section, we review the financial model that follows from the resource system. We have divided this section into three parts: (1) a review of the **revenue models** that are typically practiced by online businesses, (2) a discussion of 10 approaches to **shareholder value models**, and (3) a description of **growth models** and how firms can pursue revenue growth.

## Should the Firm Focus on Competencies or Resource Systems?

Proponents of activity (or resource) systems have clashed with advocates of core competencies in recent years. A core competency is a unique, enduring capability or resource of a firm that forms the basis for a long-term competitive advantage. Honda's small-engine capability or Wal-Mart's supply-chain management systems are examples of core competencies in the physical world.

People who support the activity system point of view argue that it is inappropriate to reduce an organization to a few competencies or resources. Rather, the key to competitive advantage rests in the organization's ability to (1) select and critically manage core activities, and (2) simultaneously manage the "fit" between activities. From this point of view, it is systems of activities that compete with systems of activities. It is not a question of simply executing on a small set of core competencies.

Core competency advocates counterargue that the large activity systems can lead to a management mindset that everything needs to be done well. As a result, the organization is unable to distinguish between the capabilities that can be considered "price of entry" and the capabilities that truly allow the organization to be differentiated.

**Types of Revenue Models.** Firms can pursue a variety of revenue models. The following are the most frequently mentioned sources of revenue:

- *Advertising.* A particular site can earn advertising revenues through the selling of ads (banner or interstitial), site sponsorships, event underwriting, or other forms of communication.

- *Product, service, or information sales.* This refers to income that is generated from the sales of goods on the site.

- *Transaction.* This refers to revenue that accrues from charging a fee or taking a portion of the transaction sum for facilitating a customer-seller transaction (as Schwab or eBay does).

- *Subscription.* This refers to subscriber fees for magazines, newspapers, or other information/service businesses.

**Types of Shareholder Value Models.** While the revenue models clearly identify the flow of money into the organization, they do not indicate how a company plans to generate cash flow or shareholder value—for either the long or short term. Profit and/or high margins originate from customers' perceptions that a given online business has provided better than competitors in a given marketspace. Recent writings have suggested that there are well over 20 alternative profit models that can be pursued in offline businesses.[18]

For example, a so-called blockbuster profit model is pursued by Disney. Profit does not originate from all of the Disney movies. However, if a blockbuster movie does emerge, Disney will aggressively pursue all potential sources of revenue, including franchising, transactional revenue, licensing, merchandising, and other revenue sources. Therefore, profit in the Disney world is based upon the exploitation of selected blockbuster movies.

# Read It and Reap

### by Peter Meyers, staff writer for tnbt.com

What's black and white and red all over? New-economy answer: most online publishers, because they're dripping red ink. Aside from *The Wall Street Journal* and various porn sites, Web publishers have been largely unable to convince readers to actually pay for their services. And though Net ad revenues have soared (up more than 140 percent from 1998 to 1999), the banner ad remains a shaky platform, with revenue-triggering click-through rates well below 1 percent.

So what's a poor content producer to do? Boston-based Zooba has one answer: create content whose express purpose is to get people to buy products. In other words, recast that long-debated question—Does content pay?—as an intriguing new proposition: Can content sell?

Launched in May 2000, Zooba lets readers sign up for free, weekly e-mails that feature original mini-essays on subjects ranging from architecture to world music. Each essay is accompanied by links to two or three books or videos relating to the reader's area of interest; for instance, an essay on Joe DiMaggio's brief marriage to Marilyn Monroe (did you know Joltin' Joe was the jilted one?) includes offers to buy a DiMaggio biography and a pair of Marilyn videos. Think the J. Peterman catalog on steroids—except Zooba's witty aperçus promote knowledge rather than colonial clothing.

"We're more of a direct-marketing company than a content company," explains Zooba's cofounder and president, Jeffrey Glass.

Zooba partners with retailers (Amazon.com, AllPosters.com, etc.) and publishers such as Henry Holt and Simon & Schuster, collecting a percentage of the sales it steers to the former and a fee for promoting products of the latter. In addition, it provides its partners with user data, including topics selected and click stream.

"The people who go deeper into the life of Abraham Lincoln are statistically more likely to buy that biography of Lincoln," Glass notes. And that's valuable information for publishers, who, Glass says, "have been starved even for high-level market research."

The firm's focus on the intersection of publishing and marketing is no accident. The 32-year-old Glass has a background in direct marketing (he was COO of Travelers/NetPlus, a CitiGroup subsidiary that sells financial-service products to consumers), while the firm's other cofounder and current CEO, Marc Bataillon, also 32, hails from the publishing world (he worked as COO of IDG Communications France).

Daniel O'Brien, a senior analyst at Forrester who recently wrote a report about Zooba, says he's impressed by the company's novel approach to the content-commerce dilemma. "I hadn't encountered this particular way of staging content and product offerings before," he says.

Zooba recently announced that it had dispatched its 1.5 millionth e-mail, and while Glass declines to disclose how many people have actually signed up for the service, he does say that he expects the number will soon reach "the multiple hundreds of thousands." But, O'Brien notes, significant hurdles remain—in particular, Zooba's challenge of sustaining itself in a niche surrounded by some fairly imposing neighbors. Those include both pure content companies like venerable encyclopedia publisher Britannica.com, which would seem to enjoy a large edge in access to high-quality content over Zooba, and e-tailing giants that produce their own product-enhancing content—Amazon, for example, with its book reviews and author chats.

The threat from e-tailers may, however, turn out to be Zooba's best opportunity, says O'Brien. The company, he suggests, should look into providing subject-specific chunks of its service to online retailers that have already established large, targeted followings—license its gardening section, for example, to Garden.com. In fact, a company spokesperson says Zooba is actively exploring several deals in this vein.

"I don't think Zooba could succeed by building an Amazon-style following; it's terribly expensive," says O'Brien. "But by partnering you can aggregate a great customer base very quickly."

*Read more articles about The Next Big Thing at www.tnbt.com*

# Who Is Making Money on the Web?

by Alex Scherbakovsky and Yakir Siegal

 Given how many once-mighty Internet companies have recently fallen, the question of how to make money on the Web has become increasingly important. Below, we discuss how various types of Internet companies have tried to make money.

**Study Methodology.** In the fall of 1999, we analyzed 190 public Internet companies that we grouped into the seven categories as follows: 1) portals: companies such as Yahoo that seek to be the user's entry point to the World Wide Web; 2) transaction: companies that take a cut of transactions conducted on their sites, such as online brokerages and auction companies like eBay; 3) commerce: e-tailers such as Amazon.com and Etoys.com; 4) content: information providers such as About.com and TheStreet.com; 5) Internet service providers (ISPs): companies such as EarthLink and Juno that provide customers with access to the Internet; 6) enablers: companies such as Cisco and Ariba that provide the hardware and software that enable communication and commerce over the Internet; and 7) advertising: companies such as DoubleClick that sell Internet advertising.

We evaluated each company on four financial metrics: gross profit (revenue minus cost of goods sold), EBIT (earnings before interest and taxes, or operating profit), net income, and EBITM (operating profit before marketing expenses). The last metric shows whether Internet companies make money before they invest in the marketing expenses necessary to participate in the "land grab" of establishing brand identity and winning market share.

**Results.** The clear winners on all four metrics are the transaction companies. Eight of the 11 stocks in this category had positive earnings, and nine had achieved operating profits. Transaction companies enjoy favorable financial performance because of their solid revenue model—they make money by taking a cut of every transaction conducted on their site. Unlike companies that focus on building a large audience with hopes to monetize those eyeballs in the future, most transaction companies extract immediate profits from their customer base.

Content providers and ISPs posted the worst numbers. Out of 34 content stocks, only four had positive net incomes. Even after adding back the amount these companies spent on marketing, only nine showed positive EBITM. Indeed, nine of the content stocks could not muster positive gross profits, showing that the cost of providing their content exceeded the revenues they were able to generate from their services. Most of these companies built their financial models around advertising revenue, which currently does not cover these companies' costs. Simply put, content companies must find alternate revenue streams—or unlock new differentiation—if they hope to achieve profitability. Even CNET, one of the few profitable content providers, derives some of its revenues from referral fees and its television programming.

ISPs struggled to show positive operating numbers. Of the 34 companies we analyzed, all but two had net losses and negative EBIT. Although 71 percent posted positive gross profits, most of these profits were spent on marketing and infrastructure investments. The ISP field is very fragmented and is ripe for consolidation. In a few years, we are likely to see most of these money-bleeding players either go out of business or get consumed by their larger peers. Even as the winners achieve economies of scale, however, they will have to adjust their business models to address the threat of free ISP services. It is unclear when, and if, the ISP companies will start making money.

Commerce companies are also struggling, with none of the 26 showing positive earnings, and only eight achieving positive EBITM. Four commerce players even failed to generate enough revenue to cover the cost of their merchandise. Most commerce companies justify their poor financial performance by claiming that they are investing in infrastructure and building their customer base. Only time will show which of these players will succeed in garnering a loyal customer base that will enable them to achieve profitability.

The performance in the rest of the categories is more varied. Portals are divided into two camps—the established brands like Yahoo are profitable, while newcomers Ask Jeeves and LookSmart are not.

*(continued on page 160)*

*(continued from page 159)*

Enablers tend to do well—like the shovel vendors during the Gold Rush. Companies such as Cisco and Check Point are making money by selling products to customers who hope to strike it rich. The advertising companies all post positive gross profits, but spend most of those profits on marketing.

Our study of the Internet stocks concludes that, for the most part, less than one in five of the companies that met the necessary requirements to go public had positive earnings. While most of the transaction companies are making money, firms in other categories are investing heavily in building their brands and customer bases. As only a fraction of these companies will eventually succeed in monetizing their customer assets, most will realize that not everyone is making money on the Web.

A second profit model is the "base and follow-on" model that is most easily understood through an example, such as razors and razor blades. That is, the base product (razors) is a "loss leader," while the real profit is extracted from follow-on products (razor blades).

In the following section, we identify 10 shareholder value models for the online world. It is important to note that for Internet-company discussion, we differ from traditional commerce theories on profit models in the following three ways:

- *Shift from profit to shareholder-value focus.* Many of the currently successful online businesses have yet to turn a profit. Significant energy is allocated to building a customer base, brand name, scaleable operations, and human-resource base. The idea is to lock in the customer base and then, as the business matures, focus on profit. In our view, shareholder value is a more appropriate metric because it considers the market capitalization of the company—that is, the share price times the number of shares outstanding.

- *Shift from supply-side language to demand-side language.* A second key feature of the current approach is the shift to demand-side rather than supply-side terms and concepts. Significant financial gain (either price of offering or price of shares) is a result of what a company does in response to a market need. Companies, or at least successful companies, focus on the core benefits that customers are looking for and respond accordingly. Hence, demand comes first, supply second.

- *Introduce new ways to create value.* Finally, this section introduces several new value-creation models that reflect the evolution of the new economy.

In this section, we describe the models, illustrate the sources of profit or value for shareholders, and discuss key success factors. As firms begin to craft and build their business models—and associated value models—they also need to consider how other firms are likely to respond to their moves in the marketplace. Thus, we not only introduce the new value models, but we also discuss the threats to the chosen model (see Table 5-2). As you read this section, keep in mind that a given company can pursue more than one model at a time.

We first consider three "company- and user-derived" value models that are based on the bringing together of large numbers of buyers and sellers. Later, we describe value models that are largely built on products and services that are provided by companies with significantly less value-added input from customers.

**Company- and User-Derived.** We term these models company- and user-derived because both the company and the user provide content and value-added services to the site. For example, eBay is a company- and user-derived site where customers provide the products, information, service, and seller ratings. The users are the ones who largely provide the content.

**Metamarkets Switchboard.** A metamarkets-switchboard model brings together many buyers and sellers based upon the activities that customers engage in to meet particular goals (see Table 5-2).[19] Examples include BabyCenter.com, VerticalNet.com, and CarPoint.com. The revenue model may include transactions, product sales, and advertising. Value comes primarily from leveraging the brand name to provide value-added services that include product information, community events, and product sales.

Consider BabyCenter.com. It sells all of the standard baby-related products—maternity clothing, toys, music, videos, and books—but also provides a gift center, baby-related expert advice from preconception through toddler stages, and community bulletin boards. It aggregates many different product providers with nonexclusive arrangements.

*Success Factors:* Key success factors for this profit model include the building and sustaining of a large number of buyers and sellers. Frequently this model results in a single, clear-winning company with multiple second-tier players. It is possible that niche markets could also emerge. Constant innovation in value-added services is necessary to sustain the customer base. Enhancing user-to-user community formation may also create switching costs.

*Threats:* The key threats to this model include the formation of an alternative switchboard at a higher level of aggregation (such as children of all ages), the same level of aggregation (such as the Planet Baby website), or a niche market. Innovative value-added services on the part of competitors who offer alternative switchboards can also threaten the profit stream.

**Traditional and Reverse Auctions.** Traditional auctions such as eBay are designed to bring together large numbers of buyers and sellers. Buyers bid up to a point where no further bidding is offered. The buyer with the highest bid takes title to the item. Reverse auctions such as FreeMarkets.com, a business-to-business site, allow suppliers to bid prices down until no further bids are received. The supplier with the lowest bid supplies the goods to the buyer. Sites that act as hubs in these situations typically take a portion of the transaction revenue. The result is often a very high margin (i.e., eBay margins are reported to be in the neighborhood of 75 percent).

*Success Factors:* Key success factors are similar to those of the metamarkets switchboard. In other words, one needs to build a large base of buyers and sellers. The current thinking is that these types of markets are often winner-take-all, with no room for the second or third players. Another critical success factor is a strong brand name—one that signals both credibility and trust. Finally, these models are most effective when there is strong back-office support.

*Threats:* Key threats to the model are similar to the metamarkets switchboard. Alternative switchboards can emerge in the market. The brand can lose credibility due to any negative factor such as site downtime, security breaches, privacy concerns, or questionable product assortments. In the case of business-to-business markets, the auction site could lose a few large suppliers and the overall model could be threatened. The auction model could also be threatened by the emergence of a pure low-price player in a particular product category. Hence, a key for firms in this market is continued innovation on value-added services.

*Category Switchboard.* The category-specific switchboard, or a category-killer type site, is somewhat similar to the metamarkets switchboard except the focus is on one particular product category. Brands are aggregated in the product category, but there is much more focus that is typically not organized by the customer activities. Indeed, it tends to be more supply-side than demand-side driven. The revenue and profit sources tend to be similar to the metamarkets switchboard.

Examples have included Chemdex, eToys, and PlanetRx. EToys focused heavily on the toy category in the face of many competitors (such as Amazon) who have entered into the toy category. Toys are broadly defined to include games, puzzles, dolls, electronic games, and a host of other entertainment products. EToys also offered a variety of innovative valued-added services including toys for children with special needs, site organization by age, brand names associated with different age levels, and a gift center.

*Success Factors:* Similar to the metamarkets switchboard, the key success factors of the category switchboard relate to the leveraging of network economics. Namely, the building of a supplier and customer base and its subsequent "lock-in" due to switching costs, such as an increasingly useful user profile, interuser communication, and experience with the site.

*Threats:* The threats are, however, distinct relative to the metamarkets switchboard. In particular, the key threat to a category-killer type site is the emergence of a metamarket player who rolls multiple-user activities into a single site (as it turned out, eToys was challenged by Amazon's partnership with Toys "R" Us). At the other extreme, it may be possible that niche players will chip away at the overall category-killer, such as a toy site that specializes in learning or development toys, a pure dot-com game site (e.g., Gamesville.com), or electronic games site (e.g., PlayStation.com). Finally, as we have seen, the brand-name strength of market leaders in the offline world may challenge the dot-com pure-play business models (e.g., ToysRUs.com).

**Company-Derived Value Creation.** The previous set of value models relied heavily on a combination of supply-side and demand-side forces to launch and defend the online competitive space. In this section, we focus on value models that are driven largely by best-of-class excellence on a key customer need or benefit (see Table 5-3). Also, as noted in the previous section, most of these models derive their value from company initiatives and products rather than from user-generated content. The exception is perhaps the model termed "broadest user network." In the following pages, we describe six such models.

*Best Information.* This value model is based on providing customers with the most timely, fresh, and credible information product or service in the online environment. Examples exist across a variety of industries including industry research (e.g., jup.com, Forrester.com), newspapers (e.g., NYTimes.com, latimes.com), magazines (e.g., Salon.com), business reporting (e.g., TheStandard.com), and entertainment (e.g., Zagat.com, Citysearch.com).

Revenue for the players comes from a mix of sources including products, services, information, and advertising revenue. Profit originates from the customer's

Table
5-2

# ALTERNATIVE SHAREHOLDER VALUE MODELS (COMPANY AND USER DERIVED)

| Alternative Models | Company and User Derived | | |
| --- | --- | --- | --- |
| | **Metamarket Switchboard** | **Auctions (Traditional & Reverse)** | **Category Switchboard** |
| *Description* | • Hub for many buyers and sellers; multiple categories | • Competitive bid hub for buyers and sellers | • Aggregates brands in product category |
| *Examples* | • BabyCenter.com<br>• VerticalNet.com | • eBay<br>• Amazon auctions<br>• FreeMarkets | • PlanetRX |
| *Revenue Model* | • Transactions<br>• Product sales<br>• Advertising | • Transactions | • Transactions<br>• Advertising<br>• Product sales |
| *Value Source* | • Perceived value-added services<br>• Brand name credibility | • Percentage of transactions | • Perceived value-added services<br>• Brand name credibility |
| *Key Success Factors* | • Build buyer database<br>• Build seller database<br>• Value-added services | • Build buyer database<br>• Build seller database<br>• Credible "hub" brand<br>• Efficient back-office support | • Build brand<br>• Critical mass of buyers and sellers |
| *Key Threat Factors* | • Alternative switchboard emerges<br>• Niche switchboard emerges<br>• Fundamental shift in core technologies | • Alternative auction<br>• Niche auctions<br>• Price of switchboard offering equal to auction<br>• Value-added services differentiate competitors | • Emergence of metamarket<br>• Niche category switchboard<br>• Brand name strength of market leaders |

perception that the particular site has the more accurate, credible, and timely information. Consider, for example, jup.com. Jupiter Communications is positioning itself as the leading provider of information and research on online commerce. A key feature of this model is the ability to hire the right analysts and staff and, in turn, provide the most up-to-date, accurate estimates of the evolution of this industry. Its news must be fresh in the sense that its predictions for the online shopping behavior for 2000 are now worthless. However, its views of the online shopping prediction for 2002 are highly valuable. Similarly, real-time stock quotes are much more valuable than stock quotes that are delayed 15 minutes. Hence, there is a price premium associated with real-time, fresh information.

*Success Factors:* The key success factors for this model include hiring the best personnel, providing the most timely and accurate information, and extracting the margins from the freshest product lines.

*Threats:* Threats to the model include customers' perceptions that other firms have similar timeliness, the price sensitivity to the freshest information is too great, and the costs associated with providing the timeliest information are prohibitive.

**Widest Assortment.** Assortment value originates from the breadth of product, service, and information coverage or inventory in the chosen product category. Within the music category this could include CDNOW.com, ArtistDirect.com, or

SecondSpin.com. For example, SecondSpin positions itself as the Internet's largest buyer and seller of used CDs, videos, and DVDs. Consumers visit the site because they expect to find the largest assortment of used CDs relative to other competitor sites.

Revenue is derived from product sales; however, the real source of profit lies in the selective premium pricing of the most desired products. Thus, customers seeking used CDs by the best-selling artists, rare CDs, classic CDs, or other hard-to-find music are likely to be charged premium prices.

*Success factors:* Key success factors involve reducing consumer uncertainty, building a strong brand presence, retaining customers who buy products frequently and share their buying experience with others, and maintaining the quality of additional information and services. For example, one feature of the SecondSpin site is that customers are automatically notified of preferred artists or music. With the site's "personal favorites" feature you can choose up to 15 of your favorite artists. Every time you visit the site, you click on personal favorites and all titles currently in stock by those artists will appear. Thus, the inventory itself must be complemented with value-added services.

*Threats:* Threats to the profit model include further specialization in the product category. For example, Drugstore.com could be out-specialized by bellisima.com, a high-end beauty product site. At the other extreme, megabrands such as Wal-Mart and Amazon could attempt to aggregate consumers at a higher level with a metamarket switchboard.

**Lowest Prices.** This model promises the customer the lowest prices online. This model may be specific to a product category (e.g., Lowestfare.com, AllBooks4Less.com) or a broader, mall-like approach (e.g., Buy.com). Revenues originate principally from product sales and advertising.

A good example of this approach is Buy.com. Buy.com positions itself as the lowest-priced superstore on the Internet. It provides products in a wide range of product categories, including computers, software, electronics, sporting goods, books, videos, games, music, and clearance items.

*Success factors:* Margins are often minimal or even nonexistent; hence, the key is to be exceptionally strong on back-office systems and leverage scale economies. In order to sustain its strategy, lowest-price sites must have outstanding supply-chain management, procurement, and overall operational excellence.

*Threats:* Key threats to the value model include the emergence of shop bots. Shop bots such as mySimon.com search the Web for the lowest-priced items in a variety of product categories. A quick search for the book *Harry Potter and the Sorcerer's Stone* by J.K. Rowling revealed a range of prices—from approximately $8.50 to $30. Interestingly, while Buy.com was toward the lower end of this continuum, it was not the lowest-priced player.

Other threats include the emergence of strong, branded players who create uncertainty in the low-priced brand, the lack of profit imperative, shifting investor confidence in low-priced business models, and the emergence of niche players who further specialize the market.

**Broadest-User Network.** A pure demand-based model is one that relies on the fast buildup of a user network. Examples include software and hardware standards that are emerging in a variety of Internet spaces (e.g., ICQ, RealNetworks) as well as demand aggregation models (e.g., Mercata.com, MobShop.com).

The revenue models are varied and may include product sales, transaction fees, and advertising. Profits begin to appear after building the user base (largely through user initiated activities such as viral marketing). If a standard emerges, premium pricing can follow.

A good example of a broadest-user network was Mercata.com. Mercata was a demand-aggregation model that entailed aggregating potential buyers into larger buyer groups and then leveraging their increased buying power for lower prices. Mercata engaged in this activity across a wide range of product categories including appliances, baby goods, gifts, electronics, lawn and garden goods, and jewelry.

*Success factors:* Key success factors included the building of a strong customer base, viral marketing by customers, and the hope of trademarked software or patents to protect the core technology (e.g., "We-Commerce" is trademarked by Mercata).

*Threats:* Threats to the model included the emergence of alternative standards, a fundamental technology shift, and backward or forward integration of complementary players.

**Best Experience.** Within every product category, it is apparent that there is room for someone who can provide the best experience, regardless of price. Within the toys category this could be FAOSchwarz.com, or within the jewelry category it could be Ashford.com. Revenue is expected to originate from products, services, or information, while profit is maintained by premium prices across the entire range of products.

*Success factors:* Key success factors include the sourcing of the best products, outstanding online service, and a comprehensive customer experience.

*Threats:* Key threats include the emergence of lower-priced offerings with similar benefits, the lack of a perceived value in the higher-priced goods, and a shift in customer preferences to emergent brand labels, as compared with the historical favorites.

**Most Personalized.** This model is based on the best customization of the consumer experience. A good recent example is Reflect.com. Its website noted that it offers "products created by you, delivered free of charge in under a week." Its products are designed to give people the power to create their own beauty-care experience. On Reflect.com's site, customers can create their own skin care, hair care, and makeup products.

*Success factors:* The key success factors for this business include deep customer knowledge and the ability to continually refresh and mine its customer database. Users have the complete ability to customize the experience and control the level of personalization.

*Threats:* Key threats include the emergence of new players who offer a richer, more personalized experience. Other threats include the emergence of new technologies that displace the incumbent or the use of older technologies that allow other companies to catch up and match the experience.

Because the business model pursued by the firm must be tightly integrated, we now consider how the previous section on the resource system is tied to the shareholder value models. Consider once again the 1-800-Flowers resource system. At

Table 5-3

ALTERNATIVE SHAREHOLDER
VALUE MODELS (COMPANY DERIVED)

| Alternative Models | Company Derived | | | | | |
|---|---|---|---|---|---|---|
| | Best Information | Widest Assortment | Lowest Prices | Broadest User Network | Best Experience | Most Personalized |
| Description | • Timely, high value–added information | • Widest assortment within the category | • Lowest prices within category | • Aggregation of users around standard | • Highest quality merchandise as perceived by target customers | • Highest level of customization |
| Examples | • Forrester.com<br>• Zagat.com<br>• NYTimes.com<br>• jup.com | • ArtistDirect.com<br>• SecondSpin.com | • Buy.com<br>• Lowestfares.com | • ICQ<br>• MP3<br>• Mercata<br>• Accompany | • FAOSchwarz.com<br>• Ashford.com | • Reflect.com |
| Revenue Model | • Product sales<br>• Subscriptions | • Product sales | • Product sales | • Varied | • Product sales | • Product sales |
| Value Source | • Premium pricing based on perception of best information | • Selective premium pricing | • Unclear | • Users drive traffic<br>• Standard emerges<br>• Price premium follows | • Level of luxury premium drives prices | • Level of customization drives premium pricing |
| Key Success Factors | • Timeliness of information<br>• Perceived quality of information | • Reduce uncertainty in offering<br>• Quality of information and value-added services | • Operational excellence<br>• Supply-chain management | • Establish standard<br>• Grow user network<br>• Network economics | • Ability to spot symbolic brands<br>• Ability to judge quality | • Deep customer knowledge<br>• Ability to mine customer database |
| Key Threat Factors | • Customers do not perceive sufficient gap in timeliness with generic offerings<br>• Competitors match market leaders<br>• Cost of freshness becomes prohibitive | • Specialization within the category<br>• Emergence of dominant brands | • Shopbots<br>• Lack of profit imperative<br>• Shifting investor confidence<br>• Reengineer total process not price<br>• Niche markets | • Alternate standard emerges<br>• Technology shift<br>• Backward or forward integration of complementary players | • Subniche markets emerge by category<br>• Symbolic brand loses appeal | • Technology advances lead to "me too" products<br>• Customers want control of personalization |

the center of the system are the four key benefits of its offering. Each of these benefits would be tied directly to one of the shareholder value models. For example, the high-quality flowers can be directly tied to the best-experience value model, while the wide assortment of gifts can be tied to the wide-assortment value model. The important point is that the central benefits of the resource system should be tied directly to the type (or types) of value model pursued.

# Financial Growth Models

A third component of a financial model is the firm's revenue growth strategy or growth model. A classic framework to understand how a company may drive revenue growth is exemplified by the Ansoff product/market matrix. Exhibit 5-6 illustrates that new revenue growth can come from deeper penetration into the current product market, new product development (i.e., new products for existing markets), new market development (e.g., existing products for new markets), or completely new products and markets. We have expanded this framework to include both online and offline activities. As a result, we will discuss eight options that a firm has to grow revenue.

Consider, once again, 1-800-Flowers. Our first observation is that 1-800-Flowers is attempting to grow revenue in a variety of ways—both online and offline. The acquisition of Plow & Hearth (plowhearth.com and Gardenworks.com) has been focused on providing new products in new offline markets. Overall, however, it appears that most growth is targeted in the area of new products for the online market (see Exhibit 5-6).

**Exhibit 5-6**

REVENUE GROWTH CHOICES: 1-800-FLOWERS

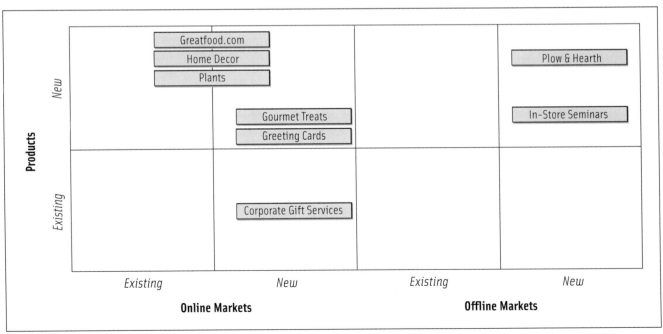

# WHAT BUSINESS CLASSIFICATION SCHEMES ARE APPROPRIATE FOR THE NEW ECONOMY?

In recent years, authors have attempted to classify generic business frameworks, or taxonomies. A good taxonomy, or framework, does two things. First, if the taxonomy is good, a reader can simply read a case study or story about a business and easily categorize the business. Second, the classification should be meaningful, meaning the classification should have business-model-choice implications. That is, placing a firm in one quadrant of the classification scheme should imply that its downstream business-model choice will be different than if it was placed in another quadrant.

In the following paragraphs, we describe three business-classification schemes. We begin with one of the most important classification schemes in strategy, the Porter model, and discuss its strengths and limitations in the new economy. Later, we describe the Sawhney and Kaplan taxonomy and the Rayport, Jaworski, and Siegal model.

## Porter Generic Strategy Model

Using a simple classification scheme, Michael Porter argued that there are three basic generic strategies: differentiation, cost, and niche. Each strategy implied a different business model. For example, differentiation strategy required constant innovation and leadership on the benefits that matter most to customers while maintaining a competitive cost position. Cost strategy, on the other hand, focused on gaining competitive advantage on costs while maintaining some level of parity on differentiation-type customer benefits. The niche strategy involved focusing the business on a particular segment of the market and then pursuing either a differentiation or cost approach.

This is an important baseline model for us to consider given the wide-ranging impact that it has had on business academics and practitioners. Some believe that Porter's model translates quite well into the new economy. They believe it is possible to isolate players in a variety of vertical industries who pursue one of the three generic strategies. For example, Travelocity.com is pursuing a differentiation strategy and Lowestfare.com is pursuing a low-cost strategy. A niche strategy is being implemented by Lastminute.com in that it focuses on travelers who are looking for good deals but who also have the flexibility of traveling on very short notice.

At the same time, Porter's model has come under attack by new-economy thinkers for a variety of reasons. First, it has been argued that many Internet firms compete on both differentiation and low cost. Due to the technological capabilities of the Internet, one no longer has to make trade-offs in strategy choices. Rather, a single company can compete in the low-cost, highly differentiated, and niche segments—all at the same time. Second, opponents argue that the Porter model focuses too heavily on within-industry competition when the great business stories of the Internet involve companies that are competing across industries based on customers' needs, goals, and activity choices.

## Sawhney and Kaplan Model

Sawhney and Kaplan have introduced the concept of electronic hubs (eHubs) and made a distinction between business-to-consumer (B2C) and business-to-business (B2B) hubs. They define the B2B eHub as "neutral Internet-based intermediaries that focus on specific industry verticals or specific business processes, host electronic marketplaces, and use various market-making mechanisms to mediate any-to-any transactions among businesses."[20] Sawhney and Kaplan argue that B2B hubs are the new middlemen that can create value by aggregating buyers and sellers, creating marketplace liquidity, and lowering transaction costs.

Further, Sawhney and Kaplan classify B2B hubs as either **vertical hubs** or **functional hubs**. Vertical hubs serve either vertical markets or a specific narrow industry focus, while functional hubs provide common business functions or automate the same business processes horizontally across different industries. Exhibit 5-7 illustrates the relation of vertical hubs to functional hubs. Vertical hubs include PlasticsNet.com (plastics) and e-Steel (steel). Examples of functional hubs are Celarix (logistics management), Adauction (media buying), and YOUtilities (energy management).

Generally, vertical hubs possess deep industry-specific knowledge but tend to lack business-process expertise. On the other hand, functional hubs possess business-process expertise, but tend to lack deep industry-specific knowledge. Unless vertical hubs find closely related domains where they can leverage their assets, they find it difficult to diversify into other vertical markets. Horizontal hubs, because of their low ability to deliver industry-specific content, run the risk of becoming back-end service providers to vertical hubs. Eventually, vertical hubs will probably form patchwork alliances with horizontal hubs or, alternatively, "metahubs" may emerge where multiple vertical hubs will share common back ends and functional services.

**Exhibit 5-7**

## SAWHNEY AND KAPLAN— CLASSIFICATION OF B2B MODELS

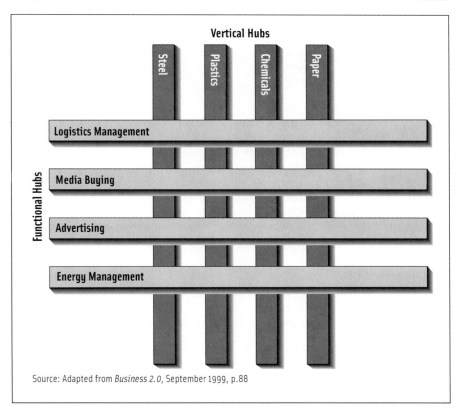

Source: Adapted from *Business 2.0*, September 1999, p.88

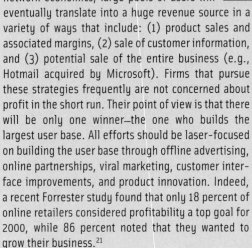
## Rayport, Jaworski, and Siegal Model

Table 5-4 provides a 2×2 categorization scheme proposed by Rayport, Jaworski, and Siegal (RJS model). Along the top axis are sources of content origination. Content in this context may refer to products, services, and/or information. The business can focus on content from a single source (e.g., Landsend.com sources only its own brands) or multiple sources (e.g., Bluefly.com carries a variety of brand name apparel). On the side axis is the focus of the business strategy, whether it is principally focused on the back-office or on supply-chain improvement and hence categorized as supply-side, or whether it is focused on a better customer experience and therefore demand-side focused. As we will describe in the following paragraphs, the options included in the taxonomy are not mutually exclusive.

**Pure Play.** Given these two axes, we can now describe alternative, "pure-play" generic approaches.

***Forward-Integrated Producers.*** Forward-integrated producers refer to single company initiatives that focus on enhancing the effectiveness or efficiency of the supply channel. We term these forward-integrated producers because they frequently refer

Table
5-4

RJS MODEL SUMMARY

| | **Sources of Content Origination** | |
|---|---|---|
| | **Single Brand** | **Multiple Brands** |
| **Supply-Side** | Forward-Integrated Producer (Wal-Mart.com) | Supply-Side Aggregator (Surplusdirect.com) |
| **Demand-Side** | Backward-Integrated User (Dellonline.com) | Demand-Side Aggregator (Accompany.com) |
| | Hybrid Integrator (Cisco.com) | Hybrid Aggregator (Amazon.com) |

*(Row label on left: Focus of Strategy)*

to companies that have decided to pursue an Internet strategy to enhance their relationships with suppliers or to reduce supply-chain inefficiencies.

A good example of a forward-integrated producer is Wal-Mart. Its online business model is designed to bring the products to market in a more efficient and effective way. The model is efficient due to shorter delivery time and lower operational costs and effective due to Wal-Mart's potential to increase revenues, and potentially, margins.

*Supply-Side Aggregators.* Supply-side aggregators are similar to forward-integrated producers in their focus. That is, they enhance the effectiveness or efficiency of the supply chain. However, supply-side aggregators do so by aggregating multiple players in the supply chain. This means they do not offer their own products, but rather, they aggregate many suppliers. A good example is the recent decision by the "Big Three" automakers to create a supply chain for their industry.

*Backward-Integrated User.* Backward-integrated user refers to a situation where a single company attempts to better serve its clients through a Web interface. The intent is to better serve existing or new clients through a single company site. An example of a backward-integrated user is Forrester.com. Forrester provides market-level reports on the evolution of technology and e-commerce, a series of online standard reports for its subscription customers, and custom analysis. It does not provide reports of competitors such as jup.com.

*Demand-Side Aggregators.* Demand-side aggregators pull together many potential buyers on a single site. MobShop.com aggregates groups of buyers to enhance their purchasing power and lower the prices to each individual consumer.

Again, an important point in the classification scheme is that these choices are not mutually exclusive. Rather, many businesses pursue hybrid approaches.

Through a hybrid model, a firm can choose to aggregate many sources of supply and many sources of demand and thus combine the supply-side aggregation and demand-side aggregation cells of the matrix (e.g., the classic metamarkets switchboard). Similarly, a firm may decide to aggregate all of its suppliers and buyers into a single hub that is firm-specific (e.g., Cisco.com).

With respect to the meaningfulness dimension, we can turn to the business implications of this taxonomy by referencing Table 5-5. This table illustrates the potential implications of the pure-play business approaches. In particular, the focus is on the potential sources of competitive advantage, potential benefits to producers, and potential benefits to users.

## MARKETWATCH.COM BUSINESS MODEL

Let us now illustrate the four components of the MarketWatch.com business model as of the end of 2000. This will help us understand what MarketWatch.com offers, how it is able to deliver it, and how it plans to become profitable through its offering.

### Value Cluster

As discussed earlier in the chapter, the value proposition or cluster consists of three components: (1) the target segments, (2) the key benefits, and (3) the supporting rationale for why the company is able to deliver these benefits better than its competitors can.

As noted in Chapter 4, the three target segments for MarketWatch.com are the savvy investors, the seekers, and the dabblers. We can derive the key benefits offered

**Table 5-5** IMPLICATIONS OF "PURE-PLAY" BUSINESS APPROACHES

| Business Implications | Forward-Integrated Producer | Backward-Integrated User | Supply Aggregator | Demand Aggregator |
|---|---|---|---|---|
| *Potential Sources of Competitive Advantage* | • Streamlined outbound logistics<br>• Producer brand<br>• Producer customer base | • Streamlined inbound logistics | • Strong brand identity<br>• Relevant strategic alliances | • Strong brand identity<br>• Relevant customer scale |
| *Potential Benefits to Producer* | • Lower cost for delivery of products, services, or information<br>• Efficiencies which translate into cost savings | • Lower cost for delivery of products, services, or information<br>• Efficiencies which translate into cost savings | • More targeted access to customers | • Expanded access to customers<br>• More targeted access to customers |
| *Potential Benefits to User* | • Lower price for products, services, or information<br>• Efficiencies which translate into cost savings | • Lower price for products, services, or information<br>• Efficiencies which translate into cost savings | • Time savings<br>• Privacy | • Connection to others who are like-minded<br>• Access to relevant information/advice |

# Who Would You Rather Be: A Dot-Com or a Bricks-and-Mortar Business?

A debate that is currently unfolding in the market is whether a particular firm is better off starting out as a pure dot-com business or whether a firm is better off starting out with bricks-and-mortar assets.

Proponents on the pure dot-com side argue that dot-com businesses are not constrained by physical world assets because those assets do not translate into the new economy. They argue that firms in this space need to operate differently—fast, with flat organizational structures, no functional boundaries, and a senior management team that understands the new economy. Furthermore, dot-com proponents point to a number of successful companies that have followed this approach, such as Amazon.com, Yahoo.com, and AOL.

On the bricks-and-mortar side, proponents counter that there are basic business issues that still apply in the new economy. Firms must be businesses—not simply customer-acquisition organizations. Furthermore, the key assets that dot-coms are attempting to build (e.g., consumer awareness, traffic, strong brands) are already possessed by the incumbent traditional businesses. Indeed, as Jack Welch recently noted, "Digitizing a company and developing e-business models is easier—not harder—than we ever imagined."[22]

to these segments from the MarketWatch.com mission statement: "To be the world-wide leader in providing fast, relevant, and accurate information to help people make and save money."[23] Thus, the three elements of the MarketWatch.com value cluster are as follows:

- *Target Segments:*

    Savvy investors (frequent financial-information users, high income)

    Seekers (sporadic financial-information users, medium to high income)

    Dabblers (financial-information newbies, all ages, moderate income, varying levels of education)

- *Key Benefits:*

    Up-to-the-minute information

    Original, in-depth, credible analysis

    Personal-finance tools

    Multiple points of access

- *Supportive Rationale:*

    Experienced editorial staff with financial experience

    Infrastructure allowing access from multiple forms of media (Web, TV, radio, print, wireless)

    Credibility of association with CBS News brand name in the United States and Financial Times brand name in Europe

# The MarketWatch.com Marketspace Offering

Let us now look at the MarketWatch.com marketspace offering, namely the combination of products, services, and information that MarketWatch.com offers to deliver its value cluster. The first step is the articulation of the scope. MarketWatch.com focused on being the best provider of financial information and analysis across a number of media.

Exhibit 5-8 illustrates the MarketWatch.com offering. In the inner circle, one can see the main steps of the personal-finance process. They include becoming educated on personal finance, planning an investment strategy, staying current with the latest developments, and performing and tracking investments. In the outer circle, we have displayed many of the services and information that MarketWatch.com offers users for each of these steps.

As part of its personal finance education, MarketWatch.com's "Getting Started" section offers educational materials ranging from a glossary of financial terms and basic facts about IPOs to recommendations of sites that parents can use to teach their children about finance. In the planning investment strategy step, MarketWatch.com offers a number of tools, such as the Home Price Checker (which displays fair property prices for different locations) and the Insurance QuickQuote (which provides competitive insurance quotes). To keep users updated on the latest financial news, MarketWatch.com offers breaking news and market figures. Breaking news is broadcast over a number of different platforms: online, as real-time headlines or in the form of personalized alerts; on television, through the *CBS MarketWatch Weekend* show or the MarketWatch.com contribution to CBS shows and to CBS NewsPath (a CBS News service to affiliate television stations); and on radio, through the MarketWatch.com reports distributed by the Westwood One Radio Network, a nationwide syndication company serving radio stations. Finally, it is accessible through wireless devices, such as cellphones and handheld devices. Detailed market figures for all investment venues are displayed on the site using the CBS MarketWatch charting technology.

One of MarketWatch.com's greatest strengths is in assisting with the next step of the personal-finance management process—developing financial insight. The site offers a number of specialized commentary columns that are produced by its experienced staff of editors and journalists. It also offers access to investment reports of established third-party sources such as Hoover's Online and Multex. The perspective of financial journalists is augmented through community tools such as message boards and personalized e-mails. MarketWatch.com does not enable investors to make online transactions, but it offers sponsored links to online brokers such as Datek and Ameritrade. MarketWatch.com focuses on helping investors manage their portfolios. It offers advanced portfolio-tracking tools, allowing users to forecast their portfolio value and adjust their investment strategy accordingly.

# The MarketWatch.com Resource System

The resource system builds on the value cluster and marketspace offering. Exhibit 5-9 demonstrates the resource system for MarketWatch.com. The four benefits that relate directly to the value proposition are the following:

- Up-to-the-minute information
- Original, in-depth, credible analysis
- Personal-finance tools
- Multiple points of access

**Exhibit**
**5-8** MARKETWATCH.COM EGG DIAGRAM

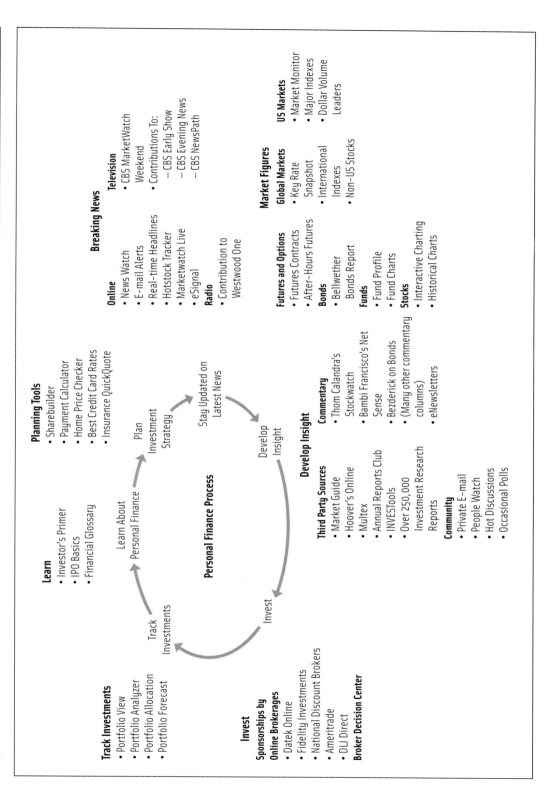

**Learn**
- Investor's Primer
- IPO Basics
- Financial Glossary

**Planning Tools**
- Sharebuilder
- Payment Calculator
- Home Price Checker
- Best Credit Card Rates
- Insurance QuickQuote

**Breaking News**

**Online**
- News Watch
- E-mail Alerts
- Real-time Headlines
- Hotstock Tracker
- Marketwatch Live
- eSignal

**Radio**
- Contribution to Westwood One

**Television**
- CBS MarketWatch Weekend
- Contributions To:
  —CBS Early Show
  —CBS Evening News
  —CBS NewsPath

**Market Figures**

**Global Markets**
- Key Rate Snapshot
- International Indexes
- Non-US Stocks

**US Markets**
- Market Monitor
- Major Indexes
- Dollar Volume Leaders

**Futures and Options**
- Futures Contracts
- After-Hours Futures

**Bonds**
- Bellwether Bonds Report

**Funds**
- Fund Profile
- Fund Charts

**Stocks**
- Interactive Charting
- Historical Charts

**Develop Insight**

**Commentary**
- Thom Calandra's Stockwatch
- Bambi Francisco's Net Sense
- Bezderick on Bonds
- (Many other commentary columns)
- eNewsletters

**Third Party Sources**
- Market Guide
- Hoover's Online
- Multex
- Annual Reports Club
- INVESTools
- Over 250,000 Investment Research Reports

**Community**
- Private E-mail
- People Watch
- Hot Discussions
- Occasional Polls

**Track Investments**
- Portfolio View
- Portfolio Analyzer
- Portfolio Allocation
- Portfolio Forecast

**Invest**

**Sponsorships by Online Brokerages**
- Datek Online
- Fidelity Investments
- National Discount Brokers
- Ameritrade
- DLJ Direct

**Broker Decision Center**

Plan Investment Strategy

Stay Updated on Latest News

Learn About Personal Finance

**Personal Finance Process**

Develop Insight

Track Investments

Invest

**Exhibit 5-9** MARKETWATCH.COM RESOURCE SYSTEM

Legend:
- ● = **Core Benefits**
- ▢ = **Capabilities**
- ○ = **Activities and Resources**

**Distribution Partnerships**
- Quicken
- Yahoo
- AOL
- Westwood One Radio Network

**Available Infrastructure**
- DBC Admin Services
- Website
- CBS Marketwatch Weekend
- Wireless Access
- Access to CBS Studios

**Multiple Points of Access**

**Association With CBS**
- Content Distribution Through CBS NewsPath
- Brand Mentions During CBS Shows
- Licensing CBS Brand Name
- TV Journalists

**Credible Analysis and Personal Finance Tools**

**Leading Technology**
- DBC Real-Time News
- E-Signal Partnership
- Big Charts Acquisition

**International Presence**
- Asia
- FT Partnership (Europe)
- U.S.

**Up-to-the-minute Information**

**Partnership With Content Providers**
- News Alert
- WSRN
- Hoovers
- INVESTools
- Multex
- Annual Reports Club
- Zachs Investment Research

**Experienced Editorial Staff**
- Award-Winning Publishers and Managing Editors
- Reporters and Editors

The next step is to identify capabilities that allow MarketWatch.com to deliver these benefits. These include the experienced editorial staff, its association with the CBS News and Financial Times brands, the technology and infrastructure to deliver content across multiple platforms, an international presence, and its content and distribution partnerships.

These capabilities are made possible through a number of MarketWatch.com activities and resources. For example, leading real-time quote technology and web-site hosting and management was originally provided by DBC, and was gradually brought in-house during 2000 by leveraging the BigCharts.com acquisition. The international presence has been achieved through the MarketWatch.com joint venture with the Financial Times, as well as by opening news bureaus in places such as London, New York, and Tokyo.

It is clear from the resource system that MarketWatch.com is able to deliver its value cluster to its users by combining its internal capabilities with those of its partners. Table 5-6 illustrates the "Give/Get Matrix," namely what MarketWatch.com gives and what it gets out of these partnerships. For example, what MarketWatch.com gets from CBS News includes brand credibility, access to its audience, access to its production facilities, and $30 million of rate-card promotion and advertising on CBS channels through October 2002. In return, MarketWatch.com gives CBS News 32 percent ownership of the company as well as reliable and in-depth coverage of world financial news generated by its experienced editorial staff.[24]

## Table 5-6 PARTNERS "GIVE/GET" MATRIX

| Partners | Benefits to Partner: "Give" | Benefits to MarketWatch.com: "Get" |
|---|---|---|
| *CBS News* | • Experienced editorial staff<br>• 24/7 international coverage of financial markets<br>• Real-time financial news<br>• Access to the Web channel<br>• 32% ownership of MarketWatch.com | • Credibility of CBS brand name<br>• Access to CBS facilities<br>• Access to CBS audience of 6.6 million homes<br>• $30 million of promotion on CBS |
| *FT.MarketWatch.com* | • Part ownership of joint venture<br>• Technology transfer | • Branding in European marketspace<br>• Traffic driven to site and increase in awareness |
| *Content Partners (e.g. Hoovers, Zacks, INVESTools)* | • Access to MarketWatch.com audience | • High-quality analysis of financial news<br>• Portion of revenue generated from sales of partner products |
| *Distribution Partners (e.g. Yahoo, AOL, Quicken)* | • Users get access to MarketWatch.com content and tools<br>• Advertising and click-through fees collected | • Increase in audience reach<br>• Increase in brand recognition |

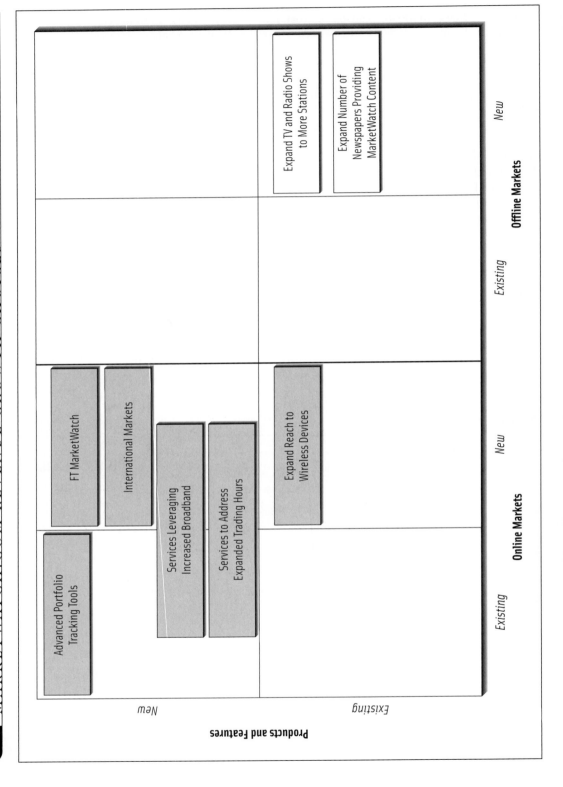

**Table 5-7** MARKETWATCH.COM REVENUE GROWTH CHOICES

Products and Features

New:
- Advanced Portfolio Tracking Tools
- FT MarketWatch
- International Markets
- Services Leveraging Increased Broadband
- Services to Address Expanded Trading Hours

Existing:
- Expand Reach to Wireless Devices
- Expand TV and Radio Shows to More Stations
- Expand Number of Newspapers Providing MarketWatch Content

Online Markets — Existing / New
Offline Markets — Existing / New

# The Financial Model

So how does MarketWatch.com make money? How is it planning to become profitable? Let us examine the MarketWatch.com financial model.

**Revenue Model.** MarketWatch.com generates revenues from the following three sources:

- *Advertising revenue* (72 percent of revenues in 1999) comes from the sale of banner advertisements and sponsorships on the company's website.
- *Licensing revenue* (21 percent of revenues in 1999) comes from two sources: (1) the licensing of its charting technology and content and (2) the sale of news content to third parties and a portion of subscriber payments from sites using MarketWatch.com content.
- *Other revenue* (7 percent of revenues in 1999) includes revenue generated during the MarketWatch.com television shows and from the paid subscription to the premium MarketWatch Live and MarketWatch RT services.

**Value Model.** Profits are primarily generated by increasing advertising revenues with small incremental cost to MarketWatch.com. This is achieved by offering advertisers a wider audience for its messages, as well as the ability to target its advertisements to select groups of MarketWatch.com users. Profits are also generated by licensing or selling the proprietary MarketWatch.com financial news and analysis content to an increasing number of third parties, at minimal additional cost to MarketWatch.com. Looking back at the different value models introduced earlier in this chapter, MarketWatch.com has a best-information value model.

**Growth Model.** Table 5-7 illustrates MarketWatch.com's potential areas of revenue growth. Growth can come from offering new services and expanding the audience for existing offerings. For example, MarketWatch.com can further develop its advanced portfolio-tracking tools, or it can develop new services that leverage the increased broadband capabilities or address new needs created by expanded trading hours. The joint venture with Financial Times creates a large opportunity for MarketWatch.com to introduce both existing and new offerings to the European markets. The expansion of the television and radio audience for MarketWatch.com programs and the increase in the number of wireless devices that could receive MarketWatch.com news and analysis further boosts the growth opportunities.

# SUMMARY

## 1. What is a business model?

A business model has four parts: a value proposition or cluster of value propositions, a marketspace offering, a unique and defendable resource system, and a financial model. The value proposition defines the choice of target segment, the choice of focal-customer benefits, and a rationale for why the firm can deliver the benefit package significantly better than its competitors. The offering entails a precise articulation of the products, services, and information provided by the firm. The resource system supports the specific set of capabilities and resources that will be engaged in by the firm to uniquely deliver the offering. The financial model details the various ways that the firm is proposing to generate revenue, enhance value, and grow.

### 2. Do firms compete on value propositions or value clusters?

Firms can compete on either or both. While offline firms may have difficulty competing on value clusters, their online counterparts can compete on either value proposition or value clusters. Firms in the online world can address consumers as "segments of one." Web businesses often attract multiple segments at the same time and compete with other firms on multiple benefits that are delivered by a single tightly conceived and implemented set of capabilities. Firms can choose to focus and primarily emphasize one critical benefit or provide multiple storefronts and clusters of benefits to multiple segments within the context of a single URL.

### 3. What are the approaches to developing an online offering, whether the business is providing a product, service, or information?

Development of an online offering requires completion of three sequential tasks: (1) identify the scope of the offering, (2) identify the customer decision process, and (3) map the offering (product, services, and information) to the customer decision process. The scope refers to the website's breadth, or the number of categories of products and services. The customer decision process can be divided into three broad stages: prepurchase, purchase, and postpurchase. The process of mapping the offering to the customer decision process (i.e., mapping the egg diagram) involves the systematic matching of product, services, and information onto each stage of the customer decision process.

### 4. What is a successful, unique resource system? What are characteristics of good resource systems?

The resource system shows how a company's value proposition is contained in a set of tailored capabilities that uniquely deliver the benefits of the proposition. A number of criteria can be used to assess the quality of the resource system, such as the uniqueness of a system and whether there are links between capabilities and benefits, links among capabilities in the system, links among resources, and links to physical-world business systems.

### 5. What are the revenue models available to firms?

Firms can pursue a variety of revenue models, including the following: advertising; product, service, or information sales; transaction fees; and subscription fees.

### 6. What business classification schemes seem most appropriate for the new economy?

Some have argued that the Porter model does not take into consideration the technology capabilities of the Internet, and hence does not allow for simultaneous pursuit of multiple generic strategies. Also, the model focuses too heavily on within-industry competition, while competition among Internet-based companies is across several industries and based on customers needs, goals, and activity choices.

The Sawhney and Kaplan model primarily concentrates on the burgeoning area of business-to-business hubs and whether these hubs are vertical or functional in nature. While this model captures important aspects of the business-to-business hubs, it fails to describe the broad landscape of the various business models that have emerged.

The Rayport, Jaworski, and Siegal model accounts for sources of content origination as well as the focus of business strategy—whether the strategy is focused on supply-side or demand-side improvements. The model options in the taxonomy are not mutually exclusive and, therefore, can accommodate "pure-play" as well as "hybrid form" business approaches. The flexibility of the RJS taxonomy accommodates both business-to-consumer and business-to-business metamarkets where the new focus is on customer needs, goals, and activity choices. While this model captures all of the Internet plays, it can be criticized for its complexity.

# KEY TERMS

| | |
|---|---|
| business model | shareholder value models |
| value proposition | growth models |
| value cluster | vertical hubs |
| egg diagram | functional hubs |
| revenue models | |

# Endnotes

[1] Kaplan, Karen. 2000. DOT-GONE? An occasional look at firms struggling in the online world: FTD.com hoped to flower on Web, but prospects are wilting. *Los Angeles Times,* 17 April, Home edition, Business section, p. C-1. URL: *http://www.latimes.com/archives/,* searchword: ftd.

[2] Market attractiveness is a function of the size of the market, growth rates of the market, weakness of competitors, strong consumer needs, supportive technology, and other forces.

[3] Lynch, John G., Jr., and Dan Ariely. 1999. Electronic shopping for wine: How search costs affect consumer price sensitivity, satisfaction with merchandise, and retention. *Marketing Science Institute Report*, pp. 99–104. URL: *http://www.msi.org/msi/publication_summary.cfm?publication*=99-104.

[4] Wyman, Tom. 1999. eTailing and the five Cs. *J.P. Morgan Industry Analysis*, 9 December.

[5] Each of these terms is independent but highly related. Interested readers may wish to consider the following sources: Prahald, C.K., and Gary Hamel. 1990. The core competence of the corporation. *Strategic Management Journal* 15 (May–June): 79–91. Collis, David J., and Cynthia A. Montgomery. 1995. Competing on resources: Strategy in the 1990s. *Harvard Business Review* 73, no. 4 (July–August): 118–28. Wernerfelt, Birger. 1994. A resource-based view of the firm. *Strategic Management Journal* 5: 171–80. Barney, Jay. 1991. Firm resources and sustained competitive advantage. *Journal of Management* 17, no. 1: 99–120. Dickson, Peter Reid. 1992. Toward a general theory of competitive rationality. *Journal of Marketing* 56 (January): 69–83. Hunt, Shelby D. 1995. The comparative advantage theory of competition. *Journal of Marketing* 59 (April): 1–15.

[6] See Collis, David J., and Cynthia Montgomery. 1995. Competing on resources, pp. 119–21.

[7] We are inferring these propositions from the websites' tag lines and communications.

[8] Sawhney, Mohanbir. 1999. Making new markets. *Business 2.0* (May): 116–21.

[9] Hoyer, Wayne, and Deborah MacInnis. 1997. *Consumer behavior.* Boston: Houghton Mifflin Company, pp. 98–100.

[10]Value chains are company-specific activities that range from raw materials acquisition through to after-sale customer service (see Porter, Michael E. 1985. *Competitive advantage.* New York: The Free Press, p. 37). Activity systems are largely derived from the value chains but focus on the key "themes" and associated activities that are the most important in the delivery of a differentiated value proposition. Additionally, activity systems focus heavily on the links between activities, reflecting the need to interweave the activities as a network rather than a linear chain. This work was an important influence on the evolution of our resource system perspective.

[11]Porter, Michael E. 1996. What is strategy? *Harvard Business Review* 74, no. 6 (November–December): 61–78.

[12]Rayport, Jeffrey F. and John J. Sviokla. 1995. Exploiting the virtual value chain. *Harvard Business Review* 73, no. 6 (November–December): 75–85.

[13]For an excellent discussion of the resource-based view of the firm, read the article by Collis, David J., and Cynthia A. Montgomery. 1995. Competing on resources.

[14]This resource system is derived largely from the Securities and Exchange Commission S1-A filing on August 2, 1999. The online version can be found at the following URL: *http://www.sec.gov/cgi-bin/srch-edgar?flowers.*

[15]Thompson, Maryann J. 1999. Net steals billions from offline retailers. *The Standard,* 4 August. URL: *http://www.thestandard.com/article/display/0,1151,5744,00.html.*

[16]Meland, Marius. 2000. Zagat takes a big byte. *Forbes.com,* 8 Februrary. URL: *http://www.forbes.com/tool/html/00/feb/0208/mu2.html.*

[17]Imitability of resources is discussed in the following: Collis, David J., and Cynthia A. Montgomery. 1995. Competing on resources.

[18]Slywotzky, Adrian J., and David J. Morrison. 1998. *The profit zone: How strategic design will lead you to tomorrow's profits.* New York: Times Business. We strongly recommend that readers review this well-regarded book on alternative profit models in the offline world. The work provided an important input into the models that are illustrated in this section.

[19]Sawhney, Mohanbir. 1999. Making new markets. *Business 2.0* (May): 116–21.

[20]Sawhney, Mohanbir, and Steven Kaplan. 1999. Let's get vertical. *Business 2.0* (September). URL: *http://www.business2.com/articles/1999/09/content/models.html.*

[21]Regan, Keith. 2000. Forrester: Most dot-coms will sink by 2001. *E-Commerce Times,* 13 April. URL: *http://www.ecommercetimes.com/news/articles2000/000412-7.shtml.*

[22]Moore, Pamela L. 2000. GE's cyber payoff. *Business Week,* 13 April. URL: *http://www.businessweek.com/bwdaily/dnflash/apr2000/nf00413f.htm?scriptFramed.*

[23]Securities and Exchange Commission, *Form 10-K for MarketWatch.com, Inc. for the fiscal year ended December 31, 1999.*

[24]Securities and Exchange Commission, *Form 10-K for MarketWatch.com, Inc. for the fiscal year ended December 31, 1999.* 32% CBS ownership as of December 31, 1999.

# 6

# Customer Interface

The purpose of this chapter is to introduce the concept of a technology-mediated customer interface. This interface can be a desktop PC, subnotebook, personal digital assistant, cellphone, WAP device, or other appliance. Within a technology-mediated customer experience, the user's interaction with the company shifts from the face-to-face encounter in a traditional retail environment to a screen-to-face encounter. As this shift from people-mediated to technology-mediated interfaces unfolds, it is important to consider the types of interface design available to the senior management team. What is the look-and-feel, or context, of the website? Should the site include commerce activities? How important are communities in the business model? To capture these design considerations, we introduce the 7Cs Framework. It is a rigorous way to understand the interface design choices that confront senior managers as they implement their business models.

## QUESTIONS

*Please consider the following questions as you read this chapter:*

1. What are the seven design elements of the customer interface?

2. What are the alternative look-and-feel approaches to design?

3. What are the five content archetypes?

4. Why be concerned with community?

5. What are the levers used to customize a site?

---

This chapter was coauthored by Bernie Jaworski, Jeffrey Rayport, Leo Griffin, and Yannis Dosios.

6. What types of communication can a firm maintain with its customer base?

7. How does a firm connect with other businesses?

8. What are alternative pricing models of commerce archetypes?

## INTRODUCTION

In Chapter 5, we detailed the four business-model choices that confront senior managers: value cluster, marketspace offering, resource system, and financial model. This set of strategy decisions significantly informs the type of customer interface choices that will confront a senior management team. For example, a decision to be a no-frills discount retailer of functional goods, such as electronics, would have very different customer interface implications compared to a high-end, trend-oriented fashion site.

Consider, for example, the different approaches of two well-regarded sports sites: Quokka.com and Gear.com. Quokka.com is concerned with immersion into sports categories such as sailing, auto racing, surfing, and the Olympics. The site focuses on the experiences that one can enjoy in each sports category, including the purchase of memorabilia, identifying event dates, and even experiencing a "sports digital network" for broadcasts. Features that encourage a sense of community are a significant portion of the Quokka site, because the primary goal is to gather sports fanatics together in one environment. Commerce is a very small portion of the site.

In sharp contrast, Gear.com is billed as "name brand sporting goods at closeout prices." Gear.com was recently purchased by Overstock.com, a liquidator that specializes in buying the inventory of distressed dot-coms. The sites of Gear.com and Overstock.com are the online equivalents of heavy-discounter specialty mall outlets in the offline world such as Filene's Basement. The entire site is focused on product offerings with a particular emphasis on low prices and good deals. No effort is made to build community or to provide "deep immersion" in the product category.

Given their distinct value propositions and associated marketspace offerings, it is not surprising that the interfaces Quokka.com and Gear.com differ in content, the look-and-feel of their layouts, degrees of commerce activity, emphasis on community, and connections to other sites.

The purpose of this chapter is to introduce, describe, and provide examples for each of the 7Cs of customer interface design. In the first section, we provide an overview of the 7Cs Framework. In addition, we also discuss two higher-order design principles to be considered when constructing a customer interface—fit and reinforcement. In the later sections, we provide a more thorough examination that includes discussion of the features or dimensions of each C along with respective sample archetypes. We conclude the chapter with an application of the 7Cs framework to MarketWatch.com.

## WHAT ARE THE SEVEN DESIGN ELEMENTS OF THE CUSTOMER INTERFACE?

### The 7Cs Framework

Exhibit 6-1 provides a simple representation of the **7Cs Framework** for customer interface design. The interface is the virtual (and, to date, largely visual) representation of a firm's chosen value proposition. Similar to a retail storefront, the virtual website provides significant information to current and prospective target-market customers. If designed effectively, the site quickly answers a number of basic questions that confront such users. Is this site worth visiting? What products or services does it sell? What messages does the site communicate: Exclusivity? Low price? Ease of use? Consistent with a tightly constructed business model, well-designed sites should simultaneously attract target segment customers and repel (or not appeal to) nontargeted customers. Compelling sites communicate the core value proposition of the company and provide a rationale for buying from and/or visiting the site.

**Definitions and Simple Illustration.** How then does the senior management team structure choices to enable the implementation of an effective site? In the following paragraphs, we briefly describe the seven design choices that form the basis of an effective interface. After this brief review, we provide a more detailed explanation of each of the Cs.

*Context.* The **context** of the website captures its aesthetic and functional look-and-feel. Some sites have chosen to focus heavily on interesting graphics, colors, and design features, while others have emphasized more simple utilitarian goals, such as ease of navigation. Exhibit 6-1 contains a webpage from Landsend.com. Lands' End

## THE 7Cs OF THE CUSTOMER INTERFACE

**Exhibit 6-1**

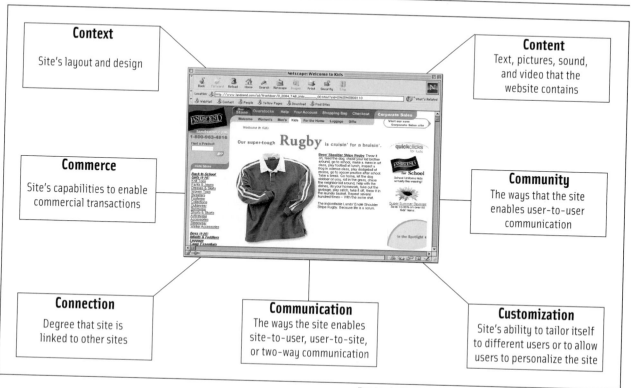

**Context**
Site's layout and design

**Content**
Text, pictures, sound, and video that the website contains

**Commerce**
Site's capabilities to enable commercial transactions

**Community**
The ways that the site enables user-to-user communication

**Connection**
Degree that site is linked to other sites

**Communication**
The ways the site enables site-to-user, user-to-site, or two-way communication

**Customization**
Site's ability to tailor itself to different users or to allow users to personalize the site

balances both aesthetic (pastel colors; simple, warm visuals) and functional (crisp, uncluttered) design elements to communicate its core benefits—traditionally designed clothing, great service, and moderate prices. In sharp contrast, Luckyjeans.com is a more hip, nontraditional brand; its website is comparatively more edgy, with bolder colors, humor (the "get lucky" slogan), and a more focused product line. Lands' End customers might not find the Luckyjeans.com site appealing, purely because of its look-and-feel. Luckyjeans.com suggests a younger, more urban, and fashion-forward target segment.

*Content.* **Content** is defined as all digital subject matter on the site. This includes the form of the digital subject matter—text, video, audio, and graphics—as well as the domains of the digital subject matter, including product, service, and information offerings. While context largely focuses on the "how" of site design, content focuses on "what" is presented. Consider again the Landsend.com site in Exhibit 6-1. The Lands' End site includes content pertaining to its product offerings (e.g., overstocks, kids, luggage, gifts), services, and offline support (e.g., 1-800 phone number). In terms of media, the site uses a combination of text, photographs, and graphics to convey its content.

*Community.* **Community** is defined as the interaction that occurs between site users. It does not refer to site-to-user interactions. User-to-user communication can occur between two users (e.g., e-mails, joint game-playing) or between one user and many (e.g., chat rooms). Landsend.com has an innovative community feature that allows two users to shop simultaneously on its site. This trademarked service termed "Shop with a Friend," enables two users to view the site at the same time, browse together, and purchase the product. It is a virtual shopping experience.

*Customization.* **Customization** is defined as the site's ability to tailor itself or to be tailored by each user. When the customization is initiated and managed by the firm, we term it tailoring. When the customization is initiated and managed by the user, we term it personalization. Let us consider two examples. On Landsend.com, the user is able to personalize the site to a limited degree, using a feature called the personal shopping account. This feature allows the user to enter basic personal information, complete an address book for potential recipients of purchases, and enter key dates in the reminder service. In turn, once personal profile data is entered and consumers begin to use the site, the site uses this data to tailor e-mail messages, banner ads, and the content of the site to the individual.

*Communication.* **Communication** refers to the dialogue that unfolds between the site and its users. This communication can take three forms: site-to-user communication (e.g., e-mail notification), user-to-site (e.g., customer service request), or two-way communication (e.g., instant messaging). Landsend.com has introduced a communication feature called "Lands' End Live" that enables the user to talk directly with the customer service representative while shopping on the site. Clicking on the Lands' End Live button results in two options: (1) connection by phone (this assumes the user has two phone lines, a direct Internet connection by DSL, or a cable modem) or (2) connection by live text chat.

*Connection.* **Connection** is defined as the extent of the formal linkages between the site and other sites. Landsend.com does not have any connections to other sites; however, it does have an affiliates program that allows other sites to connect to Lands' End. In particular, Landsend.com supplies the affiliate site with banner ads to link visitors from the site to the Landsend.com store. The affiliate partner earns 5 percent on every sale that occurs on a click-through from the site. If a customer is a first-time Lands' End buyer, the affiliate earns an additional finder's fee.

**Commerce.** **Commerce** is defined as the sale of goods, products, or services on the site. The Landsend.com site obviously has transactional capability. It has the typical shopping-basket feature along with shipping information. The shopping basket can be viewed at any point in the shopping experience. It includes such information as quantity, description, size, prices, and availability, and it also provides options to "delete the item" and "order more of this." As a summary feature, the site displays the total price of items, extra services, taxes (if applicable), shipping costs (if the shipping choice has been already selected), and the grand total. The customer can choose to check out if everything in the shopping basket is acceptable. The acceptance step accesses a secure server where the customer inputs billing information (e.g., shipping address, e-mail contact address, and daytime phone number). Finally, the customer inputs the choice of credit card along with credit-card details and submits the final order.

# Building Fit and Reinforcement

In the previous section, we provided a basic overview of each of the 7Cs. However, the success of a particular business such as Landsend.com depends on the extent that all of the Cs work together to support the value proposition and business model. Two concepts—fit and reinforcement—are particularly helpful in explaining how it is possible to gain synergy among the 7Cs.[1]

**Fit** refers to the extent to which each of the 7Cs individually support the business model. This is illustrated in Exhibit 6-2 as links between each of the Cs and the business model. Reinforcement refers to the degree of consistency between each of the Cs. This is illustrated in Exhibit 6-2 as the links between each of the Cs.

Consider, once again, Landsend.com. It largely targets the middle-class consumer, with its traditionally designed clothing, great service, and moderate prices. The content of the site "fits" this value proposition by providing mainstream and conservative fashion. Its innovative live chat "fits" with great service, and the price points of regularly priced clothing "fit" the moderate pricing strategy.

With respect to **reinforcement**—the aesthetic context of the site—the Lands' End site works well. The site's picture of a smiling customer-service representative, light-blue tones, and soft-sell approach helps to focus the customer on the ease of product searches and navigation and on the clean and clear visual displays of clothing. The elements of context, content, customization, and commerce all work well together to provide a clear, reinforcing statement of the value proposition.

Lands' End's performance ratings by third-party evaluators also suggest that they would score high on both fit and reinforcement. In Exhibit 6-3 we provide a summary of the performance of the Lands' End site according to five criteria. These criteria and the ratings were performed by Forrester Research (*www.forrester.com*).

Exhibit
6-2

## FIT AND REINFORCEMENT OF THE 7Cs

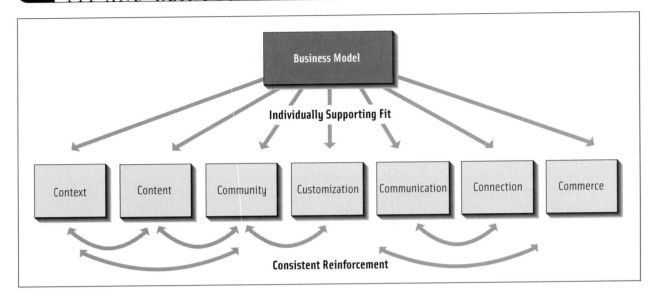

Exhibit
6-3

## PERFORMANCE OF THE LANDS' END SITE

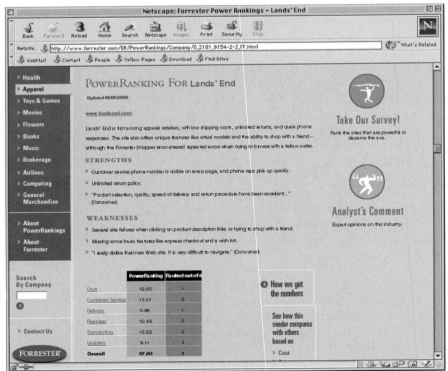

©Forrester Research, Inc.

# WHAT DETERMINES THE LOOK-AND-FEEL OF THE DESIGN?

## Context

Context is defined as the look-and-feel of a screen-to-face customer interface.

The look-and-feel of a website, PDA, or cellphone can be categorized by both aesthetic and functional criteria. A functionally-oriented site focuses largely on the core offering—whether that is product, services, or information. A good example is CEOExpress.com (*www.ceoexpress.com*). CEOExpress is an information portal that aggregates magazine, newspaper, television, and other media sites into a single destination. Its design features are simple, clean, and straightforward. The site allows for quick, no-nonsense access to information that would be relevant to CEOs—stock quotes, business periodicals, news magazines, and other content-oriented sites.

In contrast, Reflect.com (*www.reflect.com*) is a more aesthetically-oriented site. This does not mean that function is unimportant. The site has a very distinct look-and-feel that is artistic, visually appealing, and surprising in its blend of text, graphics, and photographs.

Nordstrom.com (*www.nordstrom.com*) combines both aesthetic and functional dimensions. On the aesthetic side, Nordstrom.com is a highly visual site with large photographs of products and fashion models. The fashion models not only communicate the product offering but also the type of woman who would purchase the Nordstrom product and the environment in which she resides. Recently, the Nordstrom site featured a model seated on the floor of what appeared to be an exclusive home with Spanish-influenced design. Clearly, this photograph attempted to set the tone for the kind of person who would be expected to shop at Nordstrom.

**Dimensions to Context.** In this section, we elaborate on the two key context dimensions: function and aesthetics. In particular, we define the subdimensions of function and aesthetics and provide examples of how these dimensions are evidenced in Bluefly.com (*www.bluefly.com*). Bluefly.com is a retail store positioned as "the outlet store for your home." It has a wide variety of high-end, symbolically-oriented retail goods that include clothing, household items, and gifts.

*Function.* Most sites contain much more information than can be usefully presented on a single computer screen, or page. This vast amount of information must be presented to the customer in a coherent fashion, and the customer must be able to move from interest to interest within the website. A well-designed site organizes all resident information into sets of pages and provides customers with a means to navigate from page to page. Three factors are critical in the layout of the site:

- *Section breakdown.* The section breakdown is the way the site is organized into subcomponents. Bluefly has a top-level tab structure that includes search, shopping bag, my account, and help. Beneath this general tab structure are the categories of goods—men's, women's, kids', house, and gifts. The homepage also includes clear directions to the following sections: top designers, clearance, my catalog, and selected gift items.

- *Linking structure.* The linking structure is the site's approach to linking its alternative sections. Clicking on the Prada brand on the Bluefly homepage enables one to visit the Prada fashion section. At the same time, the Prada fashion section is framed by the top-level tab structure and general categories that we noted earlier. This linking structure enables the users to move easily back and forth between sections of the site.

- *Navigation tools.* The navigation tools are the site tools that facilitate how the user moves through the site. Navigation tools for Bluefly include my catalog and two types of search (by price or by style number).

Another aspect of function relates to the performance of the site. As of this writing, the limited speed of most commonly available connections to the Internet presents a constraint to website design. Generally, with all else being equal, sites with limited graphics or multimedia features load in less time (i.e., at higher speeds), while sites with streaming video or large, richly detailed graphics take more time. We will now explore five dimensions of performance: speed, reliability, platform independence, media accessibility, and usability.

- *Speed.* Speed is described in terms of the time required to display a site page on the user's screen. For example, the Bluefly site is fast in that it has very short download times due to its straightforward design and limited use of complex graphics or sophisticated multimedia applications.

- *Reliability.* Reliability can be defined in two ways. First, reliability is based on how often the website experiences periods of downtime. Downtime is any time the website is unable to allow users access to the site, including periods of planned maintenance and unplanned system crashes. A second aspect of reliability is the percent of times that the site correctly downloads to the user. Even if the site is up, it may not download correctly to the users' screens.

- *Platform independence.* Platform independence is a measure of how well the site can run on multiple platforms that include previous versions of browsers and hardware (e.g., slower modems) and other access software. Most designers construct sites to perform on previous generation platforms.

- *Media accessibility.* As Internet-enabled devices or Web appliances proliferate, browser-based PCs will become only one of many formats to be accommodated in the design of the website. Media accessibility (the ability of a site to download to various media platforms) may become increasingly complex. Websites may need to be simplified and designed specifically for multiple platforms until standards are established and accepted by a broad audience of users. The recent introduction of XML, a meta language for describing data, has greatly improved the Web's media accessibility. XML documents contain information about their own content that allows interface devices (such as a browser) to interpret how the content will be used. For example, Tellme Networks has used XML to develop an interface that allows websites to tag content for delivery through Tellme's voice-based portal. Users can simply call Tellme from any phone to access Web-based information such as stock quotes, sports news, and flight information. Tellme promises to make the rich information of the Web accessible to everyone who has a phone.

- *Usability.* Usability is the ease with which a site can be navigated by users. Even if the content or the community of a site is wonderful, poor usability will make the site unappealing. Usability is affected by many elements of a website. For example, the speed that a site loads, the way that a site's multiple pages are structured, and the graphical design of the site all affect usability. Designing highly usable websites is part art, part science. Authors such as Jakob Nielsen have become recognized experts on usability.[2] Several sidebars in this chapter examine how some companies are working to improve the usability of their sites.

While these five performance dimensions may initially seem peripheral to a discussion on context or the look-and-feel of a site, performance can greatly affect the user's perception and judgment of this aspect, especially when that site provides slow and unreliable downloads of graphic information.

*Aesthetic.* The aesthetic nature of the site is created by visual characteristics such as colors, graphics, photographs, font choices, and other visually oriented features. Over time, as bandwidth constraints ease for consumer use of the Web, largely visual experiences will expand into so-called rich-media sites enabled by broadband services and including full use of one-way and interactive video and audio as well as text. The following bullets describe two aesthetic features and how they apply to Bluefly.com.

- *Color scheme.* The color scheme refers to the colors used throughout the site. As you might guess, Bluefly has emphasized a blue background for the site. It is a very light, pastel blue that conveys softness, freshness, and youthfulness.

# One Size Doesn't Fit All

by Keith Regan, contributor to tnbt.com

Testing a website used to be simple. If all the links worked, if people could navigate it without too much stress and if the site could stand up to a modest number of hits, it got the green light. But that was before the Internet became the place where many firms conduct most, if not all, of their business, the place where their most critical back-end systems come into play. Testing has taken on new importance in the world of e-commerce.

"There's a lot of testing going on," says Steve Caplow, director of business development at testing firm RSW Software Inc. "But the majority of it is still manual testing, which basically means taking people who happen to be in the office and asking them to bang on the site for a while."

While those hands-on tests can tell a webmaster plenty about a site (whether it makes logical sense for users, for instance), according to Caplow and other testers, it may be missing some more subtle facts—like whether the site can handle a couple thousand hits at once. RSW and Mercury Interactive lead an increasingly crowded pack of firms offering software that monitors sites for potential problems and constantly tests and retests their ability to withstand sudden barrages of traffic.

Load testing, which ensures that sites can stand up to traffic surges, became a hot topic following the rash of denial-of-service attacks that hit big-name sites in the United States and Canada in early 2000. As soon as company IT managers saw that the victim list included Yahoo, eBay, CNN.com, Amazon.com, and Buy.com, load testing came heavily into vogue, especially with e-commerce companies that rely on websites to support the business. Simply hiring a traffic cop sometimes isn't enough, however.

"Manual testing can't track every corner of the globe all the time," said Caplow. But neither, he admits, can automatic testing solve all problems. "Trying to make testing truly push-button is a dream that will never come true. Some aspects will always require somebody to look at it. You can't replace the eyeball."

In other words, while load testing and site monitoring are important, nothing replaces usability testing. For e-commerce sites, whose customers demand rapid results and whose competitors are always just a click away, ignoring the finer points of usability carries considerable risk.

Dan Bricklin, a usability expert, software engineer, and founder of Trellix Corp., which runs a website testing laboratory, says standards are beginning to emerge, with more websites having the same basic design. In fact, Internet shoppers have expectations about the language of sites. For instance, users expect the icon that moves them to the checkout to be called a "shopping cart," and a simple variation such as "shopping basket" can confuse. "You also have to take into account that you have different users, with different experience and comfort level on the Web," he says.

That fact was on the minds of the technical team at SaveDaily.com, a site that enables people to micro-invest in mutual funds with as little as $5 at a time and to get rebates from shopping at certain online merchants. The company recently spent several months redesigning and relaunching its site, reconfiguring the homepage to attract both experienced surfers and novice Internet users.

"We found that we had all the information we needed on the site so all we had to do was change the way it was presented," said Chief Technology Officer David LaVigna. The result is a page in which all of the main features are no more than two clicks away.

After the changes were made, the company set about testing its usability by having employees, friends and family test-drive the redesign. But when it came time to decide whether to continue with further testing before focus groups or additional outside consultants, LaVigna said the firm chose to trust that the early feedback was on target. Call it a different form of usability test: the leap of faith, which means hold your breath, stick to what you like, and hope for the best. Sometimes, as in SaveDaily's case, it works.

(continued on page 193)

*(continued from page 192)*

"We decided to take our chances that what we'd heard to that point would hold true," says LaVigna. "So far, what we're hearing from our customers is backing that up."

*Read more articles about The Next Big Thing at www.tnbt.com*

- *Visual themes.* Visual themes help to tell the story or stories portrayed across the site. The Luckyjeans.com site emphasizes the theme "get lucky" across many of the site pages. While the "get lucky" message is clearly a tag line, it also conveys a consistent story line throughout the site. The Bluefly brand does not appear to carry a theme or story line throughout its site.

# Context Archetypes

Context archetypes refer to broad, generic approaches to context design. There are two broad dimensions of context: function and aesthetics, which can be arrayed in a two-by-two matrix (see Exhibit 6-4). Some argue that there is an inherent trade-off between **form** and **function**. However, with the introduction of new technological capabilities, some feel that trade-offs are not fixed but are changing (i.e., new technologies introduce new techniques that then introduce new aesthetics). However, even given these varying points of view, we consider three context archetypes: aesthetically dominant, functionally dominant, and integrated.

**Exhibit 6-4**

FORM VS. FUNCTION—THE DESIGN CONTEXT FRONTIER

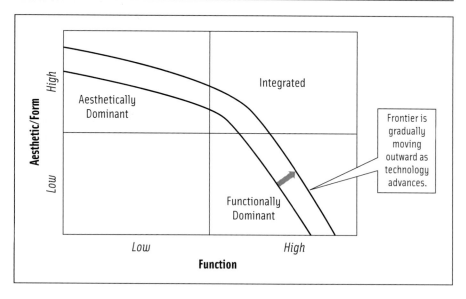

### Aesthetically Dominant.

The aesthetically dominant archetype is categorized by high form, or aesthetics, but low function. The primary emphasis is on the look-and-feel of the website. This type of site makes heavy use of multimedia or visual elements, even though this use may lead to poor performance. These sites contain pages that are visually composed with careful use and placement of the multimedia. Various art forms are frequently used to make these sites a pleasant escape for the user.

A good example of the aesthetic archetype is KMGI (*www.kmgi.com;* see Exhibit 6-5). KMGI is an advertising agency specializing in effective online advertising. It offers a variety of services ranging from Web design to advice on ways to attract audiences to a site. KMGI uses text, graphics, sound, and top-notch animation in its "Webmercials" to create a highly aesthetically pleasing product that is comparable to television commercials in quality. However, the site is slow to load, limited in information for users, and has less evident function than most sites on the Web.

### Functionally Dominant.

As Exhibit 6-4 illustrates, the functionally dominant context archetype has low form but high function. The assumption is that users care little about visual elements or themes on the site, but they care much about information. This type of site focuses on the display of textual information and limits the visual design to the bare minimum required to keep the site operational.

An example of a functionally dominant context archetype is Brint.com (see Exhibit 6-6). Brint.com is all about content (*www.brint.com*). This site is a knowledge source for people in business. It contains sections for different business areas (e.g., E-biz & Electronic Commerce Portal, Knowledge Economy Portal, and General Business Portal). Brint.com derives its success from the plethora of knowledge it makes available to people with questions related to business practices.

The site is pure text—no graphics, sound, or animation. The website is organized by areas of interest. It has a cluttered feel with an abundance of hyperlinks arranged closely to one another on each page. Although Brint.com is almost exclusively composed of textual links, many comparable sites contain content that is user-generated text in the form of chats, ratings, and reviews.

### Integrated.

The integrated archetype is a balance of form and function that creates an attractive and easy-to-use interface (see Exhibit 6-4). This type of site provides navigational tools as visual cues to allow users one-click access to any part of the site. Many times these sites have a clear and appealing theme or themes that support the underlying graphics or color schemes.

A good example of the integrated approach is Patagonia.com (*www.patagonia.com*). Patagonia.com is an online counterpart of the high-quality outdoor clothing and gear retailer (see Exhibit 6-7). Patagonia knows its athletic customers often seek gear for a specific purpose and have provided a website that features three different areas: activity (e.g., skiing), product type (e.g., jackets), and special sale items.

The site is visually pleasing and inviting with its array of outdoor pictures. Each photo tells a story of outdoor adventure and provides the customer a degree of excitement in shopping for gear. Product pages are similarly evocative with photos depicting the beauty of the outdoor activities for which the products are designed, hopefully increasing the user's desire to actively participate.

The site combines the use of a simple design theme, small images (for rapid download), and plenty of white space. Zoom-in photos and further product information are only one click away.

## Exhibit 6-5  AESTHETICALLY DOMINANT EXAMPLE—KMGI.COM

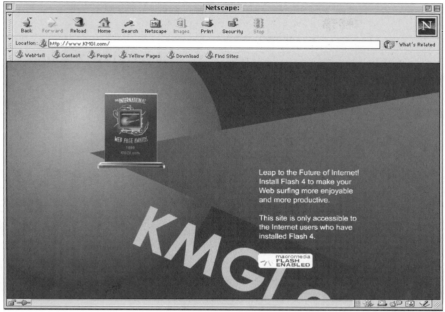

Design by Nikolai Mentchoukov, KMGI.com, Inc.

## Exhibit 6-6  FUNCTIONALLY DOMINANT EXAMPLE—BRINT.COM

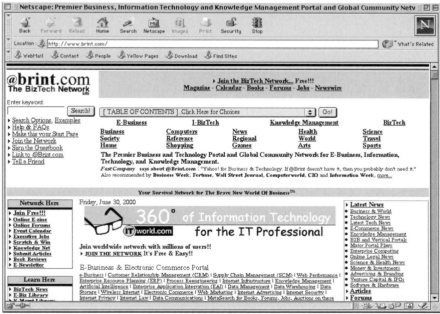

Reprinted with the permission of "@Brint.com The BizTech Network," the Premier Business and Technology Portal and Global Community Network for E-Business, Information Technology and Knowledge Management. http://www.brint.com

**Exhibit 6-7**
INTEGRATED APPROACH
EXAMPLE—PATAGONIA.COM

# WHAT ARE THE FIVE CONTENT ARCHETYPES?

## Content

Content refers to all digital information included on the site. This is broadly conceived to include audio, video, image, and text content.

**Dimensions to Content.** In this section, we consider four dimensions of content: the offering mix, appeal mix, multimedia mix, and content type. As we consider these dimensions, we apply the concepts to a now familiar example, Gear.com.

## Form Vs. Function

Prior to our discussion of content, it is important to note that our suggested context archetype is not fully representative of prevailing views of design. Jeffrey Veen, executive interface director for Wired Digital, the Web-based publisher of *Hotwired*, categorizes sites along two dimensions: form and function.[3] The form dimension is similar to our aesthetic dimension. Veen argues that there is a clear trade-off between form and function. According to Veen, it is impossible to create a site that combines both high function and elegant form. Thus, any attempt to design a site with high form or high function always results in a compromise—and therefore in a suboptimal site.

While Veen's point of view frames the context question, it does not accommodate the constant evolution toward higher function in conjunction with higher form driven by technological advances and increasing bandwidth. We could argue that designers can move sites away from a suboptimal area of low form and low function by increasing form or function or both. Hence, successful sites can be identified along a form versus function frontier. This frontier expands outward with the advent of new technology and new understandings of how to use design in the Web medium, while providing new options to include new techniques and new aesthetics as new forms and new functions.

*Offering Mix.* The content of the site can include product, information, and/or services. Frequently, sites include a mix of these three elements. Gear.com focuses almost exclusively on product content with significantly less emphasis on information or services. Product offerings include items in the outdoor shop, team sports, cycling shop, snow sports, golf shop, and others.

*Appeal Mix.* The appeal mix refers to the promotional and communications messaging projected by the company. Naturally, one would expect the appeal mix to be strongly linked to the value proposition. The academic literature has identified two broad types of appeals: cognitive and emotional. Cognitive appeals focus on functional aspects of the offering, including such factors as low price, reliability, availability, breadth of offerings, customer support, and degree of personalization. Emotional appeals focus on emotionally resonant ties to the product or brand. These include humor, novelty, warmth, or stories. Turning again to Gear.com, its tag line is "brand name sporting goods at closeout prices." This tag line suggests a very functionally or cognitively oriented appeal—good brands at low prices.

*Multimedia Mix.* The multimedia mix refers to the choices of media including text, audio, image, video, and graphics. Gear.com is largely composed of pictures of products, product information, and pricing. There is very limited use of audio, video, and graphics.

*Content Type.* Information that has been collected and presented on a website has a degree of time-sensitivity. Current content is highly time-sensitive information with a very short shelf life. Bloomberg and Reuters are examples of proprietary sources of real-time financial market data. Week-old stock data has limited value, except for archival and research purposes, as compared with stock information that is instantaneous. On the other hand, reference content is less time-sensitive information with a longer shelf life and is often historical in nature. This type of content is used as supporting or related factual material. NYTimes.com is an online publication with an archive of articles published in the past and available for reference. Gear.com provides a great deal of current content (e.g., special deals in a product category, brand, and season) but very little reference content.

## Content Archetypes

In this section, we describe five content archetypes: superstore, category killer, specialty (offering-dominant), information-dominant, and market-dominant. These archetypes are largely derived from the first content dimension, offering mix. We first describe each archetype and then provide a brief description of various sites that are representative of the archetype.

**Offering-Dominant.** Offering archetypes are store sites that sell physical goods and have analog equivalents in the physical world marketplace. In this section, we consider three store types—the superstore, the category killer, and the specialty store. In Exhibit 6-8, we classify these stores on two dimensions: number of product categories (multiple versus single) and depth of product line (narrow versus broad).

*Superstore.* A superstore is a one-stop shop where the customer can find a wide range of goods in multiple product categories. The site is commonly organized by product category and subcategory. The superstore may also offer price comparisons with additional incentives such as price discounts, coupons, and specials.

   Amazon.com (*www.amazon.com*) began as an online store for books but gradually extended its offerings to include a number of product categories including CDs, DVDs and videos, electronics, and toys. Originally, Amazon allowed users to

 **Exhibit 6-8** A FRAMEWORK TO UNDERSTAND OFFERING-DOMINANT ARCHETYPES

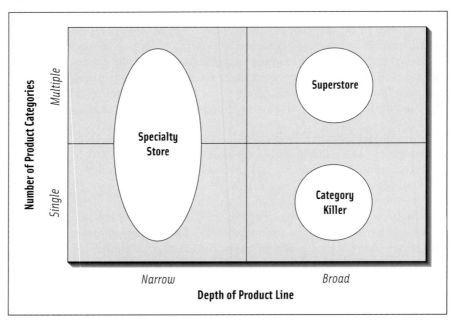

navigate between categories by placing a clickable tab at the top of the screen for each category. As the number of categories that Amazon offered grew, placing a tab on the screen for each category consumed too much space, so now the site presents about five category tabs on a rotating basis for "today's featured stores." A "Store Directory" tab allows users to select a page that allows them to choose from a list of all of Amazon's categories (Amazon had 19 different category stores at the time of writing). Within each category, a row of subtabs situated below each store tab provides immediate access to subcategories within the selected store (see Exhibit 6-9).

In addition to product categories, Amazon introduced the concept of zShops. For a monthly fee, any user can set up his or her own store online in Amazon zShops category and start selling goods. Sellers specify asking price and shipping terms while buyers can accept or reject the deal but are not provided any ability to counteroffer (i.e., no haggling). Upon buyer acceptance of a deal, Amazon contacts the seller and completes the transaction for the buyer.

*Category Killer.* A category killer exclusively provides products and services by specific product or by a customer-needs category. These sites offer a comprehensive selection of products and services but only within the specific category. Category killers also provide extensive product descriptions and recommendations along with additional incentives of price discounts and specials.

PetSmart.com (see Exhibit 6-10) is all about pets. It serves as a one-stop shop for all needs of almost all pet owners. Pets of interest are categorized as dogs, cats, birds, fish, reptiles, and small animals. Users can choose from a variety of products for each pet category. The site also provides chat rooms for interactions with licensed veterinary professionals, message boards for pet owners in each pet category, and responses to frequently asked questions in an answers section.

As the user selects a pet category, the content of the site is adjusted and the website becomes the comprehensive pet store for that particular pet. Any product that the user can think of (for the dog owner, products range from dog apparel and

## SUPERSTORE EXAMPLE— AMAZON.COM

Exhibit 6-9

# Exhibit 6-10 CATEGORY KILLER EXAMPLE— PETSMART.COM

eleven different types of dog food to dog vitamins and supplements) is categorized on the left-hand side of the site. The layout of the page makes it easy for customers to find what they need while unobtrusively presenting additional items to encourage impulse buying. The feeling one gets is, "If it's not here, it's probably not out there."

***Specialty Store.*** A specialty store focuses on exceptional quality and exclusivity while selling single or multiple categories of products. Wine Spectator (*www.winespectator.com*) is an example of a single-category specialty store. An example of a multiple-category specialty store is Frontgate (*www.frontgate.com*). These sites commonly provide high-quality imagery, photographs, and graphics. In addition, they provide extensive descriptions and background information on the products offered. Just as in the physical world, specialty stores tend to offer products or services that cater to customers shopping to fulfill part of a lifestyle need or consideration.

Frontgate is a good example of a specialty store that focuses on lifestyle positioning (see Exhibit 6-11). Frontgate carries a wide variety of home-related products, but the products have an air of traditional quality, high standards, and exclusivity. This is true across a wide range of product categories for the home, including gourmet kitchen goods, bath and outdoor furnishings, and grills.

## Information-Dominant.

Information-dominant content archetypes focus heavily on information, but a subset of these sites focuses on entertainment as well. Information-dominant sites organize and house vast archives of information and provide tools to the customer to explore areas of interest and to find answers to specific questions. These sites can be generators of content, sources of content, or aggregators of content from other sources.

## Exhibit 6-11  SPECIALTY STORE EXAMPLE— FRONTGATE.COM

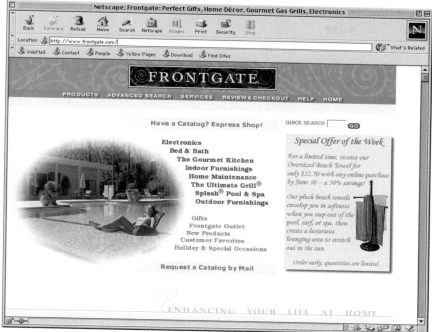

Fast Company.com (*www.fastcompany.com;* see Exhibit 6-12) is an example of an information-dominant site that focuses on providing information on cutting-edge business ideas. From old to new economy, Fast Company puts its readers on the frontier of how strategy is being implemented in dynamic marketplaces. In addition to original content by staff writers and guest columnists, Fast Company reinforces its reputation as a strategy information-dominant site by offering live events, monthly book-club chats, local discussion groups, and online discussion forums. Fast Company creates content that generally falls into one of the following themes: new ways of working, the digital domain, new logic of competition, learning, change, leadership, social justice, innovation and creativity, coping, design, and neoleisure.

### Market-Dominant.

Market-dominant sites do not directly offer goods or services for sale but create a market where buyers and sellers congregate to conduct transactions. These sites serve as brokers and act as catalysts for business deals. A vertical hub is a market site that addresses products and services associated with a single industry, while a horizontal hub serves a functional area across a number of industries. Market sites often provide product comparison tools and industry information, as well as links to supplier sites.

Founded in 1995, Commerx PlasticsNet (see Exhibit 6-13) is a vertical hub for the plastic products industry developed by Commerx, a provider of collaborative e-commerce solutions. It brings together more than 90,000 monthly visitors with over 200 suppliers. The site is not only a marketplace for plastics, but it also provides support for an online community as well as resources that include a supplier directory, material data sheets, an industry publication, job postings, and an education center. The education center is a search engine that allows users to find a

**Exhibit 6-12** INFORMATION DOMINANT EXAMPLE—
FAST COMPANY.COM

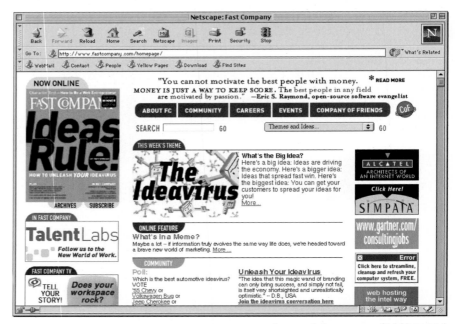

variety of educational programs, books, and seminars specific to their industry segment with one simple search.

Customers are guided through a process to select products of interest as well as their preferred type of transaction (catalog or auction). Customers can create "My Custom Catalogs" by specifying products they prefer to buy and the suppliers from whom they prefer to buy. In the catalog-sales section, the site presents a detailed list of product options with set or negotiated contract prices, and the customers can proceed to complete the transaction. Commerx Global Xchange, accessed through PlasticsNet, provides auction-style pricing where customers can bid on limited-supply products. In most cases, prices drop continually and new products sell quickly. Customers must set their preferences and check back often to complete transactions.

Content archetypes cross all offering types. Table 6-1 shows that each of the content archetypes can be illustrated with a product, information, or service example. Thus, while one has a tendency to think about physical product superstores, the reality is that there are also information superstores (e.g., *www.ceoexpress.com*) and service superstores (e.g., *www.ibmsolutions.com*). Most sites seem to offer a hybrid of these three offering types.

## WHAT MAKES A COMMUNITY?

### Community

Community includes a feeling of membership in a group along with a strong sense of involvement and shared common interests within that group. A group of people can create strong, lasting relationships that may develop into a sense

**Exhibit 6-13**

# MARKET-DOMINANT EXAMPLE—
# COMMERX PLASTICSNET.COM

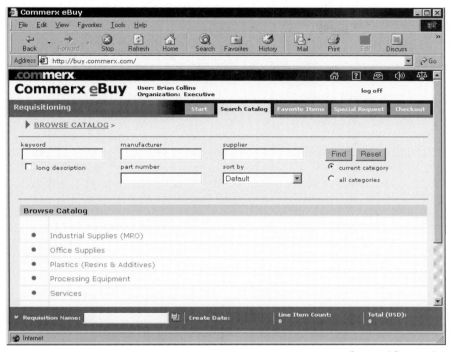

Courtesy of Commerx, Inc.

of community through an engaged and extended exchange of views focused on their shared interests. However, community not only contains elements of common interest and group acceptance. It also contains individual involvement. This sense of community can help encourage users and customers to return to a website.

Community is based on user-to-user communication. This communication can be one-to-one or one-to-many. Several authors have recently investigated community formation and maintenance within e-commerce sites. There are several ways to

**Table 6-1**

# CONTENT ARCHETYPES VS.
# OFFERING TYPES

|  | **Physical Product** | **Information** | **Service** |
|---|---|---|---|
| *Superstore* | Walmart.com | CEOExpress.com | IBMSolutions.com |
| *Category Killer* | PetSmart.com | DowJones.com | Schwab.com |
| *Specialty* | Frontgate | tnbt.com | Tradex.com |
| *Information-Dominant* | Census.gov | IFilm.com | Digitalthink.com |
| *Market-Dominant* | PlasticsNet.com | VerticalNet.com | Monster.com |

## Is Content King?

There is considerable debate concerning the role of content in the success of online businesses. There are a number of pundits who argue that content is king and that the design interface and infrastructure are significantly  less important. The argument has merit. Websites must have excellent content to compete in the targeted segment. Evidence suggests that even within a given product category (e.g., clothing), there are multiple strong content plays (e.g., Nordstrom vs. Lands' End vs. Bluelight). Users are able to discern inferior content due to negative word of mouth and network effects. This information disseminates quickly and drives out inferior content players.

Opponents of this point of view argue that content is certainly important, but it is not the only game in town. First, content is necessary for success, but it is not sufficient in its own right. Second, Web busi-

nesses appear to win more often on number of users than amount of content. Hence, some large, dominant players leverage their brand names to drive out better-content competitors. Third, the most recent information sources, even if they do not have the best content, can win out over the best content providers if the content is not current. Thus, news headline sites can be dominated by content players like *the New York Times* because NYTimes.com updates on a regular but not constant basis. However, for a segment of news junkies who want the freshest content, the Associated Press newswire may be the best source. Finally, *content* is a word that is misused and abused. If content means "just about everything" on the Web, then it loses precision and managerial relevance. Thus, content will always win because "everything is content." This circular argument results in little value.

---

 **Exhibit 6-14** COMMUNITIES—ELEMENTS, TYPES, AND BENEFITS

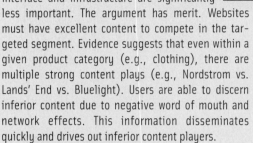

| Elements of Community | Types of Communities | Member Outcomes: Participation and Benefits |
|---|---|---|
| • Cohesion<br>• Effectiveness<br>• Help<br>• Relationships<br>• Language<br>• Self-regulation | Just Friends<br>Enthusiasts<br>Friends in Need<br>Players<br>Traders | Degree of Participation<br><br>• Need Fulfillment<br>• Inclusion<br>• Mutual Influence<br>• Shared Emotional Experiences |

categorize communities, including by elements of a community, types of communities, degrees of participation, and member benefits. Exhibit 6-14 illustrates how these components of a community can be integrated.

## Elements of a Community

The degree of community formation can be assessed along six criteria:[4]

- *Cohesion.* Sense of group identity and individual sense of belonging to the group.
- *Effectiveness.* Impact of the group on members' lives.
- *Help.* Perceived ability to ask for and receive help.
- *Relationships.* Likelihood of individual interaction and friendship formation.
- *Language.* The prevalence of specialized language.
- *Self-Regulation.* The ability of the group to police itself.

## Types of Communities

Several types of groups have been identified. In a later section on archetypes, we provide a complementary classification scheme.

- *Just Friends.* People who want to meet and socialize.
- *Enthusiasts.* People who share a special interest.
- *Friends in Need.* Support groups.
- *Players.* People who participate in game playing.
- *Traders.* People who trade possessions with one another.[5]

## Degree of Member Participation

Users can choose different levels of participation in an online community. In the book *Virtual Reality Case Book*, Randall Farmer describes the following four levels of participation:[6]

- *Passives.* Individuals who do not actively engage in but attend virtual communities.
- *Actives.* Those who participate in activities and topics created by others.
- *Motivators.* Those who create topics and plan activities of interest to other community members.
- *Caretakers.* Those who serve as intermediaries between community members.

## Member Benefits

Participants can derive a number of benefits from participation in a community, including the following:

- *Need Fulfillment.* The degree to which a participant's needs are satisfied.
- *Inclusion.* The extent to which participants are open and encouraged to participate in each other's plans and activities.

- *Mutual influence.* The extent to which participants openly discuss issues and affect one another.
- *Shared emotional experiences.* The extent to which participants include each other in sharing events that specifically arouse feeling and are typically memorable.[7]

## Dimensions of Community

**Interactive Communication.** Users or customers can directly and continually exchange responses with one another as interactive communication. Sites can provide facilities to support real-time or near real-time user-to-user interactive communication as electronic conversation in several forms that include the following:

- *Chat.* Asynchronous chat allows users to consider and formulate a response.
- *Instant Messaging or Instant Chat.* This form allows messages to be exchanged quickly, because each participant sees the message within seconds of when it is sent. Examples include ICQ.com and AOL Instant Messenger. (ICQ is now a subsidiary of AOL.)
- *Message boards.* Message boards allow a user to communicate with another by posting messages on a specific location on the website.
- *Member-to-member e-mail.* E-mail is the killer app of the Web—acting as a virtual post office for digitized messages.

**Noninteractive Communication.** Noninteractive communication does not involve the direct and continual exchange of responses between users. Many times, noninteractive communication is supported by a structure that gives the user a sense of permanence and place rather than a continuous stream of conversation.

Sites or areas of sites can present static information and only allow unidirectional communication with users. Frequently, the site information only needs to be updated periodically. Users can view online information but are not provided any means to respond. Also, users may be controlled and access may be restricted to members-only areas that contain community information. Some users may be allowed access only to public areas that contain community and member profiles that are made available to the general public.

Members make noninteractive contributions to community in two ways:

- *Public member webpages.* Community members may have the option of crafting their own webpages on a particular site.
- *Member content.* Similar to public member webpages, this is content that is generated by members.

## Community Archetypes

In this section, we consider several broad types of communities that have emerged on the Internet. As noted earlier, there are alternative ways to categorize members (recall the approach noted earlier that included "just friends"). However, it is often helpful to consider multiple ways to conceive of Web communities. Again, we borrow names from the bricks-and-mortar world to help us understand their counterparts in the digital world. In this spirit, we introduce six types of virtual communities: bazaar, theme park, club, shrine, theater, and café.[8]

The first three communities are distinguished by the number of interest areas, while the last three vary on the level of interactivity built into the site. We conclude this section with a discussion of ways these two dimensions—interest-area focus and interactivity—can be combined.

**Bazaar.** A bazaar is defined as a community that allows users to wander through a vast number of interest areas but does not provide any means for users to interact with one another in any meaningful way. This virtual space is lined with virtual shops and stalls where users can browse and wander through huge areas. The bazaar can be similar to a portal in that many times the user arrives only to be presented with links to many other destinations. Plus, users have no specific common interest to share or to focus on. The bazaar offers the user an unstructured sense of exploration but only unengaged or limited interactions with other users and a sense of community is not easily planted.

Yahoo Games is a typical example of a bazaar. Yahoo Games is a play world for Web wanderers (see Exhibit 6-15). The site is a wide collection of free, Java-based games. These are games that can be played alone or with multiple players connected to the Internet. Users wander through any of the available open play rooms and invite other room participants to play with them. Although friends might invite one another to play a game online or players might be able to comment on game results, community is not a high priority. The goal here is to have fun playing the games that the site provides.

**Exhibit 6-15**
BAZAAR EXAMPLE—
GAMES.YAHOO.COM

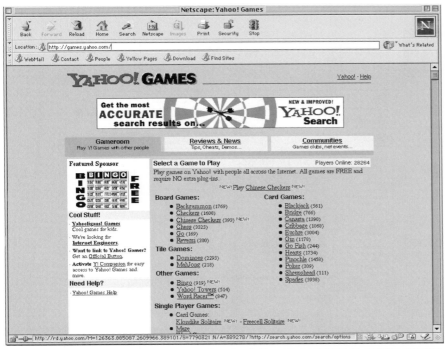

Reproduced with permission of Yahoo! Inc. ©2000 by Yahoo! Inc.
YAHOO! and the YAHOO! logo are trademarks of Yahoo! Inc.

**Theme Park.** A theme park is defined as a community that focuses on a finite number of interest areas that are organized by categories and subcategories. These sites commonly host a large number of communities. Members interact with one another, but few strong bonds are formed. SpeakOut.com (see Exhibit 6-16) is an interactive community where individuals, organizations, and businesses interact with one another to take action concerning political, civic, and social issues. It enables users to create communities around issues that include education, family, health, environment, society, and economics. Users are encouraged to share information, speak out on issues, and connect with others who have common interests to build and mobilize support for causes. Members can get informed, contribute text to newsletters and clubs, or start their own discussion group or newsletter. The site also allows members to reach out to their communities by providing e-mail links to local politicians and newspapers.

**Club.** A club is defined as a community that is highly focused on only one area of interest and promotes a considerable amount of interaction among members. These sites typically provide large volumes of information about the targeted area or the areas of interest. Gillette Women's Cancer Connection site (*www.gillettecancerconnect.org;* see Exhibit 6-17) provides a community where women can discuss all of the issues associated with any form of women's cancer. Community activities include chats, message boards, and special events. This community has a single point of focus—women learning about cancer and living with the disease.

**Shrine.** A shrine is defined as a highly focused community with minimal interaction between members. The essence of the shrine is evidence of member activities that exhibit extreme enthusiasm toward a common person or object of interest. Although these sites many times provide chat opportunities and message-board facilities, only a minimal amount of interaction occurs among members. However, the greater part of the community content is member-contributed. These commu-

**Exhibit 6-16** THEME PARK EXAMPLE— SPEAKOUT.COM

| Exhibit 6-17 | CLUB EXAMPLE—GILLETTE WOMEN'S CANCER CONNECTION |

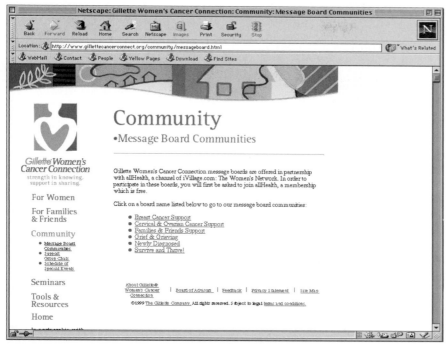

Illustration appears with permission of The Gillette Company

nities have high membership involvement, highly focused subject matter, and capabilities for interactive communication, but member-to-member exchanges are in the form of offering icons rather than conversation. The sense of community is muted by an intensely personal, rather than public, site experience.

An example is the Unofficial Dawson's Creek Web-Site (*http://dawsonsite.cjb.net*). It is composed of a number of areas that include biographies of the TV show's characters, an episode guide, still photographs, an unofficial newsletter, and links to other *Dawson's Creek* sites. There is also a news and rumors section. This site does encourage some level of interaction by including a message board and chat room.

Many shrine websites are unofficial in that the people operating the sites are not affiliated in any way with the sites' featured persons or objects of adoration. These sites often contain unauthorized copyrighted materials, but because the sites are operated by fans and do not have any commercial aspect, copyright holders have tended not to prosecute.

**Theater.** A theater is a community that is focused in a particular area but allows for moderate interaction among members. These sites present provocative and compelling content to trigger member interactions and to drive membership involvement in the form of conversation or reviews that are then used to further drive site content. IFilm.com (see Exhibit 6-18) is a film portal site that hosts independent films free of charge and provides filmmakers a previously unreachable audience. Site users download posted movies and view them online. Hosted films can receive immediate online reviews and ratings by online viewers. Although additional community-building tools are provided on the site (e.g., message boards and chat rooms), the online reviews and

Exhibit
6-18

# THEATER EXAMPLE—IFILM.COM

©IFILM Corp.

ratings are considered highly valuable community content. Because they are generated as a result of the original content on the site, they reinforce membership.

**Café.** A café is defined as a community that focuses on a common area of interest but also provides considerable interaction among members. At this type of site, the primary focus is on conversation among members, with an easily accessible and appropriately configured platform that supports the interaction. These sites also have the highest amount of interaction among community members. Typically, users are highly active in both receiving and creating content. Bolt (see Exhibit 6-19) is a popular online destination for teens and young adults (aged 15-24). The main reason users come to the site is to communicate with their peers and voice their opinions. Bolt provides a variety of free communication tools to encourage community participation such as chat rooms, message boards, clubs, photo services, instant messaging, polls, e-mail, wireless services, and homepage hosting. Ninety-five percent of site content is created by site users. Topics of discussion range from school to music to parents to dating.

At the outset of this section, we noted that community archetypes could be divided into two dimensions. The first dimension is the degree of focus—from a single area to multiple areas of interest. The second dimension is the degree of member interactivity related to the site. In Exhibit 6-20, we cross these two dimensions to create nine possible community types. Interestingly, this chart illustrates that a number of hybrid communities can form by combining interactivity and focus in unique ways.

**Exhibit 6-19**

## CAFE EXAMPLE—BOLT.COM

©Bolt, Inc., 2000.

**Exhibit 6-20**

## FOCUS VS. INTERACTIVITY

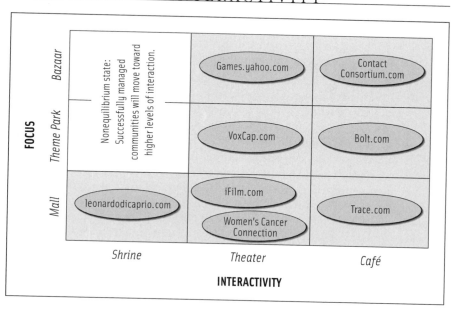

# WHAT ARE THE LEVERS USED TO CUSTOMIZE A SITE?

## Customization

Customization refers to a site's ability to tailor itself to each user or be tailored by each user. To better address individual user needs, a site can be designed to be altered by the user or by the organization. Customization can be initiated by the user, a process we term personalization, or by the organization, a process we term tailoring.

## Dimensions of Customization

*Personalization.* Some websites allow users to specify their preferences in content selection, context selection, and personalization tools. Once personal preferences have been entered by the user and saved, the site uses log-in registration or "cookies" to match each returning user to his or her respective personal setting. The site then configures itself to these preferences accordingly. To attract users and to keep them returning, the site provides a variety of features that include personalized e-mail accounts, virtual hard-disk storage, and software agents that perform simple tasks.

- *Log-in registration.* Having previously registered on a site, the user returns and enters the requisite identification information. The site recognizes the returning user and configures itself to the preset preferences accordingly.
- *Cookies.* Most website owners want to identify and understand the users of their sites and the use of their sites. These sites frequently attempt to track and gather data about the returning users' behavior by quietly saving, identifying, and tracking information on the users' local disk storage in temporary files called cookies.
- *Personalized e-mail accounts.* Many sites provide e-mail accounts free of charge to the user. Users may send and receive e-mail from the site, using a unique e-mail address.
- *Content and layout configuration.* Users can select site screen layout and content sources based on their interests.
- *Storage.* Sites provide virtual hard-disk storage space. Users can store e-mail, URLs, and other interesting content on these sites.
- *Agents.* Users can initiate computer programs, also known as agents, that are designed to perform specific simple tasks (e.g., notify them via e-mail when a product is in stock).

*Tailoring by Site.* Many sites have the ability through their software to dynamically publish unique versions of the site to address a specific user's interests, habits, and needs more appropriately. The site can be designed to reconfigure and present different content with various design layouts to individual users, depending on each user's responses and/or profile. A site can use a recommendation engine (e.g., collaborative filtering as developed by Firefly or NetPerceptions) to adapt automatically to each user's behavior and to vary the site's offering mix of products, information, and services. The site can also further recommend content or products that the user is likely to find of interest. Recommendations can be made based on past purchases by the user or based on purchases by other users with similar purchase profiles. A site can be automated to offer each user more suitable price and payment terms. Marketing messages can also be developed for the individual user based on exhibited behavior or declared preferences.

- *Tailoring based on past user behavior.* Many sites adjust themselves dynamically, based on a user's past behavior and preferences. Examples of automated adjustments include price, payment terms, and marketing messages.
- *Tailoring based on behavior of other users with similar preferences.* Some sites make recommendations to the user based on preferences of other users with similar usage profiles (e.g., collaborative filtering).

---

## DRILL-DOWN

# Customize This!
by Peter Meyers, staff writer at tnbt.com

"The customer can have any color he wants—so long as it's black," Henry Ford famously declared. Good thing Ford wasn't trying to peddle his Model T on the Internet: He wouldn't have made it out of Dearborn. When it comes to consumer goods and services on the Web, the customer rules, and customization is king. Consider the following businesses, spanning the spectrum of consumer e-commerce categories, that have made catering to individual tastes cornerstones of their enterprises:

### Products: Interactive Custom Clothes Company

You no longer have to be rich to have your clothes custom-made—just wired. The Interactive Custom Clothes Company offers shoppers the ability to custom design bags, dresses, jackets, pants, and other sartorial accoutrements, with the unique online benefit of try-before-you-buy visual sampling. The site guides you step-by-step through all the choices and measurements you'll need to create your online ensemble. Or you can simply send in a good-fitting sample, and the company will replicate it using whatever new fabrics you've chosen from their wide-ranging catalog—including faux cow fur, metallic pink vinyl and "living rubber," a fabric whose color changes according to your body temperature. (Don't ask.)

### Content: Thomson Learning's TextChoice

By now everyone's familiar with the custom homepage services offered by major portals and news providers (e.g., My Yahoo and myCnn). Educational publisher Thomson offers a slightly more elaborate variation on this theme through its TextChoice service, which lets users—mainly teachers—publish customized books comprised of content from its wide-ranging catalog of books. You get to mix and match the content you want and—voila—Thomson will publish and deliver to you a real, dead-tree book. (Actually, it takes about four weeks from creation to delivery.)

Among TextChoice's nifty features are the creation of a customized table of contents (complete with automatically generated page numbers), the ability to include one's own material in the book, and a previewing function that lets you view your creation online.

### Services: Monster

Monster, the leading online job-hunting site, offers customization features that showcase Web listings' superiority to their offline counterparts. In other words, no more eye-blearing searches through column after column of classifieds—and no forgetting where you left off when you pause for an eye-cleansing respite from four-point type. Instead, the site features the ability to post up to five different resumes, the use of search agents that continually scan Monster's job listings and e-mail users about relevant openings and the ability to provide different levels of access to your resume. (For example, if you want to job hunt without running the risk of alerting your boss, you can mask personally identifying details about your current job.)

### Online Stores: Webvan

With their huge inventories, megastores like Wal-Mart and Winn-Dixie can induce an overwhelming feeling that there's just too much to choose from.

*(continued on page 214)*

*(continued from page 213)*

Many early online stores suffered from similar short-comings, succumbing to the temptation to display every item in their inventory database because, well, they could. Now, more online stores are using the power of customization to display a much narrower selection of goods and services based partially on what shoppers say they want, partially on what technology is able to guess they'll want.

Webvan, one of the earliest of the online grocery shopping services, offers a good example of how "my store" features can make e-commerce not only more convenient, but more efficient. The site's "My Personal Market" option allows individual customers to quickly access frequently purchased goods, items from their most recent order and a listing of every item they've ever bought at Webvan. Customers can also create customized shopping lists for different events—birthday parties, dinner parties, etc.

**Marketing: MotherNature.com**

The new wave in unsolicited e-mail campaigns fore-goes that crass mass-marketing technique known as spamming in favor of targeted, personalized e-mails. For instance, MotherNature.com, which sells natural vitamins and other healthcare products, now sends out periodic electronic missives to its customers offering special deals based on what the shopper has previously browsed and purchased on the site. And traditional e-mails aren't MotherNature.com's only opportunity to make custom pitches: It uses its automated e-mail purchase receipts to get shoppers thinking about their next purchase. The customer who's just bought a couple of bottles of St. John's Wort, for instance, may find that his receipt offers him a discount on an "Anxiety Attack Pack" (including valerian root extract, kavatrol, chamomile tea and "herbal calm" capsules).

*Read more articles about The Next Big Thing at www.tnbt.com*

# Customization Archetypes

Customization archetypes are websites grouped by the source of customization—that is, either personalization by the user or tailoring by the site.

**Personalization by User.** This form of customization (**personalization by user**) enables the user to modify site content and context based on consciously articulated and acted-upon preferences. The user can make layout selections and content source selections. Users of mylook.com (see Exhibit 6-21) can toggle off or toggle on presentation of headlines from a list of news sources as well as images from a list of webcams. Configurations for four layouts are offered and depending on the layout selected, four to six webcam images can be viewed simultaneously.

**Tailoring by Site.** This form of customization (**tailoring by site**) enables the site to reconfigure itself based on past behavior by the user or by other users with similar profiles. These sites can make recommendations based on past purchases, filter marketing messages based on user interests, and adjust prices and products based on user profiles. Amazon (see Exhibit 6-22) uses collaborative filtering to compare each user's purchases with the purchases of other users with similar preferences to create a list of additional purchase recommendations. Amazon also makes recommendations across product categories. For example, based on a user's history of book purchases, the site recommends CDs or DVDs that others with similar book interests have bought.

# WHAT TYPES OF COMMUNICATION CAN A FIRM MAINTAIN WITH ITS CUSTOMER BASE?

## Communication

Communication refers to dialogue that is initiated by the organization. The dialogue may be unidirectional (one-way from the organization to the user) or more interactive.

**Dimensions of Communication.** In the following paragraphs, we describe and provide examples of three dimensions of communication: broadcast, interactive, and hybrid.

*Broadcast.* Broadcast communication is a one-way information exchange from organization to user. With this unidirectional transmission of information, organizations provide no mechanism for the user to make a return response. In general, broadcast is a one-to-many relationship between the website and its users. Below, we describe the alternative forms of broadcast communication.

- *Mass mailings.* Mass mailings are the broadcast transmissions of large volumes of e-mail targeted at relatively large audiences.

*(continued from page 214)*
alize an experience needs to have information about what you like and what you don't like or what you bought in the past or what you might buy in the future, and so there's a real tension there because people are becoming increasingly uneasy about the concept of their personal information being widely available. . . . So it's going to require a very sort of delicate balance between these issues of privacy and personalization.

*Get the full interview at www.marketspaceu.com*

---

## POINT OF VIEW

## Kamran Parsaye's Methodology for Measuring Personalization

In his article "PQ: The Personalization Quotient of a Website," Kamran Parsaye attempts to develop a methodology for calculating a site's degree of personalization. According to Parsaye's article, the Personalization Quotient (PQ) has three components:

- Customization (PQ1) measures the system's ability to customize items by allowing individual users to set their own preferences.
- Individualization (PQ2) measures the system's ability to customize itself to the user based on the user's exhibited behavior.
- Group-characterization (PQ3) measures the system's ability to customize itself to the user based on the preferences of other users with similar interests.

Parsaye then takes the average of these three quotients to derive the Personalization Quotient of a website: $PQ = (PQ1 + PQ2 + PQ3)/3$

The following presents ways to calculate each of these three quotients:

- Customization (PQ1) can be measured by taking the ratio of all the options that the user is allowed to change (call that Allowed) over all the options that could possibly be changed (call that Possible).
- Individualization (PQ2) can be measured by calculating the percentage of times that the item the site selects for a user is an item of maximum interest to him or her. If U is a user and Nj is item j on a site and match (U, Nj) gives the level of interest of item Nj to user U, then
  PQ2 = % times match (U, Nj) is maximized.
- Group Characterization (PQ3) can be measured by calculating how often similar users get shown similar pages. If $\delta U = \delta(U1, U2)$ is the difference between User 1 and User 2 and $\delta P = \delta(P1, P2)$ is the difference between Page 1 (viewed by User 1) and Page 2 (viewed by User 2), then PQ3 = 100/maximum ($\delta U/\delta P$, $\delta P/\delta U$).

Exhibit
6-21
## PERSONALIZATION BY USER
## EXAMPLE—MYLOOK.COM

Exhibit
6-22
## TAILORING BY SITE EXAMPLE—
## AMAZON.COM

- *FAQ.* Organizations post webpages with clear answers to frequently asked questions (FAQs) about the site, goods, or services.
- *E-Mail newsletters.* Regular newsletters are sent by e-mail to inform site subscribers of new features or changes to a site, special offers, letters from other subscribers, corporate news, etc.
- *Content-Update reminders.* E-mail messages can be further tailored to reflect each subscriber's interests and serve as a content-update reminder of relevant new content now available.
- *Broadcast events.* Also, events can be broadcast (or sometimes referred to as webcast) from a website that allows limited user control over variables such as camera view.

**Interactive.** Interactive communication is two-way communication between the organization and a user. The following are three alternative forms of interactive communication:

- *E-Commerce dialogue.* Organizations use two-way communication as part of the e-commerce dialogue. Organizations and users regularly trade e-mail messages regarding order placement, tracking, and fulfillment.
- *Customer service.* Organizations can provide customer service through the swapping of e-mail or through live online dialogue.
- *User input.* Another two-way communication occurs when user input is an integral part of the content of a site (e.g., user-generated articles on topics of interest, user ratings of suppliers, and user feedback to the site).

**Hybrid.** Hybrid communication, as its name indicates, is a combination of broadcast and interactive communications. These sites offer software tools as "freeware" that users can download and use at no charge for their work or entertainment. Users often pass this free software to friends and, in essence, provide free marketing to the originating site. Companies use this technique of viral marketing with the hope of rapid, broad distribution and immediate creation of brand recognition.

## Communication Archetypes

Communication archetypes are grouped by types of site-to-user communication and user-to-site communication.

**One-to-Many, Nonresponding User.** This type of site communicates with users through mass mailings targeted at defined audiences. Communications typically are in the form of e-mail newsletters or broadcast events. Site messages are announcements that users receive without needing to respond. Site content is presented with no means for customer response. Content on TheStandard.com (see Exhibit 6-23) is both exclusive to the website and from *the Industry Standard* publication. Site newsletters, 19 at the time of this writing, are broadcast to registered users. Users can select from newsletters based on their interests. However, newsletters are broadcast to readers with no one-to-one or tailored messages.

**One-to-Many, Responding User.** This type of site communicates with a mass of users who have logged on as registered users or through e-mailings targeted at specific users. Site messages are invitations to users to submit their comments and responses.

**Exhibit 6-23** ONE-TO-MANY, NONRESPONDING EXAMPLE—THESTANDARD.COM

Reprinted by permission of the *Industry Standard, www.TheStandard.com*

BizRate.com (*www.bizrate.com;* see Exhibit 6-24) is a good example of this type of communication. Customers rate their experience with online merchants on multiple dimensions and provide comments regarding their performance. BizRate.com places a pop-up survey on the receipt page of member online stores and independently invites actual online buyers to participate in the BizRate.com survey. BizRate.com uses a two-part survey to measure the online experience both at the point of sale and after fulfillment. The survey's first part is delivered immediately after a purchase is completed and the second is e-mailed shortly after the scheduled product delivery date.

**One-to-Many, Live Interaction.** This type of site allows users to interact with the site live, with information exchanged back and forth in real time. This exchange is often in the form of live chat. Accrue Software Inc. (see Exhibit 6-25), a leading software provider to online businesses, hosts Web seminars that are broadcast live to users. Users are able to register, dial in for live audio streaming, and participate in real time in the Web seminars. Users can also submit questions either online or via phone.

**One-to-One, Nonresponding User.** This type of site sends personalized messages to users to address specific user interests or needs. This information can be in the form of real-time updates or reminders. The site provides no means for customer response, and users receive site messages without any need to respond. As part of its online offering, the American Greetings site extended services from simple online cards and shopping to provide a group of tools that became a vehicle through which users could express themselves, manage their important dates and events, and manage their relationships. Americangreetings.com now offers a feature in

**Exhibit 6-24**

ONE-TO-MANY, RESPONDING USER
EXAMPLE—BIZRATE.COM

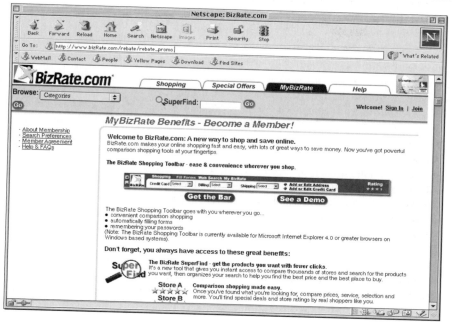

©BizRate.com

Copyright Accrue Software, Inc.

which the user provides details surrounding important events (birthday, anniversary, etc.), and the American Greetings site then later sends an e-mail reminder to the user at a user-determined time prior to each event. Apart from entering information required to enable American Greetings' personalized tools, users do not submit content to the site.

**One-to-One, Responding User.** This type of site sends users personalized messages that address specific user interests or needs. This information can include real-time updates, reminders, or information to the user. Users respond to the site by submitting content of interest or specifics of tailored transactions. Amazon.com is a hybrid communication archetype that uses one-to-one, responding-user communication. The zShops feature provides a broadcast platform that allows users to create their own storefront. For a low monthly fee, users post all information associated with their offerings and sell through the popular Amazon site. As an interactive site, Amazon allows users to check the status of their orders through queries to the site as well as automatic site transmission of e-mails. Upon order submission, Amazon sends a personal e-mail message to the customer confirming receipt of the order. Upon order shipment, Amazon sends a second e-mail message to the customer notifying him or her of the outbound order (see Exhibit 6-26).

**One-to-One, Live Interaction.** This type of site sends and receives personalized user messages or carries on chat sessions that address specific user interests or needs. Users interact live on the site with information exchanged in real time. LivePerson provides websites with a software tool that allows live customer service and sales. The software utilizes real-time text dialogue to enable sites to interact with visitors. LivePerson's

**Exhibit 6-26**

ONE-TO-ONE, RESPONDING USER
EXAMPLE—AMAZON.COM

AMAZON.com is the registered trademark of Amazon.com, Inc.

intent is to help sites provide consumers a level of personal service that is at least equal to that of traditional retailers. The goal is to make e-commerce more user-friendly and more profitable. LivePerson enabled sites present a button or pop-up window to allow the visitor to begin the dialogue. The user enters his or her name and selects from a list of available customer service representatives. This personalized chat experience allows the user to choose a familiar person. During the LivePerson chat, the user and representative exchange information in real time on a one-to-one basis (see Exhibit 6-27). Today, several companies are beginning to offer a similar service based on voice-over-IP technology, rather than text messaging technology. As bandwidth increases, sites with a customer-service focus are likely to adopt this technology.

# HOW DOES A FIRM CONNECT WITH OTHER BUSINESSES?

## Connection

Connection is the degree to which a given site is able to link to other sites through a hypertext jump or hyperlink from one webpage to another. These links are embedded in a webpage and are most commonly presented to the user as underlined and highlighted words, a picture, or a graphic. The user's click on the link initiates the immediate delivery of a text, graphic, or sound file or a webpage that can be a combination of all these types of files. Files may reside on the local server or on a server that might be anywhere in the world.

 **Exhibit 6-27** ONE-TO-ONE, LIVE INTERACTION EXAMPLE—LIVEPERSON.COM

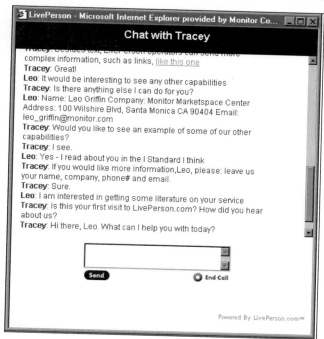

Courtesy of LivePerson, Inc.

**Dimensions of Connection.** Connections vary in type, magnitude, and direction. The following are five dimensions of connection:

*Links to Sites.* This refers to links that take the user completely outside the home site and into a third-party site. For example, users of NYTimes.com may access book reviews; in that section, a link to Barnes & Noble.com (also bn.com) appears, as it does in other parts of the site, with an offer relating to its online retail bookstore. Users who click on the bn.com logo wind up on the bn.com site, where they can then pursue their shopping interests in a new environment.

*Home Site Background.* This refers to a situation where the link takes the user to a third-party site, but the home site is noticeable in the background. Users of Ditto.com, a search engine for images on the Web, can click on any thumbnail image and examine the site from where the image was retrieved. This site opens over the Ditto.com page in a smaller frame that hovers above the full-size browser window.

*Outsourced Content.* This refers to when the site content is derived from third parties, with the source of that content labeled clearly. The user remains in the home site environment. Many sites use stock quotes and news feeds to augment their appeal to users, even as these content plug-ins are identified by their sources (e.g., Associated Press, CNN.com, *www.weather.com*).

*Percent of Home Site Content.* This refers to the percentage of content that originates from the home site. Like newspapers that make use of wire-service stories, not all the content on any given site is generated, owned, or controlled by that site. As a result, it is important to understand how content is insourced or outsourced with respect to a given site's content strategy.

*Pathway of Connection.* The pathway of the connection can lead a user outside the environment of the site as a "pathway-out." It can also lead a user to retrieval from other sites, but not by formally leaving the site, as a "pathway-in." More specifically, pathway-out is where links are absolute in the sense that the user's click causes the absolute exit from the website. Pathway-in refers to situations where links are hybrid and the user's click causes the retrieval of material from the same or other sites without an exit from the current website.

## Connection Archetypes

In this section, we consider six alternative connection approaches. We begin with a discussion of three instances of pathway-out approaches and conclude with overviews of three pathway-in designs.

**Destination Site.** **Destination sites** almost exclusively provide site-generated content with very few links to other sites. These sites frequently are valued by users for integrity and trustworthiness of content, and disclose extensive information about the providers of their content. Many times, these destination sites license their content to other sites as third-party providers. NYTimes.com, *The New York Times*' site, not only includes the daily contents of the newspaper but also publishes exclusive feature stories (see Exhibit 6-28) that appear on the site only. The site provides news updates every 10 minutes. As with the physical newspaper, content is almost exclusively site-generated and links to other websites are very limited.

**Exhibit 6-28**

# DESTINATION EXAMPLE— NYTIMES.COM

**Hub Site.** **Hub sites** provide a combination of site-generated content and selective links to sites of related interests (see Exhibit 6-29). Many times, external links are to expert or related sites on specific topics of interest. For example, IndustryCentral (*www.industrycentral.net*), a motion picture and television industry site, is a hub that provides external links to various local film commissions, production studios, and other production-related resources, as well as to film festivals. IndustryCentral serves as the primary portal to Crew-List.net, an industry resume service for film and television cast and crew. IndustryCentral also provides information concerning the production and distribution of film and television products to industry professionals. In addition, the site supplies industry news content through links to third parties such as Hollywood.com and PR Newswire, as well as to Reuters, *Rolling Stone,* and *Entertainment Weekly* through iSyndicate.com.

**Portal Site.** **Portal sites** consist almost exclusively of links to a large number of other sites (see Exhibit 6-30). Portals usually provide a vast array of links to provide the widest possible reach to other sites but present very little or no site-generated content. Yahoo is one of the most well-known and established portals (*www.yahoo.com*). Yahoo users can easily reach thousands of sites, although, as impressive as this sounds, this constitutes only a small fraction of all available sites. Yahoo carries little or no original content on its site.

**Affiliate Programs.** Websites with **affiliate programs** direct users to affiliated websites through links or through links embedded in site banners or other advertising materials (see Exhibit 6-31). Users of OnHealth shopping (*www.onhealth.com*) can

Exhibit
6-29

# HUB EXAMPLE—
## INDUSTRYCENTRAL.NET

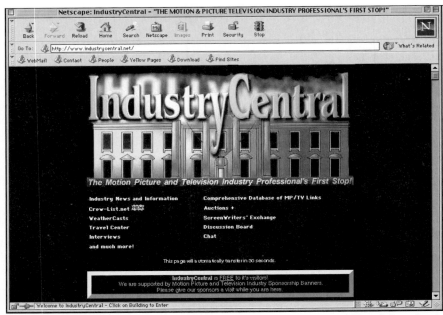

©Bruce P. Simon, Founder

Exhibit
6-30

# PORTAL EXAMPLE—
## YAHOO.COM

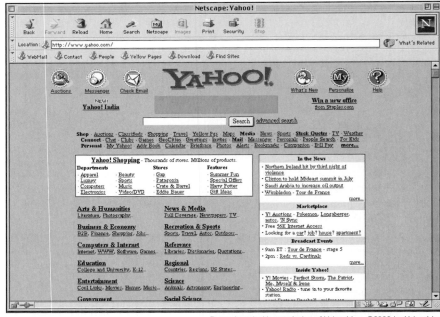

Reproduced with permission of Yahoo! Inc. ©2000 by Yahoo! Inc.
YAHOO! and the YAHOO! logo are trademarks of Yahoo! Inc.

**Exhibit 6-31**

AFFILIATE PROGRAM EXAMPLE—
ONHEALTH.COM and
PROFLOWERS.COM

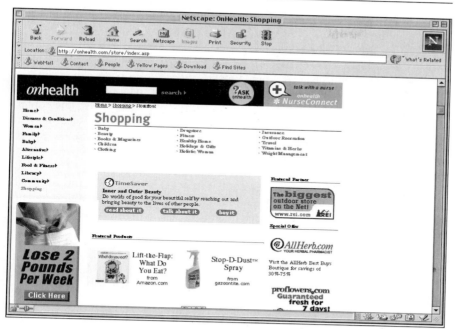

©Onhealth Network Company

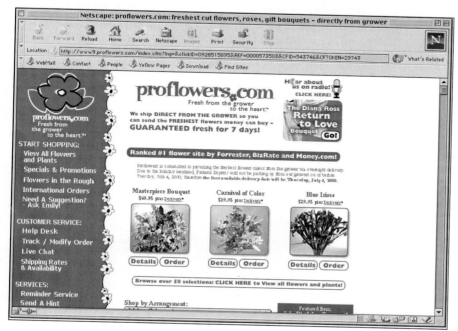

Courtesy of Proflowers.com

choose from a variety of products, some from providers other than OnHealth. For example, users who click on the proflowers.com icon on this site get transferred to the proflowers.com shopping environment where the user can make flower purchases. Although users are now shopping at proflowers.com, they remain in the OnHealth shopping environment and can easily move back to the OnHealth site by clicking on the prominent OnHealth band at the top of the page.

**Outsourced Content.** Websites often contain **outsourced content**, or content that has been generated by third parties. Many times, third-party suppliers can create content of higher quality, greater appeal, or at a lower cost than a website operation. Outsourced content can be well integrated within a website. Often, the content provider is displayed clearly with a link to its site (see Exhibit 6-32). Real.com is an established player in streaming-media technology for the Internet. The RealSystem software (including the RealPlayer) delivers content on more than 85 percent of all streaming-media-enabled webpages (*www.realplayer.com*). Real.com presents outsourced broadcast content from established content sources that include CNN Interactive, BBC News Online, and National Public Radio. By outsourcing content, Real.com focuses on its core competency to further develop software while still maintaining a stimulating and appealing site.

## Exhibit 6-32  OUTSOURCED CONTENT EXAMPLE—REAL.COM

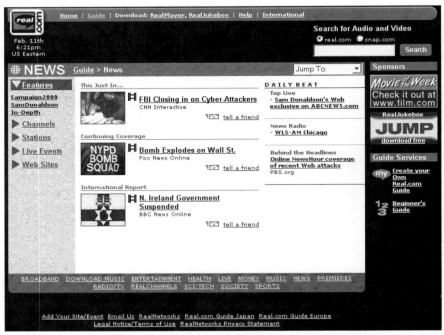

**Meta-Software.** **Meta-software** consists of utility and plug-in software applications created to assist users in narrowly defined tasks. These applications may stand alone on the user's desktop or as plug-ins to the Internet browser. Applications can be set to pop up and appear without the user requesting assistance (see Exhibit 6-33). For example, R U Sure's goal is to make online shopping less burdensome, more efficient, and more economical for the shopper (*www.rusure.com*) by offering users a free shopping agent that allows the user to easily conduct comparative shopping on the Internet for any requested product. While the user browses a supported site, the comparative shopping search engine searches other sites and notifies the user, within seconds, of any available lower prices. This task is done before the user completes a purchase and without requiring the user to leave the particular site being browsed. The R U Sure site also provides product reviews, classified ads, message boards, shop reviews, directories, auctions, e-shopping advice, and consumer comments.

**Exhibit 6-33** META-SOFTWARE EXAMPLE— RUSURE.COM

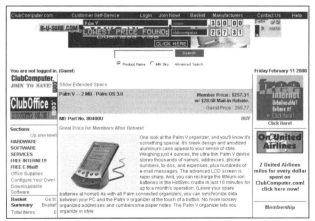

# WHAT ARE ALTERNATIVE PRICING MODELS OF COMMERCE ARCHETYPES?

## Commerce

Commerce capabilities are those features of the customer interface that support the various aspects of trading transactions. In the next section, we focus on functional tools and conclude with a discussion of alternative pricing approaches.

**Dimensions of Commerce.** Functional tools are the commerce-enabling features of a website. For a site to have e-commerce capabilities, a number of features must be present that include, but are not limited to, the following:

- *Registration.* User registration allows a site to store credit-card information, shipping addresses, and preferences.
- *Shopping Cart.* Users can place items into their personal, virtual shopping cart. Items can be purchased immediately or stored and purchased when the user returns on another visit to the site.
- *Security.* Sites attempt to guarantee the security of transactions and related data through encryption (e.g., SSL) and authentication technologies (e.g., SET).
- *Credit-Card Approval.* Sites can have the ability to receive instant credit approval for credit-card purchases through electronic links to credit-card clearance houses.
- *One-Click Shopping.* Amazon.com uses a patented feature that allows users to place and order products with a single click. Current delivery default settings are applied automatically.
- *Orders Through Affiliates.* Sites with affiliate programs must be able to track orders that originate from affiliate sites as well as determine affiliate fees for business generation.
- *Configuration Technology.* Users can put products and services together in a variety of permutations with the aid of configurator software, thus allowing analysis of performance/price trade-offs, interoperability among complex components within a system, and substitution of generic for branded products.
- *Order Tracking.* Users are provided with the ability to check the delivery status of products that they have ordered.
- *Delivery Options.* Users are presented with a choice of options to specify their desired speed and cost of delivery (e.g., next day, two-day shipping, or five-day shipping).

## Commerce Archetypes

In this section, we review a number of prototypic examples of contrasting commercial transaction models.

**Catalog Pricing.** With **catalog pricing**, the price of goods and services is preset by the seller. Users select items from displayed catalogs and pay the associated prices. These sites provide detailed pictures and other product specifications. Barnes &

# Commerce Origination Vs. Facilitation

Table 6-2 provides a more detailed review of two general approaches to generating commerce. The first approach involves commerce that originates at the site. New customer acquisition tools include online advertising, viral marketing, and offline advertising (to be discussed in Chapter 7). Commerce can also be facilitated through third-party intervention to deliver traffic to a site. This can be achieved through affiliate network relationships, "distribution deals" for ad banner and icon placement, and partnerships with related groups and third-party associations.

**Table 6-2** COMMERCE ORIGINATION VS. FACILITATION

| Commerce Origination | Commerce Facilitation |
|---|---|
| • Commerce originating at a site. It is achieved through acquisition of new customers and loyalty building among existing customers. <br> • New customer acquisition tools include <br>   – *Online advertising* <br>     – Banner ads at other sites <br>     – URL listing in industry catalogs <br>     – Sponsorships of online events or of other site activities <br>   – *Viral marketing* <br>     – Marketing with the assistance of existing customers, who pass marketing messages along to friends or colleagues <br>     – Examples include marketing footers at the end of user e-mail messages and prompts inviting users to send the site URL or the output of their activity on the site to others <br>   – *Offline advertising* <br>     – Advertisements on radio, television, and in movie theaters <br>     – Sponsorships of offline events, such as conferences on the new economy | • Commerce facilitated through the intervention of a third party directing traffic to a site. It can be achieved through affiliations and partnerships <br> • Affiliations/partnerships <br>   – *How they work* <br>     – Home site signs up other sites in a partnership/affiliation program <br>     – Affiliate sites place a link on their site that directs users to the home site <br>     – In some cases, a user gets directed to a site through an affiliate while remaining in the affiliate's URL space <br>     – Participating affiliate sites receive a percentage cut (typically 5–10%) on all sales generated at the home site as a result of click-throughs from the affiliate sites <br>   – *Incentives to affiliates* <br>     – Financial: Affiliate sites receive a percentage of the sales they generate <br>     – Brand building: Being an affiliate to a well-known brand increases visibility <br>     – Improved capabilities: By linking users to additional sites, affiliates can increase their breadth of offerings |

Noble.com provides a large variety of books at heavily discounted prices. However, product prices are set, negotiation is not allowed, and customers can only affect the total price by varying the speed and associated cost of delivery.

**Auction Pricing.** With **auction pricing**, buyers bid against each other, and the highest bid wins the supplier's products or services. The auction site provides details to each

## Online and Offline Integration of the Customer Interface

We have applied the 7Cs Framework to the online customer interface, but all the elements of the online interface also can be replicated offline. The design of mutually reinforcing online and offline interfaces provides a consistent offering and brand message to the customer. In this section, we explore how each of the 7Cs might be implemented offline and study examples of the successful integration of online and offline interfaces.

**Context** in the offline world is the look-and-feel of the physical store. Context is comprised of, among other things, the store architecture, the appearance and demeanor of the store's staff, the openness of the retail environment, the openness to light, the color, and the style selection. J.Crew stores provide a sense of spaciousness and lightness by the use of open space and abundant natural and artificial light. Store colors match store to store—and match the colors of the clothing offered in the store. The stylish and uncluttered look-and-feel of the physical store match the look-and-feel of the jcrew.com site. This look-and-feel reinforces the company's positioning as a relaxed shopping place that offers stylish and casual clothes. On the other hand, Gap stores have a consistent design to help shoppers navigate the store and to maximize sales. Customers know they can find new fashionable items at the front of the store, core lines (such as chinos and jeans) in the middle of the store, and sale items at the very back.

**Content** in the offline world includes all the products, services, and associated information about products and services offered at physical store locations. Barnes & Noble bookstores contain a very large selection of books and magazines. Customers can get large discounts on some book categories, such as bestsellers. Customers get information on books by searching through catalogs or by using in-store computer terminals. Customer service is readily available through the many customer service representatives at most stores. The Barnes & Noble physical store offering of easily accessible information on a large selection of books at discount prices complements a nearly identical virtual offering at the bn.com website. The website provides the same easy access to information and prices but through powerful search software.

*(continued on page 231)*

auctioned product: product description, starting bid price, bid start time, and bid end time. Frequently, the performance of both suppliers and buyers is rated, and the ratings are presented by the site as a benefit to current and prospective customers. CoreBin.com provides an environment where heavy-duty truck component buyers and sellers interact and conduct business. Buyers bid against each other for a variety of remanufactured automotive and truck parts (which are known as cores).

**Reverse-Auction Pricing.** With **reverse-auction pricing**, sellers bid against each other, and the lowest bid wins the buyer the business. In many cases, suppliers (sellers) must be prequalified before their bids are considered. These sites generally will have links to prospective sellers. Many times, supplier performance is rated, and these ratings are presented by the site as a benefit to current and prospective buyers. FreeMarkets.com conducts online auctions of industrial parts, raw materials, commodities, and services. Suppliers bid lower prices in real time until the auction is closed to fill the purchase orders of large buying organizations. In 1999, this site auctioned off more than $1 billion worth of purchases and saved buyers between 2 percent and 25 percent.

**Demand-Aggregation Pricing.** With **demand-aggregation pricing**, buyer demand for specific products is aggregated in order to achieve economies of scale. Prospective buyers submit product orders by a set time, at which point price is negotiated. Community tools (such as message boards) enable ordering users to encourage

*(continued from page 230)*

**Community** in the offline world is communication between customers. Community can be encouraged through store events or through store participation in and sponsoring of community activities. Borders bookstores often host events at select stores for author readings and book signings. At these events, readers can interact with each other and meet people with similar book tastes. Evite.com, an online event invitation site, recently hosted a pool bar gathering for local members in Santa Monica. The event provided users an opportunity to physically meet and build relationships. Each year in Los Angeles, Revlon sponsors the Walk for Breast Cancer to increase breast cancer awareness, raise research funds, and bring together customers and noncustomers alike.

**Customization** in the offline world comes in a number of different ways. A store can personalize products and services that customers purchase. Credit-card holders can have their pictures and signatures imprinted on the face of their credit cards and thus personalize the cards as well as reduce the risk of credit-card fraud. Levis customers can order jeans made-to-order just for them. To some degree, stores can also customize customer experience based on exhibited customer needs. Local restaurants recognize loyal customers by automatically seating them at their favorite tables. Airlines can automatically assign customers to their preference of aisle or window seating each time they travel. Stores can also send targeted marketing messages to users based on exhibited purchase behavior. Many catalog retailers send customers customized catalogs based on individual purchase history.

**Communication** in the offline world is the one-way (store-to-customer) or two-way interaction between store and customer. One-way store-to-customer communication can be in the form of newsletters or catalogs that stores send to customers. Stores can also provide personalized alerts to customers. For

*(continued on page 232)*

other users to also submit orders. MobShop.com launched its business to aggregate consumer demand in order to build bargaining power and to achieve lower prices for participating customers. Along with competitor Mercata.com, MobShop failed to build enough sales volume to make its business model work. The business has repositioned itself in an attempt to survive and it still aggregates demand in order to obtain better prices for its customers, but today its target customers are businesses, not consumers.

## Haggle Pricing.

With **haggle pricing**, users and the site can negotiate over price. Users select products and exchange offers and counteroffers with the site until a deal is reached or refused. Hagglezone.com allows users to haggle online with sales representatives. The user and sales representative make offers and counteroffers, but this is not a live interaction. The sales representative is actually a programmed response to user-based bid inputs. Frequently, agreements on price are reached, but if the difference between the bid and asking price is unlikely to be reached, the sales representative can back off and end the haggling. Users can choose among six representatives to find the one that best matches their negotiating style. By offering a variety of haggling partners the company hopes to create an entertaining and varied shopping experience (as well as saving its customers money) to keep customers coming back for more.

# CUSTOMER INTERFACE FOR MARKETWATCH.COM

In this section, we apply the 7Cs Framework to MarketWatch.com.

# Context

Exhibit 6-34 shows the homepage for MarketWatch.com. The website for MarketWatch.com pays attention mostly to function and less to aesthetics. The look-and-feel of the front page is one of a newspaper, displaying the beginnings of

(continued from page 231)

example, investors using Merrill Lynch full brokerage services can arrange for an alert by broker phone call whenever market conditions warrant. Customers can participate in two-way communications with stores by filling out and submitting surveys generated by the store. Furthermore, customers can ask for live assistance either in person (when physically in the store) or via phone. Nordstrom is widely know for excellent customer service; its representatives have even been known to deliver purchased products directly to customer homes.

**Connection** in the offline world is the degree to which a store is connected to other stores. Stores in large shopping malls are closely located to a number of other stores, and customers can quickly move out of one store and into another. A retailer can rent concession space in large department stores to provide an additional sales channel, to be associated with other nearby concessions, and to allow customers to easily move back and forth between concessions. Stores can also provide links to a large number of suppliers who offer products or services of interest to customers. Travel agencies provide links to a large number of travel providers that include airlines, hotels, and cruise-line operators. Furthermore, stores can increase their number of customers through partnerships. Coca-Cola partners with McDonald's to increase sales by making Coca-Cola available at all McDonald's locations.

**Commerce** in the offline world refers to the transaction capabilities of a store. Stores provide transaction capabilities such as shopping carts, security, credit-card and personal-check verification, custom gift wrapping, and delivery options. In addition, stores can offer a number of price determination options. Most offline stores provide products and services at catalog (predetermined) prices. However, Sotheby's, an auction house, offers members Dutch-style or English-style auctions to determine the price offered for pieces of art, jewelry, and other collectors' items. Also, haggling remains a popular way of determining price in industries. Purchasing a car at your local dealer generally involves a lengthy negotiating process where dealer and customer make offers and counteroffers and may or may not reach an agreed-upon price. Demand aggregation also occurs occasionally in the offline world. Travel agents sometimes prepurchase large blocks of airlines seats and pass through some savings to buyers of package vacations.

articles that a user can click on to access the entire story. In this sense, MarketWatch.com appears to have taken its metaphor from *the Wall Street Journal*. However, the newspaper look-and-feel makes it somewhat hard for users to navigate through all the offered information and services. One of the most functionally dominant aspects of the site is the constantly updated headlines—one-liner text messages providing the latest news developments. The site can be accessed from a variety of platforms, such as the Web, wireless telephones, pocket PCs, PalmPilots, the downloadable AvantGo system, and other Internet appliances. In addition to the functional elements, the MarketWatch.com site also contains some aesthetically pleasing features, such as animated advertisements, small photos of columnists, and a number of charts integrated into articles.

This newspaper and content-driven look-and-feel fits with the MarketWatch.com value proposition of providing "the story behind the numbers," without being slowed down by excessive graphics or other bandwidth-intensive features.

# Content

MarketWatch.com strives to be a category killer in the online personal finance industry. In addition to providing a suite of round-the-clock financial information and in-depth analyses (such as breaking news and numerous commentaries), it also provides tools and services (such as the Stock Screener and Portfolio Tracker) that investors can use to assess and plan their transactions. Even though the site does not allow users to trade, it offers links to a number of online brokers, such as Datek and

**Exhibit 6-34** MARKETWATCH.COM SITE

Ameritrade. MarketWatch.com displays its content using a number of different media, such as raw text (for example, the news headlines), pictures and charts, sound (news transmission through MarketWatch.com Radio), and video (streaming videos of topics such as interviews with new-economy leaders). The currency of the MarketWatch.com news content ranges from up-to-the-minute headlines and stock quotes to periodic updates on financial issues, such as tax laws.

The MarketWatch.com content fits well with its value proposition of "providing comprehensive, real-time business news, financial programming, and analytic tools.[9]" The wide range of information and tools that the site provides allows investors to decide on their investment strategies.

## Community

The MarketWatch.com site offers an array of community tools. Examples include personalized e-mail allowing users to exchange private messages, online chat, and participation in a number of discussion groups by reading or posting messages. MarketWatch.com believes that "providing a place . . . to meet and share ideas about investing will increase brand awareness, motivate users to return to the CBS.MarketWatch.com site frequently, and encourage our audience to spend more time on our website."[10] MarketWatch.com community members are enthusiastic, users who are eager to share opinions on financial issues. The site provides them with the stimulus for their community interactions, namely financial news and analysis. In that sense, the MarketWatch.com community can be classified as a "theater" community.

This fits well with the MarketWatch.com value proposition of empowering investors to make decisions, since the perspectives of other investors with similar interests could prove useful and insightful.

## Customization

MarketWatch.com offers a suite of personalization tools. Users can choose from a selection of e-mail newsletters, and can sign up to receive e-mail reminders with breaking news on companies that interest them. The MarketWatch.com Portfolio Tracker is a personalization tool that allows users to track up to 200 stocks on their portfolios and to analyze their performance. It also enables users to forecast their portfolio value into the future and to adjust their investment strategy accordingly. Furthermore, the MarketWatch Live service allows users to personalize their screen layout and to choose which stock information and charts get shown. It also provides users with real-time quotes, which can be delivered in different formats, such as e-mail, cellphone or pager message, audio alarm, or pop box.

MarketWatch.com is also in the process of developing a capability to customize its site to its users. MarketWatch.com is currently implementing software that will provide information on past user behavior and will allow the site to tailor its displayed content to the individual needs of each user.

The site's tiered customization, which allows power users to receive more personalized content for a fee but allows less frequent users to find the information they require without significant customization, fits well with the MarketWatch.com desire to appeal to different groups of investors.

## Communication

MarketWatch.com offers a number of communication tools to its users. In terms of broadcast communication venues, MarketWatch.com provides a variety of free e-mail newsletters (such as the MarketWatch.comer, After the Bell, the Personal Financer Daily, and Bamby Francisco's Net Sense and Net Stocks), as well as e-mail reminders with breaking company news on companies that users can specify. MarketWatch.com offers a limited number of interactive communication tools to its users for free—for example, users can submit their feedback on the site or they can send e-mail requests. Users who pay for the eSignal service (provided by DBC) can chat online with tech support representatives on business days. They can also make adjustments to their account through a secure "manage your account" area, and perform functions such as adding or removing a service or viewing their account history.

MarketWatch.com's broadcast nature fits well with its goal to be a provider of reliable and current information. Information needs to be communicated to targeted user groups, and there is little need for live interaction with the site.

## Connection

MarketWatch.com offers a number of connection venues to and from other sites. It provides links to online brokerage sites, thus allowing investors to make investment transactions. It also increases the volume and quality of financial analysis it offers by providing links to a number of content providers, such as Hoover's and Multex. Users who click on links to these sites maintain MarketWatch.com as their home site background. These links to other sites notwithstanding, the overwhelming majority of the MarketWatch.com site is developed internally, by leveraging its experienced staff of over 90 editors and journalists.

MarketWatch.com has also considerably increased its reach by partnering with major portals, and providing them with financial content and pathways to the MarketWatch.com site. Most notably, in September 1999, MarketWatch.com entered into a three-year distribution agreement with America Online to be the premier provider of business and financial news on AOL's Personal Finance Channel. MarketWatch.com and AOL have created a co-branded site that enables users to access MarketWatch.com content and tools. Furthermore, MarketWatch.com provides content and links to its site on the Yahoo Finance section, further driving traffic to its site and raising general awareness.

These connection initiatives support the MarketWatch.com goal of being a destination site for the personal finance industry.

## Commerce

MarketWatch.com offers its core service to users for free, depending on advertising and license fees for its revenue. As such, it does not offer commerce tools such as shopping carts, order tracking, and delivery options. MarketWatch.com does track the revenue from advertisements associated with MarketWatch.com content on other sites and receives a portion of that revenue. Users can register and pay for the MarketWatch Live and eSignal services in order to get a higher level of service. To facilitate the sale of these services, MarketWatch.com uses DBC's order-entry and invoicing system to offer commerce tools such as user registration, credit card approval, and security guarantees. The price of such services is preset by MarketWatch.com.

The low level of commerce tools fits well with the MarketWatch.com goal to be a provider of relevant and timely information, as opposed to selling products or services.

## Reinforcement Among the MarketWatch.com 7Cs

The MarketWatch.com site context reinforces its content. By creating a site that is mostly functionally oriented, MarketWatch.com accentuates the message that it is a destination for high quality and in-depth content on financial and business news. This message is further accentuated by the sparse presence of commerce tools. A site that is dedicated to providing comprehensive and current news and analysis does not need to provide as many commerce features.

Similarly, the MarketWatch.com site customization reinforces its communication. By providing tiered levels of service on each of these two dimensions, the site tailors itself to the main groups that it is trying to appeal to: everyday investors and highly sophisticated market players. Context further reinforces this message. At its front page, the site has a newspaper look-and-feel, appealing to everyday investors who want to be guided through the day's news. As users click to more sophisticated services and analyses, the look-and-feel becomes more functional and less aesthetically focused, tailoring the site to sophisticated investors who are more interested in the information and less on its packaging.

## SUMMARY

### 1. What are the seven design elements of the customer interface?

The seven design elements are context, content, community, customization, communication, connection, and commerce. Each of the 7Cs needs to fit and reinforce the others while satisfying the business model.

## 2. What determines the look-and-feel of the design?

The look-and-feel of websites can be arrayed on two dimensions: form, or aesthetic, and function. Aesthetic designs focus on the artistic nature of the site. Function, on the other hand, involves the pragmatic usability of the site. Some argue that these are opposing design aspects with unavoidable trade-offs, while others argue that advancing technologies lead to new techniques and new aesthetics and, therefore, fewer trade-off decisions, such that both aesthetic and functional dimensions continue to expand.

## 3. What are the five content archetypes?

The five content archetypes are superstore, category killer, specialty, information-dominant, and market-dominant. The first three content archetypes are defined by the offering mix. The information-dominant specifically relates to information goods (although physical products can be purchased as a complement). Market-dominant provides a place for transactions and brings together buyers and sellers.

## 4. Why be concerned with community?

Community includes a feeling of membership in a group along with a strong sense of involvement and shared common interests with that group. A group of people can create strong, lasting relationships that may develop into a sense of community through an engaged and extended exchange of views focused on their shared interests. However, community contains not only elements of common interest and group acceptance but also individual involvement. This sense of community can help encourage users and customers to return to a website.

## 5. What are the levers used to customize a site?

Users can personalize the site, or the site can tailor itself to users. The levers for personalization include log-in registration, personalized e-mail, content and layout configuration, storage, and agents. An organization can design its site to tailor itself to users based on either past user behavior or the behaviors of other users with similar preferences.

## 6. What types of communication can a firm maintain with its customer base?

There are three forms of communication: broadcast, interactive, and a broadcast/interactive hybrid.

## 7. How does a firm connect with other businesses?

There are two generic approaches to form connections: pathways-in and pathways-out. The pathway of the connection can lead a user outside the environment of the site ("pathway-out") or can retrieve materials from other sites without sending the user off of the site ("pathway-in"). More specifically, pathway-out refers to situations in which links are absolute and the user's click causes an exit from the website. Pathway-in refers to situations in which links are hybrid and the user's click causes the retrieval of material from the same or other sites without an exit from the current website.

### 8. What are alternative pricing models of commerce archetypes?

There are five alternative pricing approaches: catalog, auction, reverse auction, demand aggregation, and haggle.

## KEY TERMS

| | |
|---|---|
| 7Cs Framework | tailoring by site |
| context | destination sites |
| content | hub sites |
| community | portal sites |
| customization | affiliate program |
| communication | outsourced content |
| connection | meta-software |
| commerce | catalog pricing |
| fit | auction pricing |
| reinforcement | reverse-auction pricing |
| form vs. function | demand-aggregation pricing |
| personalization by user | haggle pricing |

## Endnotes

[1]Park, Choong Whan, and Gerald Zaltman. 1987. *Marketing management.* Chicago: Dryden Press. Park and Zaltman introduced the concepts of consistency and complementarity to refer to the degree to which various marketing management concepts resulted in synergy. Complementarity is equivalent to reinforcement and fit is equivalent to consistency. Given the number of concepts that begin with the letter C in this chapter, we have chosen to use the terms fit and reinforcement.

[2]Interested readers should consult the following literature: Nielsen, Jakob. 2000. *Designing web usability.* Indianapolis, IN: New Riders Publishing.

[3]Veen, Jeffrey. 1997. *Hotwired style: Principles for building smart websites.* San Francisco: Hardwired.

[4]Adler, Richard P., and Anthony J. Christopher. 1999. Virtual communities. In *Net Success.* Holbrook, MA: Adams Media, p. 42. The elements of community categorization was constructed by Teresa Roberts of Sun Microsystems.

[5]Stark, Myra. 1998. A fly on the virtual wall: Cybercommunities observed. *Digitrends Quarterly* (summer): 26.

[6]Farmer, Randall. 1994. Social dimensions of habitat's citizenry. In *Virtual Reality Case Book.* New York: Van Nostrand Reinhold, pp. 87–95.

[7]Adler, Richard P., and Anthony J. Christopher. 1999. Virtual communities. In *Net Success.* Holbrook, MA: Adams Media, p. 42. The sense of community or member benefits is based on research conducted by researchers at the Annenberg School.

[8]Figalo, Cliff. 1998. *Hosting web communities: Building relationships, increasing customer loyalty and maintaining a competitive edge.* New York: John Wiley & Sons, Inc.

[9]Securities and Exchange Commission, *Form 10K for MarketWatch.com, Inc. for fiscal year ended December 31, 1999.*

[10]Ibid.

# Market Communications and Branding

In Chapter 6, we discussed the screen-to-customer interface that brings to life the value proposition and associated business model introduced in Chapter 5. In this chapter, we turn our attention to two key levers that a firm uses to motivate consumer traffic and, ultimately, consumption: market communications and branding. Market communications can be broken down into a simple two-by-two framework based upon the audience focus (broad versus individual) and communications media (offline versus online). In particular, we describe several alternative approaches in each of these quadrants. Next, we turn our attention to branding. In particular, we discuss (1) branding basics, (2) a framework for brand equity, (3) a 10-step process to build brands, and (4) two case studies of successful online branding. We conclude with a discussion of branding choices.

## QUESTIONS

*Please consider the following questions as you read this chapter:*

1. What are the four categories of market communications?

2. What is a good brand?

3. What is the 10-Step Branding Process?

4. How does online branding compare between American Airlines and Continental Airlines?

5. What are the Point-Counterpoint arguments for leveraging an offline brand into the online environment?

This chapter was coauthored by Bernie Jaworski, Jeffrey Rayport, Nancy Michaels, Ellie Kyung, Jennifer Barron, Marco Smit, and Rafi Mohammed. Substantive input was also provided by Robert Lurie, Yannis Dosios, and Leo Griffin.

# INTRODUCTON

Chapter 6 focused on the types of interface design choices that confront the senior management team. Once these design choices are made, the team must turn its attention to building customer traffic, strengthening the brand, and locking in target customers. In this chapter, we consider how the online company communicates with its target customers and attempts to build strong brand.

We begin this chapter by introducing the link between communications and branding. Next, we introduce a simple marketing communications framework. This framework considers both online and offline media approaches as well as individualized and broad audiences. We review a number of new online approaches and traditional media approaches. We also consider the question of how to build superior, lasting brands. This requires some basic discussion of brand equity as well as a methodology for the branding processes. After introducing this methodology, we apply it to two case studies: American Airlines (*www.aa.com*) and Monster.com (*www.monster.com*). In contrast to many pundits who thought the Internet would lead to pure commoditization of products, this mini-case study discussion reveals the potential for highly differentiated, unique brands.

As in prior chapters, we conclude our discussion with an application of the market communications and branding concepts to MarketWatch.com.

# INTEGRATING COMMUNICATIONS AND BRANDING

Regardless of the source of differentiation, **branding** is about the consumer's perception of the offering—how it performs, how it looks, how it makes one feel, and what messages it sends. These perceptions are nurtured by a combination of **market communications** in the marketplace—one's interaction with the brand, others' experiences with the brand, and, more generally, mass-marketing approaches. In the offline world, these communications tend to be one-way, from the firm to the customer, while in the online world, we begin to see much more interactive, two-way communications.

Communications and brands are actually the media of which the Web is made. Old marketing notions, such as "shelf space equals market share" in retail or "mind share leads to market share" in entertainment, apply with a vengeance on the Internet. Mental space is market space, so it should come as no surprise that e-commerce or new-economy markets are realms in which we have seen an explosion in innovation in communications techniques for business and a dramatic rise in the power and impact of strong brands.

If brands are real estate owned by companies in the minds of consumers, then communications and brands on the Web represent real estate competing to attract the scarcest resource in the new economy—consumer attention. This is the critical challenge for businesses on the Web, and it links the two themes of this chapter.

Finally, it should be no surprise that approaches to claiming the real estate of the mind are varied and must take place in both the physical and virtual worlds. The opportunity to reinforce online with offline and vice versa is a profound value-creation machine for business. It is the virtual cycle of the flight simulator in which you play a video game in virtual reality to fly a real plane better, but flying a real plane also makes you better equipped to operate the simulator. This back-and-forth experience between the two worlds is what we are talking about when we introduce the hybrid approaches to marketing communications involving both offline and online worlds.

# WHAT ARE THE FOUR CATEGORIES OF MARKET COMMUNICATIONS?

Market communications refers to all the points of contact that the firm has with its customers. This includes the obvious offline communications such as television advertising, promotions, and sales calls, as well as the emergent advertising approaches on the Internet. It is important to stress that any chapter on marketing communications in the new economy must include a blended discussion of both offline and online approaches.

Consider the case of Amazon.com. In its quest to develop (and retain) its customer base, Amazon has been losing large sums of money. In 1999, Amazon lost $390 million, compared to the $74 million that it lost in 1998. However, its marketing investments (broadly defined) have been paying off. Sales increased 169 percent from $610 million in 1998 to $1.64 billion in 1999. In addition, its customer base grew from more than 6.2 million accounts in 1998 to more than 17 million in 1999.[1] Amazon is a good example of a company that has invested significantly in all four types of marketing communications, namely: (1) **general online communications**, (2) **personalized online communications**, (3) **traditional mass media communications**, and (4) to a much more limited extent, **direct communications**.

## The Customer Decision Process and Market Communications

Prior to our discussion of these four media choices, we will reflect on the objectives of the marketing communications effort and examine the so-called "hierarchy of the effects" communications model; it is difficult to think about the choice of marketing communications without first considering the objectives that one wants to accomplish (e.g., increase brand awareness, increase sales). At the same time, one also needs to consider a structured approach to moving the customer through the buying process—from early awareness of the brand through to purchase.

In Exhibit 7-1, we illustrate the buying process, which mirrors the hierarchy of effects. In traditional "big ticket" product categories, consumers are thought to pass through multiple decision stages. Each stage is a prerequisite for the next stage. That is, one cannot move through the buying process to purchase without first forming a preference for the brand. It should be noted that this buying process is a simple illustration of the egg diagram that illustrates the buying process in Chapter 5.

In the middle portion of Exhibit 7-1, we show the types of traditional marketing communications that are used to move the customer through the buying process. For example, television ads may create brand awareness, while point-of-sale promotions tend to trigger purchase.

The lower portion of Exhibit 7-1 shows the early Web market communications that can be linked to the buying process. For example, banner ads can make target customers aware of the product or service, while "daily specials" tend to be most associated with purchase.

It is important to reflect on how the marketing communications process has changed as one moves from traditional to online communications. Perhaps the

**Exhibit
7-1** EVOLUTION OF CUSTOMER BUYING PROCESS

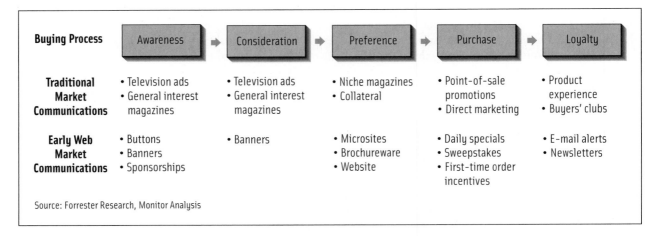

| Buying Process | Awareness | Consideration | Preference | Purchase | Loyalty |
|---|---|---|---|---|---|
| **Traditional Market Communications** | • Television ads<br>• General interest magazines | • Television ads<br>• General interest magazines | • Niche magazines<br>• Collateral | • Point-of-sale promotions<br>• Direct marketing | • Product experience<br>• Buyers' clubs |
| **Early Web Market Communications** | • Buttons<br>• Banners<br>• Sponsorships | • Banners | • Microsites<br>• Brochureware<br>• Website | • Daily specials<br>• Sweepstakes<br>• First-time order incentives | • E-mail alerts<br>• Newsletters |

Source: Forrester Research, Monitor Analysis

most important shift is from the acquisition mind-set of the traditional world to the experience, retention, and interactive (two-way) mind-set of the networked economy. In the next section, we introduce a simple framework for marketing communications that provides a backdrop to our more detailed explanation of both offline and online communications tools.

## A Framework for Online Marketing Communications

This section describes marketing communications that online companies use to attract new customers. These marketing strategies are clustered into four major categories: (1) personalized, online communications; (2) general online approaches; (3) traditional mass marketing; and (4) direct communications (see Table 7-1). In Table 7-2, we list some of the market communications options in each category.

## The Four Categories of Communications

**General Online Approaches.** The following are nonpersonalized approaches that companies take to communicate with users.

*Banner Ads.* **Banner ads** are the boxlike, graphical ads that are displayed on webpages. These ads usually display a simple message that is designed to entice viewers to click the ad. In general, this "click-through" leads to buying opportunities or to a company's website. Banner ads can be used for multiple purposes, with success being measured in several different manners.

- *Impressions.* The number of impressions (also called "gross exposures" or "ad views") is the total number of times an ad is seen by viewers. Ads are often sold based on cost per thousand impressions (CPMs). Based on the attractiveness of a site's customer base, ad CPMs range in price from $3 to $250.

**Table 7-1**

# FRAMEWORK FOR MARKETING COMMUNICATIONS

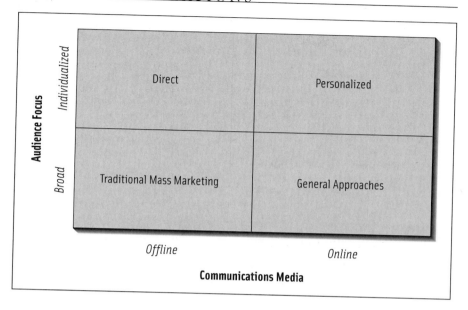

- *Leads.* A lead occurs when a viewer takes an action, such as requesting information.

- *Sales.* Firms can easily track whether click-throughs result in sales, and they can pay commissions to the site that referred the customer (we discuss associate programs later in this section). A general trend in structuring banner-advertisement fees is to use performance-based deals. Forrester Research estimates that by the year 2004, performance-based deals will account for more than 50 percent of Web advertising dollars.

- *Click-throughs.* The number of click-throughs is the number of times that viewers click on an ad. Clicking takes them to the advertiser's website or any other advertiser-specified location. Marketers try to increase the click-through rate by making banners more colorful and by adding interactivity (e.g., games, quick surveys, questions). Playing a banner game often results in a click-through, although these click-throughs are generally less effective than a click-through generated from a surfer's genuine interest.

In a related approach, John Hancock recently ran banner ads that targeted Web surfers concerned about retirement. John Hancock's banner ad asked viewers the enticing question, "I'm _ years old and I make _ a year. What will I need to retire?" Survey participants instantly received a response to this important question. They then had the option to learn more about retirement and John Hancock products. For these types of innovative banner ads, John Hancock experienced a click-through rate of almost 5 percent, which was 10 times the national average at the time.[2]

***E-Mail.*** The use of **e-mail** as a marketing vehicle is attractive to e-commerce players because of its low production costs and simplicity. In 1999, spending on e-mail

**Table 7-2**

## THE FOUR CATEGORIES OF COMMUNICATIONS

| Direct | Personalized |
|---|---|
| • Sales force<br>• Retail sales<br>• Customer service representatives | • Permission marketing<br>• Personalized recommendations<br>• Personalized advertisements<br>• Personalized webpages<br>• Personalized upsell<br>• Personalized e-commerce |
| **Traditional Mass Marketing** | **General Approaches** |
| • Television<br>• Radio<br>• Print<br>• Billboards<br>• Superior customer service | • Banner ads<br>• E-mail<br>• Viral marketing<br>• Portal sponsorship/exclusive agreements<br>• Associate programs<br>• Online and offline partnerships<br>• Provide information to entice customer purchases<br>• Leverage customer base |

marketing was $97 million, and it is expected to jump to $2 billion by the end of 2003.[3]

An early form of e-mail advertising applied a typical offline advertising method: junk e-mails (otherwise known as spam). Junk e-mails are unsolicited mass e-mailings that contain the same advertising message as one would find in a traditional mass mailing in the offline world. As stated in Chapter 3, the word spam comes from the famous Monty Python "Viking Spam Restaurant" sketch in which the canned luncheon meat Spam (which comes from "spiced ham") was pushed onto every diner regardless of whether he or she wanted it. Annoyed e-mail users picked up the term to refer to junk e-mails.

The company that is most often credited with starting the spam craze is Cyber Promotions. As Cyber Promotions soon found, Web users treat their personal e-mail accounts with greater sanctity than their postal addresses. Cyber Promotions spammed e-mail addresses, and Web users revolted making it very clear that they did not like spam. Cyber Promotions was sued by large Internet service providers that claimed that the onslaught of spam overtaxed their systems and annoyed their users. By 1997, Cyber Promotions was unable to find a company willing to supply it with the Internet connections that it needed to send spam.[4]

***Viral Marketing.*** The term **viral marketing** was introduced into the business lexicon in 1996, when Mountain Dew created an immediate word-of-mouth phenomenon by offering a deal for cheap pagers to its young customers, and then sending weekly marketing messages via the pages to these users.[5] Viral marketing occurs when company-developed products, services, or information are passed from user to user. It is analogous to a viral infection spread among people. Viral marketing gained mass fame when it turned Hotmail from a tiny upstart company into one of the first online companies with a huge valuation, which resulted in its sale to Microsoft. Hotmail provided customers with free e-mail service but also included in each sent message an invitation to e-mail recipients to obtain a free e-mail account at Hotmail.[6]

Many media-related websites allow viewers to send news items to friends. Washingtonpost.com offers such a service, which has proven to be the next step in viral marketing. This form of viral marketing is effective because marketing messages are sent between friends—consumers are more receptive to these subtle marketing messages. Readers can e-mail a specific article by simply typing in a friend's e-mail address. Washingtonpost.com benefits because new viewers are exposed to its site at a friend's suggestion, and they become regular users. Washingtonpost.com also benefits because loyal readers filter select articles from its wide product offering to a topic of exact interest to their friends. This educated filtering allows new viewers to be directed to information that is most relevant to them.

The Universal Studios theme park has created an innovative viral marketing strategy. Universal set up three user-controlled webcams for patrons to use. Using the webcams, visitors can take pictures from various vantage points in the park and send them to friends. The average webcam user sends four Web "postcards" to friends, resulting in more than 6 million park images that have been sent to potential visitors. This strategy is an unusual version of viral marketing that benefits the park, visitors, and their friends. Park visitors can easily send images of themselves enjoying Universal Studios, and the theme park is prominently featured in the image. People enjoy receiving Web postcards of their friends enjoying themselves, and Universal's brand image is either formed or reinforced in people's minds.[7]

**Sponsorship and Exclusive Partner Agreements.** Many portals offer e-commerce companies the opportunity to become a sponsor or an exclusive partner, an association that e-commerce companies have found valuable. In exclusive partnerships, portals aggressively feature and push their partner company's products. For instance, Talk.com's exclusive agreement to provide discount long-distance telephone service to AOL members has been AOL's most successful e-commerce partner program to date. Less than two years after its launch, Talk.com sold more than 1.5 million long-distance lines to AOL members. This marketing relationship enabled Talk.com to achieve the fastest market-share shift in the long-distance market's history.[8]

**Affiliate Programs.** Various forms of **affiliate programs** have been used by online firms for years. Affiliate programs refer to situations where a particular site (e.g., AOL) directs a user to an e-commerce site (e.g., Amazon) and, in turn, receives a commission on sales generated by that user (usually between 5 and 15 percent). One reason for the popularity of affiliate programs is the ease of implementation. With no more than a few clicks, websites can register, create an affiliate banner ad or icon, and start collecting commissions. In addition to this ease of implementation, the number of potential affiliates is virtually unlimited.

Although CDNOW is credited with inventing this program, Amazon is often seen as its most innovative and successful implementer. Amazon calls its affiliate program an "associates program." It allows virtually any website to promote

# Andrew Raskin–Gazooba's COO Shares his Secrets for Spreading the Marketing Bug

by Lisa Ferri, staff writer for tnbt.com

Not all viral marketing campaigns are created equal.

Just ask Andy Raskin. As co-founder and COO of San Francisco-based software and consulting firm Gazooba, he not only dreams up viral marketing strategies for other companies, but he runs their campaigns as well. And while he'll tell you that almost any company can become viral, he believes that some strategies are more infectious than others.

Here, Raskin offers five tips for producing more virulent viruses.

1. *Be careful what you wish for*
   Before you unleash a virus, make sure your system can handle it. The whole point of adopting a viral marketing strategy is to make your user base explode, right? So make sure your servers and back-office operations won't go into meltdown if you succeed. Seems simple, but too many businesses charge ahead without the proper infrastructure.

2. *Timing is everything*
   Encourage your users to tell their friends, but time it perfectly. Ever been to a website where, right off the bat, before exploring the site or buying anything at all, you were slapped with a "tell-a-friend!" button? Were you inspired to click? Not likely. Better to hit the customer with that option after she's made a purchase or—better yet, says Raskin—after the goods have been delivered and she's (presumably) delighted with the transaction.

3. *R-E-S-P-E-C-T*
   Let your users know that you respect them . . . and their friends. At its core, viral marketing is a delicate exercise in co-branding: A business tries to mix its brand with that of its consumers, usually in the form of e-mails forwarded from consumers to their circles of friends. So make sure your customers know that you respect their "brand"; for example, clearly state that a friend's e-mail address won't turn up on some opt-in spam list. And though it may be tempting, don't abuse "relationship information."

4. *What's it worth to you?*
   Want to know which incentives will motivate your customers? Ask them. Get creative with incentives. Lots of websites offer cold, hard cash to users who tell their friends about them. But there are other options that may be even better lures, like charity donations or free personalized software. How to predict what will really blow a user's hair back? Here's a radical concept: Ask.

5. *If at first you don't succeed . . .*
   If a particular viral marketing scheme doesn't make a splash, don't abandon it wholesale. Instead, run the numbers and tweak the strategy. By analyzing different components—interface designs, subject headers, etc.—you may be able to isolate and fix the problem.

   For example, how many friends, on average, do users share with you on your "tell-a-friend" page? If the number is low, it may in part be your fault: Do you allow room for only one or two e-mail addresses, forcing users who want to enter more to jump around the site or click through to another page? Simply changing the form to let users send 20 addresses instead of two may help. "When we made this change with one of our clients, the average number of friends jumped from two to six," Raskin says. "Over time, that compounds itself to exponential effect."

*Read more articles about The Next Big Thing at www.tnbt.com*

# Fifty Ways to Build Your Brand

by Leo Griffin

As online and offline companies increasingly look to the Web as a platform for building and sustaining brands, the market for Internet advertising is forecasted to explode. According to Forrester Research, U.S.-based Internet advertising will grow from approximately 1.3 percent of total advertising in 1999 to 8.1 percent, or $22.2 billion, in 2004. By that year, the global Internet advertising market will be worth $33 billion. It is not surprising that analysts expect such dramatic growth in Web advertising. In a survey by Jupiter Communications, 42 percent of respondents reported that they were spending less time watching television as a result of the Internet. As the number of Internet users rises and the average amount of time that users spend accessing the Internet increases, advertisers will need to spend an increasing proportion of their money on Internet advertising in order to capture the attention of their target audience.

Internet advertising extends three promises to advertisers:[9] accurate one-to-one targeting of ads, rich media, and interactivity (for example, banners that allow users to configure a product) and real-time detailed feedback on campaign performance, in turn allowing for adjustments to the campaign on the fly.

Despite these promises, the impact of Internet advertising has frequently proven to be a disappointment. The most common form of advertising on the Web is the banner ad—those little rectangular boxes (usually 468 pixels wide by 60 high) that contain messages from advertisers—but, in fact, there are dozens of different marketing tools on the Web. Here, we briefly examine some of the pros and cons of each.

**Banner Ads.** As users have grown more experienced with the Web, it appears that they have become more reluctant to click on Web banners. Data from Nielsen-NetRatings show that banner click-through rates continued to decline through 1999, falling below half of one percent (in other words, 1 in every 200 banners is clicked on). This does not speak well for the ability of marketers to accurately target banners at people who will be interested in them, but are there other reasons for these low numbers?

Part of the problem is probably due to the cognitive mode that people are in when they are surfing the Web. Typically, we're sitting at a desk and we have a mission. We are looking to perform a particular task or find a piece of information. So, when a banner pops up asking us to drop what we're doing and turn our attentions to something else, we're not very likely to click on it. Contrast this to the experience of watching television, where we sit back in a comfortable chair and watch what appears on the screen in front of us. This experience requires no navigation beyond choosing a channel, and we're typically much more receptive to advertising messages that temporarily interrupt our program.

Advertisers have attempted to improve click-through rates by creating interactive banners (a famous banner developed for HP by Red Sky Interactive [*www.redsky.com*] allowed users to play "Pong" in the banner). Increasingly, banners will offer the richness of television and the interaction of the Web. Free ISP NetZero recently acquired a technology that will allow it to serve television-like streaming media banners.

**Interstitials.** Visit *Fortune* magazine on the Web (*www.fortune.com*), and when you click away from the site, a new window will open in your browser inviting you to subscribe to the magazine. These windows are called interstitials, and they demand your attention because you must click on them, if only to close the window. Click-through rates are as high as 5 percent[10] (10 times the average for banners), but costs are higher too. Furthermore, research by analyst Keith Pieper (*www.keithpieper.com*) shows that most publishers and advertisers have experienced complaints or negative responses from customers who feel that interstitials are intrusive.

**Sponsorships.** Sponsorships can vary from a simple sponsorship of an e-mail list to much more sophisticated site-sponsorship deals. For example, e-retailer 800.com (*www.800.com*) sponsored a list of the top 10 videos that appeared alongside the 800.com logo on the Hollywood Stock Exchange (*www.hsx.com*).

*(continued on page 248)*

*(continued from page 247)*

By clicking on one of the video titles, visitors were transported to the 800.com site, where they could purchase the video. The advantage of sponsorships is that they can help to build a sponsor's brand by presenting it within the context of the sponsored site and by creating value for visitors to that site.

**E-Mail.** Junk mail, or spam, is an extremely common marketing tool because e-mail lists can be readily available and cheap. More recently, opt-in mail has become popular. It is offered by companies, such as YesMail (*www.yesmail.com*), that allow advertisers to send e-mail messages to a group of people who have indicated an interest in receiving e-mails about that type of product or service. YesMail has built a database of 8 million users, all of whom have opted to receive e-mails about topics of interest to them. YesMail claims that its e-mails result in a response rate between 10 and 15 percent.

**Coupons.** Companies such as CoolSavings (*www.coolsavings.com*) offer their members discount coupons that they can print out and then use for both online and offline retailers. Coupons can be an attractive marketing mechanism because they encourage product trial, and they are a way of selectively discounting prices to the most price-sensitive customers (those that are willing to go to a website and print out a coupon).

**Pay-Per-Advertising View.** Companies such as CyberGold "pay" customers to view advertisements. The approach uses the accountability of the Web to reward consumers for processing the "right" kind of information (e.g., targeted ads as opposed to generalized Web content).

**Loyalty Programs.** Companies such as ClickRewards (*www.clickrewards.com*) offer their members the chance to earn a currency, such as airline miles, by shopping at their network of partner sites (see also NetCentives, MyPoints). The economics of customer retention are well known; an existing, loyal customer is much more profitable than a new one, so rewarding existing customers to encourage them to remain loyal can be a good tactic. Beenz (*www.beenz.com*) employs a slightly different approach. It offers its members "beenz" currency in return for them registering at a site or signing up for a mailing list (as well as making purchases). This can help sites reduce their customer-acquisition costs, but it poses the risk that members will sign up just for the reward and never return to the site.

Amazon products that are relevant (or even irrelevant) to their viewers by creating a link to Amazon. Associates receive a commission between 5 and 15 percent on purchases made by customers who connect from their websites. Thus, a music-related site can promote Amazon's music inventory to its viewers and receive referral commissions. An enterprising person with a family-related website can encourage family members to order all of their books through the site's Amazon link so that he or she will reap commissions. Currently, there are more than 400,000 Amazon associates, including such well-known sites as Yahoo, Excite, AOL, Motley Fool, and MSN.

An affiliate program can offer a number of advantages to e-commerce companies. Amazon used its associate program to build over 400,000 new distribution avenues (i.e., sites that offer easy access to Amazon). Whether or not customers buy, they are exposed to Amazon banner advertising on associates' websites, which builds awareness about the site. In addition, as consumers become more familiar with Amazon, they may decide to go there directly instead of clicking through the associate's websites. Over time, Amazon can end up owning the customer without paying a commission to the associate.

*Partnerships.* While many offline companies arrange partnerships, the use of partnerships is more pervasive online. Similar to the manner in which complementary companies will collaborate to push a new technology (the Microsoft and Intel partnership is often termed Wintel), Web companies partner with complementary sites to quickly provide a more value-enhanced service to site visitors. One prevailing strategy is to select a customer niche and provide services that encompass the customer's entire needs in that area (recall our category switchboard discussion in Chapter 5).

Consider a site seeking to offer a full range of information related to retirement planning. Complementary information (and services) could be provided on topics including health care for the aging, Social Security, stocks and mutual funds, insurance, and elder law. For a site whose competitive advantage is providing retirement information, it may require too much in resources and time to provide all of these services and information. Thus, the retirement site would benefit by collaborating with complementary sites. The complementary sites receive exposure and business from the retirement site's customers, and they reciprocate by promoting the full-service retirement site with banner ads or information.

***Innovative Customer Acquisition.*** As the Internet market becomes more competitive, competitive advantage will be derived from innovative marketing. One form of innovative marketing is to ally with groups (or associations) and provide a complementary service that benefits the group's membership. By creating such an alliance, a new site can launch with a large customer base without incurring expensive and risky marketing fees. In such an arrangement, a site generally pays the group a fee to access its membership.

Such an innovative marketing concept is being used by Myteam.com. One focus of Myteam is to provide Web-based services to support Little League baseball. Myteam provides webpages for each team. These pages include team profiles, schedules, and player information. This benefits Little League's membership and saves time for coaches because, instead of calling each player about a scheduling change, each member can simply go to the team's site for updated information. Players benefit because they receive a personalized webpage that lists information such as their career highlights and statistics. In a version of viral marketing, Little League's brand is enhanced because players tell their friends and family to regularly check their personal Little League homepage. By teaming up with Little League, Myteam benefits by gaining instant access to a large group of loyal users and their family and friends. Myteam can capitalize on this large viewer base by selling targeted banner advertising and e-commerce goods (e.g., baseball equipment, team pictures, and uniforms).

***Provide Information.*** The Web allows sites to instantly offer information that is relevant to their customer base. Many sites provide instantly accessible information to their customers as a form of marketing and product differentiation. The e-commerce market for travel (airlines, hotels, etc.) is very competitive, with many well-funded players. Sites try to differentiate themselves by offering vast amounts of information to their customers. Travel information can range from top restaurant and hotel information targeted toward expense-account travelers to time-sensitive information (e.g., day-only specials, airfare updates) for budget-minded leisure travelers. Customers evaluate the information they receive and establish a relationship with the site that best meets their needs. Sites try to capitalize on this relationship by offering e-commerce opportunities like travel-reservation services.

***Leverage the Customer Base.*** As we have discussed, a primary goal of e-commerce businesses is creating a large customer base and establishing a relationship of trust with their customers. Many firms are trying to establish reputations as solid companies that are good at fulfilling e-commerce orders. Eventually, as a company establishes a large and loyal customer base, the goal is to leverage this relationship by offering an expanded selection of products and services. Amazon has successfully leveraged its customer base. Within four months of offering CDs and within six weeks of offering videos, Amazon was the top-selling site for both products.[11] Increasing the number of categories that it offers helped Amazon raise its average sales per customer from approximately $104 in 1999 to $126 in 2000.

**Personalized Online Communications.** Online companies have the opportunity to reduce mass-marketing expenses and increase response rates by personalizing their marketing for each customer. The manner in which transactions occur on the Web provides e-commerce companies with detailed information on their customers. Information can be derived from customers who register their preferences and demographic information, as well as by analyzing past purchases and Web surfing habits. This information gives e-commerce companies the opportunity to create one-to-one marketing relationships. In addition, many companies use their sites to establish a two-way dialogue with customers, and this dialogue provides additional information regarding product desires and avenues. We categorize personalized marketing into five primary forms: (1) permission marketing, (2) personalized recommendations, (3) personalized advertisements, (4) personalized webpages, and (5) personalized e-commerce stores.

*Permission Marketing.* Seth Godin coined the term **permission marketing** to describe how successful e-mail campaigns can result from creating relationships with customers. Permission marketing has become the rage among online marketers and has led to increases in marketing response rates.[12]

Permission marketing presumes successful marketing campaigns can be created by establishing a mutually beneficial and trusting relationship between the firm and its customers. In exchange for some offered benefit, customers volunteer information about themselves and, in essence, ask to be marketing targets. Once customers initiate this relationship, they anticipate e-mail messages because they know that these messages will be on relevant topics. By using the permission-marketing philosophy, online firms create a valuable database of customers who have given the firm permission to market to them and are receptive to marketing messages.

Permission-marketing e-mails must be relevant to the consumer. Response rates and trust can increase by sending permission-marketing e-mails that are highly specific to customers' interests. Many online firms ask their permission-marketing customers for detailed personal information when they sign up for e-mails. This information allows them to send more targeted e-mails to specific segments of the firm's customer base. Customers appreciate these targeted e-mails, and this increases their relationship level with the firm. The associated increased trust level may also induce customers to reveal additional information about themselves.

Estée Lauder's marketing campaign for its Clinique "Stop Signs Anti-Aging Serum" reveals the effectiveness of targeted e-mail campaigns. Clinique has a database of more than 600,000 people who have registered to receive product updates via e-mails. To register, customers have to fill in a brief survey that provides Clinique with opportunities to send them more personalized e-mails. The company sends a monthly newsletter that contains beauty tips and information on new products.

In March 1999, Clinique introduced its "Stop Signs Anti-Aging Serum" with a two-tiered offline/online marketing strategy. By using data from its e-mail registration survey, Clinique initially sent a sample of its new product to every registered woman who was over 35 or had listed that she was worried about wrinkles. A few weeks after the sample was sent, Clinique followed up with an e-mail message inviting the recipient to purchase the product. About 8 percent of the targeted customers bought the product online. This is a very high response rate, and does not include customers who purchased the product from retail outlets.[13]

***Personalized Recommendations.*** Many e-commerce sites have personalized services that make specific merchandise recommendations for each user based on past purchases, site pages viewed, and survey information that the user has provided. As noted earlier in the book, the recommendations that work best rely on collaborative-filtering technologies sold by companies such as NetPerceptions and Firefly (now a unit of Microsoft). These services use sophisticated algorithms that utilize information specific to each customer to find the best matches of additional products that may be of interest to the customer. Without this information, customers may not otherwise have known about these recommended products. This can increase revenues and loyalty from the all-important repeat customer. When Music Boulevard test-marketed its personalized recommendation service, it found that the recommendations prompted customers to buy CDs 10 percent to 30 percent of the time. This purchase rate is much higher than the 2 percent to 4 percent general purchase rate realized on the rest of the site.[14]

***Personalized Advertisements.*** Websites increasingly are using personalized-technology software to determine dynamically, in real time, which Web advertisements should be shown to viewers. ZDNet uses personalization technology that is based on an analysis of five user-profile and impression-environment variables. Variables used include the user's past click behavior, time of day, the page, recency/frequency of visits, and search keywords. Based on these variables, users are given a relevancy score (i.e., indicator of the probability of a click), and ads that are most likely to be of interest to the viewer are displayed. During a test run of this technology, ZDNet realized an impressive 20 percent to 100 percent increase in click-through results.[15] Yahoo collects 400 billion bytes of information a day (the equivalent of a library with 800,000 books) on how its customers use the Yahoo site.[16] This personalized information helps Yahoo better understand each customer. By using this information to target ads to individual customers, Yahoo has realized higher ad rates and e-commerce sales.

***Personalized Webpages.*** Many portals and e-commerce sites allow users to create their own personalized webpages, encouraging users to return more often and increasing the user's familiarity with the site. This leads to users spending more time on the website, thereby increasing advertising exposure time. Since a creator/user of a personalized webpage reveals detailed personal information, the site sponsoring the personalized webpage can deliver more targeted consumers to advertisers. This results in an opportunity to charge increased ad rates to reach specific customer groups. At the portal Excite, users can create personalized portal pages using the MyExcite service. Excite found that users who create a MyExcite page come back five times as often and view twice the number of pages as users who do not have a personal page. This has allowed Excite to reap higher advertising revenues.[17] In addition, personalization increases users' switching costs.

***Personalized E-Commerce Stores.*** One of the goals of online merchants is to use Internet technology and their knowledge about individual consumers to tailor their products and services for each customer. Jeff Bezos, Amazon's chairman, has stated that one of his goals is to have his "store redecorated for each and every customer."[18]

However, he cautions that it could take up to 10 years to achieve such individual customization. Office Depot offers its small-business customers personalized catalogs, allowing businesses to create real-time unique catalogs for their employees—based on their buying authority.[19] In addition to making their customers' shopping experience more pleasant, personalization is a key tool for increasing switching costs. If a customer is satisfied and becomes dependent on a site that offers personalized services, it will be more costly to switch sites. Even if a competing site offers superior services, inertia that often slows users from switching sites.

### Traditional Mass Media Communications.
As the online environment has grown more competitive, it has become increasingly difficult for Web companies to make a (cost-effective) marketing splash. Online companies increasingly turn to the primary advertising forum of bricks-and-mortar companies: television. In their quest to rapidly attract customers and stake out their niche, a growing number of online companies seem to feel that, while expensive, television advertising can quickly transmit their marketing message to a large audience. Moreover, in many cases, the offline media is necessary to bring new customers onto the Internet or, for existing Internet users, to make them aware of the brand.

According to Competitive Media Reporting, in 1998 Internet companies accounted for $323 million in television-advertising spending. In 1999, Internet companies were expected to spend more than $1 billion on television advertising. Spending on television advertising by Internet companies reached a peak with the 2000 Super Bowl. In 1999, 30-second ads for the Super Bowl averaged $1.6 million, but for the 2000 Super Bowl, the average 30-second ad sold for $2 million.[20] This 25 percent average increase has been attributed in part to demand from Internet companies. After that peak in January 2000, however, television-advertising spending by dot-coms declined as the focus switched from customer acquisition to cost management and profitability.

Today, the general opinion is that online advertising is becoming less effective. In the early days of e-commerce, it was easier for a company to make a big splash through low-cost, innovative online advertising. As often happens in business, many saw new opportunities and jumped into the market. As more e-commerce companies inundated surfers with heaps of (often innovative) online ads, effectiveness dropped. In response, Internet companies are trying to better leverage more traditional marketing channels (e.g., television, radio, print).

Priceline believes that radio is the most effective medium for reaching potential customers. In 1999, Priceline allocated two-thirds of its $60 million marketing budget to radio. Jay Walker, Priceline's founder, claims that the radio campaign has helped Priceline increase sales by 5 percent a week.[21]

Many cited eToys' initial success as an example of the effectiveness of television advertising. In eToys' first year of business (the site launched in October 1997), its total revenues were $2 million. During the 1998 holiday season, Visa USA ran a co-branded television ad that featured parents using the eToys site to purchase holiday presents for their children. Due in large part to the effectiveness of these television ads, eToys' fourth-quarter revenues skyrocketed to $23 million.[22] Despite this early growth, eToys was unable to sustain its early momentum. In December 2000, eToys announced that it had retained Goldman Sachs to sell the business.[23]

Monster.com found that using traditional television marketing fueled explosive growth of its business. In its quest to establish a brand as the best place for job seekers to post their resume, as well as a brand for employers of being the easiest way to find people online, Monster.com invested heavily in television advertising. Despite having estimated profits of $1.2 million in 1998, advertising spending for 1999 was estimated at $60 million.

**Direct Communications.** Direct communications can take many forms, including the use of the classic business-to-business sales representatives, retail sales clerks, and telephone customer sales representatives, as well as the use of direct marketing and telemarketing.

*Sales Representatives.* One of the most interesting developments on the Web is the reemergence of the *traditional sales representative.* When properly managed, the Web can paradoxically lead to the increased effectiveness of sales representatives, rather than making sales representatives obsolete. Dell Online found that sales leads increased in quality because of its website. As a result, sales representatives could be more efficient, and their satisfaction increased after the online channel was added.

*Direct Marketing.* A second form of offline marketing communication is **direct marketing** through the postal system. Of course, a key difference is that with the new information gained online, firms are able to target and customize the mailings to a much more significant degree. Firms such as 800.com and Amazon.com send coupons through the mail to select customer groups. For instance, people who purchase a DVD at Amazon may receive a discount voucher for DVDs through the mail, followed by a reminder e-mail a few days later.

*Telemarketing.* A third option is the use of a **telemarketing** sales force. We have all received those wonderful sales pitches near the dinner hour. The aim of telemarketing is clearly to increase sales—not to strengthen brand awareness or image.

As noted at the beginning of this section, online companies must consider how to manage their entire mix of communications (as implied in Table 7-1) to influence both consumer behavior and the brand-building process. In the next section, we turn our attention to the building of strong brands.

# WHAT IS A "GOOD" BRAND?

According to the American Marketing Association, a brand is a "name, term, sign, symbol, or design, or a combination of them intended to identify the goods and services of one seller or group of sellers and to differentiate them from those of competition." The term "product" simply describes the general category of the goods (e.g., books), while the brand (e.g., Amazon.com) refers to both the product and the additional "wrap-arounds" (e.g., easy customer interface, one-click shopping, collaborative filtering) that differentiate it from other products in the category.

## Branding Basics

Exhibit 7-3 provides a few key insights into what constitutes good online branding. At the center of the exhibit is the core product or service. In the case of American Airlines (*www.aa.com*), this means safe, on-time transportation from location A to location B. The wrap-arounds for American Airlines include superior service, the AAdvantage frequent-flier club, the Admirals Club, in-flight service, and the comfort of the environment. Its market communications emphasize the benefits of membership, which can be functional (e.g., arrive at location on time), symbolic (e.g., communicates your social status versus Southwest Airlines), or experiential (e.g., comfort of chairs).[25]

# Quotes on Online Branding

"E-branding is more important [than e-commerce]. And it must come first. Because few people will buy your stuff—online or off—unless you are top-of-mind."

—Annette Hamilton, Executive Producer, ZDNet

"Brand is the price of entry [to the Internet], not the winning strategy."

—Dylan Tweney, InfoNet

"By the time your potential customers log on, they already know what they're looking for, and they often know from whom they want to buy it. . . . They're just not listening to branding messages anymore."

—Michael Fischler, Principal, The Pubs Group

"Brands stand as comfort anchors in the sea of confusion, fear, and doubt. In dynamic markets, strong brands have more value than ever, precisely because of the speed with which these markets move."

—Chuck Pettis, Technobranding

"It took more than 50 years for Coca-Cola to become a worldwide market leader, but only five years for online search engine Yahoo to gain market dominance. The role of the brand has changed dramatically and has created a vacuum between offline and online brands."

—Mark Lindstrom, Executive Director, ZIVO

"A company's website IS the brand. It's the hub of consumer experience, the place where all aspects of a company, from its annual report to its products to its support, intersect. It's the company in a nutshell, all there in a way that just is not possible in the analog world."

—Sean Carton, Carton Donofrio Interactive

A fascinating development of the Internet has been the importance of branding. Perhaps due to the limited "real estate" that a screen-to-customer interface provides, or to a desire to build consumer goods companies quickly, or to the perception that this is a winner-take-all environment, it is abundantly clear that branding in the e-commerce arena is receiving a great deal of management attention.

Several key concerns are apparent in these quotes:

- Branding is a necessary but not sufficient condition for success.
- Branding may be more important in the online than the offline environment.
- Brands serve to add value in each step of the decision process—at prepurchase (e.g., driving traffic to the site), purchase (e.g., erasing doubt), and postpurchase (e.g., assurance).

Good brands provide a clear message to the market about the core offering, the wrap-arounds, and the communications. All not only provide a signal about the functional offering, but are simultaneously differentiated by their emotional, symbolic, and experiential benefits—for both the firm and target customers.

**A Simple Conceptual Model of Brand Equity.** Exhibit 7-4 provides a simple framework for understanding the effects of the brand (core, wrap-around, and communications) and brand equity. The exhibit has three basic parts: the brand, customer responses, and benefits (both to the firm and the customer). **Brand equity** has a wide variety of definitions in the academic literature.[26] According to David Aaker, brand equity is a combination of assets that can be viewed from both the firm's and the customer's perspectives. In other words, Aaker views brand equity as a combination of consumer responses and benefits (firm and customer). In particular, he notes that brand equity is "a set of assets (and liabilities) linked to a brand's

# What Is an Advertising Network Manager?[24]

by Leo Griffin

Advertising network managers such as DoubleClick, L90, Engage, and 24/7 aggregate and represent websites, selling (either to individual advertisers or to the media-buying arms of advertising agencies) banner impressions on websites belonging to their network members. Typically these firms keep 35 to 50 percent of the sales revenues for ads that they serve, passing the balance on to the site on which the banner actually appeared. The advantages of advertisers being able to buy from an aggregator are considerable—rather than making hundreds of phone calls and purchase decisions, media buyers can make just one. DoubleClick, which has one of the most extensive networks, has operations in over 20 countries and represents over 1,500 sites; 24/7 represents over 3,500 small and medium traffic websites.

Network managers do much more than just aggregate websites. They also provide technology and systems that allow advertisers to accurately target advertisements to relevant customer segments, to track click-through rates, and to monitor where and when and to whom their ads are being displayed.

DART (Dynamic Advertising Reporting and Targeting) is DoubleClick's ad serving and reporting system. It is used by sites in the DoubleClick network as well as by websites that manage their own banners but contract with DoubleClick to use the application, such as Ask Jeeves *www.ask.com*. The technology uses cookies (small data files placed on the hard disks of visitors to a DoubleClick network website) to individually identify each user whenever he or she visits a DoubleClick affiliate, and to record where he or she goes and what he or she does. DART has the ability to track people's click-stream and ad-viewing behavior across the DoubleClick network (sites such as Autobytel [*www.autobytel.com*], MTV [*www.mtv.com*], and Comedy Central [*www.comedycentral.com*]). To date, DoubleClick has built up over 50 million user profiles. The software allows advertisers to show their ads across the whole network, or on specific sites or categories of sites (e.g., entertainment sites). They can also target users based on variables such as their computer operating system, their zip code, and even their business name. Companies can also serve customized ads to users who have, for instance, visited their site but not made a purchase, or who have viewed a specific page on their website. So don't be surprised if you visit an e-commerce site, check out albums by your favorite artist, and the next day see an ad on a different site offering you a discount on CDs for that very same artist.

DoubleClick has recently made moves to expand its tracking capabilities beyond online click stream data to include offline purchase data. In June 1999, DoubleClick announced the acquisition of Abacus Direct Corporation, which manages the largest database of catalog purchasing behavior in the United States. This database contains purchase information taken from 1,500 catalogs and 3.5 billion transactions and includes information such as name, address, and the dates, amounts, and categories of purchases for 90 million U.S. households. DoubleClick's original intention was to merge the Abacus database with its own data to create an incredibly powerful database on people's online and offline behavior; however, public outcry over privacy concerns has caused it to agree to suspend its matching efforts, pending the agreement of industry standards.

L90 has taken a different approach to the advertising market. It focuses primarily on selling sponsorship-based advertising rather than banner ads. Sponsorships are attractive to advertisers and content creators alike. Advertisers like them because they can often create a more effective ad by integrating the message into the site's content. Websites like this approach because an advertising success does not automatically mean that the user will be transported away from the host's website. Sponsorship deals can also result in higher CPMs, which translate into more revenue for website owners.

## Do Strong Online Brands Matter?

As the discussion in the previous section implies, a strong brand can be viewed as essential to the growth of an online business. In particular, with the introduction of so many brands, a strong brand name provides a clear presence in the market. Furthermore, strong brands attract customers, and, hence, in the long run, firms may be able to decrease marketing expenditures once the brand is established. In effect, a strong brand is an instant message that contains a wide variety of associations on the part of target customers. Clear brands are also associated with higher conversation rates. Finally and most importantly, all current online "winners" have strong brands.

Opponents of the strong brand line of reasoning argue that history will prove this assumption to be lim-

ited. They believe that alliances are the key to locking up a market—and these alliances can be accomplished with strong venture backing. Second, third-party evaluators such as Gomez Advisors and BizRate will increasingly influence consumption—much like *Consumer Reports* does today. However, unlike *Consumer Reports,* the BizRate data is easily available, easy to access, and, hence, can drive consumption behavior during the purchase process. Third, speed to market may be more important than branding. Also, the meaning of brands is changing. Because all experiences are increasingly becoming customized, the meaning of a "mega-brand" is no longer relevant. Finally, while it is true that all winners have strong brands, a number of "big losers" also have strong brand names.

---

**Exhibit 7-3**

WHAT IS A GOOD BRAND?

**Marketing Communications**

**"Wrap-arounds"**

**Core Product/ Service**

**AmericanAirlines®**

- Mix of offline and online advertising
- Emphasizes advantages to AADVANTAGE memberships, including nonexpiring miles and online services

- Superior service
- AADVANTAGE frequent flier mile club
- Award-winning Admirals Club lounges
- Comfortable chairs
- Portable defibrillators on every flight

- Safe, on-time transportation from A to B

**Brand** ⟶ **Prestige**

name and symbol that add to (or subtract from) the value provided by a product or service to a firm and/or that firm's customers."[27]

Other authors tend to focus heavily on the customer responses only: "Customer-based brand equity is defined as the differential effect that brand knowledge has on consumer response to the marketing of that brand."

Others tend to focus only on financial criteria, such as the dollar value of the brand. Similar to Aaker, we tend to divide brand equity into two key components: (1) intermediate customer responses and (2) the benefits—to both the customer and the firm. Thus, the framework has three basic parts: the brand, customer responses to the brand (awareness and associations), and benefits (to both the firm and the target customers).

***Consumer Responses.*** Consumer responses can take two broad forms: brand awareness and brand associations. Brand awareness refers to the strength of a brand's presence in the consumer's mind. A brand with high brand awareness (e.g., Monster) is more likely to be recalled—either prompted by an advertisement or unaided.

Brand associations refer to the connections that consumers make to the brand. These associations can be categorized in terms of (1) strength, (2) valence, and (3) uniqueness. Consider the Amazon brand. **Strength of association** refers to the intensity with which the target consumer links a particular word, phrase, or meaning to a particular brand. Thus, if one were to cue the customer to reflect on the meaning of Amazon, the customer might say "big company," "Jeff Bezos," "they sell books," "it was my first Internet purchasing experience," "it is easy to use," or "they are unprofitable." Strong associations tend to be those that are "top of mind" for the customer. Measures of strength include:

 **Exhibit 7-4** A SIMPLE CONCEPTUAL MODEL OF BRAND EQUITY

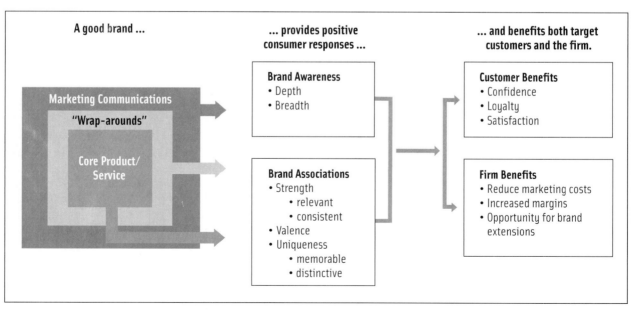

Sources: Kevin Keller, *Strategic Brand Management* (Saddle River: Prentice-Hall, 1998); David Aaker, *Building Strong Brands* (New York: The Free Press, 1995); Strategic Market Research Group; Marketspace Analysis.

number of times an association was mentioned, ranking of the association, and speed of recall. Our hypothesis is that "Jeff Bezos" would be a strong association to the Amazon brand name, compared to the association of it being a "Seattle-based" company.

**Valence** refers to the degree to which the association is positive or negative. Again, consider the Amazon associations above. "Easy to use" is a positive association, "unprofitable" is a negative association, and "they sell books" is a neutral association. **Uniqueness** captures the degree to which the association is distinct, relative to other brands. "Jeff Bezos" is an association that is unique to the Amazon brand.

Consider the American Airlines example again. A customer may have strong associations to the brand name (e.g., large carrier, the AA slogan). Strength of the association is often divided between two criteria: relevance and consistency. Relevance is defined as the degree to which the brand is perceived as meeting the needs of the target customer. Is the tag line relevant to the needs of the airline's key target segment—the business traveler? Consistency is the degree to which each element of the brand reinforces the brand intent. Does the AA symbol reinforce the airline's positioning as an airline for the business traveler? This is, of course, debatable. All else being equal, brands that are highly relevant and highly consistent tend to produce strong associations.

Companies hope these associations will be positive ("I had a great time flying American Airlines" versus "that is the airline that always is late"). Hence, associations can be rated on the degree to which they produce positive or negative associations—that is, their valence. Finally, associations can be rated on their uniqueness. Uniqueness also can be subdivided into distinctiveness and memorability. Distinctiveness captures the degree to which the brand is differentiated from competitors (e.g., Jeff Bezos is distinctive), while memorability captures the brand's ability to provide a lasting communication effect (e.g., does the tag line create memorability?). A memorable brand association leaves an impression in the mind of the customer, which enables easy recall.

***Firm and Consumer Benefits.*** Returning to Exhibit 7-4, positive consumer responses in turn produce benefits for both customers and the firm. Customer benefits include the increased confidence in the purchase decision, loyalty to the brand, and satisfaction with the experience. Firm benefits translate into top-line revenue growth, increased margins, and lower marketing costs. The firm also has the opportunity to extend the brand into new categories—such as Amazon's expansion into home improvement.

## Types of Brands

***Pure Offline and Online Brands.*** Early in the evolution of the Internet, brands were categorized as pure offline or online brands. Table 7-3 provides a sampling of these brands. Classic offline brands included the Gap, UPS, OfficeMax, and Disney. New-to-the-world online brands included Amazon, Yahoo, GeoCities, and Priceline. However, as the Internet expanded, we observed the crossover of offline brands into the online world, and the transition of online brands into the offline world (e.g., *Yahoo Internet Life* magazine).

***Blurring of the Distinction.*** The end result is a blurring of the distinction between pure offline and pure online brands. Consider the following developments:

- Brands such as Yahoo were established online but use offline promotional activities to grow brand awareness.

- Brands such as *Yahoo Internet Life* magazine are traditional brands in the sense that the product is established in the physical world, but they are extensions of the online brands—and thus a mixture of the two.
- Brands such as Egghead.com have completely shifted from an offline brand to a purely online brand.
- Brands such as WingspanBank were established in the virtual world but by a traditional brand.
- Brands such as Schwab have successfully bridged the gap between online and offline activities.
- Brands such as Ragu were established offline but use online promotional activities to grow brand awareness and loyalty.

Exhibit 7-5 provides a simple diagram to capture the movement of brands. In particular, the figure has two basic dimensions: mix of promotion (online versus offline) and initial product establishment (online brand versus offline brand). This figure illustrates that Schwab was initially a traditional brand—and has now moved toward the center of the figure to reflect its hybrid nature. Also, Schwab is doing both online and offline promotion—hence, the circle is quite wide. Egghead.com initially was a traditional, offline brand but has moved to an online brand with heavy online promotion activities.

# What Is the 10-Step Branding Process?

There are a number of well-known frameworks to build brands. In this section, we provide a simple, managerially relevant **10-Step Branding Process** (see Exhibit 7-6). In addition to the broad review of each step, we also discuss how the branding process may differ in the online environment. Broadly, these steps include the following:

**Table 7-3**

## TYPES OF BRANDS

| Traditional Brands | Online Brands |
|---|---|
| • The product/service with which the brand is associated was established offline in the bricks-and-mortar world. | • The product/service with which the brand is associated was established in the online world. |
| *Examples:* | *Examples:* |
| • The Gap<br>• UPS<br>• Dell<br>• J. Crew<br>• McDonald's<br>• OfficeMax<br>• Ragu<br>• Coca-Cola<br>• Disney | • Amazon<br>• Yahoo<br>• ZDNet<br>• AOL<br>• Priceline<br>• CDNow<br>• WingspanBank<br>• E*Trade |

**Step 1: Clearly Define the Brand Audience.** In Chapter 4, we discussed the need to specify the target audience for the offering. A clear picture of the target customer segment is critically inportant.

As noted in Chapters 4 and 5, it could be argued that a larger number of segments can be effectively addressed in the online environment than in the offline environment. This is due to a number of factors, including the firm's ability to reconfigure its storefront in a real-time fashion for each customer.

**Step 2: Understand the Target Customer.** After defining the brand audience, it is frequently useful to describe a typical customer who can bring the target segment to life.

Both online and offline environments require deep understanding of customer behavior. Indeed, firms building brands exclusively in one environment still need to be aware of consumer behavior in the other environment. As noted in Chapter 4, it is clear that a great deal of information can be collected online through click-stream data. However, this information is not sufficient to infer the process of consumption (e.g., attitudes, knowledge, brand image). Hence, a blending of traditional and online research is often necessary.

**Step 3: Identify Key Leverage Points in Customer Experience.** While target customers may share many of the same behavioral characteristics, this step forces the firm to consider the key organizational levers—prices of products, customer interface, mix of online versus offline communications—that will activate the customer to behave

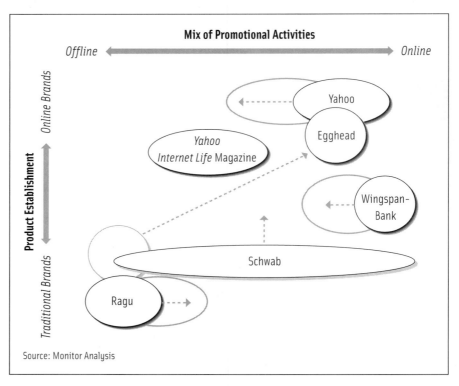

**Exhibit 7-5**

BRAND PRESENCE

Source: Monitor Analysis

in a manner that is consistent with the objectives of the firm. Consumer research should focus heavily on these key organizational levers that can motivate consumption.

The customer decision process involves prepurchase, purchase, and postpurchase decisions in both the online and offline environments. In the offline environment, it is the retail salesperson or the telephone customer service representative who guides the customer through the buying process. In the online environment, the store can be reconfigured—much like a chess match—to guide or direct consumers. It is a more subtle form of selling.

### Step 4: Continually Monitor Competitors.
Building a brand is tough even when there are no competitors in the space. However, competition in the online world is incredibly intense. It is not unusual for a firm to develop a clear business plan only to have competitors emerge before its launch date. Hence, it is critical that emerging and existing competitors are constantly monitored.

Competitors must be monitored in both online and offline environments, but the online environment is distinctive in two respects. First, the degree of competitive intensity is different. Numerous new firms can emerge both within the product category and across product categories. Second, it is much easier to analyze competitors given the emergence of sources such as Hoover's Online (*www.hoovers.com*), the Securities and Exchange Commission (*www.sec.gov*), and financial sites (MarketWatch.com).

### Step 5: Design Compelling and Complete Brand Intent.
The brand intent brings to life the value proposition. Value propositions, or clusters, tend to focus on the high-level customer benefits. The goal is a customer-friendly description of how the brand should be interpreted from the customer's viewpoint. The intent should be both compelling (i.e., provide the positive brand associations) and comprehensive.

While the brand intent is important in both environments, there is more opportunity for customization in the online environment. In general, the brand intent tends to be more segment-focused in the offline environment, while the online environment allows individuals within the segment to customize the offering.

**Exhibit 7-6**  BUILDING AN ONLINE BRAND

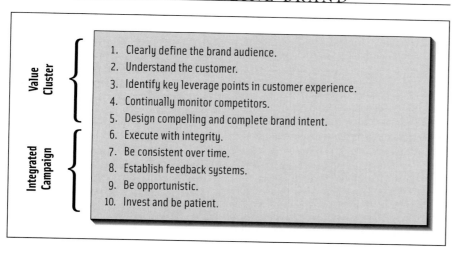

**Value Cluster**
1. Clearly define the brand audience.
2. Understand the customer.
3. Identify key leverage points in customer experience.
4. Continually monitor competitors.
5. Design compelling and complete brand intent.

**Integrated Campaign**
6. Execute with integrity.
7. Be consistent over time.
8. Establish feedback systems.
9. Be opportunistic.
10. Invest and be patient.

**Step 6: Execute with Integrity.** This step refers to the quality of the implementation choices and the extent to which the firm provides a clear, trustworthy message.

Historically, in the offline environment, building a brand took consistent, long-term investment. Most of the well-known Internet brands have been introduced since 1995.

**Step 7: Be Consistent Over Time.** Strong brands take time to develop. Of course, on Internet time, this may be months or years rather than decades. Regardless of the time line, the key is a consistent message.

While consistency is important, it is also clear that, given the interactive nature of the Internet, each consumer can have a slightly modified experience with the brand. Hence, while both environments attempt to be consistent, the Internet allows customers to experience the brand in unique ways.

**Step 8: Establish Feedback Systems.** Market communications and reactions in the marketplace rarely work out exactly as planned. Hence, it is important to have regular feedback systems in place.

The effects of branding can be measured more quickly and more precisely in the online environment. Sophisticated tools exist to track customer responses to the brand, marketing communications, and marketing.

**Step 9: Be Opportunistic.** Brand-building opportunities present themselves in unexpected ways. For example, Monster.com has always attempted to be one of the first in its category to try communicating in new ways, including Super Bowl commercials and blimp advertising.

Opportunism typically occurs at the segment level in the offline environment and at the individual level in the online environment.

**Step 10: Invest and Be Patient.** While the stock market's valuation of dot-coms may vary considerably, it is also evident that brands need to be nurtured and managed over time. Careful investment, long-term patience, and the ability to focus on the long run are critical.

Both environments require long-term investments in a consistent, compelling message. While it could be argued that online brands have the potential to generate loyalty more quickly—due principally to the newness of the experience for many consumers—both environments require significant long-term investment (see Table 7-4).

## A Framework for Branding

Table 7-5 illustrates a simple categorization scheme for brands. On the top row, we divide brands into two categories according to whether they were established as traditional or online brands. We subdivide the traditional category into "branding online" and "branding and selling online." For online brands, we classify them into two categories: intermediaries and e-commerce sites. Along the column, we note that these categorizations can apply to both business-to-business and business-to-consumer sites.

## Branding Choices

A firm's online branding choices depend upon its communications objectives. Exhibit 7-7 illustrates the types of decisions that influence the ultimate choice of communications elements. In the middle of Exhibit 7-7, we note that a firm can have at least six communications objectives.

**Brand Creation.** The objective may be to build a new-to-the-world brand name. Under such a scenario, it is likely that the firm will focus on brand awareness rather than brand loyalty. This choice, in turn, would lead to a mix of choices that emphasize brand-name awareness rather than communications that provide detailed information on the brand, such as comparative advertising.

**Table 7-4** SIMILARITIES AND DIFFERENCES IN OFFLINE VS. ONLINE BRANDING

| Branding Element | Offline | Online |
|---|---|---|
| 1. Clearly define the brand audience | • Limited to manageable number of segments to prevent inconsistent messaging | • Could include larger number of segments, with customer-driven messages |
| 2. Understand the customer | • Requires understanding of environment, desired purchase and usage experience | • Requires more thorough understanding of desired purchase and usage experience in an interactive environment |
| 3. Identify key leverage points in customer experience | • Buying process is typically a simplified representation of customer segment behavior with static leverage points | • Buying process tends to be more dynamic and flexible |
| 4. Continually monitor competitors | • Requires monitoring of competitor advertisements and activities | • Competitor advertisements & activities can be monitored online |
| 5. Design compelling and complete brand intent | • Brand intent (desired positioning) is designed to address the needs and beliefs of target segments | • Greater opportunity for customization of key messages |
| 6. Execute with integrity | • Strong, positive brands are built up over time | • Online interactions bring in added concerns of security and privacy<br>• Limited familiarity with online brands makes fostering trust more difficult |
| 7. Be consistent over time | • Brand intent guides marketing communications<br>• Image reinforced through variety of offline media | • Brand intent guides marketing communications<br>• With the ability to customize, one customer's brand image may be different than another customer's brand image |
| 8. Establish feedback systems | • Collecting and analyzing customer feedback is more time-consuming | • Sophisticated tools exist for tracking online; allow for anonymous, interactive, quick feedback |
| 9. Be opportunistic | • Marketing strategy includes plan for sequenced growth and adjustment of brand based on changing customer needs | • Customization for multiple segments and opportunity for early recognition of the changing customer requires a corresponding tailoring of brand intent |
| 10. Invest and be patient | • Building brand awareness requires significant investment<br>• Building brand loyalty takes time offline, especially because early customer receptivity to brands is difficult to assess (and usually involves market research) | • Building brand awareness requires significant investment, especially for those competitors who are not first in their category online<br>• Brands have the potential to generate loyalty more quickly, especially if customers are targeted effectively |

**Table 7-5** CASE STUDIES OF SUCCESSFUL ONLINE BRANDING EFFORTS

| | Established as Traditional Brand | | Established as Online Brand | |
|---|---|---|---|---|
| | **Branding Online** | **Branding and Selling Online** | **Intermediary/ Vertical Portal** | **e-Commerce** |
| *Business-to-Consumer* | Ragu | American Airlines | Monster.com | CDNow |
| *Business-to-Business* | FedEx | Cisco Systems | Healtheon | Ventro |

**Sales Leads.** The company may decide that the Internet will be used to facilitate the sales-lead process. Dell Online and others have found that their Web presence actually builds qualified leads in a quicker, more effective way than traditional sales approaches. Hence, in sharp contrast to the view that the sales force will decrease as the Web expands, this finding suggests that the focus of the sales force will change from lead generation to "closing the sale."

**Exhibit 7-7** ONLINE BRANDING CHOICES

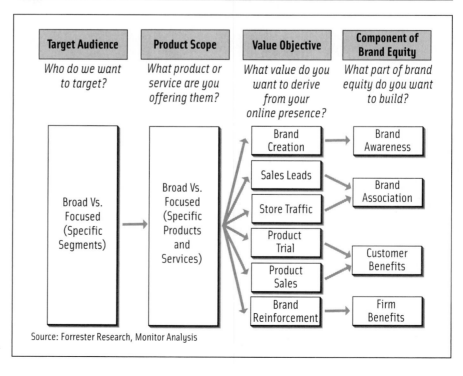

Source: Forrester Research, Monitor Analysis

**Store Traffic.** The principal objective for some sites is store traffic. That means the effectiveness of the campaign will be judged by the increase in unique visitors.

**Product Trial.** A fourth objective may be trial usage of the product. For example, *The Wall Street Journal's* interactive edition provided two weeks of free access to Palm VII users to encourage trial adoption of the newspaper.

**Product Sales.** The company can also measure the success of a campaign based upon the actual increase in product or service sales.

**Brand Reinforcement.** Finally, it is possible that the communications effort is focused largely on reinforcing a brand image that is already widely accepted in the marketplace.

These communications objectives, in turn, can produce effects on the brand awareness, brand recognition, and firm/customer benefits. Finally, the particular choice of brand equity that is targeted will naturally lead to the selection of certain communications elements.

# HOW DOES ONLINE BRANDING COMPARE BETWEEN AMERICAN AIRLINES AND CONTINENTAL AIRLINES?

In the following section, we consider two case studies about online branding—one for American Airlines and one for Monster.com. In order to understand the branding process and show how branding can be differentiated on the Internet (an equally important topic), these companies are compared to average performers in their product categories.

## Case Study: American Airlines

American Airlines is an excellent example of a bricks-and-mortar company that increased brand recognition and cemented customer loyalty by successfully taking its brand online. American had been a pioneer in the industry since developing the SABRE computer-reservation system in the 1960s and initiating the first frequent-flier program in the 1980s.

**Overview of Online Branding Efforts.** American Airlines was the first airline to establish a website; it did so on May 17, 1995. It is now one of the top airline sites in terms of unique visitors and awards. By February 2000, it was logging more than 1.9 million unique visitors per month. It receives upwards of 300,000 visits on peak days, with 25 million page views per month. It has 2.1 million subscribers to its weekly Net SAAver Fares™ e-mail list (the most popular e-mail travel product on the Web). Gross sales were $575 million in the 1999 calendar year.

A key to American's success in creating an online brand has been its ability to differentiate itself from competitors by consistently being first. American was

- First to have a service-oriented website (May 1995)
- First to launch an e-mail service of discounted fares, Net SAAver Fares™ (March 1996)
- First to offer real-time flight information (Spring 1996)
- First to offer flight information on competitors (Spring 1996)

## Should Offline Firms Create New Brands or Use Their Existing Brands?

There is considerable debate in the practitioner community on the value of leveraging an existing brand name into the online environment. Simply put, should companies such as Lands' End, Wal-Mart, American Airlines, and Kmart use their existing brand name in the online environment, or should they create a new-to-the-world brand name? Consider the following examples:

**Wal-Mart Vs. Kmart.** Wal-Mart has decided to use its existing brand name to launch walmart.com (*www.walmart.com*) while Kmart, a clear bricks-and-mortar competitor, has decided to use a new brand name (*www.bluelight.com*). BlueLight.com is using a brilliant approach that involves the offer of free ISP service available to all through its site. If that is not a direct pitch to Middle America, we do not know what is. And it worked. After just a few months in the market, more than a million people have registered for the service, which is fast and easy to download.

**American Airlines Vs. Travelocity.** Until this year, American Airlines owned SABRE. SABRE, in turn, owned over 80 percent of Travelocity. Hence, American was able to see the clear advantage of using a different brand name in its attempt to become the dominant company in the entire category of travel.

Proponents of the "keep the same brand" school argue that it takes an enormous amount of time and money to build a strong brand name. People in the

venture-capital community claim that it costs $50 to $100 million to launch a new consumer brand on the Web. Hence, it makes a great deal of sense to continue using the offline brand name for the online brand. Second, customers who decide to purchase online can be assured that services can occur offline (e.g., the ability to return product to a physical store, phone calls can be made to service centers). Third, it is difficult to uncover interesting new brand names. Fourth, the online and offline brands can have a synergistic effect—one that is greater than either brand operating alone. Finally, target customers will not be confused by brand offerings that appear on new sites (e.g., Kmart brands appearing on BlueLight.com).

Opponents argue that using an existing brand limits the growth of the user base. That is, it is easier for customers to believe that Travelocity or Expedia is the most comprehensive travel site as compared to their majority stockholders (i.e., American Airlines and Microsoft, respectively). Second, existing offline brands "don't get the Net." Their user interfaces are likely to be less useable, hip, and interesting than those of true dot-com brands. Third, it is possible to sign up more partners—potential competitors, collaborators, and others—when a third-party name is used. For example, General Motors, Ford, and Chrysler selected a new brand name for their announced B2B exchange.

- First to offer airline reservations online (June 1996)
- First to offer paperless upgrade coupons and stickers (Spring 1997)
- First to send e-mail confirmation of itinerary and ticket purchase (Fall 1997)
- First to offer high personalization for consumers (June 1998)
- First airline to partner with AOL to create AOL AAdvantage Rewards Program (Fall 2000)

American's online strategy and brand are tightly aligned with its offline objectives: to provide the best possible product to the consumer and, in turn, increase the profitability of the company. Online resources not only provide an additional customer base and an additional medium for branding but also reduce the need for costly phone transactions.

Exhibit
7-8

W W W . A A . C O M

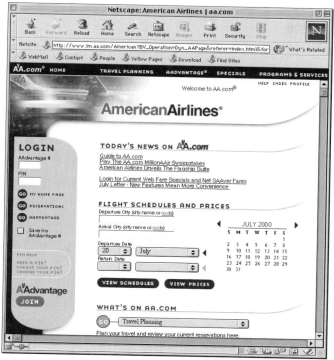

Courtesy of AA.com and American Airlines, Inc. (www.aa.com)

Several other features of the American effort are worth noting. American's online initiative was set up as a separate entity with its own profit-and-loss statement to allow for flexibility and speed of responsiveness. It constantly attempts to anticipate and fulfill the needs of customers—to the point of offering competitor information and fares. It develops and adopts new technologies to respond to customers' needs, including such innovations as database synchronization to provide a single, integrated consumer database; a combined BookSmart and SABRE system; and new design features for an interactive, visual appearance.

**Comparison to Average Performer.** In Exhibit 7-9 we compare the American Airlines site to Continental Airlines by using the 10-Step Branding Process. Again, keep in mind that Continental is by no means the worst performer in the category. Indeed, Forrester Research ranked the site eighteenth in terms of reach, tickets booked, and revenue—and first in its travel-category ratings. However, Media Metrix does not list Continental in its top 10 travel sites.

In order to interpret this exhibit, it is necessary to understand the key at the bottom of the exhibit. One can think of the circles as a visual way to express a five-point scale by which a clear circle (one-point score) indicates poor performance and a completely black circle is the highest rating (five-point score).

It would take a very long time to highlight every point illustrated in Exhibit 7-9. Hence, we focus only on the most important lessons. A quick visual scan of the exhibit reveals that American Airlines systematically outperforms Continental on

**Exhibit 7-9**

## ASSESSMENT OF KEY BRANDING ELEMENTS

| Key Elements | Online Branding Best-in-Class American Airlines | | Comparison Continental | |
|---|---|---|---|---|
| | Rating | Rationale | Rating | Rationale |
| 1. Clearly define the brand audience | ● | • Specifically targets AADVANTAGE members—highly profitable and loyal customers familiar with travel (and thus more likely to buy tickets online) | ◑ | • Targets both high-spending business customers as well as Onepass members and non-Onepass members |
| 2. Understand the customer | ● | • Constantly anticipates and innovates to meet the needs of the customer | ◕ | • Tends to be a "follower" in the industry, late in launching its website (6/97) |
| 3. Identify key leverage points in customer experience | ● | • Net SAAver Fares™ and new customization program leverage consumers' desire for finding cheap fares into transaction by sending out e-mails each week | ◑ | • Sends C.O.O.L. e-mails similar to Net SAAver Fares™ and added a personalization feature to site, but late identification of this leverage point resulted in significantly lower subscription rates |
| 4. Continually monitor competitors | ● | • If a competitor adopted a technology before American; it was quick to follow | ◑ | • Tends to follow what competitors are doing at a slower pace, launching "copy-cat" initiatives many months after competitor roll-out |
| 5. Design compelling and complete brand intent | ◔ | • Focus, streamlining, and ease of use of website all convey American's message of customer needs first | ◑ | • Unclear target segment (business travelers? OnePass members?) causes lack of clarity with brand intent |
| 6. Execute with integrity | ◕ | • Trust fostered in the offline world carries over into the online world | ◕ | • Trust fostered in the offline world carries over into the online world, with extensive information for members on privacy and use of provided information |
| 7. Be consistent over time | ● | • Although constantly innovating new technologies and features, stays true to its tag line | ◑ | • Different URLs for different portions of the site do not convey message of consistency |
| 8. Establish feedback systems | ◑ | • Customer service offered as a service at the top of each page in small letters but is not labeled as a specific menu item | ● | • Very easy to access, prominent feature for obtaining customer feedback on the website |
| 9. Be opportunistic | ● | • Leader in its industry in innovation and development | ◔ | • Follower in the industry |
| 10. Invest and be patient | ● | • Invests significantly in technology for the future | ◑ | • Has a tendency to wait too long to make changes to its site |

○ = Very Low   ◔ = Low   ◑ = Moderate   ◕ = High   ● = Very High

almost all of the relevant elements. On seven of the elements, American has a "very high" score, while Continental received this score for only one element.

A few particular elements are worth examining in depth. With respect to the target audience, the *www.aa.com* site targets its frequent-flier group, while Continental's targeting client base is much less clear (it appears to have three target groups). While American tends to be an innovator, Continental is a consistent laggard. One key leverage point for American is the Net SAAver Fares™ program. Its early debut of an e-mail newsletter for last-minute fare discounts enabled it to grow a user base very quickly. While Continental eventually followed with a similar e-mail discount program, the late entry led to significantly lower subscription rates.

Overall, American is providing a more consistent brand image over time. It has invested in its key constituent base—the business traveler. It has provided consistent technology and customer-facing innovation for well over 20 years. Finally, with respect to brand recognition, the American site receives high marks for relevancy, distinctiveness, consistency, and memorability (see Exhibit 7-10).

# Case Study: Monster

Monster.com (see Exhibit 7-11) is a good example of an online company that has succeeded by branding itself in both online and offline environments. Monster is a metamarket switchboard that offers employment services to job seekers and employers. For job seekers, Monster aims to serve as a "lifelong career network," offering not only job and resume postings but also chats, message boards, and

**Exhibit 7-10**

## ASSESSMENT OF KEY BRAND ATTRIBUTES

| | | **Online Branding Best-in-Class**<br>*American Airlines* | | **Comparison**<br>*Continental* |
|---|---|---|---|---|
| **Key Attributes** | **Rating** | **Rationale** | **Rating** | **Rationale** |
| 1. Relevant | ● | • Up-to-date flight and gate check information<br>• Personalized information based on AAdvantage profiles<br>• PDA applications with flight information | ◔ | • Offers only information for Continental Airlines, but does not offer bookings for rental cars and hotels<br>• Allows travel preferences to be saved in profiles |
| 2. Distinct | ● | • Availability of competitor information<br>• Offers highly personalized experience<br>• First to offer tie-in with PDA applications | ◔ | • Offers extensive online customer service options<br>• Offers customized services for the business traveler |
| 3. Consistent | ● | • Portrays a consistent online image throughout the site | ◕ | • No key messages online associated closely with the offline campaign |
| 4. Memorable | ● | • Provides a unique service others cannot offer (in terms of personalization)<br>• Net SAAver Fares™ is the most well-known and effective e-mail marketing tool | ◑ | • Multiple URLs associated with the site and lack of online/offline message association fail to create a cohesively memorable brand for the consumer |

○ = Very Low ◔ = Low ◑ = Moderate ◕ = High ● = Very High

**Exhibit 7-11**

# WWW.MONSTER.COM

courtesy monster®.com

expert advice on career management. For employers, Monster provides value-added solutions including resume-skills screening, resume routing, and real-time recruiting, in addition to access to its database of more than 4 million job seekers.

**Overview of Branding Efforts.** Launched in 1994 as the 454th website in the world, Monster was a true early entrant in the commercial world of the Internet. According to Media Metrix, it has well over 50 percent of the online-recruitment advertising market.[28] Revenue increased from $6.9 million in 1996 to $133.5 million in 1999.[29] The site's traffic—averaging 3.6 million unique visitors in January 2000—translates into a reach of more than 5 percent of all U.S. Internet users. At the end of 2000, Monster had 7.2 million resumes on file and more than 273,000 registered recruiters.

Some have argued that a large part of Monster's early success was its ability to brand itself both online and offline. Its offline advertising and associated Monster logo provided a distinctive branding message. Its Super Bowl advertising showed young children discussing their desired futures: "I want to file all day," "I want to claw my way up to middle management," and "I want to have a brown nose." These provided a clear message of what Monster could deliver—good jobs, challenging careers, and rapid advancement.

These somewhat risky ads produced immediate results. The 24 hours following the February 1999 ads generated 2.2 million job searches—a 450 percent increase in traffic from the previous week. A considerable jump in job searches also followed the 2000 Super Bowl's ad. More than 4.4 million job searches were conducted within a 24-hour period—twice the number of job searches that Monster received the day after the 1999 Super Bowl.

Monster pursues an "Intern to CEO" strategy, providing recruiting solutions globally in a wide range of industries at all levels of experience. It has formed alliances to expand its online career service offerings to include health care, technology, telecommunications, temporary work, and, more recently, free-agent talent markets. Advertising targets a wide array of individuals, attracting the largest and most diverse pool of job seekers for employers using the site.

To further its branding efforts, it has also signed alliances with Yahoo, as well as a $100 million four-year agreement with AOL to be the online service provider's exclusive career-information provider.

### Comparison to Average Performer.
Exhibit 7-12 compares Monster to HotJobs on the 10 steps of branding. At first glance, it is apparent that Monster is outperforming HotJobs on a number of elements—although the gaps in performance are not as wide as the gaps between American and Continental. Indeed, HotJobs is strong in a number of areas, including customer focus, specialization by entry-level positions, and privacy screens/policy. It is comparatively weaker on the interactive nature of the site, the compelling nature of its brand intent, and opportunity for feedback. Similar to Monster, it is clearly willing to take advertising risks—both with Super Bowl placement and with its various ad copy (e.g., "all the hottest jobs at all the hottest companies").

Exhibit 7-13 shows a comparison of Monster versus HotJobs on four brand-recognition criteria. Our analysis reveals that the brands are similar on relevancy and distinctiveness, but that Monster outperforms HotJobs on consistency and memorability.

# MARKETWATCH.COM MARKET COMMUNICATIONS AND BRANDING

As discussed in earlier chapters, MarketWatch.com tries to appeal to a broad audience interested in financial information. In order to reach that audience and to communicate its marketing message, it uses a number of methods. Table 7-6 uses the marketing communications framework to classify those methods into four categories: general approaches, traditional mass marketing, personalized marketing, and direct marketing.

In terms of *general online approaches,* MarketWatch.com aggressively advertises on sites with broad reach, such as Yahoo, Lycos, and Excite. In addition, it is a recommended link on the CBS site and the sites of CBS partners. One very successful way of communicating its message online is to offer financial content to other sites in exchange for advertising and exposure. For example, MarketWatch.com is the premier provider of business and financial news for AOL's Personal Finance channel, with links on the AOL site leading to MarketWatch.com. It also has a content-licensing agreement with online brokers such as E*Trade and Fidelity.com. In addition to agreements with other parties, MarketWatch.com offers the majority of its content and tools for free, encouraging users to explore the site and to return to it regularly. MarketWatch.com has also pioneered innovative online communications, such as the "Financial Survivor" contest that was planned for the end of 2000. Selected investment clubs would compete for the highest end portfolio value, with the

**Exhibit 7-12**

# ASSESSMENT OF KEY BRANDING ELEMENTS

| Key Elements | Online Branding Best-in-Class *Monster.com* | | Comparison *HotJobs.com* | |
|---|---|---|---|---|
| | Rating | Rationale | Rating | Rationale |
| 1. Clearly define the brand audience | ◕ | • Within the employer market, targets all types of companies, from startups to large corporations | ◕ | • Appeals to a wide range of job seekers, but specializes in the intern and entry-level positions |
| 2. Understand the customer | ● | • Offers highly personalized services for job seekers, addresses security concerns, and offers value-added services (resume help, advice, interactive communication with other job seekers) | ● | • Only site to offer privacy feature that allows job seekers to select which companies have access to their resumes |
| 3. Identify key leverage points in customer experience | ● | • Provides interactive career information for customers who are not necessarily "looking," thus increasing the probability that they will become job seekers | ● | • Allows recruiting process to become internal through Hotjobs.com and its proprietary Softshoe technology, eliminating concerns about adding an additional venue for recruiting |
| 4. Continually monitor competitors | ◔ | • Currently a leader in providing unique services to its consumers, but lacks some features that competitors have | ◑ | • Adopts successful features of the Monster.com site, but usually on a lesser scale |
| 5. Design compelling and complete brand intent | ● | • Message of "there's a better job out there" combined with diversified strategic alliances and "intern-to-CEO" strategy to convey the idea that Monster.com can find you that better job | ◑ | • Message of "all the hottest jobs at all the hottest companies" was overshadowed in spring 2000 with controversy over tastefulness of ads that were rejected by networks |
| 6. Execute with integrity | ◕ | • Offers password and ID protection, as well as some ability to selectively decide when and where your resume can be seen | ◑ | • Offers most specialized security measures for individual users (prevents current employers from viewing resume) |
| 7. Be consistent over time | ● | • In the short time since "there's a better job out there," messages have been consistent | ◑ | • Recent "Hottest Hand on the Web" campaign different from past branding messages |
| 8. Establish feedback systems | ● | • Offers extensive feedback system for users, allowing users to even select categories of information/feedback | ◕ | • Also offers feedback mechanism for users, although less specialized |
| 9. Be opportunistic | ● | • Partners with firms that could potentially be competitors rather than trying to eliminate competition | ◕ | • Took a risk with Super Bowl advertising, even without a compelling ad campaign, to raise brand awareness |
| 10. Invest and be patient | ◕ | • Willing to invest heavily in the offline world to gain brand recognition | ◕ | • Also willing to invest in the offline world to gain brand recognition |

○ = Very Low      ◔ = Low      ◑ = Moderate      ◕ = High      ● = Very High

Exhibit
7-13

## ASSESSMENT OF KEY BRAND ATTRIBUTES

| Key Attributes | Rating | Online Branding Best-in-Class Monster.com — Rationale | Rating | Comparison HotJobs.com — Rationale |
|---|---|---|---|---|
| 1. Relevant | ● | • For job seekers: Provides information for individuals regardless of whether they are actively pursuing a new position, including career information and chats with other members on various career topics | ● | • For job seekers: Provides information geared more specifically for those individuals who are seeking positions |
| 2. Distinct | ● | • For job seekers: Aids in resume building, personalization with "My Monster" pages and enhanced privacy options; also offers opportunity for interactive communication with other members | ● | • For job seekers: Allows selection of companies that view posted resumes |
| 3. Consistent | ● | • Recent partnerships have been consistent with Monster.com's aim to provide the most diverse set of individuals with the most diverse set of employment opportunities | ◐ | • New "Hottest Hand on the Web" campaign, although new and catchy, has not been consistent since the company's beginning |
| 4. Memorable | ● | • Witty and award-winning offline advertising has allowed Monster.com to cement itself as the best-known online career site on the Web | ◐ | • Although also one of the most well-known online career services on the Web, has not been as successful as Monster.com in creating a uniquely memorable advertising campaign and message |

competition being covered by the MarketWatch.com site and on television by the CBS *Early Show.*

MarketWatch.com also uses a variety of *traditional mass-marketing media.* It leverages its relationship with CBS News to extend its communications to television and radio. On television, it has its own weekly show, *CBS MarketWatch Weekend,* and it provides financial content for popular CBS News programs (such as the *Early Show* and *CBS Evening News*) as well as for CBS NewsPath, a CBS news service for affiliate stations. In radio, MarketWatch.com contributes content that is aired through the Westwood One Radio syndication company across the country (154 stations, including the top 10 markets in the nation, with a reach of 11.5 unduplicated listeners each week). In addition to placing ads in business trade journals, MarketWatch.com communicates through the print medium by providing financial content to newspapers, such as the *Daily News Express.* This allows MarketWatch.com to target people interested in financial news and who have varying degrees of knowledge of financial concepts. MarketWatch.com also targets its offline marketing through bus advertisements in target cities and by participating in conferences related to online finance issues.

MarketWatch.com does not personalize its marketing communications, online or offline. It does, however, perform online permission marketing using opt-in e-mail lists. As it collects more information on its users, it is likely that it will be able to better target its marketing communications to individual users.

# Brand Loyalty

by Elizabeth Millard, staff writer for tnbt.com

*Shot in gritty black and white, the scene is bleak: a young child, his expression blank and humorless, stares into the camera and declares, "I want to be forced into early retirement."*

Remember the ad? Even though it first aired during the 1999 Super Bowl, Monster.com is betting that you do: Like many Internet players, Monster.com has embraced old-school branding for its new e-commerce model, investing heavily (to the tune of $60 million) in the notion that name recognition will translate into page hits, revenue, and ultimately, staying power as a powerhouse online brand. But despite the commercial's success—it was seen by some 100 million people, and still enjoys buzz as a best-of-breed dot-com ad—Monster.com is hardly home free. According to a pair of intriguing new studies, when it comes to establishing and maintaining dominant brands on the Web, many companies—even ones that break fast out of the branding gate—may face a bleak scenario of their own.

The first problem: The vast majority of Internet branding initiatives to date seem to have left consumers distinctly underwhelmed. A recent Harris Interactive poll revealed that while consumers are well-acquainted with a few online superbrands—Amazon, eBay, and Egghead topped the name-recognition list—respondents were unable to name a single Web retailer in the insurance, fitness, or online electronics categories, despite the slew of advertising for Buy.com, Netmarket, and other companies that fit the bill.

"The sheer lack of penetration in the minds of most Americans is really stunning," says Ben Black, director of business development at Harris Interactive.

Still, Julia Resnick, product manager for the company's eCommercePulse division, says, "From our perspective, we look at unaided brand awareness among websites and there seems to be a correlation between brand awareness and high performance. It's kind of a chicken and egg thing, though. I don't think branding alone is what's causing the success, but it's really interconnected with performance."

If a company establishes its brand successfully, that means they've conquered the branding problem and are here to stay, right? Maybe not. A study done by Peter Golder, a marketing professor at New York University's Stern School of Business, reexamines a 1923 benchmark NYU study of top brands in 100 product groups and shows that only 23 were still leaders in 1997.

"I'm not here to bash brands, I certainly agree that they're important," Golder says. "What my study suggests is that the staying power of brands is a lot less than what people may believe." In the dot-com world, he says, the lack of staying power is particularly relevant as Internet companies try to build brand awareness quickly in a busy marketplace. Golder suggests an alternative tack: "In the Internet environment, there's confusion over brand awareness versus brand equity. I think the primary emphasis of too many Internet companies is on just getting people to be aware of their name, but it's the equity that resides in the brand that insures success."

So, if you can get consumers to your site, but have difficulty filling orders or providing customer service, you can kiss those branding dollars good-bye. Golder says, "If the customer's experience at the site is consistent with your advertising message, then branding works, but if it's inconsistent, it'll ruin whatever efforts you've made."

If awareness is bolstered with equity, it's time and money well spent. "With branding, people build associations. If the entire usage experience for the customer reinforces those good associations, then you'll have staying power in an Internet environment that's constantly evolving."

*Read more articles about The Next Big Thing at www.tnbt.com*

**Table 7-6**

## MARKETWATCH.COM MARKETING COMMUNICATIONS

| | Direct | Personalized |
|---|---|---|
| **Individualized** | | • Permission marketing e-mails sent to groups from opt-in lists |
| | **Traditional Mass Marketing** | **General Approaches** |
| **Broad** | • Television<br>  –Advertising on CBS<br>  –Mentions and scrolls during CBS shows<br>  –*CBS MarketWatch Weekend*<br>  –Contributions to CBS NewsPath<br><br>• Outdoor Advertising<br>  –Outdoor placards<br>  –Bus advertisements in target cities<br><br>• Radio<br>  –Contributions to Westwood One Radio Network<br>  –Spots during NFL radio broadcasts<br>  –Mentions on CBS owned and operated radio stations<br><br>• Print<br>  –Limited ads in trade journals<br><br>• Conferences<br>  –Participation in online finance, online journalism, and Internet-related conferences | • Advertising on major portals (e.g., Yahoo, Lycos, Excite, AltaVista)<br><br>• Advertising on CBS site and other CBS Internet partners (e.g. CBS SportsLine.CBS HealthWatch)<br><br>• Advertisements on targeted sites (e.g. other online financial sites)<br><br>• Provision of content and tools to sites (e.g., AOL, Quicken.com)<br><br>• Licensing content arrangements<br><br>• CBS MarketWatch Survivor contest<br><br>• Free information onsite |

**Audience Focus** (left axis)

*Offline*        *Online*

**Communication Needs**

# Key Branding Elements and Brand Attributes for MarketWatch.com

Earlier in this chapter, we introduced a 10-step process for building a successful brand. In Exhibit 7-14, we assess the performance of MarketWatch.com using these steps. We can make some interesting conclusions by looking at areas where MarketWatch.com performs very strongly and where there seems to be the most room for improvement. MarketWatch.com's ability to execute its branding message of providing "the story behind the numbers" with integrity, through its staff of experienced journalists and its association with CBS News, makes the MarketWatch.com

**Exhibit 7-14** ASSESSMENT OF KEY BRANDING ELEMENTS FOR MARKETWATCH.COM

| Key Elements | Rating | MarketWatch.com Rationale |
|---|---|---|
| *Clearly define the brand audience* | ◑ | • Three target groups cover a wide range of the population: savvy investors, financial information seekers, and "dabblers" (users with little financial knowledge) |
| *Understand the customer* | ◕ | • Understands the different needs of savvy investors versus less sophisticated investors and provides offerings accordingly |
| *Identify key leverage points in customer experience* | ◕ | • Focuses primarily on providing breaking news and analysis, rather than enabling investors to make transactions<br>• Has developed a community that shares knowledge and encourages frequent returns to the site |
| *Continually monitor competitors* | ● | • Continuously tracks studies on demographics, behavior, and brand awareness of its users versus competition |
| *Design compelling and complete brand intent* | ◕ | • Message of "get the story behind the numbers" captures most of the value offered to users—relevant and in-depth financial information and analysis; it does not fully capture the tools and education that the site offers |
| *Execute with integrity* | ● | • The message of the CBS MarketWatch brand is trustworthy; its credibility is enhanced by the association with the CBS News brand name and its staff of over 90 experienced journalists and editors |
| *Be consistant over time* | ◑ | • Initial branding message was "your eye on the market"; switched to "get the story behind the numbers" in 1999; the new message was designed to appeal to a broader user group |
| *Establish feedback systems* | ◕ | • Rigorously tested site and message effectiveness with focus groups half-way through the new marketing message campaign, at a time when the market was in turmoil; results were highly positive |
| *Be opportunistic* | ● | • Establishing CBS MarketWatch brand over a number of different media, including Web, TV, radio, print, and wireless |
| *Invest and be patient* | ◕ | • Investing a large percentage of the company budget to sales and marketing activities–patiently waiting to become profitable, even with a market that currently demands profitability |

○ = Very Low  ◔ = Low  ◑ = Moderate  ◕ = High  ● = Very High

brand stand out from its competitors, many of whom do not have the staff to generate their own financial content. The opportunistic nature of its marketing strategy, communicating its branding message across multiple media (TV, radio, Web, print, wireless), has allowed MarketWatch.com to broaden its reach and to appeal to new target groups, such as people who are not as knowledgeable but are still interested in financial news and analysis (the "seekers" and "dabblers" segments that were introduced in Chapter 4). Furthermore, the close monitoring of its competitors allows MarketWatch.com to tailor its branding message so that it remains unique and memorable in a very competitive market.

There are also some branding elements where it appears that MarketWatch.com could improve. By trying to appeal to a very wide audience (including savvy investors, people interested in financial news and analysis, and people new to financial concepts), MarketWatch.com may be trying to satisfy the needs of too many types of users, leading to a potential loss of focus. Also, even though the decision to change its brand message to "get the story behind the numbers" from "your eye on the market" was successful in expanding the target audience, it may have been confusing to savvy investors who were used to a site that focused on providing breaking news. MarketWatch.com may need to evaluate which of the two groups (savvy investors versus people marginally interested in financial news) it needs to target and focus its efforts on that group.

In terms of key brand attributes, the MarketWatch.com brand message is both distinct and memorable compared to those of its competitors. Recent TV advertisements, which start with the end market result of a news announcement and trace it back to the unlikely events that led to the announcement, greatly contribute to the memorability of the MarketWatch.com brand. Competitor sites do not communicate messages that are as catchy or as clear. Finally, the MarketWatch.com brand is highly relevant. It determines the needs of distinct user groups for financial information and guidance, and addresses them with different levels of sophistication. Exhibit 7-15 includes a detailed assessment of the MarketWatch.com brand, along with the key brand attributes, and helps explain its popularity and success.

# SUMMARY

### 1. What are the four categories of market communications?

Market communications can be categorized into a simple two-by-two framework based upon the audience focus (broad versus individual) and communication media (offline versus online). The four categories of communications are direct, personalized, traditional mass marketing, and general online approaches.

### 2. What is a "good" brand?

Good brands provide a clear message to the market about the core offering, the wrap-arounds, and communications. All provide a signal about the functional offering, and are simultaneously differentiated by their emotional, symbolic, and experiential benefits—for both the firm and target customers.

### 3. What is the 10-Step Branding Process?

The 10-Step Branding Process can be broken down into two general stages: building the value cluster and the integrated campaign (see Exhibit 7-6). The steps are as follows:

**Exhibit 7-15**

ASSESSMENT OF KEY BRAND ATTRIBUTES
FOR MARKETWATCH.COM

| Key Attributes | Rating | MarketWatch.com |
| --- | --- | --- |
| | | **Rationale** |
| 1. Relevant | ● | • Directly addressing the needs of different user groups for savvy investors, providing real-time quotes, in-depth analysis and tools; for financial information seekers and users new to financial concepts, providing headline news and analysis as well as education tools |
| 2. Distinct | ● | • Brand message "get the story behind the numbers" is distinct from competitor messages; it focuses on the unique MarketWatch.com capability of providing new-to-the-world, relevant, in-depth content |
| 3. Consistent | ◑ | • The initial brand message was "your eye on the market," which changed to "get the story behind the numbers" in mid-1999; the intent was to appeal to a wider group of users, shifting the focus toward less sophisticated investors and people new to financial information<br><br>• The main offering message of providing quality market analysis has remained relatively consistent |
| 4. Memorable | ● | • The Marketwatch.com brand message is highly memorable<br><br>• This has been aided by appealing and memorable TV advertisements, which start with the end market result of a news announcement and trace it back to the events that led to it<br><br>• As a result, the CBS MarketWatch brand rose 10 points in aided awareness in one year |

○ = Very Low     ◔ = Low     ◑ = Moderate     ◕ = High     ● = Very High

1. Clearly define the brand audience.
2. Understand the customer.
3. Identify key leverage points in target customer experience.
4. Continually monitor competitors.
5. Design compelling and complete brand intent.
6. Execute with integrity.
7. Be consistent over time.
8. Establish feedback systems.
9. Be opportunistic.
10. Invest and be patient.

## 4. How does online branding compare between American Airlines and Continental Airlines?

Exhibit 7-9 illustrates that American Airlines systematically outperforms Continental Airlines on almost all of the relevant elements. On seven of the elements, American Airlines received a "very high" score, while Continental received this score for only one element.

5. **What are the Point-Counterpoint arguments for leveraging an offline brand into the online environment?**

Arguments for the use of existing brands are that they (1) are known, (2) are less costly to develop, (3) provide assurance to the target segment, and (4) provide an integrated online and offline experience. Opponents argue that using an existing brand limits the growth of the user base. Second, existing offline brands "don't get the Net." Third, it is possible to sign up more partners—potential competitors, collaborators, and others—when a third-party name is used.

## KEY TERMS

branding

market communications

general online communications

personalized online communications

traditional mass media communications

direct communications

banner ads

e-mail

viral marketing

affiliate programs

permission marketing

direct marketing

telemarketing

brand equity

strength of association

valence

uniqueness

10-Step Branding Process

## Endnotes

[1]SEC Form 10-K for Amazon.com, Inc. filed on March 5, 1999, and March 29, 2000.

[2]Petersen, Andrea. 1999. You can have the greatest e-commerce site on the Web; The trick is to get people to come to it. *The Wall Street Journal,* 12 July.

[3]Anderson, Diane. 2000. E-Mail or me-mail. *Industry Standard*, 6 March.

[4]Weber, Thomas E. 1999. The Spam king is back, and his new recipe clicks on changing net. *The Wall Street Journal,* 13 December.

[5]Rayport, Jeffrey. 1996. The virus of marketing. *Fast Company,* issue no. 6 (December-January): 68.

[6]Jurvetson, Steve. 2000. Turning customers into a sales force. *Business 2.0,* March.

[7]Butt, Joseph L., Jr. 1999. Universal Escape Webcams turn images into marketing. In The Forrester Report (October): p. 18.

[8]Talk.com Investor Relations. 1999. America Online and Tel-Save.com announce extension of AOL Telecommunications Marketing Agreement. Press release newswire, 5 January. The URL for this citation is as follows: http://www.corporate-ir.net/ireye/ir_site.zhtml?ticker5talk&script5410&layout5-6&item_id522775.

[9]Segrich, J. 2000. L90 Inc.: Initiating coverage. Analyst report. CIBC Worldmarkets Corporation, 25 February, p. 5.

[10]Sourced from the following online article: Cavoli, Brian. What really is beyond the banner. URL: http://adsonline.about.com/aa062199.htm

[11]*Economist.* 2000. Amazon's amazing ambition, 26 February, E-Commerce Survey, p. 24.

[12]For further information, see: Godin, Seth. 1999. *Permission Marketing: Turning strangers into friends, and friends into customers.* New York: Simon & Schuster.

[13]Petersen. 1999. You can have the greatest e-commerce site. *The Wall Street Journal,* 12 July.

[14]Hof, Robert D., Heather Green, and Linda Himelstein. 1998. Now it's your web: The Net is moving toward one-to-one marketing—and that will change how all companies do business. *Business Week,* 5 October.

[15]For further clarification, please go to the following URL for the January 4, 2000, press release from Net Perceptions entitled: Net Perceptions to provide realtime ad targeting to ZDNET. *http://www.netperception.com/press/indiv/0,1032,163,00.html.*

[16]Green, Heather. 1999. The information gold mine: New Software—and the Net's legions of cybersurfers and shoppers—are starting to hand companies opportunities they've only dreamed of. *Business Week,* July 26.

[17]Hof, Green, and Himelstein. 1998. Now it's your web. *Business Week,* 5 October.

[18]Green. 1999. The information gold mine. *Business Week,* 26 July.

[19]Hof, Green, and Himelstein. 1998. Now it's your web. *Business Week,* 5 October.

[20]Kaufman, Leslie. 1999. Web retailers empty wallets on advertising. *The New York Times,* 2 November.

[21]Petersen. 1999. You can have the greatest e-commerce site. *The Wall Street Journal,* 12 July.

[22]Kaufman. 1999. Web retailers empty wallets. *The New York Times,* 2 November.

[23]This sidebar draws from data presented in several analysts' reports including an ING Barings report on DoubleClick dated March 31, 2000, and CIBC World Market's report on L90 dated 25th February 2000.

[24]Bannon, Lisa. 2001. Slowing sales left eToys in lurch as costs continued. *The Wall Street Journal,* 22 January.

[25]Functional benefits capture the intrinsic advantages of the product. They tend to be correlated with the features or attributes of the product. Symbolic benefits relate to social approval and personal expression. Experiential benefits relate to what the product feels like to use, and tends to capture various sensory pleasures. See the following article for further elaboration: Park, Choong W., Bernard J. Jaworski, and Deborah J. MacInnis. 1986. Strategic brand concept-image management. *Journal of Marketing* 50, no. 4 (October): pp. 135–45.

[26]Keller, Kevin Lane. 1998. *Strategic Brand Management.* Upper Saddle River, NJ: Prentice-Hall, Inc., p. 43.

[27]Aaker, David. 1996. *Building Strong Brands.* New York: The Free Press, pp. 7–8.

[28]Media Metrix. 2000. January. Cited in Dickson L. Louie and Jeffrey Rayport, Monster.com (Boston: Harvard Business School Publishing, 2000), p. 1. Fifty percent market share refers to percentage of eyeball minutes among career sites.

[29]As of December 1999. Brean Murray Institutional Research Report, 2 December. Cited in Dickson L. Louie and Jeffrey F. Rayport, Monster.com (Boston: Harvard Business School Publishing, 2000), p. 1. "Revenue increased from $6.9 million in 1996 to $133.5 million in 1999."

# Strategy Implementation

This chapter provides a review of two key components of strategy implementation—the delivery system and the innovation process. Implementation answers the general question, "How do we go to market?" The delivery system is defined as the people, systems, assets, processes, and supply chains that enable the company to bring its offering to market. However, the delivery system alone is not sufficient to guarantee successful implementation. A comprehensive view of implementation must also consider innovation, because the Internet requires continual revision of strategies, offerings, and interfaces. Later in the chapter, we illustrate the differences between innovation in the online and offline domains, as well as introduce several new frameworks for innovation.

## QUESTIONS

*Please consider the following questions as you read this chapter:*

1.  What is online implementation?

2.  Why does implementation matter?

3.  What is the delivery system?

4.  What are the categories of offline innovation?

This chapter was coauthored by Marco Smit, Rafi Mohammed, Bernie Jaworski, and Jeffrey Rayport. Sharon Grady and Lisa Ferri provided considerable substantive input on the online/offline integration issues.

5. What is the offline innovation process?

6. What is the new logic behind online innovation?

7. What are the online innovation frameworks?

8. What are the online innovation processes?

# INTRODUCTION

In Chapter 6, we considered the Web interface choices that brought to life the firm's business model. In Chapter 7, we discussed the market communications and branding decisions designed to draw customers to the site. However, a highly usable interface and a strong brand are not sufficient to deliver the brand to target customers; rather, the firm must develop a strong organization, hire and train the right talent, and build an infrastructure (e.g., structures, systems, processes) that will move the physical (or digital) products from suppliers through to the end customer.

The purpose of this chapter is to introduce the firm-specific infrastructure that must be created and configured to achieve the firm's strategic goals. In particular, we discuss two broad categories of infrastructure—the delivery system and the innovation process. The delivery system is defined as the sum of the people, systems, assets, processes, and supply chains that enable the company to bring its offering to market. In addition to the delivery system, the firm must develop a clear point of view on how innovation related to its offering, as well as to the infrastructure itself, will unfold.

## WHAT IS ONLINE IMPLEMENTATION?

We begin our discussion by introducing the general implementation framework. Then we consider why implementation is important and the consequences of poor implementation. Following this discussion, we turn to the five key components of a delivery system: people, systems, assets, processes, and supply chains. We conclude with a discussion of offline and online innovation, and an application of these concepts to MarketWatch.com.

## A Framework for Implementation

Exhibit 8-1 provides an overview of the connection between the communications and branding concerns of top management and the implementation process. In particular, this exhibit illustrates that implementation follows from and is informed by branding, communications, and customer-interface choices. The **online implementation process** involves two phases. In the first phase, the firm is concerned with the delivery of the offering. In the second phase, the firm is concerned with the extent to which both the offering and the infrastructure are modified to fit the evolution of the market.

Once the customer interface has been developed, the company must configure the infrastructure to deliver on the site's brand promise. In particular, we consider two broad categories of infrastructure: (1) the configuration of structure, systems,

**Exhibit 8-1**  MARKETSPACE EVOLUTION AND NEED FOR CONTINUOUS INNOVATION

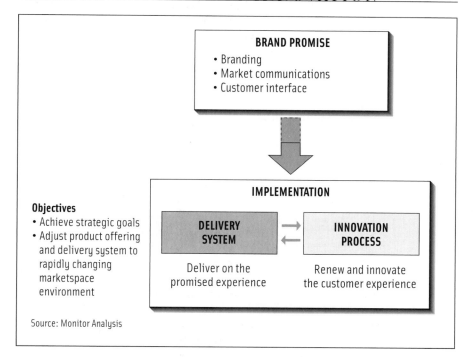

Source: Monitor Analysis

and processes that form the basis of company organization, and (2) the supply chain.

Today's supply-chain models focus on rapidly changing structures in B2C, B2B, C2B, and C2C markets. These new supply-chain options have significantly changed the ways in which customers and suppliers interact with manufacturers.

The fast pace of change in the marketspace is driven by the evolution of technology, changes in customer preferences (and demographics), new competitors, and new collaborators. To continue to execute and adapt strategy in this fast-changing, competitive environment, firms can no longer separate innovation from implementation. In this section, we contrast the different innovation categories and processes in new-economy and old-economy companies, and discuss archetypes of processes and organizations for innovation emerging in the online domain.

# WHY DOES IMPLEMENTATION MATTER?

Exhibit 8-2 provides a simple illustration of the importance of solid implementation. On the horizontal axis, we observe two conditions: appropriate and inappropriate strategy. On the vertical axis, we consider both good and poor implementation. When crossed, we can view the following four conditions that can be experienced by firms in the marketplace: success, roulette, trouble, and failure.

In this chapter, we are particularly concerned with conditions that steer firms into the trouble quadrant. A firm in this quadrant has made all the right strategy choices related to the business model, interface, brand, and marketing communica-

**Exhibit 8-2** WHY DOES IMPLEMENTATION MATTER?

**Strategy**

| | Appropriate | Inappropriate |
|---|---|---|
| **Good** (Implementation) | **Success**<br>• All that can be done to ensure success has been done | **Roulette**<br>• Good execution can mitigate poor strategy<br>or<br>• Same good execution can hasten failure |
| **Poor** (Implementation) | **Trouble**<br>• Poor execution hampers good strategy<br>• Management may never become aware of strategic soundness because of execution inadequacies | **Failure**<br>• Difficult to diagnose—bad strategy masked by poor execution<br>• More difficult to fix—two things are wrong |

Source: Modified version of materials in *The Marketing Edge* by Thomas V. Bonoma. 1985. New York: The Free Press

tions, but its implementation is poor. As a result, the firm will likely perform poorly in the marketplace, with senior management unable to distinguish whether inappropriate strategy or poor implementation is responsible for the company's poor performance.

## Implementation Challenges for Online Firms

Exhibit 8-3 provides an overview of the implementation challenges that confront online businesses. In particular, it has been argued that increased speed and intensity of competition in the online environment means that implementation mistakes will be punished much more severely and quickly than in the offline world. In the following sections, we articulate six implementation challenges exemplified by online firms.

**Higher Visibility to Errors.** Due to investors' infatuation with Internet firms, the media closely monitors and reports on them. The Web also offers consumers a wide variety of easily accessible sources of information on e-commerce companies, and many ratings services have been established to help consumers choose reputable companies. In addition, Web bulletin boards give disgruntled customers the opportunity to vent their feelings and experiences to a large audience. Some consumers become so frustrated by failed implementations that they create websites to share (and invite others to share) their experiences.

**Exhibit 8-3**

CHALLENGES OF ONLINE IMPLEMENTATION

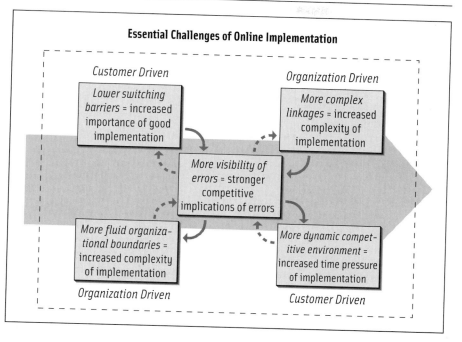

**Essential Challenges of Online Implementation**

**Lower Switching Costs.** It can be argued that **switching costs** for consumers who shop on the Internet are significantly lower than for consumers who shop at bricks-and-mortar firms. Should a consumer have an unsatisfactory experience shopping at a bricks-and-mortar company and decide to shop elsewhere, switching costs could include additional driving, new constraints on method of payment, and time spent learning about a new retailer. In another scenario, a switching cost of convenience to a consumer could arise if a consumer became dissatisfied with only a particular shop in a shopping mall, full of satisfying and often-used shops.

As the Internet further evolves, there will be a wider variety of competitive offerings in each product category. A recent survey revealed low switching costs in the Web retail book market. This market is relatively mature and has three well-funded companies (Amazon, Barnes & Noble.com, and Borders.com) as well as a host of smaller niche players aggressively vying for customers. The survey found that more than 73 percent of online book shoppers indicated no retail brand preference for their next purchase.[1]

Switching costs involve a simple click of the mouse. If a retail site disappoints an online shopper, there are several other sites offering similar goods or services that can be easily accessed. This lack of loyalty reflects low switching costs and a willingness to switch online retailers for any reason, no matter how trivial the implementation error.

**More Dynamic Competitive Environment.** Due to the low barriers to entry, poor implementation by incumbent firms provides opportunities to potential entrants as well as to current competitors. It can be relatively easy for new entrants and competitors to gain advantage from a company's implementation errors and problems.

**More Fluid Organizational Boundaries.** The lack of clear dividing lines between parties partnering and collaborating creates fluid organizational boundaries. While this fluidity increases contact and community between partners, it also increases the complexity of interactions.

**More Dynamic Market Environment.** The speed of change in the market places a significant burden on firms to respond quickly to changing developments. Netscape went from being the absolute dominator of the Web-browser market to an also-ran struggling to be a significant player in the market—over a period of barely three years. The speed of evolution and its implications for strategy implementation are clear. Even the best company cannot afford to implement too slowly or in a fashion that will inhibit it from adjusting to changing marketspace conditions.

**More Complex Linkages.** Complexity of linkages refers to the number of linkages among various partners. The more linkages, the more likely that decisions will be slowed, become prone to miscommunication, or become more bureaucratic. In *The Mythical Man-Month*, Fred Brooks illustrates the effects that an increase in the number of communication linkages can have on an organization. He uses an example of a team writing software: "If each part of the task must be separately coordinated with each other part, the effort increases as $n(n - 1)/2$. Three workers require three times as much pair-wise intercommunications as two; four require six times as much as two." In the online world, the number and nature of the linkages frequently change, adding another layer of complexity.[2]

## The Effects of Poor Implementation

The 2000 holiday season overwhelmed many e-commerce businesses: 12 percent of all e-commerce orders were not delivered on time, and 67 percent were not received as ordered. The previous holiday season was even worse, with 26 percent of all e-commerce deliveries failing to arrive by the promised delivery date.[3] Such questionable service created a legion of unsatisfied customers, and led them to question the ability of e-commerce companies to deliver on their promises. It is no surprise, then, that product fulfillment is one of the top e-commerce consumer complaints. Consider the following two high-profile implementation breakdowns.

**EBay's Network Shutdown.** EBay is the world's largest personal online-trading community, with over 2,900 auction item categories and over 400,000 new items up for auction each day. EBay's popularity and positive reputation provide confidence to both sellers and bidders. Sellers gain confidence to list their items on eBay because they feel high volumes of user traffic will translate to a higher probability of selling their items through the site. Likewise, buyers feel confident that high volumes of user traffic ensure a robust marketplace that will increase the likelihood of finding items of interest, relative to visiting other auction sites. EBay earns a small commission from every sales transaction on its site.

In June 1999, eBay suffered a 22-hour site outage due to technical difficulties. When this shutdown occurred, investors panicked and eBay's stock immediately lost over 20 percent of its value. In addition to this market-capitalization loss, eBay lost significant revenues. To appease angry sellers, eBay waived all listings fees for items offered during the service outage. EBay officials estimated that the shutdown cost the company $3 million to $5 million in revenue—a sizeable loss considering that the company's first quarter 1999 revenue was $34 million. Also, this service shutdown affected auction sellers' confidence in eBay's abilities. Rival auction sites operated by Yahoo, Amazon, and Auction Universe gained significant additional business and media exposure as a result of eBay's troubles.[4]

### Buy.com Pricing and Fulfillment.
Buy.com is a retail website that primarily offers computer equipment, which it sells at extremely low, sometimes negative, gross margins. For example, in the first nine months of 1999, Buy.com's net revenues were $3 million less than the $401 million worth of goods that it sold.[6] The goal of the company's pricing strategy is to attract a lot of attention to the site, then monetize that attention by selling advertising targeted at its customer base.

Buy.com utilizes a business model that outsources most of its infrastructure services (e.g., customer support, fulfillment). While outsourcing can be advantageous because it requires a relatively low capital investment, it has a crucial implementation downside. Buy.com does not control elements critical to its brand promise. It has developed a reputation for advertising products that languish in back-order for weeks. A Securities Exchange Commission (SEC) filing by the company even acknowledges that the methods that Buy.com uses to update its prices may result in future pricing errors, which may result in significant future litigation.[7] Buy.com's implementation problems have created negative publicity and shaken both consumers' and Wall Street's confidence in the company. Buy.com's February 2000 Initial Public Offering (IPO) was initially encouraging, with the company's stock price reaching as high as $33 per share. By spring of 2001, Buy.com's stock was hovering below $1—a level at which the Nasdaq market initiates delisting proceedings. Investors do not believe that Buy.com's audacious business model will succeed.

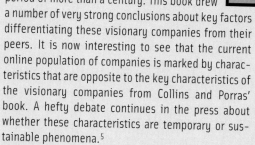

## POINT-COUNTERPOINT

# Built to Last or Built to Rebuild?

In 1995, James Collins and Jerry Porras published *Built to Last*, an analysis of visionary companies in the offline world that were more successful than peer-group companies over a period of more than a century. This book drew a number of very strong conclusions about key factors differentiating these visionary companies from their peers. It is now interesting to see that the current online population of companies is marked by characteristics that are opposite to the key characteristics of the visionary companies from Collins and Porras' book. A hefty debate continues in the press about whether these characteristics are temporary or sustainable phenomena.[5]

For advocates of "built to last," the argument is that growth is largely organic—coming from careful and systematic analysis of chosen markets. The firm scales up over a period of years and repeatedly leverages its brand in the marketplace. Brand assets and equity take many years to build and must be carefully nurtured over a long period of time. Finally, these companies are often not led by visionary leaders with strong personalities.

In sharp contrast, there is no time for elaborate planning and analysis in the online world. Rather, firms act very quickly. While growth can be organic, it is just as likely to be from acquisitions of competitors and complementors. The challenge is not finding opportunity—it is choosing the right opportunity.

# Smoothed Sale-ing

**Sun Microsystems's personalized intranet helps its sales team tame the info-glut**

by Peter Meyers, staff writer for tnbt.com

 What's the ultimate killer app? Scott Claypool knows. "It's e-mail," declares the rookie sales rep for Sun Microsystems. "Because it literally kills my time."

Like many new-economy foot soldiers, Claypool is swimming—or, more accurately, drowning—in information. "With 800 e-mails a day, where do you start?" he asks, his weary voice making him sound as if he's exaggerating only slightly. To add insult to injury, many of those missives come from Claypool's own company, informing him of new product developments and sales tips that may—or may not—be of use to him.

And it's not just e-mail: There are company-produced white papers, third-party market research reports, product spec sheets, corporate slide presentations—in all, over 115,000 documents Claypool could potentially cite in his sales efforts. Any one of them could contain information vital to Claypool's job selling to Internet service firms such as Scient and Razorfish.

"The good news is there's lots of information," says Michael Douglas, Sun's director of e-marketing. "The bad news is there's lots of information."

Until recently, all of Sun's sales-support information was stored in an unwieldy and motley collection of printed manuals, e-mails, and, as Douglas says, "in a collection of many, many, many static websites." But then the company devised a solution: a customizable intranet site dubbed MySales that's designed to make all that information work for, not against, sales reps like Claypool.

What's notable about MySales, which launched within the company in early February of 2000 is its innovative use of personalization technology—technology that is most typically deployed on mass-market websites like Amazon and Yahoo to provide individually tailored information and recommendations to consumers. Sun, which currently has 3,200 of its salespeople and engineers trying out the system, is one of the first companies to make extensive use of this technology to provide better service to its own employees.

MySales is designed to consolidate information that used to be scattered throughout the company and help salespeople manage that information by selecting the specific products, services and industries they want to track. Like consumers using My Yahoo or some other personalization tool, salespeople first establish their preferences; then, every time they visit the site, their homepage displays links to custom-selected documents ranging from product information to relevant news articles.

Though the intranet is still in its early stages, it already appears to be helping overwhelmed salespeople—especially new employees like Scott Claypool who face the daunting task of quickly mastering the company's sprawling offerings. "Instead of just a monster," Claypool says, assessing MySales' impact, "it's now a manageable monster."

There is a certain irony in the fact that a veteran technology company like Sun should have trouble managing its internal information flow. But the fact is, much of what's helped Sun to become one of the industry's leading hardware and software manufacturers has also made it difficult for the company to streamline information.

Take decentralization. Employees throughout the firm describe with almost uniform ambivalence the leeway that separate product groups have in developing sales literature to support their products. On the one hand, this lack of centralization has encouraged a rich culture of communication, unstructured enough to allow, for instance, product engineers to construct their own internal websites touting the high-tech wizardry they've developed. But that same freedom has made it difficult for those selling Sun's products to know exactly where to go to find the information they need to support a sales call.

"The information was really spread all over the place," says Jonathan Green, a district sales manager who's been with the company for almost five years. "You really had to develop a knack about which sites to check."

*(continued on page 289)*

*(continued from page 288)*

Compounding this information sprawl was a tendency to document and promote the attributes of individual products rather than describe the ways that customers were most likely to use those products. While that may work well for engineers, for salespeople, it's less than ideal.

"Customers don't say, 'Tell me about your Enterprise 450 because I think it's a great box,'" notes Bob Lewis, area marketing director for Sun's western U.S. territory. "Instead, it's, 'Tell me about the products relevant to my needs.'"

*Read more articles about The Next Big Thing at www.tnbt.com*

# WHAT IS THE DELIVERY SYSTEM?

In this section, we discuss how each online company must configure its delivery system to create an infrastructure that can effectively serve online customers. We first provide a framework for the delivery system, then define and describe each of its components. In the next section, we focus on the evolution of the delivery system. The final section concludes with specific online/offline integration issues that can be particularly challenging for many online companies.

## A Framework for the Delivery System

Once the company has succeeded in attracting customers to its website, it must deliver the total customer experience that the brand communication has promised. Not only must the customer experience satisfy interactions through the customer interface, but the company must be able to correctly execute transactions initiated through the customer interface.

For example, if a customer has ordered flowers through the company's website to be delivered to a certain address on Valentine's Day, then the company cannot make any mistake with the delivery of the flowers. Potential execution mistakes could come in the form of incorrect processing of payment, delivering to the wrong person or on the wrong date, delivering the flowers with the incorrect accompanying note, or delivering the wrong flowers. In short, the delivery system has a direct bearing on the total experience that the customer equates with his or her beliefs about the brand. It also has a major impact on customer retention, and, therefore, on the lifetime value of the customer base.

A company's **delivery system** is the most detailed and concrete expression of the company's value proposition. The value proposition, product offering, and business model each determine the requirements for the resource system's construction. The delivery system translates the resource system from a conceptual structure into a concrete configuration of resources, processes, and supply chains. Once the strategy has been defined and necessary capabilities identified, the structures, processes, reward systems, and human-resource practices that will produce the needed competencies and capabilities must be defined.[8] It is at this stage of the strategy process that strategic intent is turned into a configuration that produces consumer and financial results.

## The Five Components of the Delivery System

The five components of a delivery system include people, systems, assets, processes, and supply chains (see Exhibit 8-4).

**Exhibit 8-4**

# THE DELIVERY SYSTEM NEEDS TO SUPPORT AND REINFORCE THE RESOURCE SYSTEM

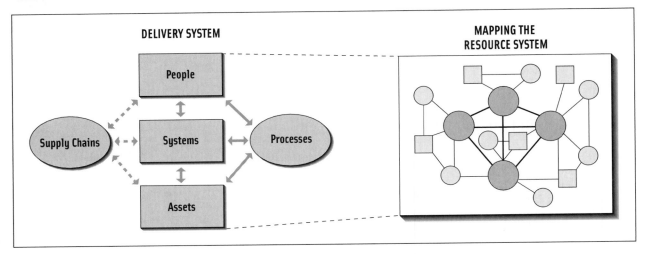

1. *People.* A key characteristic of many successful Internet companies is a human-resource system and an associated culture that places an exceptionally high value on the recruitment, selection, training, development, and evaluation of key personnel.

2. *Systems.* Systems are defined as routines or established procedures for the organization, and can be related to any aspect of the organization. In the current context, there is an obvious emphasis on information technology (IT) systems. These include database systems, website support systems, management information systems, and other digital data-based approaches.

3. *Assets.* Assets can be either physical or information-based. Physical assets are those that are so often found in the offline world: buildings, warehouses, offices, and equipment. Information-based assets, on the other hand, are assets constructed from data—including databases, digital content, and customer-behavior data. As so much recent literature has pointed out, one of the most influential developments has been the replacement of physical assets as value generators with information-based assets.

4. *Processes.* Processes are defined as the patterns of interaction, coordination, communication, and decision-making that employees use to transform resources into customer value. The online firm can potentially play a number of roles, including that of a pure manufacturer and distributor of products, a mere facilitator (e.g., AOL was originally a pure facilitator of chat among community members), or anything in between. The following processes must be configured by online firms during implementation:

   • *Resource-allocation process.* With vast areas of opportunity still to be developed in the online environment, there are often more opportunities available than a company can pursue in a sustainable manner. The **resource-allocation process** is the formalization of the trade-offs and the prioritization that the company uses when making choices about which opportunities to pursue. It goes without saying that this process needs to be very tightly aligned with the value proposition and the business model.

- *Human-resource management processes.* Online companies need to scale-up and adjust quickly to keep growing with the market. Upgrading the **human-resource management process** in a manner that is in line with the value proposition, resource system, and market evolution is essential in such an environment.

- *Manufacturing and distribution processes.* The **manufacturing and distribution processes** have been defined as the supply chain and will be the subject of a later section in this chapter.

- *Payment/billing processes.* It is clear that without proper functioning of the **payment and billing processes,** the online company will have difficulty producing anything other than virtual profits. However, billing processes are not equally important for all online companies. For ISPs, it can be a strong strategic advantage to produce one integrated bill for the customer's telecom, television (cable), online services, and other services it delivers. For most online companies, however, these processes are more of a minimum performance requirement and can have a mainly negative impact if they are not functioning properly. For example, B2C payment processes are typically credit card based, and many online companies experience problems with smooth, comprehensive billing.9 B2B payments take place in a more complex manner, and enabler companies have recently launched new billing products focusing specifically on this market.

- *Customer support/handling processes.* The customer may have questions when he or she is on the website, as well as after a transaction has been completed. Questions may arise regarding a simple request for tracking the delivery progress of the order, a change of the order in process, or help with problems once the product has been received. The **customer support/handling processes** should address these questions. Usability firm Creative Good describes on its website (www.creativegood.com) how as many as four customer support calls (and a lot of persuasion from the customer's side) were required to conclude an order for an Apple G3 Tower that Creative Good wanted to buy from the Apple website. It is hard to imagine that such a customer handling process actually reinforces the resource system. It is more likely to hamper the system and cause the loss of transactions and customers in the longer term.

5. *Supply chains.* The online environment has radically changed the structure of business supply chains and the options available to retailers and manufacturers. We first focus on B2C supply chains and several different **supply-chain models** that have arisen to serve B2C companies. Next, we review B2B supply chains and reveal how the online environment is creating significant efficiencies and opportunities in the B2B market. Finally, we discuss developments in the C2C (or P2P) and C2B markets (see Exhibit 8-5).

## Business-to-Consumer (B2C) Supply Chains.

One reason for the many supply-chain options available in the **business-to-consumer (B2C)** market is that online retailers (or e-tailers) do not need to have products physically in stock in a network of retail outlets to sell directly to consumers. Unlike bricks-and-mortar retailers, which must maintain stock on hand in retail outlets, as long as the e-tailer fulfills its promise to deliver goods in a specified time period, consumers do not care how the order is fulfilled. This provides the e-tailer significant flexibility in designing its supply chains.[10] On the other hand, the B2C supply chain for marketspace companies is significantly more complex than for offline companies. Web-based deliveries

Exhibit 8-5

## FOUR TYPES OF SUPPLY CHAINS FOUND ONLINE

| B2C—Business-to-Consumer |
| --- |
| • Stock-it-yourself<br>• Outsource warehousing<br>• Drop ship<br>• Fulfillment intermediaries |

| B2B—Business-to-Business |
| --- |
| • Customer-centric<br>• Vertical hubs |

| C2C—Consumer-to-Consumer |
| --- |
| • Much like a vertical hub, many sites (e.g., eBay) have created consumer-to-consumer sales<br>• Provides a forum for buyers and sellers to meet<br>• Buyers and sellers trade directly (eliminating an intermediary)<br>• A global marketplace with a large and interested trading company |

| C2B—Consumer-to-Business |
| --- |
| • Individual consumers place bids with businesses (e.g., Priceline) and businesses decide whether to sell<br>• C2B chains also include consumers group-buying, as in Mercata.com |

are often small, time-sensitive (overnight, two to three days) deliveries to individuals about whom the company might have very limited information. This is very different from periodically delivering to an established network of shops with which the company has long-term relationships. In addition, a physical outlet network provides the outlet supplier with a predictable expectation of needed routes and volumes. Such a predictability is certainly absent when it comes to delivering goods to a changing volume of both new and existing consumers every day.

One of the weakest links in the B2C implementation chain is fulfillment. Late or unfulfilled orders are the leading source of e-commerce complaints. A recent Forrester study found that half of the customers who had an unsatisfactory online buying experience stopped doing business with the offending company. Given the high costs of customer acquisition and the knowledge that disgruntled customers will relay their poor experiences to friends, poorly executed orders are costly to B2C firms. The cost of handling a return is generally three to four times the cost of shipping a product. In addition to refining fulfillment processes to satisfy customers, many firms are beginning to use expedited fulfillment as a means to product differentiation. For example, in an effort to prove its superior fulfillment capabilities in 1999, Amazon.com guaranteed Christmas delivery to its customers if orders were received by December 22.

In today's B2C market, there are four primary supply-chain models: stock-it-yourself, outsource warehousing, drop ship, and fulfillment intermediaries.

- *Stock-it-yourself.* For a bricks-and-mortar company that also sells online, this model typically involves maintaining an integrated warehouse that is able to handle shipments to stores as well as shipments to Web customers. This is often very difficult, if not impossible, to implement. Systems and processes must handle both large deliveries to physical stores and small, individual orders to online customers.

For purely online companies, the **stock-it-yourself** model generally involves an automated warehouse that can directly fulfill online orders. A primary benefit of this model is that it gives the online firm control over its fulfillment process. Control over fulfillment is a major concern for online companies. The primary reason that Barnes & Noble tried to purchase the Ingram Book Group, the nation's largest book wholesaler, was to improve its book distribution system. This purchase was ultimately not completed due to antitrust concerns, but if the purchase had gone through, 80 percent of Barnes & Nobles' online and offline customers would have been within overnight delivery distance from the combined companies' 11 distribution centers.[11] The only disadvantage of this model is that the whole supply chain is no longer likely to be a strategic asset that the firm can shape in a proprietary way. Hence, it could be argued that such a structure commoditizes the supply chain.

- *Outsource warehousing.* **Outsourcing warehousing** generally involves the use of logistics specialists like Federal Express (FedEx) or UPS to stockpile and ship Web orders. Hewlett-Packard (HP) uses FedEx to handle all of its fulfillment orders from its retail website; FedEx warehouses HP inventory in Memphis, Tennessee (one of its hubs). Once an order comes in through HP's site, it is automatically transmitted to FedEx's Memphis facility. Orders are packaged at its warehouse and directly shipped to the customer via FedEx.[12] HP thereby has a very efficient distribution system to handle fulfillment to its distributors. However, its distribution system is simply not configured to handle small, individual shipments. It is not a trivial task to reconfigure its system to be able to handle both distributor and individual order fulfillment.

  FedEx also handles all of the fulfillment duties for proflowers.com. When orders come into proflowers, the order is routed directly to flower growers using FedEx technology. These growers create the floral arrangement, and FedEx picks it up and delivers it directly to the customer. In this case, proflowers.com's role is strictly focused on marketing, assembling a network of quality growers, and overseeing the production process.[13]

- *Drop shipping.* **Drop shipping** requires an e-commerce company to depend on its manufacturers or distributors to pack and ship its retail Web orders. Drop-shipper specialists even go as far as placing the e-tailer's name and logo on all shipped orders. Direct-mail catalog companies are benefiting greatly from the growth of e-tail drop shipping; they are experienced in fulfilling individual mail-order catalog purchases and are applying this experience to e-commerce fulfillment. The general design of a drop-shipping fulfillment warehouse is one in which shipments from manufacturers are unloaded at one end, merchandise is organized throughout the warehouse, and individual customer orders are shipped out via U.S. Mail or by an overnight service through the other end of the warehouse. One reason Federated Department Stores purchased Fingerhut, a mail-order house, was to help Federated with its e-commerce supply-chain strategy. In addition to working on Federated fulfillment orders, in 1999, Fingerhut won contracts to do order fulfillment for other well-known companies such as eToys and Wal-Mart. Fingerhut has strongly benefited from the drop-shipping boom. Fingerhut's revenues in 1999 were expected to be $40 million and were forecasted to increase to $100 million in 2000.[14]

- *Fulfillment intermediaries.* **Fulfillment intermediaries** take care of all back-office operations for e-commerce companies. They handle order processing, direct orders to suppliers, keep customers updated on their order progress, handle order cancellations, and process product returns. These types of systems afford e-commerce entrepreneurs the opportunity to focus on developing their businesses, and also reduce the initial set-up costs. One fulfillment intermediary, OrderTrust, estimates that it would cost the average e-commerce firm at least $1.5 million a year to build and operate an order-processing system; OrderTrust claims to sell the same fulfillment capabilities for between $25,000 to $100,000 a year.[15] Fulfillment intermediaries allow e-commerce companies to start operating almost immediately.

  Outsourcing order fulfillment also minimizes risk. In the rapidly changing online environment, e-commerce companies that outsource do not have to commit to a specific type of supply chain. Shipper.com hopes to capture business from this growing trend of providing same-day service by investing $150 million to build fulfillment warehouses in 10 markets. The company plans to focus on becoming an e-commerce facilitator rather than an e-commerce retail business, with the core of its business focused on fulfilling orders for e-commerce companies. Innovative fulfillment companies such as Shipper.com may give firms without a proprietary supply chain an advantage over rivals who have invested resources in a supply chain that cannot provide same-day service.[16]

***Example: Dell Online.*** When Dell moved to sell personal computers over the Internet, it identified two primary areas in which it could achieve cost savings: **sales force efficiency** and **service efficiency**.[17]

- *Sales force efficiency.* By allowing consumers to order directly over the Internet, fewer transactions needed to be routed through the sales force, which resulted in increased sales force efficiency. Also, sales force personnel that handled calls originating from the website had a higher close rate. Dell found that the website sales team could handle 1.5 times the quota of the traditional sales force.
- *Service efficiency.* Dell saved considerably because its consumers used the Web to check on their order status, seek technical service FAQs, and download files. In a typical quarter, Dell Online's website had 200,000 order status checks, 500,000 technical service inquiries, and 400,000 file downloads. Each of these transactions would have cost between $5 and $15 if they had been handled by telephone.

## Business-to-Business (B2B) Supply Chains.

Buyers reduce costs by creating an environment in which sellers are more competitive. Sellers can use **business-to-business (B2B)** sites to instantly advertise their products to potential customers. Gartner Group estimates the worldwide B2B Internet trade was $109 billion in 1999. Gartner predicts that by 2004, the worldwide B2B Internet trade will be a $7.29 trillion market.[18] The potential B2B market is estimated to be 3 to 10 times the size of the B2C market.[19] B2B customers generally spend more than B2C customers. W.W. Grainger, the leader in MRO supplies, had an average order size of $240 in 1999; estimates put Amazon.com's average order size in the $30 to $50 range.[20]

The B2B supply chains in the online space are somewhat different from other supply chains. Whereas other supply chains are truly new to the industry, B2B supply chains are rooted in more than a decade of enterprise-level expenditures in various technology, including computing, networking, and client/servers.[21] Thus, companies may have had existing supplier relationships, and the parties simply converted the relationship into an electronic format.

Investment bank Goldman Sachs refers to an evolution from electronic data interchange (EDI) via virtual private networks (VPN) to intranets and, finally, to the Internet itself:

> Prior to the existence of e-markets, large (buyer) businesses had 1:1 relationships with other (seller) businesses, using EDI or other mechanisms (like VPNs, ed.). These were primarily focused on direct materials and production goods. (For many suppliers, ed.) . . . the cost of doing business electronically was prohibitive and it was difficult enough to get the attention of the large buyers (Hubs).[22]

There are five main reasons that big buyers (e.g., automobile companies) push such systems on their suppliers:

- Lower costs compared to offline management of suppliers and transactions
- Improved transaction speed and control (allowing for dependable global production of cars, for example)
- High security of the system, as it was purely proprietary and often supervised by the buyer
- Proprietary nature of the system created a strong switching barrier for participating suppliers
- Good reliability of capacity to process the transaction volume as the buyer was the key driver behind capacity management of the system

The evolution of computing and communications technology has made the Internet an increasingly attractive alternative to these proprietary, expensive systems due to the following advances:

- Improved security
- Increased transaction-handling capacity (hardware and software)
- A much broader supplier base, based on open standards

B2B sites are revolutionizing manufacturers' supply chains by allowing manufacturers the opportunity to realize lower input prices, reduced inventory and transaction costs, faster delivery, and improved customer service.

- *Lower input prices.* Manufacturers use B2B sites to conduct auctions from prequalified bidders for their supply-chain inputs. The ease of bidding expands the universe of potential supplier bidders and takes favoritism out of the buying equation. Increased competition coupled with decreased supplier overhead pushes suppliers to offer lower prices. One negative effect of the use of the auction process for procurement is that suppliers may become less inclined to invest in customizing products for a manufacturer if they have to bid against others for contracts at purchase time. In many dynamic industries, it is necessary for manufacturers to create partnerships with suppliers to achieve fast product-development cycles.
- *Reduced inventory.* B2B supply chains establish a closer communication-process with suppliers regarding input needs and procurement time frames. This allows manufacturers to reduce their inventory stock, warehousing costs, and inventory carrying costs, and to increase return on assets. At 3Com, in an effort to make its inventory process more efficient, expanded

product production automatically triggers additional orders for input supplies such as cardboard boxes.

- *Reduced transaction costs.* By using the Internet to announce order requests and to receive bids, both manufacturers and suppliers reduce the transaction costs associated with supply procurement. AMR Research reports that buyers in the B2B market can expect to realize a 15 to 20 percent drop in maverick purchases, $50 to $100 transaction savings per order, and a 2.5 to 10 percent price savings due to competition brought on by B2B sites.[23]

- *Faster delivery.* Because procurement transactions are no longer processed through multiple internal departments or entered in several different data systems, the time between supply request and supply delivery can be greatly reduced.

- *Better customer service.* General Motors (GM) is trying to use B2B supply chains to provide better service to its customers (the current order-to-delivery time of a new car is up to eight weeks) by connecting its factories and suppliers via the Internet. This connection will provide suppliers with real-time notification of needed materials and delivery deadlines. Prequalified suppliers can instantly submit a bid to provide supplies. This system allows GM to better coordinate with suppliers. GM hopes the system will reduce the order-to-delivery time of new cars to four to five days.[24]

GM began to move its purchasing process to the Web by establishing its TradeXchange site, and announcing its intention to do all of its purchasing (some $500 billion per year) over this site by the end of 2001. In February 2000, GM and Ford merged their online purchasing efforts with those of DaimlerChrysler, Renault, and Nissan to form Covisint, a B2B exchange whose partners include Oracle and Commerce One.[25]

***Example: Boeing's B2B Site.*** Until recently, 90 percent of Boeing's spare-parts customers had to go through a tedious and time-consuming process to order aircraft parts. Customers ordering spare parts were required to search through a catalog, find the spare-part order number, relay requests to their purchasing departments, make phone calls to check part availability, and, finally, send the order by fax. Once Boeing received the fax, an employee would have to input the order into Boeing's order system—occasionally causing delays and mistakes. Boeing now uses a Web-based spare-parts ordering system through which customers can instantly check product availability and, if the product is available, simply click to place the order. The Web-based process reduces transaction costs, as well as the time needed to process and deliver each order. In the airline industry, this speed of order delivery can result in significant overall cost savings; it is very expensive to have an out-of-service aircraft awaiting a part. Boeing benefits because this new process lowers transaction costs and provides better service to its customers.

### Consumer-to-Business (C2B) Supply Chain.

The **consumer-to-business (C2B)** concept was well-illustrated by the Mercata.com business model. Mercata.com tried to organize consumers together and harness their group-buying power when dealing with suppliers. The company aggregated customers who were interested in buying in volume and reaping lower prices; it then negotiated with suppliers to provide discounts on their merchandise based on the volume of goods sold. Mercata offered goods for sale on its website with a group buying incentive—as more purchases were made, the selling price would decrease. By creating an online group of customers interested in gaining group buying power, Mercata aimed to create a "win-win" for both consumers and suppliers. Consumers benefited by receiving lower prices and sellers won by quickly selling a large amount of merchandise with a low transaction cost.

While group buying is common in the bricks-and-mortar world, it is often very cumbersome to organize online. Mercata tried to eliminate many of the obstacles associated with old-economy group buying. By establishing a large and varied group of buyers interested in participating in group deals, suppliers offered their merchandise to Mercata's price-conscious group-buying crowd and the crowd participated without costly negotiations. In return, Mercata received a small fee for each product sold over its site. Ultimately, the C2B company was unable to aggregate enough consumer demand to allow it to negotiate meaningful discounts with manufacturers before its $90 million of funding ran out. In January 2001, Mercata announced that it would cease trading due to a lack of funds.

**Consumer-to-Consumer (C2C) Supply Chain.** The eBay business model clearly illustrates a **consumer-to-consumer (C2C)** supply chain. The auction site's mission is to help people trade practically anything tradable—it is a platform to facilitate person-to-person trading. EBay allows sellers to place individual items up for sale on which interested buyers can bid. EBay has created the largest online community of individual buyers and sellers in the world, as well as an efficient platform on which members of this community can interact and complete business. The platform provides a forum for buyers and sellers to meet and trade directly (as opposed to hiring an intermediary), uses the Internet to create a global marketplace, and offers convenience to the community. EBay offers over 450,000 new items for sale each day. It receives between 1.5 and 5 percent of the final sale price of each item successfully auctioned.

# Online and Offline Integration

As noted earlier, many companies in the online environment not only have significant difficulty creating a smooth integration between the front end of the customer experience and the delivery system, but also with integrating their online and offline front ends (e.g., retail outlets and websites). This integration is most complex for hybrid companies. Exhibit 8-6 provides a simple matrix illustrating the formation of hybrid companies. A pure online or pure offline company is not considered a hybrid; hybrid companies combine both online and offline systems, whether it be customer interface, fulfillment, or both. Borders is an example of a hybrid. The book retailer started as an offline firm, with bricks-and-mortar bookstores serving as its primary interfaces with customers. Later, it created a website to allow customers to shop and buy books online (*www.borders.com*). Gazoontite.com (*www.gazoontite.com*) is another example of a hybrid. Gazoontite provides specialty products to online allergy sufferers via its website and offline through bricks-and-mortar retail stores.

For bricks-and-mortar–based sites, the mix of products offered on the Web may significantly differ from the product selection offered at retail stores. Consider drugstores, for example. Many of the items bought at a physical drugstore are impulse or convenience items. Therefore, retail stores stock many items targeted toward convenience-related demand. Because shopping over the Web is not very conducive to the purchase of impulse convenience items, drugstore websites stock items not normally sold at drugstores that are nonetheless important to their Web customers. In addition, the economics of shopping on the Web versus shopping in a retail store are very different due to the low prices of many items in drugstores, vis-à-vis the shipping costs of delivering Web-ordered goods to customers. Consequently, the average sale to customers at Drug Emporium's website is two and

**Exhibit 8-6**

# WHERE TO PLAY ONLINE AND OFFLINE

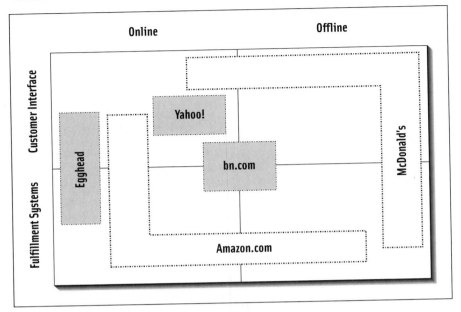

a half times the average sale at its retail stores.[26] Also, bricks-and-mortar–based companies must consider the demographic composition of their online customer base; their online customers may have significantly different motives or purchase patterns than their offline customers. Online and offline product mixes, as well as selling approaches, need to reflect the differences between customer bases.

Due to their dual-interface nature, hybrid firms face issues that do not concern pure online firms. One key decision the hybrid firm must make is how the company should be organized: Should the online part of the business be housed in the same organization as the offline business, or should it be spun out as a separate firm or operating unit?

### Single-Organization Hybrid—Advantages.

There are a number of advantages to housing the online and offline interfaces in the same organization.

- *Customer benefits.* Tightly coupled online/offline back-office support systems benefit the customer as well as the firm. The more integrated the two interfaces, the more likely customers will be able to migrate back and forth between the online and offline platforms during their interactions with the company. For instance, The Home Depot's website tries to make it easy for customers to interact with the company how they want, when they want. Website visitors can browse online listings of The Home Depot's products, assemble a shopping list, pay for their purchases online, and have the merchandise shipped to their home. Alternatively, they can choose to send the order to their nearest Home Depot store, where it will be packaged and left for them at a checkout station for purchase.

  Contrast the flexibility offered by The Home Depot to that offered by jcrew.com, the online operation of clothes retailer J.Crew. Customers who order clothes from jcrew.com must receive the clothes at home; they cannot pick up their purchases at a J.Crew store. Should they decide to return the clothes, they must be shipped back to jcrew.com because products purchased online cannot be returned to the physical stores.

When traditional retailers first launched websites, many did not allow customers to buy products through the Web channel and return them to a store. Sometimes this was due in part to the organizational structures of the firms. For example, Barnes & Noble.com was launched as a separate entity from Barnes & Noble. The two maintained separate inventory and cost-accounting systems, and revenues and sales were tracked separately as well. Thus, a book purchased from Barnes & Noble.com and returned to a bricks-and-mortar store would pose a number of difficulties. First, the physical store would record the return against sales it had not made; as a result, its profit would be understated. Second, the online operation would have made the sale but not recorded the return and would appear to be more profitable than it really was. In time, retailers such as Barnes & Noble realized that, integration between their channels gave them a competitive advantage against pure-play e-tailers. Today, many companies such as Wal-Mart— whose online division is a separately capitalized entity—allow Web customers to return product to their stores.

- *People.* The single-organization structure can be a recruiting advantage for firms that begin offline and expand to the online platform. Because e-commerce is still an attractive field at present, offline firms become more attractive to many candidates when they add an online interface.

- *Taxes.* In cases in which one interface is operating at a loss and the other is profitable, combining the operations into a single entity can provide significant tax benefits. The profit of one venture is reduced by the loss of the second, immediately lowering the tax liability of the profitable venture. As a separate organization, the unprofitable venture would amass its losses for application against future profits, in effect postponing the benefit that could be gained immediately in a single organization.

- *Valuation.* During 1999 and the first quarter of 2000, Wall Street was awarding enormous valuations to many online ventures. Even after the crash of Internet valuations in April 2000, many companies were very highly valued according to traditional valuation measures. In an online firm, a company's ability to lock in alliance partners, acquire competitors, and attract top talent is strongly related to its market capitalization. Shareholders of offline firms stood to gain when their firms built or bought online capabilities and housed the two interfaces in the same organization.

- *Systems.* The ability of any interface, online or offline, to deliver value to a customer depends in large part on the back-office infrastructure (e.g., IT infrastructure, order processing and fulfillment systems, inventory control, etc.) that supports it. Online and offline interfaces that are housed in a single organization can potentially rely on a single set of back-office systems. This is particularly true for firms that start out as hybrids and therefore can design their back-office systems specifically to support two different types of channels.

When the online and offline interfaces are housed in different organizations, it is unlikely that they will be supported by a single set of back-office systems. At best, the two organizations may attempt to link their systems at critical points—an endeavor that can be costly and is not always successful.

### Single-Organization Hybrid—Disadvantages. The principal challenges associated with single-organization hybrids are as follows:

- *Coordination and cooperation processes.* Achieving the cost savings and customer benefits that derive from a single set of back-office systems requires considerable coordination between the online and offline operations. If managers of the two interfaces do not work cooperatively, they will be unable to leverage a single set of back-office systems. As a result, the firm will not realize the potential cost efficiencies and customer benefits of the single-organization structure.

- *People.* While some workers will be attracted to a single-organization hybrid, others may be repelled. In an interview with *Fortune* magazine, Jim Tuchler, a project manager working on Sears' website, conceded that recruiting new-economy workers to an old-economy employer can be difficult. "Telling people you work at Sears doesn't elicit oohs and ahhs," he explained.[27]

- *Allocations.* When both interfaces are housed in the same organization, they compete for critical resources such as funding, staffing, and mindshare with senior management. Managers of the new interface may find themselves spending as much time negotiating for resources as applying them. Given the interdependencies between the offline and online parts of the organization, as well as the potential difference in drivers of competition, unambiguous resource-allocation processes may be very complex to design and difficult to manage.

### Dual-Organization Hybrid—Advantages. A dual-organization structure has its own advantages:

- *Coordination processes.* With coordination processes there is no need for the company to simultaneously grow two organizations driven by different skills and evolution speeds. Women.com is one of many online companies that experienced significant problems with the coordination of very different types of organizations under one roof. Women.com opted for the dual-organization structure, but then quietly closed its online store for women's clothing and accessories just three months after launching. Instead of adding to its revenues, Women.com found that its e-commerce site was detracting from other revenue sources—especially banner ads. The company decided that its new partner for women's books e-tailing, Harlequin Enterprises, would handle the customer service and fulfillment of orders placed on eHarlequin: "It is an integrated partnership in which they do what they do best, and we [Women.com] do what we do best: driving traffic and sales."

- *License to cannibalize.* A cannibalistic strategy is easier to execute when the new interface is housed in a separate organization. Few organizations have the will or strength of leadership to cannibalize themselves.

- *People.* Housing the interfaces in two separate organizations can be a recruiting advantage for the online operation; some workers prefer a pure online environment.

- *Allocations.* When the new interface is housed in a separate organization, it does not have to fight with the offline interface for senior management time, funding, or staff.

- *Taxes.* As this book went to press, most online sales were exempt from sales tax. If the online and offline interfaces are legally separate entities, sales on the offline interface are subject to sales tax, but sales on the online interface are exempt. If the two stores are housed in a single corporation, sales on both stores are taxed.

- *Valuation.* Investors may prefer to see the online interface incorporated as a separate organization and valued at e-commerce multiples rather than risk having its value diluted by merging with an online firm.

## Dual-Organization Hybrid—Disadvantages.
The principal challenges associated with dual-organization hybrids are as follows:

- *Avoiding customer confusion.* A lack of consistency between online and offline interfaces can create confusion for customers. One author of this book is an executive platinum member of the American Airlines system. He is quite satisfied with the offline interface—namely, the phone operations, service personnel, gate attendants, and Admirals Club staff. However, he was quite dissatisfied with the American's website prior to 1999 site modifications. First, attempts to visit the site during a major site relaunch often failed and required multiple attempts. Second, there was no password storage; one needed to remember the password on each occasion. Third, there was no clear integration of the offline and online services.

- *Consistent integration of online and offline customer service.* Good customer service can build customer trust in the company managing the website. Customer service can be a significant portion of the customer experience; for example, eBay receives between 40,000 and 75,000 customer support e-mails per week.[28] However, a survey by *The Industry Standard* of the top 10 e-commerce sites found that the average customer-service response time of surveyed companies on the Internet was over a day and a half. Amazon.com was the quickest to return a personalized response—in 34 minutes.[29]

A particularly illustrative example of the potential backlash of insufficient integration between online and offline customer service is offered by usability firm Creative Good's review of the Apple website (*www.store.apple.com*). After the check out process accidentally terminated the site evaluator's attempt to buy a G3 Tower, the evaluator called the Apple customer service department to get the order processed. Creative Good's summary of the interaction is as follows:

*We eventually were able to complete the buying process, after we called Apple's 800 number no fewer than four times trying to figure it out. During the phone conversations, it became clear that the Apple [customer service] staff had little knowledge of the customer experience on the website.[30]*

Such a lack of integration between online and offline customer interfaces and service can easily damage the company brand and hinder its ability to implement its strategy successfully.

- *Managing a consistent brand.* Maintaining a consistent brand image across stores requires cooperation and communication between managers of the online and offline channels. Together, managers must answer questions such as the following: How similar should the look-and-feel of the two channels be? How much consistency should there be between the online and offline versions of customer activities such as product selection, purchase, and returns? Coming to an agreement on these decisions is enough of a challenge when online and offline managers are part of a single organization; it is especially difficult in dual-organization hybrids, in which managers may have less contact with colleagues, less mutual trust, and fewer incentives to cooperate. Even when managers of the two stores share a common vision, their ability to execute it may be hampered by separate back-office systems with differing capabilities and limitations.

## WHAT ARE THE CATEGORIES OF OFFLINE INNOVATION?

In this section, we explore the different ways in which offline and online firms produce **innovation**. First, we discuss innovation categories and the innovation process in the offline world. Then, we discuss how the online environment has affected the drivers underlying the offline approach to innovation. Finally, we review new classifications of innovation categories and processes online.

Long considered a leading innovator in the offline world, technology firm 3M has classified types of innovation into three categories: **line extensions, changing the basis of competition,** and **new industries** (see Table 8-1). Each of these developmental categories has a different research process and product timeframe. Most offline companies use a similar categorization of innovation.

### Line Extensions

Line extensions are incremental advances to an existing product—in other words, they are new and improved versions of an existing product (e.g., an advanced release of a software package). To create line extensions, 3M established research units called "division laboratories." These research units work closely with customers to

**Table 8-1** INNOVATION USED TO BE SLOW AND GRADUAL IN THE OFFLINE WORLD

| 3M's Research Paradigm | | | | Key Takeaways |
| --- | --- | --- | --- | --- |
| **Laboratories** | **Primary Activities** | **Time Frame** | **Innovation Type** | |
| Division Laboratories | • Product development <br> • Product control <br> • Technical service | • Today's business 0–3 years | • Line extension | • Traditional offline innovation took years and emphasized sustainable/gradual innovation <br> • Marketspace still offers room for incremental innovation, but emphasizes shifts to more drastic innovations <br> • High information content of innovation objects increases speed of innovation from years to months or even less <br> • Short history of marketspace means new collaborators/complementors become available frequently |
| Sector Laboratories | • Sector technology development | • 3–10 years | • Changing the basis of competition | |
| Central Research | • New technology development | • 10+ years | • New industries | |

Source: Gundling, Ernest. 2000. *The 3M Way to Innovation*. Tokyo, Japan: Kodansha Int. Ltd., New York, USA: Kodansha America, Inc.

determine their needs and develop variants of current products to meet these needs within a project timeframe of zero to three years.

## Changing the Basis of Competition

Other innovations create a new competitive position or niche in a market. In their rush to gain overnight-service market share, UPS and FedEx constantly offer service innovations. Both companies offer 8AM service between select cities; FedEx also offers Saturday and Sunday service. Each innovation does not necessarily need to be a profit center, but the fact that one service offers delivery in one category that the other does not (i.e., weekend delivery) may sway a client company to give all its business (including lucrative overnight service) to the more innovative service. Thus, these types of incremental innovations have the ability to change the basis of how delivery services compete. 3M set up sector laboratories to develop this type of innovation. The goal of sector laboratories is to create innovations within a timeframe of three to 10 years.

## New Industries

Still other innovations can lead to the creation of an entirely new industry. These types of innovations are quite common in the pharmaceuticals field. For example, Upjohn's introduction of Rogaine, a medical advance in growing scalp hair, created a lucrative new market. At 3M, central research labs were established to develop this type of major innovation. The timeframe within which the central research labs create new industry products is considerably longer—a minimum of 10 years.

## WHAT IS THE OFFLINE INNOVATION PROCESS?

An underlying reason for the significant time required to innovate in the offline world is the complexity of the standard "funnel process." 3M has described three distinct and successive phases in the **innovation funnel process** (see Exhibit 8-7): **innovation by doodling, innovation by design,** and **innovation by direction.** During this three-stage process, an increasing number of innovations are eliminated until only the most promising remain and are brought to market.

This funnel process is also sometimes referred to as the **waterfall concept of new product innovation.** The purpose of the funnel is to streamline the process of making internal choices about innovations that the company should pursue, and to ensure that the company launches only the innovations with the highest probability of succeeding. 3M's three phases reflect the initial supportive focus on the generation of a host of ideas and the following shift toward the screening of these ideas. The screening tightens as the ideas move through each phase of the funnel. The process becomes complex because these screenings are done within the organization, they are based on expected customer behavior, and the perspective of the screening criteria are very broad in nature. Indeed, as Gundling points out, "Full scale innovation success—the proverbial hit product—requires streetwise market acumen and staying power to select the right application, accurately forecast demand, and implement a sales strategy that gets the product into the hands of paying customers."[31]

Exhibit 8-7 THE OFFLINE INNOVATION PROCESS
WAS INTERNAL TO THE FIRM

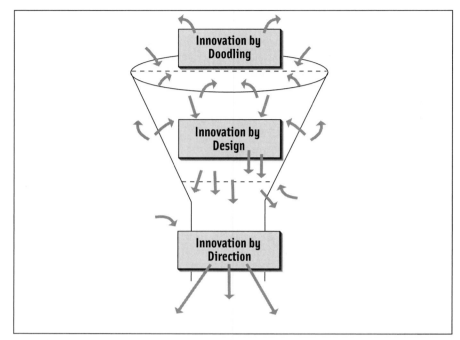

Source: Adapted from 3M's Innovation Funnel, in Ernst Gunding's *The 3M Way to Innovation.*
(Banyo-ku, Tokyo: Kodansha America, 2000.)

## Innovation by Doodling

The enterprising manager knows that her staff has a great deal of experience, knowledge, and interesting ideas. She gathers them into a conference room for an afternoon meeting, and announces that she wants to create a free-form brainstorming session during which no idea is dumb. At the end of the brainstorming session, the manager has several pages of innovative marketing ideas.

## Innovation by Design

The manager and a subset of her staff select several of those brainstorming ideas that appear cost effective and show promise in consumer acceptance. As a team, they reduce the initial set of ideas into a smaller, commercially viable set.

## Innovation by Direction

Working from the commercially viable set, the staff undertakes market research and further tests implementation viability. After reviewing the results of these tests, the staff further narrows the commercially viable idea set into a final set of marketing concepts to fully implement in the market.

# WHAT IS THE NEW LOGIC BEHIND ONLINE INNOVATION?

The fundamental logic behind the offline innovation process is significantly altered by the dynamic nature of online business. This is the topic of the first subsection. In the second subsection, we illustrate how new innovation frameworks try to incorporate the coevolution of technology and customers. Finally, we consider new innovation processes that are emerging as applied versions of these new innovation frameworks.

Innovation in the networked economy shares a similarity to the 3M innovation funnel process. However, key differences between the nature of new-economy and old-economy innovations affect the innovation process. These differences change several crucial trade-offs underlying the offline (funnel-based) innovation process (see Table 8-2). We describe several of these differences in the following sections.

## High Investment Costs as Key Constraint in Innovation Selection Process

In general, the size of the investments required to launch innovative services and products are significantly higher in the offline world than in the online world. The implication is that the offline focus on "picking the big hit" loses its relevance, because smaller innovations requiring lower investments can prove just as effective in implementing a company's strategy.

**Table 8-2**

## OFFLINE INNOVATION PROCESS VS. ONLINE INNOVATION PROCESS

| Offline Trade-Offs/Principles Supporting Funnel Approach | Online Principles |
|---|---|
| • Investments required to launch new innovation are high | • Investments required to launch new products and services are moderate |
| • Limited resources force trade-offs/choices of which innovations to pursue or not | • Choices about future of new innovations can easily be made by markets; no need to make these choices internally |
| • Trade-offs/choices are made inside the organization before product hits the market | • First-mover imperative can be aligned with gathering (more) customer input |
| • Time-to-market/first-mover imperative needs to be traded off with extensive time required to gather customer input | • Launching beta-versions allows for revisioning/customization, actually benefiting innovator |
| • Launching early increases risk of flops, and flops need to be avoided at all times:<br>– Costs of flops very high<br>– Significant damage to brand equity | • Key drivers determining success of innovation/implementation are<br>– Customer base<br>– Customer data analysis<br>– Knowledge management |

## Innovation No Longer an Optimization Within Given Constraints

For many offline companies, the innovation process focuses on an intense screening of innovation options. The primary reason for this is that the companies have limited capital and human resources and, hence, have to optimize the potential use of these limited resources. The fluid nature of online companies means they do not need to focus on such an optimization. Instead, online companies can experiment much more and rapidly increase or decrease investments to launch marketing innovations.

## Locus of Innovation Selection Moving Outside the Firm's Boundaries

As noted earlier, in the offline world, all trade-offs regarding innovation are generally made internally. The management of the company or business unit decides which innovations to pursue, how to market them, when to launch, and how to extract revenue. These decisions are based on expectations about likely customer behavior gathered from testing prototypes or other forms of market research. In the online environment, the focus of innovation decision-making moves outside the boundaries of the organization and into the market. That is to say, the organization can launch a series of innovations or versions of innovations, and customers provide direct feedback by either adopting them or not. The online company can actually gain customer buy-in by adjusting its innovations based on adoption behavior.

## Adaptive Innovation Instead of Trying to "Guess It Right the First Time"

Online commerce is relatively young. As such, many online companies have developed a "sense and respond" approach to innovating and serving customers.[32] This means that online companies toss into the marketplace many early versions of products and innovations (so-called beta versions), which are then rapidly improved upon based on measured customer feedback. In general, online customers are much more open to this form of innovating/marketing than traditional offline customers.

As a result, it could be argued that innovation is fundamentally different in the online world. Offline firms tend to be risk averse because of the high cost of launching innovations. But also, once an innovation is launched, old-economy companies do not have the infrastructure in place to immediately fix glitches and incorporate feedback ideas in real time—further exacerbating the potential downside of an early launch. These constraints, coupled with concern over the potential negative impact of a failed innovation on a well-established old-economy brand name (e.g., Cherry Coke), limit offline firms' appetites for rapid-cycle innovation launches.

In contrast, online companies are eager to launch new innovations and are more tolerant of imperfections that can be quickly fixed. If the innovation proves ineffective, it is often very easy to undo. In addition, some have argued that online customers are more understanding of innovation glitches and derive some satisfaction in helping fix glitches and providing insights to sites for future evolution.

# WHAT ARE THE ONLINE INNOVATION FRAMEWORKS?

In the networked economy, several factors are thought to speed up the innovation process. These factors include the observation that innovation decisions are cheaper and easier to implement; the market is actively seeking innovation; customers are willing to tolerate glitches and provide feedback; and online firms are well suited to immediately incorporate findings from customer feedback. This leads to rapid innovation and an innovation cycle that is measured in months, compared to years in the old economy.

The need to rapidly and continuously adapt and improve has led to frameworks for innovation that focus less on product innovation and more on the coevolution of technology and customers. Two leading models of innovation have emerged to address this challenge.

## Disruptive Technologies

Clayton Christensen defines **disruptive technologies** as innovations that create an entirely new market through the introduction of a new kind of service or product. Though these disruptive technologies can initially be inferior to established technologies, their performance levels progress faster than market demands and more fully fulfill consumer expectations later in the product's lifecycle.[33]

> *Most technologies foster improved performance. I call these sustaining technologies. . . . What all sustaining technologies have in common is that they improve the performance of established products, along dimensions of performance that mainstream customers in major markets have historically valued. Disruptive technologies . . . result in worse performance, at least in the near-term. Generally disruptive technologies underperform established products in mainstream markets. But they have product features that a few fringe (and generally new) customers value.*[34]

Exhibit 8-8 illustrates Christensen's approach. As examples of disruptive offline-world technologies, Christensen lists sectors that were surprised or upset by disruptive technologies: DEC was surprised by the rise of personal desktop computers; Sears did not anticipate the rise of discount retailing; and conventional health insurers were surprised by the rise of HMOs.

The Internet has proven to be a disruptive innovation for many companies and industry sectors. Yahoo, Schwab.com, and Amazon.com are examples of organizations whose very reason for existence is a disruptive innovation. In the early days of the Internet, portals such as Yahoo were mainly extended search engines that served as an entry onto the World Wide Web. These search engines were an innovation to the buying process and were initially difficult and inconvenient to use, with very specific input formats that must have made more sense to programmers than users. Also, search engines had limited reach—the universe of online users was small and consisted mainly of hobbyists. However, the sophistication of search engines has evolved to a level at which natural-language words can be used and searches can be tailored much more precisely.

The same evolution goes for Amazon. At its launch, Amazon only sold books online at a discount without many frills or value-added services. As such, it was a relatively simple innovation in the world of the traditional book-buying market.

Over time, Amazon upgraded its bookselling product offering by adding the following:

- Reviews by customers
- Easier purchase process (1-Click)
- Personalized recommendations for new book purchases based on the customer's previous purchases
- Opportunity for customers to personalize their own account page

In addition, Amazon used its strong position in bookselling to initiate additional buying process innovations in a host of other categories (e.g., music, electronics, and even lawn and patio) as well as other forms of commerce (e.g., zShops and auctions).

However, an additional challenge arises for players in the online environment. Because so much of the online product offering is technology-driven, increased technological innovation can set expectations and affect performance levels demanded by consumers. There could be a tighter link between technological innovations and performance demanded by online customers than in the offline world. The continual upgrades of Amazon, MP3, and, to a lesser extent, My Yahoo are examples of this.

## Dorothy Leonard Innovation Framework

Next, we consider the **Dorothy Leonard innovation framework**.[35] While this framework was developed in an offline context, many of the principles apply in the online environment. First, we review Leonard's five distinct categories of innovation: (1) **user-driven enhancement**, (2) **developer-driven development**, (3) **user-context development**, (4) **new application or combination of technologies**, and (5) **technology/market coevolution** (see Exhibit 8-9).

### Exhibit 8-8 CHRISTENSEN INNOVATION FRAMEWORK

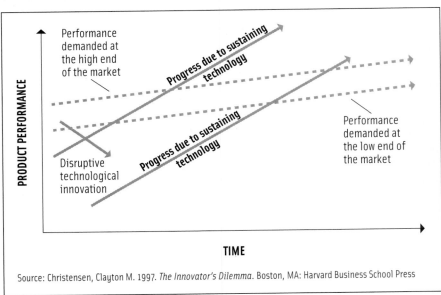

Source: Christensen, Clayton M. 1997. *The Innovator's Dilemma*. Boston, MA: Harvard Business School Press

**Exhibit 8-9**

## LEONARD INNOVATION FRAMEWORK

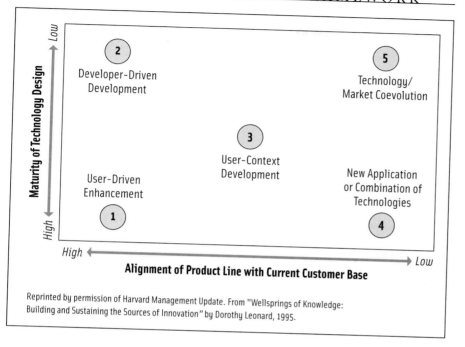

Reprinted by permission of Harvard Management Update. From "Wellsprings of Knowledge: Building and Sustaining the Sources of Innovation" by Dorothy Leonard, 1995.

**User-Driven Enhancement.** Innovations of this type are generally features that are no-risk improvements to a product. Common types of user-driven enhancements include lowering product price; adding low-cost, high-value feature enhancements; and introducing cost-efficient quality improvements. Crest has a long-standing reputation for offering high-quality toothpaste products. In recent years, competitors have created a new line of toothpaste products specializing in teeth whitening. These products often use baking soda as a whitener and have been very popular. Crest's entry into the premium whitening toothpaste market through development and sale of a baking soda and peroxide whitening product is an example of a user-driven enhancement.

**Developer-Driven Development.** This type of innovation occurs when a firm develops a new way of meeting an existing consumer need. The PalmPilot is a great example of a developer-driven development. There has been a long-standing need for personal organizers. For the most part, paper-based companies produced pocket diaries and desktop rolodexes to meet these needs. While simple handheld organizers did exist, Palm revolutionized the market by finding a new way to meet consumers' organizing needs. Palm produced a handheld device that incorporated most (if not all) of the important features that users need to organize themselves. As a result, Palm products have fueled the worldwide market for electronic personal companions and, as of May 1999, held 68 percent of the worldwide market share.

**User-Context Development.** This type of innovation occurs when firms develop products to meet a previously unexpressed need. In many cases, careful market research revealed these needs and firms have built products to meet them. A good example of user-context development is the positioning and further development of sport utility vehicles (SUVs) as spacious family vehicles. In today's SUV market, very few purchasers actually use SUVs for off-road travel or utilize their four-wheel-drive features. Although consumers apparently do not use many of the original design functions of SUVs, producers discovered that SUVs met the personal expressive needs of many consumers buying large, family-size vehicles.

### New Application or Combination of Technologies.

This type of innovation occurs when an established technology is applied to a new industry. Broadcast Data Systems (BDS) is a radio monitoring service that implemented this type of innovation. Music companies are always interested in learning when music from their artists is being played on the radio (to monitor airplay success, channel marketing promotions, etc.). Prior to BDS entering the market, radio airplay information was compiled by survey companies that called radio stations and asked what songs they played. There has always been a general concern over data integrity and frustration over the amount of play-list detail; the best result survey takers could get was a top-40 list. To meet the needs of the music industry, BDS retooled existing technology to revolutionize the music-reporting business. BDS uses a sophisticated monitoring system that involves feeding snippets of record samples into a computer. Every few seconds, this computer scans thousands of radio stations in the United States to make song matches. Every 24 hours, BDS provides clients detailed lists of the titles and exact playing times of songs played on specific radio stations. The BDS monitoring service is based on a version of advanced technology used during the Vietnam War to monitor troop movements along the Ho Chi Minh Trail.

### Technology/Market Coevolution.

This type of innovation stands at the very frontier of innovation. The customer base is not clearly known, nor is the technology well-established. These products sometimes appear to have a more or less accidental growth path, but they can be the beginning of entire new markets. The Post-it Note is an offline example of technology/market coevolution. This form of coevolution innovation is quite common in the online domain for three reasons:

- *Marketspace is undeveloped.* To a large extent, the online domain is still undeveloped with much white space, new players emerging, and industry boundaries blurring.
- *User behavior is not well-defined.* User behavior is still in a much more embryonic stage than in the offline world.
- *Large influence by technology.* Product offerings in the marketspace are heavily influenced by technological evolution and content.

## WHAT ARE THE ONLINE INNOVATION PROCESSES?

The erosion of traditional constraints on innovation does enable a faster, cheaper, and more adaptive innovation process. At the same time, the need for the innovation process to be adaptive increases sharply because uncertainty surrounding innovation has intensified dramatically, as new innovation frameworks have tried to capture. Two fundamentally different process models that attempt to accommodate this additional uncertainty are emerging in the online world.

## Napster as an Example of Technology and Market Coevolution

Napster is an example of recent technology and market coevolution in the online music arena. Until fairly recently, the cost of the necessary computer hardware capacity that would allow easy downloading and playing of music files was prohibitive. Music buyers relied on traditional offline distribution channels to fulfill their music-buying needs.

By filtering out all humanly inaudible sounds from the music track, Layer 3 technology increased the ability to compress music files by a factor of 10. In 1988, Layer 3 was adopted as an international standard by MPEG (Moving Pictures Expert Group). In 1995, Windows-compatible Winplay was released, enabling users to download music files easily and quickly from the Internet. In 1999, MP3 was so successfully adopted that it overtook *sex* as the most-searched-for term on the Internet. *[The Men Behind MP3, The Industry Standard, April 24, 2000]*

The Napster proposition is simple: Users download free software that indexes MP3 files on the user's hard drive and makes the hard drive visible to other Napster users when connected to the Internet. From there, a simple title or artist search results in locating the requested MP3 file on other users' hard drives from which it can be downloaded. *[Napster Grows Up, Red Herring.com, March 10, 2000]*

Napster's technology was not intended to be a major commercial product. Because the central concept is to allow users to share files with one another, paying for files is not currently required or possible. The technology was introduced into the online world, much like 3M's Post-It Notes, and has been adopted exponentially by the sheer demand of enthusiastic end users. According to Jupiter Research, in 1999 (the year Napster was inadvertently launched), an estimated 1 million of the 10 million online music buyers were Napster users!

There are two final notes the reader should keep in mind on co-innovation of technology and markets. First, the behavior of music buyers changed as a result of this new technology. According to the same Jupiter report, music retailers saw a spike in album sales for artists like Beck and the Beastie Boys, who often release music in MP3 form. This could create a new form of advertising or promotional revenue opportunity for online music providers like MP3 or Napster. Second, the Napster indexing technology was originally developed for MP3 files but has already been extended to other applications. Recently, Scour offered the same type of functionality for all media-related files: pictures, music files, or any other media files.

## Flexible Development Process

In discussing product development on the Internet, professors Marco Iansiti and Alan MacCormack of Harvard Business School introduced a model that emphasizes the integration of technology with customer preferences.[36] Exhibit 8-10 illustrates their model. The key point is that concept development and implementation of the ideas in the field need to overlap and be tightly integrated. Beta testing begins shortly after the product is developed and continues well into the implementation phase. The benefits that have been associated with the **flexible development process** include the following:

- *Reduced time-to-market of innovations cut from years to months.* This simultaneous development and feedback process reduces the time to launch.

- *Multiple versions of an innovation can be launched without significant risk or additional cost.* As customer feedback is received, new versions of the product can be launched.

**Exhibit 8-10** INTEGRATING NEW TECHNOLOGY WITH CUSTOMER PREFERENCES

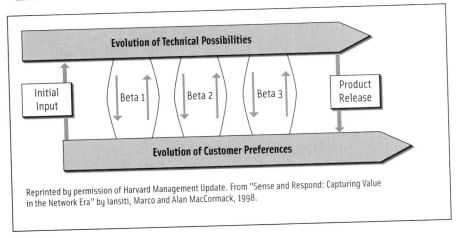

Reprinted by permission of Harvard Management Update. From "Sense and Respond: Capturing Value in the Network Era" by Iansiti, Marco and Alan MacCormack, 1998.

- *Increased flexibility to adjust direction of innovation.* The Netscape 3.0 product innovation process, illustrated in Exhibit 8-11, is a good example of the flexible development process. Netscape began the process of developing Netscape 3.0 shortly after Netscape 2.0 was released in January 1996. As Iansiti and MacCormack note, the first two beta versions were released internally in February and March; the first public release (Beta 3) was in March. From that point on, Netscape was able to gather a tremendous amount of user feedback for the full release in August.

## Distributed Innovation Model

The flexible development process can be considered a dramatically improved version of the traditional funnel process. The **distributed innovation model** (see Exhibit 8-12) is an additional step away from the classic funnel process. This process model puts continuously maintaining a fit between the organization and the evolution of the online domain at the very heart of the innovation process. In order to do this successfully, the organization tries to tap into the sources of online evolution: technology, collaborators, customer preferences, new entrants, and even competitors. The organization can be viewed as the center of the (innovation) web, or like an octopus with its tentacles connecting the inside of the organization with the sources of online evolution.

The innovation process is therefore no longer a funnel process with a fixed beginning and end; rather, it becomes a fluid, organic process. This innovation process is the ultimate expression of the "sense and respond" strategy. The benefits that have been associated with the distributed innovation process include the following:

- Maximizes use of both internal and external experts/sources
- Minimizes chances of the organization being surprised by external changes
- Highly interactive and much more flexible process than funnel process
- Reduced time-to-market

Exhibit
8-11

## THE DEVELOPMENT OF NETSCAPE 3.0

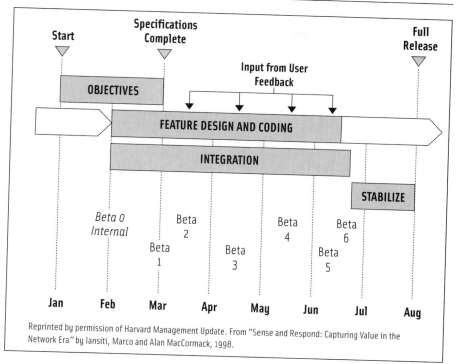

Reprinted by permission of Harvard Management Update. From "Sense and Respond: Capturing Value in the Network Era" by Iansiti, Marco and Alan MacCormack, 1998.

Linux distributor Red Hat is an example of a company that adopted the distributed innovation process. The innovation of the Linux product is driven by an explicit interaction between market evolution and Red Hat's reactions to these evolutions. The main drawback of this innovation process is that its fluidity can make it more difficult to manage. As we noted, it links the competitive environment and

Exhibit
8-12

## DISTRIBUTED INNOVATION

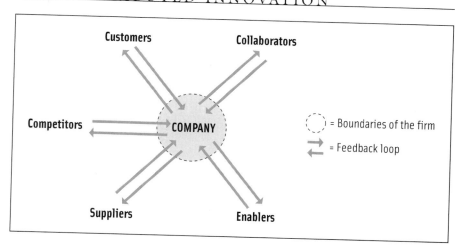

the inside of the organization tightly together. The innovation process is partly steered by forces outside the boundaries of the firm, which makes it difficult to control. Also, participants outside the boundaries of the firm know more about what is going on inside the firm than in the usual (internal) innovation process. The firm must find a way to work effectively with this new fluidity. Which model proves to be most effective is likely to depend on the difficulty of consistently implementing the process models. So far, neither model has proven to be more effective than the other, although the flexible development process currently seems to be more widely adopted.

# MARKETWATCH.COM'S IMPLEMENTATION

We now examine the use of technology and innovation in the implementation of MarketWatch.com's delivery system.

## Marketwatch.com Delivery System

As we discussed earlier in the chapter, the five components of the delivery system are assets, people, systems, processes, and supply chains. Here, we examine these first three components as they had developed for MarketWatch.com by the beginning of 2000.

**Assets.** MarketWatch.com's physical assets consist primarily of 10 news bureaus, located in San Francisco, New York, Washington, D.C., Boston, Chicago, Dallas, Los Angeles, London, Hong Kong, and Tokyo. The worldwide presence of MarketWatch.com offices allows for 24-hour coverage of global financial news. The main administrative, sales, marketing, and news facilities are located in San Francisco in 11,000 square feet of office space leased from CBS; the engineering, development, and licensing sales groups are located on leased space in Minneapolis, Minnesota. In addition, MarketWatch.com has colocated its broadcast productions in the CBS Broadcast Center in New York. This provides MarketWatch.com with access to the CBS television production facilities, producers, and support staff, saving it the expense of developing these assets on its own. This is a good example of a successful online/offline synergy between CBS News and MarketWatch.com: CBS provides the physical assets, while MarketWatch.com provides the experienced staff and knowledge of the Internet space.

In terms of intangible or information assets, in the last quarter of 2000, MarketWatch.com had an average of 8.4 million unique visitors per month, according to DoubleClick.[37] The site continuously collects information on its users, and is able to convert this information into its main revenue source by providing targeted advertising to interested providers. The site does not give advertisers individual information, but allows them to target messages geographically and at different times to MarketWatch.com's audience. In addition to its information on users, MarketWatch.com maintains an archive of news stories that were generated either internally or by other content providers. In June 1999, the company acquired BigCharts.com, a leading provider of licensed online financial-charting content. This provided MarketWatch.com with a proprietary technology that it could leverage in its news reporting.

**People.** MarketWatch.com's experienced staff of 90 professional journalists and editors sets it apart from its online competitors, and it is one of the main reasons that CBS News found MarketWatch.com such an appealing partner. MarketWatch. com's

CEO, Larry Kramer, was formerly the executive editor of *The San Francisco Examiner,* and metro editor and assistant managing editor of *The Washington Post.* Other members of the MarketWatch.com editorial staff previously worked for companies such as Bloomberg News, Associated Press, UPI, CBS Radio News, and Dow Jones Television. Most members of MarketWatch.com's news staff specialize in particular financial topics, such as IPOs or investment conferences. Based on his prior experience, Kramer believes that the ideal newsroom should have no more than 100 journalists, regardless of the audience it caters to. This allows for a highly scalable people model that can lead to increasing levels of profitability as the site's audience grows.

At the end of 1999, MarketWatch.com had 48 sales and marketing professionals; over 20 of them specialized in selling advertising space on the MarketWatch.com site. The company's salespeople had considerable experience in Internet sales and traditional media, and developed and implemented advertising strategies for existing and new advertisers. Finally, MarketWatch.com had 17 people responsible for website operations, 22 people in general administration, and a number of people dedicated to new product development.[38]

**Systems.** Until recently, DBC (one of MarketWatch.com's primary stakeholders) provided the company with most of its systems capabilities, including hosting services, software programming assistance, data communication lines, office space, network operations, and website management services. DBC's data center in Hayward, California, hosted the MarketWatch.com site. MarketWatch.com has now brought most of its systems in-house.

The current MarketWatch.com technology infrastructure is centralized in a primary data center in Minneapolis, Minnesota; there are two additional data centers located in New York and California. The three data centers are networked through Virtual Private Network connections, and the 10 MarketWatch.com offices are connected to the central Minneapolis data center through a direct line. The MarketWatch.com system could comfortably run on just one and a half data centers, but having three data centers allows the systems to continue to function properly in the event of a localized malfunction, and allows the company to turn off one of the centers independently for maintenance work.

Within each data center, there is a four-tier infrastructure with multiple points of redundancy. Each data center has 60 Web servers, and there are systems in place to balance the information load between them. Internet access in the California area is maintained through multiple connections with three different ISPs, and the computer equipment used to operate the MarketWatch.com website is powered by multiple uninterruptible power supplies. This configuration further ensures against system failures and site malfunctions. Any content generated by journalists in any of the 10 offices gets submitted to the data centers, and from there can be distributed to any interested party, including users, content licensees, and other partners.

# Marketwatch.com Innovation

Since its launch on October 30, 1997, MarketWatch.com has brought about a number of innovations (see Exhibit 8-13). They can be grouped into three categories: innovations in infrastructure, innovative Web offerings, and new ways of delivering offerings across multiple media platforms.

**Exhibit 8-13** TIMELINE FOR MARKETWATCH.COM INNOVATION

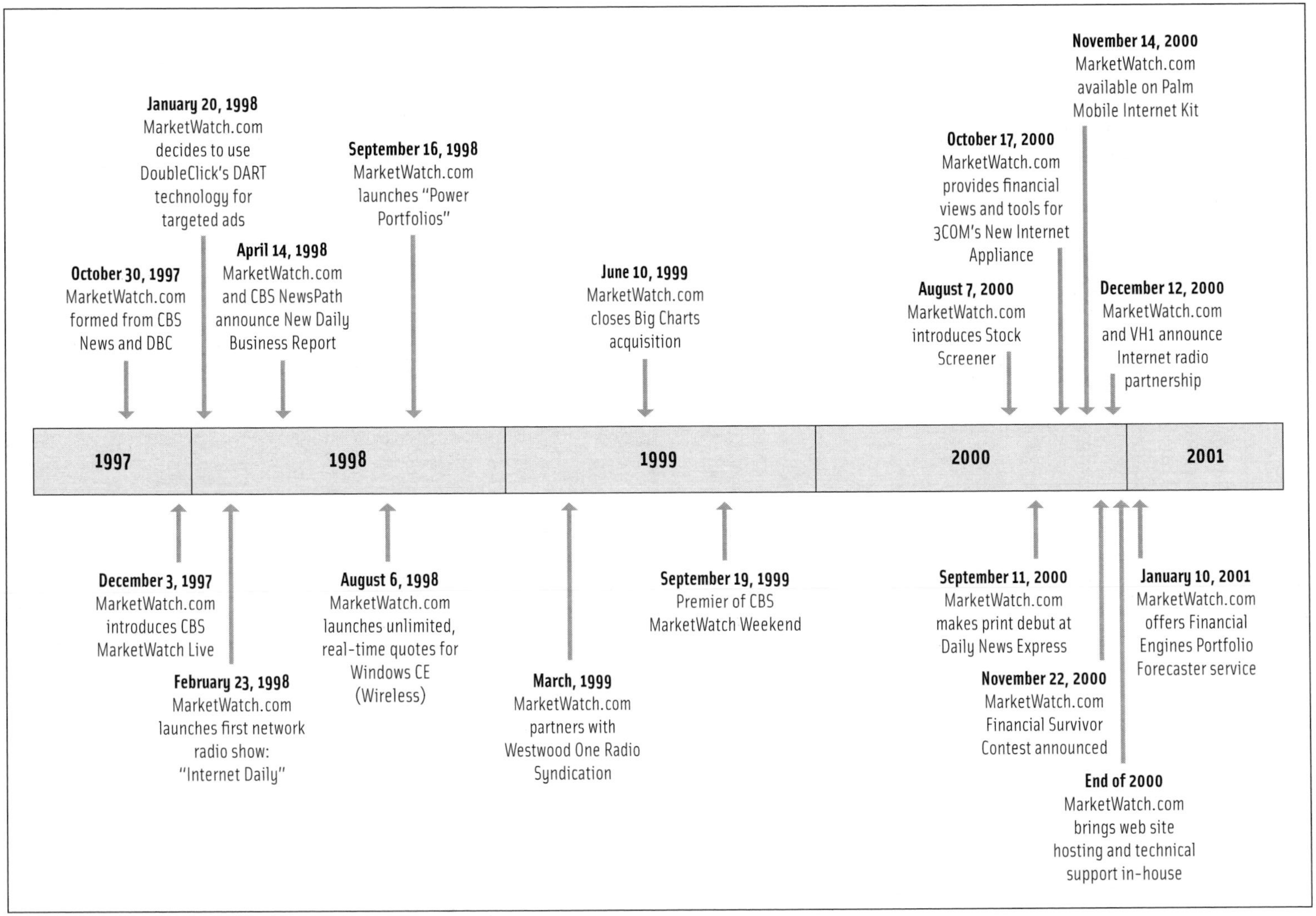

**October 30, 1997**
MarketWatch.com formed from CBS News and DBC

**December 3, 1997**
MarketWatch.com introduces CBS MarketWatch Live

**February 23, 1998**
MarketWatch.com launches first network radio show: "Internet Daily"

**January 20, 1998**
MarketWatch.com decides to use DoubleClick's DART technology for targeted ads

**April 14, 1998**
MarketWatch.com and CBS NewsPath announce New Daily Business Report

**August 6, 1998**
MarketWatch.com launches unlimited, real-time quotes for Windows CE (Wireless)

**September 16, 1998**
MarketWatch.com launches "Power Portfolios"

**March, 1999**
MarketWatch.com partners with Westwood One Radio Syndication

**June 10, 1999**
MarketWatch.com closes Big Charts acquisition

**September 19, 1999**
Premier of CBS MarketWatch Weekend

**August 7, 2000**
MarketWatch.com introduces Stock Screener

**October 17, 2000**
MarketWatch.com provides financial views and tools for 3COM's New Internet Appliance

**November 14, 2000**
MarketWatch.com available on Palm Mobile Internet Kit

**September 11, 2000**
MarketWatch.com makes print debut at Daily News Express

**November 22, 2000**
MarketWatch.com Financial Survivor Contest announced

**December 12, 2000**
MarketWatch.com and VH1 announce Internet radio partnership

**End of 2000**
MarketWatch.com brings web site hosting and technical support in-house

**January 10, 2001**
MarketWatch.com offers Financial Engines Portfolio Forecaster service

1997  1998  1999  2000  2001

## Innovations in Infrastructure.
One of the most important MarketWatch.com innovations was the development of a media-agnostic system for managing editorial content. All content, regardless of its media type (text, audio, video), can be entered into the MarketWatch.com data centers from any office. Once entered, that content can be accessed by third parties through the MarketWatch.com website, or it can be used by the MarketWatch.com television, radio, or print programs. This streamlined content distribution system leads to considerable time and resource savings. MarketWatch.com's competitors have attempted to build similar systems, but were not successful; MarketWatch.com was a pioneer in effectively implementing such a system.

## Innovative Web Offerings.
MarketWatch.com has gradually but steadily expanded its suite of Web tools and services. In December 1997, the company introduced its MarketWatch Live service, offering real-time financial news and data, charting capabilities, and stock alerts; in April 1998, it introduced another feature called the New Daily Business Report. Realizing that advertising would be its main source of revenue, MarketWatch.com started using DoubleClick's DART technology for targeted advertising. MarketWatch.com also complemented its information services by offering customization tools with which users could personalize the site; for example, the Power Portfolios tool, launched in September 1998, allows investors to track portfolios with up to 200 stocks, get personalized views, and review their transaction history and capital gains reports. The Power Portfolio service was further enhanced in January 2001, when MarketWatch.com announced that it would team up with Financial Engines to offer the new Portfolio Forecaster, a service that allows investors to estimate the potential value of their portfolios 1 to 30 years into the future, and also offers personalized investment recommendations.

Additionally, the June 1999 acquisition of BigCharts.com added cutting-edge charts technology to the MarketWatch.com site, which it could license to third parties and incorporate into its offerings; the acquisition also provided MarketWatch.com with the technical expertise to move its website hosting and network-support operations in-house. The company planned to complete this transition by the end of 2000, further limiting its dependence on DBC. MarketWatch.com also pioneered innovative marketing campaigns: On November 20, 2000, it launched the Financial Survivor Contest with 14 investor-club participants. Each club started with a fictional $100,000 portfolio; the club with the largest portfolio at the end of the contest was to be awarded the value of its investment (up to a certain limit). The contest was covered extensively on the *CBS Early Show* and the MarketWatch.com site.

## New Ways of Delivering Offerings Across Multiple Media Platforms.
MarketWatch.com also leveraged its relationship with CBS News to gradually offer its information and services across multiple platforms. On February 23, 1998, MarketWatch.com launched its first network radio show, *Internet Daily*. MarketWatch.com's participation in radio continued in March 1999, when it partnered with the Westwood One radio syndication. By the end of 2000, MarketWatch.com content aired on 154 radio stations including the top 10 U.S. markets, reaching 11.5 million unduplicated listeners each week. MarketWatch.com also began making its content available through wireless devices by launching unlimited real-time quotes for Windows CE in August 1998. MarketWatch.com began providing content for 3Com's Internet appliance in October 2000; the following month, it began providing content on Internet-connected PalmPilots. MarketWatch.com also

provided television content, both through short segments on CBS News programs and through content contribution to the CBS NewsPath network. MarketWatch.com debuted its own television show, *CBS MarketWatch Weekend*, on September 19, 1999. The show met with great success, airing on 131 stations representing more than 80 percent of the United States by year-end 2000. Finally, the site made its content available through the print medium by providing the financial content for *The Daily News Express,* the evening edition of *The New York Daily News,* in September 2000.

## SUMMARY

### 1. What is online implementation?

The online implementation process can be divided into two phases. In the first phase, the firm is concerned with the delivery of the offering through the five key components of a delivery system—people, systems, assets, processes, and supply chains. In the second phase, the firm is concerned with the extent to which the offerings and infrastructures are innovative and modified to fit the evolution of the market.

### 2. Why does implementation matter?

It has been argued that increased speed and intensity of competition in the online environment means implementation mistakes are punished much more severely and quickly than in the offline world. Online firms face six primary implementation challenges: (1) higher visibility to errors, (2) lower switching costs, (3) more dynamic competitive environment, (4) more fluid organizational boundaries, (5) more dynamic market environment, and (6) more complex linkages.

### 3. What is the "delivery system"?

The delivery system of a company is the most detailed and concrete expression of the company's value proposition. The value proposition, the product offering, and the business model each determine the requirements for the construction of the delivery system. The delivery system translates the resource system from a conceptual structure into a concrete configuration of resources, processes, and supply chains. Once the strategy has been defined and necessary capabilities identified, it becomes a matter of defining the structures, processes, reward systems, and human-resource practices that will produce the needed competencies and capabilities. It is at this stage of the strategy process that strategic intent is turned into a configuration that produces actual consumer and financial results. The five components of a delivery system include: people, systems, assets, processes, and supply chains.

### 4. What are categories of offline innovation?

Most offline companies classify types of innovation into three categories: (1) line extensions, (2) changing the basis of competition, and (3) new industries. Each of these developmental categories has a different research process and product time frame.

## 5. What is the offline innovation process?

The offline world typically views innovation in a funnel process with three distinct and successive phases: (1) innovation by doodling, (2) innovation by design, and (3) innovation by direction (see Exhibit 8-7). This three-stage process functions like a funnel in that an increasing number of innovations are eliminated during each phase until only the most promising remain and are brought to market.

## 6. What is the new logic to online innovation?

Online innovation shares a similarity with the innovation funnel process but key differences remain: (1) high costs make offline firms risk averse but online innovation costs can be dramatically lower; (2) the fluid nature of online companies and the abundance of external capital allow online companies to experiment much more; (3) online organizations can launch innovations and have customers provide direct feedback; and (4) online companies can launch early versions of innovations, which are then rapidly improved based on measured customer feedback.

## 7. What are the online innovation frameworks?

The ability to rapidly and continuously adapt and improve has led to frameworks for innovation that focus more on the coevolution of technology and customers. Christensen frames disruptive technologies as innovations that create an entirely new market through the introduction of a new kind of service or product. Though these disruptive technologies initially can be inferior to established technologies, their performance levels progress faster than market demands and more completely fulfill consumer expectations later in the product's lifecycle.

Dorothy Leonard developed a framework in the offline context, but many of the principles apply in the online environment as well. Leonard categorizes innovation into five groups: (1) user-driven enhancement, (2) developer-driven development, (3) user-context development, (4) new application or combination of technologies, and (5) technology/market coevolution.

## 8. What are the online innovation processes?

The erosion of traditional constraints on innovation enables a faster, cheaper, and more adaptive innovation process, but intensified uncertainty also increases the demand to innovate. Two fundamentally different process models attempt to accommodate this additional uncertainty: (1) the flexible development process is one in which the key point is concept development, and implementation of the ideas in the field need to overlap and be tightly integrated; and (2) the distributed innovation model is one in which the company tracks the evolution of each source of uncertainty and uses this to guide innovations while bringing all sources of market evolution inside the organization to maintain a continuous fit between the current online offering and the latest innovations.

# KEY TERMS

online implementation process

switching costs

delivery system

resource allocation process

human-resource management
    processes

manufacturing and distribution
    processes

payment/billing processes

customer support/handling
    processes

supply-chain models

business-to-consumer (B2C)

stock-it-yourself

outsource warehousing

drop shipping

fulfillment intermediaries

sales force efficiency

service efficiency

business-to-business (B2B)

consumer-to-business (C2B)

consumer-to-consumer (C2C)

innovation

line extensions

changing the basis of competition

new industries

innovation funnel process

innovation by doodling

innovation by design

innovation by direction

waterfall concept of new product
    innovation

disruptive technologies

Dorothy Leonard innovation
    framework

user-driven enhancement

developer-driven development

user-context development

new application or combination
    of technologies

technology/market coevolution

flexible development process

distributed innovation model

## Endnotes

[1]Butt, Joseph, L., Jr. 1999. Empowered consumers. In *The Forrester Report* (October): 12.

[2]Brooks, Fred. 1995. *The Mythical Man-Month*. Reading, MA: Addison-Wesley Publishing, 18.

[3]Lawrence, Stacy. 2000. e-Commerce spotlight: Hard numbers on e-Christmas in 1999. *Industry Standard*, 24 January.

[4]Anders, George. 1999. eBay struggles to repair image after big crash. *Deseret News*, 16 June, Business section.

[5]Collins, James. 2000. Built to flip. *Fast Company* (March): 131–43.

[6]*Economist*. 1999. Playing i-ball, 6 November, 65.

[7]Securities and Exchange Commission. 1999. *BUY COM INC. S-1 filing*, 27 October. For those who are not within close proximity of Washington D.C., please consider the convenient online version of this document, located at the following URL: *http://www.sec.gov/Archives/edgar/data/1097070/0001017062-99-001796-index.html*.

[8]Morhman, Susan A., Jay R. Galbraith, Edward E. Lawler III et al. 1998. *Tomorrow's organization: Crafting winning capabilities in a dynamic world*. San Francisco: Jossey-Bass Publishers.

[9]Please see the following article that provides a singular exemplification of a B2C complication: large-scale credit-card frauds by customers of an online company. Helft, Miguel. 2000. The real victims of fraud. *The Industry Standard*, 6 March.

[10]Technically, many of these retailers, such as Amazon, do have large warehouses with stock on hand. However, companies such as Amazon are able to take advantage of significant cost differences relative to other retailers since they do not need to maintain expensive retail locations.

[11]Piller, Charles. 1999. Most net retailers all sale, no service. *Los Angeles Times*, 28 June, Home edition, Business section.

[12]Goldman, Abigail. 1999. e-Commerce gets an F without the 'D' word retailing. *Los Angeles Times*, 25 July, Home edition, Business section.

[13]ibid.

[14]ibid.

[15]Dorsey, David. 1999. The people behind the people behind e-commerce. *Fast Company*, issue no. 25 (June): 184.

[16]Li, Kenneth. 1999. Instant delivery. *The Industry Standard*, 10 September.

[17]For further information, please see: Rangan, V. Kasturi, and Marie Bell. 1999. *Dell on-line*. Case no. 9-598-116, 26 March. Boston: Harvard Business School Publishing.

[18]King, Julia. 2000. How to do B2B. *Computerworld*, 28 February.

[19]Hill, Miriam. 2000. A new net craze is on the way: Business-to-Business firms hold tremendous potential, but the investing risks are steep. *Philadelphia Inquirer,* 18 January.

[20]Cass Information Systems: The State of Logistics Report 2000.

[21]As the following recent Goldman Sachs report on B2B put it: Goldman, Sachs and Co. 1999. B2B: 2B or not 2B? Version 1.1, 12 November.

[22]Goldman, Sachs and Co. 1999. B2B: 2B or not 2B? Version 1.1, 12 November, 14.

[23]Grygo, Eugene. 2000. A buy-sell revolution. *InfoWorld*, 6 March.

[24]Gerdel, Thomas W. 2000. Industry takes to the Web; Internet fast reshaping traditional supply chain. *Plain Dealer Reporter*, 27 February, final edition.

[25]Tait, Nikki, Louise Kehoe, and Tim Burt. 1999. U.S. car monoliths muscle in on the Internet revolution: Ford and GM plans to buy from suppliers online may reduce costs further. *Financial Times*, 8 November, International Companies & Finance section.

[26]*Drug Store News.* 1999. The burgeoning e-retail frontier, 25 October, Technology section.

[27]Brown, Eryn. 1999. Big business meets the e-world. *Fortune*, 8 November.

[28]Rafter, Michelle. 1999. Customer disservice. *The Industry Standard*, 10 May.

[29]Ibid.

[30]Hurst, Mark. Chapter 2: Apple store. In *In search of e-commerce*. This chapter exists in online form and can be accessed at the following URL: *http://www.goodexperience.com/reports/isoe/apple/index.html.*

[31]Gundling, Ernest. 2000. *The 3M way to innovation: Balancing people and profit*. Tokyo, Japan: Kodansha Int. Ltd.; New York, USA: Kodansha America, Inc., 180.

[32]Bradley, Stephen P., and Richard L. Nolan. 1998. *Sense and respond*. Boston: Harvard Business School Press.

[33]Christensen, Clayton. 2000. Meeting the challenge of disruptive change. *Harvard Business Review* 78, no. 2 (March-April): 72.

[34]Christensen, Clayton. 1997. *The innovator's dilemma*. Boston: Harvard Business School Press, xv.

[35]Leonard-Barton, Dorothy. 1995. *Wellsprings of knowledge*: *Building and sustaining the sources of innovation*. Boston: Harvard Business School Press, 180–212.

[36]See: Iansiti, Marco, and Alan MacCormack. 1998. Product development on Internet time. In *Sense & respond*. Boston: Harvard Business School Press. See also: Iansiti, Marco, and Alan MacCormack. 1999. *Living on Internet time: Product development at Netscape, Yahoo!, NetDynamics, and Microsoft*. Case study, no. 9-697-052, 30 June. Boston: Harvard Business School Publishing. URL: *http://www.hbsp..harvard.edu/hbsp/prod_detail.asp?697052.*

[37]MarketWatch.com year-end Press Release, January 30, 2001.

[38]Source: MarketWatch.com Annual Report 1999.

# Metrics

This chapter focuses on how companies can assess the progress and health of their online businesses. To determine their financial progress, most companies routinely analyze benchmarks such as sales, margins, profit, and market share. However, to judge the strategic health of the company, senior executives must analyze metrics that reflect the entire strategy of the company—how customers perceive the value proposition, the marketplace offering, and the effectiveness of implementation. In this chapter, we introduce the concept of a Performance Dashboard that senior managers can use to assess the overall strategic health of the company. The Performance Dashboard is composed of five categories of metrics: (1) opportunity, (2) business model, (3) branding and implementation, (4) customer interface and outcomes, and (5) financial metrics. We conclude the chapter with an overview of the firms that provide metrics services for online companies. These metrics can be used to make a comprehensive assessment of the strategic as well as the financial health of individual companies.

## QUESTIONS

*Please consider the following questions as you read this chapter:*

1. Should senior managers be concerned about metrics?

2. How can we assess the health of online firms?

---

This chapter was coauthored by Bernie Jaworski, Jeffrey Rayport, Leo Griffin and Yannis Dosios.

3. What are the steps to implement the Performance Dashboard?

4. What sources of metrics information can firms use to chart their progress?

## INTRODUCTION

In Chapter 8, we analyzed the key components of business-model implementation. In this chapter, we turn our attention to the **metrics** that senior managers can use to evaluate the progress of their businesses. This is not a straightforward issue because senior and stock-market analysts tend to have a bias toward financial metrics. Clearly, this emphasis is important. However, focusing only on financial measures is limited in two fundamental respects. First, while financial measures reflect the performance history of the company in the marketplace, they do not provide managers with an early warning system by which to take corrective action before disappointing returns are realized.[1] Financial results are essentially a measure of the success of past strategies.

Second, financial measures are output measures that do not reflect the strategy of the company. In order to assess the progress of an online company, one needs to develop company-specific metrics that precisely track the strategy of the company.[2] To return for a moment to our flower example from Chapter 5, the value proposition of 1-800-Flowers focused on freshness of flowers and reasonable prices. Hence, one of the early warning metrics for 1-800-Flowers would be the degree to which customers in the company's target segment perceive that 1-800-Flowers is outperforming competitors on freshness and reasonable prices. Because the value proposition is only one component of the overall strategy, other metrics would also need to be developed for each strategy component, such as the offering, resource system, and implementation.

The purpose of this chapter is to provide a framework by which one can assess the health of an online business. The framework is composed of five categories of metrics—opportunity, business model, branding and implementation, customer, and financial. Opportunity metrics focus on the conditions in the customer and competitor environments. Business-model metrics include topics related to the value cluster, marketspace offering, resource system and capabilities, and partnerships. Branding and implementation metrics focus on supply-chain performance, organizational dynamics, and marketing communication effectiveness (including branding). Customer metrics focus on output measures that relate to the customer experience (e.g., overall satisfaction, average dollar amount of purchases, stickiness) as well as metrics that relate to the customer interface. Finally, financial metrics capture the financial performance of the company, including such measures as sales, profit, and margins.

The chapter is organized as follows: In the first section, we address the question of why metrics matter. In the second section, we introduce the Balanced Scorecard as a reference framework, discuss its potential limitations, and introduce the Performance Dashboard. In the third section, we focus on a five-step process by which to implement the Performance Dashboard. In the fourth section, we apply this five-step implementation process to MarketWatch.com. We then conclude with an overview of the alternative sources of information that firms can use as inputs to the metrics process.

# SHOULD SENIOR MANAGERS BE CONCERNED ABOUT METRICS?

Before we discuss alternative metric frameworks, it is important to consider whether metrics are significant to an organization. On the one hand, we could argue that organization metrics are always important, because they represent the performance targets of the company. That is, each month any particular dot-com company might look at a handful of metrics to guide its progress, including such measures as percent increase in revenue, percent increase in unique visitors, length of time that visitors remain on the site, and cost of customer acquisition.

However, it is vital that we stress that metrics only matter to the extent that they are used by senior management to either reward employees or take strategic action (e.g., change processes, strategy, product offerings). In other words, metrics devoid of follow-through action by senior management are of limited value.

## Metrics Drive Behavior in a Number of Ways

Metrics can produce very positive results for an organization. In this section, we isolate five ways in which metrics can have a positive effect on the growth and vitality of an organization.[3]

**Help Define the Business Model.** The act of specifying concrete goals with precise measurement can help senior management define the business model of a company. Companies often struggle with their choice of value proposition or cluster. Focusing attention on measurement can help increase the precision of the value proposition.

A good example is Dell Online Premier. Users from large accounts can access their password-protected company-specific site on Dell Online Premier to search, select, purchase, track shipping, and receive service. Moreover, the entire process is electronically enabled through interorganization applications (e.g., order tracking, funds transference, and shipping).

Should Dell's value cluster focus on price, speed of delivery, level of custom configuration of the PC, customer service, or assurance of reliability? Certainly, one could implement metrics that reflect all five of these benefits. At the same time, one could ask which is the most important. Our point is simply to note that focusing on the measurement of key targets helps management clarify its strategic priorities.

**Help Communicate Strategy.** Clearly documented performance targets can go a long way toward communicating the particular goals and strategy of a company. Once performance metrics are specified, they should be communicated as widely as possible within the organization. Communicating the strategy to the workforce helps employees understand and appreciate the metric-setting process.

**Help Track Performance.** One of the unique features of the online world is the availability of instantaneous site-performance feedback. Metrics concerning usage, visitors, length of time on site, average sales, page views, and so on are constantly available. Thus, in sharp contrast to traditional offline models, firms are able to track performance in real time and make appropriate modifications in tactics or strategy.

**Help Increase Accountability.** Companywide metrics need to be linked to the performance appraisal system. If the metrics are tied to the reward system, then the metrics have weight behind them. Importantly, individual performance appraisals can be tied to companywide, team-specific, and individual metrics. That is, general performance measures such as sales growth and amount of sales are likely to have companywide accountability. On the other hand, specific measures related to site usability can be tied to the interactive design function, while customer service metrics can be tied directly to the customer service department.

**Help Align Objectives.** Finally, clear, precise metrics can help align individual objectives, departmental functional goals, and companywide strategic activities as a whole. For example, understanding that one's firm has made it a priority to increase its look-to-book ratio (the number of customers who buy relative to the number who visit, often expressed as a ratio of 100 visitors; a site with a look-to-book ratio of 5:100 has 5 buyers per 100 visitors) enables various departmental functional groups and individual employees to adjust their behaviors accordingly.

# Current Challenges to Specifying Metrics for Online Businesses

While it is clear that there are important benefits in articulating metrics that link to business strategy, many online firms do not have a systematic approach to developing, assessing, and applying metrics. In this section, we explore the reasons why some firms have not made an explicit commitment to metrics.

**Companies' Strategies Change Rapidly.** One classic argument against the use of metrics relates to doing business on "Internet time." It is now common for business models to change often and quickly, given the emergence of new competitors and rapidly evolving customer tastes. In this environment, it is difficult to think of a long-term commitment to a strategy, much less the metrics that follow. Free PC is a recent example. Initially, the revenue model of Free PC was to give away PCs for free—in exchange for the forced viewing of advertisements. However, as Bill Gross, founder of Idealabs, admitted, the growth of new users could not sustain the business model. Hence, the business was sold and a new strategy emerged.

**Measurement Is Resource-Intensive.** While the Internet has made customer data much more available, making the data usable and actionable remains a significant issue. In many cases, capturing metrics data requires the setup and maintenance of systems and procedures that require significant capital investment and human resources. Moreover, once the data is mined, management must set aside time to review the data closely and then react accordingly. Each of these issues—data capture, data mining, and information use—requires the time and commitment of senior executives.

**Online Measurement Systems Are Vulnerable.** There is some evidence to suggest that online data capture (e.g., page views, usage data, demographics) can be compromised. Examples include sites artificially boosting their number of unique users (e.g., employees' access to sites), users submitting false demographic data, and hackers tampering with system data.

### Soft Metrics Are Not Valued by the Investment Community.

Generally, the investment community is most comfortable with the reporting of hard numbers related to revenues, margins, number of visitors, length of time on site, customer acquisition costs, and other easily quantifiable measures. Not as highly valued are the softer metrics of customer perception such as ease of use of site versus that of competitors' sites, belief that the site provides the best value, and other market research measures. But, curiously, these softer measures that reflect customers' perceptions of the site are frequently the best early indicators of site performance.

### Meaningful Metrics Change on Internet Time.

Metrics considered relevant and appropriate to use in tracking a site's success often change. Less than two years ago, companies used "hits" as the basic metric of success. The basic metric then shifted to page views. Now conversion rates are considered the appropriate measure. The point is, while traditional financial metrics remain timeless, customer metrics tend to change as firms better learn to interpret the data.

One small case in point: The concept of stickiness, or length of visitor time on the site, makes perfect sense as a measure of success for eBay. However, the same measure would not be true for American Airlines (*www.aa.com*). Indeed, frequent travelers want to book tickets, cash in travel stickers, and check mileage. The last thing these travelers want is to stay on the site for an extended period of time. Moreover, the number of page views would probably be a measure of a frustrated consumer rather than an interested one. Our point is that even well-regarded customer metrics need to be carefully assessed when applied to the particular site.

## HOW CAN WE ASSESS THE HEALTH OF ONLINE FIRMS?

In this section, we introduce the Performance Dashboard as a framework with which to judge the progress and health of an online business. We use the dashboard metaphor to describe the real-time navigation task that confronts the management team of a dot-com enterprise. Analogous to an automotive dashboard, the framework provides vital business performance feedback to the firm, which enables quick confirmation of success or the immediate identification of corrective actions needed. We begin our discussion by reviewing Robert Kaplan and David Norton's seminal work on the Balanced Scorecard.

## The Balanced Scorecard

Kaplan and Norton introduced the **Balanced Scorecard** in response to their perception that managers overwhelmingly focus on short-term financial performance. To address this concern, they argued that firms must balance their financial perspective by analyzing other domains of the business, including internal business processes and customer responses. In particular, they introduced four categories of metrics that they believed more accurately captured the performance of companies (see Exhibit 9-1): financial, customer, internal business systems, and learning and growth. This approach not only added perspective to a restricted financial focus but also provided managers with an early warning system that allowed for corrective measures to be taken before poor financial results were realized. A key feature of the

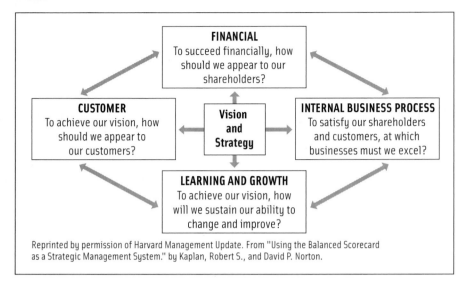

Kaplan and Norton approach was to start with the strategy of the firm and then derive the metrics in the four areas. In the following paragraphs, we describe each of the four areas in detail.

**Financial Metrics. Financial metrics** are designed to assess the financial performance of the company. Typical financial measures include revenue, revenue growth, gross margins, operating income, net margin, earnings per share, and cash flow. Financial measures reflect strategic choices from the most recent planning period and, to some degree, an accumulation of all previous planning periods. Hence, Amazon's financial performance in 2000 is a function not just of 12 months but of the previous five years, since its launch in 1995. Finally, financial measures are used by all stakeholders of the company, including employees, customers, and partners. However, these metrics are the most heavily weighted and analyzed by the investment community.

**Customer Metrics. Customer metrics** are intended to assess the management of customer relationships by the firm. With the Kaplan and Norton scheme, these measures typically focus on a set of core measurements, including market share, customer acquisition, customer satisfaction, and customer profitability. These are general measures that reflect the overall health of the customer base. Kaplan and Norton also point out that these measures need to be customized to the target segment. To return to our Dell example, a large client, such as Boeing, would probably have fairly large customer acquisition costs but high profitability if the relationship is solidified. In contrast, smaller clients may have lower acquisition costs but also a lower total lifetime value of the customer.

**Internal Business Process Metrics. Internal business process metrics** focus on operations inside the company. In particular, this set of metrics focuses on the critical value-adding activities that lead to customer satisfaction and enhanced shareholder value. Kaplan and Norton divide these metrics into three broad groups: innovation, operations, and postsale service.

- *Innovation.* Innovation metrics measure how well the company identifies customer needs and creates associated new products. Innovation measures could include customers' perceptions of the innovativeness of the company or quantitative measures of innovativeness (e.g., percent of product sales from new products, percent of new products versus competitors).
- *Operations.* Operations metrics measure the quality of the entire supply-chain process through to delivery of products to the customer. This could include measures that reflect customer order processing, order cycle time, delivery time, and order error percent.
- *Postsale service.* Postsale service metrics measure the quality of the service the company is offering to its customers. This includes return processing, warranty processing, turnaround time for e-mail questions, and payment processing.

## Learning and Growth Metrics.

**Learning and growth metrics** broadly cover employee, information systems, and motivation metrics. Employee metrics relate to selection, training, retention, and satisfaction. Information system metrics capture the quality of the infrastructure that must be built to create long-term growth and improvement; measures would include timeliness, accuracy, and utility of data. Motivation broadly captures employee motivation, empowerment, and alignment. Metrics would relate to alignment of company goals and incentives with personal employee goals.

## Limitations to the Balanced Scorecard

The Balanced Scorecard has become a classic tool for senior managers; however, it becomes less useful as one attempts to apply its framework to the online world. The following examples are some identified shortcomings:

- *No clear definition of strategy or business models.* A key theme of the Balanced Scorecard is that the entire scorecard is based on the strategy of the firm. However, Kaplan and Norton do not clearly define the strategy or business model. Without this definition, it is difficult to assess whether the four categories of metrics accurately capture the critical aspects of the business strategy or the business model.
- *Unclear location of organizational capabilities or resources in the framework.* Organizational capabilities and resources span a variety of domains, including internal business processes, customer relationships, partnerships, and the unique selection of markets (e.g., market-sensing capabilities).[4] Thus, capabilities often extend beyond internal business processes. It is unclear where capabilities are located in the framework.
- *Unclear where partnerships reside in the framework.* Strategic partnerships are a critical measure of a firm's ability to compete in today's market. However, partnerships are not addressed in the Balanced Scorecard framework.

In sum, the Balanced Scorecard has taken the important first step toward the development of a set of metrics to assess the effectiveness and efficiency of businesses. In the next section, we introduce a framework that accounts for the issues not addressed by the Balanced Scorecard.

## The Performance Dashboard

Similar to the Balanced Scorecard, the **Performance Dashboard** is intended to reflect the health of a business. Below, we address each of the Balanced Scorecard's limitations through features of the Performance Dashboard. We also review the five categories of metrics that reflect the strategy framework of this book.

### The Strategy Framework Drives the Necessary Metrics.
While the Balanced Scorecard offers no clear definition of strategy or business model, the Performance Dashboard utilizes the strategy framework to derive the necessary metrics. In Chapters 4 through 8, we articulated a strategy process that is captured in an organizing framework for the textbook (see Exhibit 1-7). In the proposed framework, there are six critical steps to the strategy process: (1) opportunity assessment, (2) business-model specification, (3) customer-interface design, (4) market communications and branding, (5) strategy implementation, and (6) evaluation.

These six steps represent a strategy process for online businesses and can be used to identify the categories that map onto and directly link to the strategy. Relevant metrics categories include: (1) opportunity metrics, (2) business-model metrics, (3) customer-interface and outcome metrics, (4) branding and implementation metrics, and (5) financial metrics (see Exhibit 9-2).

### Capabilities Are Featured in the Resource System of the Business Model.
While the Balanced Scorecard is unclear in specifying the location of organizational capabilities or resources, the Performance Dashboard identifies the capabilities featured in the resource system of the business model. Firm-level capabilities are defined dur-

**Exhibit 9-2** THE PERFORMANCE DASHBOARD

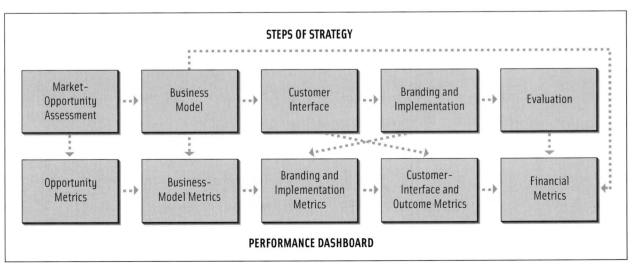

ing the third step of the business model. Hence, capabilities of the firm are highlighted and integrated into the Performance Dashboard metrics. Recall that the isolation of these capabilities is essential and key to determining the drivers of the customer benefits.

**Partnerships Are Featured in the Resource System of the Business Model.** While the Balanced Scorecard is unclear about where partnerships reside in its framework, partnerships are featured in the resource system of the business model in the Performance Dashboard. It explicitly includes partnership measurements in the business-model metrics. Recall that in Chapter 3 we isolated the firm-level capabilities that related to the various benefits. We also noted that it is at this step that partnerships need to be considered to fill in where the firm does not have the requisite capabilities. Hence, partnerships are explicitly considered in the Performance Dashboard measures.

## Components of the Performance Dashboard

The Performance Dashboard is composed of five categories of metrics: opportunity, business model, customer interface and outcomes, branding and implementation, and financial.

**Opportunity Metrics.** Recall that we defined market-opportunity analysis as the firm's ability to discern an unfulfilled need in the marketplace. The ability to discern unserved needs is critical to the strategy process. This is not a one-time event within the strategy process, but rather a continual process, because market conditions ceaselessly evolve. For example, by constantly expanding its offerings to include complementary gifts, the 1-800-Flowers site extended its segment focus beyond the core offerings.

Market-opportunity metrics assess the degree to which the firm can accurately gauge the market opportunity. Generic indicators include the ability of the firm to target the most attractive segments, the ability of the firm to understand and map competitors' strategy evolution, and the ability of the firm to track the evolution of target-segment needs.

**Business-Model Metrics.** Business-model metrics capture the subcomponents of the business model: the value proposition, egg diagram, resource system, and financial metrics. In this section, we review the metrics that would capture the value proposition, egg diagram, and resource system. The financial metrics are critically important to the firm and, as such, represent an entire category of metrics in their own right (see discussion below).

*Value Proposition or Cluster Benefits Metrics.* The value proposition is composed of three parts: target segment, benefits offered, and capabilities that drive the benefits. Metrics for this assessment would focus on customer perceptions of the benefits that a given site offers relative to competitors. Capabilities in the value proposition will be addressed in our discussion of the resource system.

Thus, to return to 1-800-Flowers, the key customer benefits are lower prices, fresh flowers, a broad assortment of gifts, and widespread access. Here, management would be concerned about the firm's performance relative to its competitors' on these four benefits, as perceived by target customers.

*Marketspace Offering Metrics.* This phase of the business model is captured in the egg diagram reviewed in Chapter 5. Metrics should capture all phases of the customer decision process as well as the features and attributes of the offering.

Customer decision-process metrics would reflect the entire decision process from prepurchase (e.g., customer acquisition costs, satisfaction with selection), purchase (e.g., satisfaction, site usability), and postpurchase (e.g., loyalty, customer response rates, percent of returns, percent of shopping carts filled versus products purchased, lifetime value of the customer). Offering metrics focus more on the nuts-and-bolts features, attributes, and functionality of the site. Thus, to return to our egg diagram, the offering metrics would capture performance on the products and services ring of the egg diagram. For 1-800-Flowers, this would include customer evaluations of the gift recommendations section, FAQs, ease of commerce transaction, and member specials.

*Resource-System Metrics.* The resource system is based on the benefits offered to consumers. From these benefits, the firm would analyze the capabilities that are necessary to supply the benefits. These benefits can be offered by the firm or its partners.

In this phase of metrics building, the firm should track its performance on the most critical capabilities and associated activities. In the context of 1-800-Flowers (see Exhibit 5-3), the capabilities include logistics, sourcing, brand name, multiple contact points, media partnerships, product partnerships, and an online gift center. At this stage, the firm would want to track performance on each of these key capabilities. Also, recall that capabilities are provided by both the firm and partners and, therefore, the firm would also want to consider performance metrics for these critical partnerships.

*Financial-Model Metrics.* Given the significance of financial measures, we address them as a separate category in the dashboard.

## Customer-Interface and Customer-Outcome Metrics.

**Customer-interface** and **customer-outcome metrics** capture two forms of metrics. The first class of metrics measures the customer's experience with the technology interface; that is, the customer's response to the 7Cs of the interface. The second class of metrics captures output metrics such as the overall levels of satisfaction, average order size, and customer profitability. Next we review each class of metric.

*Customer-Interface Metrics.* In Chapter 6, we provided a detailed review of the 7Cs of the customer interface. In this chapter, we are concerned with customer perception of the firm's performance on each of the seven characteristics. For example, how would customers rate the level of customization on the firm's site versus the levels of competitors' sites in the category? Is the content adequate? Is the level of community adequate? Obviously, a host of specific measures could be created for each C. The challenge for managers is to select a subset of the most critical interface metrics. A starting point for this winnowing exercise is the value proposition of the firm.

*Customer-Outcome Metrics.* The customer-interface metrics capture the process measures that the firm believes will produce favorable customer responses such as satisfaction and loyalty. Thus, a great community site will lead to more favorable overall levels of satisfaction with the site. Here, we focus attention on both the subjective and objective customer-outcome metrics. Subjective measures include customer satisfaction and, in regards to the site, an overall evaluation of the customer's experience at the site. Objective, quantitative measures include customer acquisition costs, average order size, customer profitability, and number of visits per month. These latter metrics can be aggregated into an overall lifetime value of the customer measure.

### Branding and Implementation Metrics. Branding and implementation metrics
focus on supply-chain performance, organizational dynamics, and marketing-communication effectiveness (including branding). In Chapter 7, we introduced approaches to developing branding; and in Chapter 8, we discussed implementing the plan through developing the delivery system and by creating an organization capable of continuous innovation. Fulfillment of the brand promise could include metrics related to the brand's strength—widespread customer awareness of the brand, for example. Delivery-system metrics track business processes, internal organization, and supply-chain management. Finally, innovation metrics could capture the firm's ability to rapidly innovate, even in a potentially discontinuous fashion.

### Financial Metrics. Financial metrics capture the revenues, costs, profits, and balance-sheet metrics of the firm. These are the most critical metrics for the long-term success of the firm. However, as noted at the outset, these results are a function of the accumulated strategy decisions of the firm. Hence, while they focus management attention on what results need to be correct, they offer no guidance to factors that can influence their correction.

## Life Cycle of a Company

Exhibit 9-3 illustrates that online firms pass through four stages of development in the **life cycle of a company**. These stages are identified as **startup, acquisition of customers, monetization,** and **maturity.** Some authors have argued that the relative weight of the metrics vary by the stage of the business. For example, in the startup phase, the market-opportunity metrics and the articulation of the business model are critical. In the customer acquisition stage, customer acquisition is critical and financial metrics are not as critical. However, at the maturity stage, customer retention and cost control become comparatively as important as customer acquisition costs.

*(continued from page 332)*

So what do you have left over to actually build the infrastructure of your business? And there is actually significant correlation. If you look for instance at Yahoo!, Yahoo! on an annualized basis generates about six dollars per customer in this personal profitability, gross margin minus sales and marketing expense per customer. Lycos generates about a dollar per customer after sales and marketing expense.

Interestingly, if you then look at the market caps on those stocks, more often than not, the value that the market places on each Yahoo! customer is six times [what] they place on Lycos. So there is some rationality out there. Does it work all the time? No. But it's a step in the right direction."

*Get the full interview at www.marketspaceu.com*

### Exhibit 9-3

LIFE CYCLE OF A COMPANY

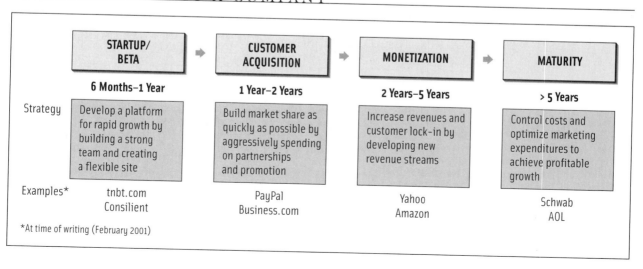

| | STARTUP/ BETA | CUSTOMER ACQUISITION | MONETIZATION | MATURITY |
|---|---|---|---|---|
| | 6 Months–1 Year | 1 Year–2 Years | 2 Years–5 Years | > 5 Years |
| Strategy | Develop a platform for rapid growth by building a strong team and creating a flexible site | Build market share as quickly as possible by aggressively spending on partnerships and promotion | Increase revenues and customer lock-in by developing new revenue streams | Control costs and optimize marketing expenditures to achieve profitable growth |
| Examples* | tnbt.com Consilient | PayPal Business.com | Yahoo Amazon | Schwab AOL |

*At time of writing (February 2001)

POINT OF VIEW

# Gurley on Customer Conversion Rates

Bill Gurley, a well-respected venture capitalist at Benchmark Capital, believes that the single most important metric of website performance is the "conversion rate."[5] Conversion rate is defined as the number of visitors who come to a website and take action (i.e., make a transaction) as a proportion of the total number of visitors to the site. This number has also been termed the look-to-book ratio.

According to Gurley, average conversion rates are in the 3 to 5 percent range. The very best websites achieve conversion rates of 10 percent or more. Gurley argues that the conversion rate captures information on many qualitative aspects of the sites (in our terminology, on the effectiveness and efficiency of the 7Cs). He believes that "no other single metric captures so many aspects of the quality of the website in a single number."

In particular, Gurley asserts that five variables affect the conversion rate: user interface, performance, convenience, advertising, and word of mouth. When a user interface is easy to use, conversion rates increase. Gurley's performance variable is similar to our Chapter 4 performance dimension—namely, sites

that are extremely slow will tend to have lower conversion rates. Convenient functionality, such as Amazon's patented 1-click shopping, also increases conversion. Finally, two key forms of marketing communication, standard online and offline advertising and word of mouth (both viral and offline), are particularly important in enhancing the conversion rate.

The impact of conversion rates on customer acquisition costs can be enormous. Table 9-1 shows the impact that increasing the conversion rate from 2 percent to 4 percent or 8 percent can have on marketing costs for a typical e-commerce site.

Consider the following example. A successful advertising campaign costing $10,000 might result in 5,000 unique visitors to a company's website. A site with a conversion rate of 2 percent will make 100 transactions as a result of these visits, while a site with an 8 percent conversion rate will make 400 transactions from the same number of visits. The site with a 2 percent conversion rate spends 100 percent of its revenues on marketing, while a site with 8 percent conversion spends a much more sensible 25 percent of its revenues on marketing.

**Table 9-1** BILL GURLEY ON THE POWER OF CONVERSION RATES

|  | Conversion Rate | | |
|---|---|---|---|
|  | 2% | 4% | 8% |
| Advertising Costs | $10,000 | $10,000 | $10,000 |
| Visitors | 5,000 | 5,000 | 5,000 |
| Transactions | 100 | 200 | 400 |
| Cost/Transaction | $100 | $50 | $25 |
| Revenue | $10,000 | $20,000 | $40,000 |
| Marketing/Revenue (%) | 100% | 50% | 25% |
| Average transaction size = $100 | | | |

Source: Gurley, J. William. 2000. The Most Powerful Metric of All. CNET News.com, 21 February
URL: http://www.news.com/Perspectives/Column/0,176,403,00/html?tag5st.ne

# WHAT ARE THE STEPS TO IMPLEMENT THE PERFORMANCE DASHBOARD?

In this section, we provide an overview of how a company would implement the Performance Dashboard. As noted above, it is important to develop these metrics based on the strategy of the firm. The strategy, however, is likely to be influenced by the life cycle of the company.

Exhibit 9-4 provides a blueprint or road map to the metric development process. The five steps of the process are illustrated on the top row of the figure. Next, we show a more detailed flow of the types of questions, sample metrics, leading indicators, and specific performance targets. Keep in mind that this is simply an illustration and any metrics that followed would need to be tied specifically to the strategy.

## Step One: Articulate Business Strategy

The first step in the process is to articulate the business strategy. The business strategy is composed of six stages: market-opportunity assessment, business model, customer-interface design, branding, implementation, and evaluation. The business strategy was the focus of Chapters 4 through 8.

## Step Two: Translate Strategy into Desired Outcomes

The second step in the process is to specify key actions and desired outcomes in specific performance areas. For example, we have identified five areas where desired outcomes can be targeted. Consider, for example, the customer-interface design and the outcomes area. Here we may target increased levels of customer conversion, retention, and customer profitability. Note, we are not setting the performance target levels (e.g., increase conversion rates from 2 to 4 percent); rather, we are simply specifying the outcome that we want to effect.

## Step Three: Devise Metrics

Step three takes the outcome areas and identifies specific metrics that reflect the desired outcomes. Thus, during this step, one would specify the exact measurement (or often a set of metrics) that one would use to track the desired outcome. Again, we are not specifying the exact level of the metric that we desire (that will occur in step five) but rather isolating the metrics that can be gathered, measured, and tracked over time.

Take, for example, the conversion rate. We noted earlier that the conversion rate is typically measured in terms of look-to-book ratios—that is, how many customers buy, relative to the number of visitors. This is seemingly straightforward in that it entails tracking the log files of the website and simply calculating how many people conducted e-commerce transactions relative to the number of site visitors.

However, this conversion rate metric can be complicated in several ways. First, does the firm want to separate completely new users from previous users and buyers? What is a reasonable look-to-book ratio of all completely new visitors versus a look-to-book that includes all visitors? Should this look-to-book vary by sections

**Exhibit 9-4** BLUEPRINT TO THE PERFORMANCE DASHBOARD

**Step One:**
Articulate Business Strategy

**Step Two:**
Translate Strategy into Desired Outcomes

**Step Three:**
Devise Metrics

**Step Four:**
Link Metrics to Leading and Lagging Indicators

**Step Five:**
Calculate Current and Target Performance

Define goals and value proposition

Develop resource system required to deliver the strategy

**Market Opportunity**
- Opportunity size?
- Competitive environment?

**Market Opportunity**
- Market size and growth
- Average age and income
- Competitor concentration

**Business Model**
- Unique value proposition?
- Capabilities vs. competition?

**Business Model**
- Customer perceived benefits
- Exclusive partnerships
- More invested in technology vs. competition

**Implementation and Branding**
- How to develop brand?
- How to go to market?

**Implementation**
- Customer brand awareness
- System uptime percentage
- Number of IT staff
- % inaccurate orders

**Customer**
- How to acquire customers?
- How will customers change?
- The customer experience?

**Customer**
- Market share
- Purchases/year
- Success rate
- Service requests/customer

**Financial**
- Financial consequences in terms of revenue, profit, cost, and balance sheet?

**Financial**
- Revenue
- Profit
- Earnings per share
- Debt to equity ratio

- For each metric, determine the metrics that it affects and that affect it
- Map the linked set of metrics, indicating leading and lagging indicators
- Ensure that there is a balance between leading and lagging indicators

- For each metric, calculate current level of performance
- Determine target level required to meet outcomes described in Step Two
- Ensure that targets are consistent with each other

of the site? For example, should the look-to-book ratio be the same for each product category? Does the firm need to target different look-to-book ratios depending upon the level of site traffic?

Note that look-to-book is a rather straightforward metric. It gets more complicated when one looks at qualitative measures, such as employee or customer satisfaction. Let us say a company targets an increase in customer satisfaction from 80 to 95 percent. How does the firm translate this desired outcome into metrics that everyone in the organization buys into? Should it be a general measure of "how satisfied are you with the site?" Or should it ask a series of questions about satisfaction with the site's usability, content, products, ease of use, and so on, and then aggregate these measures into a customer satisfaction index?

Our point is not to make this process more complex. Rather, while it seems straightforward to link outcomes with desired metrics, the selection of metrics requires a great deal of management attention. Metrics must be established for all the desired outcomes targeted across the stages of business strategy.

## Step Four: Link Metrics to Leading and Lagging Indicators

Step four is to determine the leading indicators of a particular metric and to map the entire set of metrics, including focal and leading indicators. Thus, if conversion rate is the target metric, one also needs to identify leading indicators such as levels of advertising expenditure and degree of positive (and negative) word of mouth. More often than not, the financial measures are lagging measures of business performance.

## Step Five: Calculate Current and Target Performance

Step five is to calculate the current level and the target level of performance for selected metrics. Thus, the firm identifies the current conversion rates, advertising expenditure, and degree of positive word of mouth. At this stage, one also attaches specific numeric levels with each of the key desired outcomes. For example, one might state that the customer conversion rate should move from 2 to 4 percent, that customer retention or repeat use should increase from 15 to 20 percent, and that one should move from 10 to 30 percent customer profitability in the ensuing time period.

## WHAT ARE SOURCES OF METRICS INFORMATION THAT FIRMS CAN USE TO CHART THEIR PROGRESS?

We will now discuss sources of industry standard metrics and benchmark values. As noted earlier, traditional financial metrics are common and easy to acquire, while more qualitative metrics can be more difficult to obtain. Firms are often in a position to collect metrics on many of the targeted areas noted above. That is, firms are likely to track their value proposition versus competition, customer satisfaction with the site, site usability, and financial outcomes. However, it is also useful for the firm to complement these internal data sources with market-level data from third-party sources. Acquisition of external industry data allows the firm to compare its performance relative to the performance of other sites. For example, Forrester publishes detailed ratings on all the flower websites. Each flower site can obtain this objective data that compares its site to others on ratings devised and scored by Forrester, an objective third-party information provider.

In this section, we review three types of data sources for the metrics assessment. Following this discussion, we map the available Internet research sources to the various metric categories. Finally, we conclude with an overview of a firm in each of the three data source categories.

# Online Information

*Market Research.* Online **market research** firms collect primary customer data through online surveys or customer submissions. These firms tend to have a strong emphasis on site usability, customer satisfaction, and traffic level. Examples include BizRate (*www.bizrate.com*), Media Metrix (*www.mediametrix.com/landing.jsp*), and AC Nielsen (*www.acnielsen.com*).

Table 9-2 is an example of the type of market-level findings produced by Media Metrix. The table shows the top 25 websites ranked according to the number of unique visitors to the site in a given month (unique visitors are counted only once). AOL is the top site, with over 60 million unique visitors each month.

*Analyst Reports.* **Analyst reports** are data sources that blend primary market data on a particular topic with an analyst's view of the market. Thus, for example, Jupiter Communications (*www.jup.com*) produces a series of reports on the Internet. These reports cover topics such as network infrastructure (e.g., broadband applications report), media convergence (e.g., AOL Time Warner Alliance), and trend data on Internet use (e.g., European use of online banking). Typically, analysts conduct primary research and/or use site traffic information to produce their reports. Firms in this space include the Aberdeen Group, Forrester, Frost & Sullivan, and IDC.

**Financial Information.** These data sources principally provide statutory filings of **financial information** on particular companies or aggregated financial data across industries. Reports may appear with or without accompanying analyst commentary. The data collected generally includes income statement, balance sheet, and statement of cash flow information. Among the providers are Hoover's Online (*www.hoovers.com*), Edgar Online (*www.edgar-online.com*), and broker/analyst reports from leading brokerage houses (e.g., DLJ Direct [*www.dljdirect.com*]).

To provide a richer feel for available Internet data services, we turn to a more detailed look at three companies. First, we focus on BizRate.com, which bills itself as the "people's portal" to e-commerce and rates e-businesses by asking tens of thousands of customers about their shopping experiences. BizRate.com asks every customer at participating online stores to take part in a survey, immediately after completing a purchase, to provide input on the quality of the experience. Follow-up queries ensure that the customer received the order as scheduled and that the overall experience met expectations.

In particular, BizRate.com asks consumers to rate the performance of an online store on its "ten dimensions of service." These are briefly noted in Exhibit 9-5 and include ease of ordering, product selection, product information, website navigation and looks, and on-time delivery.

**Table 9-2** U.S. TOP 25 WEB & DIGITAL MEDIA PROPERTIES (DECEMBER 2000)

| Rank | Digital Media/Web | Unique Visitors (000) |
|------|-------------------|------------------------|
| 1 | AOL Network | 60,562 |
| 2 | Yahoo Sites | 54,626 |
| 3 | Microsoft Sites | 53,809 |
| 4 | Excite Network | 30,819 |
| 5 | Lycos | 29,965 |
| 6 | About the Human Internet | 21,279 |
| 7 | Amazon | 21,053 |
| 8 | Walt Disney Internet Group | 20,469 |
| 9 | CNET Networks Digital | 19,953 |
| 10 | eBay | 19,536 |
| 11 | Alta Vista Network | 18,718 |
| 12 | Infospace Impressions | 18,042 |
| 13 | Time Warner Online | 17,027 |
| 14 | NBC Internet Site | 15,921 |
| 15 | eUniverse Network | 15,134 |
| 16 | Look Smart | 13,647 |
| 17 | Grab.com | 13,479 |
| 18 | Real.com Network | 12,753 |
| 19 | The Weather Channel | 12,461 |
| 20 | The Uproar Network | 11,889 |
| 21 | Ask Jeeves | 11,853 |
| 22 | Viacom Online | 11,825 |
| 23 | American Greetings | 9,355 |
| 24 | Network Commerce | 9,150 |
| 25 | AT&T Websites | 9,121 |

Source: Media Metrix (*www.mediametrix.com/press/releases/20010116.jsp*) January 16, 2001

Forrester (*www.forrester.com*) provides some of the most well-regarded reports on the e-commerce industry. It offers comprehensive coverage of a wide range of markets. Similar to our market-opportunity analysis chapter, Forrester's reports tend to cover the competitors, consumers, and technology evolution in a particular segment of the industry. More recently, it has teamed with Greenfield

**Exhibit 9-5**

# MARKET RESEARCH SOURCE—
# BIZRATE.COM

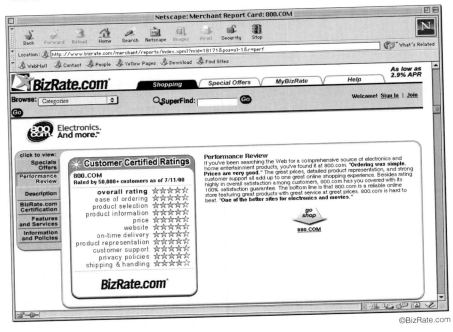

©BizRate.com

Online (*www.greenfieldonline.com*) to offer "power ratings" for various sites. These ratings are based on six factors: cost, customer service, delivery, features and content, transacting ability, and usability. Forrester ratings are based on expert reviews and customer surveys, as opposed to the pure user reviews of BizRate.com (see Exhibit 9-6).

Hoover's Online is a leading provider of financial and market information for a variety of offline and online companies. Hoover's provides company profiles, financials, and industry research for all major companies.

Exhibit 9-7 provides a quick overview of the products and services of Hoover's. Company profiles include company overviews, history, press releases, products and operations, competitors, financial information, and research reports. Company financial data include annual and quarterly financial data, SEC filings, stock market data, and comparison data by industry and market. Finally, industrywide information is provided to put the entire analysis in proper context.

## Mapping Internet Research onto the Performance Dashboard

In Exhibit 9-8, we provide a mapping of the Internet research sources onto the business strategy framework for this book. This analysis reveals that each data source specializes in a different type of data. That is, Media Metrix and AC Nielsen tend to emphasize market information and traffic while Hoover's Online specializes in financial information. It is rare that a single source covers all types of data. However, Forrester captures a large number of the data categories.

Exhibit
9-6

# ANALYST SOURCE—
# FORRESTER

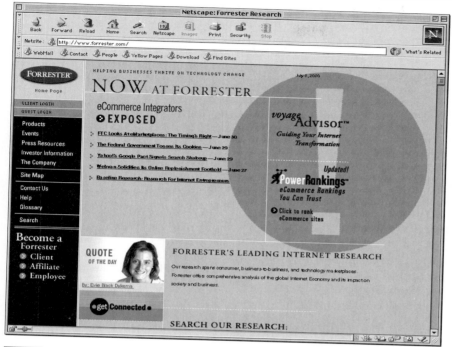

©Forrester Research, Inc.

Exhibit
9-7

# FINANCIAL INFORMATION SOURCE—
# HOOVER'S ONLINE

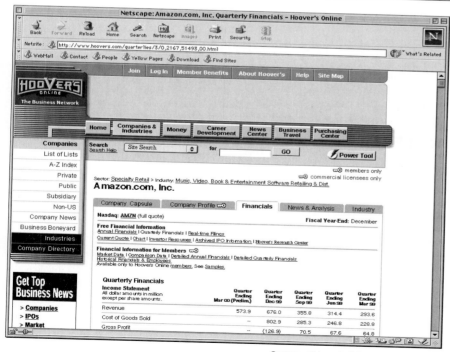

Courtesy of Hoover's Online (*www.hoovers.com*)

# Which Is Better? Online or Offline Data Sources?

With the emergence of online metrics, an interesting debate is unfolding on the advantages and disadvantages of online data collection as compared to the older, more traditional forms of market research.

Traditional market research has advantages of allowing for richer real-time interaction with respondents, deviations from planned scripts, and a rigorous sampling plan. For example, consider the real-time, one-to-one interview process that many market research firms use. Here, the interviewer can adjust the script as needed to delve deeper into issues and is able to detect the interviewee's body language and tone of voice input, all of which helps to provide a richer interpretation of the interviewee's responses. As a result, the interviewer can give a true "thick description" of the phenomena of interest.

At the same time, the traditional research approach has several drawbacks. The sampling process is typi-cally lengthy and resource intensive. Data collection is very costly and there are few economies of scale. Once the data is collected, there is an additional step of data entry and storage. This approach is quite good for assessing attitudes, preferences, viewpoints, and purchase intent, but it is not as strong for measuring actual behavior. In general, traditional market research is very human-resource intensive at each step in the process.

Interestingly, online research reverses many of the advantages and disadvantages of traditional market research. It is less time intensive, allows for automatic data capture, and, most importantly, allows for real-time data tracking. Its disadvantages relate to potential sampling biases, issues of privacy, and more difficult real-time adjustments to unexpected responses.

# Which Is Better? User-Based or Expert-Based Research Content?

A second interesting debate in this area concerns the sources of research information. Of the sources noted earlier in the chapter, some focus on user responses while others focus on analysts' viewpoints.

User-based data sources rely on the input of consumers. Consumer-oriented data sources are often very up-to-date, may have a large customer base for input, and tend to be viewed as trustworthy by other users. In contrast, when experts rate a site, they tend to be more episodic in their reviews, can offer the input of only one expert, and provide information often viewed as objective. On the other hand, expert sites typically are reviewed by people whose responsibility is to know how to evaluate the features and functionality of a site, who have deep knowledge of competitor sites, and whose annual performance reviews are based on the soundness of their analysis. Hence, they have an enormous incentive to provide the best information to their customer base.

**Exhibit 9-8**

MAPPING INTERNET RESEARCH ONTO
THE PERFORMANCE DASHBOARD

|  |  | Market Research | | | | Analyst | | | Financial Information |
|---|---|---|---|---|---|---|---|---|---|
|  |  | Media Metrix | AC Nielsen | BizRate | Forrester | Gomez | Jupiter | Creative Good | Hoover's |
| **Market** | Market Info | ● | ● |  | ● |  | ● |  | ● |
|  | Traffic | ● | ● |  |  |  |  |  |  |
| **Implementation** | Fulfillment |  |  | ● | ● |  |  |  |  |
|  | Implementation |  |  |  | ● |  | ● |  |  |
|  | Privacy |  |  | ● |  |  |  |  |  |
| **Customer** | Usability |  |  | ● | ● | ● | ● | ● |  |
|  | Content |  |  | ● | ● | ● | ● |  |  |
|  | Customer Satisfaction |  |  | ● | ● | ● |  |  |  |
|  | Customer Service |  |  | ● | ● |  |  |  |  |
| **Financial** | Financial Performance |  |  |  | ● |  |  |  | ● |

---

## DRILL-DOWN

# Online and Offline Integration Metrics

The metrics described so far refer primarily to a firm's online strategy and operations. We can also use the Performance Dashboard, with its five areas of market opportunity, business model, branding and implementation, customer interface and outcome, and financial, to determine appropriate measures of performance for offline company operations. Obviously, metrics must be adjusted to reflect a change of focus from the digital to the physical world. An extensive body of literature exists on the subject; in particular, Kaplan and Norton's Balanced Scorecard provides a comprehensive approach for offline companies. We find no need

to go into further detail concerning that subject. Instead, we focus on metrics that measure the successful integration of online and offline presence and operations.

A well-integrated online and offline operation exhibits two major attributes: a seamless customer experience (front end) and a seamless set of internal business processes and operations (back end). We examine each of these in greater detail.

**Seamless Customer Experience.** A seamless customer experience refers to the customer's ability to have a consistent experience while moving between online and offline channels. The customer purchase

*(continued on page 344)*

*(continued from page 343)*

process framework (introduced in Chapter 4) is a useful tool for identifying metrics for a seamless customer purchase experience.

Exhibit 9-9 outlines steps of the customer purchase process and lists associated metrics to measure the consistency between the online and offline channels at each step. As discussed in Chapter 4, the customer purchase process has three stages: the prepurchase stage (includes brand awareness, knowledge, and evaluation of alternatives), the purchase stage, and the postpurchase stage (includes satisfaction, loyalty, and disposal).

In the step to evaluate alternatives, a consistent availability and selection of products through the online and offline channels would provide the customer access to the same pool of offerings regardless of channel. Wal-Mart, the world's leading retailer, offers nearly the same selection of products and services through its offline stores and its

website, Walmart.com. However, differences exist. For example, travel planning services are available to customers through the online store but not at offline stores.

In the purchase step, consistent security and privacy standards in offline and online stores allow users to feel equally comfortable in providing sensitive information when purchasing online and offline. ToysRUs, one of the largest toy retailers, offers a consistent level of security through its stores and its toysrus.com site. To prevent unauthorized viewing, toysrus.com uses "secure socket layers" technology to encrypt all order-related information in transit to the company server. If a user's browser does not support this encryption technology or if the user does not want to send his or her credit-card information over the Web, the site urges customers to call its guest relations department to complete the order securely over a phone line.

*(continued on page 345)*

## Exhibit 9-9 METRICS FOR SEAMLESS ONLINE/OFFLINE CUSTOMER PURCHASE PROCESS

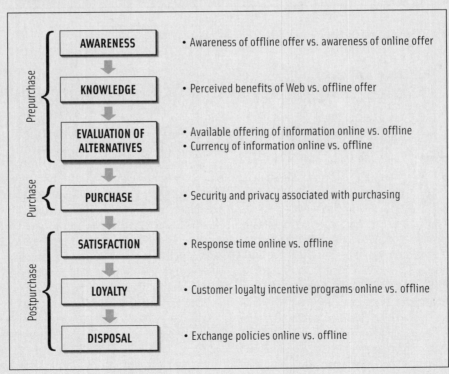

**Prepurchase**
- **AWARENESS** — • Awareness of offline offer vs. awareness of online offer
- **KNOWLEDGE** — • Perceived benefits of Web vs. offline offer
- **EVALUATION OF ALTERNATIVES** — • Available offering of information online vs. offline
  • Currency of information online vs. offline

**Purchase**
- **PURCHASE** — • Security and privacy associated with purchasing

**Postpurchase**
- **SATISFACTION** — • Response time online vs. offline
- **LOYALTY** — • Customer loyalty incentive programs online vs. offline
- **DISPOSAL** — • Exchange policies online vs. offline

(continued from page 344)

In the satisfaction step, consistent response time to a customer service request through online and offline channels allows customers to get assistance online or offline promptly and equally. 1-800-Flowers provides live customer service seamlessly. Customers can receive live assistance through a private online customer service eQ&A chat with a website representative, a toll-free telephone call, or a visit to one of over 1,500 stores in the 1-800-Flowers retail network.

**Seamless Internal Business Processes and Operations.** Seamless internal business processes and operations refer to a company's ability to perform all internal processes and operations, regardless of whether a customer is interacting with the company through its online or offline channel.

Table 9-3 outlines metrics that can be used to assess seamless internal business processes and operations. Most metrics refer to capabilities that are clearly "available" or "not available" and, therefore, the metric value will be either a "yes" or a "no." We can group these metrics into two categories: information sharing and fulfillment systems.

Information-sharing metrics measure the site's ability to collect and analyze information on customers or products seamlessly between online and offline channels. For example, a company's ability to have customers access their accounts online and offline is an essential part of a company's integrated back-office operations. Merrill Lynch customers can open and access their accounts through the Merrill Lynch website. Alternatively, they can access their account by calling a customer service representative or by visiting one of the Merrill Lynch branches.

Fulfillment-systems metrics refer to a company's ability to deliver seamlessly on a customer order, regardless of whether that order was placed online or offline. For example, a company's ability to provide seamless order tracking allows customers to check their order status online or offline, regardless of which channel they used to place their order. Federal Express customers can get information about the delivery status of a package by logging on to the FedEx.com site and entering the package delivery confirmation code. Alternatively, they can call a Federal Express customer service representative and get the same information over the phone.

## Table 9-3 METRICS FOR SEAMLESS INTERNAL BUSINESS PROCESSES AND OPERATIONS

| **Information Sharing** | • Ability to open accounts online and offline<br>• Ability to access accounts online and offline<br>• Integrated customer databases |
|---|---|
| **Fulfillment Systems** | • Seamless order processing<br>• Seamless order tracking<br>• Integrated inventory keeping |

# MARKETWATCH.COM METRICS

Let us now apply the five-step process used in implementing the Performance Dashboard to MarketWatch.com. As we have discussed, strategy can change very quickly as an Internet company moves through its different life stages. Hence, it is important that we apply the process to a particular stage in the MarketWatch.com life cycle. In late 2000, the company found itself in a challenging situation. The Nasdaq market had witnessed a significant downturn, and it was unclear whether there would be a rebound or whether the economy would slowly move into a recession. MarketWatch.com's competitors and their alliances had been growing at a steady pace. MarketWatch.com needed to defend itself against competitors and maintain and extend its lead in the online financial news market. It also needed to become profitable within a reasonable time frame, to address the market expectations.

In order to successfully apply the methodology, we use outcomes of the MarketWatch.com analysis that we performed in previous chapters. The Performance Dashboard for MarketWatch.com reflects aspects of the company performance at each step in the strategy process.

## Step One: Articulate the MarketWatch.com Strategy

The first step is to clearly articulate the MarketWatch.com business strategy. As was discussed in Chapter 5, a company's business strategy requires four choices: (1) a value proposition (or cluster) for targeted customers, (2) an offer (egg diagram), (3) a unique defendable resource system and (4) a financial model. At this first step, we will use the first three of the four choices (the financial model choice will be reflected in steps two and three).

**Value Proposition.** The value proposition for MarketWatch.com was "to be a leading Web-based provider of comprehensive, real-time business news, financial programming, and analytic tools."[6]

**MarketWatch.com Offer.** The egg diagram contains a wide variety of information and services aimed at delivering the three key benefits to users: real-time information, comprehensive and in-depth analysis and tools, and multimedia access.

**Resource System.** The MarketWatch.com resource system consists of three layers. The first layer is the core benefits delivered to users, as they are described in the company's offer. The second layer is the capabilities that must be in place for the company to be able to deliver the core benefits to its customers. These include capabilities that the company has developed in-house (such as an experienced editorial staff, leading technology, a solid and versatile infrastructure, and an international presence), as well as capabilities that it has acquired through partnerships (such as the relationship with CBS News and partnerships with content providers and distribution partnerships). The third layer is the activities and resources that need to be retained to deliver these capabilities. For example, the leading technology capability was originally achieved through the association with DBC, and later was developed in-house, leveraging the technology expertise of BigCharts.com. Other actions for MarketWatch.com include hiring and training an experienced group of journalists and editors, leveraging the CBS News relationship by accessing the CBS studios, licensing the CBS News brand name and distributing content through CBS networks, and forming distribution partnerships with companies such as AOL, Yahoo and Quicken. (For a more detailed description of the MarketWatch.com resource system, please see Figure 5-2 in Chapter 5).

# Steps Two and Three: Translate Strategy into Outcomes and Metrics

The next two steps are easier to perform concurrently because they are closely related. For each of the five categories of the Performance Dashboard, we need to translate the strategy articulated in step one into a set of desired outcomes and associated metrics. An effective way to generate these pairings is by asking key questions for each of the five categories.

## Market Opportunity.
In the market opportunity category, we establish metrics for the attractiveness of the market opportunity for MarketWatch.com and the degree of market competitive intensity.

### Is the Opportunity Significant?
*Desired Outcome #1: Identify a significant market opportunity in the financial services industry.* MarketWatch.com chose to play in the financial media industry. With online financial advertising accounting for 20 percent of the $2 billion online advertising market in 1998,[7] and with projections for total online advertising to reach more than $8 billion by 2002, this looked like a very promising opportunity. This opportunity was also reflected by the rapid growth in online brokerage accounts, from 6 million in 1998 to a projected 15 million by 2002.[8]

*Metrics to Track:*
- Online advertising market size
- Percentage of online advertising that is finance content-related
- Online financial advertisements CPMs (cost per thousand impressions)
- Number and percentage growth of online brokerage accounts

### How Intense Is the Competition?
*Desired Outcome #2: Serve segments where competition is not very intense.* MarketWatch.com competed in a crowded market, including Web portals (such as Yahoo and AOL), traditional media companies (such as CNN and NBC), online brokers (such as Fidelity and Schwab), and niche sites (such as Motley Fool and TheStreet.com).

*Metrics to Track:*
- MarketWatch.com versus competition
- Unique visitors
- Page views
- Time spent on site
- Rate of competitor entry and exit in the market
- Number of mergers/acquisitions within the market
- Competitor advertising expenditures

Exhibit
9-10   MARKETWATCH.COM STRATEGY

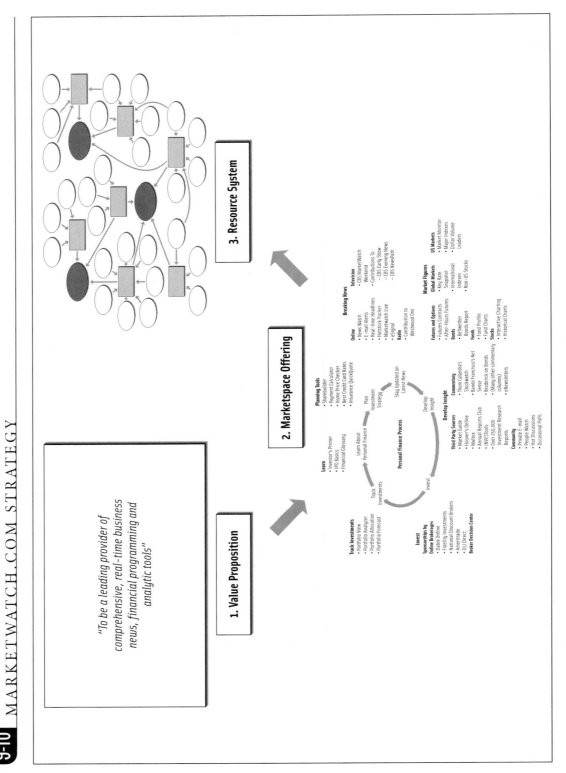

1. Value Proposition

"To be a leading provider of comprehensive, real-time business news, financial programming and analytic tools"

2. Marketspace Offering

3. Resource System

**Personal Finance Process**

Learn → Learn About Personal Finance → Plan Investment Strategy → Stay Updated on Latest News → Develop Insight → Invest → Track Investments

**Learn**
• Investor's Primer
• IPO Basics
• Financial Glossary

**Planning Tools**
• Sharebuilder
• Payment Calculator
• Home Price Checker
• Best Credit Card Rates
• Insurance QuickQuote

**Develop Insight**

**Third Party Sources**
• Market Guide
• Hoover's Online
• Multex
• Annual Reports Club
• INVESTools
• Over 250,000 Investment Research Reports

**Community**
• Private E-mail
• People Watch
• Hot Discussions
• Occasional Polls

**Commentary**
• Thom Calandra's StockWatch
• Bambi Francisco's Net Sense
• Bedderick on Bonds
• (Many other commentary columns)
• eNewsletters

**Track Investments**
• Portfolio View
• Portfolio Analyzer
• Portfolio Allocation
• Portfolio Forecast

**Invest**

**Sponsorships by Online Brokerages**
• Datek Online
• Fidelity Investments
• National Discount Brokers
• Ameritrade
• DLJ Direct
• **Broker Decision Center**

**Breaking News**

**Online**
• News Watch
• E-mail Alerts
• Real-time Headlines
• Hotstock Tracker
• Marketwatch Live
• eSignal

**Radio**
• Contribution to Westwood One

**Television**
• CBS MarketWatch Weekend
• Contributions To:
  − CBS Early Show
  − CBS Evening News
  − CBS NewsPath

**Futures and Options**
• Futures Contracts
• After-Hours Futures

**Bonds**
• Bellwether
• Bonds Report

**Funds**
• Fund Profile
• Fund Charts

**Stocks**
• Interactive Charting
• Historical Charts

**Market Figures**

**Global Markets**
• Key Rate Snapshot
• International Indexes
• Non-US Stocks

**US Markets**
• Market Monitor
• Major Indexes
• Dollar Volume Leaders

**Business Model.** In the business models category, we establish metrics for the uniqueness of the MarketWatch.com value proposition, the strength of the company's capabilities relative to competition, and the sustainability of the value proposition over time.

### How Unique Is the MarketWatch.com Value Proposition Relative to Competition?

*Desired Outcome #3: MarketWatch.com value proposition is unique relative to competition.* Despite the large number of providers of financial information, the MarketWatch.com offering had the unique advantage of being the No. 1 online financial news source, leveraging its staff of experienced journalists. However, competitors were slowly trying to develop similar capabilities through partnerships, such as The Street.com partnership with *The New York Times* and FoxNews.

*Metric to Track:*
- Customer perceptions of MarketWatch.com key benefits versus competition

### Are the MarketWatch.com Capabilities and Partnerships Significantly Better than the Competition's?

*Desired Outcome #4: Market perceives MarketWatch.com capabilities and partnerships are superior to competition's.* Analyst reports cited the experienced editorial staff of MarketWatch.com and the credibility associated with its relationship to CBS News as two key reasons why MarketWatch.com was better positioned to deliver on its value proposition than the competition.

*Metrics to Track:*
- MarketWatch.com versus competition
- Number of journalists on staff
- Average journalist's experience
- Number of markets where the company has operations
- Cumulative reach of distribution partnerships
- Percentage of outsourced content
- Production capacity

### How Sustainable Is the MarketWatch.com Value Proposition Relative to the Competition's?

*Desired Outcome #5: Key resources are well maintained.* Factors such as an experienced staff of journalists are highly sustainable over time. However, factors such as an exclusive relationship to CBS News or to distribution portals are more subject to change and introduce uncertainty.

*Metrics to Track:*
- Exclusivity and length of MarketWatch.com partnership agreements versus competition
- Number of MarketWatch.com patents on tools and services

**Implementation and Branding.** In the implementation and branding category, we establish the metrics measuring the effectiveness of MarketWatch.com establishing its brand and implementing its strategy.

### How Is the MarketWatch.com Brand Perceived in the Market?

*Desired Outcome #6: Users are aware of the MarketWatch.com brand and make positive associations with it.* The association to CBS News and the strong focus on marketing led to MarketWatch.com having strong brand recognition among users.

*Metrics to Track:*
- Aided user awareness of MarketWatch.com brand name
- User associations with MarketWatch.com brand versus competition
- Percentage of MarketWatch.com users that fall into the company's target segments

### Does MarketWatch.com Have an Infrastructure That Enables It to Reliably Distribute Financial Content Across Multiple Platforms?

*Desired Outcome #7: The MarketWatch.com infrastructure enables reliable content distribution across multiple platforms.* The innovative MarketWatch.com IT infrastructure allowed it to seamlessly communicate financial information both internally and externally.

*Metrics to Track:*
- System percentage uptime
- Average download time
- Maximum percentage of servers down at any point in time
- Maximum response time
- Maximum information volume that system could handle
- Number of articles produced each day
- Percentage of site that gets updated each day

**User Interface and Outcomes.** In this category, we determine the metrics for the users' perception of the usability and effectiveness of the MarketWatch.com site as well as their usage behavior, satisfaction, and loyalty.

### How Effective and Efficient Is the MarketWatch.com New User Acquisition?

*Desired Outcome #8: MarketWatch.com has a lower user acquisition cost versus the competition.* MarketWatch.com has a large number of unique visitors, however to achieve this it also has a large marketing budget.

*Metrics to Track:*
- User acquisition cost
- Number of unique visitors versus competition*
- Percentage of users coming to MarketWatch.com from other sites
- Percentage of revenues spent on marketing versus competition
- Percentage of visitors who register on the site
- Percentage of visitors who purchase services on the site
- Percentage of visitors who return to the site
- Frequency of user visits

*Indicates a metric that has been mentioned before

### What Is the Perception of the Online User Experience?

*Desired Outcome #9: The MarketWatch.com site is usable and attractive to users.* One way to measure the effectiveness of the MarketWatch.com site is by evaluating its performance along the 7Cs (see Chapter 6). Another way is to deduce it through the online behavior of the site users.

*Metrics to Track:*
- Site evaluation by users on the 7Cs versus competition
- Average minutes spent on site per user[*]
- Popularity of individual articles
- Average time to complete a task
- Number of negative feedback items received over a certain time frame

### How Satisfied and Loyal Is the User Base Vs. Competition?

*Desired Outcome #10: MarketWatch.com has the highest satisfaction and loyalty in the industry.* Satisfied and loyal users are a significant source of long-term profitability. MarketWatch.com regularly tracked user loyalty using innovative measuring techniques by companies such as Digital Ideas.

*Metrics to Track:*
- User loyalty (measured by the Dial Score by Digital Ideas)
- Overall user satisfaction with the site versus competition, as well as on a number of key attributes, including information relevance and timeliness, and tool effectiveness
- User churn rate

**Financial.** In this category, we establish metrics for the financial performance of the company in terms of revenue, profit, and cost.

### When Will MarketWatch.com Become Profitable?

*Desired Outcome #11: MarketWatch.com will become profitable soon.* Following the technology market slump during the spring of 2000, investors had become increasingly cautious, looking for company profitability as quickly as possible. Consequently, even though MarketWatch.com was on a clear path to profitability, its stock had witnessed a significant drop, reflecting investor requirements for profitability. However, the company's strong fundamentals and its plan to be profitable in the following one to two years provided optimistic indications for the company's future financial performance.

*Metrics to Track:*
- Revenue
- Revenue breakdown by advertising, licensing, subscription, other
- Total revenue per page view
- Profit
- Total loss and percentage decrease of loss over time
- First expected profitable quarter
- Cost
- Total cost
- Customer acquisition cost[*]
- Percentage of revenues spent on marketing and sales[*]
- Balance sheet
- Stock price

- Available funds in liquid assets
- Cash burn rate
- Average days receivables

Exhibit 9-11 provides a summary of the desired outcomes. For each desired outcome, we have identified a number of metrics in the analysis above. While it may seem large at first glance, management must be able to track all the relevant metrics in order to be able to read early signs of problems with the company strategy or its implementation. We turn to the issue of leading and lagging indicators in the next section.

## Step Four: Link Metrics to Leading and Lagging Indicators

Now that we have a list of useful metrics to track MarketWatch.com performance, the question becomes, "How do we link them to each other?" There can be three possible relationships between two metrics (let us call them A and B). A could

### Exhibit 9-11   MARKETWATCH.COM DESIRED OUTCOME SUMMARY

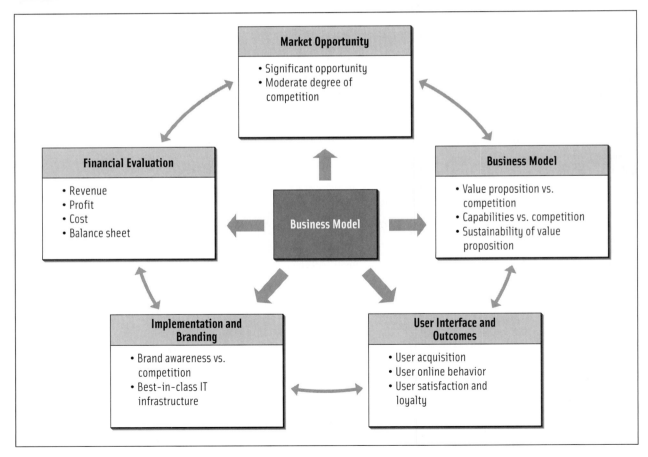

affect B (A would then be called a leading indicator with respect to B), A could be affected by B (A would then be called a lagging indicator with respect to B), or A and B could not affect each other. In order for management to be able to use these metrics effectively, it needs to understand which metrics (or groups of metrics) are leading or lagging indicators for which other metrics.

Knowledge of this interrelation will help management understand which groups of leading indicators it needs to focus on in order to achieve its target performance on lagging indicators. For example, if a company has a revenue target, then knowledge of the fact that revenue targets are affected by new customer acquisition, website usability, and high levels of customer service will signal to management that these are the metrics it should focus on in order to achieve its revenue target. The interrelation between leading and lagging indicators for MarketWatch.com is demonstrated in Exhibit 9-12 (p. 354). Let us trace just one flow of leading and lagging indicators in this exhibit.

Metrics tracking competitive intensity and the degree to which competitors are underserving the market help determine a value proposition that is unique. A unique value proposition that is marketed successfully will lead to the creation of a strong brand and high brand awareness among users. This will stimulate usage, which will lead to an increase in ad revenue because there will be more users viewing more pages. Such an increase in ad revenue, associated with marginal incremental cost, will lead to an increase in profitability.

# Step Five: Calculate Current and Target Performance

Knowledge of the appropriate use of each metric is of little help if management does not know the current and target value of these metrics. A successful strategy needs to be implemented by setting targets and taking actions to reach those targets.

MarketWatch.com tracks its performance on key metrics and compares it to the performance of its competitors. In many cases, the target performance is to become the best performer in a metric. For example, since advertising revenue is so important to MarketWatch.com, being the best performer in its category in the number of unique visitors to the site is very important, hence unique visitors to MarketWatch.com versus competitor sites is closely tracked. Monthly fluctuations in performance are very important, since they can indicate trends and help to promptly identify areas where changes need to be made.

Table 9-4 illustrates the MarketWatch.com performance versus its competitors for two consecutive months on some key metrics. MarketWatch.com was the top performer in terms of unique visitors, but it was considerably behind its competitors when it came to time spent on the site or unique pages viewed per visit. One possible explanation for this outcome was that other sites (such as the best performers CNBC.com and MoneyCentral.com) also had content that was nonfinancial. For example, MoneyCentral.com had a shopping and entertainment section and CNBC.com had a career and living section. If MarketWatch.com wanted to maximize its revenue from advertisers, it needed to increase the number of pages its users viewed on its site to levels similar to those of the top performers in this category. It could achieve this by increasing its brand awareness, which could be achieved through a stronger brand and a clearer and more appealing value to users. This could help management by pointing to the levers it needed to pull to achieve the desired results.

**Exhibit 9-12** CUSTOMER ACQUISITION STAGE
LEADING/LAGGING INDICATORS FOR MARKETWATCH.COM

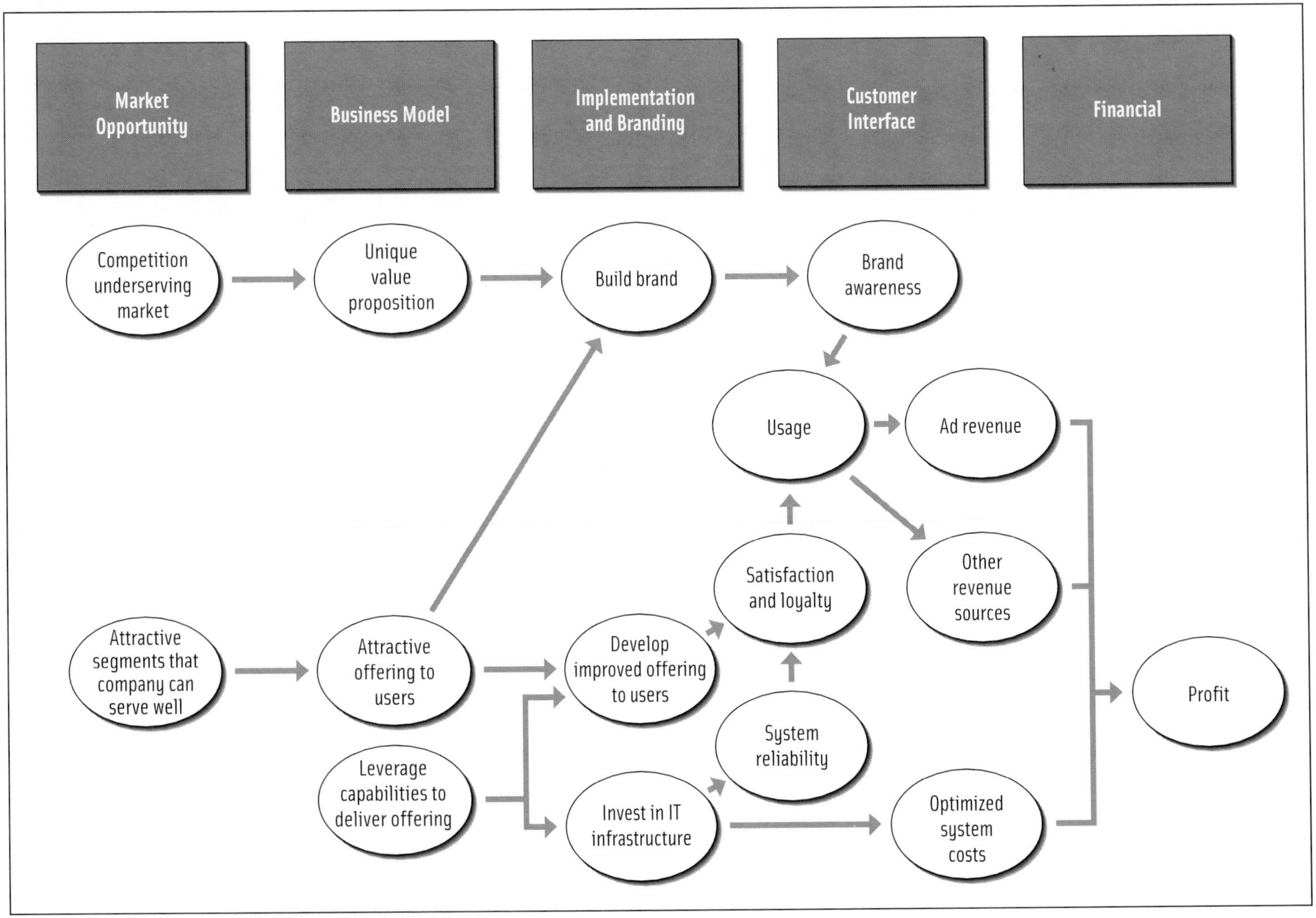

Market Opportunity | Business Model | Implementation and Branding | Customer Interface | Financial

Competition underserving market → Unique value proposition → Build brand → Brand awareness → Usage

Usage → Ad revenue → Profit

Usage → Other revenue sources

Satisfaction and loyalty → Usage

System reliability → Satisfaction and loyalty

Optimized system costs → Profit

Attractive segments that company can serve well → Attractive offering to users → Build brand

Attractive offering to users → Develop improved offering to users → Satisfaction and loyalty

Leverage capabilities to deliver offering → Develop improved offering to users

Leverage capabilities to deliver offering → Invest in IT infrastructure → System reliability

Invest in IT infrastructure → Optimized system costs

| Metric | September 2000 | | | October 2000 | | |
|---|---|---|---|---|---|---|
| | MarketWatch Value | Market Position | Best Performer | MarketWatch Value | Market Position | Best Performer |
| Unique Visitors (000s) | 3,698 | 1 | N/A | 3,724 | 1 | N/A |
| Reach | 4.8% | 1 | N/A | 4.7% | 1 | N/A |
| Average Minutes Spent per Usage | 8.8 | 9 | 35.6 (CNBC.com) | 12.6 | 9 | 28.5 (CNBC.com) |
| Average Unique Pages per Visitor | 7.1 | 10 | 28.9 (CNBC.com) | 10.4 | 7 | 23.0 (Money Central.com) |

Source: MarketWatch.com, Media Metrix

# SUMMARY

### 1. Why should senior managers be concerned about metrics?

Managers should be concerned about metrics because metrics drive organizational behavior in a number of ways, which include defining the business model, communicating the strategy, tracking performance, increasing accountability, and aligning objectives.

### 2. How can we assess the health of online firms?

The Balanced Scorecard assesses the health of a business in four categories of metrics: financial, customer, internal business process, and learning and growth. While this framework may be appropriate for some firms, it is also limited in three respects: It does not offer a definition of strategy, capabilities of the firm are not clearly articulated (instead, the focus is on internal business processes not linked to customer benefits), and partnerships are not explicitly included.

### 3. What are the steps to implement the Performance Dashboard?

There are five steps to implement the Performance Dashboard. They include (1) articulate the strategy, (2) translate strategy into actions, (3) devise metrics, (4) link metrics to leading and lagging indicators, and (5) calculate current and target performance levels.

## 4. What sources of metrics information can firms use to chart their progress?

Market-research data sources tend to focus on customer perceptions of sites and site performance. Analyst reports often combine primary data collection along with a strong analyst point of view on the issue at hand. Financial sources focus heavily on the investment community and tend to include in-depth financial information. Each approach has its strengths and limitations, but all are complementary. Firms often need to acquire data from all three areas in order to obtain a complete picture of their markets.

## KEY TERMS

metrics

Balanced Scorecard

financial metrics

customer metrics

internal business process metrics

learning and growth metrics

Performance Dashboard

market-opportunity metrics

business-model metrics

customer-interface metrics

customer-outcome metrics

branding and implementation metrics

life cycle of a company

startup

acquisition of customers

monetization

maturity

market research

analyst reports

financial information

## Endnotes

[1] Readers are encouraged to review the seminal work of Robert Kaplan and David Norton on the Balanced Scorecard. The starting point should be Kaplan, Robert, and David Norton. 1996. *The balanced scorecard*. Boston: Harvard Business School Press.

[2] See: Kaplan & Norton. 1996. Chap. 2 in *The balanced scorecard*.

[3] See: Kaplan & Norton. 1996. *The balanced scorecard*, 10–19.

[4] Day, George. 1994. The capabilities of market-driven organizations. *Journal of Marketing* 58, no. 4 (October): 37–52.

[5] Excerpt from the following: Gurley, J. William. 2000. The most powerful Internet metric of all, *CNETNEWS.COM*, 21 February. URL: *http://www.news.com/Perspectives/Column/0,176,403,00.html?tag5st.ne.*

[6] Securities and Exchange Commission, *Form 10-K for MarketWatch.com, Inc. for the fiscal year ended December 31, 1999.*

[7] Source: Jupiter Communications

[8] Source: Jupiter Communications

# 10

# B2B Grows Up

## OVERVIEW

The explosive growth of business-to-consumer (B2C) websites in the late 1990s demonstrated that businesses could utilize the Internet to sell products and services to individual consumers. B2C Web businesses also proved that smaller businesses could effectively compete with larger ones, as the cost to create a Web presence and participate in e-commerce could be relatively low. Business leaders realized that if they could enable their employees to utilize the Internet in performing business tasks in the same manner as B2C websites did for consumers buying online, businesses could buy and sell the goods and services needed to operate online. Furthermore, commerce along the entire demand chain could be potentially Internet enabled—beyond just the purchase of finished goods by end consumers. Indeed, both the sell-side and buy-side of a business could be moved online. This epiphany triggered the subsequent explosion of business-to-business (B2B) e-commerce.

## QUESTIONS

*Please consider the following questions as you read this chapter:*

1. What are the four stages to the evolution of B2B capabilities?

2. What are three categories of B2B?

3. Describe the four major steps of the B2B sell-side evolution.

---

This chapter was written by Breakaway Solutions.

357

4. Describe the major challenges to implementing systems for indirect e-procurement.

5. Describe the major challenges to implementing systems for Net marketplaces or Net exchanges.

## INTRODUCTION

To facilitate B2B e-commerce, businesses first had to make the required investment in IT infrastructure and provide employees with the tools and connectivity to access the Internet. Early business adopters of the Internet began utilizing e-mail as an important mechanism for communicating not only internally with employees, but externally with customers, suppliers, and partners. Although e-mail did not allow a customer to create an order online, it did facilitate relationships and interaction between buyers and sellers that directly resulted in commerce activities. However, e-mail was only the beginning of the use of the Internet to enable commerce. The use of the World Wide Web and the Web browser would prove the more significant breakthrough in B2B e-commerce.

B2B's coming-of-age coincided with a period when most large businesses had invested tremendous time, effort, and money in implementing client/server-based **enterprise resource planning (ERP)** applications. Although ERP applications provided significant improvements by integrating all internal applications and processes, these applications were not built to provide Web-based access or functions to work with external trading partners. Like traditional business applications, they were built for internal use only. In fact, businesses with existing mainframe and client/server business applications in place realized that significant time, effort, and investment would be required to either replace these legacy systems with Web-based applications or to develop Web front ends for existing applications—and to integrate the Web-based sales channel with the other traditional channels.

The advent of B2B saw new businesses turning to the Internet as their primary or sole sales channel. It also ushered in new Web-based business applications that could be used to support all business operations. These new businesses had a distinct advantage over larger, established businesses with traditional sales channels and legacy applications, and they developed their processes and associated applications with the Internet in mind. Web-based applications integrated with the traditional client/server and mainframe back-office capabilities could be implemented from the start. As a result, B2B has increased competition between companies of all sizes and given tremendous advantage to Internet-based newcomers.

## WHAT ARE THE FOUR STAGES TO THE EVOLUTION OF B2B CAPABILITIES?

A business will typically go through a basic evolution of Web-based business application capability, and, if successful, will emerge with the greatest capability: collaboration. The evolution of B2B capability involves four stages: **broadcast, interact, transact,** and **collaborate.** However, a business does not necessarily need to start the broadcast stage before moving to later stages. Aggressive businesses implement some aspects of all four stages simultaneously from the beginning of their e-commerce efforts.

## Broadcast

The first application of the Internet within a business is to create a webpage for the organization that provides primarily static information to the customer, such as company financial information, company contact information, and information about the products and services offered. The more sophisticated early adopters created product catalogs and provided detailed product information such as technical-support documentation or material safety data sheets online. The first capability in the B2B sell-side evolution is to broadcast this relatively static information in one direction—from the organization to the customer.

## Interact

The next step in the evolution is for information to flow both ways, from the organization to the customer and back. Organizations realize that the Internet has fostered the creation of Web-based applications and mechanisms that facilitate interaction. One simple and primary mechanism is e-mail. Organizations use the Internet to interact with their customers for customer support. E-mails can be submitted to different business units or groups within the organization. Web-based applications have been created to administer customer surveys and gather customer feedback, which can be analyzed and measured for management and utilized for process improvement.

One arena in which commercial Web-based applications have been particularly successful is customer relationship management (CRM). New CRM vendors and applications that provided Web-based customer support have appeared. These applications provide **content management** capability to create and administer static help content for a website; they also provide Web-based case management, which enables the user to submit questions and issues via e-mail or Web-based forms and also track and manage the status of multiple cases. Administration capability allows the customer-support organization to manage the Web-based support channel and the cases submitted. Queues can be established to ensure that certain cases are managed by certain groups in certain geographies. Workflow capability can allow the customer-support organization to route cases and approve resolutions before they are sent back to the customer. Today, Web-based CRM applications have integrated the Web-support channel with the traditional support channels of phone and fax to create a fully integrated support mechanism. In addition to customer-support capability, Web-based CRM applications can support the sales and marketing efforts of an organization using the Internet.

To provide information to customers using a Web interface, organizations have turned to back-office ERP systems. Before customers could access information via the Web, customer-support organizations spent a significant amount of time on the phone with customers, confirming order, shipping, and fulfillment status. Early B2B adopters experimented with integrating the customer storefront to the back-office ERP applications to provide order status online, which meant significant process efficiencies for customer service representatives who may have spent 25 percent of their time giving out this information on the phone.

## Transact

The next step in the sell-side evolution is to take, manage, and support commerce transactions with customers using the Internet. Like the basic B2C capability, organizations implement Web-based catalogs of the products or services available and implement order-processing capability to allow the customers to add products and services to a shopping cart and place an order. In the transact phase, organizations begin to understand the complexities of Web-enabling capabilities that were traditionally back-office functions.

## Collaborate

The core value of Web-based applications is to provide inter-enterprise functionality that is accessed and utilized by an organization and its trading partners. Examples of collaboration on the sell-side include collaborating with customers to generate sales forecasts and gathering and utilizing point-of-sale information. More details on and examples of B2B collaboration will be described in the next chapter.

## WHAT ARE THE THREE CATEGORIES OF B2B?

In their brief history, as B2Bs have been conceived, built, modified, and sometimes dissolved, these businesses have clustered around three broad categories of B2B activities: sell-side solutions, **indirect e-procurement,** and Net marketplace and Net exchange activities. While we will describe all three categories in more detail later in this chapter, we will concentrate on the category of Net marketplaces and Net exchanges, the most complex category of the three.

### B2B Sell-Side Solution

Because B2C gained momentum before B2B, early adopters of B2B focused on the use of the Internet to sell products to end consumers, and eventually other businesses. Businesses began to develop sell-side capability or new Web-based applications to provide buyers with product and service information, as well as the ability to allow buyers to place orders for products or services (see Exhibit 10-1).

B2C best practices, such as searchable online catalogs and shopping-cart functions, were developed and implemented as B2B sell-side transactional capabilities.

**Exhibit 10-1**

THE B2B SELL-SIDE SOLUTIONS ACTIVITIES

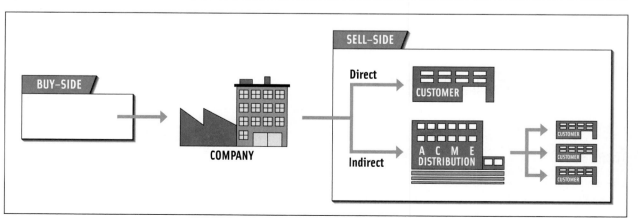

Also, a sell-side capability typically included online access to fulfillment data informing the customer of expected ship date, delivery date, and shipping status, provided either by the seller or a third-party logistics provider.

## Indirect E-Procurement

Once Web-based sell-side applications were implemented and businesses began using the Internet to sell merchandise to customers, businesses quickly realized they could Web-enable their buy-side by implementing Web-based e-procurement capabilities (see Exhibit 10-2).

Initially, the focus on e-procurement was for the purchase of nonstrategic products and services—often referred to as indirect materials, or maintenance, repair, and operations (MRO) materials, for manufacturing companies. E-procurement capabilities to facilitate MRO procurement are the mirror-image of sell-side capabilities, including **catalog management,** which allows the buying organization to store and search supplier catalogs and transaction processing—and in turn, allows the buyer to create a purchase order to be sent to the supplier for products or services. The same fulfillment-status capability required on the sell-side to enable the supplier to provide order and shipping status to the buyer is required on the buy-side for e-procurement.

## Net Marketplaces and Net Exchanges

With buy-side and sell-side capabilities implemented, businesses were now able to interact with their trading partners directly using the Internet and to facilitate commerce transactions. Meanwhile, a new wave of Internet-based businesses was emerging. **Net marketplaces** and **Net exchanges** were created to provide Web-based capabilities to facilitate the interaction and exchange of commerce transactions among buyers, sellers, and other trading partners (see Exhibit 10-3).

Net marketplaces integrated with and enhanced the buy-side and sell-side capabilities implemented by buyer and seller businesses. Net marketplaces were created in a wide range of industries, with a wide range of capabilities, and using a wide

**Exhibit 10-2**

INDIRECT E-PROCUREMENT ACTIVITIES

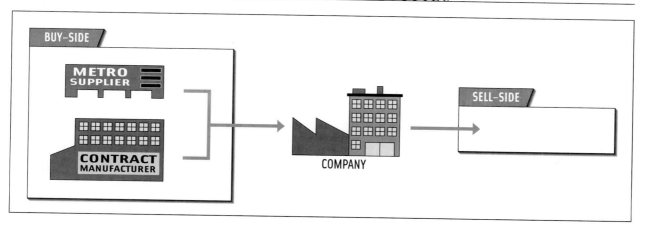

### Exhibit 10-3

NET MARKETPLACE AND NET EXCHANGE ACTIVITIES

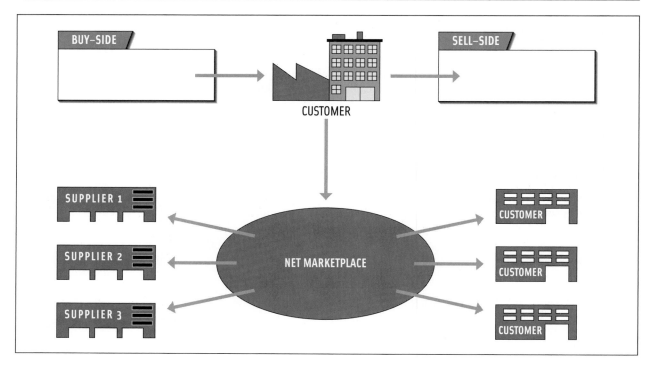

range of business models. The Net marketplaces provided an alternate Internet sales channel for buyers and sellers.

## B2B SELL-SIDE SOLUTIONS

The concept of B2B was initiated when businesses realized the potential value of applying the basic B2C concepts of commerce to business. The early B2C capabilities—an online storefront with product information, a searchable product catalog, a shopping cart to pool desired items, and an order placement process—are applicable to any business selling products or services. Initially, this concept was applied by the businesses and industries that sell products or services that can be cataloged and purchased without physical interaction with a customer service representative.

Because the concept of utilizing the Internet for business was new, the adoption and implementation of sell-side B2B capability was evolutionary for early adopters. Today, because of the adoption and proven value of the Internet, any organization can begin at any of the four stages (see Exhibit 10-4).

### Early Mover

**Grainger.** A 70-year-old Midwestern maintenance, repair, and operations (MRO) supplier, Grainger was one of the first distributors to see the potential of the Internet and to create online fulfillment capability. Before the Internet, like most

**Exhibit 10-4**

THE EVOLVED SELL-SIDE SOLUTIONS ACTIVITIES

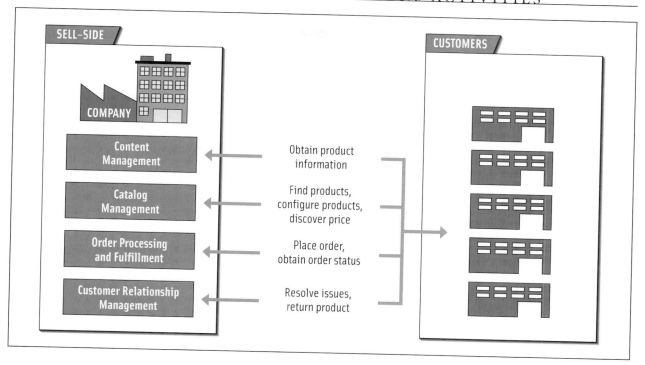

traditional MRO suppliers, Grainger relied on paper catalogs and traditional mail and phone orders. Grainger was one of the first MRO suppliers to transfer its paper catalog of over 200,000 MRO products into a format that could be displayed and distributed to customers and intermediary sales channels via the Web. By late 1995, Grainger had a brochureware website. Today, customers can view the Grainger catalog, place an order, and view fulfillment and shipping status online.

Grainger was one of the first bricks-and-mortar businesses to understand the organizational complexities of establishing an online presence. It built a separate organization of more than 80 people to create and support its online capabilities. As a result, Grainger is the largest distributor of MRO products to commercial and industrial customers in the United States. Grainger offers other value-added services, such as the ability to participate in auctions of Grainger's slow-moving and excess inventory, access to other service providers, and technical support. Although Grainger has first-mover advantage, it will experience severe competition as additional MRO suppliers Web-enable their catalogs and move their businesses online.

## Technology Components

Early B2B adopters provided customers with an online storefront analogous to a physical storefront. From a technology-capability perspective, the necessary components included a content management system to present marketing and broad product information for identifying the organization and its offering, a catalog management system to provide a product catalog and specific product information, an order-processing system to receive and process orders, a fulfillment system to provide order status, and a Web-based customer relationship management system to support the customer relationship.

### Content Management.

The content management system allows the organization to create, aggregate, store, maintain, and present the content contained and presented on its website. Types of content include text, pictures, graphics, and sound. Many content management systems include catalog information as a type of content. In this chapter, however, catalog content will be described separately, as the capability and skills required to manage the two types of content are completely different.

A content management system might not only involve the creation and maintenance of content, but also the ability to manage organizational control and approval of that content—that is, manage the content workflow. This tool can also provide an interface to reach external sources to dynamically and/or periodically pull in content to the site. An additional personalization capability would allow the organization to present content specific to a customer's preferences, demographics, interests, or activity. Content management tools provide the following specific capabilities: document management, control and approval, access and distribution, search, personalization, and external content.

### Catalog Management.

A catalog management system provides the following basic capabilities: taxonomy, population and load, and search. The catalog management system allows the organization to load and manage a Web-based product or service catalog. Catalog management requirements are generally much simpler in facilitating sell-side activities than buy-side or exchange activities—selling organizations only need to create and manage a catalog of their own products, not those of their suppliers or other trading partners. Although sell-side catalog management may be simpler, like content management, catalog management has its technical, business process, and organizational challenges. Catalog management is time consuming, requires new and specific skills, and is ongoing for new and existing products.

A primary complication to catalog management is the **normalization** of data for catalog presentation to the customer. The customer view of a normalized catalog should allow the buyer to select a product category and drill-down through subcategories to the actual desired product. A denormalized catalog would not be organized by logical product categories and subcategories. Ideally, an organization uses an internal taxonomy to understand and manage its products, and this taxonomy perfectly coincides with the product organization that is naturally and logically used by a customer to find and purchase a product. If so, the internal taxonomy is transferred to the online catalog. If not, extensive and specialized effort is required to define the external taxonomy and to organize the online catalog for customers to easily find items for purchase. In some industries and for some types of products, standard categorizations exist, such as the UNSPC specification. An organization could utilize an industry standard instead of creating its own taxonomy, but the industry standard may not be applicable or exist for all products or services purchased. The maintenance of the taxonomy must be ongoing for new products and services sold.

Once the taxonomy is defined, the next challenge within an organization is to map the products or services sold through the taxonomy. In many cases, a single product will have different unique identifiers, descriptions, and information in different product management systems across a large organization. This information must be collected, aggregated, and scrubbed before a single online catalog can be loaded to the website. The process requires extensive manual effort for each individual product or service sold. Ideally, an internal taxonomy already exists, as does the mapping of the product to the taxonomy.

Establishing a taxonomy and mapping catalog data to a single online format are the greatest catalog management challenges. Once these challenges are met, the data must be loaded into a database where the catalog information is stored. Depending on the number of products or services in the catalog, different technologies exist to store and present large volumes of products with reasonable performance—such as object-oriented technology. Search capability is required to allow the customer to search the online catalog in real time using a number of different mechanisms including free text, category drill-down, and search on specific attribute values. Search mechanisms have begun to include use of artificial intelligence to take users through a series of questions and, based on the answers, help find the desired product or service. Also, more complex buying-assistance capabilities exist, but they are typically specific to industry or type of product sold.

## Order Processing and Fulfillment.

Early sell-side B2B adopters created Web-based order processing to allow customers to place online orders for products or services. This capability was modeled after the B2C capability, which allowed users to search a catalog, find desired products, add products to a shopping cart as order line items, and complete an order with billing, shipping, delivery, and payment information. The seller would then provide delivery date information.

Automation of the customer service representative (CSR) process is a primary challenge for many organizations providing online order processing. This automation requires real-time integration with the back-office systems that CSRs use for order processing and the intelligence of inventory allocation, or the available-to-promise (ATP) process. Many back-office systems and business processes are not capable of providing real-time integration; as a result, orders placed at a website are "order requests," not orders. The order-request information must be passed to back-office systems in some form of non-real-time interface or manually typed in by a CSR. Then an order acknowledgement must be sent back to the customer indicating whether the product can be delivered in the desired time-frame and, if necessary, with what exceptions.

Once customers place orders, the ability to obtain order status through a web-site becomes a great benefit to the customer. Before B2B sell-side capabilities were developed, customers had to call a CSR for order status. Again, depending on the same integration issues and complexities described previously, a website may or may not be integrated with order processing, warehousing, and logistics applications to provide real-time order and shipping status.

## Customer Relationship Management (CRM).

Early B2B sell-side adopters created basic capabilities to support online customers. In many cases, customer support on the website involved static help text and an ability to submit an e-mail message to the customer-support organization, which would then designate someone in the organization to respond with a resolution. Today, a more complex CRM capability is available to selling organizations to provide customer-support capability.

The current capability offers a Web-based mechanism for customers to acquire and manage support requests. Web-based CRM provides customers with static-help knowledge bases, which users can search for answers to fundamental support questions (i.e., frequently asked questions, or FAQs). If needed information is not found on the static help pages, CRM provides the user with a case-management capability, or the ability to create, maintain, and submit "cases" or questions to the customer-support organization of the marketplace using the Web interface. The administrative tools of the CRM capability allow the customer support representatives to receive, route, resolve cases, and communicate the resolution to the submitting user. As a website evolves, the CRM application can also provide Web-based sales and marketing and salesforce automation capabilities that are integrated with the customer-support capability.

## Challenges

Implementing new technology is relatively simple compared to changing and challenging business processes or organizations. Sell-side B2B capabilities present the business challenges of content ownership, customer data access and visibility, and channel integration, as well as the technical challenge of integrating real-time and non-real-time processes and systems.

**Content Ownership.** A sell-side website provides sales and marketing information as well as product catalog and technical-support information. Only one website exists, and only one set of content is required for site presentation. Typically, this content is a combination of content managed by a number of different groups within the organization. Business challenges in site content management include identifying the source of all of the different content and establishing a single point of contact and responsibility for the site content. Organizational conflict can occur between different groups that believe they own and manage the site. A good content management capability addresses this issue with workflow functions to centrally manage the gathering, aggregating, approving, and presenting of content.

**Customer Data Access and Visibility.** The primary goal of creating B2B capabilities is to give trading partners access to information and to collaborate in business processes using that information. Before the Internet and B2B software, companies only shared information with trading partners through direct interaction with employees or through predefined reporting. B2B capabilities make it possible to share information with trading partners through a Web-based user interface. This is a blessing and a curse for most organizations.

Many organizations have discrete internal applications and systems that present inaccurate information—forcing employees to gather and interpret data manually. Here, automating the presentation of information to trading partners would not be accomplished without manual intervention—contrary to the general benefits of B2B. To determine whether a product can be delivered by a specific date or to place an order, customers normally call a customer service representative. The CSR takes the order over the phone, accesses the order processing system, enters the order, and may or may not have visibility to inventory allocation or be able to provide real-time, available-to-promise (ATP) information. If system capabilities cannot provide this information in real time to the CSR, the same systems cannot be made real time to customers placing orders through a website. Internal inefficiencies would now become obvious external inefficiencies to trading partners.

**Channel Integration.** The creation of Web-based sell-side capabilities also creates a new sales channel for an organization. This sales channel needs to be integrated with other sales channels from customer support, marketing, sales, salesforce automation, and fulfillment perspectives. If a Web-based channel is treated separately, customers will become frustrated with multichannel interactions with the organization. Customers want to be able to call a CSR after placing an order on the Internet, or return merchandise bought online to an offline store. Therefore, the Web channel needs to be treated as a separate channel, but integrated with all the other sales channels.

**Systems Integration.** The primary technical challenges for organizations implementing sell-side or Web-based transactional applications in general is the ability to integrate the Web-based capability with legacy back-office applications in real time. In the order-processing section, an example was provided where, without real-time integration for inventory availability or ATP information, an online order is nothing more than an "order request"—until the process can be integrated with the back office. Development of a B2B capability presents an opportunity to provide trade partners with Web access to traditionally internal information. But if this information is not available real time internally, it cannot be made available real time to trading partners. To participate in B2B collaboration, an organization's back-office systems must be integrated and efficient.

# INDIRECT E-PROCUREMENT

A typical business must purchase a wide variety of products and services in order to operate, and they can be divided into two main categories: direct and indirect materials. Indirect materials are nonstrategic materials used to support the business. Direct materials are the raw or intermediate materials that are used in the manufacturing process to make the products that are core to the business. Direct materials vary by industry, company position in the supply chain, and types of products sold.

## Indirect Procurement Us. Direct Procurement

In most cases, the procurement of indirect materials is highly manual, involving an employee's submission of a purchase request or requisition to a purchasing department, where all requisitions are then aggregated into purchase orders and sent to contracted suppliers to fulfill. The indirect purchasing cycle tends to be drawn out by the control and approval process. Typically, employees have spending privileges limited by type of product or amount of dollars. Requisitions for certain products or over specified threshold dollar amounts require approval by organization management before the requisition is submitted to the purchasing department and purchase orders are generated.

Because direct materials are important to the core business, very often the requirements for direct procurement are automatically generated by core planning and transaction systems, such as MRP systems in manufacturing. Delivery, receipt, and quality of direct materials are more closely monitored and managed to ensure that dependent manufacturing schedules are not compromised.

## Indirect or MRO E-Procurement

Early B2B adopters realized that Web-based business applications would be better suited, at least initially, to streamlining the manual indirect procurement process. As a result, e-procurement capabilities focused on indirect procurement. The purchasing department of a typical business performs multiple functions that include the following:

- *Supplier relationship management*—establish and maintain supplier relationships, source and negotiate contracts, monitor performance, catalog management
- *Transaction processing*—research products, requisitioning, control and approval, purchase-order processing, fulfillment, billing and invoicing, receiving, settlement
- *Third-party service provider management*—logistics providers, couriers, purchasing card settlement

Web-based procurement capabilities were designed to facilitate the catalog management and transaction processing functions of the purchasing process (see Exhibit 10-5).

## Product Vs. Services

E-procurement can be utilized to purchase both products and services. Product procurement requires a catalog of items for sale. Procurement of services typically involves a request for information or proposal (RFI or RFP) process. Initially, the focus of e-procurement was on the purchase of products.

**Exhibit 10-5** INDIRECT OR MRO E-PROCUREMENT

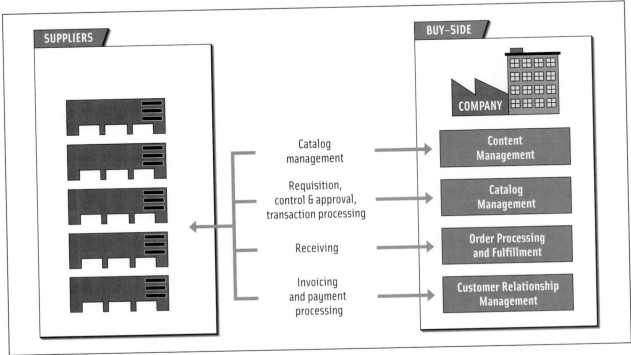

# Early Movers

**Ariba.** Founded in 1995, Ariba was one of the original providers of B2B software. It was also the first to build software that enabled companies to procure goods and services online. Ariba's e-procurement software allows users to view an online catalog of goods and services available from partner suppliers, to create a purchase requisition online, to route a requisition throughout the organization for control and approval, and to create and send an associated purchase order to the supplier. Ariba's software has helped its customers achieve tremendous ROI by streamlining the procurement process for indirect goods and services.

After tremendous growth, Ariba moved from providing indirect e-procurement software to providing software for creating and managing Net marketplaces, then to operating its own Net marketplace for indirect MRO purchasing, and then to providing software that enables direct procurement. Ariba achieved much of its growth and expanded capability through its acquisitions of Aspect Technologies (catalog services), Tradex (Net marketplace software), and Agile (supply-chain management software). Today, Ariba's customers include over 40 of the Fortune 100.

# Technology Components

E-procurement applications provide Web-based functions that allow employees of a buying organization to purchase goods and services and allow suppliers to manage and communicate the fulfillment of the purchase orders submitted. E-procurement capability includes the following: catalog management (basically the same as sell-side sites), requisitioning, control and approval, receiving and exception processing, and financials and payment processing.

**Requisitioning.** Requisitioning capability allows the buyer to create a purchase requisition for the products or services desired. In addition to specifying the desired merchandise for purchase, the system allows the buyer to include information specific to the requisition, including buyer name, billing address, shipping address, cost accounting codes, and desired delivery date. This information may be stored with the user profile and prepopulated with the requisition for the buyer to modify as necessary.

**Control and Approval.** Once a purchase requisition is created, the system automates the control and approval process. The catalog and user-management capabilities of the system allow the buying organization to define for each specific user what they can or cannot purchase and from which suppliers. As a result, when a buyer searches a catalog, he will only see the products and services he is "allowed" to purchase as configured by the buying organization. In addition, the system allows the buying organization to define and configure spending limits for individual buyers, which may include limits on dollars per requisition or type of product or service. A more sophisticated e-procurement application provides for complex approval workflow, which may (1) allow the buying organization to define multiple approvers in the process, (2) allow serial as well as parallel approval to take place with multiple approvers, and (3) allow the approvers to forward and consult other employees in the approval process.

**Transaction Processing.** The transaction processing capability of the e-procurement application accepts all of the purchase requisitions created by a buying organization and creates purchase orders to be sent to the suppliers. Depending on the buying organization's business requirements, there may be a one-to-one relationship between requisitions and purchase orders, or the system may consolidate multiple requisitions into a single purchase order—simplifying the fulfillment for the supplier. The system utilizes a message-delivery mechanism to deliver the purchase order to the supplier, or allows the supplier to manage his or her purchase orders using a Web-based user interface. Delivery mechanisms include fax, e-mail, HTTP, **Electronic Data Interchange (EDI)**, and MQ Series among others. The supplier is then responsible for providing fulfillment status on the purchase order, including acceptance acknowledgement and shipment and logistical information. This information is used by the buying organization to understand delivery status of the order. In some cases, third-party logistics providers may be integrated with the e-procurement system to provide shipping information as well.

**Receiving and Exception Processing.** Once the supplier ships the products and they are received by the buying organization, e-procurement applications allow the buying organization to record receipt of the goods. Capability is required to address any potential exceptions that may occur, including differences among items originally ordered by the buyer, shipped by the supplier, and finally received by the buyer. Is is also required to address partial shipments, partial payments, and returns.

**Financials and Payment Processing.** Finally, the e-procurement application includes or integrates with other applications for financials and payment processing. At minimum, e-procurement applications include the ability for the buyer to purchase merchandise using a credit or corporate p-card. Credit card information is entered with the purchase requisition and sent to the supplier for processing. Integration with a financial application is typically required for accounts payable to provide supplier invoice information to the buyer in the e-procurement system and to indicate supplier invoice payment.

## Challenges

As with any technology implementation, business and organizational challenges can affect the ability to implement the technology as well as to achieve the benefits and ROI on the investment. Business challenges of e-procurement include strategic sourcing, as well as adoption and compliance, while technical challenges include catalog content management, supplier integration, and back-office systems integration.

**Strategic Sourcing.** Before implementing an e-procurement application, an analysis of an organization's spending is required to understand what products or services are being purchased and from which suppliers. Implementation of e-procurement is an iterative and ongoing process. An organization should phase the implementation over time by categories of spend, organizational geography, and suppliers. The analysis of spending allows the buying organization to understand which categories of spend would provide the greatest benefits from e-procurement and which are the high-volume, low-dollar transactions. The analysis also allows the buying organization to perform product and supplier rationalization before implementing e-procurement.

**Adoption and Compliance.** For a buying organization to achieve the maximum ROI from an e-procurement implementation, the organization must ensure that its purchasing agents and employees submit requisitions using the new application. This sounds fundamental and simple, but in many cases buying organizations are slow to turn off old mechanisms in place for purchasing and, as a result, buyers do not change buying habits and begin to use the new system. A buying organization should also address the organizational changes associated with an e-procurement implementation. Training and role clarity must be provided to the purchasing agents who will do less requisitioning creation and approval and more strategic sourcing.

## Catalog Content Management.

Buying organizations quickly realize that loading and managing catalog content is a time-consuming effort, requiring new and specific skills and an ongoing effort for new products and suppliers. The buying organization is responsible for acquiring and loading the catalog information that its individual buyers view online for creating requisitions. The buying organization must rely on the supplier or third-party catalog provider for the content that is loaded into the application. In addition, the buying organization is responsible for determining the presentation of catalog content to the individual buyer, which requires transforming catalog content into some other appropriate format before it is loaded into the application.

If a normalized catalog is desired by the buying organization, a **catalog taxonomy** must be created, and then the contents of individual supplier catalogs must be mapped to that taxonomy. The buying organization must define the product categories and subcategories of the catalog. For example, if a supplier sells a product with a description of "8 1/2-by-11 inch paper," a link must be created in the e-procurement catalog between the product and the categories and subcategories of "office suppliers" and "paper." Then, when the buyer selects "office supplies" and "paper," she will see "8 1/2-by-11 inch paper" and an associated price. Ideally, an industry standard is utilized and the supplier provides the UNSPC code of the product sold, allowing automated mapping to the taxonomy. The maintenance of the taxonomy is ongoing for new products or services purchased.

In addition to taxonomy standardization and mapping, different suppliers selling the same product may describe the product differently or store different information about the product. As a result, the normalization effort requires not only mapping to the taxonomy, but also comparing and scrubbing the associated product or service information to ensure similar information is stored and presented to the buyer when comparing two different suppliers. This further complicates the acquisition, transformation, and loading of catalog content. In many cases, e-procurement applications do not provide the necessary tools to address catalog content management, and additional software is required to transform data from the supplier format to the format required by e-procurement application. For faster e-procurement systems implementation, many buying organizations begin with a denormalized catalog and normalize their catalog over time.

The complexity of catalog management created an opportunity for a new breed of e-businesses that provide catalog taxonomy, catalog mapping, and catalog content services to buying organizations. The e-procurement vendors themselves, such as Ariba and Commerce One, took this opportunity to develop relationships with common suppliers, create a taxonomy of their own, map supplier data to their taxonomy, and offer a catalog content subscription service to their buying organization customers. This provided a new revenue stream for e-procurement vendors. Other new e-businesses appeared to provide these services to buying organizations as well. This was also the impetus behind the creation of, and one of the value-added services provided by, the new Net marketplaces or Net exchanges, as we later describe.

**Supplier Integration.** Beyond working with each new supplier to acquire and load catalog content, the buying organization and supplier must work together to determine the business process for business document exchange. Business documents typically include purchase orders, advanced shipping notices (ASN), and invoices. Smaller suppliers without ERP systems to manage their order processing and fulfillment processes can utilize the user interface of their e-procurement application to manage the business process, and do not require electronic integration for business document exchange. Most e-procurement applications provide out-of-the-box integration with fax and e-mail servers as the simplest method for business document exchange with suppliers. Most Fortune 500 buying and selling organizations require a more sophisticated message-delivery mechanism to further automate and integrate business document exchange as well as ensure guaranteed delivery of documents. In the past, EDI served this function, but use of the Internet has displaced EDI as the de facto message-delivery mechanism. Today, mechanisms such as HTTP and MQ Series are utilized. Buying and selling organizations must determine and implement the message-delivery mechanism to be utilized.

Not only must the method of messaging be determined, but the format of the data exchange must be determined as well. For example, the format of the purchase order exported from an e-procurement application may not be in the same format as the purchase order that the supplier expects and utilizes. As a result, either the buyer or the seller must map the buyer format to the supplier format and perform a translation before the message is delivered. This process requires effort for each business document and for each new supplier relationship. The organization with the most leverage typically dictates who performs the mapping and translation. In some cases, the buying and selling organizations agree to exchange business documents in an industry standard format, which eliminates the need for document translation. Multiple industry standards exist with new ones being developed all the time. EDI has an industry standard format and multiple **Extensible Markup Language (XML)** standards now exist for B2B business document exchange, including Rosettanet, cBL (Ariba), CXL (Commerce One), MM XML (Internet Capital Group), and others. The need for supplier integration created by B2B business document exchange has introduced a new breed of e-business software and service companies that provide tools and services for messaging and data transformation.

**Back-Office Integration.** Depending on the size of the buying organization, an installed e-procurement application does not stand alone. Integration with other existing legacy and ERP systems is required to automate the procurement process with other business processes. Like any systems implementation, integration with other systems is one of the greatest challenges. The following systems typically integrate with an e-procurement application:

- Purchasing—PO creation
- Inventory and warehousing—receiving
- Financials—A/P, invoicing
- MRP and planning—PO requirements

Larger buying organizations commonly have an existing back-office purchasing system in place to manage the overall procurement process. And when an ERP already exists, it probably has been integrated with other major systems used to run the operation. If this is the case, the purchasing system is the "owner" of any purchase orders generated for suppliers. As a result, purchase orders generated by the e-procurement application need to be populated in the purchasing system.

Once created, the purchasing system may also be integrated to provide the status of the order back to the e-procurement system, or this may come from other systems. For example, if the buying organization records receipt of supplier shipments in an inventory or warehousing system, this system might be integrated with e-procurement to display receipt information to the buyers and suppliers. Integration may be required between e-procurement and the financial applications to display invoice and payable information to the buyers and suppliers—indicating receipt of invoice and invoice payment. Finally, for direct procurement, integration between e-procurement and MRP or planning systems may be required for the planning systems to communicate manufacturing requirements for direct materials and for the PO to generate automatically in the e-procurement system. Direct procurement is described in more detail in the following chapter.

The complexity of the integration effort normally depends on the complexity of the existing back-office systems environment of the buying organization. Different systems reside on and utilize different technical platforms and are managed by different organizational groups—all of which adds to the complexity of interface design and implementation. A larger organization may have different back-office and legacy systems for different business units and in different geographies. If multiple purchasing systems exist across the company, multiple interfaces are required for each system for each type of integration.

# NET MARKETPLACES AND NET EXCHANGES

Early B2B movers demonstrated that businesses could sell products or services to other businesses over the Internet. This movement facilitated point-to-point interaction and integration between buying and selling organizations that use the Internet for commerce transactions. However, both the buying and selling organizations quickly realized that time, effort, and money were required on an ongoing basis to continue to implement and facilitate point-to-point interaction and integration with each newly established trading partner relationship. As a result, many organizations realized that **point-to-point integration** with trading partners was not cost effective and was only worthwhile for strategic relationships involving large volume and dollar transactions. A more cost-effective means of integrating with nonstrategic trading partners was required.

E-procurement vendors were the first to realize this market trend and to offer a solution. They already had relationships with buying organizations that had implemented their e-procurement software. With each implementation, these vendors were working with and establishing relationships with suppliers. The e-procurement vendors realized they could create an online marketplace that would bring together their existing buyers and suppliers, who could then exchange catalog information and commerce transactions. The buyers and suppliers quickly realized that by integrating into this marketplace, they were integrating with all the other trading partners without having to spend the time, effort, and money to facilitate the point-to-point integration.

At about the same time, a new e-business had been established to facilitate non-commerce interaction between trading partners in specific industries. VerticalNet

Exhibit
10-6
## NET MARKETPLACES AND NET EXCHANGES

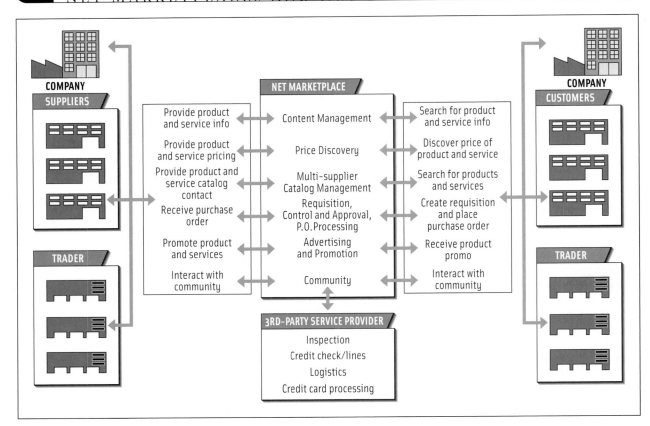

created a website where people with like minds and interests within a specific industry or "vertical" could congregate and interact to exchange ideas and information and build relationships. Mechanisms such as bulletin boards, e-mail, and instant messaging were utilized for community interaction. Storefronts were established to allow suppliers to advertise to buyers, facilitating new buyer-seller relationships. Content management capability was implemented to allow trading partners to access and exchange industry information and content. The concept of a vertical community quickly gained momentum; within a very short period of time, VerticalNet had hundreds of vertical communities in multiple industries and hundreds of thousands of users (see Exhibit 10-6).

As a result, new kinds of Internet-based businesses were created. Net marketplaces and Net exchanges facilitated the interaction and exchange of commerce transactions, industry content, and communication between buyers, sellers, and other trading partners with similar needs, within similar industries. E-procurement enabled a one-to-many (buyer-to-suppliers) model; Net marketplaces and Net exchanges enabled a many-to-many (buyers to suppliers) model. The capability of these new marketplaces integrated with and enhanced the buy- and sell-side capabilities implemented by buyer and seller organizations. The Net marketplaces provided an alternative to the direct sales channel for buyers and sellers.

## Vertical Vs. Horizontal Marketplaces

In general, Net marketplaces are either vertical or horizontal in focus. A horizontal marketplace creates a community for, and provides products and services required by, all industries (examples of horizontal Net marketplaces include Ariba, Commerce One, and Grainger). Vertical Net marketplaces create a community for, and provide products and services specific to, a particular industry or vertical marketplace. These marketplaces focus on the buying and selling of direct materials for the specific industry, as well as provide industry-specific content and enable industry-specific interaction between trading partners (examples include VerticalNet, ChemConnect, and eHitex). While horizontal marketplaces typically only focus on commerce, vertical marketplaces are better able to take advantage of community and content capabilities, such as industry news and literature, product specifications, and technical-support documents.

## Buyer-Centric, Seller-Centric, or Neutral

Net marketplaces can be categorized as buyer-centric, seller-centric, or neutral in approach and business model. Buyer-centric marketplaces focus on providing benefits to the buying organizations. For example, a marketplace that pools and aggregates buyer-spend and uses high volume as leverage in negotiating lower prices with suppliers for all the buyers is a buyer-centric model. Similarly, a seller-centric marketplace primarily focuses on providing suppliers with benefits of participation, which may include providing storefront capability and the ability to outsource or provide services to support fulfillment. A neutral marketplace provides capabilities and benefits to both buyers and suppliers equally without favoring one or the other.

The type of business model or owner of the Net exchange would give some indication of which trading partners are benefiting the most. If the participation cost is assumed by either the buyer or seller and not shared, the marketplace is either buyer- or seller-centric. In theory, neutral Net exchanges and business models have the best chance for survival over time. When a Net exchange is either buyer- or seller-centric, one party will always feel at a disadvantage and look for other channels through which to buy and sell—including other marketplaces. A neutral Net exchange has a better chance of obtaining customer loyalty and achieving liquidity for the vertical or targeted market. Both buyers and sellers see benefit in participating and are less inclined to seek alternative channels.

## Public Vs. Private Marketplaces

Early-mover Net marketplaces were primarily dot-com startups backed by venture capital. These early marketplaces initially targeted specific buyer and seller organizations, but were fundamentally open to any buyer or seller who wanted to participate. Since the market correction in the spring of 2000 and the resulting decrease in venture capital for dot-com startups, many marketplaces being established today are spinoffs or consortia of existing bricks-and-mortar companies partnering with each other to create private Net exchanges for their particular industry. These private marketplaces target and allow only strategic buying and selling partners to participate in the Net exchange, giving them strategic advantage over competitors and the rest of their industry or supply chain. The business models and participants of public and private marketplaces may differ, but the technical and functional capabilities of the two are typically very similar.

# Industry Dynamics

Each industry or vertical market has greatly varying dynamics that determine whether or not a vertical Net marketplace is necessary and viable. Net marketplaces are most successful in industries in which the following conditions exist:

- There are large volumes of low-cost transactions.
- There is fragmentation, meaning that a large number of buyers and sellers with an insufficient or inefficient mechanism find each other as well as multiple participants and intermediaries in the supply chain.
- There is a high cost of obtaining, selling to, and retaining buyers and suppliers.
- Products and services are a commodity, and the goal is to reduce the transaction costs as a percentage of sales.
- The markets are inefficient so a large portion of the cost of goods sold is in process and distribution.

The most important industry dynamics that affect the business model of the Net marketplace are power structure, existing relationships, and channel conflicts. If the sellers in a particular industry have the power and leverage, the Net marketplace is best suited to provide a seller-centric solution. This might include aggregation of buying demand for the sellers; providing new sales channels for slow-moving merchandise; protecting the supplier margins, brands, and positions; and putting the burden of transaction costs on the buyer. If the buyers in a particular industry have the power and leverage, a Net marketplace is better suited in implementing a buyer-centric approach. This might include pooling buyer demand to negotiate lower prices, facilitating price comparison and seller competition, and putting the burden of transaction costs on the seller. If existing intermediaries in an industry, such as distributors, have the power and leverage, a Net marketplace is better suited to either partnering with, complementing, or supplementing the intermediary offering. This might include combating the business model of bricks-and-mortar sellers in selling directly to buyers. In a truly healthy industry, there is balance of power and leverage, which is supported and facilitated by the Net marketplace.

The specific industry dynamics impact and determine the business model and marketplace requirements. Regardless of industry, the value of participating in the marketplace must be real and clear to all participants.

# Early Movers

**FreeMarkets.** FreeMarkets understood early the value of providing dynamic commerce or pricing mechanisms to improve transaction efficiency and to facilitate price elasticity. FreeMarkets provides online bidding services and purchase consulting through a reverse-auction capability for industrial buyers of custom-engineered parts. Suppliers compete in real time for large purchase orders from large industrial manufacturers. Access to new, prequalified suppliers allows buyers to streamline the purchasing process and reduce costs (advertised as 10 to 15 percent savings for large industrial buyers). FreeMarkets provides reverse-auction, supplier identification, contract negotiation, and supplier selection capabilities. In addition, FreeMarkets provides value-added services to further facilitate transactions, including decision support and auction preparation services.

**VerticalNet.** VerticalNet was one of the first companies to understand and exploit the B2C concept of Internet communities. Founded in 1995 as an industry trade magazine, VerticalNet is now the leading developer and operator of industry-specific communities on the Internet, with over 600 employees worldwide. Community capability brings people of like mind and interests together. VerticalNet enabled this capability for specific verticals or industries, bringing together customers, suppliers, manufacturers, and end-users for each vertical. Today, VerticalNet hosts hundreds of different vertical communities in aerospace, food and hospitality, consumer packaged goods, oil and gas, healthcare, high-tech, construction, discrete and process manufacturing, scientific equipment, and telecommunications.

Now with millions of users, VerticalNet has moved from providing community capability to offering commerce or transactional capability to participating buyers and sellers within each community, originating with an online bookstore for access to industry content. Commerce capability and services available today include the ability for suppliers to advertise to the industry, catalog and order processing, auctions for used equipment and excess inventory, and training services. With more than 60 Net marketplaces, VerticalNet has become the de facto "horizontal" vertical marketplace on the Internet. VerticalNet's challenge will be to continue to add verticals, commerce capability, and ultimately, users. VerticalNet will experience severe competition from individual vertical marketplaces with greater industry expertise—in some cases initiated by a major player in the industry.

# Technology Components

The technical approach for creating a Net marketplace or Net exchange has evolved over time. Until 1999, there were few commercial applications available to operate Net marketplaces. In mid to late 1999, commercial software to power Net marketplaces began to appear. The concept of a Net marketplace was relatively new, as was the perception of the capabilities that a Net marketplace should provide. Excellent point solutions for Net marketplaces became available in late 1999. In 2000, commerce, content, and community capabilities began to appear in commercial software solutions.

The major e-procurement vendors perceived the industry shift toward Net marketplaces and Net exchanges and began to either transform their existing e-procurement software or build new software to power Net marketplaces. For many e-procurement vendors, this transformation is still taking place into 2001. Even now, no single commercial solution provides all capabilities required by Net marketplaces.

Other new e-businesses saw the opportunity for Net marketplaces and created service organizations for outsourcing the technology to power them. Application service providers (ASP) for Net marketplaces began appearing in 2000.

The approach to implementing the marketplace varied by industry because of market trends in Net marketplace software and services as well as the diversity of Net marketplaces being created. The operator of a new Net marketplace must first make a fundamental choice between outsourcing the technology and operation of the marketplace to an ASP or developing and operating the marketplace independently. The implementation of a robust Net marketplace typically involves a combination of custom development, integration of best-of-breed point commercial solutions, and outsourcing and integration with third-party service providers.

The capability required to operate a Net marketplace varies greatly. Three general capability areas evolved from the early movers: commerce, content, and community. Most Net marketplaces begin by implementing and focusing on one of these three capabilities as an initial core competency and then evolving to provide all three over time. For example, VerticalNet focused solely on providing and facilitating community for multiple vertical industries in its initial years, but by 2000 began providing support for enabling commerce transactions. By contrast, most MRO marketplaces initially focused on enabling commerce transactions—but because of the lack of community and content capability, MRO marketplaces found difficulty in differentiating themselves from the competition.

## Commerce Capabilities

Commerce capabilities provide the ability for products and services to be bought and sold in the Net marketplace. For most Net marketplaces, facilitation of commerce is the goal, as this is typically the revenue-generating mechanism. Enabling commerce transactions requires a wide variety of capabilities and services, which include catalog management, order processing, and payment processing. The capabilities required to facilitate commerce transactions in a Net marketplace vary by business model and industry.

**Catalog Management.** To facilitate the purchase of products and services, the Net marketplace must provide the ability for the buyer or supplier to find or specify what is desired for purchase or sale. Typically, this involves allowing the operator and suppliers to define, populate, and maintain a marketplace catalog with all of the products and services available. To simplify initial marketplace capability, catalog management may not be utilized early in the evolution if the user can define the products or services to be bought or sold at the time the transaction is initiated. For example, if the Net marketplace provides request-for-information (RFQ) capability, the buyer may describe the types of products or services desired in the creation of the RFQ, instead of selecting them from a catalog. However, if the marketplace requires any fixed-price capability, allowing the suppliers to enter prices for specific products, a catalog is also required.

The capabilities needed to manage all aspects of a marketplace catalog include the following: access to external catalog information, catalog database, catalog taxonomy, catalog search, catalog mapping, aggregation, and load capability.

The fundamental decision a marketplace operator must make about catalog management is the source of the catalog content. This includes the information that describes the products or services listed for purchase in the catalog, such as name, description, price, color, and size. The content can come from suppliers, manufacturers, or third-party catalog-content service providers. Once the source of the content has been identified, next the marketplace operator must decide where the content will reside. The content can reside within the physical architecture of the marketplace or externally with the supplier, manufacturer or third-party service provider. The catalog management capability required by the marketplace will depend on these fundamental decisions.

If the marketplace operator chooses to have catalog content physically reside external to the marketplace with the suppliers, manufacturers, or third-party service providers, a "punch-out" capability is required. When buyers search the marketplace catalog for desired items, the punch-out capability allows the search to execute through external catalogs, select external items, and add externally selected items to a shopping cart internal to the marketplace. Punch-out capability requires integration with the site of the external catalog content provider. Net marketplaces compliant with the Open Buying Interface (OBI) industry standard support punch out of external content. XML industry standards now support punch-out access as well.

For catalog content that is managed internal to the marketplace, the catalog management capability requires a database in which the catalog content will reside. For catalogs that approach or exceed a million items, scalability quickly becomes an issue. The marketplace operator must decide if catalog content will be presented in a normalized manner. If normalization is desired, significant effort is required by the operator to define the ontology or taxonomy of the Net marketplace catalog and to map supplier catalogs to the taxonomy.

The catalog management capability should provide multiple search mechanisms to allow buyers to find the products or services they seek—including the ability to drill-down through categories in a normalized catalog, and to search by free-text or by parametric values and other intelligent search mechanisms, such as natural language or artificial intelligence.

Catalog management capability requires not only a storage database for content, presentation capability to display the content, and search tools to search the database, but also tools to map, transform, and load catalog content into the database. These tools allow the operator to accept a file of catalog information, to map the input file to the taxonomy and format of the Net marketplace catalog using a Web-based user interface, and to transform the data from the input format to the destination format. Once transformed, a tool allows the operator to load the content to the catalog. This process is executed for each new supplier catalog and periodically updated for existing suppliers.

## Price Discovery.

While catalog management capability helps the buyer or supplier find or specify what is desired for purchase or sale, price discovery capability helps the buyer or supplier determine the buying price or selling price of the product or service. The two fundamental price discovery categories are fixed and dynamic.

A fixed-price capability allows the supplier to assign a set price to a particular product or service for sale. Multiple types of fixed pricing exist, and the specific price can vary depending on the relationship among the buyer, supplier, product or service, and set of pricing rules. For example, a supplier may specify a "list" price at which any buyer can buy a product or service. A "contract price" is a specific price for a product or service for a particular buyer and supplier relationship, as maintained by the supplier. In between list and contract pricing, there are multiple types of "discount" pricing, including the following: percentage or dollar amount above cost, percentage or dollar amount under list, volume discounts, tiered pricing, rebates, transaction fees, and bundled discounts.

Fixed-price capability can be very complex and require a pricing engine depending on the different types of discount pricing supported. The price for a particular product or service can be dependent upon the buyer and supplier relationships as well as the volume of the order, purchasing history, and existing contracts in place. Integration with other components of the Net marketplace may be required to support complex pricing, such as contracts or prior purchasing history.

## Dynamic Pricing.

In most cases, Net marketplaces enable the buyer and supplier to negotiate a price where a fixed price may not exist. Multiple dynamic pricing mechanisms can be facilitated by the Net marketplace, including: request for information (RFI), request for proposal (RFP), request for quote (RFQ), auction, reverse-auction, and bid/ask exchange.

**Negotiated Exchange.** The RFI, RFP, and RFQ mechanisms are all examples of negotiated exchange. Although traditionally buyer-initiated, negotiations to buy or sell can be initiated by either a buyer or seller. These mechanisms allow the buyer or seller to create a transaction specifying products or services desired for purchase or sale. Many times there is a sequence from RFI to RFP to RFQ. An RFI involves a buyer or seller requesting general information from potential trading partners; an RFP involves a buyer or seller asking for a proposal from potential trading partners specific to the desired product or service; and an RFQ involves a buyer or seller asking for a quote or price from trading partners for specific products or services desired for purchase or sale.

Under this system, the initiator can create and define the transaction or document. The initiator specifies the details of the transaction, including which attributes are negotiable, and can specify to which trading partners in the marketplace the transaction will be delivered for response. Delivery and notification capability allow a trading partner to know when a transaction has been created and sent to him. The capability allows the trading partner to bid on the transaction by the attributes specified as negotiable. The bids are then returned to the initiator for review; the initiator can accept, reject, or respond. Accepting a bid awards the transaction to the bidder. Rejecting a bid eliminates the bidder from the negotiation. Responding to a bid continues the negotiations, which can go back and forth between initiator and bidders as many times as required. Ultimately, one bidder is awarded the transaction.

Negotiated exchanges may include an optimization capability to help the initiator analyze multiple bids for multiple products and services. The initiator may find it difficult to manually analyze multiple bids when a single transaction includes multiple products or services, the bidder is allowed to bid on some or all items, and multiple products or services can be bundled into various single bids. Bid optimization allows the initiator to specify award criteria and to understand the associated optimum award scenario.

In many cases, an RFI, RFP, or RFQ results in a contract and contract pricing for the associated product or service. In this case, integration with the contract management capability is required to store the terms of the transaction. Integration is also required with the catalog management and pricing engine of the procurement capability to store contract pricing for later use during order processing.

**Auction and Reverse-Auction.** The auction and reverse-auction are additional types of dynamic pricing mechanisms. The difference between the two mechanisms depends on who initiates the transaction—traditionally, auctions are seller initiated, while reverse-auctions are buyer initiated. The auction capability allows a single seller to offer products or services to multiple buyers, with buyers dynamically competing to arrive at a price. In most cases, auctions are used to sell excess or obsolete inventory, one-of-a-kind items, limited capacity or inventory, perishable goods, or capital assets. This capability differs from the negotiated exchange mechanisms described earlier in that there is typically no negotiation. Auctions and reverse-auctions usually are specified to automatically close at a particular time or price. Negotiations for RFP, RFI, and RFQ are not typically completed until the initiator manually awards or closes the transaction.

Types of auctions include the following:

- English auctions involve a single seller and multiple buyers in which bids continually increase the price for an item for a predetermined period of time.
- Dutch auctions involve a single seller and multiple buyers. The product is offered at a specific price, which is reduced by a certain amount in specific time increments until a bidder accepts the price.
- Sealed-bid auctions involve a single seller and multiple buyers. Each bidder makes a secret bid with the highest bid winning once all bids are received.
- Japanese auctions are the opposite of Dutch auctions because the price is set when bids are collected. The price is then raised a certain amount in specific time increments until only one bidder remains.

**Bid/Ask Exchange.** A third type of dynamic pricing mechanism is the true bid/ask exchange capability. This capability supports a many-to-many, multiparametric marketplace where participants negotiate on predefined attributes of the product or service until a match between buyer and seller is achieved. The market maker for this capability typically defines the different markets or exchanges and the associated products or services that are traded. This capability provides stock-market-like conditions in which buyers create "bids" and sellers create "asks," both specifying the attributes of the products or service desired. A negotiation capability described previously may be utilized to refine specification of the product or service. In this case, a matching engine automatically matches bids and asks when the specifications are aligned. Streaming technology is utilized to allow users to view real-time market activity, including bid, ask, matching activity, and market-price fluctuations. The bid/ask exchange capability is commonly utilized by Net marketplaces that facilitate the buying and selling of true commodity-type products and services that can be universally defined and standardized by the market.

**Procurement, Fulfillment, and Settlement.** The same e-procurement capability that is implemented on the buy-side to enable requisitioning, control and approval, and purchase-order creation is required for a Net marketplace. This capability allows the buyer to search an online catalog, fill a shopping cart with desired products or services, and create a purchase requisition. The capability routes the requisition to appropriate individuals in the buying organization for approval. Once approved, requisitions are aggregated, turned into purchase orders, and sent to the appropriate suppliers.

Once the purchase order has been generated, the marketplace can allow buyers and sellers to manage the fulfillment process. Many marketplaces initially focused on purchase-order creation, but not the fulfillment process—as with operators of B2C sites in late 1999. Operators of marketplaces learned that the fulfillment process must be enabled to ensure order delivery. The marketplace can also provide Web-based capabilities to the supplier to view and manage purchase orders, including acceptance or rejection of POs, modification of shipping status, generation of invoices, and management of exception processing. The buying organization can use these capabilities to understand delivery status of orders through integration with third-party logistics providers for in-transit shipping status. Once the supplier ships the products and they are received by the buying organization, e-procurement applications allow the buying organization to record receipt of goods.

Finally, as with e-procurement, marketplace capability integrates with other applications for financials and payment processing. At the very least, e-procurement applications include the ability for the buyer to purchase merchandise using a credit card and require integration with a financial application for accounts payable to provide supplier invoice information to the buyer in the e-procurement system and to indicate invoice payment status.

**Advertising and Promotion.** Early B2C business models were based on revenue from advertising and product promotion. Initially, the B2B Net marketplaces followed the B2C lead and B2B business models relied on advertising revenues as well. Online advertising in its current form has proved to be not very effective in delivering an intended audience, and many question its viability and capability to drive revenues. Nevertheless, Net marketplaces must enable suppliers and third-party service providers to place advertisements to buyers in the marketplace. However, providing this capability presents a chicken-and-egg dilemma. It is not a first-phase requirement—most marketplaces begin with only a few strategic buyers and suppliers and facilitate existing relationships. As more and more buyers and sellers join the marketplace and discovery becomes a value-added service of participating in the marketplace, the ability for sellers to advertise to buyers becomes increasingly important. Multiple mechanisms for advertising and promotion include the following:

- *Supplier storefronts.* One of the first value-added services a Net marketplace can provide suppliers is the ability to advertise themselves in a supplier storefront, which lets buyers view a list of all of the participating or interested suppliers. The suppliers are given "real estate" on the site that can be accessed by the general public. The storefront allows buyers to find new suppliers and allows suppliers to introduce themselves and the products they sell. The capability is simple, as there is little or no integration required to the transactional activity of the exchange.

- *Banners and product promotion.* An early, and still widely used, B2C advertising mechanism is the banner. A Net marketplace can also utilize banner capability to advertise itself or allow suppliers within the marketplace to advertise themselves, the products they sell, or special promotions. Banners can be targeted to a specific audience based on profile, interest, or activity. The banner advertising mechanism can also be used for product promotion or for suppliers to specify products for promotion and to integrate the promotion into their procurement process.

- *Campaign management.* A campaign management capability provides advertisers with Web-based user interfaces to manage the advertising process. A campaign is a specific instance of advertising defined by the advertising content, target audience, and delivery mechanism. Typically, tools are provided to analyze the performance of a campaign after delivery or completion.

- *Target advertising.* B2C sites and advertisers quickly realized that users were not happy with unsolicited or irrelevant advertising. As a result, Net marketplaces now allow the advertiser to target ads to a specific type of marketplace user. In its simplest form, targeting can be based on user profiles or interests. The advertiser can specify that an ad only be served to users with specific profile characteristics such as role, geography, or user interests. A more sophisticated campaign management capability would allow the advertiser to target ads based on user activity. For example, a banner might be defined to serve only users who have bought a particular product in the last month.

- *Cross-sell and up-sell.* A more sophisticated advertising capability would allow advertisers to cross-sell and up-sell. The cross- and up-sell capability informs a buyer when an order is placed for a particular item with complimentary (cross-sell) or higher quality (up-sell) substitute items. For example, if a buyer elects to purchase a computer, the advertising capability could suggest a better computer than the one selected or complimentary accessories such as a modem or mouse pad. This requires a great deal of maintenance on the part of the marketplace administrator or the seller to develop and maintain item relationships.

## Content Management Capabilities

Content management capability involves the storage, management, and presentation of non-catalog content to the users of the Net marketplace. Types of content include documents, text, graphics, pictures, sound, and video. A Net marketplace might provide value to users by aggregating and furnishing access to industry-specific content and services sold in the marketplace.

**Document Management.** Document management allows the marketplace operator or users to create, aggregate, store, maintain, and present the content contained on the website screens. Each distinct piece of content is managed as an individual entity. Document management capability provides text-editing tools to create, aggregate, and maintain text to be presented on a webpage. Document management tools store all types of content in a database for ease of access, maintenance, and safety. This capability provides traditional document version control allowing multiple versions of a piece of content to exist, but ensuring the same piece of content is not maintained by two separate people at the same time and that versions of content are not overwritten or lost. Audit trails can be maintained to understand the maintenance history of a piece of content, to support editorial control and tracking, and to allow restoration to previous versions of content.

**Control and Approval.** Content management allows the organization managing the marketplace to perform document management across multiple individuals responsible for content management. The capability allows the organization to ensure accurate version control by permitting individuals to "check out" and own content—preventing anyone else in the organization from simultaneously accessing the content. The capability also allows content to be routed to specific individuals for approval of changes. For example, there may be a group of individuals who have to approve all content changes before they are actually presented on the site.

**Access and Distribution.** Content management allows the operator to define different mechanisms for accessing content and different methods of delivery. In addition to the traditional presentation of content on the site page, with this capability the operator can specify content to be downloaded on-demand by users (e.g., product brochures, MSDS, Certificates of Analysis). The capability can allow users to download content in multiple formats (e.g., HTML, MS Word documents,

Acrobat files) and ensure the download occurs in a secure environment. The operator may define content subscriptions, which allow users to sign up for a subscription that delivers specific content on a periodic basis. For example, the marketplace operator may create an industry newsletter, which the user can subscribe to and receive periodically by e-mail. The operator can define the number and types of subscriptions (e.g., MRO Purchasing Trends, Managing Hazardous Waste) and the delivery frequency.

Content management can also allow users of the marketplace to upload content to the marketplace. The marketplace operator might solicit content from the marketplace community to be stored on the site and presented to all users—allowing the operator to take advantage of multiple sources of industry- or marketplace-specific content. Before uploaded content is made accessible to others, it goes through document management, which scrubs the content and ensures it is appropriate to display on the site.

**Search.** Users of a marketplace site must be able to search and find specific or relevant content. Search capability includes the ability to search within the site (internal content) as well as other related or partner sites (external content). The following types of search mechanisms allow users different ways to find specific content:

- *Free-text search*. The ability to enter and search for word strings. Also, this search provides the ability to specify "and/or" for multiple words.
- *Fuzzy-text search*. The ability to search for words similar in spelling to the word entered but not necessarily including all characters in the search string.
- *Synonym search*. The ability to search for word synonyms.
- *Thesaurus search*. The ability to search for words of similar meaning.
- *Time constraints*. The ability to enter time constraints for a particular search (e.g., only search content as of a certain date).
- *Content types*. Ability to search multiple types of content sources including URLs, document titles, document bodies, graphics, Adobe files, Microsoft Office documents, HTML, etc.

**Personalization.** The personalization capability allows the marketplace operator to create relationships between specific content or groups of content and user demographics, interests, or activity, as well as present content by these relationships. For example, the marketplace user profile might capture information about the user's gender and address (demographics). The content management capability could allow the operator to indicate that a particular type of content is specific to male users living in Europe. When a male user from Europe selects a URL to take him to a specific page, the content management capability would know the user is a male from Europe and present the specific content as a displayed result. Users of a different gender or geography may see a different piece of content specific to their demographics. Similarly, the user profile may contain information about user interests to which content could be personalized. The more sophisticated sites personalize based on user activity. In this case, a relationship would be maintained between specific content and types of activity, such as buying specific products or downloading specific content. For example, if a user buys work tools at the marketplace, the capability could be utilized to maintain a relationship between this activity and a written article about maintaining tools, and then present this article to the user the next time he logs into the marketplace.

The capability provides the ability to store and analyze the relationship between content and user, creating an audit trail of content a user has seen. Personalization begins with a new user and becomes more intelligent with time and user activity. The content management tool could allow the operator to analyze customer preferences and content popularity to determine what content to keep, what to change, and when to change it.

The personalization capability utilizes the knowledge of a member to deliver personalized content and services, which creates a unique user experience designed to attract, engage, and retain users. The more specific the operator desires target-user demographics and granularity of content to be personalized, the more complex and time consuming it makes the activity of personalization.

**External Content.** The content management capability not only allows the marketplace operator to store, manage, and present content that resides locally with the marketplace site, but also allows the operator to identify, extract, and present information from external sources of content, such as other websites or even internal systems of marketplace participant companies. The operator must identify the specific external sources of content, the specific desired content from within each source, and the format of the content to be obtained. The content management capability can dynamically (e.g., upon user request) or on a periodic basis (e.g., nightly) reach out to the external source and retrieve the desired content. The capability can access multiple types of content including HTML (e.g., other websites), XML (e.g., content from a third-party service provider such as industry news), databases, flat files, or legacy applications (e.g., the ERP system of a distributor for shipping information). Content management provides for the initial loading of the external content and is intelligent enough to only incrementally update content that has changed since last downloaded.

In addition to the operator defining external sites and content to be utilized in the marketplace, users search the external sources for desired content. The operator registers the valid external sources of content with the search engine to inform the engine of their spheres of limitation. The user identifies the external sources to search, searches by the provided search types, and the search engine returns real-time results. Similar content from multiple external sources may display in different formats when retrieved. Once the external content has been obtained, the content management tool allows the operator to aggregate and translate the variously formatted content into the desired standard format to be stored in or presented at the marketplace site.

# Community Capabilities

Net marketplaces can facilitate user interaction in an effort to build relationships, develop contacts, develop networks of like-minded individuals, collaborate and build consensus on topics of interest, share knowledge, and educate and be educated in a virtual environment.

The community capability provides multiple mechanisms including discussion forums, online chat, and instant messaging. Traditional customer relationship management (CRM) capability utilized by the marketplace operator is a community building capability for the marketplace to manage customer relationships with buyer, sellers, and third-party service providers. The marketplace operator can use community capabilities to build business relationships between the marketplace operator and its customers or between the marketplace operator and its trading partners participating in the marketplace. Community interaction encourages users and members to return to the site. The community capabilities could also allow users to generate content for the site without commercial implications. For example, if a discussion forum about a topic generates responses with valuable insight, the marketplace operator could harvest this information, reformat it, and either post it in a knowledge base for any user to access or, in some cases, sell it to the marketplace users.

**Discussion Forums.** Discussion forums provide bulletin-board type capability allowing marketplace users to post and respond to messages about a particular common topic of discussion. Multiple discussion forums can exist as defined by the marketplace operator or, if desired by the operator, the user community can develop discussion forums itself. For example, the operator may create multiple forums for each industry or business function that participates in the marketplace (a forum or discussion for waste management, one for MRO purchasing, etc.). A discussion forum can be open to the general public or password-protected for selective involvement. The operator needs to determine the level of moderation the discussion forums require.

Discussion forums typically provide the following capabilities:

- *Subforums*—a forum related to a specific topic can have subforums on related select subtopics.
- *Threads*—once a user posts an original message, other users can create responses to the original message with multiple responses creating a "thread."
- *Search and sort*—the ability to search through and sort messages by author, date, thread, subject, and content.
- *Database and archive*—the ability to store forum messages for immediate and ongoing retrieval, and to manage database space requirements without losing the older content.
- *Messaging*—the ability for members to be informed by e-mail or other mechanisms when an activity has taken place specific to their message.
- *Administration*—the tools that allow the operator to create and manage the forums, such as managing passwords and moderating discussion by removing inappropriate messages.
- *Attachments*—the ability for files, graphics, and other types of information to be attached to a message for other members to access.

Traditional B2C discussion forum capability has B2B applications that can be utilized by Net marketplaces and their operators. For example, a Net marketplace could hire industry experts to create, moderate, and support specific discussion forums relevant to the marketplace and their individual industry expertise. A simple discussion forum could become an "ask the expert" capability in which the participating industry expert generates interest and participation among users, resulting in the attraction of new users and the retention of existing users for the marketplace. Another example would be to utilize the discussion forum capability as a means for participating companies and individuals to submit and respond to open job postings.

**Online Chat.** Online chat allows users to communicate in real time. Users congregate in peer groups and participate in online discussion specific to a certain topic of interest. The marketplace operator either has the ability to predefine public chat rooms or to allow the users to create private chat rooms dynamically, which allows selective congregation and discussion. The operator needs to determine which chat rooms require moderation.

Some of the specific capabilities provided by online chat include the following:

- *Administration*—gives the operator the ability to create, maintain, and delete chat rooms, specify public versus private, manage member access, and define moderation requirements.
- *Peer tracking*—provides the ability for members to recognize and track other members.
- *Archive*—provides the ability for a chat session to be saved for future reference.
- *Moderation*—allows the operator to moderate activity by filtering all messages through a user before posting to the general public.
- *Overflow*—allows the operator or users to dynamically take tangent discussions to a separate chat room.

Like discussion forums, this basic B2C capability can be utilized in a B2B environment to facilitate commerce. For example, a private chat room could be established and utilized by specific users to facilitate the negotiation of an RFP. The marketplace operator could create and operate a public chat room for user technical support. A CSR could chat with any interested member about how to use the site or how to order products.

## E-Mail and Instant Messaging.
Other mechanisms for facilitating marketplace community interaction include e-mail and instant messaging. The marketplace could issue e-mail IDs for all marketplace participants to provide a sense of participation. Similar to online chat, the marketplace could provide instant messaging to the users, which allows users to send real-time messages to other users logged into the marketplace.

## Customer Relationship Management (CRM).
A marketplace operator could utilize a traditional CRM application to provide customer support, sales, and marketing capability for the organization supporting the marketplace. The capability would provide a mechanism for marketplace users to acquire and manage support requests. Web-based CRM would provide the users with static help information that the users could search for answers to fundamental support questions. If answers are not found in the static help pages, the CRM capability might provide the user with case management capability, or the ability to create, maintain, and submit "cases" or questions to the customer support organization of the marketplace. The administrative tool of the CRM capability would allow the CSRs to receive, route, and resolve cases and communicate resolution to the user. Ideally, the Web-based CRM capability would be integrated with other support channels (e.g., cases submitted by call center, fax, or e-mail) so that the user can utilize the Web interface to manage and view all customer support cases they submit through any channel. The customer support capability of the marketplace is essential in building user confidence in the site, and the user interaction with the marketplace operator helps build a sense of marketplace community. The operator can manage relationships with all types of marketplace users including buyers, sellers, and third-party service providers.

**Community Building.** The challenge of developing a sense of marketplace community involves enticing the members to not only utilize the site for placing an order, but also build relationships with other users. Each marketplace operator must make business-development decisions regarding the best use of community capabilities, facilitation of community building, and enticement of members to interact. Community capability is most effective when there is participation from both novice members looking for insight and expert members who provide the insight. Little effort is necessary to entice novices to look to the marketplace site for insight because they are motivated to get their questions answered. The difficulty is enticing experts to provide insight without any return on their time or investment. To provide the expert insight and answers to novice questions, the operator will need to do one of the following: (1) provide the independent expert users commercial incentives, (2) hire experts, or (3) develop third-party business relationships with industry experts.

**Third-Party Service Providers.** Many times, Net marketplaces are established through custom development or implementation of commercial software to provide some subset of the commerce, content, and community capabilities. The first capabilities implemented are, in most cases, commerce-related and either fixed-price procurement (catalog management and order processing) or dynamic pricing (RFP or auction). The actual marketplace architecture may physically reside with the marketplace operator or may be outsourced to a third-party service provider or application service provider (ASP). Once some aspect of core capability is in place, the capability of the marketplace can be extended through integration with third-party service providers. The B2B marketplace has exploded with companies that provide Internet-based services to marketplace operators to facilitate B2B commerce, content, and community.

The integration of third-party services into the marketplace can be complex. These services can be integrated with a marketplace site without software implementation or custom development, but rather through simple HTTP integration. For example, a service could be utilized in which a simple HTTP request for a currency conversion rate could be passed from the marketplace to a third-party service provider that provides a simple HTTP integration with a real-time exchange rate. This would be invisible to the user. Other third-party service integration can be more complex. In some cases, the integration requires the user to physically go from the marketplace to the third-party service provider site to execute some function related to the task the user is performing. If the integration is in real time, the method of integration will typically still be HTTP; however, the third-party service provider may actually modify the look-and-feel of its site to match the marketplace, which makes the integration invisible to the user. In other cases, the integration with third-party service providers may not be real time and executed by the user, but instead performed offline in a batch process. In this case, the integration may be more traditional, using methods such as HTTP, EDI, e-mail, MQ Series, or some other messaging capability.

There are vast numbers and types of third-party services available to operators of marketplaces including, but not limited to, the following:

- *Content providers.* Like the B2C market, there are a number of content service providers who will provide text, sound, and graphics related to the specific theme of the marketplace. For example, if the marketplace is focused on direct ad spot purchasing of plastics, there are content providers who can provide content specific to plastics, such as news specific to the plastics industry, product specifications, technical support documents, material safety data sheets (MSDS), labeling information, and more. Content providers allow the operator of the marketplace to simplify or outsource the content management function of the marketplace by utilizing experts in content management specific to the particular industry or theme of the marketplace.

- *Community management.* The marketplace operator can utilize or even outsource third-party service providers who specialize in building community within the marketplace. These service providers can provide the experts to manage the expert forums, which provide the novice marketplace users with industry or technical insight. These service providers are paid and given incentives to increase the interaction in the user community.

- *Payment processing.* Among the original third-party service providers for B2C were the credit card processing vendors. The processing of credit cards for a B2B marketplace is only slightly different and more complicated, and many of the original B2C vendors now provide this service to B2B marketplaces. The primary difference is that corporate purchasing is not usually performed with personal credit cards, but instead with a company-issued credit card called a purchasing card, or p-card. The issuers and payment processes for p-cards involve a different group of service providers. A marketplace must be able to accept p-cards for payment.

  There are also service providers to which a marketplace operator can outsource the entire billing and invoicing process. If the marketplace is the merchant of record, which means that the suppliers invoice the marketplace and the marketplace invoices the buyers for all purchasing transactions, the marketplace requires an invoicing capability. The marketplace can integrate to a service provider who accepts order information, shipping and fulfillment information from the supplier, and receipt information from the buyer, and performs the two- or three-way match on this information to ensure that what was ordered is shipped and received. The service provider manages the exception processing and generates the appropriate invoices. Another Net marketplace payment-processing service offered by third-party providers is tax calculations.

- *Trade finance.* A wide variety of third-party service providers from the bricks-and-mortar financial market also facilitate the financial aspects of a marketplace. Some of the services these companies provide include credit checks and approval, credit limits and trade finance, and escrow and settlement.

  Dun & Bradstreet provides a service for electronic integration in which the marketplace can perform a credit validation of the D&B rating for a company registering to buy or sell in the marketplace. Other providers perform a similar service to integrate with financial-service institutions, such as banks and insurance companies, for high volumes of credit-check information.

  Many credit-check service providers also provide integration with functions to establish a buyer's credit limit with banks and the follow-up steps needed to completely finance transactions—marketplaces that facilitate small-volume, high-value transactions typically require this type of capability. For example, a marketplace of manufacturing equipment that costs hundreds of thousands of dollars would provide this service to assist its buying organizations in establishing credit limits and facilitating finance transactions with a bank. In some cases, the marketplace may establish a credit limit with the bank and finance the transaction itself. This aids the marketplace operator in determining the risks of each transaction and whether it is best to provide financing or allow a third-party bank to do so.

Some service providers exist to facilitate transaction settlement. Buying organizations can deposit funds into an interest-bearing escrow account established with a third-party service provider from which large transaction payments are settled. Alternatively, the service provider can manage the settlement or transfer of funds from the buyer bank to either the marketplace or supplier bank through an electronic funds transfer (EFT) mechanism.

- *Logistics.* There are a number of third-party service providers focused on providing Internet-enabled logistics services. In some cases these companies are the actual third-party logistics providers that own and provide or contract with other companies for truck, rail, and ocean freight services. There are also new B2B companies that have created an exchange where all traditional third-party logistics providers have integrated to form a logistics marketplace. In either case, a marketplace can integrate with these service providers to procure logistics to support a transaction. When integrating with a logistics marketplace, logistics can actually be dynamically sourced using a RFP or auction mechanism to lower costs. Once logistics have been procured, the third-party logistics providers pass shipping status information in real time to inform marketplace buyers the status and location of their shipment.

- *Other third-party services.* Many B2B third-party services and providers exist in the market today. Other significant services that exist include the following:

  - *Inspection*—Depending on the particular industry or vertical, primarily in the perishable-goods industries, service providers exist to inspect and validate quality of material before it is shipped to the buying organization.

  - *Import and export*—Service providers exist to facilitate the import and export of goods. This includes the ability to complete customs documentation and submit it through integration with the appropriate government agencies. These companies also facilitate the calculation of tariffs.

# Challenges

Creation of a Net marketplace presents substantial challenges, as demonstrated by the current state of the B2B market in early 2001. Early marketplace adopters severely underestimated difficulties—but these challenges tended to be business related and not technical. The technology available is still relatively immature, but sufficient to get a Net marketplace established with a manageable number of buying and selling organizations participating and supporting substantial numbers of transactions. This has been proven by a few marketplace success stories. The business challenges need to be addressed through the enlightenment and education of marketplace operators and companies investing in the marketplaces. Some larger business challenges for Net marketplaces are described in the following section.

**Catalog Content Management.** As described previously in both the buy-side e-procurement discussion and the Net marketplace catalog content management section, acquiring and managing catalog content is one of the primary challenges for a Net marketplace operator. The same catalog management challenges that exist for buy-side e-procurement also exist for Net marketplaces. However, if a Net marketplace is utilized, the catalog management challenge transfers from the buying organization to the operator of the marketplace—providing a value-added service to buying organizations. The challenges of catalog management for the marketplace operator include the following:

- Internal storage versus external access to catalog content
- External content—quality, search, and normalization
- Taxonomy definition and maintenance
- Mapping to taxonomy
- Supplier updates

As described earlier, the fundamental catalog management decision a marketplace operator must make is the source of catalog content—from suppliers, manufacturers, or third-party catalog content service providers. Once the source of the content is identified, the marketplace operator must decide the residing location of the content. The content could reside within the physical architecture of the marketplace or could reside externally with the supplier, manufacturer, or third-party service provider. The catalog management required by the marketplace will depend on these fundamental decisions. These decisions are critical to marketplace operations and affect site usability as well as the level and effort of support.

Reliance on external content simplifies the catalog management effort. If a supplier or manufacturer already has an electronic catalog that can be accessed from the marketplace, the operator does not need to manage this catalog information internally. Similarly, there are third-party service providers that can facilitate content to either be loaded into the marketplace or accessed through punch out from the marketplace—then the catalog management effort is minimized. However, outsourcing catalog content has limitations—from the catalog of the marketplace, content cannot be normalized across external sources. Typically, the search mechanism of the marketplace is limited to searching one external source at a time and is unable to search across multiple external sources with a single query. This has usability implications for the user. For example, if a buyer looks for a hammer, she will have to search each external source of content for the hammer instead of being presented with one, aggregated catalog search result. Also, when a Net marketplace operator relies on the supplier or manufacturer for catalog content, she lacks control over the quality of the data and information.

If the marketplace operator decides to have catalog content physically reside within the marketplace, a number of issues need to be addressed. First, if the operator determines that catalog content will be presented in a normalized manner, there is significant effort associated with taxonomy definition and maintenance because the operator must define the ontology or taxonomy. Standard taxonomies exist for certain industries, which can be bought and utilized by the operator to minimize this effort. If not, the operator needs to have the knowledge and staff to define and maintain the taxonomy specific to products and services sold in the marketplace. This requires a specialized skill that many marketplace operators do not have.

Second, once the taxonomy is defined, significant effort and specialized skills are required to take each supplier or manufacturer catalog provided and map its content to the taxonomy. For example, if the marketplace defines a hammer in the taxonomy as "maintenance—tools—hammer," and the first supplier defines a hammer as "ball point hammer," and the second supplier defines a hammer as "mallet," the operator needs to map the two different catalog entries to its taxonomy. Unless there is a common reference point in the information, this process is manual. Intelligent tools exist to support this process, but for nearly 40 percent of the items in a supplier catalog this process is manual. This mapping needs to take place for every product or service in each supplier catalog. Unfortunately, this is an ongoing process and needs to be updated every time a supplier catalog is changed.

**Internationalization.** A significant challenge for Net marketplace operators is to create capabilities that users anywhere in the world can use to facilitate commerce transactions across geographical boundaries—the ultimate goal of any marketplace is to facilitate global commerce. As such, the marketplace must support multiple languages and currencies.

The content management capability of the marketplace must be able to provide textual content in multiple languages. The content management capability should allow the operator to translate and deliver content in multiple languages based on user preference. The early reaction to the multilanguage requirement was to create a whole separate version of the marketplace website, translate it into the appropriate language, and allow the user to select his desired language upon accessing the marketplace URL. This concept is called *localization,* and is utilized when a site's architecture was not initially built with multilanguage in mind. A marketplace site with the multilanguage requirement built into the architecture allows the user organization or individual to specify a language preference; then the site recognizes the user through login or client site certificate, and dynamically presents the site in the preferred language.

The technical approach to addressing the multilanguage requirement is only part of the issue. Regardless of which technical approach is utilized, a substantial effort is also required to translate all aspects of the site into each language to be supported. For every language supported, every piece of text on every screen has to be translated and stored in the database with an appropriate language identifier.

Despite the marketplace site being localized for multiple languages, the marketplace site is not or, typically, cannot be responsible for the information the user enters. If the user specifies German as his language preference, the site will be presented in German. But should the user then make entries in English, the site cannot detect the entered English, nor translate the information into English without significant effort or intelligence. This type of capability is not widely available in B2B sites and software today.

Similar to the language detection issue, multiple currencies must be supported by the marketplace architecture. Wherever currency is utilized, the architecture must support the ability to store the type and amount of currency. This is the easy part. The difficulty comes when one currency needs to be converted into another currency. Currency exchange rates can be stored and managed in the marketplace, but a difficulty arises because exchange rates are continuously changing. Most marketplaces rely on integration to a third-party service provider to receive real-time exchange rates, and the user can use these rates to request a conversion of an amount from one currency to another, anywhere in the business process. The challenge comes with determining the exchange rate at various points of time during the transaction process—at bid, transaction awarding, and settlement.

For example, a seller initiates an auction for an item in U.S. dollars, the marketplace allows interested buyers to bid in any currency, and a buyer places a bid in German marks. At the time of the bid, given the exchange rate, the bid was worth so many U.S. dollars, but the exchange rate continues to fluctuate during bidding. A business rule must be established for the exchange rate to fluctuate or be locked during bid time. If the exchange rate changes with time, does the bid amount change? To simplify the process, most international commerce sites provide the calculation as only indicative information, but any activity associated with a transaction is executed in the initiating currency. The challenge for the Net marketplace operator is to implement a marketplace architecture that supports these dynamic and varied business processes.

## Business Model.

Possibly the greatest challenge to the marketplace operator is to find a business model that provides enough value to trading partners to justify the effort and cost of participation. Net marketplaces have experimented with transaction fees, subscription fees, advertising fees, and many other methods of charging for their service. Part of the challenge is to determine to whom the fees should be charged and for what activities. Either buyer or seller or both could be charged a fee—but most importantly, the operator must understand the dynamics of the market and must craft a business model that entices trading partners to want to participate.

The following is a list of services for which Net marketplaces have charged: participation, advertising, lead generation, transaction, fiduciary services, content and subscriptions, marketplace analysis and intelligence, licensing and hosting, and value-added services.

The most commonly utilized marketplace charge is the participation fee, which usually includes a flat fee to permit participation in the marketplace for a designated period of time. This type of fee requires users to understand and appreciate the value of participation before even being allowed in. For some, understanding only comes with time, and this fee does not help to entice participation.

Early B2B marketplaces utilized banner advertising with little success in revenue generation. B2B marketplace users were not interested in unsolicited banner ads for products or services irrelevant to their reason for participating in the marketplace. Some operators found the screen real estate more valuable for functions other than banners. If banners were utilized, operators found greater success in using the banners to advertise the marketplace itself or by selling banners to participating suppliers to advertise product promotions tied to user-buying activity.

Fees are often charged for value-added activities, which help suppliers and third-party service providers of the marketplace sell their products and services. Fees can be charged for a storefront or site page for the supplier to advertise and sell. Also, lead generation based on analysis of user demographics, interests, and site activity can be sold and provided to suppliers.

Another type of charge is the transaction fee. The challenge to charging transaction fees is determining whether or not the buyer or seller holds enough value in marketplace participation to be charged these fees. The other challenge is to determine how much to charge and for what activities. The most common transaction fee is levied as a flat percentage of each purchase order. However, this percentage may translate to an amount greater than the participant wants to pay for large-dollar transactions. Another challenge with levying the purchase-order fee is the fact that there is no charge for other types of transactions such as auctions, RFPs, change orders, invoicing, and exception processing.

Many marketplace operators experiment with making money on the fiduciary aspects of managing the marketplace. If the marketplace is the merchant of record, some operators expect payment from the buyer within a certain term and negotiate to pay the supplier in a greater term. The operator of the marketplace makes money on the interest on the balance for the difference between terms.

Marketplace participants may be willing to pay for specific types of content provided by the marketplace. More specialized content or subscriptions could be provided at a fee, instead of being available to any marketplace user. Many marketplace participants are also willing to pay for marketplace analysis and intelligence. As a marketplace becomes liquid with buyers and sellers, the operator is in a unique position to analyze and anticipate market activity. This information is valuable to marketplace participants. The operator needs to ensure the anonymity of information sold.

Marketplaces have begun to license their software or infrastructure to other marketplace operators. Some operators package their technology and sell it as software (e.g., VerticalNet). Marketplaces can provide private brands for new marketplaces or sub-marketplaces for buyer or supplier groups (consortiums) for private use within existing architecture and infrastructure of an original marketplace (e.g., Commerce One).

Marketplaces typically charge additional fees for the value-added services available to the marketplace user. The marketplace operator needs to negotiate and manage these additional fees for users to ensure the total fee per transaction or use does not exceed the value of participating in the marketplace.

**Adoption and Liquidity.** The final indicator of marketplace success is the ability of a Net marketplace to attract buyers and sellers. The Holy Grail is to attain marketplace liquidity—which means the Net marketplace is the sole source of trade for a particular category of goods or services, and buyers and sellers do not or cannot look elsewhere for sourcing alternatives. Very few marketplaces in the world ever achieve this status. EBay, a B2C marketplace for the sale and purchase of collectible goods, is the best marketplace example of high liquidity—few other marketplaces have achieved the volume and user base.

Unfortunately, the "build it and they will come" mantra does not work for B2B marketplaces. Buyers and sellers seek economic incentive for participating in a marketplace. However, even with the proper economic incentives, the process of convincing an organization to participate is long and expensive. The greatest challenge for the new Net marketplace operator is to assemble the first group of strategic buyers and sellers into the marketplace and to execute the first set of commerce transactions. Early buyers and suppliers must provide the greatest impact in the marketplace—such as buyers or sellers with great leverage over their supply chains. Many early marketplaces took a buyer-centric approach and partnered with the large and powerful buyers. Once influential buyers became participants, their participation was leveraged to entice the current smaller suppliers of the buyer to participate. This method has shown only modest success because most suppliers are not willing participants, and they are always looking for sourcing alternatives to the marketplace. Marketplace operators have also experimented with a number of methods for enticing early participation including equity participation.

Once a buying or selling organization has joined a Net marketplace, the subsequent challenge is to ensure that individual employees of the organization adopt and utilize the marketplace for buying activities. This can be a challenge equal to enticing the organization to initially participate.

# SUMMARY

### 1. What are the four stages to the evolution of B2B capabilities?

A business will typically go through a basic evolution of Web-based business application capability, which, if successful, will ultimately result in the greatest capability—collaboration. The evolution of B2B capability involves the following four stages: broadcast, interact, transact, and collaborate. A business does not necessarily need to start the broadcast stage before moving to later stages. Aggressive businesses implement some aspects and all four stages simultaneously from the beginning of their e-commerce implementation efforts.

## 2. What are three categories of B2B?

In their brief history, B2Bs have clustered around three broad categories of activities: sell-side solutions activities, indirect e-procurement activities, or Net marketplace and Net exchange activities. Because B2C gained momentum before B2B, early adopters of B2B focused on B2C best practices, such as online searchable catalogs and shopping cart functions. Once Web-based sell-side applications were implemented and businesses began using the Internet to sell merchandise to customers, businesses quickly realized they could Web-enable their buy-side or procurement process by implementing Web-based e-procurement capabilities for nonstrategic products or indirect e-procurement. With buy-side and sell-side capabilities implemented, businesses interacted with their trading partners directly, using the Internet to facilitate commerce transactions. Net marketplaces and Net exchanges were created to further provide Web-based capabilities, which facilitated the interaction and exchange of commerce transactions among a broad group of buyers, sellers, and other trading partners.

## 3. Describe the four major steps of the B2B sell-side evolution.

The early B2B sell-side capability gave businesses the ability to send relatively static information in one direction to its customers. Then information flowed both ways—organizations and their customers used the Internet to interact through e-mail messages, and, later, through elaborate, commercial Web-based applications for customer relationship management (CRM), which also provided content management, case administration, workflow management, and, still later, integration with back-office ERP systems. Next, the ability to transact arrived, and B2Bs were able to take, manage, and support commerce transactions with customers using the Internet. And, finally, the ability to collaborate was provided by Web-based applications for inter-enterprise activities between an organization and its trading partners.

## 4. Describe the major challenges to implementing systems for indirect e-procurement.

Business challenges of e-procurement include strategic sourcing as well as adoption and compliance, while technical challenges include catalog content management, supplier integration, and back-office systems integration.

To determine strategic sources, an organization must gather and analyze spend data, rationalize suppliers by reevaluating current supplier contracts, determine which suppliers provide the greatest value for each specific category of spend, and create leverage for contract negotiation.

To ensure adoption and compliance, an organization must require purchasing agents and employees to submit requisitions using the new application. Also, the organization should disable the old purchasing system and provide role clarity, as well as employee training, for those who will make desktop requisitions and approvals with the new e-procurement system.

Catalog content management is a time-consuming effort, requiring new and specific skills and an ongoing effort for new products and suppliers. The buying organization is responsible for acquiring and loading the catalog information in the e-procurement system as well as determining the catalog content presentation to the individual buyer, which typically requires transforming catalog content into some other appropriate format before it is loaded into the application.

Supplier integration may become daunting when the buying organization must integrate with each supplier's business process for business-document exchange. A method of messaging, as well as the format of data exchange, must be determined—this process must be repeated for each new supplier relationship and each business document.

Difficulty with back-office integration depends on the complexity of the existing back-office systems environment of the buying organization. Different systems may reside on and utilize different technical platforms, while being managed by different organizational groups—all of which add to the complexity of interface design and implementation.

### 5. Describe the major challenges with implementing systems for Net marketplaces or Net exchanges.

Large business challenges for Net marketplaces are catalog content management, internationalization, business models, adoption, and liquidity.

The catalog management challenges that exist for buy-side e-procurement also exist for Net marketplaces. However, when a Net marketplace is utilized, the catalog management challenge transfers from the buying organization to the operator of the marketplace. The marketplace operator must determine and implement the most effective solutions to the following areas of concern: internal storage versus external access to catalog content, external content (quality, search, and normalization), taxonomy definition and maintenance, mapping to taxonomy, and supplier updates.

Another significant challenge for the Net marketplace operator is to create capabilities that users anywhere in the world can use to facilitate commerce transactions across geographical boundaries. The capability of the marketplace must support multiple languages and currencies.

Possibly the greatest challenge to the marketplace operator is to find a business model that provides enough value to trading partners to justify the effort and cost of participation. Net marketplaces have experimented with transaction fees, subscription fees, advertising fees, and many other methods of charging for their services. Part of the challenge is to determine to whom the fees should be charged and for what activities. Either buyer or seller or both could be charged a fee—but most importantly, the operator must understand the dynamics of the market and craft a business model that entices trading partners to want to participate.

Once a buying or selling organization has joined a Net marketplace, the subsequent challenge is to ensure individual employees adopt and utilize the marketplace for buying activities.

The final indicator of marketplace success is the ability of a Net marketplace to attract buyers and sellers. The Holy Grail is to attain marketplace liquidity—which means the Net marketplace is the sole source of trade for a particular category of goods or services, and buyers and sellers do not or cannot look elsewhere for sourcing alternatives. Unfortunately, very few marketplaces in the world ever achieve this status.

# KEY TERMS

Enterprise Resource Planning
   (ERP)

broadcast

interact

transact

collaborate

indirect e-procurement

catalog management

Net marketplaces

Net exchanges

content management

normalization

Electronic Data Interchange
   (EDI)

catalog taxonomy

Extensible Markup Language
   (XML)

# Collaborative Commerce

In the next three to five years, collaborative commerce, or "c-commerce," will be as broadly conceived and defined as e-commerce was in the past five. It has the potential to enjoy the same notoriety, mystery, and speculation that e-commerce did in its early days. Its roots are, however, more grounded because its proponents are bricks-and-mortar companies rather than dot-coms. While e-commerce has had some teething problems, there is little doubt that the Internet as a medium for collaboration is here to stay.

## QUESTIONS

*Please consider the following questions as you read this chapter:*

1. What is collaborative commerce?

2. What is buy-side collaboration?

3. What is sell-side collaboration?

4. What is collaboration with competitors?

5. What are collaborative service chains?

---

This chapter was written by Breakaway Solutions.

# WHAT IS COLLABORATIVE COMMERCE?

**Collaborative Supply Chains.** Collaborative supply chains are intracompany and intercompany collaborations that span all core functions of manufacturing organizations. Some of these collaborative supply-chain functions include collaborative design, planning, inventory management, and bundling of multivendor products and services.

**Collaborative Communities.** Community collaboration makes B2C and B2B sites stickier. The collaboration allows community participants to provide the "human glue" to discover and trust each other and thus make transactions. This collaboration includes online community solutions, groupware/workflow, knowledge management, and project management solutions that allow community members to share information and coordinate tasks.

**Collaborative Service Chains.** Collaborative service chains refer to collaboration up and down the service chain for companies in industries such as professional services, insurance, and finance executed in order to manage communication with their distribution channels and subscriber base. Collaborative service-chain functions include document management and workflow, collaborative proposal management, contract management, project management, extended enterprise personnel management, and subscriber base management.

C-commerce is actually all of the above—and therein lies the problem and the opportunity. As the authors of *The Cluetrain Manifesto: The End of Business As Usual* wrote: "Markets are conversations." The Internet is here to enable these conversations and to redefine the existing boundaries and information flow between companies, suppliers, distributors, and customers.

This chapter introduces the collaborative communities where c-commerce was born. However, it primarily focuses on collaborative supply chains as they apply to manufacturing companies and the collaboration between a company and its supply-chain partners, which include suppliers, contract manufacturers, distributors, and end customers. Finally, the chapter introduces collaborative service chains and advanced collaboration to complete the landscape of what lies ahead for c-commerce over the next three to five years.

# CASE STUDY: COMPUTER CORPORATION OF AMERICA— A BRIEF HISTORY IN INTERNET TIME

In order to best demonstrate the opportunities and limitations associated with collaborative commerce, we will take you through a case study of a fictitious company—Computer Corporation of America ("Computer Corp.")—throughout the rest of this chapter.

In 1995, Computer Corp. started out as a reseller of used computers, with a simple static website and a toll-free telephone number to take orders. Encouraged by its early success, Computer Corp. decided to implement a B2C site so that it could take orders electronically. By 1996, it had implemented a robust B2C site that was hosted at Exodus. It was still selling used computers, but it had also started selling new and refurbished computers as a distributor for Compaq. In 1996, Computer Corp.'s revenues exceeded $10 million. With encouragement from Compaq, it decided to focus its growth on business customers. By 1997, Computer Corp. was selling directly to businesses, not just consumers, over the Internet. In 1997, Computer Corp.'s revenues rose to $50 million.

In 1998, Computer Corp. raised significant financing and decided to step up and become a serious computer manufacturer competing directly with Dell, Compaq, and others. Over the next two years (1999–2000), it used the Internet to integrate suppliers, distributors, retailers, and large-business customers into a seamless web, creating a company that was an Internet e-commerce powerhouse as much as it was a leading computer manufacturer.

By early 2001, Computer Corp.'s Internet systems were the best in the industry, which allowed it to explore options such as outsourcing a significant portion of its design and manufacturing functions for new product introductions (NPI) while still maintaining control of the process. In February 2001, Computer Corp. released new high-end servers in a record cycle time that was 40 percent faster than its nearest competitor. This milestone confirmed that it was well on its way to transforming its business from a computer manufacturer into a company focused on the management and coordination of outsourced supply-chain information.

Computer Corp. is now in the process of completing this transition. It is unbundling core organization functions and outsourcing design, manufacturing, and distribution capabilities, which will make it a company focused on brand and information management. Throughout the chapter we will use Computer Corp. as an example of the "model collaborative e-business" to explain and explore the present and future of c-commerce.

## Online Communities

Community is one of the 7Cs of the Internet—context, content, community, customization, communication, connection, and commerce. While the "C" for "community" has begun to be replaced by the "C" for "collaboration," community is where Internet c-commerce was born. Internet newsgroups, one of the oldest forms of an online community, and VerticalNet, one of the early B2B companies, are all two examples.

Community solutions provide synchronous and asynchronous collaborative solutions. These solutions can be used to enable group, project, and user-to-user collaboration. They leverage community knowledge and interests to empower members, and the process increases member loyalty and stickiness on both B2C and B2B sites. Computer Corp. used a number of community solutions for collaboration: bulletin boards, chat, calendaring/scheduling/file sharing, and collaborative presentations.

### Bulletin Boards.
Computer Corp. provided a bulletin board application with threaded discussions as well as integrated search and e-mail alerts. These were designed to fulfill knowledge sharing and customer interaction needs. Computer Corp. created online communities for design where its engineers and suppliers could share information as members of one extended enterprise. This further allowed Computer Corp. to provide a forum to explore design ideas and to gather information to determine whether or not to outsource the design or manufacturing of certain subassemblies.

### Chat.
Computer Corp. provided a chat room application that allowed live user-to-user and customer service interaction. It used chat in addition to e-mail to provide customer service interaction, to respond to questions related to FAQs, and to share pricing for key business customers.

**Calendaring/Scheduling/File Sharing.** Computer Corp. provided a calendar application that allowed user-group collaboration, task scheduling (e.g., order fulfillment), and group or personal organization capabilities. Computer Corp. used calendaring and scheduling extensively for NPI, where it works with its contract manufacturers to coordinate design, prototype releases, and new product pilot runs in the early stage of a new product's life cycle.

**Collaborative Presentations.** Computer Corp. provided a Web-based application that allowed users to collaboratively create and review slide show-type presentations, eliminating the need for client-side presentation applications. It used these presentations to work on new product introductions for distributors and marketing strategies, among other things.

One of the key benefits that Computer Corp. saw from the use of community solutions was a 6 percent decrease in NPI cycle time due to interaction of the extended enterprise design community. It also saw a 9 percent increase in online transactions from distributors as increased trust from community interaction resulted in more transactions.

# A BRIEF HISTORY OF COLLABORATIVE SUPPLY CHAINS

The current collaborative supply chain grew out of the manufacturing resource planning (MRP) in the 1960s and 1970s. MRP was focused on tracking and reconciling transactions within a business to manage the manufacturing and distribution activities. These were early attempts to use technology for collaboration within a company to deliver "the right product, at the right place, at the right time, and at the right cost."

One can divide the functions of a manufacturing organization into the following categories: planning, execution, and control. MRP was focused on the execution functions, such as production planning and master scheduling systems.

Enterprise resource planning (ERP) was born to address industry needs for a better set of transaction systems to manage the physical movement and accounting of goods. Despite the "P" in MRP and ERP, each had little to do with planning. ERP was primarily focused on the execution and control associated with the physical movements of goods—but not on planning. The ERP transaction set was later expanded to include financial control via accounts receivable (AR) and accounts payable (AP) functions.

Supply-chain management (SCM) was the next wave to follow ERP. Technically, SCM predated ERP. The terms *supply* and *logistics* became prevalent during World War II and encompassed the planning process and physical movement, or logistics required to get supply to the front lines and intermediate points in enemy territory. As originally defined, SCM focused on the flow of information and products between trading partners. Unlike ERP, SCM did not focus inward but on processes between trading partners. A core SCM function—APS (advanced planning and scheduling)—had to do with collaborative demand and supply planning with trading partners. While ERP primarily focused on the efficiencies of asset utilization in a large organization based on a premise that large organizations needed a single view of their business, SCM focused on the effectiveness of asset utilization, with a greater emphasis on planning and collaborating with suppliers and customers in the supply chain.

Finally, collaborative supply chains became the new hot category. Collaborative supply chains define the confluence of e-commerce, supply chain, and CRM/SRM (customer relationship management and supplier relationship management). The concept is about changing organizational behavior, about information sharing, and about promoting "co-opetition" over competition. Collaborative supply chains allow large organizations to be more nimble by externalizing information and processes from SCM and ERP systems to enable collaboration with trading partners. They also allow smaller suppliers to bundle their product and services and compete with large suppliers.

# WHAT ARE THE VARIOUS TYPES OF SUPPLY CHAINS?

Before we can explore the collaborative supply chain, it is important to explain the different types of supply chains that exist.

## Discrete and Repetitive Manufacturing Supply Chain

*Discrete manufacturing* is defined as the making of products such as motor vehicles and computers through the assembly of discrete parts. In contrast, *process manufacturing* is the making of products such as chemicals or foods from a mix of ingredients. Discrete manufacturing supply chains focus on engineer-to-order products (e.g., engineering equipment, heavy-construction equipment, oil rigs) on one end of the spectrum. Repetitive production of products (e.g., phones, computers, clothing) over longer time periods is on the other end of the spectrum.

## Process Manufacturing Supply Chain

The primary characteristic that sets apart process industries from other industries is the fact that they are asset intensive. Process manufacturing plants are large and costly. Also, due to the continuous nature of most processes, product changeovers in process manufacturing plants are more complex and less frequent than changeovers in discrete manufacturing facilities.

## Service Chain

While the term *supply chain* is reserved for manufacturing industries, **service chain** is applicable to industries such as professional services, insurance, and finance. Since there is no physical movement of goods involved, service chains are more focused on the delivery of "information value." The challenge to managing the service chain includes productizing services, managing distribution channels (e.g., Hancock managing insurance brokers and representatives) to consistently represent an organization's services, and managing the subscriber base proactively for cross-sell or retention-centric opportunities.

## The Value Chain

The original definition of **supply chain** focused on the flow of information and products between trading partners. More recently, the terms *supply chain* and *demand chain* are frequently used. The **demand chain** is focused on the activities (e.g., plan, execute, control) related to an organization's customers, channels, markets, and other external factors. The supply chain, on the other hand, is focused on the activities related to meeting needs based on a combination of an organization's capacity and its suppliers' capacities. Together, the supply chain and demand chain form the **value chain**—the series of synchronized value-added steps from raw materials to end product.

The collaborative supply chain as discussed in this chapter is focused on collaboration across a manufacturer's entire value chain (i.e., between a manufacturer and its suppliers, its partners, its channels, and its customers).

# LEVELS OF SUPPLY-CHAIN COLLABORATION

In the e-business world, the organization that can make informed decisions faster than its competitors will leave its competitors at the starting gate. In the information age that we live in, competitive advantage is achieved by making consistently good decisions quickly.

It is often necessary to involve the various stakeholders, both within and outside a company, in operational decisions. Collaboration ensures that multiple perspectives are considered simultaneously. Collaborative decision-making provides concrete savings across the board.

- Collaboration provides a contribution of up to 40 percent to the improvement of the supply chain.
- Collaborative scheduling alone provides up to 15 percent reduction in inventory.
- Forecast accuracy is increased by as much as 15 percent.
- Expediting is reduced by 20 percent to 30 percent.
- Transport costs are reduced by 3 percent to 5 percent.

Collaboration increases the sense of ownership for process changes, transfers key business knowledge from one business function to another, focuses the internal organization on external goals, and decreases lost information as it is passed from department to department by as much as 30 percent.

## Barriers to Collaboration

Fundamental issues must be resolved before an organization can be profitable with the collaborative paradigm.

### Integrating Organizational Product Objectives. Because different organizations have different goals, they view data at many different levels of aggregation. For example, the sales organization may prefer to look at data from a regional and customer point of view. On the other hand, manufacturing may be primarily interested in product families and production assets. To foster collaboration, there must be an agreed-upon mechanism for translating the inputs from one organization's view to another's. To put it simply, there must be a way of translating a product's change in demand to its capacity, even if the product can be made on different machines at different rates.

### Metrics That Are Not Internally Consistent. Different internal organizations have different goals because they are judged differently. Metrics focused on internal performance, such as measures of utility or yield, are quite often in conflict with an organization's overall objectives.

**Constantly Changing Data.** Contrary to popular opinion, the most up-to-date data may not be the best for making decisions. A *consistent* set of data is more important for planning than the most up-to-date data available.

The easiest way to reduce exceptions is to properly define information within an organization and between organizations and then make it available online to all interested parties.

## The Collaboration Pyramid

Collaboration is neither an event nor a goal. Collaboration is a process that is executed at different levels of effectiveness and can be illustrated with the **collaboration pyramid** (see Exhibit 11-1). In a typical organization, collaboration evolves from information gathering to consultative decision-making. At the simplest level, collaboration may start with an organized and periodic exchange of information on shutdowns and planned product promotions. Over time, the process evolves to structured sales and operations planning (S&OP) in which the S&OP process becomes the default process for resolving all operational issues.

Collaboration cannot be achieved through better systems alone or through organizational decrees. However, it can be facilitated through effective systems and modeling. To reconcile conflicting perspectives, businesses have found it effective to evaluate alternatives within a common framework. Quantitative models of a business can provide an effective mechanism for conflict resolution. The basic supply-chain model represents in an integrated manner the capacity, inventory, bills of material, routes, demand and demand prioritization, and transport resources. With

**Exhibit 11-1**

THE COLLABORATION PYRAMID

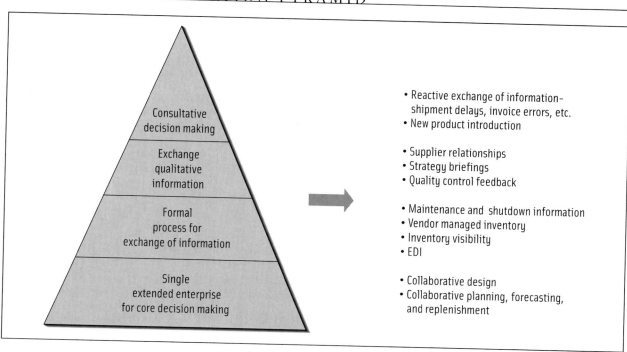

- Reactive exchange of information—shipment delays, invoice errors, etc.
- New product introduction

- Supplier relationships
- Strategy briefings
- Quality control feedback

- Maintenance and shutdown information
- Vendor managed inventory
- Inventory visibility
- EDI

- Collaborative design
- Collaborative planning, forecasting, and replenishment

Consultative decision making

Exchange qualitative information

Formal process for exchange of information

Single extended enterprise for core decision making

such a model, the business can look at the effect of parameter changes on capacity, revenue, production and distribution costs, and internal metrics.

Collaboration with customers and suppliers also typically evolves over time. Initially, information may be shared through regular e-mail or through EDI transactions. As confidence grows, the entire process may reach a stage where the customer and supplier supply chains meld into an extended enterprise that is planned and executed within one chain.

# CASE STUDY: COMPUTER CORPORATION OF AMERICA

## Core Functions

As in most traditional manufacturing organizations, the core functions in Computer Corp.'s value chain include designing, planning, sourcing, marketing and selling, manufacturing, fulfilling, and servicing (see Exhibit 11-2).

**Design Function.** The design function includes product conception and design for new product introductions (NPIs) for make-to-stock (MTS) products. Make-to-stock products constitute 75 percent of Computer Corp.'s products and would compete head-to-head with Dell and Compaq. In addition, it would design and manufacture **make-to-order (MTO)** products based on orders from key business customers. Twenty-five percent of Computer Corp.'s products were MTO and were focused on expensive servers.

The engineering bill of materials (BOM) for the products were handed over to the planning function to determine the procurement quantities (product mix) of the components required in manufacturing make-to-stock and make-to-order computers.

**Exhibit 11-2** CORE FUNCTIONS OF THE COMPUTER CORP.

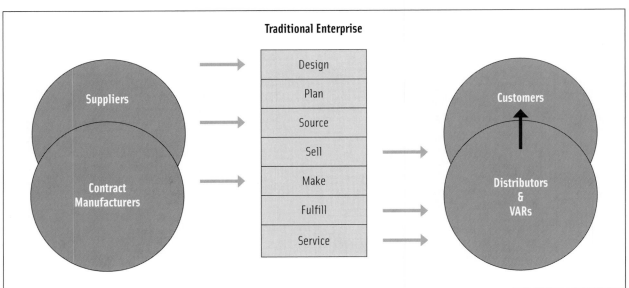

## Planning Function.
Planning is an iterative process that needs to be continuously modified based on demand and supply events.

The core planning for a NPI starts with master planners creating high-level plans to determine product mix and quantities based on high-level demand forecasts, manufacturing capacity constraints, and historical information. For example, for every 10 PCs, 10 Intel CPUs are required, but only every 2 PCs need a DVD player. Commodity and noncommodity requirements for NPI and engineer-to-order products are then handed off to the procurement division to source the products from suppliers.

Supply planning identifies where to make or buy products based on profit maximization and cost minimization. Supply planning comprises functions, such as ATP (available-to-promise) and CTP (capable-to-promise) functions, in which suppliers provide varying levels of commitment to fulfill orders. It includes the ability to evaluate stock storage and transportation constraints to optimize a supply plan. It also includes replenishment planning based on inventory and service levels that need to be maintained and on current orders and commitments.

## Sourcing Function.
Sourcing was responsible for identifying and selecting suppliers and negotiating and establishing purchase contracts with suppliers. Sourcing was also in charge of tracking purchases against contracts and monitoring supplier performance against service level agreements (SLAs) specified in contracts.

The sourcing department at Computer Corp. was composed of commodity managers and noncommodity managers. Commodity managers were specialists focused on procuring a commodity like "memory" at the lowest price and highest quality to meet Computer Corp.'s manufacturing requirements.

Noncommodity managers worked with contract manufacturers to manufacture noncommodity SKUs to entire subassemblies required by Computer Corp.

## Marketing and Sales Function.
Marketing and sales were responsible for marketing and demand creation for existing and new products. Sales managers managed the RFP/RFQ process and established long-term sales contracts with distributors and big business customers.

Marketing and sales worked together to determine the most efficient sales channels. They were responsible for the entire demand planning, forecasting, and execution process for each sales channel to maximize Computer Corp.'s sales. Forecasting and demand planning is based on "demand pull" versus the "supply push" environment. Demand planning reconciles high-level business forecasts with low-level product forecasts that are generated from multiple demand points, such as point-of-sale (POS) bookings and shipments.

Required activities, such as creating promotions for excess inventory, marketing and sales activities, and channel management programs, are determined based on integration of supply and demand planning. Computer Corp.'s sales channels were based on 60 percent direct Internet sales and 40 percent distributor and VAR sales.

## Manufacturing Function.
Manufacturing was responsible for working with sourcing to maintain low inventory levels and manage an efficient just-in-time (JIT) manufacturing process. Inventory planning is focused on managing stock for MTO and MTS requirements while maximizing inventory turns and confirming JIT programs. Manufacturing is focused on creating tactical and long-term capacity plans for central schedules or individual plants. The goal is to maximize constrained resources while supporting long-range strategic plans through sequencing and inventory allocation.

**Fulfillment Function.** The fulfillment function is responsible for delivering products to the channel or to the end customer. This includes the function of logistics (warehouse, shipping), and order management for the entire sales order-to-payment cycle. Coordinating the third-party logistics involved in product delivery and, finally, managing returns (reverse logistics) from the end customer and the channel are also part of the fulfillment function.

**Service Function.** Computer Corp.'s service function was focused on servicing customers, distributors, and suppliers. Treating all participants in the value chain as customers has allowed Computer Corp. to gain the loyalty of suppliers and distributors. Computer Corp.'s customer service functions include field service, repairs, and warranty management. Service functions for distributors included lead distribution, joint marketing, and spare-part planning. Service functions for suppliers focused on invoice error resolution to pay suppliers on time.

## Computer Corp.'s Approach to Collaborative Supply Chains

When it comes to early technology adoption, innovators such as Cisco are usually two to three years ahead of the industry. Not surprisingly, in 1996, Cisco was doing more B2B commerce on the Web than the rest of the industry put together. These innovators have taken a particular approach, as described in the following:

- Redefine the boundaries of their supply chains by making internal procurement, supply-chain, and ERP infrastructure accessible to suppliers, distributors, and customers.
- Provide trading partners seamless access to real-time information to each link of their supply chains.
- Consider "total supply-chain profit" as costs of design/production, costs of poor quality, and two new related variables—costs of longer cycle times and costs of poor management of trading partner relationships. Total supply-chain profit affects all trading partners in a supply chain.

By providing their trading partners seamless access to their internal systems, these innovators reduce the time it takes information, such as demand signals, to propagate through the supply chain from end customers to suppliers (see Exhibit 11-3). The net results were lower inventory costs, higher supply-chain responsiveness, and higher total supply-chain profit.

## Cost Impact of Information Flow

Again, take the example of Computer Corp., the PC manufacturer. In a very simple world where it produces one SKU—a computer, there are only two links in its supply chain—its distributor and a single retailer. Assume the retailer orders product once a week from the distributor, who in turn places an order, also once a week, to the manufacturer. The retailer's weekly order is based on the customer demand it sees and its ability to meet that demand from its own inventory. The manufacturer takes one week to build and send the product to the distributor. The manufacturer in this example never sees market demand directly but fulfills whatever the distributor orders. Exhibit 11-4 illustrates the relatively mild variation in actual product demand, the results in variation in orders placed by the retailer, and, finally, the demand as seen by the manufacturer.

**Exhibit 11-3**

## AREAS OF THE COLLABORATIVE ENTERPRISE

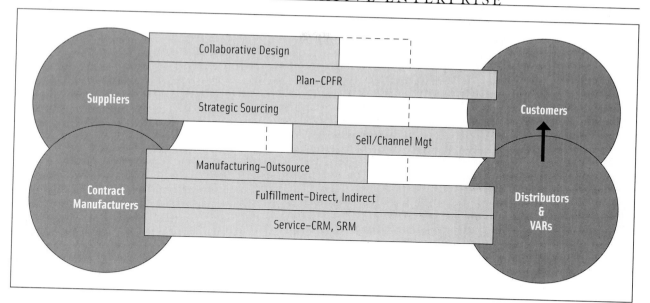

**Exhibit 11-4**

## SIMPLIFIED EXAMPLE OF IMPACT OF LIMITED INFORMATION ACROSS SUPPLY CHAIN

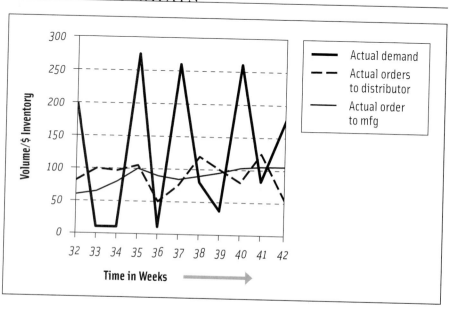

Why has this variation occurred? The short answer is because of the lack of information across the supply chain. Each link in the chain "saw" a different "demand" placed on it from the link ahead (there was a week's delay in the system). Each player—the retailer and the distributor—always overcompensated for what they thought the actual market demand was going to be. The real world is much more complicated than this example, and the net results are more links and more information flow to keep the supply-chain activities synchronized.

## Total Supply-Chain Profit

Once again, consider the Computer Corp. Any one or combination of the following reasons could cause excess costs in production and inventory:

- *Manufacturing management:* The manufacturing cost is too high due to a flawed process such as assembly line failure or issues of worker skill level.
- *Supply management:* Supplier sent defective disk drives resulting in returns and an unexpected shortfall and, thus, increased cycle time.
- *Demand management:* The forecasting of customer demand was too high, resulting in a rise in finished-goods inventory. In fact, in the last quarter of 1998, Computer Corp. was giving away free monitors and keyboards for this exact reason.
- *Supplier management:* The cost of raw materials and components, such as disk drives, is too high because the company has too many suppliers and no bargaining power over them.
- *Customer management:* Raw materials and component inventory (e.g., microprocessors) were too high because the order entry process did not "talk" to the fulfillment process accurately and in a timely manner.

**Total supply-chain costs** for Computer Corp. are as much a function of its ability to manage the cost effectiveness of its manufacturing and order entry processes as they are dependent on business decisions and processes of each link in their extended supply chain.

The net result is, if Computer Corp. encounters variations in distributor, retailer, or end-user demand, it typically will be left stranded with too much or too little raw material inventory, based on orders it has placed in the past. Therefore, companies resort to ordering raw materials and components by rules of thumb and often overcompensate their production costs by 10 to 20 percent to accommodate poor information flow.

# WHAT IS BUY-SIDE COLLABORATION?

## Outsourced Manufacturing

The use of contract manufacturers is fundamental to high-tech companies. This phenomenon is evident from the growth of electronics contract manufacturing. Companies such as Solectron and Jabil more than tripled in revenues between 1992 and 1997. There are three principal modes of contracting between a contract manufacturer and an OEM such as Computer Corp.:

- *Capacity:* In this mode an OEM will typically reserve production capacity owned by the contract manufacturer. The OEM will provide the necessary components and materials and use the ability of the contract manufacturer to efficiently transform the components into an assembled product.

- *Capacity and material:* In this mode the OEM company will commit to placing a certain volume of orders. On the basis of a forecast and actual orders, the company is purchasing both production capacity and materials management from the contract manufacturer.

- *Hybrid:* In this more typical form, a OEM company will provide certain components while allowing the contract manufacturer to furnish other components and capacity.

In each case, the order-to-payment process captures all steps from creation of an order by an OEM, in this case Computer Corp., through shipment of the order by the supplier and receipt of payment by the supplier. A sequence of document-based transactions supports the order-to-payment process. It necessitates the creation and management of purchase orders, invoices, and receiving documents (see Exhibit 11-4). Many of the transactions require labor-intensive human intermediation—processing invoices and reconciling POs are typical tasks performed by staff throughout the supply chain.

On average, Computer Corp. was spending $150 per purchase order processed. In addition, delays in order-to-payment resulted in the contract manufacturer bearing the burden of increased working capital requirements, which in turn restricted the amount of new orders the contract manufacturer could accept from Computer Corp.

Computer Corp. implemented a supplier portal where Computer Corp. and contract manufacturer employees could have a single view of order status and a single platform for reconciling exceptions. It significantly reduced the PO costs and the order-to-payment cycle duration. The net result was savings to Computer Corp. and to the contract manufacturer, increasing total supply-chain profit.

 **Exhibit 11-5**
## TRADITIONAL ORDER-TO-PAYMENT PROCESS BETWEEN OEM AND SUPPLIERS

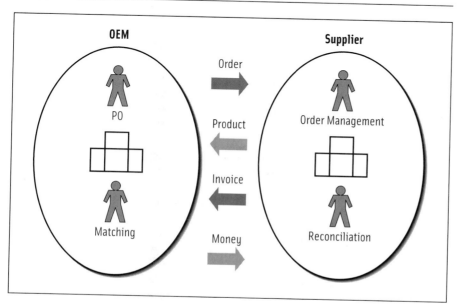

## Collaborative Design

For Computer Corp., the *collaborative design* goals are well understood: reduce cost and cycle time for NPI by 25 percent and manage the execution of ECNs (engineering change notices) quickly and accurately by communicating with manufacturing and the suppliers that are affected. To achieve these goals, Computer Corp. used collaborative product commerce (CPC) to work with its suppliers and contract manufacturers. CPC is a new category of collaborative commerce defined by Parametric Technologies, a leader in this area. Manufacturers use CPC to leverage the Internet to link up with their suppliers and customers and to build better products faster. Two recent industry trends make CPC important:

- Higher level of new product introductions (NPIs) activity and increased focus on make-to-order (MTO)
- Increased level of outsourced design and manufacturing to suppliers

The result of this shift toward make-to-order and outsourced design is a considerably higher degree of collaboration within and across an enterprise. Some of the leading technology vendors in this space include Agile (in the electronics components segment), MatrixOne, and Parametric Technologies. In a world moving toward mass customization, globalization, and solution selling, collaborative product commerce is ripe for growth and innovation in the next 10 years.

Computer Corp. used CPC for total product data life-cycle management that was not limited to engineering but allowed customers and partners to collaborate on the make-to-order life cycle. It allowed sales to manage complex configuration and outsourced manufacturing and design firms to function transparently as internal divisions of Computer Corp.

## Exhibit 11-6    DEGREES OF COLLABORATION

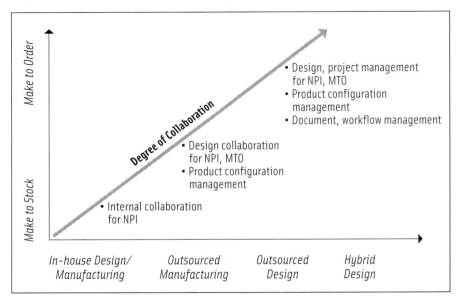

# New Product Introduction

Computer Corp.'s **new product introduction (NPI)** process follows a plunger model (see Exhibit 11-7). The strategy and planning phase (the funnel of the plunger) is concerned with exploring new product ideas. A cross-functional product team studies the feasibility of the idea in terms of manufacturability, product cost, and market demand. At this stage, the concept is yet to be validated. Once validated, the idea moves into execution. During this phase a Computer Corp. cross-functional internal team and contract manufacturers get involved.

The execution phase involves several iterations of prototype and pilot builds to be ready for deployment. Each iteration reveals valuable information regarding reliability, manufacturability, and build process for the product under design. However, the iterations cost Computer Corp. time and money. In the past, it required as many as three to four iterations of prototype building, with each iteration on average taking between one to two weeks. The iterations were on the critical path of NPI and, therefore, had direct impact on time to market. Reduction in the number of prototype turns and the duration of each prototype was a key operational goal.

One of the biggest drivers of costs and time delays in the prototype phase was the labor-intensive process for gathering and disseminating information. Engineering and production information on new products was spread across disparate systems—none of which were integrated. To aggregate and prepare the necessary files for an iteration of prototyping, an engineer needed to manually sift through the systems, often taking as long as an entire day. If the engineer collected and sent the wrong information to a contract manufacturer, the pilot would then be built to the wrong specifications and rejected, creating the need for yet another iteration.

To reduce the time delays and costs of the execution phase, Computer Corp. automated the process for gathering product data information. With information-gathering now automated, the engineers can more actively participate in the core NPI process itself. Next, it provided the collaborative platform for engineers and contract manufacturers to define the commodity and noncommodity components in an NPI bill of materials (BOM).

Two major benefits quantified from the collaboration between Computer Corp. and contract manufacturers were the following:

- Reduction in time for information gathering and correct specification of BOM and reduction in number of prototype turns and, hence, time-to-market.

- Reduction in the number of noncommodity items and new commodity items resulted in lowering the overall cost of an NPI. When all the sourcing activities, such as contract negotiation and finalization, were completed, sourcing every new commodity product was costing Computer Corp. between $15,000 and $25,000. Sourcing every noncommodity item was even more expensive as there was no benefit, as from economies of scale, in pooling commodity item requirements across products. Collaboration with the contract manufacturer who could make recommendations to find "like parts" resulted in cost savings for NPI.

Time is money, but when it comes to new product introduction, time is more important than money. If a new product is six months late, a company stands to lose a substantial portion of its profits as compared to only incremental profit losses from large overspends. Given this, managers should "manage out" time in the innovation cycle with networked applications.

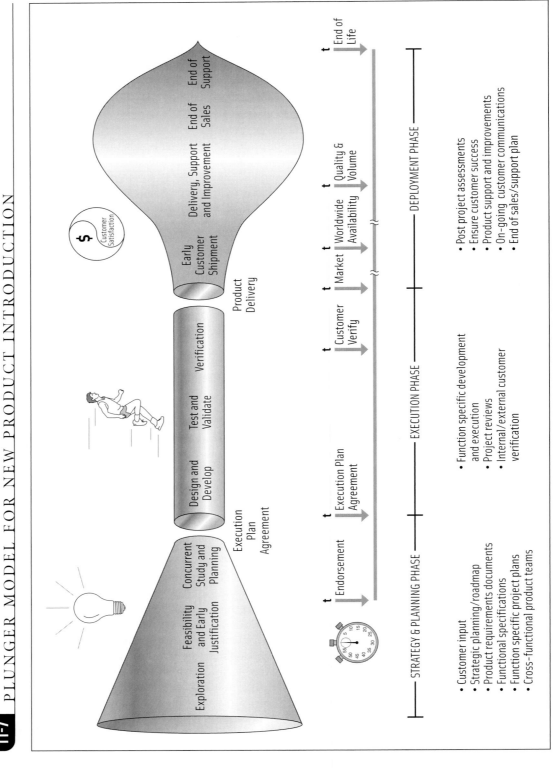

**Exhibit 11-7** PLUNGER MODEL FOR NEW PRODUCT INTRODUCTION

Exploration

Feasibility and Early Justification

Concurrent Study and Planning

Execution Plan Agreement

Design and Develop

Test and Validate

Verification

Product Delivery

Early Customer Shipment

Delivery, Support and Improvement

End of Sales

End of Support

$ Customer Satisfaction

t Endorsement

t Execution Plan Agreement

t Customer Verify

t Market

t Worldwide Availability

t Quality & Volume

t End of Life

—— STRATEGY & PLANNING PHASE ——

—— EXECUTION PHASE ——

—— DEPLOYMENT PHASE ——

- Customer input
- Strategic planning/roadmap
- Product requirements documents
- Functional specifications
- Function specific project plans
- Cross-functional product teams

- Function specific development and execution
- Project reviews
- Internal/external customer verification

- Post project assessments
- Ensure customer success
- Product support and improvements
- On-going customer communications
- End of sales/support plan

# Direct Fulfillment

As Computer Corp. shifted more and more manufacturing to contract manufacturers (CMs), the *direct fulfillment* process became a two-step *indirect fulfillment* process: first from the contract manufacturer to Computer Corp. and then from Computer Corp. to the customers. The added shipment step to this indirect fulfillment approach obviously contributed to increased unit cost: The expense of the additional leg was not recoverable, inventory was locked in transit for three additional days (the average duration of a leg), and certain tax advantages were forgone.

To Computer Corp., direct fulfillment was a natural extension of the collaborative supply-chain initiative. Contract manufacturers (CMs) had access to the necessary order information to allow them to actually ship the products directly. The CM enters the shipment transaction directly into Computer Corp.'s ERP application upon which a series of other transactions is triggered. One is a transaction to bill the customer, while another is a transaction to pay the contract manufacturer.

Advanced logistics can be as much of a competitive differentiator as a company's products and services. Direct fulfillment and other state-of-the-art logistics techniques, such as merge-in-transit and cross-docking, have become key capabilities in many supply chains.

## Exhibit 11-8  INDIRECT FULFILLMENT VS. DIRECT FULFILLMENT

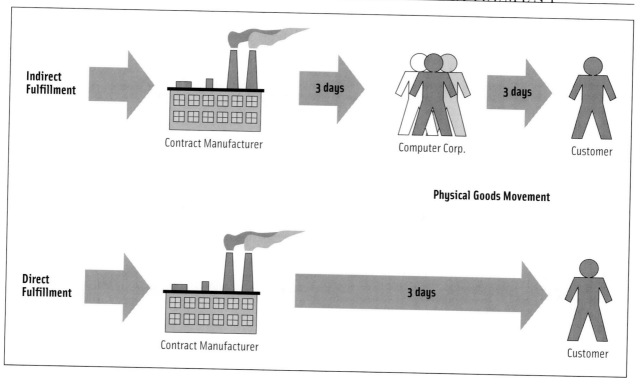

**Indirect Fulfillment**

Contract Manufacturer → 3 days → Computer Corp. → 3 days → Customer

**Physical Goods Movement**

**Direct Fulfillment**

Contract Manufacturer → 3 days → Customer

# Dynamic Inventory Replenishment

The lack of real-time demand and supply information forced suppliers to respond to internally generated signals that were distorted and inaccurate. Inventory levels and overhead were higher than acceptable. By allowing market signals to propagate downstream instantaneously, Computer Corp. doubled inventory turns. Recognizing shortcomings of the asynchronous replenishment model, it gradually adopted **dynamic inventory replenishment**, a fundamentally different model that allows the market demand signal to flow directly through to the contract manufacturer without any distortion or delay. To collect the market demand signal, Computer Corp. integrated all direct customer and distributor demand signal creation points via its collaborative supply-chain platform. Contract manufacturers then tracked Computer Corp.'s inventory levels in real time. Armed with real-time demand and inventory signals, contract manufacturers were able to entirely manage replenishment of subassemblies and components.

Dynamic replenishment was initially rolled out to one product family with impressive results. The inventory turns more than doubled from 15 to 30 over a 15-week period, lowering annual carrying cost by $500,000 on this product family. Computer Corp. has since rolled out dynamic replenishment to all product lines.

Dell's supply chain has 11 days of inventory. Its closest competitor requires 50 to 60 days. Why? Dell's entire supply chain builds to order. In most supply chains, build-to-order is fashionable but often practiced only in downstream stages. When pushed further upstream, build-to-order can be extremely powerful. In the continuum of demand response models, dynamic replenishment shifts the entire supply chain toward a make-to-order approach. Networked applications break down barriers to real-time communication and allow all stages of the supply chain to build closer to customer demand. As a result, the entire supply chain becomes more competitive.

 **Exhibit 11-9** RECEIPTS TRACK SHIPMENT AND INVENTORY DROPS

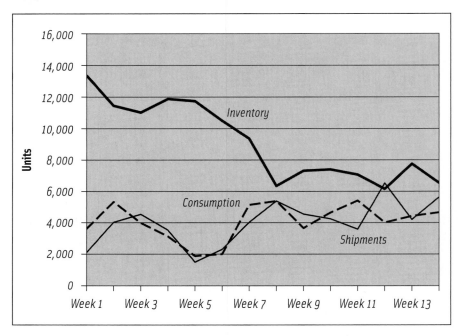

## Collaborative Planning, Forecasting, and Replenishment (CPFR)

After completing the implementation of dynamic inventory replenishment, Computer Corp. is in the process of implementing the next-generation solution—**collaborative planning, forecasting, and replenishment (CPFR)**. CPFR is the latest trend among supply-chain software vendors. CPFR emerged as a strategic initiative of the VICS (Voluntary Interindustry Commerce Standards) Association. Twenty-six industry leaders such as Wal-Mart were part of the VICS effort to define CPFR standards for trading partners to improve the flow of goods from producer to end consumer.

Over the Internet and through intranets, CPFR enables collaboration and is essential to synchronize supply-chain planning across multiple plants and to support extended supply-chain efforts such as just-in-time, quick response, vendor managed inventory, and continuous forecasting and replenishment. All trading partners in the supply chain benefit from increased sales, improved cash flow, and improved return-on-assets (ROA).

How does CPFR work? It begins with an agreement between trading partners to develop a market-specific plan based on sound product category management principles. The key to success is that trading partners agree to own the process and plan of which they are part. Using CPFR, value-chain participants establish a jointly agreed-upon plan to define how goods will be sold, merchandised, and promoted and in what timeframe. Either party can adjust the plan within defined parameters. Other changes require negotiations between trading partners. With CPFR, the collaborative forecast can be used to accurately represent demand and reduce days of inventory from the extended supply chain.

The network of trading partners uses the Internet to exchange forecast data in the demand chain and reconcile to a manufacturer's product category forecast with its distribution channel's forecast for the same product category. The channel forecast is based on the channel's understanding of end-consumer demand and on data such as point-of-sale (POS) and order data that are collected in the channel.

The reconciled CPFR forecast is then, in turn, used to execute replenishment plans through collaboration between manufacturers and suppliers. Manufacturers and suppliers who may be managing vendor-managed inventory or comanaged inventory and other continuous replenishment programs can ensure that stock is made available in response to the end-customer demand signal.

Success stories using CPFR are relatively new. For example, Nabisco and Wegmans yielded a 16.7 percent increase in sales in the nuts category, while Sara Lee tested CPFR with Wal-Mart to increase sales by 45 percent and reduce weeks-in-hand inventory by 23 percent in the women's underwear/hosiery category. Computer Corp. has completed rolling out its CPFR pilot for its entry-level consumer PCs in December 1999. Encouraged by the 20 percent reduction of inventory, Computer Corp. is now in the process of rolling out CPFR across all product categories.

# WHAT IS SELL-SIDE COLLABORATION?

## Customer Self-Service

To improve collaboration with customers, distributors, and value-added resellers (VAR), Computer Corp. created the Computer Corp. Customer Portal (CCCP) to accommodate *customer self-service* as part of its collaborative supply-chain effort.

Through CCCP, customers are linked to Computer Corp.'s internal operational systems and databases and can access a wide variety of support materials and applications, including product and technical information, assistance from technical support engineers, software downloads, order tracking, and electronic commerce services.

CCCP is a comprehensive suite of networked commerce applications that enables users to configure, price, route, and submit electronic orders directly to Computer Corp. Orders are placed directly into its database where they are immediately queued for scheduling. They are then processed and readied for shipment, reducing product delivery lead times by an average of two to three days domestically and three to five days internationally.

For its large corporate customers, Computer Corp.'s provides software tools to integrate CCCP into its procurement and intranet applications. Its customers have also reported that their own purchasing productivity has increased by up to 25 percent by using these tools.

In addition to its online ordering system, a series of tools called "supply-chain agents" allow customers and partners to access vital information about the status of their orders, such as purchase order numbers, order date, expected ship date, and shipping carrier. The tools even allow users to directly connect to the Federal Express tracking site to determine the exact location of their order.

The results of deploying these systems have been dramatic. Error rate for processing orders has declined from 20 percent to 2 percent. Furthermore, as a result of shifting account executive focus from handling administrative tasks to proactively managing accounts, sales productivity was estimated to have increased by 15 percent. Networked applications can provide for superior customer management and order management capabilities. Because they can alter the company's product and service offerings and create a point of competitive differentiation, networked applications are a must-have in customer management.

## Channel Management

In the early days of e-commerce (1996-1997), *disintermediation* was all the rage. Dell was an early advocate for use of e-commerce to disintermediate the channel with its "sell direct" strategy. While this approach was highly successful for Dell, B2B commerce recognizes the channel is an integral part of the manufacturer's method to deliver products to the end customer. Companies expect that channels will be responsible for the majority of their sales in the next few years. The right distribution strategy would employ a combination of channels and *channel management* to avoid conflict among direct sales, one-/two-tier channels, VARs and OEMs, depending on the complexity of the product/service, the industry, and the type of geography into which the product is being sold.

When Computer Corp. sells personal computers and PDAs to Latin America, it uses a two-tier distribution model. The first tier is composed of country distributors, and the second tier is made up of local distributors and retailers. Computer Corp. must address issues of channel pricing and virtual inventory management in implementing and managing the correct channel strategy.

**Channel Pricing.** Channel pricing is driven by the total cost of managing a channel and the margins that justify its use. The net result is pricing varied by product, channel, quantity ranges, and more. To manage channel pricing, Computer Corp. implemented a channel pricing engine that maximized revenues for both Computer Corp. and the distributor. The pricing rules included discounts tied to channel performance and end-customer satisfaction, creating a virtuous feedback loop from the channel to the distributor.

**Virtual Inventory Management.** The second challenge that Computer Corp. had to address was managing the virtual inventory in its channel based on the demand signals it received. This required implementing a distributed inventory management and order capture system that provided Computer Corp. with visibility to stock availability at each point in the channel to determine whether inventory levels had to be replenished based on new orders or whether the channel orders had to be fulfilled directly. The net result was order-to-delivery cycles shortened by as much as 40 percent for the channel and lower inventory levels in the channel resulting in increased total supply-chain profit.

In addition to addressing the channel pricing and inventory management, Computer Corp. has implemented a collaborative platform for returns, repairs, spare parts, and warranty management. The net effort of collaborating with the channels is higher end-customer satisfaction, happier channel partners, and an efficient channel that is synchronized with Computer Corp.'s supply chain.

# WHAT IS COLLABORATION WITH COMPETITORS?

## Consortia

Competing companies have recently joined as collaborators in consortia to realize gains through combined efficiencies. Covisint, in the automotive industry, and Transora, in the packaged goods industry, are showcases for collaborative commerce with competitors in action. Covisint's members include GM, Ford, and Chrysler. As a group, they wield $240 billion in annual spending power. With $400 billion in annual spending power, Transora's founding members include Coca-Cola, Procter & Gamble, Kraft Foods, and Unilever.

The auto supply chain is the most complex supply chain in the industry, comprising dealers, OEMs, and four tiers of suppliers. Initially, Covisint signed on tier-one suppliers such as Dana and Lear, which sell completed assemblies such as axles and brake systems. Key services that Covisint provides its members today include the following:

- *Procurement services to buy completed parts and parts suppliers to purchase their own raw materials through online catalogs and auctions.* Procurement promises two types of savings: pricing efficiencies through vehicles such as auctions and lowering the cost of processing transactions. Other consortia even pool the buying power of buyers to drive supplier costs even lower.

- *Virtual product design and development.* Collaborative design tools allow engineers to share CAD drawings, schedules, and communicate changes. Product development takes two to four years; a single change takes five weeks to filter through engineers and managers. Covisint's Virtual Project Workspace is a collaborative design platform for any member to leverage.

- *Supply-chain tools for demand forecasting, capacity planning, and logistics.* Sixty-six percent of the savings will be achieved by increasing efficiencies between the OEM and tier-one suppliers. Eventually, as Covisint provides a collaborative platform for all members in the supply chain to share orders (demand) and forecast (anticipated demand), it will significantly reduce inventory and provide logistics to ultimately create the make-to-order automobile.

Covisint's big promise is to cut as much as $2,000 to $3,000 of cost from every $19,000 car. The long-term vision is a massive upheaval of the industry that will allow delivery of make-to-order cars, much in the way that Dell produces mix-and-match models of personal computers.

# WHAT ARE COLLABORATIVE SERVICE CHAINS?

A number of different links, relationships, and processes exist among business partners. As discussed, the supply chain describes the process of moving goods through the raw materials, supply, and production stages as well as the distribution of products to the consumer. Years ago, software vendors realized many of the business processes that make up supply chains could be automated and with automation came reduced costs and increased efficiencies. The resulting supply-chain management (SCM) and enterprise resource planning (ERP) applications have had a huge impact on the manufacturing and distribution sectors.

The service industries—government, telecommunications, energy, finance, healthcare, independent consulting, and professional services organizations —differ dramatically from traditional manufacturers. Still, like supply-chain companies, service organizations have their own set of integrated processes and dependencies for selling, managing, and delivering services, often referred to as the service chain.

Service-chain software differs from its supply-chain automation counterpart. Supply-chain automation focuses on a process that can be summarized as "buy, build, distribute, and sell" for manufactured products. On the other hand, service-chain software accomplishes the same for human resources and information.

What factors have contributed to the birth and high expectations for the professional services automation market at this particular time? One contributing factor is that Industrialized countries have been rapidly moving from a manufacturing-based economy to one that is mostly services-based.

## Service Chain for Professional Services (PSA)

The term *services industry* denotes a wide variety of business types across an equally wide-ranging number of vertical market segments. Currently, most products that are recognized as **professional services automation (PSA)** software are designed to support independent IT consultants and professional services organizations. As the market becomes saturated, PSA software suites will target other service-oriented vertical markets.

It is easy to understand the growing interest in the PSA market, particularly with regard to the IT services market. The IT professional services market is huge and is expected to exhibit continued strong growth. Market research firm Dataquest, based in San Jose, California, estimates that the market will exceed $630 billion by 2002 in the United States alone.

Solutions for core processes of a services organization include automating the process of managing human resources and information capturing, storing, and sharing among service professionals, their managers, and customers. A more detailed look includes the following:

- Opportunity and proposal management
- Resource allocation and scheduling
- Project management
- Time and expense management
- Knowledge management

It is clear that PSA is a niche collaborative service-chain solution that automates many business processes and whose value proposition is extremely compelling. For any sizable services firm, increasing efficiencies even slightly across sales, resource allocation, project management, and any other service-chain business process produces a substantial return on investment.

# Advanced Service-Chain Solutions

Efficiencies and productivity can be increased and costs can be reduced when intra- and interenterprise business processes in the service chain are automated. PSA solutions are a precursor to service-chain solutions focused on professional services industries where the work primarily revolves around contracts/custom engagements and where contract life-cycle management and personnel management are the core components of the solution.

For service companies in the financial and insurance industries with information products such as mutual funds or life insurance, service-chain solutions must focus on additional functions, such as subscriber base management and distribution channel management. As the global economy increasingly becomes a service economy, expect service-chain software companies to provide complete solutions to allow for all the following:

- *Mass customization.* Collaboration with the end customer and collaboration with distributor of the end customer. An example is Foliofn that allows customers to build their own mutual funds and index funds.

- *Contract and project management.* Collaboration with partners to deliver custom/turnkey solutions to a common end customer. An example is Cisco, AT&T, and Exodus partnering to provide a complete Virtual Private Network solution to a large customer such as Ford.

- *Combining products and services.* Collaboration with partners to deliver combined products and services. An example is Hallmark partnering with a flower delivery company to deliver a Valentine's Day greeting card and a bouquet of roses.

- *Proactive subscriber management.* The existing CRM solutions are being used for subscriber management, but expect this to evolve into a new set of solutions unto itself. For example, a subscriber's life events could result in cross-selling or changes in life insurance policies.

- *Distribution channel management.* The existing document management and workflow solutions are being used for managing the information flow between a service company and its distributor, such as an insurance and its brokers. Again expect this to evolve into a new set of solutions unto itself.

An insurance broker representing a company such as Hancock will need to provide a cobranded website, provide access to forms, allow brokers to participate in the introduction of new products, and empower brokers to sell custom policies to individuals and businesses, among other things. All these activities need to be synchronized with the parent insurance company, Hancock in this case, for reasons ranging from basic channel empowerment to tracking legal compliance requirements.

## Advanced Collaboration Topics

A key take-away from the market correction in 2000 is the near death of "pure e" e-commerce businesses. E-commerce is going mainstream and will be measured by the same metrics by which traditional businesses have been measured. However, there are key trends around c-commerce solutions that will be created in the next few years. Some of these trends include supply webs, commerce nets, continuous planning supply chains, and outsourcing of the supply chain.

**Supply Web.** The term *supply chain* implies a series of serial steps that make up a chain. Today, both information and physical goods tend to flow along the supply chain. The Internet allows for control and flow of information to manage the flow of goods that compose more a web than a chain. Rather than a demand signal flow from tier one to tier two and then from tier two to tier three, the demand signal can simultaneously flow to both tier two and tier three, reducing the demand signal distortion and communication time significantly. The net result is better management of the flow of goods and the associated costs.

Examples are direct fulfillment of spare parts from supplier to customer, bypassing the manufacturer, or a merge-in-transit of monitors (from Viewlogic) and speakers (from Polk), managed by Federal Express for Computer Corp. so that it can avoid one step in the supply chain. Another example is Cisco requesting that its contract manufacturer Solectron use a specific commodity, such as memory chips from a specific supplier with whom Cisco has a purchase contract in place. This

**Exhibit 11-10** SUPPLY CHAIN VS. SUPPLY WEB

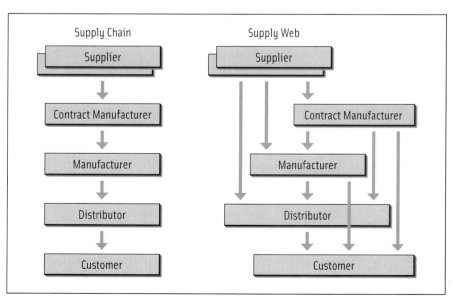

leads to a triangular relationship where Solectron's ability to meet Cisco's requirements is dependent on Cisco's relationship with a third commodity supplier.

The emergence of the supply web will be dependent on c-commerce solutions that will enable scenarios such as those described above. In the past, information using EDI followed the moving path of physical goods. In the future, we can expect physical goods and money to follow the most efficient paths as determined by information. It is conceivable that, in the future, every time an online payment of $125 is made for a shirt at Polo.com, the payment will be split, and $50 would be delivered to Ralph Lauren and $75 delivered directly to the shirt manufacturer in New England, avoiding the delay of capital that occurs in traditional businesses today.

**Commerce Nets.** So what is the vision for the round-one winners of e-commerce, such as Ariba and i2? Other than the central theme of elevating e-commerce to c-commerce, the goal is to create a network of buyers and sellers that are connected to each other via a **commerce net**. Ariba or i2 could then broker a customer order for direct materials to the constituent suppliers in the commerce net and then coordinate the fulfillment of the order. It is conceivable that infomediaries will emerge on commerce nets that specialize in different vertical industries to either manage the brokering of orders to suppliers or the pooling of customer orders to increase buying leverage. These commerce nets and infomediaries could coordinate the collaboration between buyers and sellers and the host of service providers that provide settlement and fulfillment.

How far are we from this vision? At a minimum, this vision is a few years away. The existing consortia or vertical e-hubs (another term for commerce nets) are focused on MRO products such as pen, paper, and furniture—not direct materials. Private exchanges, such as the recent Atlas Commerce–Wal-Mart announcement, have focused on direct materials that are managed by large organizations at the hub. So c-commerce will go mainstream when commerce nets becomes a reality.

**Continuous Planning Supply Chains.** If one develops a detailed plan to drive to work, the plan needs to adapt to the sequencing of traffic lights, changes in driving patterns, and changes in the weather, or the plan is unlikely to be implemented successfully.

The traditional paradigm for supply-chain management was to develop a plan at intervals of a month or more and then execute the plan within the month. The underlying assumption was that the plan had enough buffers in it to account for the variability. In the old planning paradigm, planning and execution were recognized as two distinct steps. The short-term part of the plan was then made more precise for execution, and the exceptions and market changes were reconciled at the end of each planning period.

Continuous planning does not mean the plan is constantly changed. It does mean that the planning process considers the changes in the environment *when* they occur. In the companies that have implemented this approach, a number of small minor adjustments to the plan take the place of a major overhaul at the end of the month. Continuous planning is achieved by creating a collaborative environment in which information flow, such as demand signals, can be quickly reconciled with a forecast. The collaborative environment requires the ability to proactively identify key events (changes in market demand) and exceptions (fulfillment exceptions such as backorders, partial shipments, returns, substitute products, incorrect orders, and changed SKUs) that affect the plan and to make appropriate planning changes.

The easiest way to reduce exceptions is to properly define the information once, online, and make it accessible to all interested parties. For instance, orders configured online can be checked by a configurator to see if all the components work together. The billing and shipping address data can be filled in from the customer number, eliminating data entry errors. The buyer can check order status, cutting down on double orders. Bringing more transparency to the fulfillment process makes it more efficient and easier to coordinate.

Direct procurement is unforgiving. Out-of-stock conditions and back-orders translate directly into lost market share, idle factories, lower profits, and poor customer satisfaction. To proactively manage key events and exceptions against plan, a new category of solutions called supplier relationship management (SRM) has emerged. These solutions are analogous to their CRM counterpart in that SRM solutions allow proactive management of events and exceptions between a manufacturer and its suppliers, similar to CRM systems' handling of service trouble tickets. However, unlike their CRM counterparts, SRM solutions rely on collaborative workflow between buyers and sellers to resolve exceptions.

The potential payback for use of these SRM solutions is enormous. They allow just-in-time planning to become a reality by providing a solution that manages exceptions in the execution of direct procurement orders for a just-in-time plan. They provide new options for collaboration such as outsourced design and manufacturing while still providing visibility and control over the process to the manufacturer.

**Supply-Chain Outsourcing.** It is all in the brand and the coordination of information to manage the outsourced supply chain. By the year 2006, Computer Corp. will not touch the product in the entire value chain. All it will do is generate the demand and coordinate the manufacturing, fulfillment, and service. All products will be make-to-order, and there will be no inventory to manage.

Nike does this today for shoes. Computer Corp. will do this tomorrow for home computers, servers, storage systems, and more. In 10 years, Computer Corp. will have arrived, at the end of a long journey, right back where it started in 1996, as an Internet company with a webpage and a toll-free telephone number—no assets, no inventory, and managing only information. The difference will be billions of dollars in revenues, incredibly aggressive NPI cycle times, and an ultimate goal of every order being a make-to-order request, with the most competitive price depending on market conditions.

## SUMMARY

### 1. What is collaborative commerce?

Collaborative commerce combines aspects of collaborative supply chains, collaborative communities, and collaborative service chains. Collaborative supply chains are intracompany and intercompany collaborations that span all core functions of manufacturing organizations. Community collaboration makes B2C and B2B sites stickier and allows community participants to provide the "human glue" to discover and trust each other and thus make transactions. Collaborative service chains refers to collaboration up and down the service chain for service companies such as professional services, insurance, and finance to manage their communication with their distribution channels and their subscriber base. The Internet enables cooperative conversations and redefines the existing boundaries and information flow between companies, suppliers, distributors, and customers.

## 2. What is buy-side collaboration?

Buy-side collaboration focuses on suppliers, contract manufacturers, and logistics and can include outsourced manufacturing, collaborative design, new products introduction, direct fulfillment, dynamic inventory replenishment, and collaborative planning, forecasting, and replenishment (CPFR). Manufacturing can typically be outsourced to contract manufacturers on a capacity, capacity-and-materials, or a hybrid basis.

## 3. What is sell-side collaboration?

Sell-side collaboration focuses on collaboration with customers, distributors, and value-added resellers, and includes customer self-service and channel management. Customer self-service activities can be allowed through networked commerce applications that enable users to configure, price, route, and submit electronic orders directly. Channel management involves determining and using the right distribution strategy, which is usually a combination of direct sales, one-/two-tier channels, VARs, and OEMs, depending on the complexity of the product/service, the industry, and the type of geography into which the product is being sold.

## 4. What is collaboration with competitors?

Competing companies have recently joined as collaborators in consortia to realize gains through combined efficiencies in pricing and lowering costs to processing transactions through shared procurement services, to shorten cycle times for new product introduction through virtual product design and development, and to realize savings by increasing efficiencies through use of supply-chain tools for demand forecasting, capacity planning, and logistics.

## 5. What are collaborative service chains?

The service industries—government, telecommunications, energy, finance, healthcare, independent consulting, and professional services organizations—differ dramatically from traditional manufacturers, but like supply-chain companies, service organizations have their own set of integrated processes and dependencies for selling, managing, and delivering services, often referred to as the service-chain. Supply-chain automation focuses on a process that can be summarized as "buy, build, distribute, and sell" for manufactured products while, on the other hand, service-chain software accomplishes the same for human resources and information. Solutions for core processes of a services organization include automating the process of managing human resources and capturing, storing, and sharing information among service professionals, their managers, and customers. A more detailed look would include opportunity and proposal management, resource allocation, and scheduling, project management, time and expense management, and knowledge management.

## KEY TERMS

collaborative supply chains

collaborative communities

collaborative service chains

service chain

supply chain

demand chain

value chain

collaboration pyramid

make-to-order (MTO)

total supply-chain costs

new product introduction (NPI)

dynamic inventory replenishment

collaborative planning, forecasting, and replenishment (CPFR)

professional services automation (PSA)

supply web

commerce nets

# Early-Stage Business Development: Human and Financial Capital

In the strategy section, we walked through the basic elements of creating solid e-commerce strategies for businesses. In this chapter, we go one step further, adding a basic understanding of human and financial capital to our thinking about how to build a new business. We introduce business planning as an iterative process of developing an early-stage business using human and financial capital. The critical sources of human and financial capital during these early stages of development will be discussed in detail, both in terms of human capital that can be leveraged to build the business and the potential financial capital sources that can be utilized. We then look at the pitch process the entrepreneur must engage in to ultimately secure financial capital. In the following chapter, we will take a close look at the mechanics of obtaining financial capital, valuation of the startup, negotiation, and potential liquidity events.

## QUESTIONS

*Please consider the following questions as you read this chapter:*

1. What are the key considerations in the business planning process?

2. What are the different sources of human capital that can play a role in a startup business?

---

This chapter was coauthored by Bernie Jaworski, Jeffrey Rayport, Dorsey McGlone, and Ellie Kyung.

3. What are the typical sources of funding for an early-stage startup business?

4. What elements are needed for a successful pitch to investors?

# INTRODUCTION

In earlier chapters, we discussed how solid business strategies create new opportunities in the market. The preceding Technology Infrastructure and proceeding Media Infrastructure sections survey the key components of technology and media that have changed the way we do business today, and will continue to change how we do business in the future. This knowledge can spark ideas around creative business concepts or technological innovation, but turning these ideas into viable businesses requires capital—both human and financial. The next two chapters will examine the mechanics of how to manipulate these sources of capital in the development of an e-commerce business.

Rather than pursuing the linear step-by-step approach from concept to IPO often pursued by trade books, this chapter provides a basic understanding of the components involved in the relationship between human and financial capital for an early-stage business. First, we introduce business planning as a dynamic process of testing a business' resources today against what it hopes to achieve tomorrow, and how it will bridge gaps between the two with human capital. We will describe the key considerations for a solid business planning process. Next, we detail the human capital that the entrepreneur can leverage to create a compelling offering that will attract the financial capital needed to make the business come alive. We also overview the common sources of financial capital and how they play into the business planning process. Finally, we bring these concepts together to think about the pitch entrepreneurs must make to investors to receive financial capital.

Given the expansive nature of the topics we will be covering, it is worth mentioning how we will focus our attention on these topics in this chapter:

1. *We will concentrate specifically on online businesses*, rather than on businesses in general. While many of the principles of success remain the same, we approach the topic from the perspective of a company that will need to grow quickly and will require larger amounts of initial capital to ensure market success. Consequently, we will spend considerably more time discussing equity sources of financing rather than debt financing, as equity sources are more likely to grant online businesses the type of capital outlay necessary.

2. *We will focus on the early stage of the company's development.* Exhibit 12-1 provides an overview of the financing needs during the life of a new company. By early stage, we are referring to the seed and startup phases of financing. This is when the startup is engaged in activities to validate the business concept and ready the product or service for launch. The next chapter includes a discussion of the expansion and later stages of the business, as well as the types of financiers involved at each stage. (The discussion regarding the expansion phase will be limited to the financial capital context since the human capital context requires a more in-depth study of organizational behavior and design than can be covered in one chapter.)

3. *We will introduce the sources of funding.* However, we will not discuss in detail the logistics of financing, which will be addressed in the next chapter,

Exhibit 12-1 STARTUP BUSINESS INVESTMENT STAGES

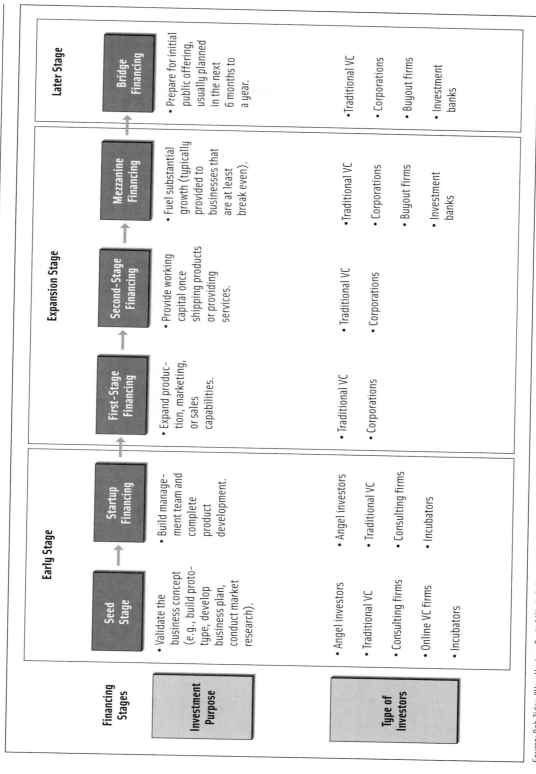

**Financing Stages**

**Investment Purpose**

**Type of Investors**

**Early Stage**

**Seed Stage**
- Validate the business concept (e.g., build proto- type, develop business plan, conduct market research).

  - Angel investors
  - Traditional VC
  - Consulting firms
  - Online VC firms
  - Incubators

**Startup Financing**
- Build manage- ment team and complete product development.

  - Angel investors
  - Traditional VC
  - Consulting firms
  - Incubators

**Expansion Stage**

**First-Stage Financing**
- Expand produc- tion, marketing, or sales capabilities.

  - Traditional VC
  - Corporations

**Second-Stage Financing**
- Provide working capital once shipping products or providing services.

  - Traditional VC
  - Corporations

**Mezzanine Financing**
- Fuel substantial growth (typically provided to businesses that are at least break even).

  - Traditional VC
  - Corporations
  - Buyout firms
  - Investment banks

**Later Stage**

**Bridge Financing**
- Prepare for initial public offering, usually planned in the next 6 months to a year.

  - Traditional VC
  - Corporations
  - Buyout firms
  - Investment banks

Source: Bob Zider, "How Venture Capital Works," *Harvard Business Review*, November–December, 1998.
*The Gold Book of Venture Capital Firms* (New Hampshire: Kennedy Information), vii.

especially with regard to three primary sources of equity financing—bootstrapping, angels, and venture capital.

Chapter 13 will also describe the logistics of working with funding sources, including an explanation of mixing funding, basic concepts of valuation, the process of negotiating a deal, and potential exit-strategy options.

## BUILDING A BUSINESS

There is a vast amount of existing intellectual capital and literature on the subject of building businesses, including nearly every book and business school class on strategy, marketing, finance, organizational behavior, or human resources. Although there are various schools of thought on all these subjects, one universal truth has held true: building a business is hard work.

For a time, the Internet boom of the 1990s seemed to flout this conventional wisdom. Companies had initial public offerings within months of being founded with multibillion dollar market capitalizations. Founders made fortunes overnight. Not to trivialize the blood, sweat, and tears of those startup employees, but building a business almost seemed easy. Then, of course, everyone was brought to their senses with the Nasdaq crash in April 2000 and its steady decline through the rest of the year.

What happened? Previous chapters touched upon a number of possible reasons, including fundamentally flawed business models and improper execution. Essentially, more emphasis was placed on *starting*—rather than *building*—a business. Launching quickly to gain the first-mover advantage was valued over thoughtful business strategy. However, laying a good foundation during the early stages of a business is critical for sustained future success, even in the networked economy, and the Internet startups that rushed toward IPO were often prepared insufficiently on an operational level. Strategic management of human and financial capital during this startup stage is essential.

However, it is important to emphasize that there is no one formula or step-by-step process for assured success—whether success is defined as obtaining funding, going public, or building a business that lasts through the next millennium. Factors both internal and external to the business—as well as luck—play a role. The principles outlined in this chapter are necessary for internal alignment, but are by no means guarantees for entrepreneurial success.

First, we begin by addressing a more fundamental question: What is a startup?

## What Is a Startup?

The word **startup** seems like a word of modern origin, but the term was officially coined back in 1845, to describe any business enterprise in the early stages of development.[1] The new economy experienced an onslaught of new businesses as each sought to capitalize on new Internet technology. Tangibly articulating what constitutes a startup becomes even more difficult as one considers the rapid growth of online companies, many of which had headcounts in the hundreds within a year. Boo.com, the much overhyped B2C site that sold luxury goods online, hired nearly 400 people in the United States and Europe during its first two years in business, but closed its doors in 2000 long before turning a profit. While the company seemed to be a startup defined by its relatively young age (and inexperience), it also acted as a business that had moved into an expansionary phase beyond that of a typical startup. How is one to define a startup given the many variations and anomalies?

While there is no absolute delineation between a startup business and a "grown-up" business, startups of all genres, online or otherwise, are in the process of developing the underlying infrastructure needed to support future growth. We define a startup as a business engaging in these three basic processes:

**1.** Developing and refining the offering and strategy to go to market
**2.** Obtaining initial funding to begin operations
**3.** Building a capable management team to handle operations

Engaging in all three simultaneously makes the business of entrepreneurship a challenge.

In the e-commerce world, dot-com companies conjure the image of entrepreneurs taking on this challenge. But even online, there are different types of companies making a start, again bringing to question what constitutes a startup. Specifically, there is the question of whether the online ventures of bricks-and-mortar companies can also be considered startups. These initiatives are like startups in many ways. They have separate management teams seeking outside funding, and they are setting up a business that requires a separate infrastructure and technology. Some even cannibalize existing offline sales channels. They are set up as separate entities to avoid red tape within the organization. However, corporate ventures have access to one luxury that pure dot-com startups do not: the deep pockets of a corporate parent. These deep pockets can constrain the strategic initiatives of online ventures when they clash with the objectives of the parent company. While one might be less inclined to view these corporate initiatives as startups *per se*, they are faced with the same challenges in building a solid business, and the market fall hit both dot-com startups and corporate initiatives alike. (See Point-Counterpoint "Bricks-and-Mortar Ventures Online: Are They Startups?" for more on this debate.)

Why are failure rates for young businesses so high? Any number of external forces come into play: general market conditions, the state of capital markets, inflation, interest rates, and even government regulation. Entrepreneurs have no control over these forces and can only act—or react—according to the outside context. However, much of what we observed in the Nasdaq decline was due to poor business planning, rather than unfavorable external conditions. Indeed, with the abundance of venture funding and a strong economy, external conditions were quite favorable at the time. In theory, a startup should be structured to adapt to change—able to foresee and maneuver through difficult external circumstances. (In the case of insurmountable external conditions, the entrepreneur should decide in the business planning process not to pursue the opportunity at all.) Building a business like this requires a solid understanding of the relationship between human and financial capital.

# Understanding the Relationship Between Human and Financial Capital

As discussed previously, the entrepreneur is subject to a number of internal and external factors that can make starting a business difficult, and the risk of failure is quite high. Consider the data in Exhibit 12-2.

# Bricks-and-Mortar Ventures Online:
## Are They Startups?
## The Toysrus.com Example

At the height of the Internet boom, bricks-and-mortar companies were blasted as cumbersome, slow-moving organizations incapable of moving in "Internet time." Traditional retailers such as Barnes & Noble and Toys "R" Us scrambled to make amends as the dot-com startups Amazon and eToys took over their retail markets online. The solution: set up separate business units with separate sources of funding, management, and strategy, and hope for a separate ticker one day. What was this separate business unit? Could it indeed be viewed as a startup and compete with its counterparts online? Let us consider this question in the context of the highly publicized Toysrus.com venture.

After the 1998 Christmas season, Toys "R" Us was hit with a double blow to its position as leading toy retailer. By not having an online offering, it missed the boat in the first "e-Christmas," strengthening the position of eToys as the leading online toy retailer. Offline, it lost out in sales to discount retail chain Wal-Mart. In 1999, Toys "R" Us was determined to make a come back and become the leading online toy retailer by the Christmas season. Thus, the launch of Toysrus.com.[2]

The Toysrus.com online venture resembled a startup in many key aspects. It was set up as a separate business unit under separate management—management that proved to be difficult to find, as in the case of many startups. Robert Moog, the first choice to head up the division, declined the position over disagreements in the online strategy.[3] The venture went without any leader at all until John Barbour stepped in at the end of August—with half the year already gone. Outside funding also proved difficult to find and negotiate, again, as is usually the case for startups. In August, negotiations with Benchmark Capital fizzled when no agreement could be reached on how much of Toysrus.com Benchmark should receive in exchange for $10 million dollars in capital,

aid in pulling together a management team, and the formulation of an online strategy.[4] Toys "R" Us was hoping for the expertise of seasoned venture capitalists to lead their enterprise to entrepreneurial success (Benchmark Capital had previously backed companies such as eBay and Ariba). They did not reach this entrepreneurial success, but experienced many of the common startup hang-ups.

On the other hand, Toysrus.com was unlike a true startup in several ways due to its corporate parentage. There was, of course, the added benefit of $80 million allocated from the corporate parent to the online venture. But there were problems associated with this blessing as well. Although it was, in theory, set up as a separate unit, Toysrus.com had to answer to several important Toys "R" Us constituencies—shareholders and offline store managers. Neither wanted to see traditional sales lines cannibalized by the new online company, and Toysrus.com could not offer the heavy discounts of its online counterparts. Prevented from acting in its own interest, it ended up being a venture in no one's interest at all.

So what happened to Toysrus.com? Not surprisingly, it missed the boat again in e-Christmas '99, with a fiasco of late deliveries that had to be remedied with expensive rebates. It lumbered in at $39 million in sales, compared to eToys' $106 million and Amazon's $95 million. But in February 2000, it obtained $57 million from Softbank Venture Capital and Softbank Capital Partners in exchange for 20 percent ownership and a seat on the board.[5] In August, it struck a deal with online retail giant Amazon to provide toy sales through the Amazon site. Things are not looking nearly so grim for Toysrus.com now. Whether a "true" startup or not, one wonders whether corporate parentage is such a liability online as eToys' files for chapter 11.

**Exhibit 12-2**

PROBABILITY OF STARTUP "SUCCESS"

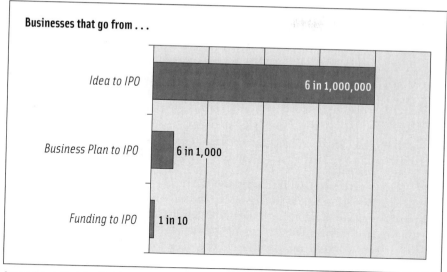

**Businesses that go from . . .**

Idea to IPO — 6 in 1,000,000

Business Plan to IPO — 6 in 1,000

Funding to IPO — 1 in 10

Source: John L. Nesheim, *High Tech Start Up* (New York: Free Press, 2000), p. 8.

While not meant to imply that an IPO is the sole determinant of success, the data of Exhibit 12-2 point directionally to where startup businesses fall out along the path to development. While the number of ideas culminating in an IPO seems discouraging, two observations should give the entrepreneur some hope. One is that putting together a business plan increases the chance of success dramatically. The other observation is that obtaining funding increases the prospect of success even further. This underscores the importance of understanding the mechanics of how human and financial capital function in the business planning process, because they are the primary assets over which the entrepreneur has some degree of control when attempting to overcome these two significant milestones.

Exhibit 12-3 visually summarizes the relationship between human and financial capital with the business planning process. The left side of the diagram details the human capital resources available to the entrepreneur during the business planning process. While introduced here, each resource is discussed in further detail in the next section. **Human capital** resources include the following:

1. *Entrepreneur* (or entrepreneurs): The **entrepreneur** is usually the person with the "big idea" who puts the startup in motion—whether the idea is a piece of technology, the identification of a market inefficiency, or a concept about unmet customer needs.

2. *Management team:* The **management team** is the group of people (which may or may not include the founding entrepreneur) that orchestrates the strategic direction and operations of the startup. While there are a number of different roles that can be included here, an early-stage company commonly includes a CEO (someone to spearhead operations overall), an individual with expertise in the consumer market to identify and manage the customer base, and an individual with technology expertise to determine what is or is not technologically feasible.

3. *Strategic advisors and partners:* These include the advisory board, board of directors, and companies with which the startup forms strategic alliances. **Strategic advisors and partners** can be an asset to the startup by providing strategic direction and advice through their own experiences (especially in areas where a fledging management team may be lacking) and, with the right names, serve to attract the eye of potential investors.

4. *Logistical advisors and partners:* These include paid outsourced parties—either through fees or equity—that can fill missing skill sets on an as-needed basis. While they can be involved in determining the strategic direction of the startup, they differ from strategic advisors and partners in their level of involvement in the day-to-day operations of the firm. Necessary **logistical advisors and partners** include legal counsel and accountants. Secondary logistical advisors and partners include intermediaries, consultants, and incubators, but can include a host of other parties as the startup continues to develop and grow.

The arrows between these resources and the business planning process go both ways, as each can influence the business plan and, in turn, be influenced by the business plan. For example, an entrepreneur with a heavy technology background may realize a need for marketing expertise in a particular customer segment in order to launch a product, and he may look to fill this need for marketing expertise when hiring a management team. Another example is a younger management team that may try to compensate for its inexperience by convincing industry heavy-hitters to join their advisory board.

 **Exhibit 12-3** THE RELATIONSHIP BETWEEN HUMAN AND FINANCIAL CAPITAL

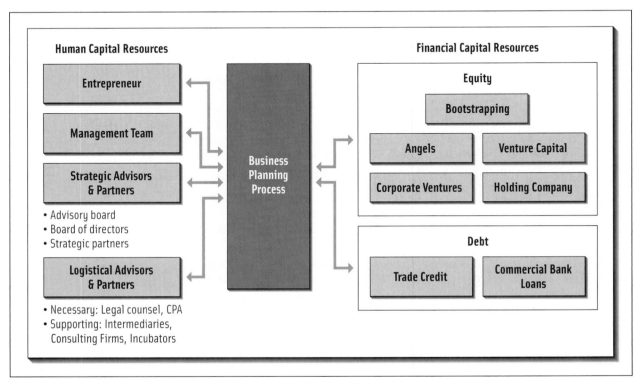

Financial capital is also involved in the business planning process. The most common sources for entrepreneurs in the early stages of business development are detailed on the right side of the diagram in Exhibit 12-3. Sources for financial capital include the following:

1. *Debt financing:* **Debt financing** is when a business borrows a certain amount of money for a specified time period and repays the principal with interest in regular payments. While there are many forms of debt financing, we will primarily address trade credit and commercial bank loans–the most likely sources for the e-commerce entrepreneur.

2. *Equity financing:* **Equity financing** involves a business exchanging a portion of ownership for cash, with the investor expecting financial return in the future as the value of the business goes up. The most common sources of equity financing for startups are through bootstrapping, angels, venture-capital firms (VCs), corporate ventures, and holding companies.

Each source can be influenced by—and, in turn, influence—the business plan. As indicated by the arrows going to the right from the business planning process to funding sources, good business plans attract financial capital. As indicated by the arrow extending to the left, many funders, such as venture-capital firms, also provide industry expertise and contacts to further aid the startup in its business planning process, even filling key management team positions. The actual dollar amount of funds obtained will also influence the business planning process. If a startup cannot raise the originally intended amount of financial capital, it must look for places to revise operations or develop a plan to attract other investors.

The significance is in understanding that business planning is not merely putting together an attractive, color-printed document for potential investors. **Business planning** is the constant iterative process of building and evaluating a business to lay the foundation for a solid organization. Early identification of strengths and weaknesses allows the entrepreneur to determine how and where to leverage resources. The number of dot-com startups that declared bankruptcy in 2001 underscores the importance of solid planning.

We will now detail the key elements of a solid business planning process, the human capital resources available to the entrepreneur, and the more prevalent sources of funding.

# ELEMENTS OF A SOLID BUSINESS PLANNING PROCESS

The business plan of any startup has two primary objectives: (1) to serve as a "resume" for potential investors and (2) to provide a framework for testing the business from conception through early development to capitalize on strengths and compensate for weaknesses. Because of the first objective, entrepreneurs tend to focus the business planning process on what the investor wants to see, rather than objectively fleshing out strategy. We later will address the issue of making the business plan a document appealing to investors, but we will first focus on elements that should be considered in a solid business planning process. Using the words of Harvard Business School professor William A. Sahlman, the entrepreneur (or management team) should evaluate whether they have the means to "just do it" and, if not, have the sense to "just say no."[6]

In the Strategy Formulation section, we described the different components of e-commerce strategy, and the principles from these chapters should be used when formulating a business plan for an e-commerce business. Clearly, there are numerous schools of thought on the formulation of successful business strategy, but regardless of frameworks or theories utilized, the **business planning process** outlines the following:

### Define the Value Proposition.
Quite simply, what is the product or service the business proposes to provide for customers, and why would they want it?

### Frame the Market Opportunity.
To turn an idea into a viable business there must be a need for the proposed offering. Potential customers should be identified, segmented, and sized to determine their attractiveness. Market-growth potential is also an important factor, as is timing when entering a growing market. The five conditions detailed in Chapter 4 (Framing the Market Opportunity) come into play here. To briefly review, these five conditions require the business to (1) seed opportunity in an existing or new value system; (2) uncover an opportunity nucleus, an unmet, or underserved need(s); (3) identify and choose priority customer segment(s); (4) declare the company's resource-based opportunity for advantage; and (5) assess competitive, technological, and financial opportunity attractiveness.

### Detail How to Reach Customers.
In other words, how do you bring the offering you defined to the market? Customer acquisition in any market is difficult, even more so for a new entrant. What marketing plan or strategy will the business employ to attract customers in the noisy online world? How much will this cost? How will customers get access to the product? How will the business develop a continued relationship with the customer? Before the markets demanded profitability, many e-commerce sites heavily discounted products—sometimes below cost—to attract customers. Rather than serving as a mechanism to retain customers, heavy discounts fostered the bargain-hunting, rather than loyal, consumer. Solid marketing, sales, and customer relationship strategies are essential for the viability of the business.

### Develop an Implementation Plan.
For a product-oriented business, how will the product be designed and manufactured? For an e-commerce site, what are some of the basic principles of site design that may be employed in the customer interface? What aspects of the business will be pursued in-house versus outsourced to other parties? What type of facilities will be needed to house the operation? The preliminary operational strategy should think through the basics of how day-to-day business will be done by the startup and determine the necessary players and components. Implementation made all the difference between Apple's failed attempt at a handheld organizing device—the Newton—in 1993 and Palm's extraordinary success with the Palm 1000 and Palm 5000 in 1996. In spite of its intended functionality, technical bugs plagued Apple's device, which became a technological laughingstock. In contrast, the Palm organizer, a device of the same functionality with superior organizational execution, created a billion-dollar handheld computing industry.[7]

### Evaluate Potential External Influences.
What activities in the macroeconomic environment could potentially have an effect on the business? Market conditions, inflation, exchange rates, interest rates, and government regulations can all play a role. The infrastructures described in the sections of this book—technology, capital, media, and public policy—also play a role. Consider the role of copyright laws in the businesses of online music sites, such as Napster and MP3.com. Although both offered services highly valued by consumers—convenient access to digitized, down-

loadable music—both were crippled by copyright lawsuits from the major record conglomerates. Entrepreneurs need to acknowledge potential hindrances in the external environment to prepare appropriate responses.

## Articulate the Revenue Model.

How will the business make money? Chapter 5 described key components for a successful business model. This has clearly been the stumbling block for many a rushed dot-com startup. The strategy of acquiring customers first, and addressing profitability later, was not rewarded long term. All of Porter's five classic forces should be considered when evaluating potential threats to profitability: existing rivalry in the market, bargaining power of suppliers, bargaining power of customers, threat of new entrants, and threat of substitutes. At the end of the day, how will the business turn in profits, and what aspects of this business model are sustainable advantages? Many of the online businesses that are leaders in their industry in terms of users are still struggling with the question of translating a user base into profits: iVillage with its huge base of women users (especially after the Women.com acquisition), Amazon.com as the leading online retailer, and drkoop.com as a leader for medical information. All these businesses have significant user bases, but continue to struggle with the question of profits.

## Identify People Needed.

Who is going to run or help run the business? These parties are the human capital previously identified. There is the entrepreneur, who has the idea and the vision; the management team, which operationally runs the business; and the board of directors and advisory board, which—as their names indicate—direct and advise the fledgling enterprise. There can also be strategic alliances that help provide a sustainable advantage for the business, whether through aiding in customer acquisition, supplying an auxiliary service, or providing industry experience. As the company continues to expand beyond the startup stage, staffing plans, headcount, compensation, and culture will need to be considered.

## Calculate Preliminary Financial Projections.

Preliminary financials have come to be ridiculed as the overinflated delusions of overenthusiastic entrepreneurs. Because of this view, potential investors often discount the calculations, which leads to "padding" by the entrepreneurs, further compounding the problem. True, these numbers are necessary for the funding process, but they should be seen as a way to check the financial viability of the business. Base numbers and assumptions should be as realistic as possible. Calculations must be made to determine how much money is needed at what intervals to make the business happen, as well as what types of returns investors may expect. These financial projections should include a list of underlying assumptions, five-year forecasts, an income statement, a balance sheet, and cash-flow statements.

## Establish Critical Milestones.

Although the many variables involved in starting a business make predicting an exact development path impossible, some milestones should be identified. These milestones can include an estimated timeline for product or site development and launch and projections for future headcount or revenues. While not intended as an inflexible commitment for the organization, milestones provide a documented benchmark for future evaluation of progress. Many investors will require some evidence of success to continue funding, and establishing and passing milestones can demonstrate this success.

**Summarize the Advantage.** In the end, some combination of the previous elements should constitute the startup's advantage vis-à-vis current and potential players. What are the driving principles that will make the organization different? What is the startup's vision for the future, and what will it do to reach its aspired vision? Most importantly, what is the organization's core competency or competitive advantage, and how will it be maintained?

A realistic assessment of these components helps the entrepreneur create an overall picture of the business venture's feasibility. This is an evolutionary process as potential weaknesses and needs are assessed and filled. We will now look at the human capital resources we introduced in the previous section and how they contribute to completing a compelling picture.

## HUMAN CAPITAL

While human capital is necessary for any operating business, its role in a startup business is especially critical because, for a time, it is the only resource available. A true startup has no assets to speak of, and typically begins with the entrepreneur and her idea. When funders consider investing in an early-stage company, they look for answers to questions regarding the startup's human capital. Who is the entrepreneur? Does she have the drive to see this business through? Who is on the management team? Will they be able to execute? The human capital attracts the financial capital. To that end, it is important to understand the role and contributions of each human capital resource: the entrepreneur, the management team, strategic advisors and partners, and logistical advisors and partners.

## The Entrepreneur

Although difficult to believe at times, every company in existence today was at one point a startup. Coca-Cola, Hewlett-Packard, Nike, FedEx—all very different companies that began in the same place: with an entrepreneur and an idea. E-commerce startups are no different in this sense: the entrepreneur is critical to the startup's early development. The entrepreneur has the idea that evolves into a vision for a business. And although the Internet boom made entrepreneurship seem commonplace, the subsequent crash illustrated the difficulties of *successful* entrepreneurship. Here we consider some of the challenges of entrepreneurship, characteristics consistent with successful entrepreneurs, and the link between the entrepreneur and the idea.

**The Trials and Tribulations of the Entrepreneur.** From the outset, the entrepreneur is faced with reconciling several difficult paradoxes. An entrepreneur must stay true to the vision for the business, but also attract financial capital. This is especially true for the e-commerce entrepreneur who requires equity funding at some point to quickly scale the business.

*Being Visionary Vs. Being Realistic.* In the past, the most successful entrepreneurs (old and new economy alike) have been visionaries—people who fundamentally changed the way people work and play, often creating or filling a need that people never knew existed. In 1964, Fred Smith received a "C" on his Yale economics paper, which examined the notion of a premium, overnight delivery service for certain types of products. He still went ahead to found FedEx in 1971. Today, FedEx has become an essential part of how companies do business.

The new economy has seen its share of visionaries as well. Israeli high-school dropout Arik Vardi and his three friends, Yair Goldfinger, Amnon Amir, and Sefi Vigiser, invented an instant Internet messaging system allowing users to communicate real-time across the globe. The service was launched for free in 1996 with absolutely no marketing budget, and the founders concentrated on creating a site with community and services to appeal to youthful tech-savvy users. The result was ICQ, a platform that grew through viral marketing to include 12 million users by June 1998, at which point it was acquired by AOL for $407 million—although it never grossed revenues more than $30,000.[8] The vision of the four young entrepreneurs drove the company's success.

In retrospect, any investor would have wanted to be involved in these endeavors, but the reality of every investment is risk. Louis Borders, cofounder of the successful Borders book retail chain, started the company now known as Webvan with the aim of using the Web and its own proprietary technology as mediums for selling groceries online. At one point, Webvan had a staggering valuation of over $6 billion and over $400 million in funding from a bevy of the most reputable of sources, but as of March 2001 Webvan's stock languishes at less than a dollar, facing the very real possibility of closure.[9] Even with technology to optimize delivery, a previously successful entrepreneur, and a group of experienced investors, the online delivery service simply did not take off the way investors expected.[10]

While investors are looking for "the next big thing," they are also looking for ideas grounded in reality. The entrepreneur is faced with the challenge of coming up with unique ideas, while not seeming too far off base. True, not every successful new business is a new-to-the-world idea, but the big ideas that most enthusiastic entrepreneurs dream of are those that will change the world—or at least some small subsegment of it.

***Generating Quick Returns Vs. Investing in the Future.*** Building an organization that will last takes time, patience, and investment in growth. Investors, in an almost contradictory fashion, are looking for companies that will last as investment prospects, but will require a return on their investment in a relatively short three- to five-year time frame. The entrepreneur is challenged with staying the course to build the organization while meeting the demands of the investors that are needed to build the organization in the first place. Balancing the two can prove quite challenging. Jeff Bezos had stood by a policy of aggressive growth, no matter what the cost, since Amazon.com's founding in 1995. He was criticized on all sides but stayed with his policy, which enabled him to cement Amazon's position online as a leading retailer and amass a large, loyal user base. However, in the end, even Bezos had to give in to the cry of the investor as the public markets began to demand that online companies show profits. In early 2001, he was forced to lay off 1,300 employees and close two facilities to cut costs and accelerate the path to profitability.[11] Imagine the challenge for less-known entrepreneurs in the face of demands from investors.

***Optimism Vs. Pragmatism.*** The entrepreneur must truly believe in the validity of his business idea and that it will truly succeed (or they should not be starting the business). Enthusiastic and optimistic belief in the venture—usually instilled by the entrepreneur—drives the culture and motivation of employees in these early stages. However, while this optimism is an essential motivating force, it must be balanced with the pragmatism to evaluate potential weaknesses and pitfalls that may come along the way. In some instances, insurmountable obstacles or challenges can prevent a good idea from becoming a reality. The excitement of "Yes, we can do it!" must be balanced with "But, really, can we do it?" Overexuberance brought down many an entrepreneur in the Internet boom.

In 1998, Greg McLemore and Eva Woodsmall founded Pets.com with the aim of making it the leading pet-supply retailer online. However, even with a brilliant advertising campaign (involving the infamous Pets.com sock puppet), a host of reputable financial backers, and a top-notch management team, Pets.com closed its doors in less than two years. A critical sticking point for the business: shipping for products like a 50-pound bag of dog food costs as much as the dog food itself.[12] Without a workable business model, profits were not forthcoming. Although in retrospect this seems like common sense, optimism and excitement over creating the premier online pet retailer overshadowed the practicalities of running the business.

The trial of satisfying investors while building the business does not diminish as the startup ages. If the startup becomes a public company, it will have to answer to a host of analysts, investors, and shareholders that will scrutinize financial returns. Keeping the vision and articulating it in a way that reassures investors will continue to be a challenge for the entrepreneur.

**Characteristics of Successful Entrepreneurs.** While there are dangers to generalizing across any population, there are certain key characteristics common to successful entrepreneurs. Though the characteristics seem intuitive, they are worth mentioning.

*Natural Problem Solvers.* By definition, businesses fill some market need. The best entrepreneurs are those who are able to make observations about industries, markets, and everyday life and find the best way to meet these needs—or create them. Most are constantly on the prowl for ideas. In 1994, Jeff Bezos read a report that claimed access to the World Wide Web was growing at 2,000 percent per year. Recognizing the audience potential, Bezos drew up a list of 20 types of items he could potentially sell on the Internet. He then settled on books because of the large number of titles readily available and the potential to offer samplings electronically online.[13] A seemingly simple problem-solving approach lead to Amazon.com, the dot-com that beat out traditional booksellers online.

*Willingness to Take Risks.* Entrepreneurs are willing to leave stable jobs and situations for their enterprises. In the early stages, this can mean not only leaving the stability of a position at work, but also risking the savings of family and friends to try their new idea. That said, smart entrepreneurs always take calculated risks (i.e., they make a realistic assessment of the chances of success). But they are willing to take a gamble and risk failure, oftentimes failing at their first few enterprises before finding success. Before his phenomenal success with the Internet instant messaging service ICQ, Arik Vardi had dropped out of high school intent on becoming an entrepreneur, and had unsuccessfully tried his hand at creating ISP software and selling T-shirts. Although neither of these endeavors grew into full-fledged businesses, his entrepreneurial spirit carried through to his success with ICQ.[14]

*Drive.* Starting a business is hard work, especially in the early stages when cash is short and the entrepreneur may be bootstrapping his way to the next level. The entrepreneur is willing to put in long hours and make sacrifices in his personal life to bring the business to life. The entrepreneur's personal drive is especially critical in the early stages, when his enthusiasm spurs the drive of other employees. In its early days, the Yahoo mystique and energy was conveyed primarily through its founders, Jerry Yang and David Filo, made famous not only for their vision but also for "taking one with the troops," forgoing corner offices for standard cubicles, and staying late nights with everyone else, often the last to leave themselves.

*Flexibility.* The ability to react quickly to changes and adapt vision are especially important in the networked economy, where the market changes in extra-speedy Internet time. The entrepreneur must be prepared to react to new entrants, as well as heavy hitting bricks-and-mortar companies defending their space. Even though the entrepreneur develops the plan, the plan is never adhered to exactly as it stands. If the next round of funding is smaller than expected, adjustments need to be made. If a key person in management decamps for the nearest competitor, contingencies must be in place. Flexibility and ingenuity are critical in an environment that will likely throw a few curveballs.

*Vision.* In the end, the entrepreneur's vision for his idea drives the startup. History has shown that the most successful entrepreneurs were not driven by money (which is a nice byproduct of success), but by a vision or a passion consistently pursued. This pursuit, and not one for wealth at large, is what ends in a successful business enterprise. Joseph and Jimmie Boyett summarize this point from the perspective of successful entrepreneurs in their *Guru Guide to Entrepreneurship*:

> *One reason for not having money as your primary goal . . . is that the single-minded pursuit of personal wealth will very likely make it impossible for you ever to gain real wealth . . . Ted Turner explains why: "If you think money is a real big deal . . . you'll be too scared of losing it to get it."*[15]

Netscape founder and serial entrepreneur Marc Andreessen states, "Money is not the motivator or even the measure of my success."[16] He was motivated by the desire for a better piece of software to access the wealth of information available on the Internet. His first Internet interface, Mosaic, was developed in conjunction with the National Center for Supercomputing Applications (NCSA) at his university, the University of Illinois at Urbana-Champaign. It was released on the Internet for free. At age 23, he was offered the opportunity to start a new company with James Clark, the founder of Silicon Graphics, and Netscape was born.[17] Ironically, those pursuing visions, rather than financial returns, often end up with the most lucrative success.

These are a few characteristics common to entrepreneurs. Some have another characteristic as an asset—charisma. This type of entrepreneur is the driving force behind the organization, even as it grows. He can articulate the vision and convey his excitement to the employees. Jeff Taylor created the leading online job-recruitment site with Monster.com, but was also intent on creating an environment where employees would be motivated and excited to work. He held hip recruiting parties aimed at young crowds to encourage employees to bring friends into the fold. The Monster.com offices in Maynard, Massachusetts, boast a free breakfast bar with snacks and refreshments, an employee gym, and a comfortable employee lounge— all at the express wishes of the CEO.[18] In March 2000, the Monster.com CEO water-skied 3.3 miles across Florida's St. Andrews Bay pulled by the company blimp in an attempt to break the previous world record[19] (which, incidentally, he more than doubled). The result was not only increased publicity for the business, but yet another example employees could point to to remind themselves, "Hey, our CEO is cool!" Charisma is a great asset for entrepreneurs, but is not a substitute for business sense or an assurance for success. Dependence on any one individual in an organization can be dangerous.

While all of these characteristics are assets for the entrepreneur, it is the idea that makes the entrepreneur.

## The Entrepreneur and the Idea.
What are some characteristics of the entrepreneur's idea? Thinking back to the elements of the business plan, the entrepreneur's idea

defines the product offering, and her continued thinking will preliminarily evaluate market need and begin articulating the revenue model. At minimum the entrepreneur must work through these issues before asking others to join her and bear the burden of risk.

Although we mentioned that the entrepreneur may not be driven primarily by a desire for personal financial gain, the idea itself must make money in some way. What is this idea? The idea can start the company, or actually be the company, depending on its type. Some ideas are applications, or a way of doing business. Some ideas develop around creating and meeting new market needs. The idea should embody the competitive advantage the startup hopes to retain. Outlined in the following sections are some of the more common types of business ideas. These types are not mutually exclusive.

**Introduce a New Product.** Most new products are based on a technology-oriented concept. This is the business idea that is the company, at least in the startup stages. New products can be classified by how they affect existing products on the market. *Products that enhance* increase the functionality or lengthen the lifecycle of existing technology. Software upgrades are examples of enhancing products. *Products providing alternatives* to existing technology provide another means of doing the same thing without completely displacing existing products. MP3 is such a product, providing an alternative to the previously existing Liquid Audio format—a digitizable technology for downloading music from the Web. Based on different core coding, MP3 allowed for a more flexible and ubiquitous digital format than Liquid Audio, which was a proprietary format with digital watermarks and strong encryption keys.[20] While the Liquid Audio format continued to exist, MP3 provided an alternative format.

*Products that displace* provide an entirely new means of doing something that has already been done. The development of audio-on-demand is such an example. This technology could turn CD tracks into digital files, which could be downloaded and e-mailed online, and its development threatens to displace traditional music distributors such as Sony Music Entertainment, Universal Music Group, and BMG Music. (The result was a rash of copyright lawsuits on the part of the industry giants.) While it is arguable whether this technology would entirely displace traditional music distributors and how long this displacement may take to occur, the implications of audio-on-demand as a displacing product are clear.

Finally, *products that transform* fundamentally change the way people do business or the way they live. These types of new products are few and far between. The invention of the PC is an example, giving computational power (and entertainment) to the individual user beyond anything previously available. The advent of the Internet is also an example, allowing the instantaneous transfer of and access to information among people around the globe.

**Introduce a New Service.** Ideas for new services can come either through identifying previously unmet needs in an existing market or as the result of new technology. FedEx is an example, bringing the service of overnight delivery to businesses that often have last-minute paperwork or products that need immediate shipment.

New technologies can create the need for a whole host of services to supplement or leverage them. Because technology typically requires expertise often difficult for companies to source in-house, service businesses provide a way for companies to bridge missing skill sets. The Internet brought the birth of a number of different types of service-related companies. Companies such as Razorfish, Agency.com, and Organic offered services to build and design Internet sites. Companies such as

Verio, Exodus, and Navisite hosted and managed websites for companies. Services ranging from network management to developing online strategy cropped up with the popularization of the Internet. New services can prove to be very successful business ideas if the entrepreneur has the right expertise to provide the service.

***Improve an Existing Model of Business.*** This is the classic "faster, better, cheaper" improvement to existing industry paradigms. There are several types of ideas along this vein. One idea is to capitalize on new technology. This includes the rash of retail sites that sprouted up on the Web selling everything from pet supplies (Pets.com) to books (Amazon.com) to toys (eToys). On the business-to-business side, exchanges bringing together buyers and suppliers in industry-specific areas provided a means to simplify a previously time-consuming matching process. FreeMarkets helped industrial buyers sort through numerous suppliers available for each product purchase by providing product specifications and proprietary bidding platforms. Many exchanges allowed access to larger bases of both suppliers and customers online, and the 24/7 access to these groups provided a faster, better, and cheaper alternative to their offline counterparts. (Indeed, many of the casualties of the 2000 fallout were retail sites that had discounted their prices so much, they could not turn a profit.) Many e-commerce companies started with this goal: to do it faster, better, and cheaper online than offline companies do it. Some companies were more successful than others.

Another way to improve an existing model of business is to capitalize on the weakness of current players. Established players are often older, larger, and unable to react as nimbly to market changes as a smaller startup. In these industries, opportunities exist through improved execution. Consider the way Schwab transformed the brokerage business. Although not a new venture *per se*, it essentially transformed itself into an entirely new business. By taking the traditionally phone-based financial services online and fully integrating these new online services with traditional offline businesses, Schwab was able to create an entirely new type of discount brokerage service. It was able to gain marketshare from traditional brokerage houses that could not sufficiently integrate their offline and online services, and also provided a significant advantage over online brokers that did not have a significant real-world presence.

***Create Demand.*** These business ideas seek to meet needs that consumers may not know they even have, often for some type of luxury or convenience product or service. Although an old-economy heavy hitter, DeBeers provides a prime example. DeBeers engaged in an advertising campaign that convinced consumers that diamonds are the ultimate expression of love, while it single-handedly controlled the supply and, thus, the pricing. A kind of variation on creating a new product, OXO Good Grips also provides an interesting example. By adding large rubberized grips to otherwise mundane kitchen utensils, Good Grips is able to charge $9.99 for an ice-cream scoop that might otherwise be $3.99. Customers suddenly found themselves needing the "good grips" when faced with an otherwise indistinguishable array of products at Lechters. Some recent attempts at these types of ideas failed to catch on. Kozmo.com launched the procrastinating, lazy man's service—free delivery of a variety of videos, snacks, meals, and gifts in an hour's time for orders placed online. The business was a novel concept and planned to roll out in major urban centers across the United States, but failed to catch on in cities other than New York and San Francisco, where operations were profitable. Even with free delivery, demand could not be created in large enough volume to make business efficient.

***Build a Brand—the First-Mover Advantage.*** This notion drove most e-commerce business activity through 1999—entrepreneurs rushing to be the first online with their business idea in the hopes of shoring up their brand name and creating the first-mover advantage. In an environment competitive for customer "eyeballs," substantial investments were made in advertising, marketing, and catchy URLs. However, the fallout shows that this principle alone cannot drive a business. Those new-economy first-mover legends that made names for themselves—such as eBay and Yahoo—were the first online with novel business concepts. The flood of retail sites online, each seeking to be the first online to sell pet supplies (Pets.com), toys (eToys), party supplies (eParty.com), and other retail goods, found that being first was not enough, which was one of the important lessons of the new economy.

**The Entrepreneur, the Idea, and the Business Plan.** In summary, the entrepreneur contributes to the beginning stages of the business planning process through formulating an offering, identifying a market need, and thinking through the business model. In some instances, the entrepreneur himself can often provide the largest source of human capital to strengthen the business plan and attract investors. An entrepreneur with a proven track record and an idea can be more attractive to investors than an inexperienced entrepreneur with what he believes is the next "killer app." After his success with Netscape, top-notch venture capitalists were more than willing to fund Marc Andreessen's new endeavor, putting more than $200 million into Loudcloud, an Internet infrastructure management company.[21] Investors constantly seek entrepreneurs that have shown the ability to execute successfully—whether the actual venture succeeded or not. One learns from failure as well as success. However, experienced or not, the entrepreneur's concept needs to be tested for merit as a business.

For a time, the new economy seemed to break many of the basic principles of doing business (such as valuation based on earnings), and, in the subsequent market correction, we learned several lessons. *Not every good idea will make a good business.* Consider the Kozmo.com example we discussed previously. Although conceptually a great, convenient service, low margins in retail challenged the online business. *Even good entrepreneurs can sometimes have unsuccessful business ideas.* And perhaps one of the most important lessons of all—*there is no substitute for solid strategy.* An entrepreneur alone does not make a business. An idea alone does not make a business. The importance or necessity of the charismatic entrepreneur and the big idea in building a solid business has often been the topic of debate. (See Point-Counterpoint "Does the Entrepreneur Matter or Not?") The concept is most succinctly summarized by Amazon's Jeff Bezos: "Ideas are easy. It's execution that's hard."[22]

And with that, we begin to examine the next element of human capital that moves the business on the path to execution—the management team.

# The Management Team

Building a solid management team is critical for startup success. In the early stages of the company, these are the people who work to architect fully the entrepreneur's idea into a functional business. They also can be the individuals that make or break investor decisions about financing. Management teams are scrutinized intensely by investors along multiple facets—most importantly skills, drive, and experience. Because business plans and markets are never static, the management team must be able to handle and operate within change. Well-seasoned management teams with a past history of success are difficult to come by, and investors place a premium on experience. In instances where specific experience or reputation may be lacking, investors will screen management team individuals for qualities that will make

# Does the Entrepreneur Matter or Not?

In many ways, the new economy ushered in a new period of the cult of the entrepreneur: Jeff Bezos, Jerry Yang, Marc Andreessen, Meg Whitman, and a host of others—each entrepreneur's name synonymous with their creation.

Venture-capital money followed the big names, the big ideas, and the big vision. Yet in *Built to Last*, James Collins and Jerry Porras' six-year research study of visionary companies revealed that neither a charismatic leader nor a big idea was central to success. What does this mean for the new economy? Does the entrepreneur matter or not?

On one hand, every company begins as a startup. At some point, there was an individual or a group of individuals that decided to start a business, and this business revolved around some sort of notion of what the business should be. In the tough early days when cash is short and times are hard, the blood, sweat, and tears of the entrepreneur, and those he can motivate, build the company from the ground up. Without the vision of the entrepreneur, the startup would proceed without much-needed direction to focus efforts. Especially in the days of the new economy, the entrepreneur is also the salesman for the organization, obtaining much-needed cash for operations from investors. Yet Collins and Porras imply that it is neither an entrepreneur, nor his idea, that builds a visionary organization. A visionary organization is defined as one that meets the following criteria:[23]

1. It is a premier institution in its industry.
2. It is widely admired by knowledgeable business people.
3. It has made an indelible imprint on the world in which we live.
4. It has had multiple generations of chief executives.
5. It has been through multiple product (or service) life cycles.
6. It was founded before 1950.

Examples of these organizations range from 3M to IBM to Procter & Gamble to Sony. These organizations survived multiple CEOs and a variety of market conditions through a combination of solid organizational principles and operational policies. These principles make a visionary company, not the original entrepreneur, which is one of Collins and Porras' 12 "shattered myths" associated with building a company.

*Myth: Visionary companies require great and charismatic visionary leaders.*

*Reality: A charismatic visionary leader is absolutely not required for a visionary company and, in fact, can be detrimental to a company's long-term prospects. Some of the most significant CEOs in the history of visionary companies did not fit the model of the high profile, charismatic leader—indeed, some explicitly shied away from that model. Like the founders of the United States at the Constitutional Convention, they concentrated more on architecting an enduring institution than on being a great individual leader. They sought to be clock builders, not time tellers.*[24]

What does this mean for the entrepreneur and his business? Ultimately, both points of view are true. In the early stages of development, the entrepreneur is critical to getting the business started—to come up with the vision, to motivate his employees, to hold operations together. But eventually, to create a lasting organization, the business needs to be grounded in solid operational principles and core values that will endure beyond the lifetime of the entrepreneur. This is a failing that we have seen in the new economy already—too many entrepreneurs focused on starting, and not building, a business, and many of these businesses have already fallen. Which new-economy business will be "built to last"? Only time will tell.

them assets to the business. Quality human capital is a scarce resource, and those startups that are able to secure it are at a significant advantage.

A startup is seldom able to begin operations with a full management team in place. The management team is formed through an evolutionary process of finding and bringing the right people on board as they are needed. In some instances, experienced funding sources aid in pinpointing the right individuals for the job. This brings an ironic paradox, as management teams are needed to attract investors while investors and the promise of financing are needed to attract the right individuals for the management team. It begs the question of which comes first—the management team or the financing. The answer is that the exact sequence depends on each startup's capabilities and weaknesses, rather than a stylized set of rules. In most instances, this ends up being a somewhat simultaneous process. The management team coalesces as the funding process is finalized, oftentimes consisting of individuals recommended by investors.

Regardless of whether the management team comes before or after funding, an incomplete management team will slow a startup's development. Certain individuals are necessary at critical developmental milestones.

**The Core Team.** These are the individuals essential to the early formative days of the startup. Their exact titles or positions are not as critical as their roles. The entrepreneur usually fills one of these roles according to his area of expertise and may be replaced if more experienced management can be brought on board when funding is secured. However, independent of funding in these infant stages, three roles need to be filled:

1. *Technology specialist.* In a product-oriented business, this is the person who understands the specific mechanics of how the product works, how it is manufactured, and how it can be utilized. For e-commerce businesses, this is the person who determines the technology platforms that will be utilized or need development in order to make the business possible. He knows what is in the realm of technological feasibility to support the business and understands how to develop what is lacking. This individual is often called the chief technology officer (CTO) or chief intelligence officer (CIO).

2. *Sales & marketing specialist.* This is the person with an in-depth understanding of the startup's customer. His expertise lies in segmenting the potential customers, selecting the most attractive targets, and understanding the target's wants and needs. This process enables him to understand how to position the company to capture the customer's attention. His primary responsibility is successful customer acquisition and retention. This individual can be the VP of sales, VP of marketing, or VP of business development, often holding several of these titles at once in the early stages of the business.

3. *Execution specialist.* This person keeps everything in perspective in the startup's development, from ensuring the sensible connection between the technology and the market to securing funding for continued operations, essentially making the vision for the business a reality. This individual is the chief executive officer (CEO).

It is also to the startup's benefit to have a financial specialist, or chief financial officer (CFO), involved as early as possible to make sure the company remains financially solvent and fully understands its financing needs. While this job can be outsourced, having an internal team member intimately familiar with the startup's financials is extremely helpful when the startup enters into negotiations with an investor.

**Extended Management Team.** Once the core management team is in place and the seed round of financing is underway, other members of the management team can be added on an as-needed—and as-found—basis, depending on how quickly the startup is growing and how far along product and business-model development have come.

1. *Chief Operating Officer.* This person serves as leverage for the CEO, especially as the organization grows, taking care of the day-to-day business operations and making sure that customers receive their products or services. If the company is product oriented, the VP of manufacturing can assume this role, overseeing a seamless production process.

2. *Chief Financial Officer.* (If not part of the core team outlined previously.)

3. *VP of Marketing.* (If not already filled in the core team.) While the three marketing and sales-related functions can be served by a single person in the early stage of the startup's development, as the company grows additional people will be required to fill these roles. The VP of marketing is responsible for creating and maintaining the company's brand image and creating the positioning strategy for the market.

4. *VP of Sales.* (If not already filled in the core team.) The VP of sales is responsible for generating revenues and creating and maintaining a network of direct sales channels for the organization.

5. *VP of Business Development.* (If not already filled in the core team.) The VP of business development acts to further enlarge the customer base and business opportunities through indirect channels. These opportunities come through developing strategic partnerships, seeking potential acquisition targets, and looking for new areas in which to expand the business.

6. *Chief People Officer.* In an environment where quality human capital is scarce, creating a company culture that fosters learning, growth, and appreciation for the individual is central to retaining talent. The chief people officer is responsible for creating this culture, sorting through recruiting issues, and considering potential effects of rapid growth on maintaining a consistent culture.

7. *General Counsel.* Having in-house legal staff to deal with immediate legal questions and issues is beneficial and cost efficient for organizations as they grow, especially if the business is involved in a number of strategic alliances or requires complex contracts from its customers. While hired legal firms may deal with more complicated issues, such as a large acquisition, general counsel can deal with the day-to-day legal issues affecting the organization.

With the addition of the management team to make the business operational, the business-plan issues detailed previously should be clearly sorted out—at least preliminarily—as these markets tend to change quickly. However, given the difficulty of hiring competent and experienced management and the uncertain timing for obtaining funding, it is entirely feasible that key areas of the business plan remain weak even with a preliminary management team. These weaknesses can be strengthened through strategic advisors and partners, discussed in the following section.

# Strategic Advisors and Partners

Even with a strong management team in place, a startup always can benefit from the expertise and advice of seasoned industry veterans. Strategic advisors and partners provide the startup with strategic direction, advice, and in many instances

# What Is More Important—the Idea or the Management Team?

This is a question that became especially relevant in the new economy, where it seemed (at least for a time) that any twenty-something with a bright idea could obtain funding and set up shop online. What was more important to investors—the idea or the management team? The entrepreneur's idea is the driving impetus of the organization without which there would be no business venture at all. In the online environment where speed to market can make or break an organization, investors were willing to take risks on the business ideas of inexperienced entrepreneurs. Some of the most novel concepts brought to the Web were through these young entrepreneurs with a bright idea. Shawn Fanning was 18 years old when he founded Napster— the music exchange that threatened old recording industry giants. (Although the value of Napster as a financial investment is currently questionable post-copyright lawsuits.) Twenty-somethings Jerry Yang and David Filo built Yahoo into one of the Internet's most recognized brands around the concept of organizing online content. These young entrepreneurs and their ideas seem to be the investor's key to finding "the next big thing." However, these were also entrepreneurs who were unlikely to attract the expertise of skilled management teams on their own, and in many instances, investors had to be willing to take a risk on an idea alone.

On the other hand, the collapse of the Internet economy has shown the importance of execution and solid business experience, even in operating e-commerce startups. The collapse of a host of retail sites, from eToys to Pets.com, demonstrated the importance of management with the financial and strategic experience to operate a company within its financial means. The management team description is one of the first sections read in a business plan, and the makeup of this team can make or break a deal. Investors are comfortable betting their money on people who have experience, as they are more likely to build organizations that are operationally sound.

So in the end, which is a better bet—banking on the idea or on the management? The answer, in most instances, will probably be both, but it will depend on the taste of the individual investor.

(depending on the individual) credibility for the organization as a whole. A reputable individual or business in a particular industry would not want to risk their reputation or waste valuable time on a venture without merit. These are individuals and organizations that the management team should target specifically based on areas of need assessed in the business planning process. They are usually involved with the startup through the advisory board, board of directors, or strategic partnerships—all of which are disclosed to investors in the business plan. For example, if the entrepreneur is new to a particular industry and an individual with deep industry experience could not be found for the early-stage management team, finding a reputable industry player to sit on the advisory board can strengthen the startup's position. While not a substitute for finding the right individual for the management team, the presence of an advisory board member can allay fears on the part of investors that the entrepreneur is proceeding blindly into an industry.

**Advisory Board.** Advisory board members typically receive options in exchange for their expertise, serving as an outsourced resource to fill a particular need. There is no specific number of individuals needed or recommended for an advisory board. Selection of individuals should be based purely on necessity. While advisory boards are involved with the company in its startup stages, the need for and presence of advisory board members diminishes as the company grows. Few public companies have advisory boards.

## Board of Directors.

The board of directors consists of individuals who will be responsible for the well-being of the company, as well as holding the management team accountable for its actions, when the business formalizes operations. In a public company, shareholders vote for these individuals, but in a startup individuals on the board of directors are selected by the management team and entrepreneur, and later by investors in the startup. Venture-capital firms that make substantial investments in a company will require that an individual in their firm be on the board of directors. Members of the board of directors usually have an equity stake in the startup venture. Like advisory board members, they also provide strategic expertise and advice for the startup but have voting power of approval over key decisions, such as investments, mergers, acquisitions, offerings, and management team selection or replacement. Once the startup becomes incorporated, the board of directors will be legal liable for the well-being of the company. (Incorporation refers to the process by which a company receives a state charter allowing it to operate as a corporation.) Unlike the role of advisory boards, which tends to diminish as the startup develops, the power of the board of directors increases if the company goes public.

## Strategic Partnerships.

The value of a strategic partnership to a startup depends on its type. A *strategic association* is the partnership with the least commitment and can consist of a verbal or written agreement for two entities to work together. The purpose of the partnership is a mutual exchange of expertise between companies in areas where they lack core competencies. For example, one company may promise exclusive access to a particular customer group in exchange for discounts on particular services. The partnership between drkoop.com and MedAdvantage Corporation is an example of this type of partnership. A MedAdvantage banner ad on the drug-checking tool on drkoop.com's site linked drkoop users to MedAdvantage's site for discounts on mail-order prescriptions. Drkoop was able to offer users access to a money-saving program, while MedAdvantage was able to gain access to drkoop's extensive user base.

In a *strategic alliance*, the parties draw up a legally binding contractual agreement to share resources on a project for a particular timeframe. The numerous AOL partnership agreements are examples of strategic alliances. In each case, a potential partner offers AOL some large sum of cash in exchange for exclusive access to a particular service for its customer base for a specified period of time. AOL has made a business of crafting these partnerships: 1-800-Flowers paid $25 million, plus agreed to share revenue for a four-year period, to offer its service to AOL customers; Barnes & Noble.com paid $40 million to serve as exclusive bookseller on AOL's proprietary network; drkoop.com committed $88.5 million to an AOL partnership shortly after raising $89 million in its IPO.[25] Each partner hoped to gain competitive advantage through access to AOL's 25 million-plus user base.

In a *strategic joint venture*, the businesses each contribute resources to create an entirely separate business entity capitalizing on the strengths of both organizations. The formation of Ralph Lauren Media, with its flagship site Polo.com, is such an example. A collaboration between Ralph Lauren and NBC, the Polo.com site is expected to offer commerce and content. NBC and its affiliates will own 50 percent of the venture for a combination of cash, on-air promotion time, and the use of customer-service facilities. Ralph Lauren will own the other 50 percent of the venture in exchange for agreeing to sell Ralph Lauren goods to Ralph Lauren Media at cost, allowing returns and exchanges through offline stores throughout the country, and attaching the Polo.com logo to its famous advertisements.[26] In these instances, the strategic joint venture is the startup organization itself.

A thoughtful strategic partnership can provide another venue to bolster weak spots in the business plan. Having examined the strategic advisors and partners that can strengthen a startup's offering, we turn to those that can help on a more operational level with the business planning process.

## Logistical Advisors and Partners

These sources of human capital aid with the nuts and bolts of pulling the business together. They can be involved in strategy formulation, but differ from strategic partners and advisors in that they are—at least for a time—more involved in the down-and-dirty day-to-day operations of the business. They can be advisors in the sense that these entities can work for a fee, or partners because they sometimes work for an equity stake in a company they believe will succeed. These advisors and partners can be classified as *necessary* versus *supporting* to the startup in the early stages of development.

**Necessary Logistical Advisors and Partners.** Necessary services include those essential in the startup's development. These parties include *certified public accountants (CPA)* and *legal counsel.*

The CPA is responsible for compiling the financial history of the business and can be valuable in the process of validating and checking assumptions made for financial projections. The CPA also processes and prepares all tax and finance-related documents and is familiar with relevant legal regulations. A reputable CPA can even serve as an advocate to investors as someone intimately familiar with the company's financials. Once the funding processes become more formalized, venture-capital firms and investment banks require CPAs. On the path toward an initial public offering, a CPA will review and audit financial statements with regulators to ensure accurate reporting. Examples of firms that offer these services and have experience in the technology realm include Arthur Andersen, Ernst & Young, PricewaterhouseCoopers, KPMB, and Deloitte & Touche.[27]

Legal counsel is another necessity for startups, handling general legal issues and, in the case of more technology-oriented business, intellectual-property issues. Depending on the expertise of the individual firm, two separate attorneys may need to be engaged. The attorney, like the CPA, can aid the startup in both logistical and strategic issues. From a logistical standpoint, the attorney prepares and processes all legal documents from the offering to incorporation. Having an attorney on hand to deal with these legal issues and coordinate with the CPA and investment bankers allows the management team to focus on more important strategic issues. A reputable attorney with experience in the startup's field can provide credibility, and even contacts, with investors.

**Supporting Logistical Advisors and Partners.** Supporting advisors and partners serve as outsourced, human-capital leverage for the startup. While not functional necessities, they serve as an economical way to fill specific skill sets on an as-needed basis, as startups are chronically understaffed. The most prominent supporting advisors and partners include *intermediaries, consultants,* and *incubators.* Consultants and incubators can also serve as a type of funding for startup businesses. An entrepreneur can exchange equity in the startup for services he might otherwise pay for in cash. We address them here as logistical advisors and partners, rather than sources of funding, because they are more involved in the basics of building the business than as financial partners, and the startup will usually still need funding even with the help of one of these sources.

**Intermediaries** are well-connected individuals in the investment community who match a startup with the right investors and, in some instances, acquisition targets. They act as paid middlemen between startups seeking funding and funding sources seeking good investments, and can be particularly helpful in locating difficult-to-find business angels and strategic corporate investors, as well as venture-capital firms. From the startup's standpoint, intermediaries can help in the preparation of presentation and pitch documents, as they are familiar with what investors expect. In an environment in which few unsolicited business plans are even read, the intermediary can provide an entrée for the entrepreneur who does not have many connections of his own. Entrepreneurs with attractive business plans are invited to join the stable of businesses the intermediary keeps for review by investors. From the investor standpoint, the business broker serves as an outsourced screener for quality business plans—an attractive alternative to digging through the deluge of business plans they normally receive. In return for these services, the intermediary receives a percentage of the startup's funding (anywhere from 2 to 10 percent depending on the intermediary and the deal) and sometimes has the right to purchase an investment stake in the startup itself. (See the Drill-Down "Garage.com" for further information.) Investment banks also can serve in this type of role, typically called placement agents, helping the startup hone its pitch and secure investors.

**Consultants** can provide expertise on multiple fronts, depending on the specialty area of the individual or firm. Consultant has traditionally been an umbrella term for a number of types of outsourced advisors. Corporate financial advisors are consultants that help specifically with finance-related decisions, especially for early-stage companies that have yet to find a CFO. They provide expertise in determining the right types of funding sources for the startup to pursue and the ideal mix of funding. Valuation consultants, sometimes called business brokers, aid in determining the startup's valuation in the funding process. Traditional strategy consulting firms provide expertise in the articulation and development of the venture's strategy and the preparation of business plan documents. Well-connected strategy consulting firms with experience in the industry also can provide investor leads,

## DRILL-DOWN

# Case Example: Garage.com

 Garage.com was founded by Guy Kawasaki in 1999 as an online intermediary. It used the Internet as a forum for matching startups seeking $500,000 to $10 million in funding with potential investors. Since its founding in 1999, Garage.com has arranged 67 transactions totaling over $240 million in equity financing. In 2000, Garage.com received approximately $2.5 million in placement fees for arranging these transactions, as well as an equity stake in each company that obtained funding (an average 5 percent stake in each). In addition to matching services, Garage.com also offers "bootcamps," which prepare prospective entrepreneurs for the startup process, and extensive online information.

sometimes having corporate venture funds themselves. Consultants should not replace the management team in thinking through the business plan and fundamental strategy, as the management will need to know the intricacies of their own business when approaching investors, but consultants can provide advice and expertise to inexperienced or overstretched management teams. Market-research consultants can perform industry research and analysis to bolster the business plan's market opportunity rationale. These are the types of consultants that are most frequently hired by startups, but consultants of any specialty can provide expertise in specific areas of a startup's particular needs.

**Incubators** help new businesses start without having to worry about many of the operational issues that plague startups. Some of the more common services offered are coaching, information technology, public relations, recruiting, office space, and legal and accounting services. More reputable incubators also offer opportunities for networking, as well as pooled purchasing power with the other portfolio companies. In some instances, they also offer a small amount of seed capital, but primarily they aid startups through services. The entrepreneur will have to give up an equity stake, pay fees, or both, and the equity stakes run high, averaging 30 percent. Today, there are few stand-alone incubators, as they proved to have poor business models of their own. The most effective incubators are run through large corporations, such as Bertelsmann and IBM, or venture-capital firms, such as Benchmark Capital and Klein Perkins Caulfield & Byers, to help portfolio companies in which they have invested. Tapping venture-capital resources will be further addressed in the next chapter. (See Drill-Down "Cambridge Incubator" for further information.)

As the startup continues to develop and gets closer to the initial public offering process, investment bankers, public-relations firms, and other logistical advisors will be become involved.

Now, with these human capital resources in place—the entrepreneur, the management team, strategic advisors and partners, and logistical advisors and partners—the startup needs to clearly articulate the vision developed in the business planning process to catch the eye of the investor. First, however, we look at the potential investors for the business enterprise.

## DRILL-DOWN

# Case Example: Cambridge Incubator

 By the end of 2000, over half of all incubators had either gone out of business or completely changed their business models. One of the survivors of the dot-com fallout is Cambridge Incubator (CI), which learned that incubators could not survive on equity stakes alone. CI provided startups with office space, recruiting support, product-development advice, and network operations. After the Nasdaq crash, CI began charging startups for these services in addition to receiving an equity stake. It has also readjusted expectations for success. While incubating 10 to 12 startups per year, it now expects only a 50 percent probability of success. Since its founding in 1999, CI has launched five startups: Veritas Medicine, Peoplestreet, BrandStamp, Job Rewards, and the nonprofit startup Secure Sponsorship.[28]

# FINANCIAL CAPITAL

The Internet boom of the late 1990s brought an unprecedented demand for **financial capital** as startups clamored to stake their claim in the online space, and, for a time, availability of investor capital seemed plentiful. Venture-capital spending soared from $11 billion in 1997 to $69 billion in 2000.[29] Investments by angels were estimated to be nearly $50 billion in 1999. Investments by corporate venture funds were estimated at $4.3 billion in the third quarter of 2000 alone, well into the Nasdaq downswing.[30] There was also an increase in the number of businesses, such as consulting firms, incubators, and intermediaries, willing to offer services to startups in exchange for equity.

The subsequent market crash has not changed the amount of financial capital available as much as the criteria used to define an attractive investment opportunity. The basic sources of financial capital remain the same. From an entrepreneur's perspective, the strategy for determining the ideal mix of financing also remains the same, although certain types of business opportunities may become more difficult to fund.

In this section, we discuss the primary sources of debt and equity funding utilized by e-commerce businesses. Table 12-1 details the common sources of funding for startups at large, e-commerce and otherwise, according to Federal Reserve data.

While we will address two of the more prominent sources of debt financing—trade credit and commercial bank loans—it is important to keep in mind that these sources are less common among e-commerce startups, which have few tangible assets to serve as collateral. Among the equity sources, we examine bootstrapping, angels, venture-capital firms, corporate ventures, and holding companies. With the exception of some bootstrapping sources (e.g. friends and family), these financial sources are able to provide e-commerce companies with several key assets: large amounts of cash needed to move the business quickly, networks needed to form

**Table 12-1 COMMON SOURCES OF DEBT AND EQUITY FINANCING FOR STARTUPS**

| Source | Percent |
|---|---|
| *Debt* | 52.33% |
| Commercial Banks | 19.94% |
| Trade Credit | 17.01% |
| Other Debt Sources | 15.38% |
| *Equity* | 47.67% |
| Owner's Equity | 27.12% |
| Angels | 4.89% |
| Venture | 2.42% |
| Other Equity (Primarily Friends and Family) | 13.24% |
| *Total* | 100.00% |

Source: "Venture Capital and Angels Provide Just Over 7% of Funding for Private Companies." *Business Wire*, April 23, 1999.

management teams and partnerships, and publicity needed to attract attention in a noisy online market. We will also touch on major debt and equity financing programs available to startups through the U.S. government.

Each of these financiers has different objectives when evaluating an investment opportunity, and understanding these objectives will help the entrepreneur to decide where to focus his attention when looking for financial capital. For each source, we provide an overview of factors that can influence an entrepreneur's decision to pursue a particular type of financial capital:

1. What the source is and why they are in the game
2. Criteria for investment selection
3. General pros and cons for utilizing this source from an entrepreneur's perspective

Where applicable, we will also detail key players and provide example profiles. Chapter 13 will take a much closer look at the three most common sources of equity financing for e-commerce companies—bootstrapping, angels, and venture capital—in the context of further information that should be considered in the negotiation and valuation process. Exhibit 12-4 provides a summary of the information to follow in this chapter.

## Financial Vs. Strategic Investing

Individual funders within a particular category have different objectives when evaluating investment opportunities, and these are critical for an entrepreneur to research. An entrepreneur starting a retail e-commerce business should not waste his time approaching a computer manufacturer interested in software startups. Similarly, an entrepreneur developing a product with a lengthy research and development cycle should not approach angels and venture-capital firms looking for quick return on investment.

While each source does have its own criteria for selection and different internal objectives, one distinction common to investors is the degree to which their investments are primarily strategic or financial in nature. When a purely financial investor evaluates an opportunity, she is concerned with return on investment (ROI),[31] internal rate of return,[32] cost of capital,[33] return on equity,[34] and incremental revenue (e.g., the bottom line). When a purely strategic investor evaluates an opportunity, he is concerned with how the business complements his current activities. This can include seeking exposure to cutting-edge technology or business models, collaboration in research and development for a product, or gaining access to new products, marketing, or manufacturing practices.[35] Having an understanding of whether an investor is primarily financial or strategic will facilitate the entrepreneur's process of locating appropriate funding sources.

## Debt Financing

The two most common sources of debt financing for startup companies are trade credit and commercial bank loans, which account for 71 percent of debt financing among startups at large.[36] The remainder of debt financing comes from numerous sources, which include using credit cards, mortgaging property, and borrowing

Exhibit 12-4

SUMMARY OF PRIMARY FINANCIAL CAPITAL RESOURCES

| | Source | What Is It? | Primary Criteria for Investment Selection | Key Advantages & Disadvantages of Use | |
|---|---|---|---|---|---|
| | | | | Pros | Cons |
| Debt Financing | Trade Credit | Credit extended to a business by its suppliers | • Those buyers with an established track record of making prompt payments | • Can provide an interest-free loan | • Certain terms could carry a costly implied interest rate<br>• Difficult for e-commerce startups to obtain |
| | Commercial Bank Loan | Typically installment loans where business borrows a specific amount of money with an interest rate for a specified length of time to be repaid in installments until paid in full | • Likelihood of loan repayment<br>• Amount of cash on hand<br>• Existence of positive cash flow<br>• Current burn rate | • Provide cash without losing equity | • Difficult for e-commerce startups to obtain given criteria for investment |
| Equity Financing | Bootstrapping | Using personal resources to finance the early stages of a startup | • Entrepreneur's belief in his own business | • Retain firm equity<br>• Gain valuable operational experience | • Unlikely to provide enough cash to sustain extended growth |
| | Angels | Wealthy individuals who invest personal capital in startups | • Referral through network connections<br>• Businesses in early stages of development<br>• Personal objectives for investment<br>• Market potential<br>• Nature of the business concept<br>• Quality of management team (if any)<br>• Track record of the entrepreneur | • Angel can provide expertise, networks, and credibility to help the entrepreneur build the business<br>• Can provide referral to additional funding sources<br>• Tend to negotiate terms more favorable for entrepreneurs than VCs | • Difficult to locate<br>• Investors can decide to get very operationally involved with the startup, creating potential conflicts with the entrepreneur<br>• One angel alone is unlikely to provide enough capital for operations<br>• Dealing with multiple angels can cause operational and logistical complications |

*(continued)*

**Exhibit 12-4** SUMMARY OF PRIMARY FINANCIAL CAPITAL RESOURCES cont.

*Equity Financing*

| Source | What Is It? | Primary Criteria for Investment Selection | Key Advantages & Disadvantages of Use | |
|---|---|---|---|---|
| | | | **Pros** | **Cons** |
| *Venture Capital* | Private partnerships or closely held corporations that raise money from investors, which is invested in companies that hold promise for a liquidity event | • Referral through network connections<br>• Potential return on investment in three to five years<br>• Firm's strategic objectives<br>• Existence of proprietary technology or concept for sustainable advantage<br>• *Plus items italicized for angels* | • Able to provide large amounts of cash to sustain growth<br>• Expertise in particular industries can provide coaching expertise and industry contacts to create a management team<br>• Quality firm provides name brand recognition and publicity | • Objectives are primarily financial, which can create conflicts with the entrepreneur's vision for the company<br>• Requires high equity stake<br>• Entrepreneur must give up a certain degree of control<br>• Difficult to locate and obtain |
| *Corporate Ventures* | Venture funds set up by large corporations | • Degree to which business complements corporation's current strategic objectives<br>• Right to utilize technology developed in the venture<br>• *Plus items italicized for angels* | • Provide operational expertise<br>• Provide credibility and visibility for the business through corporation's brand name<br>• Provide large amounts of cash<br>• Financing terms tend to be more favorable than that of VCs<br>• Patient capital | • Potential conflict of interest with parent company can cause problems<br>• Complicated intellectual property rights discussions if business later seeks VC funding<br>• Slow to make investment decisions |
| *Holding Company* | Company that offers cash in exchange for equity in companies with an operational, rather than financial, focus. Equity stakes typically range from 25–50%. | • Usually defined by particular focus of the holding company<br>• *Plus items italicized for angels* | • Patient capital due to operational focus<br>• Ability to learn from other portfolio companies<br>• Investors usually very experienced in specific industry | • Requires a large equity stake, and thus control |

Note: There are additional sources of financing that provide services in exchange for equity rather than cash for equity (incubators, consulting firms, etc.). Items italicized for angels are those criteria common to multiple sources of funding.

against insurance policies. We will only discuss the first two forms of debt financing available to the startup business. The other forms can be used by the entrepreneur to raise cash against any personal collateral. This will be further addressed in the discussion of bootstrapping.

## Trade Credit. **Trade credit** is credit extended to a business by its suppliers. It is an interest-free loan covering the time period from when supplies are delivered to when the invoice is due. For example, if a business were to purchase supplies on net 30-day terms, it would receive the supplies today, but not have to pay for the supplies for 30 days. This is effectively an interest-free 30-day loan.

*Criteria for Selection.* Suppliers typically offer trade credit to buyers with an established track record of making prompt payments.

*Pros and Cons.* While a 30-day interest-free loan may sound attractive to an entrepreneur as an opportunity to hold on to cash, the fine print could prove costly. Under different terms, this "interest-free" loan could have an implied interest rate. For example, if a supplier provides a business with the terms 2/15 net 30, the business will receive a 2 percent discount from the invoice if payment is received within 15 days, but otherwise it has to pay the invoice within 30 days. Initially, this seems attractive either way to the business—a zero percent loan if payment is made in 30 days, and an additional 2 percent discount for early payment. However, by not making payment within 15 days, the business is, in effect, borrowing the amount of the invoice for 15 days at 2 percent interest. This 2 percent implied interest rate over the 15 days translates into an enormous 62 percent annual interest rate (annual interest rate $= [(1 + \text{discount percent})^{365/\text{credit period}} - 1]$). The firm could save more money by borrowing money from a bank at a lower interest rate and paying the supplier within the 15-day time frame (assuming, of course, that it would be able to obtain a bank loan).

While trade credit can be a useful tool to manipulate cash flow, it is typically not available to an early-stage startup without a track record or other outside source for cash. In most cases, the power to request beneficial terms for financing lays with the stronger player, which, unfortunately, is not the early-stage startup.

## Commercial Bank Loan. A **commercial bank loan** typically takes the form of an installment loan in which the business borrows a certain amount of money for a specified length of time—usually one to five years—with either a fixed or variable interest rate. The payments are made on a monthly basis until the loan is paid in full. The commercial bank makes money on the interest when the loan is repaid.

Businesses that do not meet the bank's lending criteria for an installment loan can qualify for the SBA 7(a) loan guaranty program. An SBA loan is a loan offered through a commercial bank, guaranteed by the Small Business Administration (SBA)—a government association established in 1953 to help individuals who operate small businesses. The business must meet certain criteria established by the SBA in order to receive the loan. Commercial bank loans guaranteed by the SBA were granted to 43,700 businesses in 2000, totaling $10.5 billion in value.[37] (See Drill-Down on SBICs for further information on other government-backed financial capital.)

*Criteria for Selection.* Commercial banks evaluate a business' loan application by assessing the likelihood of loan repayment. This involves determining how much cash the business has available through equity financings or positive cash flow, neither of which an early-stage startup is likely to have. In the absence of these indicators, the bank will also look at the amount of cash the business uses on a monthly basis (burn rate), its current cash balance, planned amounts of equity financing in the future, and level of investor support.

While SBA loans tend to have less stringent criteria for qualification, they look at the type of business, the size of the business, and the intended use of funds when making an investment decision. While almost any type of business can qualify for the loan, the maximum allowable size for the business depends on the industry. For a retail or service business, revenues cannot exceed $13.5 million in a given year.[38] However, like all loans, the most important factor considered in a SBA loan is repayment ability, which is determined by the cash flow of the business—a burden of proof difficult for e-commerce startups to meet.

***Pros and Cons.*** Bank loans provide an attractive option for a startup business, as long as the monthly payments are not larger than the startup can handle. However, they can be relatively difficult to obtain, especially for early-stage businesses with little collateral and no positive cash flow. Entrepreneurs can bolster their business' credit attractiveness in several ways. One way is to offer personal assets as collateral as a display of commitment to the business. Another way is applying for a small loan, even if the business does not require it at the time, and repaying the loan on schedule to establish a reputation as a safe loan candidate with the bank. With an established relationship at a commercial bank, the entrepreneur can gain access to a host of other loan products, such as capital equipment leasing programs or revolving credit, and even sources of equity financing, depending on the individual.

Although both trade credit and commercial bank loans are attractive sources of financial capital, an e-commerce startup that needs a large amount of cash to boost operations in a short amount of time will have difficulty surviving on these sources alone. The dollar value of loans offered by these sources is too small to be helpful to the startup beyond the very early stage—the stage when they are least likely to qualify. Loans to small business are seldom more than $250,000, as the lenders seek to make money through interest earned, rather than the larger return on investment sought by equity financing sources. These lenders are more risk averse, and thus less suited for e-commerce startups.

# Equity Financing

In contrast to debt sources, equity sources are willing to take a gamble on the future value of a business, exchanging cash for ownership of some portion of the firm today, hoping for significant returns on their shares at some point in the future. Valuation of a startup for this type of financing will be addressed in Chapter 13. The most common sources of equity financing are through bootstrapping, angels, venture capital, corporate ventures, and holding companies, which we will discuss here. Keep in mind the logistical advisors and partners that we discussed in the human capital section as people with whom the entrepreneur might exchange equity for services, rather than cash, especially if they are services for which they would have expended cash.

**Bootstrapping.** **Bootstrapping** is the art of using personal resources to finance the early stages of a startup. For the entrepreneur, this may include taking a personal loan, mortgaging a home, using credit cards, or draining savings accounts—essentially, taking on personal debt financing through some of the sources we discussed earlier. If these personal sources are not enough to get the company started, the entrepreneur turns to friends and family for additional cash. In exchange, of course, the entrepreneur is able to keep the ownership of the business between himself and the friends and family members that contribute.

***Criteria for Selection.*** Bootstrapping provides the most viable option for the entrepreneur when the startup is in the earliest stages of business, especially during the stages that involve proving the business concept. Many companies—regardless of their performance—are not qualified for other sources of funding, which seek specific types of investments, or are not yet at a stage of development to attract outside funding.

***Pros and Cons.*** Bootstrapping provides several benefits to the entrepreneur. In addition to holding on to firm equity, bootstrapping requires that the entrepreneur be intimately involved with the finances and mechanics of running the company. He learns valuable operational experience that can provide credibility when later working with outside investors. Bootstrapping also allows the entrepreneur to refine his business strategy without pressure from outside investors seeking quick financial returns.

The disadvantage of bootstrapping is that it is unlikely to provide sufficient cash for a good business concept to grow quickly beyond the earliest stages. For an e-commerce company with an intended global reach far beyond that of the local doughnut shop, the startup will need to turn to additional sources of equity to maintain growth.

## Angels.

**Angels** are wealthy individuals who invest personal capital in startups in exchange for equity, and sometimes a seat on the board of directors. Investments typically range up to $200,000, although it is difficult to get true amounts since many angels do not disclose figures.[39] Angels are interested in early-stage companies that have not developed enough to seek venture-capital financing. Some angels are former Internet entrepreneurs who invest in promising enterprises to retain entrepreneurial excitement or fulfill the dreams of others like themselves. Some are from other industries, lured by the sexiness of the Internet. Each individual has his or her own reasons for investing in certain enterprises and, thus, slightly different criteria for investment.

While the exact dollar amount of angel investments is unknown because of the personal nature of the source, estimates run from $20 billion[40] to $50 billion[41] per year, significantly higher than the $5.8 billion total investment by venture-capital firms in seed-stage companies.[42]

Individual angels sometimes come together to form a firm that finances startup businesses. "Angel firms" allow the entrepreneur to receive larger amounts of capital without having to go through the logistics of dealing with multiple angel investors.

***Criteria for Selection.*** Angels, like venture-capital firms and other prominent sources of equity financing, seldom look at unsolicited business plans. It is critical for the entrepreneur to develop a network of individuals within the industry to gain introductions to potential financiers, whether through an investor's friend, family member, business associate, or even an entrepreneur from an angel's prior investment.

Once the entrepreneur has developed a network that will allow his business plan to be read, an angel evaluates the idea and the management team against his own individual criteria, depending on his objectives. Like most investors, he will be interested in the quality (or existence) of the management team, market potential for the business idea, and the track record of the entrepreneur. However, angels do tend to be less interested in scrutinizing balance sheets than whether or not they find the business intriguing. They are inclined to be more emotional investors than venture-capital firms, which seek a specific ROI.

Given the size of the investments angels make, they look for startups in their early stages, often providing the seed-round of financing (see Exhibit 12-1 for information on seed-round financing).

***Pros and Cons.*** A good angel investor can provide several advantages to the entrepreneur. A well-connected angel will have other friends or associates that he can interest in a business, either as investors or as members of the management team. He has industry knowledge and expertise to draw from to coach the entrepreneur and the management team. As individuals, and not firms, angels have the flexibility to be "patient capital" if everything does not go according to plan. They also tend to work in financial terms that are more favorable for the entrepreneur than venture-capital firms. Established angels will also have contacts at venture-capital firms, and, in certain instances, a name can serve as a stamp of approval for the startup.

In addition to being difficult to locate, there are two primary disadvantages to receiving angel funding. Depending on the amount of capital the entrepreneur needs, he may need the investment of multiple angels. This can significantly complicate logistics for the entrepreneur from the perspective of filing paperwork, negotiating a deal, and dealing with multiple investors on an operational level. Angels tend to be more involved in the day-to-day operations of startups because the investment is in an early-stage company, and thus by nature more risky. Depending on the angel's past experience, this could cause problems if the angel and entrepreneur have different visions for the company. Imagine the further complications if there are multiple angel investors.

In the end, the advantages and disadvantages of using angel investment depend on the individual making the investment. An angel who is well connected and has deep industry expertise will be of far greater help to an entrepreneur than an angel who simply has money. However, for any good business idea, angel funding—like bootstrapping—will prove insufficient in time, and the entrepreneur will need to look for a larger source of funding.

***Sample Players.*** While there is no definitive directory of individual angel investors, there are some known groups of angels. They include: Band of Angels, Angel Investors, Alliance of Angels, Tech Coast Angels, Silicon Alley Venture Partners, Common Angels, and The Angel's Forum. (See the Drill-Down "Band of Angels.")

## Venture Capital. 
Venture capital is the most widely publicized financial capital source for startups. **Venture-capital firms** are usually private partnerships or closely held corporations that raise money from a group of private investors. These investors consist overwhelmingly of pension funds, and also include funds from corporations, individuals, financial and insurance companies, endowments, foundations, and foreign investors. Each allocates a small percentage of its total capital to the VCs to diversify its investments.

A venture-capital firm typically invests $250,000 to $10 million[43] in a business in exchange for a 30 to 40 percent equity stake and a seat on the board of directors. In

## Case Study: Band of Angels

Band of Angels is a "firm" of angels consisting of 150 former and current high-tech executives from companies such as Hewlett-Packard, Intel, and 3Com. They invest in startups seeking seed-stage or early-round financing. As current and former executives of high-tech companies, they are able to provide entrepreneurs with expert advice and a diverse set of contacts, in addition to financial capital. As of June 2000, they had invested nearly $75 million into more than 125 different companies. These investments include companies such as GlobalCast, NetBuy, and Wit Capital.

addition to receiving cash, the entrepreneur receives guidance for building the startup, which could include industry expertise, contacts with potential management team members, and further strategy development.

Venture capitalists make money on their investments in two ways: management fees and profits on investments. Management fees are typically 1 to 5 percent of the capital investment in a startup, payable as long as the company remains in business and the VC has equity in the startup. Profits on investments come through a liquidity event, such as a merger, acquisition, or initial public offering, when the VC can sell its equity stake. (This is explained in further detail in Chapter 13.) A VC seeks opportunities that will return 10 times the original investment within five years, but realizes that each investment is a gamble and that only 10 percent are likely to succeed. For a typical VC, the success of that one investment should outweigh the failure of the other nine, with a net ROI of approximately 25 percent.[44]

Although most venture capitalists invest in technology-related businesses as a whole, investments have become increasingly Internet related. In 1997, only 37 percent of venture-capital dollars went into Internet-related ventures, compared with 83 percent in 2000.[45] This corresponds to a dollar amount increase of $4.2 billion to $56.9 billion.[46] However, only 10 percent of these investments were in early-stage companies.

In addition to venture-capital funding available through private sources, over $5 billion is available through small-business investment companies (SBICs). SBICs use their own capital and funds borrowed from the SBA to invest in companies in the early stages of development, as defined by the SBA. (For further information, see the Drill-Down on SBICs.)

***Criteria for Selection.*** While venture-capital firms are looking for a rather large return on their investment, and would therefore seem more inclined toward risk, they are actually quite risk averse. (Indeed, they cannot afford substantial amounts of risk with institutional funding involved.) They look for companies in their expansion phase—companies with developed business concepts that are in the process of assembling their management team, but not yet at the point of product launch. The vast majority of VC investments are in these types of companies.

An ideal investment candidate for a VC would have the following: (1) a large and growing market potential, (2) some proprietary or revolutionary product or strategy to sustain competitive advantage, and (3) an experienced and driven management team. The VC will look at a startup's business plan, preliminary management

# SBICs—Government-Backed Private Equity

In 1958, Congress created the Small Business Investment Company (SBIC) Program to encourage private, venture-capital investments in small businesses in startup and growth situations. SBICs are privately owned and managed investment firms that use their own capital for investment and are able to borrow funds at favorable rates guaranteed by the Small Business Administration (SBA). During 2000, investments in small business through SBICs totaled $5.5 billion. Over 60 percent of businesses receiving financing were less than two years old.

All SBICs are licensed and regulated by the SBA. The only requirements are a management team with some venture-capital expertise and at least $5 million in private capital. The SBA can provide leverage of up to 300 percent of this private capital if the SBIC has a demonstrated need for additional funds. An SBIC can be organized as a corporation, limited partnership, or limited liability company, depending on the investors, which are typically small groups of local financiers or bank-owned entities.

Like venture-capital firms, SBICs offer cash in exchange for equity, but can also offer startups long-term loans, which would otherwise be difficult to obtain. Loans can have a maturity of up to 20 years, and can be used for "financing, growth, modernization, and expansion"—as defined by the SBA. The average loan size for SBICs to startups in 2000 was $1.2 million.

Eligibility for SBIC financing, as defined by the SBA, can depend on industry, but is generally defined as a business with a net worth of less than $18 million, with an average after-tax income of the preceding two years of less than $6 million. There are no industry-specific criteria or restrictions, and SBICs tend to invest in a broad range of industries depending on the expertise of the management team.

Why does the government invest in such programs? Every new business created, no matter how small, expands the U.S. economy and increases the availability of new jobs. In terms of cost, the program more than pays for itself through tax dollars collected from the new businesses. Often overlooked for the glitz and glamour of venture-capital funding, the SBIC program provides a significant capital source for small startups that would otherwise have to bootstrap to the point at which they could approach traditional VCs.[47]

team, and the entrepreneur himself when evaluating how well the business meets the basic criteria. Because VCs tend to be far more active investors, offering expertise in operations and management team contacts, they look for individuals with which they share a certain degree of compatibility on a personal level. Each VC also has different strategic objectives and areas of focus, whether by industry, technology, or geography, and these individual criteria will also be evaluated.

Investment criteria can sometimes depend on the general market climate and trends. The Internet boom saw a great deal of this trend-like investing, with VC dollars moving from B2C to B2B to P2P, and on and on, depending on whatever area seemed hot at the time. Exhibit 12-5 shows the significant shift in venture-capital investments between 1999 and 2000, both in terms of total spending and the mix of investments. Even with VC spending exploding in 2000, there was a noticeable shift away from strictly e-commerce businesses after they fell from grace in the Nasdaq crash. However, the crash also brought investors back to old evaluation criteria, with VCs more likely to evaluate each business based on its merits, rather than some market fad.

Like angel investors, venture capitalists seldom review unsolicited business plans. The entrepreneur must utilize network connections to gain access to a ven-

**Exhibit 12-5**

# INDUSTRY COMPARISON OF VENTURE-CAPITAL INVESTMENTS IN INTERNET-RELATED BUSINESSES

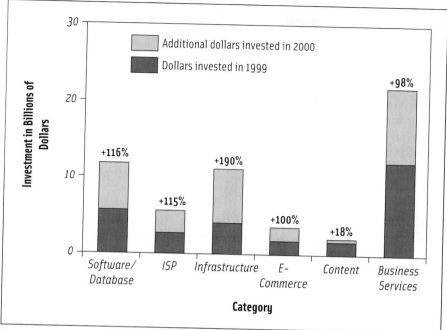

Source: PricewaterhouseCoopers Money Tree Report

ture capitalist, even to get a business plan read. If a business plan catches the eye of an investor, the entrepreneur may be invited to pitch his business to the firm as a potential investment opportunity.

***Pros and Cons.*** Venture-capital firms are able to provide startups with large amounts of cash that cannot be obtained from other sources that are not willing to take the associated risk. Obtaining funding from a high-profile, reputable venture-capital firm will also give the startup credibility, publicity, and industry networks. The investments of high-profile VCs are routinely covered in trade magazines and online publications. This is especially critical for e-commerce companies because mass-consumer awareness is key to success. Individuals being courted for management team positions look to a startup's VC backing as an indication of potential success. Experienced VCs can also help a startup hone its market strategy and smooth operational processes.

The biggest disadvantage to VC funding is the source's concern with the bottom line. The venture-capital firm is looking for a certain return on investment, and when strategic imperatives clash with financial constraints, the entrepreneur is often unable to exercise total control, especially when a VC sits on the board of directors. If a VC believes that his investment is in danger of failure, he can choose to replace the management team and take over the company. The tension between short-term profit and long-term interest often proves problematic for entrepreneurs.

Venture-capital firms also require a relatively large equity stake in exchange for cash, with financing terms that are often less favorable for the entrepreneur.

However, depending on which venture-capital firm this may be, the benefits of the VC's name can outweigh the cost of equity. In the end, the total value of the business matters much more than the entrepreneur's share of the business. It is better to own a small share of a business valued at several hundred million dollars than to retain total control of a business worth only a few million dollars.

*Sample Players.* Table 12-2 summarizes the key venture-capital firms by number of investments in 2000.

**Corporate Ventures.** Large corporations sometimes set up venture funds as a subsidiary that can make investments on behalf of the parent company, referred to as either **corporate ventures** or "direct investors." While venture-capital firms invest primarily for financial reasons, corporate-venture funds invest in complementary businesses for primarily strategic reasons. In exchange for cash, they will seek an equity

**Table 12-2** FIRST QUARTER 2000 TOP 20 VENTURE DEAL MAKERS

| | | |
|---|---|---|
| BancBoston Capital and Ventures | Boston, MA | 45 |
| Chase Capital Partners | New York, NY | 45 |
| Bessemer Venture Partners | Wellesley Hills, MA | 33 |
| New Enterprise Associates | Baltimore, MD | 29 |
| Oak Investment Partners | Westport, CT | 28 |
| Accel Partners | Palo Alto, CA | 26 |
| US Venture Partners | Menlo Park, CA | 26 |
| Sprout Group | New York, NY | 23 |
| Norwest Equity Partners | Minneapolis, MN | 22 |
| Crescendo Venture Management LLC | Minneapolis, MN | 21 |
| Crosspoint Venture Partners | Woodside, CA | 21 |
| Sequoia Capital | Menlo Park, CA | 21 |
| Battery Ventures L.P. | Wellesley, MA | 20 |
| Canaan Partners | Rowayton, CT | 20 |
| CMGI Ventures | Andover, MA | 20 |
| Mayfield Fund | Menlo Park, CA | 20 |
| Charles River Ventures | Waltham, MA | 19 |
| Mellon Ventures Inc. | Pittsburgh, PA | 19 |
| Technology Crossover Ventures (TCV) | Palo Alto, CA | 19 |
| Draper Fisher Jurvetson | Redwood City, CA | 18 |

Source: PricewaterhouseCoopers MoneyTree Survey Q1 2000.

## Case Study: Charles River Ventures

Charles River Ventures (CRV) was founded in 1970. It has managed 12 funds and invested in over 200 companies since its founding, focusing investments on e-commerce, software, and communications companies. Some investments are also made in the nonprofit sector, including funding of medical foundations and universities. CRV's average initial investment in a startup is $3 million, typically investing from $10 million to $25 million over the lifetime of the company. In May 2000, it founded CRVelocity, a provider of incubator-type services such as recruiting, law advice, IT services, and other operational services. Investments include Excite, Sybase, Ciena, and Be Free. A $1.2 billion fund was closed in early 2001.

stake in the company and access to the company's technology or product. Investments made by corporate-venture funds can include investments in outside businesses as well as business ventures within the corporation. In 1999, corporate-venture funds invested almost $8 billion in over 900 companies[48] in various stages of development; in 2000, spending in the third quarter alone topped $4 billion. In some instances, investment in these companies can result in acquisition by the corporate entity.

***Criteria for Selection.*** The criteria used by a corporate-venture fund to evaluate an investment opportunity will depend on the strategic objectives of the firm and the type of firm. In addition to a solid business idea, qualified management team, and driven entrepreneur, investors will be looking for a startup that will bolster the parent organization through complementary technologies, customer bases, distribution systems, or services.

***Pros and Cons.*** Corporate-venture funding provides several significant advantages for entrepreneurs. Established corporations can offer the operational expertise, as well as the credibility and visibility that come from associating with an established high-profile parent. Because the investments are strategic rather than financial, the pricing of deals with corporations tends to favor the entrepreneur more than deals with venture-capital firms. Investors are also more patient than venture-capital firms because they are more interested in the business' success through its product than an immediate financial return.

On the flip side, there are a number of challenges associated with working with a venture fund with corporate parentage. Large corporations tend to be slower moving in general, and thus slower to make investment decisions. Changes in the financial situation of the parent can affect the amount of money in the fund, and funding can be curtailed if revenue numbers need to be met. Corporate funding can also cause complications if the startup later needs to seek venture-capital funding. In addition to complicating funding terms, conflicts of interest can arise if the startup has developed technology that could compete with the parent firm. Hammering out access agreements with the corporate parent can seriously hamper additional funding discussions with other sources.

***Sample Players.*** Although VC investments are expected to slow in the future, with stricter criteria for investment, corporate venturing is expected to grow since it is based on strategic need rather than financial returns. Table 12-3 shows some corporate-venture funds that were set up in fourth quarter 2000, well into the Nasdaq freefall. Corporate-venture funds continue to grow in spite of the market slowdown. (See the Drill-Down, "Intel Capital.")

**Holding Company.** Similar to the other equity sources discussed previously, a holding company also offers cash in exchange for equity to a startup company. The distinction between a **holding company** and a venture-capital firm is the nature of the investment as defined by the U.S. Securities and Exchange Commission. Venture-capital firms have more of an investment focus, while holding companies have an operational focus. The distinction is made by how much of the business the firm owns. A holding company usually owns 25 to 50 percent of its portfolio company—often the majority stake holder—for an extended period of time that exceeds that of a venture-capital firm.

*Criteria for Selection.* Holding companies have criteria similar to those of other investors—looking at the quality of the idea, business plan, management team, and entrepreneur. However, holding companies usually have a particular focus or area of expertise that they use to select potential investments.

*Pros and Cons.* Because holding companies are operational—rather than financial—investors, they are more patient with their capital than venture-capital firms, which expect returns in a specified time frame. The startup can also benefit from the experience of the individuals running the holding company in their industry, and also learn from the experiences of other businesses in the portfolio.

The biggest disadvantage of receiving capital from a holding company is that the substantial amount of equity usually results in a loss of control for the entrepreneur.

 **Table 12-3** FOURTH QUARTER 2000 CORPORATE-VENTURE FUNDS

| Company | Amount of Fund (MM) | Target Sector |
|---|---|---|
| Compaq | $100 | Data storage hardware, software, and services |
| Corning | $50 | Fiber-optic networking technologies |
| Intel | $300 | Network infrastructure, wireless |
| Koor Industries (KOR) | $250 | Israeli-based information technology |
| Liberante Technologies (LBRT) | $50 | Interactive television |
| Merck | $100 | Health-care information technology |
| Nokia | $500 | Wireless applications and hardware |
| Qualcomm | $500 | Digital-wireless technology and services |

Source: Jim Evans. "Corporate Venture Grows Bold." *The Industry Standard.* January 10, 2001.

***Sample Players.*** The most high-profile holding companies have a clear focus to their investments. The Internet Capital Group (ICG) focuses investments in B2B Internet enterprises. CMGI focuses investments in the B2C space. Communicade, a division of the advertising company Omnicom, manages a variety of interactive-marketing companies, which include Agency.com, Organic, Razorfish, and Red Sky Interactive.

## Hybrid Sources of Funding.
The new economy brought attention not only to new types of business, but also to new sources of funding. Although here we have delineated different types of funding sources, in reality, many sources of funding are a hybrid of these types. For example, although CMGI is by definition a holding company, it is also an incubator, providing many operational services to its port-folio of startup businesses. Many of the top-notch venture-capital firms, such as Softbank and Benchmark Capital, also provide incubating services; many corporate-venture firms also do the same. Another example is a firm that is set up similar to venture-capital businesses, but offers debt financing. Sand Hill Capital, which functions as a cross between a bank and venture-capital firm, specifically offers additional short-term debt financing through bridge loans[49] and lines of credit[50] to those startups with venture-capital dollars. This provides additional capital without further equity dilution. (See "Sand Hill Capital" Drill-Down for further information.) As the financial needs of startups continue to evolve, other sources of hybrid financing are likely to develop.

Now, with a basic understanding of how human capital and the sources of financial capital can be managed to create a compelling business, we will discuss how to approach these funding sources with a business idea.

# PACKAGING YOUR OFFERING: PREPARING THE PITCH

# The Business Plan

At some point after thinking through the critical elements of the business planning process discussed in the previous section, a physical business plan document must be prepared to summarize the company for potential investors. While there are different sources of investor funding, and each may be looking for something specific,

## Case Example: Sand Hill Capital

In 1996, William Del Biaggio cofounded Sand Hill Capital with Daniel Corry. Frustrated with the difficulty of lending to startups, he wanted Sand Hill to serve as a "venture lender," somewhat of a cross between a bank and a venture-capital firm. Like VC firms it has a general partnership and limited partners, and receives about 20 percent of profits and a 2 percent management fee. But, because it is not a chartered bank, it is not subject to federal regulations, making most of its money from fees on loans and discounted warrants to buy stock in companies to which it lends. The money for the loans is obtained through limited partners.

Although Sand Hill did offer lines of credit and subordinated debt offerings, it has focused only on bridge loans since the market downturn in April 2000, lending money to startups that need cash to keep operations going while additional funding is found. Sand Hill finds its investments from among the 20 venture-capital firms it works with, which have investments in around 2,500 companies. It reviews 40 to 50 deals a month, and make six to eight loans. This is up from the IPO heyday when VC money was plentiful—then it saw only 10 to 15 deals per month and made loans to two to three companies. In light of the market downturn, more startups are desperate for short-term cash until additional funding can be secured. By the end of 2000, Sand Hill had $98 million in outstanding loans.[51]

preparation of the business plan document is largely the same, although it should be directed towards a specific audience. Here we will consider the objectives of the business plan, information that should be included in the document, and important document qualities.

The objective of the business plan is to pique the interest of investors. Similar to a resume, it should engage the curiosity of the investor enough to give the entrepreneur the opportunity to present the business in person. And, as with resumes, unsolicited business plans are largely ignored by investors. Good preparation of the document is important, but only networking on the part of the entrepreneur will get the business plan read—whether it is a referral to a VC from a friend or a match-up to a corporate-venture fund through an intermediary.

To that end, when investors actually read a business plan, they are looking for a concise justification of the startup's business opportunity and its advantage vis-à-vis other players that are pursuing this opportunity and they are looking for something compelling within three to four minutes of reading. A spectacular executive summary—a few pages that succinctly summarize all the poignant aspects of the business developed in the planning process—is the key to engage the reader. While the exact content will depend on each individual business, the following should be included:

1. Description of the product or service that will be offered and the value proposition for the customer
2. Summary of the size and nature of the market opportunity
3. Explanation of the revenue model
4. Profiles of the management team, advisory board, and board of director members describing specific relevant skills and experience (the first section most investors turn to in the business plan)

**5.** Clear articulation of the startup's core competencies and sustainable competitive advantage

**6.** Summary of financials and financing needs

The purpose of an executive summary is to interest the potential investor enough to ask further, more specific questions about the business. An example of a brief executive summary is included in Appendix A.

Visual presentation, quality writing, and honesty are important complements to the previously outlined content. Everything about the business plan should embody the type of organization the startup aspires to be. Graphics design does not need to be complex, but should be neat. Clear, straightforward writing will ensure that it is the business, rather than the composition, that attracts attention. Realism and honesty are important both for conveying the market opportunity and for underlying financial assumptions. While enthusiasm is important, investors are well conditioned to each entrepreneur believing he will easily conquer a new market with unprecedented returns. Unsubstantiated or exaggerated claims will detract from the entire business plan.

With a well-prepared business plan and a network of contacts, the entrepreneur may have an opportunity to present his business to an audience in person and actually pitch his idea.

## The Pitch

Closing a deal for funding to the point where all parties sign on the dotted line is a challenging, and usually lengthy, process. While the process is different depending on the startup, funding source, and market conditions, the basic succession of steps is the same. The entrepreneur must put on his salesman hat.

With a solid business plan in hand, the entrepreneur should launch a campaign to reach investors—after determining the ideal investors to target. However, before embarking on this quest, the entrepreneur should decide on a reasonable time frame to pursue funding sources (after which the business may fold, or need to look for alternative means) and how much time he will devote to the process. Although it is essential for the entrepreneur to participate, he should not lose sight of running the business and making sure it moves forward while funding is being sought.

After a great deal of persistence and thorough use of a network of personal contacts, an investor will review the entrepreneur's business plan. If interested, the investor will arrange an hour-long personal meeting with the entrepreneur to determine if the business is worth further research. At this point, the entrepreneur should prepare a concise PowerPoint presentation that summarizes the key aspects of the business, particularly addressing the business' competitive advantage and realistic estimates of return on investment. The level of detail should not bore or confuse the investor, but provide enough information to interest her in another meeting. The second meeting will usually run at least two hours, and should again involve a professional-quality presentation. At this point, if the funding source involves multiple individuals, such as a VC firm or a band of angels, more members of the entrepreneur's firm will be involved.

At both meetings, the entrepreneur should be prepared to answer difficult questions about his business plan, particularly questions about any proclaimed sustainable advantage that distinguishes the startup from other players and any assumptions made to determine return on investment. The entrepreneur will also need to play the role of salesman and advocate for the business, but not in an overly aggres-

*(continued on page 470)*

sive fashion. He wants the business to be valued on its merits, but needs to sufficiently interest the investor.

More often than not, some investors reject the entrepreneur during the quest for cash. However, these experiences help the entrepreneur learn what aspects of the business plan and pitch need to be tweaked for the next investor. Feedback from sources that have rejected the business is extremely valuable for iterating the business plan. If, on the other hand, the investors decide they are interested, they will most likely engage in some form of due diligence, depending on the type of funding sources and the resources available. Due diligence is a careful process on the part of the investor to check on the validity of the business plan and expertise of any individuals involved. References are checked, management team individuals interviewed, and business ideas tested. Potential customers may be interviewed on the likelihood of purchasing or using the product or service offered. When the investors are satisfied with what they find, they will preliminarily agree to fund the business enterprise.

However, nothing is final until the documents are signed and the cash is in the bank, and this comes only after a valuation for the firm is negotiated and determined (see Chapter 13).

# SUMMARY

### 1. What is a startup?

A startup is a business in the process of developing the underlying infrastructures needed to sustain future growth, specifically (1) developing and refining its offering and strategy to go to market, (2) obtaining initial funding to begin operations, and (3) building a capable management team to handle operations.

### 2. What are the key considerations in the business planning process?

Business planning is the dynamic process that brings together the elements of human and financial capital needed to build a business. It serves as an iterative template to constantly test the business and ensure a solid foundation for the future. A solid business plan should do the following:

1. Define the value proposition
2. Frame the market opportunity
3. Detail how to reach customers
4. Develop an implementation plan
5. Evaluate potential external influences
6. Articulate the revenue model
7. Identify people needed
8. Calculate preliminary financial projections
9. Establish critical milestones
10. Summarize the advantage

### 3. What are the different sources of human capital that can play a role in a startup business?

There are four key sources of human capital that can play a critical role in building an early-stage business: (1) the entrepreneur with the idea who begins the business; (2) the management team that transforms the entrepreneur's idea into an operational reality; (3) the strategic advisors and partners who provide direction, advice, and advantage through their own experiences; and (4) the logistical advisors and partners consisting of individuals and organizations that can fill missing skill sets within the nascent startup. Each plays a role in developing the business plan and also attracting financial capital.

## 4. What are the typical sources of funding for early-stage startup businesses?

The most typical sources of debt financing for startup businesses are trade credit and commercial bank loans. On the equity side, bootstrapping, angels, venture-capital firms, corporate ventures, and holding companies are the most common sources of financing. The government supports sources through the Small Business Administration (SBA), including SBA 7(a) loan guaranty programs and small-business investment companies (SBICs). Hybrid sources of funding, combinations of some of the previously mentioned sources, are also becoming more prevalent. Other sources of funding can include those that exchange services for equity rather than cash, such as potential logistical advisors and partners.

## 5. What elements are needed for a successful pitch to investors?

A successful pitch requires a solid business plan based on reality, but even more importantly, it requires that the entrepreneur make the right contacts in the industry that will get his business plan read. The business plan document should be brief, with a short and compelling executive summary. The pitch itself should be concise, clear, and convey the business' sustainable competitive advantage and financing needs, piquing the investor's interest in further meetings. Both the business plan document and the pitch should be grounded in truth and honesty, so as not to cloud the message and mission of the startup.

# KEY TERMS

| | |
|---|---|
| startup | intermediaries |
| business plan | incubator |
| business planning process | trade credit |
| entrepreneur | commercial bank loan |
| management team | bootstrapping |
| strategic advisors and partners | angel |
| logistical advisors and partners | venture-capital firm |
| debt financing | corporate venture |
| equity financing | holding company |
| human capital | pitch |
| financial capital | |

# Endnotes

[1]Merriam-Webster's online dictionary, Collegiate Dictionary copyright © 2001 by Merriam-Webster, Incorporated.

[2]Werner, Bernhard, and Miguel Helft. "How culture clash sank the Toys 'R' Us deal," *The Industry Standard,* 29 August, 1999.

[3]Evans, Jim. "Offline companies stalk Sand Hill Road," *The Industry Standard,* 23 July, 1999.

[4]Warner, Bernhard, and Miguel Helft. "Toysrus.com plays with Softbank," *The Industry Standard,* 23 February, 2000.

[5]Warner, Bernhard, and Miguel Helft. "Toysrus.com plays with Softbank," *The Industry Standard,* 23 February, 2000.

[6]Sahlman, William A. "Some thoughts on business plans," Case Study. Harvard Business School Publishing, 1996.

[7]Daly, James. "The death of ambition," *Business 2.0,* 9 January, 2001. *www.business2.com/content/insights/opinion/2001/01/02/23662.*

[8]Akst, Daniel. "Mirabilis dictu," *The Industry Standard,* 17 January, 2000.

[9]Davey, Tom. "Webvan is starving for cash," *Red Herring,* 2 January, 2001.

[10]Thomas, Susan L. "Skeptics eye Webvan," *Business 2.0,* 25 January, 2001.

[11]Helft, Miguel. "End of an era at Amazon.com," *The Industry Standard,* 5 February, 2001.

[12]Hellweg, Eric. "The Pets.com lesson," *Business 2.0,* 9 November, 2000.

[13]Boyett, Joseph H., and Jimmie T. Boyett. *The Guru Guide to Entrepreneurship* (New York: John Wiley & Sonsa, Inc., 2001).

[14]Akst, Daniel. "Mirabilis dictu," *The Industry Standard,* 17 January, 2000.

[15]Boyett, Joseph H., and Jimmie T. Boyett. *The Guru Guide to Entrepreneurship* (New York: John Wiley & Sonsa, Inc., 2001).

[16]Hamm, Steve. "The education of Marc Andreessen," *Business Week, Industrial/Technology Edition,* 13 April, 1998, 92.

[17]Boyett, Joseph H., and Jimmie T. Boyett. *The Guru Guide to Entrepreneurship* (New York: John Wiley & Sonsa, Inc., 2001).

[18]Louis, Dickson L. *Monster.com.* (Cambridge: Harvard Business School, 2000).

[19]Barack, Lauren. "Wanted: decent job site ads," *Business 2.0,* 26 September, 2000.

[20]Hellwab, Eric. "The sound of money," *Business 2.0,* 1 September, 1998.

[21]Shreve, Jenn. "Marc Andreessen: the valley's blank check," *The Industry Standard,* 16 February, 2000.

[22]Hazelton, Lesley. "Profile: Jeff Bezos," *Success,* July 1998, 60.

[23]Collins, James C., and Jerry I. Porras. *Built to Last* (New York: Harper-Collins, 1997).

[24]Collins, James C., and Jerry I. Porras. *Built to Last* (New York: Harper-Collins, 1997).

[25]Johnston & Johnston Development Corporation presentation.

[26]Li, Kenneth. "NBC, Ralph Lauren to fashion media venture," *The Industry Standard,* 7 February, 2000.

[27]Necheim, John L. *High Tech Start Up* (New York: The Free Press, 2000).

[28]Red Herring.com, *www.redherring.com/vc/2001/0103/vc-incubators1013001.html.*

[29]PricewaterhouseCoopers and VentureOne. "PWC moneytree survey 2001," PricewaterhouseCoopers 2001. *http://pwcmoneytree.com/aggregatemenu/asp.*

[30]Evans, Jim. "Corporate venture grows bold," *The Industry Standard,* 10 January, 2001.

[31]Return on investment: the ratio of after-tax operating income to the net (depreciated) book value of assets. (Richard A. Brealey and Stewart C. Myers. *Principles of Corporate Finance* (New York: McGraw-Hill, 1996.)

[32]Internal rate of return: Discount rate at which an investment has zero net present value (same source as above).

[33]Cost of capital: Expected return that is forgone by investing in a project rather than in comparable financial securities (same source as above).

[34]Return on equity: Equity earnings as a proportion of the book value of equity (same source as above).

[35]J&J Presentation.

[36]"Venture capital and angels provide just over 7% of funding for private companies," Business Wire, 23 April, 1999.

[37]7(A) Loan Guarantee Program Small Business Association. *www.sba.gov/financing/fr7aloan.html.*

[38]7(A) Loan Guarantee Program Small Business Association. *www.sba.gov/financing/fr7aloan.html.*

[39]American Express Small Business Services. "Angels," *http://home3.americanexpress.com/smallbusiness/resources/expanding/financing/angels.shtml.*

[40]Center for Venture Research at the University of New Hampshire.

[41]Ehrenfeld, Tom Ehrenfeld. "The angel's share," *The Industry Standard,* 19 June, 2000.

[42]Seed stage investments by venture capital in 1999. First round financing investments totaled $36 billion. *Venture Economics,* 2000 National Venture Capital Association Yearbook.

[43]American Express Small Business Service. "Venture Capital," *http://home3.americanexpress.com/smallbusiness/resources/expanding/financing/venture_cap.shtml.*

[44]Nesheim, John L. *High Tech Start Up* (New York: Free Press, 2000).

[45]PricewaterhouseCoopers and VentureOne. "PWC moneytree survey 2001," PricewaterhouseCoopers 2001. *http://pwcmoneytree.com/aggregatemenu/asp.*

[46]PricewaterhouseCoopers and VentureOne. "PWC moneytree survey 2001," PricewaterhouseCoopers 2001. *http://pwcmoneytree.com/aggregatemenu/asp.*

[47]Small Business Association Homepage. *www.sbaonline.sba.gov.*

[48]Rabinovitz, Jonathan. "Venture capital, Inc," *The Industry Standard,* 10 April, 2000.

[49]Bridge loan: Short-term working capital loan designed to bridge a company to its next liquidity event, typically with a maturity schedule of three to six months (*www.sandhillcapital.com*).

[50]Lines of credit: Longer-term working capital with a maturity schedule of about twelve months (same source as above).

[51]Aragon, Lawrence. "Getting into debt," *Red Herring,* 17 January, 2001.

13

# Working with Funders

In the previous chapter, we discussed the beginnings of building a business, from the idea to the business plan to formulating the pitch. In this chapter, we continue our exploration of the capital infrastructure. We begin with a more in-depth discussion of the equity financing most commonly used by e-commerce companies: bootstrapping, angels, and venture capital. We then cover the different methods available for valuing a company, the basics of negotiation, different methods of exit (liquidity events), and future trends in the capital market. The previous chapter focused on putting business elements together to attract financial capital and make basic decisions about selecting appropriate sources of funding. In this chapter, we walk through the mechanics of obtaining financial capital, providing the information needed to raise financing, protect a company from a bad deal, and follow through to a liquidity event for the company.

## QUESTIONS

*Please keep the following questions in mind while reading this chapter:*

1. What are the major sources of equity financing, and how do these sources differ from one another?

2. How is the value of a startup determined?

3. What are the steps involved in negotiating with investors?

4. What is an IPO? What process must an entrepreneur undertake to complete an IPO successfully?

---

This chapter was coauthored by Bernie Jaworski, Jeffrey Rayport, Dorsey McGlone, and Ellie Kyung.

# INTRODUCTION

Once an entrepreneur has an idea, a great management team, a concise and compelling business plan, and an overview of the landscape of potential funding sources, she has to decide from whom to take the money that her company needs to grow and prosper. Before jumping headlong into raising funds for her business, she must ponder the sobering statistics presented in Exhibit 13-1. Venture capital is not as easy to obtain as it was in the years preceding 2000. VCs are investing more money in expansion rounds for existing portfolio companies, rather than funding seed and early rounds.

According to Michael Gerber, the author of *E-Myth,* "businesses start and fail in the United States at an increasingly staggering rate. Every year, over a million people in this country start a business. Statistics tell us that by the end of the first year, at least 40 percent of them will be out of business. Within five years, more than 80 percent of them will have failed." Of those that survive in the first five years, 80 percent of these businesses will fail within the next five years.[1]

**Exhibit 13-1**

## VENTURE CAPITAL PYRAMID

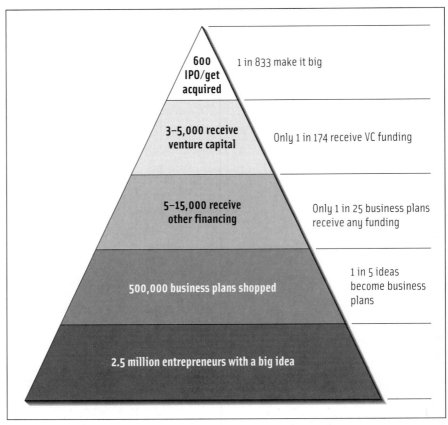

Source: Andrea Hamilton, Debra Aho Williamson, and Maryann Jones Thompson, "High Noon," *The Industry Standard,* June 12, 2000.

While starting a successful company is certainly not impossible, the market for e-commerce business certainly cooled in the year 2000 with the return to more sane valuations for Internet companies. The Nasdaq, once at a high of 5048.62 on March 10, 2000, closed at a low of 2117.63 nearly a year later on March 2, 2001—a 58 percent loss of value. The interesting question is whether value was destroyed (which presupposes that value existed in the first place) or if the market simply got smart. We may never know. However, considering the slowdown of venture-capital cash infusions into startups and the dizzying devaluation of top e-companies, the pendulum may have swung too far in the opposite direction. Table 13-1 illustrates the valuation downturn for several companies once considered leaders in their industry.

All of this is clearly bad news for entrepreneurs seeking funding from venture capitalists, but, as was discussed in the preceding chapter, venture capitalists are not major players in financing the majority of startups. However, because this book concentrates on e-commerce companies, we take a closer look in this chapter at venture capital and two other sources of equity financing: bootstrapping and angels. As indicated by Exhibit 13-2, the allocation of venture-capital dollars to Internet-related ventures has increased steadily in the past five years, accounting for 83 percent of investments in 2000. While it is important to have a general understanding of the most popular forms of debt financing and when they may be appropriate to include in a company's funding mix, debt financing is appropriate only when the startup business has some sort of stable cash-flow cycle, and it is safe to assume that it will not default on the terms of financing.

After taking a closer look at the three main sources of equity financing, we detail the basics of valuation, including the primary methods used in the industry as well as the method most often employed by venture capitalists. Next, we explore the process of negotiating with a venture capitalist, with special emphasis on the basics of a terms sheet and the securities most commonly used to structure deals. This discussion includes a simple but detailed explanation of dilution and pre- and post-money valuations. The next section covers liquidity events, concentrating specifically on the basics of initial public offerings (IPOs)—including the step-by-step process that every company must go through to become public—with a quick overview of mergers and acquisitions. In the final section, we take a stab at predicting future trends.

 **Table 13-1**

## DIZZYING DEVALUATION

| Company | High | Current Status |
|---|---|---|
| eToys (ETYS) *Leading online toy retailer* | $84.25 (10/11/99) | $0.0938 (2/26/2000: Last day traded) Filed for chapter 11 March 7, 2001 |
| Pets.com (IPET) *Leading online pet retailer* | $11 (2/11/00) | $0.125 (2/21/2001:Last day traded) Stockholders voted for liquidation and dissolution January 16, 2001 |
| drkoop.com (KOOP) *Leading online medical content site* | $36.86 (7/6/99) | $0.25 (3/6/2001) Stock hovered around $0.21 to $0.25 during February and March. |

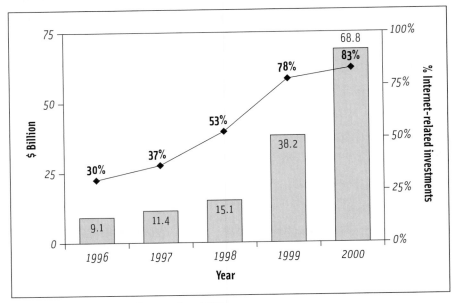

Source: PricewaterhouseCoopers Moneytree Report 2000

# EQUITY FINANCING

The previous chapter provided an overview of the different sources of funding, explaining the basics of what they are, their criteria for investment, and their key advantages and disadvantages for the entrepreneur. Because we will go into the mechanics of working with funders in this chapter, we provide further information about what the entrepreneur or management should consider when using the three most common equity sources. For bootstrapping, angels, and venture capital, we will detail the following:

1. Recent industry facts and figures regarding the market attractiveness of the source
2. Key considerations for the entrepreneur or management when thinking about using the source

## The Art of Bootstrapping

**Recent Industry Facts and Figures.** Every true entrepreneur, at one time, has probably bootstrapped a company in its early years. As explained in Chapter 12, bootstrapping is the act of using personal resources to get the beginning stages of a business off of the ground. While this may seem like a piecemeal process, it is often necessary and, more importantly, successful. According to garage.com, "Interviews with the founders of 100 companies on a recent Inc. 500 list attributed their initial success to bootstrap financing. More than 80 percent of these Inc. 500 fastest-growing private companies were initially financed solely by bootstrapping. The median startup capital of these 100 companies was approximately $10,000. Bootstrapping is a viable and often necessary form of financing for entrepreneurs."[2]

Bootstrapping produces over 40 percent of all financing used during the course of starting a business. Several prominent companies have been created through bootstrapping (Microsoft and Apple, just to name two). However, bootstrapping was not very popular in the late nineties. When *Red Herring* magazine selected the best bootstrap of 1999, the award went to: "Nobody." The magazine stated, "With venture capitalists practically throwing money at young companies and valuations continuing to soar, startups have little incentive to go it alone anymore."[3]

Although this was true in 1999, the climate certainly changed the next year. With venture-capital money more difficult to find, entrepreneurs might once again have to return to bootstrapping their ventures through the proof-of-concept phase. Indeed, many companies, regardless of their performance, simply are not qualified for venture-capital funding, which seeks out very specific types of investments.

## Key Considerations.
Bootstrapping sounds like a very difficult process, and it is, but there are some real benefits to bootstrapping a company. "Bootstrapping in a startup company is like zero inventory in a just-in-time system: It reveals hidden problems and forces the company to solve them."[4] In other words, there is a downside to receiving funding too early in the process of starting the venture. Cash in the bank covers up problems that would otherwise become apparent, financing terms can restrict flexibility (many outside investors will not stand by as a startup tries an iterative approach to strategy), and an entrepreneur who receives funding too early in his career might not have the tactical, day-to-day management experience or the credibility to stand up to investors should there be differences of opinion on what is best for the company.

***Some Guiding Principles.*** How does an entrepreneur decide when bootstrapping is right for him? Obviously, each opportunity and company is unique, and the path of financing taken during the bootstrapping years is going to be as individual as the entrepreneurs themselves. However, according to Bhide's work on entrepreneurial ventures, there are some common principles to follow while trying to start a company.[5] When starting a new company, entrepreneurs should keep the following principles in mind:

- *Get operational as soon as possible.* New ideas and winning strategies are often formed while working on another problem within the company. Running the company will not only generate revenues, but will also allow the entrepreneur and any management team that has been assembled to gain some quick wins. These wins will establish a pattern of success that will increase the confidence of investors in future rounds. In addition, the management team can assess how well they work together, what holes exist within the current team, and the best ways to leverage complementary talents.

- *Take on cash-generating projects, even if they are not in line with the written strategy.* While this tactic is usually disastrous for large companies, a small company is flexible enough to take on these quick, one-off projects, and positive cash flow will give the entrepreneur and his company added credibility with customers, suppliers, employees, and future financiers. Sometimes a bootstrapper has to take on one job that is not in his focus in order to pay for development of the product/service that his company wants as its future business focus.

- *Go the extra mile.* Bootstrappers must put in the sweat needed to deliver a product successfully to those first clients who take a chance on them. This means going above and beyond the call of duty to satisfy customers, which are among the greatest assets of a company and necessary for references.

- *Growing too fast can be just as dangerous as not growing at all.* There is a natural sustainable growth rate that the entrepreneur's business should not pass. The trick is to grow at a steady pace and keep an eye on cash flow. Consider the trade-credit example from the previous chapter. If customers are not paying their bills on time, they are, in essence, being extended an interest-free loan. Most startups cannot afford to float cash to their customers. If the customer base grows too rapidly, and too many of the customers decide not to pay on time, the company can quickly run out of cash. Accounts receivable, while they may be assets on the balance sheet, are not the same thing as money in the bank.

- *Get comfortable with being cheap, but do not skimp on the essentials of the business.* For example, a company should set up a no-frills office, but buy the best computer equipment possible if that equipment is essential to the success of the business.

- *Establish a relationship with a bank as soon as possible.* Even if the entrepreneur is not getting a loan, he should make sure that his books are neat and accurate from day one. And, as stated before, even if he does not need a loan right away, it is not a bad idea for the entrepreneur to apply for one and pay it off promptly to show the bank that he is a safe investment.

Last and most importantly, when bootstrapping a startup, an entrepreneur must always remember these three words: *cash is king.* This phrase should be the mantra of the entrepreneur. If his idea is a good one, the entrepreneur will eventually need more cash than he can provide to the venture through personal resources. Indeed, in the fast-moving world of e-commerce, sometimes the entrepreneur simply cannot take the time to build a company alone from the ground up. With competitors moving at lightning speed and a market that changes so fast that today's newest technology can slip into obsolescence overnight, obtaining substantial amounts of capital usually makes the difference between a great idea that never makes it to market and an idea that builds a strong and lasting company. Therefore, we will cover equity financing, from both angels and venture capitalists, in detail. Keep in mind, however, that many of the principles that help entrepreneurs start a company through bootstrapping are still extremely important, even with an outside infusion of cash.

## Angels

### Recent Industry Facts and Figures.
As described in the previous chapter, angels are wealthy individuals who invest their own capital in startup companies they find intriguing and potentially lucrative as investment opportunities. In a study by Genesis Technology Partners commissioned by Harvard Business School and the MIT Entrepreneurial Center, angel investors were broken down into four groups: guardian angels (industry veterans), professional-entrepreneur angels (angels who are less-experienced), operational-expertise angels (large-company senior executives), and financial-return angels (wealthy individuals).[6] Depending upon several

factors (including internal management expertise, strength of relationships with key suppliers and customers, structure of the industry in which the company plans to compete, and the company's financial strength), different types of angels will be more or less suitable as investors in a company.

Although the press has focused much of its attention on the venture-capital community, the dollar investment made by angels in seed-stage companies in the United States is nearly twice that of venture capitalists. We mentioned previously that estimates for angel investments range from $20 billion to $50 billion, but this actually represents only a fraction of potential angel financing. Given the large number of people with investable assets over $1 million, angels can prove to be an even larger source of investment in the future (depending, of course, on how the current market downturn has affected personal portfolios).

## Key Considerations.
According to Ron Conway, cofounder and general partner at Angel Investors, "We're willing to help a company that needs less than $1 million. A top-tier VC won't even consider these companies. They've got bigger fish to fry. Just during this year, the minimum investment by a top-tier VC has gone from $2 million to $5 million. It's unbelievable. So who's going to fund companies that need less than a million bucks?"[7] The answer is that angels will fund these companies, and provide valuable expertise, in addition to cash, as part of the deal.

### What to Look for in an Angel.
What qualities should an entrepreneur look for in an angel? Ron Conway tells the entrepreneur to ask these questions:

- What is their track record?
- Have they funded other successful startups in similar spaces?
- How available are they?
- With whom do they coinvest?
- Will they bring in a really good group of angels besides themselves?
- Who is in their Rolodex, and are they willing to open it up to help the company?[8]
- How many deals do they invest in per year?
- Will they roll up their sleeves and work with the entrepreneur (and management team) to build the company, or are they more "hands-off" in their approach? Which is preferred?

### Advantages and Disadvantages of Angel Financing.
As with any other source of investment, there are positive and negative aspects to investing with angels. While we discussed some of the more general pros and cons of using angel financing in the previous chapter, we expand here on those aspects in the context of actually structuring a deal.

**Pros**

- Angels tend to be more flexible on their exit strategy.
- A term sheet from an angel tends to favor the entrepreneur more than a term sheet from a VC.
- Taking less money from an angel provides the company a chance to prove the concept (through prototyping, market testing, etc.), focus the strategy, round

out the management team and, therefore, improve the valuation before approaching a VC later.

**Cons**

- Because angels are individual investors, backing out of deals at the last minute occurs more frequently than with traditional VCs or other funding sources.
- Inexperienced angels might put together poorly structured deals that have to be restructured by VCs investing in later rounds.
- If the investment sought is rather large for an angel network (e.g., $2 million) the company might have difficulty finding the required number of investors that can be pooled together to create the needed investment. In addition, it will be harder to manage this large group of investors after the investment has been made. Investors should be chosen wisely, and the entrepreneur should think seriously about how he will manage a large pool of investors. Investors will have approval on all future rounds of financing, so the entrepreneur needs to make sure that he does not get locked into a situation from which VCs will shy away.

However, most angels are savvy enough to construct deals that will be attractive to future financing from VCs. After all, if a VC invests in the deal, the company has a greater chance of success, and therefore the angel has a greater opportunity to increase the value of his initial investment. "The biggest milestone for an angel is to get the company funded by a top-tier VC."[9]

*Angels and Equity.* On average, angels will receive between 4 percent and 5 percent of the company (an average deal might be a $200,000 investment at a $5 million valuation). Of course, valuations will be higher based upon the quality of the management team (if there is one in place), the clarity of the pitch, the nature and size of the market that the idea addresses, and the general track record of the entrepreneur. Entrepreneurs should not worry too much about valuation, though. Ron Conway says, "A CEO who's completely stuck on valuation is a warning sign. That's a CEO who's confused about his role. The bottom line: if the idea is great, you'll end up with a multibillion dollar market cap and everyone will make more money than they can ever spend. Rather than focusing on valuation, focus on execution."[10]

In addition, just like valuation, the entrepreneur should not worry too much about dilution, since 100 percent of nothing is nothing. (In the Negotiations section we will discuss points to remember about dilution when constructing a deal.) In the same vein, too much energy should not be spent worrying that someone will steal the idea. The entrepreneur must be open about explaining his idea to others to try to raise interest in funding the company. Top angels and VCs explain that an entrepreneur who is overly worried about secrecy is not concentrating on the right things. If he is too concerned with confidentiality, the entrepreneur will not be focused on building the company.[11]

There is a symbiotic relationship between angels and venture capitalists, because the structure of a venture-capital firm makes it less likely that the two groups will be competing for the same deals. Angels fulfill the important role of closing the "capital gap" that exists between an entrepreneur who is bootstrapping his company and one who needs a larger investment (e.g., in the $5 million range) from a venture-capital firm. Angels will invest sums from a few thousand dollars to a few million, and (the good ones) will help the company get to its next round of financing by talking to venture capitalists in their network.

# The Venture-Capital Community

## Recent Industry Facts and Figures.
As previously described, VCs are in the business of finding companies with the potential for great economic return, nurturing them, then "cashing out" to make a return on their investment. The venture-capital community controls more than 500 funds, managing increasingly larger sums each year. In 1998, venture-capital investments totaled $15 billion; in 1999, $38 billion; in 2000, a staggering $69 billion. The average investment per company (both startups and later-stage companies) in 2000 was $15.2 million, with a slight dip in the fourth quarter when 1,345 companies received an average of $14.2 million each. The majority of investments are in expansion-stage companies, with estimates ranging from 54 percent to 80 percent in 2000.* Internet-specific companies received a total of $56.9 billion in funding in 2000.[12] The amount of money invested in entrepreneurial ventures increased dramatically from $4.1 billion in the second quarter of 1999 to $19.6 billion in the second quarter of 2000. The number of Internet-related deals nearly tripled from 1,085 to 3,197 between 1998 and 2000.[13]

**Exhibit 13-3**

VENTURE CAPITAL—MARKET SIZE

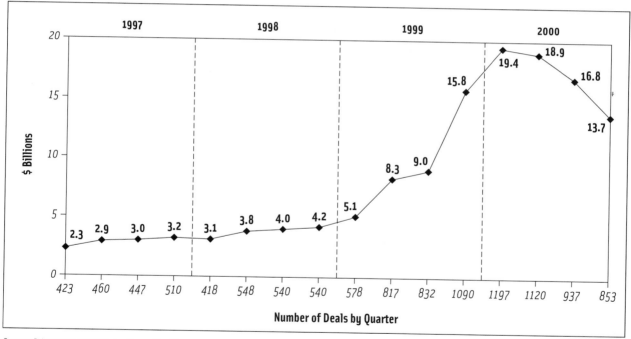

Source: PricewaterhouseCoopers Money Tree Report 2000

---

*It should be noted that one of the confusing things about researching numbers in the venture-capital industry is that the two main sources, VentureOne and Venture Economics, which supplies numbers to the NVCA, have different approaches to counting VC firms. VentureOne does not include any SBICs or corporate ventures, whereas Venture Economics does. PricewaterhouseCoopers, another major source, has numbers closer to those of VentureOne. This leads to vast differences in the numbers given by each firm, and the range of numbers that we have available here. Be sure to check the data source when comparing numbers related to the venture-capital industry.

Yet even with this huge influx of cash, receiving venture-capital funding does not always guarantee success. According to VentureOne, of the 3,018 Internet companies that received venture-capital funding between 1994 and the first quarter of 2000, only about 600 have gone public or been acquired.

**Key Considerations.** Given the prominence of venture-capital investments in Internet-related ventures, we delve in some detail into the industry to provide further context for valuation and deal structuring in future sections.

***Structure of Venture-Capital Funds.*** While we briefly reviewed venture-capital firms and how they make money in the previous chapter, it is necessary to have a deeper understanding of how they are structured to further understand their motivation when making investments. Venture-capital funds are organized as limited partnerships consisting of general partners and limited partners. The venture-capital firm serves as the general partner, and private investors are known as limited partners. (These private investors are the pension funds, corporations, individuals, financial and insurance companies, endowments, foundations, and foreign investors we discussed in the previous chapter.) In general, because of the long-term nature of the investment and the significant capital requirement, VC funds do not serve as vehicles for the average individual investor. VCs also invest some of their own money into the fund, which is beneficial to both the VC and the limited partners. For the VCs, the investment provides them with additional monetary gain, and for the limited partners, an investment on behalf of the VCs ensures that the VCs' incentives are in line with those of the limited partners. Exhibit 13-4 details the breakdown of investors in venture-capital funds.

***How Venture-Capital Firms Make Money.*** As mentioned in the previous chapter, venture-capital firms make money through a combination of profits on investments and management fees. The VC uses the money raised to invest in private companies with a potential for great economic return, hoping to guide the investment to a liquidity event—normally an initial public offering (IPO), merger, or acquisition—allowing them to cash out and provide a significant return on their investment. The VC then split the returns with the limited partners. The VC (or general partner) receives an annual management fee to cover salaries and expenses, also known as "committed capital," and a percentage of profit from investment, also referred to as "carried interest." (This percentage of profits, or "carry," generally ranges between 20 percent and 25 percent, although in recent years, VCs have been able to increase their carry because of the enormous success of venture-capital investing, due in large part to the hot IPO market.) The limited partners receive their original investment, plus their share of the profits, after the general partners have taken their carry. The average life of a fund is 10 years, but VCs target companies that will make a return in about five years.

***How Funds Are Created.*** Venture-capital funds come in all shapes and sizes, and each venture-capital firm might have several funds under management simultaneously. Each fund is a legally separate entity, with different groups of investors and different strategies for investment. The pool of money in the fund is fixed, meaning that once the venture-capital firm has raised a predetermined amount of money, the fund is closed and cannot receive any additional capital infusions. Average venture-capital fund sizes continue to grow. In the third quarter of 2000, the average fund size closed was $259 million (an increase of 65 percent over the previous quarter),[14] but funds from a few million dollars up to billions of dollars

**Exhibit 13-4**

## 1999 CAPITAL COMMITMENTS BY LIMITED PARTNER TYPE

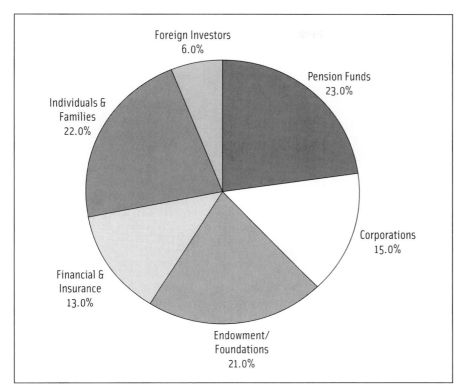

Foreign Investors
6.0%

Pension Funds
23.0%

Individuals & Families
22.0%

Corporations
15.0%

Financial & Insurance
13.0%

Endowment/ Foundations
21.0%

Source: 2000 National Venture Capital Association Yearbook

exist. The venture-capital industry has four main players: startups who need funding, investors who want high returns, investment bankers who need companies to take public, and the venture capitalists who make money for themselves by making a market for the other three.

***Where Venture-Capital Firms Make Investments.*** Each venture-capital firm has a unique personality. A few invest primarily in seed or early-stage companies; others reserve their investments until a company has begun to succeed and is entering into a growth or expansion stage. Still others wait until the company is about to have a liquidity event (usually an IPO or a merger or acquisition). The majority of venture-capital investments are in companies that have entered an expansion phase: those that need money to expand current production capabilities or sales forces, need financing to provide working capital, or are about to enter a substantial growth phase (Exhibit 13-5). This does not include the majority of startups that need money just to get an idea off of the ground or to recruit a management team.

As mentioned in the previous chapter, venture-capital firms participate in all stages of a startup, but most of the venture capital recently invested has been in the expansion stages, as more large VC firms focus on those companies to speed up time to exit and concentrate on higher, investment-dollar opportunities (see Exhibit 13-7, page 488). In the first quarter of 2000, 85 percent of all VC investments went

**Exhibit
13-5**  HOW THE VENTURE-CAPITAL INDUSTRY WORKS

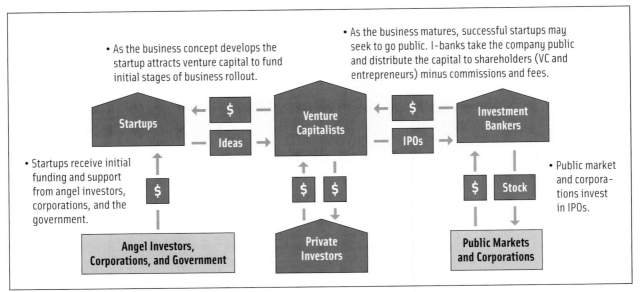

• As the business concept develops the startup attracts venture capital to fund initial stages of business rollout.

• As the business matures, successful startups may seek to go public. I-banks take the company public and distribute the capital to shareholders (VC and entrepreneurs) minus commissions and fees.

• Startups receive initial funding and support from angel investors, corporations, and the government.

• Public market and corporations invest in IPOs.

Source: Reprinted by permission of *Harvard Business Review*. From "How Venture Capital Works" by Bob Zider, Nov–Dec 1998.

to companies in early or expansion stage versus 65 percent in the first quarter of 1999. Expansion-stage companies received the largest percentage of investment in the first quarter of 2000, with 62 percent of invested money.

Some VCs target their investments in particular industries, technologies, or geographic locations, while others take a more generalist approach to their investments. However, the majority of VC investments are in the high-tech industry. VCs differ in the amount of average investment, which can range from as low as a few million dollars all the way up to tens of millions of dollars for the larger venture-capital firms and strategic investors—some may invest even more. VCs are normally very active investors, helping to guide the invested companies by providing network contacts, management help, or industry expertise. Almost all will take a seat on the board as a minimum level of involvement. In recent years, however, many VCs have taken a more hands-off approach to investing—that is, until the entrepreneur misses a milestone or if the company seems to be faltering under current management. In the land grab for deals, many spread themselves too thin and were not able to spend the requisite amount of time with their invested companies. The consequence of this lack of attention was that many promising companies that could have been helped, had the VCs been more involved, ended up faltering and even failing.

Yet, because of the structure of their industry, almost all VCs are only interested in certain variables: large market, proprietary or revolutionary product, and a competent and winning management team. In addition, it is likely that a company will deal with more than one VC. Syndication within the industry is the norm, allowing VCs to spread the risk involved in any one venture, and provides valuable networking within the industry.

# Why VC Investing?

Because it is profitable. Between 1989 and 1999 venture capital outperformed all the major equity classes, as well as fixed income. Over the course of that period, venture capital (represented by 800 venture pools) outpaced large-, mid-, small-, and micro-capitalization U.S. stocks and international equities.[15]

**Exhibit 13-6**

## ROI ON VC INVESTMENTS

| What $1 Invested in Different Markets in 1989 Grew to Be Worth in 1994 and 1999 | | | |
|---|---|---|---|
| | **1989** | **1994** | **1999** |
| VC–Venture Economics Pooled | $1 | $1.90 | $7.61 |
| S&P 500 Index | $1 | $1.87 | $6.08 |
| MSCI Eafe Index | $1 | $1.55 | $4.70 |
| Lehman Gov./Corp. Bond Index | $1 | $1.87 | $3.69 |

Source: Red Herring.com

***Recent Trends in Venture-Capital Investments.*** In the past few years, venture-capitalist funding flowed in increasingly large proportions to early-stage companies. The venture capitalists swooped in on these early-stage companies hoping to fund the next Yahoo or eBay, but with recent market corrections venture capitalists are returning to the basics. A report from the National Venture Capital Association and Venture Economics found that investments in new ventures have been dropping steadily for the past three years. In 1998, 43 percent of venture-capital dollars went to early-stage companies; in 1999 it was 34 percent. The level of investment fell to 33 percent for all of 2000, and only 26 percent in the fourth quarter of 2000. Venture capitalists are decreasing funding of early-stage companies and turning their energies to investing more money in the stronger companies in their portfolios, hoping to salvage returns for their funds. According to Steve Lazarus, a partner in ARCH Venture Partners and a board member of the National Venture Capital Association, "We have slowed down and the watchword right now is *caution.*" Mr. Lazarus also stated that the pullback in investing did not represent an anomaly, but rather a return to a more traditional state of affairs after the dot-com boom.[16]

Most analysts believe that once VCs get their houses in order, they will begin investing in technology again, and they expect the tech sector to respond with another wave of innovative products. Kirk Walden, director of venture-capital research at PricewaterhouseCoopers, says that even with a decline in funding in the

**Exhibit 13-7** VENTURE-CAPITAL INVESTMENTS—BREAKDOWN BY STAGE

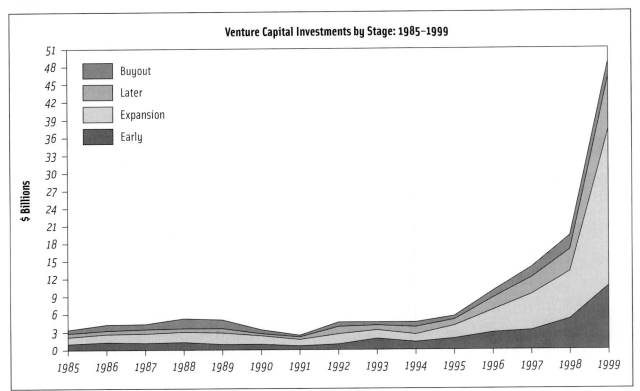

Venture Capital Investments by Stage: 1985–1999

Note: 1998 was atypical because Warburg, Pincus Equity Partners (NY) raised $5BB to start its fund
Source: 2000 National Venture Capital Association Yearbook

fourth quarter of 2000, venture capitalists invested about $70 billion for the year, or double the 1999 figure. "There will be fewer deals and less money invested this year," Walden says. "That's a virtual certainty, but investments could still be triple what was invested in 1998."[17]

***The Final Word for Entrepreneurs.*** Venture-capital dollars will be harder to come by, but the VCs will still be looking for smart investments in early-stage companies that show the potential for rapid growth and superior returns. The new climate will mean that entrepreneurs will have to have better business plans, better management teams, and more profitable business models to receive venture-capital dollars. The entrepreneur will have to be smarter than his predecessors of just three years ago.

Table 13-2 shows a summary of all the sources of financing over the life of a new venture. We covered the most frequently used sources in the early stages of business development in Chapter 12. Those that we have not discussed in detail are defined briefly in Table 13-3. We will offer a further explanation of IPOs and acquisitions later in this chapter.

# VALUATION

**Valuation** is the act of trying to determine a company's worth. Valuation forms the basis from which an entrepreneur and a venture capitalist will determine what percentage of the company the financier would ask to own, based upon the cash that the financier is willing to give. There are many different methods that can be used to value a company, and each method may produce a different result. As with many seemingly mathematical approaches, valuation is as much an art as it is a science. The goal of valuation is to determine a reasonable range of values for the company as a starting point in negotiations. We will not attempt to discuss all of the intricacies of valuation (indeed, that would take several books); rather, we will explain the most commonly used methods of valuing a company, provide easy-to-understand examples, and point out the strengths and weaknesses inherent in each valuation technique.

The three most commonly used methods of valuing a company are based on: comparison with similar companies (the comparables method), future income streams (financial performance method) and assets (asset-based valuation).

## The Comparables Method

Valuing a company with the **comparables method** essentially means placing a price on the company by comparing it to other companies (both privately and publicly held) that are similar. The first item of business is to find several companies similar to the startup to use as a basis of comparison. The comparison companies should be similar in as many respects as possible, especially in the following areas: industry focus, income statement ratios (e.g., sales to costs), location, relationship with suppliers, customer base (e.g., number of customers, diversification of customer base), potential growth (types of cash flows expected over a given time period), growth rate, and capital structure (the percentage of debt and equity in the company).

Obviously, no two companies will be identical (or at least one should hope that there are no identical, established companies in the marketplace). Therefore, it is the management team's job to look for the best matches and then make intelligent changes to the value placed on those companies to more closely reflect the business. One of the weaknesses of the comparables method is that it may be extremely hard to gain information on private companies, which are more likely to resemble the startup than a public company; therefore, it is difficult to value the startup. In addition, if a public company is used for comparison, the major difference between the startup and the public company is that there is a market for the public company's shares (i.e., they are "liquid"). Due to this difference, whenever using a public company as a basis for comparison for valuation, the amount of the valuation must be discounted to compensate for illiquidity. For example, if a public company is worth $10 million, the startup might be valued at only $7.5 million, even if the two companies are identical. This is because the startup's shares are not traded publicly yet (they are "illiquid"), and therefore are worth less than shares that can be sold easily in the public market. Surveys suggest that the discount for illiquidity is normally between 25 percent and 30 percent.[18] Another major difference is that a public company will have a different capital structure, and adjustments will have to be made for this as well.

Generally, most of the information that is used in calculating a valuation based on comparables is accounting based. For example, some of these accounting-based measurements include: a company's PE ratio (market price per share divided by

**Table 13-2**

SUMMARY OF SOURCES OF NEW VENTURE FINANCING

| Sources of New Venture Financing | | | | | |
|---|---|---|---|---|---|
| **Financier** | **Development** | **Startup** | **Early Growth** | **Rapid Growth** | **Exit** |
| Entrepreneur | ■ Primary | ▨ Secondary | | | |
| Friends and Family | ■ Primary | ▨ Secondary | | | |
| Angel Investors | ■ Primary | ■ Primary | ▨ Secondary | ▨ Secondary | |
| Strategic Partner | ■ Primary | ■ Primary | ■ Primary | ■ Primary | |
| Venture Capital | ▨ Secondary | ■ Primary | ■ Primary | ■ Primary | |
| Asset-based Lender* | | ■ Primary | ■ Primary | ■ Primary | |
| Equipment Lessor | | ■ Primary | ■ Primary | ■ Primary | |
| SBIC | | ■ Primary | ■ Primary | ■ Primary | |
| Trade Credit | | | ■ Primary | ■ Primary | |
| Mezzanine Lender | | | | ■ Primary | ■ Primary |
| IPO | | | | | ■ Primary |
| Acquisition, LBO, MBO | | | | | ■ Primary |

■ **Primary focus**   ▨ **Secondary focus or focus of a subset of investors of that type**

Source: From *Entrepreneurial Finance* by Richard L. Smith and Janet Kilhom Smith (John Wiley & Sons, Inc. 2000). This material is used by permission of a subsidiary of John Wiley & Sons, Inc.
Note: *Asset-based lenders are the debt-financing sources that include commercial bank loans. Further definition of sources not covered in the chapter are available in Table 13-3.

earnings per share), the market-to-book ratio (market value of the company's equity divided by the book value of shareholder's equity on the balance sheet), and comparisons of EBIT (earnings before interest and taxes).

However, these accounting-based measurements are not as useful when attempting to value an early-stage company, because the company has not yet posted a profit and is experiencing rapid growth. For an e-commerce company, it makes sense to look for more valid means of comparison. For instance, what are the key drivers of success in the startup's industry? Is it the number of Web hits? Number of registered users? The relationship with suppliers? Whatever the key metrics are, they should be the measurements used when attempting to create a valuation based on comparables.

## The Financial Performance Method

The **financial performance method** of valuation uses a company's earnings or potential earnings to project future cash flows and then applies a discount rate to determine the present value (PV) of those cash flows. It is therefore known as the

**Table 13-3**

## DEFINITIONS OF OTHER SOURCES OF FUNDING

| Funding Source | Definition |
|---|---|
| Equipment Lessor | Equipment lessors finance various equipment types generally costing $1 million or more (production equipment, R&D equipment, etc.) for midsize companies and large corporations, for lease terms of three to seven years. |
| Mezzanine Lender | A mezzanine lender (like the VC professional) employs active investment professionals who negotiate the purchase of privately placed securities in venture-capital/private equity transactions, such as buyouts; but the securities purchased are normally from the portfolio company and are predominantly debt securities, such as a slice of common stock, warrants, or conversion rights. |
| Leveraged Buyout (LBO) | An LBO is a takeover of a company using borrowed funds. Most often, the target company's assets serve as security for the loans taken out by the acquiring firm, which repays the loan out of cash flow of the acquired company. |
| Management Buyout (MBO) | An MBO is the purchase of all a company's publicly held shares by the existing management, which takes the company private. |

Source: Jack S. Levin. *Structuring Venture Capital, Private Equity, and Entrepreneurial Transactions.* (Panel Publishers, 2000) John Downes & Jordan Elliot Goodman. *Dictionary of Finance and Investment Terms.* (New York: Barrons, 1995).

discounted cash-flow (DCF) method. In theory, if the net present value (NPV—the PV minus the potential investment) is positive, an investment will occur. Conversely, if the NPV is negative, an investment will not occur. Most discounted cash-flow analyses are projected for at least a five-year time period, roughly corresponding to the projected date of a liquidity event (e.g., an IPO or a merger or acquisition). Before determining the DCF, the proforma income statement, free cash flow, and terminal value must be determined.

## POINT OF VIEW

# Startup Questions

Shawn Neidorf, who writes a column called "Term Sheet" for *The Mercury News*, discussed the thought process potential entrepreneurs should go through before starting a business. He suggests each entrepreneur consider the following questions:

1. *Could a $500 million-plus company be built around my idea within a few years? . . .*
2. *Who would my customers be? Would my product or service solve a sizable problem for them? Would they pay for it? . . .*

3. *How many competitors are there, and how well established are they? Can I really beat them? . . .*
4. *Do I have the temperament and experience to be an entrepreneur? Am I comfortable taking on the risks and demands? . . .*
5. *Am I willing to give up, over time, majority ownership in my company to get the money and assistance venture capitalists provide? Can I accept that I might not be CEO, at least not for very long?[19]*

**Proforma Income Statements.** The first step in creating a DCF is to project the company's future income statement (this projection is also known as a **proforma income statement**). The projections for the income statement will be based on growth assumptions for costs and revenues. These growth assumptions should be based upon growth rates of similar companies in the same industry. However, in the case of many startups, the industry for the product or service has not been fully formed yet, and similar companies are hard to find. If no similar companies or products exist, the entrepreneur must project growth rates based upon the foreseeable market in which the company will play (size, structure, expected competition) and the size of the market that the company expects to own (which will result in projections for sales figures). Above all, assumptions must be made explicit, as these assumptions will serve as the basis for negotiations with the financier. If, for example, a company expects its sales to grow by 20 percent per year, the logic behind this assumption must be well thought out and defensible.

**Free Cash Flow.** The second step in determining a DCF is to calculate the company's free cash flows—the amount of cash a company has at its disposal after normal operations. **Free cash flow** will be based upon the proforma income statement produced in the first step.

There is a relatively simple formula to determine free cash flow (FCF):

$$
\begin{array}{l}
\text{EBIAT (earnings before interest but after taxes)} \\
+ \text{ depreciation} \\
- \text{ the change in operating working capital}^\dagger \\
\underline{- \text{ capital expenditures}} \\
= \text{Free cash flow}
\end{array}
$$

**Terminal Value.** The third step in producing the company's DCF is to determine a terminal value (sometimes called a "residual" or "continuing" value) for the company. The **terminal value** is the expected value of the company at the end of the projected period (for our purposes, five years). It is, essentially, a dollar amount attached to a possible selling price for the company at the time of a liquidity event. There are two main ways to determine a terminal value for the company.

The first way of estimating a terminal value is to use free cash flow in the last year of the projection as a starting point. Next, an assumption must be made about the terminal growth rate. This is just a fancy term that produces an answer to the question, "If the company were to continue to grow forever, at what rate would it grow?" A good rule of thumb is to use 3 percent as a terminal growth rate. In this case, the terminal value is equal to the free cash flow in the last year of the projection, divided by the total of the discount rate used minus the terminal growth rate. The **discount**

---

†Operating working capital=accounts receivable + inventory + prepaid expenses − accounts payable − taxes payable. If the working-capital requirement of the company decreases, then the negative amount of this change from one statement to the next is subtracted from EBIAT. In other words, if working-capital requirements decrease, a positive number is added to EBIAT, increasing the free cash flow of the company. This makes sense: If less money is needed to keep the company running, there will be more free cash available.

# Present Value

The concept of **present value** can seem complex, but it is really simple. Essentially, cash today is worth more than cash tomorrow. For instance, if someone were offered $50 today in exchange for paying $100 five years from now, should they take the deal? First, they would have to determine an appropriate rate of return on their money (how much could they get for the $50 over five years if they invested it) and perform a present-value calculation. Assume that someone determined that they could invest the $50 and receive a compounded return of 15 percent over five years.

They would take the $100 and divide it by the total of one plus the rate of return, raised to the power of the number of years over which they would invest, to determine what that $100 is worth today.

$$100/(1.15^5) = \$49.71$$

In this case, the $100 that they would have to pay out in five years is only equal to $49.71 today. So they should take the offer, because the $50 is "worth" more than the present value of the $100. In other words, the offer has a positive NPV.

---

**rate** does just what it says: It discounts future earnings to determine an appropriate present value for those earnings. The higher the discount rate, the lower the present value of the earnings and, thus, the lower the present value of the company.

Discount rates used by VCs will be discussed next, but for this example let us assume that the discount rate is 20 percent, the terminal growth rate is 3 percent, and the free cash flow in the last year is projected to be 100. Then the terminal value of the company would equal:

FCF / (the discount rate − the terminal growth rate)
100 / (20% − 3%) = 588

**Determining a DCF.** Once the proforma income statement (and from that, projections of the company's free cash flows), a terminal value for the company, and a discount rate have been determined, the entrepreneur has all of the information needed to calculate the company's value. (One additional note on terminal value: If the company is completing a five-year projection, it must project FCF for one additional year [in this case, for year six] and use this FCF value to determine the terminal value in year five.)

The present value of a cash flow stream equals:

[Year 1 FCF/(1+discount rate)] + [Year 2 FCF/(1+discount rate)$^2$]
+ [Year 3 FCF/(1+discount rate)$^3$] + . . .
+[(Year N FCF+Year N terminal value)/(1+discount rate)$^n$]

In Table 13-4, we present an example, using a discount rate of 20 percent and the terminal value calculated previously over a five-year period.

In this case, the total value of the company is equal to the sum of all of the calculated present values (i.e., the present value of all of the FCF plus the present value of the terminal value). The total present value of the company equals $378 million.

# The Venture-Capital Method

Venture-capital firms, however, rarely use the method described previously; they use somewhat of a hybrid method, looking both at comparables and future free cash flows. The **venture-capital method** values a company by determining a terminal value for a potential investment by using either a "multiple" or the terminal-value technique just described, but with a much larger discount rate. VCs typically use a price to earnings (PE) multiple (market price per share divided by earnings per share) to multiply the earnings in the last year of the projection. This terminal value is then discounted back to the present using a very high discount rate.

Venture capitalists determine the discount rate that they will use in valuations by assessing what kind of compounded rate of return they desire on their investments. While the most desirable rate of return varies, most VCs are looking for companies that will multiply their investment by either five times in three years (ROI = $5^{1/3}$ = 71%) or ten times in five years (ROI = $10^{1/5}$ = 59%).[20]

Discount rates employed by venture capitalists typically range from 30 percent to 70 percent, depending upon the stage of the company, the industry in which the company plans to operate, the management team, and a host of other factors.

The discount rates applied by venture capitalists are very high, and vary by the potential investment's stage of development. For example, an early-stage company is extremely difficult to value because of a high risk of unknowns. In these companies there are so many variables to consider that if even one of these variables takes a negative turn (e.g., a late product delivery, loss of a major client, an unforeseen competitor entering the market) the value of the company can be diminished severely. To try to compensate for some of this increased risk, a venture capitalist will apply an enormous discount rate to the terminal value of an early-stage company to determine its present value, and from that, what percentage of the company the VC will want in exchange for the investment.

Here is an example. Let us say that the company is projecting earnings in year five of $20 million, and similar companies are trading at ten times earnings. The terminal value for the company is calculated to be $200 million ($20 million times ten). In this case, the company is a startup, and the VC decides that he should use a 60 percent discount rate on the terminal value to calculate the present value. The discounted terminal value equals the terminal value in year five divided by one plus the discount rate (which is also the VC's target rate of return on the investment) raised to the power of the year of the projection. In this case, the discounted terminal value equals $200 million/$(1 + 60\%)^5$ or $19 million.

Further, let us assume that the VC plans on investing $5 million. The required percent ownership for this investment would be 26 percent (the $5 million investment/$19 million value of the company). Thus, for its investment, the VC will

**Table 13-4** EXAMPLE OF A DISCOUNTED CASH-FLOW ANALYSIS

|  | Year 1 | Year 2 | Year 3 | Year 4 | Year 5 | Year 6 |
|---|---|---|---|---|---|---|
| FCF (in Millions) | 10 | 50 | 50 | 75 | 85 | 100 |
| Terminal Value |  |  |  |  | 588 |  |
| Present Value | 8 | 35 | 29 | 36 | 270 |  |

## Table 13-5  DISCOUNT RATES

| | |
|---|---|
| Startup | 50% to 70% |
| First Stage | 40% to 60% |
| Second Stage | 35% to 50% |
| Third Stage | 30% to 50% |
| Fourth Stage | 30% to 40% |
| IPO | 25%–35% |

Source: James L. Plummer, "QED Report on Venture Capital Financial Analysis" (QED Research, Palo Alto, CA), 1987

demand a little more than a quarter of the company. However, the 26 percent ownership stake that the VC demands now will only yield the target rate of return (60 percent) if the company does not raise any more money. If the company does participate in future rounds of financing, which it almost certainly will, the VC will demand a higher-percent ownership to compensate for the dilutive effect of future financing rounds. (We will cover dilution in detail in the next section.)

To compensate for dilution, the VC will calculate what is referred to as a **retention ratio**, and use this ratio to determine a new, higher-percent ownership required for the current investment. For example, let us assume that the company plans to have one more round of financing in which it will sell shares representing an additional 20 percent of the company's equity, and then plans an IPO in which it will sell shares representing an additional 35 percent of the company's equity. In this case, if the VC owns 26 percent today, his stake in the company after the two planned rounds of financing will be 26 percent divided by (1+20%) divided by (1+35%) or 16 percent. The retention ratio is then determined by dividing the diluted stake in the company (16%) by the initial stake (26%). The retention ratio equals 61.7 percent. Next, to determine the new, higher required percentage of ownership in the company, the VC will divide the required final percentage ownership (26%) by the retention ratio (61.7%). The VC determines that he must own 42.1 percent of the company now in order to receive his targeted rate of return.

The valuations produced by the preceding methods, however mathematical, are necessarily subjective. Changing the underlying assumptions in any method changes the value placed on the company, which can result in a wide range of valuations. The smart entrepreneur will develop several different valuations, based upon best-case, worst-case, and base-case scenarios, and use these valuations to assess the range of possible values for the company to conduct sensitivity analysis on the business.

## The Asset Valuation Method

The **asset valuation method** is most appropriate if the company seeking financing has a high, fixed asset value, implying that it is, most likely, a fairly mature company. An asset valuation can serve as a baseline for negotiations (i.e., the entrepreneur would never sell his company for less than the value of the underlying assets). However, in general, it simply does not make sense for startups in the e-commerce space to use the asset valuation method, because the majority of the assets are intangible, therefore making objective valuation extremely difficult. Furthermore, a valuation based upon assets is historical by its very nature (i.e., it is based upon what the startup has) and does not take into account the possibility of future growth and success, which is where the value of any startup is contained.

## Options Analysis

Another potential way of valuing a company is through the use of options analysis. This technique takes into account that a company has the flexibility during its operation to make choices about how to run the company—this flexibility is not taken into account with a simple financial analysis. Still, the methods listed previously are the most frequently employed valuation techniques used within the industry.[21]

The purpose of creating valuations for the company is to produce a reasonable range of values as a basis for negotiation with an investor. Keep in mind, however, that if a company is truly early stage, the numbers and the projections are not going to be very important to a venture capitalist, because these numbers simply cannot be trusted. There are too many variables in the model for it to be reliable. One venture capitalist stated that as a benchmark, she expects that any early-stage deal is going to be worth between $2 million and $6 million, and that where the valuation falls has more to do with the entrepreneur and the presentation than any numbers that he or she can produce. Which leads us to our next point: An entrepreneur is, first and foremost, a salesperson.

## NEGOTIATIONS

## Principles for Entrepreneurs

We reviewed the basics of putting together a pitch in Chapter 12. Before negotiating with potential investors, the entrepreneur has to get them interested in the idea. The investors have a limited amount of time and invest in only a few deals. Venture capitalists generally invest in only about 1 percent of the opportunities presented.[22] Investors really want to know only two things: what is the opportunity, and why is this management team the best to pull it off. The most effective way of making an investment opportunity stand out is to make the pitch concise and compelling. The following guidelines should be emphasized for pitching specifically to the angels and venture capitalists we have discussed in this chapter:

- *Know the audience.* Knowing what investors want will help the entrepreneur hone the pitch to the individual audience. Remember, each venture capitalist has unique needs and specific areas of investment, so a single pitch will not be suitable for all audiences. The target investors should be investigated: What is their average deal size? What type of return do they normally seek? Are they hands-on with the management of the enterprise, or do they prefer to keep a low profile, only stepping in when the company misses a predetermined milestone? How can the specific investor complement the company and management team? Does the investor prefer to invest in early- or later-stage companies? The answers to these questions will not only help customize the pitch, but also help determine if the investor should even be a target.

- *Keep the presentation concise.* These investors are especially hard-pressed for time, receiving volumes of unsolicited business plans daily. Ideally, the presentation should consist of no more than 25 slides. Investors will say if they would like more information on a specific topic. The goal is to get them interested enough to ask questions.

- *Talk about the management team.* Especially in an early-stage company, investors are interested in the management team as much as in the idea itself. They have to be convinced that the management team assembled will make the company successful. To accomplish this, the background of each of the key members of the team should be highlighted, focusing on how the team members complement one another and explaining how their experience is relevant to the industry in which the company will compete. The management team's past wins—Did they get a product to market ahead of schedule? Were they able to negotiate a particularly good deal with an important supplier?—will also be a factor in receiving financing.

## Term Sheet

If the pitch is successful, the parties will produce a **term sheet**, which is a nonbinding description of the proposed deal between the financier and the entrepreneur. In his book *The Fundamentals of Venture Capital*, Joseph Bartlett writes, "The term sheet is analogous to a letter of intent, a nonbinding outline of the principal points which the stock purchase agreement and related agreements will cover in detail."[23] The advantage of a term sheet is that it is a fairly short document that can be produced quickly, expediting the entire negotiation process. It provides both parties with a baseline to begin further negotiations. However, a term sheet does not mean that a deal is imminent. Venture capitalists will still be conducting due diligence even after the term sheet is signed, and since it is nonbinding, the investors can pull out if they uncover something about the company that they find unacceptable, or if the two parties fail to reach a compromise.

A term sheet generally includes the following information:

- Names of the investors and the proposed amount of the investment
- The type of security to be used in the transaction, including rights associated with those securities, such as antidilution rights, terms of conversion, liquidation preferences assigned to the security, and redemption rights
- Pre-money valuation (the valuation of the company prior to the investment; see the insert on pre- and post-money valuations)
- Voting rights of the shareholders
- Board of directors composition
- Rights of the investors (including, but not limited to, registration rights and rights of first refusal)
- Information on options and vesting, dividend payments (if applicable), affirmative covenants and financial statements, and performance

Most of the negotiations surrounding the structure of the transaction will center on the valuation of the company and what type of security to use. In the last section, we provided the basics of valuation. Now, we will turn to a general overview of the types of securities that exist and how these securities differ.

# Securities

An easy way to think about securities is by picturing a spectrum, with debt securities on one end and equity securities on the other. As an investor moves from left to right on the spectrum (from debt to equity) the riskiness of the security increases, as does the reward.

Generally, securities will fall into one of the categories listed on the spectrum. The security chosen by the company and the investor for the transaction will reflect the risk/reward appetite of each, terms of previous rounds of financing (if there are any), and the anticipated terms of any future rounds. Securities will differ vastly from each other depending upon the terms and rights attached to those securities. The basic types of securities used in a transaction are

- *Zero coupon bonds (debt securities with warrants attached).* **Zero coupon bonds** are the ultimate in protecting the investor. Upon maturity of this security, the investor will redeem the initial investment and interest upon that investment at a predetermined rate. The investor also has some upside benefit because warrants (rights to buy shares at a predetermined price) have been included in the deal. Essentially, the investor protects the original investment, receives interest on that investment, and has the option to buy stock.

- *Convertible debentures.* **Convertible debentures** are loans that are convertible into equity. Investors will ask for this type of security if the company is perceived to be extremely high risk. Through use of a convertible debenture, the investor maintains a high liquidation preference (e.g., the investor will be paid before other stockholders in the case of bankruptcy) and is considered to be a creditor until the company is past its risky stage. The convertible debentures are "converted" (thus the name) into common stock based upon the conversion rights associated with the security.

**Exhibit 13-8**

THE SPECTRUM OF SECURITIES

| Zero Coupon Bond | Convertible Debentures | Participating Convertible Preferred | Redeemable Preferred | Convertible Preferred | Common |
|---|---|---|---|---|---|
| *DEBT SECURITIES* *Highest Liquidation Preference/Can Force Liquidation* *Safest* | | | | | *COMMON* *Lowest Liquidation Preference* *Riskiest* |
| With warrants attached—must wait one year after debt is redeemed and warrants are exercised to sell underlying stock. Zero Coupon Bond is the ultimate in locking in a return: upon maturity get interest at a fixed rate and interest on interest. | Essentially loans convertible to equity shares. Can sell immediately upon conversion as long as not deemed an affiliate. Investor profile: likes upside potential leavened with downside protection. | Receive FV and conversion to common. Term usually in event of sale or liquidation. Typically used in later rounds when investors have to pay a higher price to play. (Essentially preferred stock bundled with common.) | No convertibility into equity, only face value (FV) plus any dividend. Always carries a term specifying when redemption occurs, usually at the option of the shareholder. Not considered outstanding for EPS purposes. | Converted at shareholder's option into common. Usually a mandatory conversion at IPO. Usually includes a provision to redeem par plus some form of ROIC, as if dividends had been declared but not paid. | Each share has one vote. Class A common is a form of preferred. |

Sources: Joseph Bartlett. *The Fundamentals of Venture Capital* (New York: Madison Books, 1999); Howard Stevenson and Michael Roberts, *Deal Structure* (Note), (Harvard Business School Publishing); G. Gelda Hardymon and Josh Lerner, *A Note on Private Equity Securities* (Harvard Business School Publishing); Josh Lerner. *Venture Capital and Private Equity: A Casebook* (New York: John Wiley & Sons, 1999); *The Entrepreneurial Venture*, Edited by William Sahlman (Boston: Harvard Business School Press, 1999)

- *Preferred stock.* **Preferred stock** is the security most commonly used in a transaction with a venture capitalist. Preferred stock affords the VC preference over common stock (such as antidilution provisions, redemption rights, and special voting privileges) while providing an upside to the investor. There are three main types of preferred stock. Although as mentioned before, securities come in many shapes and sizes depending upon the rights attached to those securities. The three common forms of preferred stock are

  *Convertible preferred.* This security is converted at the shareholder's option into common stock, although a mandatory conversion at IPO almost always exists. If the company is sold for less than a favorable price, the investors get the money they invested back before the common stock holders get anything. Obviously, if the company is sold at a favorable price, the investors will convert their shares into common stock and share in the upside.

  *Redeemable preferred.* This security is not converted into equity. The investor receives the face value of the stock plus a dividend.

  *Participating convertible preferred.* For investors, this is the most prized security. Participating convertible preferred is also known as "double dipping" because the investors not only get their original investment back (as in the case of redeemable preferred), but also get to convert their securities into common stock (as is the case with convertible preferred) to share in the company's upside.

- *Common stock.* VCs will use **common stock** to structure a deal only in rare circumstances because this security does not provide investors with any of the protections of the other securities. Common stock does not provide investors with a fixed return on investment, special voting rights, or privileges or liquidation preference.

Determining the securities that will be used in the transaction is only the first step in structuring the details of the term sheet.

# Rights and Privileges of Investors

Several other factors will have to be considered, such as the rights and privileges of the investors and how these rights and privileges will be attached to the securities. Some of the most common rights that investors demand are

- *Right of first refusal.* **Right of first refusal** safeguards the investor by locking in the opportunity to invest in future rounds. With a right of first refusal, the current investor has the right to meet any offer of outside financing.

- *Preemptive right.* **Preemptive right** gives an investor the right to maintain his percentage of ownership by investing additional funds in the next round of financing.

- *Redemption rights.* **Redemption rights** give the investor the right to achieve liquidity if the company has not been sold or undergone a public offering within a predetermined time period. Upon redemption, the investor generally receives the original investment plus any dividends that have accrued.

- *Registration rights (demand and/or piggyback).* Registered shares can be freely traded on the market, whereas unregistered shares cannot. Investors with piggyback **registration rights** will have their shares registered automatically any time the venture registers its shares. Demand registration rights give the investor the power to demand registration of shares, thereby forcing the company into a liquidity event, in this case, a public offering.

- *Covenants.* There are both affirmative and negative **covenants**, and both are designed to make sure that the money provided by the investor is used in a manner that is consistent with the agreement between the entrepreneur and investor. Affirmative covenants are actions that the entrepreneur promises to take in exchange for the investment. Examples of affirmative covenants can include: maintaining certain financial ratios, sending financial statements at predetermined times to investors, maintaining adequate insurance, granting board seats to investors, and a host of other promises. Negative covenants are actions that the entrepreneur promises not to take without consent of the investor, such as agreeing not to change the nature of the business, management team, or compensation structure without first gaining the approval of the investor.
- *Antidilution provisions.* **Antidilution provisions** protect the investor from dilution in ownership that might occur in future rounds of financing.

Of all of these rights, antidilution provisions can be the most vexing to the entrepreneur, because while the investor generally gets some type of antidilution protection, the entrepreneur does not. So, what exactly is dilution, and why are some antidilution provisions so harmful to the entrepreneur?

**Dilution.** Before we talk about antidilution provisions, let us first define **dilution**. Percentage dilution occurs whenever the company issues new shares of stock. It is called percentage dilution because the percentage of a company that is owned decreases with any new share issuances. Quite simply, if an investor owns 25 percent of a company with 100 shares outstanding, he owns 25 shares in the company. If the company then issues 25 new shares, his percentage ownership will decrease from 25 percent to 20 percent [25/(100+25)]. It is important to note, however, that just because your percentage stake in the company is less than it was before the new shares were issued, it is entirely possible, indeed it is hoped, that this 20 percent stake in the company represents a higher *value*. If the company is doing well, it will issue these new shares at a higher valuation. For example, if the company was worth $100 before the new shares were issued, the value of 25 percent ownership was $25. If, after the 25 new shares are issued, the company is valued at $200, then the 20 percent stake is valued at $40.

But what happens if the company is forced to raise additional funds by issuing new shares at the same or a lower valuation? In this case, not only would the investor's percentage ownership of the company decrease, but the value of that percentage ownership would decrease as well. For example, if the company issues 25 new shares at a total company valuation of $80, then the investor's 20 percent stake in the company is only worth $16. Thus, not only has his percentage ownership decreased by 5 percent, but also the value of that percentage ownership has decreased by $9. Clearly, a wise investor wants protection from this type of dilution, which is why antidilution provisions are written into the terms of investment.

**Antidilution Provisions.** There are two types of antidilution provisions that typically are written into the terms of an investment: *full-ratchet* and *weighted average* antidilution provisions. Of the two, full-ratchet antidilution provisions provide the most protection to investors, but can be extremely punitive to entrepreneurs. If at all possible, the entrepreneur should avoid any full-ratchet antidilution provisions in favor of the weighted-average provisions.

- *Full-ratchet antidilution.* A **full-ratchet antidilution provision** will kick in when a subsequent round of financing is raised at a lower price per share than the round in which the investors with the provision participated. The provision will increase the number of shares owned by the original investors to the number of shares that the investor would have received had he invested at the lower price per share. Let us turn to an example.

  Say an investor bought 20 preferred shares convertible into common at $10 per share, for a total investment of $200 in the first round of financing. Then, in a second round of financing, the company can raise money only if it issues new shares at a $5 per share conversion price. If the investor has full-ratchet protection, he will be issued 20 new shares without any additional investment. This is because, at a $5 price per share, the $200 initial investment would have bought the investor 40 shares, not the 20 that he initially received. Therefore, 20 new shares must be issued to make up for the difference. The problem the entrepreneur faces with this type of provision is that the investor gets 20 new shares regardless of how many shares were issued at the $5 price per share in the second round. This means that if the company must raise money at a lower valuation, original investors end up with proportionately more of the company than the entrepreneur does, because the additional shares given to the investor are taken out of the pool of total shares outstanding, and this means that his claim on that pool of shares has decreased.

- *Weighted-average antidilution.* **Weighted-average antidilution** provisions are more fair to the entrepreneur, while still protecting the investor. Weighted-average provisions take into account how many shares were sold at the lower price, and subsequently adjusts the number of new shares the investor receives proportionally. If the company sells a lot of stock at the new, lower price per share, then the original investors will receive a lot of shares to make up for it. If the company sells only a little stock at the lower price per share, then investors will only receive a few additional shares. The number of new shares issued is based upon a formula. Joseph Bartlett says, "There are various ways of expressing the formula, but it comes down to the same central idea: the investors' conversion price is reduced to a lower number, but one that takes into account how many shares (or rights) are issued in the dilutive financing. If only a share or two is issued, then the conversion price does not move much; if many shares are issued—that is, there is in fact real dilution—then the price moves accordingly."[24]

  Let us turn to an example, using a common formula for weighted-average antidilution, which is expressed as follows:

$$(A + C) / (A + D) \times \text{Old Conversion Price}$$

A = Total number of shares outstanding prior to the dilutive financing
C = Number of shares issued if old conversion price had been used
D = Number of shares actually issued at new conversion price

Now, we will fill in this equation with the numbers used in the description of full-ratchet antidilution, assuming that the total number of shares outstanding prior to the dilutive financing was 500, and that the company issued 50 new shares at the conversion price of $5 per share.

$$[(500 + 25) / (500 + 50)] \times \$10$$

A=Total number of shares outstanding prior to the dilutive financing (500).

C=Number of shares issued if old conversion price had been used. In this case, 50 new shares were issued at $5 per share for a total cash infusion of $250. If the shares had been issued at $10 per share, as in the previous round of financing, the total number of shares issued would have been 25 ($250/$10).

D=Number of shares actually issued at new conversion price. In this case, 50 new shares were issued.

Because the financing round was dilutive (i.e., the shares were issued at a lower price than in a previous round of financing) the old conversion price of $10 per share is multiplied by a number that is less than one, resulting in a new conversion price. The result of the equation is $9.55. In other words, the original investor will be issued new shares as if the original investment had been priced at $9.55 per share, rather than $10 per share. In this case, the investor will receive only one additional share because, if the investment had been made at the lower price per share, the investor could have purchased 21 shares instead of the 20 that he received ($200 original investment divided by $9.55 per share equals 20.9, which we will round up to 21).

If a full-ratchet provision had been used, the investor would have received 20 new shares instead of one new share, significantly diluting the founder. Clearly, it is in the entrepreneur's best interest to negotiate a deal that uses weighted-average antidilution, rather than full-ratchet antidilution provisions.

**Founder's Dilution.** While investors can protect themselves from dilution, there is little an entrepreneur can do to protect himself from dilution. The founder of a company is diluted with every round of financing. Though he starts out owning 100 percent of the company, with every round of financing he loses a piece of the company in exchange for the cash that is needed to help it grow. This dilution occurs even if the company has a higher valuation from one round of financing to the next. Yet, as discussed before, it is hoped that this new, lower percentage of ownership will actually be worth more in terms of real dollars.

# Stages of Investment

A venture capitalist will invest in stages, rather than giving the entrepreneur all of the necessary cash up front. This is because an investor wants to give a little bit of cash, see how the company is doing, and then invest more cash at a later time if the company is doing well. By staging the investments in the company, the investor retains his "option to abandon" the investment if the company is not performing up to expectations. The investor may decide not to invest any additional funds in the company, or will invest additional funds but only at a renegotiated, lower company valuation. Venture capitalists look at their investments in terms of pre- and post-money valuations for the company. A **pre-money valuation** is the value that the investor puts on the company before his investment, and a **post-money valuation** is the value of the company immediately after the investment. Simply, if a company is determined to be worth $3 million immediately before the investment and the investor puts in $2 million, the company will be worth $5 million immediately after the investment. In this case, the pre-money valuation is $3 million and the post-money valuation is $5 million. The founder's ownership in the company is diluted, because at each round of financing, the founder must give up a percentage of equity in the company to the investor in exchange for the cash investment.

Table 13-6 illustrates this. In this case, let us assume that the company receives three separate investments. In the first round, a seed-stage investment, the investor gives the company $1 million for proof of concept. In exchange for this $1 million investment, the investor asks for 40 percent of the company. The implied post-money valuation for the company is $2.5 million dollars (the $1 million investment divided by the percentage ownership obtained from the investment). The entrepreneur now owns only 60 percent of the company, instead of the 100 percent with which he started.

In the next stage, the company is doing well, but needs more money to expand production and sales. The investor decides to invest an additional $4 million to help the company expand in exchange for 20 percent of the company. The investor now owns 52 percent of the company: the original 40 percent plus 20 percent of the outstanding equity, which is the 60 percent that the entrepreneur still holds. That is, 40 percent plus 20 percent of 60 percent, which equals 12 percent (40% + 12% = 52%). In the final stage of financing, in this case the third round, the company is still performing well and needs additional funds to expand. The investor decides to give the company $15 million to aid in expansion efforts for an additional 20 percent of the company. The investor now owns 62 percent of the company: the 52 percent from the second round plus 20 percent of the outstanding equity (20 percent of 48 percent equals 9.6 percent, which we will round to 10 percent).

As demonstrated through this example, at every stage of the investment, the founder's share is diluted. The founder starts with 100 percent of the company, but after the third round of investment he owns only 38 percent. Yet the entrepreneur is worth more. After the first round, the entrepreneur's 60 percent stake was worth $1.5 million (60 percent of the post-money valuation). After the third round of financing, the entrepreneur owns only 38 percent of the company, but his stake is worth $28.5 million (38 percent of the post-money valuation). So, even though the entrepreneur has been diluted on a percentage basis, his worth has still increased. Remember that at every stage, the entrepreneur will have to renegotiate the company's valuation with the investors, and the higher the valuation of the company, the more the diluted percentage of ownership is worth.

## Table 13-6 — PRE- AND POST-MONEY VALUATIONS MADE EASY

| Round of Financing | Amount Invested This Round | % Received This Round | Cumulative | | |
| --- | --- | --- | --- | --- | --- |
| | | | VC's Share | Founder's Share | Implied Valuation (Post Money) |
| Seed-Stage Round | $1,000,000 | 40% | 40% | 60% | $2,500,000 |
| First Round | $4,000,000 | 20% | 52% | 48% | $20,000,000 |
| Second Round | $15,000,000 | 20% | 62% | 38% | $75,000,000 |

## EXIT (THE PATH TO LIQUIDITY)

After an entrepreneur successfully negotiates with a venture capitalist for outside funding to finance the growth of his business, his next step is to have some sort of liquidity event through which he, his employees, and the outside financiers can obtain a return on investment in the company. Normally, venture capitalists will expect a liquidity event in three to five years. While there are many different ways to obtain liquidity—including management buyouts, which normally take place in later-stage companies, and selling equity to an employee stock option plan, or ESOP—we will cover the two liquidity events most common for e-commerce companies: the initial public offering (IPO) and mergers and acquisitions (M&A). Both the IPO market and M&A market experienced large increases from 1998 to 1999. Year 2000 estimates, however, were not as clear-cut. While M&A activity will most likely take a huge jump in the number of deals, the total number of VC-backed IPOs will most likely rise at a much slower rate than in previous years. VC-backed IPOs decreased in the second quarter of 2000, but still represented half of all IPOs.

## The Initial Public Offering (IPO)

IPOs received much attention in the past few years, as entrepreneurs took their companies (most of which had no profits, and no plans to be profitable in the near future) to market to tap into the vast wealth of a new shareholder: the public. Venture capitalists who backed these companies were ecstatic; investment bankers were desperate to get in on the hottest deals, and the public swallowed up shares at an alarming rate. It seemed as if the market for IPOs would exist forever and that if a company could go public, then by all means it should. Then the walls came crashing down, and the market experienced a correction.

In recent months, IPOs have stagnated, and the public seems to have lost its once voracious appetite for Internet-related offerings. In the fourth quarter of 2000, only 16 companies completed IPOs, raising about $1.4 billion. This seems like a lot of

---

### DRILL-DOWN

## VC Speak—What Are They Saying?

In their article "Going Public," Constance Bagley and Craig Danchy point out that venture capitalists often confuse new entrepreneurs by speaking their own language. When making an offer they might say,

*"I'll put in $2 million based on three pre-money."*

*"I'm thinking two-thirds based on three pre-; that will get you to five post."*

*"I'm looking for two-fifths of the company post-money, and for that I'll put up the two."*

*Each of the above statements is a different way of expressing exactly the same proposal. The venture capitalist is proposing that the company is worth $3 million before the investment of $2 million and is therefore worth $5 million immediately after the investment. The amount of ownership being requested is equivalent to 66 2/3% of the equity based on the pre-money number (i.e., $2 million/$3 million), which is 40% of the company measured immediately after the closing (i.e., $2 million/$5 million).[25]*

**Exhibit 13-9**

EXIT STRATEGIES OF VC FIRMS—IPOS AND M&A

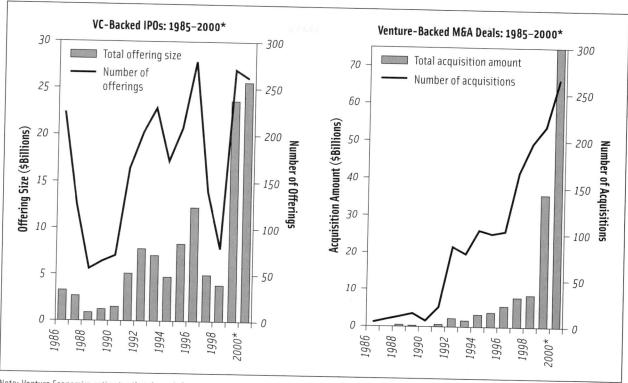

**VC-Backed IPOs: 1985–2000***

Legend:
- Total offering size
- Number of offerings

**Venture-Backed M&A Deals: 1985–2000***

Legend:
- Total acquisition amount
- Number of acquisitions

Note: Venture Economics estimates that through Q2 2000, there were 131 VC-backed IPOs for a total of $12.8B. Through Q2 2000, there were 132 M&A transactions of venture-backed firms for $37.5B (the 2000 numbers above simply double the current available numbers through Q2 2000).
Source: *Venture Economics and 2000 National Venture Capital Association Yearbook*

money to raise in the public market, but this "is the smallest number of IPOs since the fourth quarter of 1998, and far below the $6.6 billion raised in 70 offerings during the third quarter of 2000."[26] Yet, even in this slumping market, Internet firms still account for 59 percent of all IPOs, and they go public in about half the time of non-Net companies.[27] So what is an IPO, and how does a company decide when an offering to the public is appropriate?

An **initial public offering** is the sale of shares to public investors of a company that has never been traded on a public stock exchange. It is a way of tapping the greater public for investment dollars when either a) the original investors are pushing towards a liquidity event, or b) the company is about to experience rapid growth and needs more money than the original investors or new investors are willing to provide. It may also be a very emotional time for the founders, to whom an IPO represents the ultimate success. However, before rushing headlong into an IPO, the management team should first decide if its company is even a good candidate for a public offering. If it is, then it is necessary to understand the IPO process, as well as both the positives and negatives of becoming a public company, before proceeding.

**Determining the Right Time for an IPO.** Many factors will influence the decision a company makes when contemplating a public offering. First, there should be a review of the general health of the company to assess whether the timing is right for an IPO. Should the company wait until it has launched its next killer product? What is in the R&D pipeline? Will there be a better valuation from the public markets if the company waits for a year? Does the company need cash right now to fuel the expansion needed to crush its nearest competitor? The CEO and board will be the ones to answer these questions. If they decide that the company is ready for an IPO, they will have to assess if the market is ready to accept their offering. When the market sours on a particular industry or business model, the company has to fight an uphill battle to receive a fair valuation. If the market is not right for an IPO, and the company needs the money to grow, merging with another company or looking for a buyer for the business should be considered.

**The IPO Process.** If the timing is right both internally and externally, the company will enter into the 10- to 14-week process necessary to complete an IPO. This process will affect almost everyone in the firm, and will need the full attention of top management and their advisors (in-house counsel, accountants, etc.). There are seven major steps in the IPO process, all of which have many components. Chronologically, these steps are[28]

- Selection of the underwriters
- Preparation of the registration statement (including the prospectus) for the U.S. Securities and Exchange Commission (SEC), the government entity that serves to protect investors and maintain the integrity of the securities markets
- Distribution of the preliminary prospectus (or "*red herring*")
- Preparation for and completion of the "road show"
- Incorporation of the comments from the SEC into the registration statement
- Agreement on a final price and number of shares for the offering
- Close of the offering and distribution of the final prospectus

*Selection of the Underwriters.* The selection of the underwriters is one of the most important decisions made during the IPO process. The underwriters are investment bankers who arrange for the purchase of stock for a commission. (The underwriter buys a company's stock at a discount, normally 6 percent to 7 percent, and then sells it to the public at full price. The difference between these two prices is the underwriter's commission.) The underwriters will not only be responsible for taking a company public, but also for making sure that once public, the company will have the analyst coverage it needs to receive favorable attention from the market.

Many entrepreneurs will actually make the investment bankers compete for the chance to take their company public. In this competition, often referred to as "bake-offs" or "beauty contests," each prepares an evaluation of the company and explains why they would be best suited to become the "lead underwriter." In most cases, the lead underwriter will work with one or more additional investment banks in a syndicate to spread risk and increase sales and distribution capabilities.

When choosing an underwriter, there are certain questions that should be asked:

- Will this investment bank give a firm commitment to sell the newly issued securities, or will it just employ a best-efforts approach? A firm commitment means that the investment bank will actually buy the securities from a company and then make its money by reselling them. *Best efforts* simply means that the investment bank will try its hardest to sell all of the securities, but if it does not, the company has no recourse.

- Does the investment bank have the ability to syndicate with other top banks?

- What kind of analyst coverage will the company have after it is public? What investment bank has the best analyst in the company's field? When the management chooses an investment bank, it also chooses an analyst—the person who will be most responsible for providing coverage to the firm long after it has become public and the investment banker has forgotten its name, so it should choose wisely.

- Does the investment bank have knowledge of the company's industry? Has it taken other companies public in that industry, and what were the results? The investment banker will be responsible in large part for explaining the company's fundamentals to potential investors and convincing these investors that a company has the right business model/technology/management team to succeed in the marketplace. This will be a difficult task if the investment banker is not an expert in the industry.

- What is the investment bank's reputation? Is it a new kid on the block that has brokered a few good deals and will likely give the company great analyst coverage and service because it is trying to prove itself? What kind of bench strength (marketing, analysts, distribution) does it have?

- If all other things are equal, the management team should ask, "Do I like this bank?" After all, the team is going to have to work closely with the bank over the next three months on one of the most important projects the company will ever undertake, so it is best to make it an enjoyable experience.

***Preparation of the Registration Statement for the SEC.*** The company will have to file a form S-1 with the SEC. As part of preparing this registration statement, the company will create a prospectus, which is a document that outlines the company's business and financial fundamentals. During this time, due diligence, which is an extensive review of the company to check for accuracy and completeness of the preliminary prospectus, is conducted. It is extremely important that the prospectus is a completely accurate representation of the business because affiliates (directors, managers, and underwriters) are civilly liable for any errors in the prospectus and are usually named as the defendants in any lawsuits that might ensue. The company will submit this preliminary prospectus to the SEC for review at the same time it distributes the preliminary prospectus to its underwriters, who can then pass it on to potential investors.

The preliminary prospectus is also known as the **"red herring"** because of the red marks on the front of the prospectus warning investors that it has not yet been approved by the SEC and, therefore, is preliminary. Every prospectus contains the following main sections:

- *Box summary.* The box summary is a one-page summary of the offering, which includes a description of the business and an overview of the most recent financials.

- *Risk factors.* The risk-factors section lists all of the possible challenges and risks that the company faces or may face. All risks, even outside market risks that the company cannot control, are listed. This section is not intended to present the company in a favorable light—it is meant to make every potential risk explicit to the investor, and can protect the company in the event of a lawsuit.

- *Use of proceeds.* The use-of-proceeds section does just what it says: describes how the company plans to use the proceeds of the IPO.

- *Management's discussion and analysis of financial conditions and results of operations.* This section includes an analysis of the financial state of the company for the past three years on an annual and period-to-period basis. All material changes in the company's statements must be discussed and explained.
- *Business.* This is a description of the business that includes the company's strategies, goals, research and development, marketing efforts, and anything else that is material to the business. This section should also include risk factors (such as reliance on a sole supplier or customer, any new or dangerous competitive threats, any technology risk, etc.). It will be the management team's job to make sure that this section clearly states all of the threats that could hinder success of the company, while still managing to show the company in a favorable light to the investor.
- *Management.* The management section describes the key employees in the management team.
- *Audited financial statements.* The statements include income statements from the past three years and balance-sheet statements for the last two.

Every prospectus is written using the same outline and type of language, and reading a prospectus is invaluable. (See *http://www.sec.gov/edaux/formlynx.htm* and enter "S-1" into the appropriate box. This SEC site can access any prospectus that has been filed.)

***Distribution of the Preliminary Prospectus (or Red Herring).*** After the prospectus has been written and the registration statement has been filed, the red herring is then distributed to potential investors through the underwriters that have been chosen to represent the company. This is the period when the underwriters attempt to locate any potential investors and drum up support for the IPO.

***Preparation for and Completion of the Road Show.*** The road show is probably one of the most time-consuming activities of the IPO process. Essentially, the road show is the time in the process when a company's offering is presented directly to potential investors. It usually lasts for two to three weeks (occurring in many cities) and demands a huge time commitment from top management. However time-consuming and stressful, though, this is the opportunity for management team members to present themselves to investors firsthand. No matter how adept the underwriters chosen are, many potential investors will want to meet and feel comfortable with the management team before they invest. The only material that can be presented during the road show is material from the red herring, and it is the only document that can be distributed to potential investors.

***Incorporation of Comments from the SEC into the Registration Statement.*** While the road show is occurring, the SEC should be reviewing the red herring and making comments. If the underwriters have timed the event well, the company should receive comments from the SEC as the road show is entering its final stages. Once the comments from the SEC have been received, these comments must be incorporated into the red herring by filing "pre-effective amendments" with the SEC. These amendments address any issues flagged by the SEC, and should be filed within a week of receiving the SEC comments. If the SEC is satisfied with the pre-effective amendments, the company will then file an acceleration request to make the registration statement effective. Once the SEC has declared the registration effective, the company is then allowed to trade its shares on the stock market.

***Agreement on a Final Share Price and Number of Shares for the Offering.*** The company and the underwriters must agree on the number of shares to offer to the public, as well as a price per share. The parties in this negotiation are the underwriters and representatives of management (usually a special committee composed of members of the board of directors). The negotiation should not be too complex, as an initial range of share prices has already been determined and printed on the cover of the red herring. The range of share prices is determined by previous valuation discussions between management and the underwriters (typically priced between $10 and $20 per share), but can change before an offering depending upon market conditions, success of the road show, and myriad other external factors. This final negotiation typically takes place the night before trading will commence, and if all goes well, the stock will trade on the selected market (usually the Nasdaq) the next day.

***Close of the Offering and Distribution of the Final Prospectus.*** The close of the offering normally takes place three days after trading has begun. Closing involves delivering the stock certificates to investors and receiving the funds from the offering.

## Pros and Cons of the IPO Process.
As seen from the previous summary, the IPO process is long and complicated, with many moving parts and potential pitfalls. Before deciding if going public is the right thing to do, a company should think carefully about the pros and cons of such a process. In particular, an IPO does not mean that the founder will have immediate liquidity. Insiders (founders, directors, some employees, and the VCs) hold what is referred to as "restricted stock." *Restricted stock* is stock that is not offered to the public through the IPO process, but can be traded under certain circumstances. Insiders are restricted for a certain time period from trading this stock after a public issuance. This "lock-up" period usually lasts 180 days after the effective date of the IPO. In addition to this lock-up period, there are several other rules (SEC Rule 144, in particular) that further restrict when and how much stock insiders can sell. Furthermore, the sale of large quantities of stock by insiders can send a negative signal to the market (the market thinks that the insiders know something potentially damaging to the stock price, and are trying to cash out), causing the price of the stock to drop.

Table 13-7 outlines some of the major benefits and disadvantages of becoming a public company, and these should be considered and weighed before entering into the process. The market conditions of the past few years made going public extremely romantic and seemingly easy, but this is not a decision that should be undertaken without a great deal of thought and preparation.

# Mergers and Acquisitions

If an IPO is not the right path for a company, there are certainly other options. In fact, the IPO process is laborious and often influenced by factors outside of the management's control. Mergers and acquisitions can often accomplish the same goals as an IPO (e.g., liquidity and increased valuation) with lower potential risk.

In fact, in certain industries or markets where only a few public companies can be supported, many companies have discovered that they can often achieve 80 percent of an IPO valuation by being acquired. Since acquisition is often much less risky than going public, more and more growing firms are choosing that option.[29]

Mergers and acquisitions have become increasingly popular in the present economy (and are likely to become even more popular as an exit route, considering the

**Table 13-7**

## IPO PROS AND CONS

| Pro | Con |
|---|---|
| Provides founders and shareholders with liquidity (although not immediate liquidity because of lock-out periods, signals to the market, etc.) | IPOs are expensive and time-consuming. An unfavorable market (something that the company can not control or predict) might necessitate pulling the IPO at the last second |
| Provides capital to fuel expansion and growth within the company | Strict SEC reporting requirements |
| Possibility of attracting and retaining employees at lower than market rates because of granting of stock options and promise of eventual liquidity | Pressure to produce quarterly numbers for analysts |
| The price of the company's shares should increase dramatically with an IPO, providing (at least paper) wealth to the founders and other shareholders | Increased officer and director liability |
| As long as the company is performing well, it can return to the market to raise additional cash | Hostile takeover is possible |
| The ability to use stock as currency | Does not necessarily provide a liquid market for all shareholders because of restrictions on trading the stock |

recent downturn in IPO activity), where speed to market and rapid growth are considered crucial to survival. One of the easiest routes to quick growth is to buy the assets of, or combine assets with, another company. This can be done before or after a company has gone public. In 2000, there were a total of 365 mergers valued at approximately $96 billion, but the top-grossing mergers were reserved for semiconductor and software companies.[30]

It sounds like a logical approach to growth, and in some cases it is, but the process is far from easy. Entrepreneurs will have to consider the potential downside of combining with another company, including the structure of the deal and the often overlooked cultural disconnects. So what exactly is a merger? What is an acquisition? And how does a company determine which exit strategy is most attractive?

The major difference between a merger and an acquisition boils down to who is in control of the resulting company. In a merger, two companies are combined to achieve a financial and/or strategic objective, usually through an exchange of shares. In an acquisition, one company buys another, usually with cash and/or stock. In recent years, we have seen an increase in mergers and acquisitions by new-economy companies, as these Internet companies use their stock as currency to acquire or merge with other companies to expand.

Consider the case of one of the most famous recent acquisitions: the AOL-Time Warner deal. AOL acquired Time Warner (although most reports call the transaction a merger) using its valuable stock as currency. This was to be the dream merger, the largest Internet service provider (ISP) merging with the largest media company in the world. The merger was announced in January 2000, and following some rough rides from the FCC (Federal Communications Commission) and FTC (Federal Trade Commission), the merger was completed on January 11, 2001. Shareholders from each company received stock in the new, combined entity, AOL Time Warner. In this stock-for-stock merger, AOL shareholders received one share in the new company for every share that they owned in AOL. Time Warner shareholders received 1.5 shares in the new company for every share of Time Warner stock that they held. AOL ended up with 55 percent of the new company. When the deal was announced on January 10, 2000, it was valued at $164.7 billion. However, as of December 12, 2000, the value placed on the deal had decreased by over 35 percent, as both companies suffered from the downturn in the stock market.

However, even with the decrease in the value of the deal, analysts predict that mergers and acquisitions will become increasingly popular, as once powerful but now struggling dot-coms fight for survival. In addition, as foretold by the AOL and Time Warner merger, it seems that Internet pure-plays may increasingly merge with old-economy companies, forming new ventures that integrate the online and offline experience.

Additionally, new rules were introduced in December 2000 governing the accounting practices for mergers and acquisitions, and these rules make it likely that M&A activity will increase in the future. Essentially, the Financial Accounting Standards Board (FASB) changed the procedure for accounting for goodwill, which is the difference between the book value of an acquired company and the price paid in the acquisition. Until this new ruling was passed, the acquiring company would have to amortize the cost of goodwill over a period of 20 years, meaning that for each of these years that the amortization occurred, the acquiring company would take a hit to its earnings. Under the new ruling, amortization will only occur if

## DRILL-DOWN

# The Fate of a Bad Marriage—AOL and Time Warner

 Sometimes mergers turn out to not be as good an idea as they seemed at the time. Dan Ackman at Forbes.com had the following opinion about the AOL Time Warner merger:

*Time Warner must feel like a girl who agreed to marry a guy for his money, found out he wasn't nearly as rich as she thought, and then noticed he's ugly, too. On the other hand, the couple will move into the biggest house in town, AOL Time Warner, as it's now called, being the world's largest media company.*

*The success of the merger, analysts say, will depend on the "cross marketing" of the company's products—movies, music and mag-azines—on the Web and through traditional channels. Others say it depends on creating a whole new communications "platform" to rival the television and the telephone. But there is no reason for the Time Warner companies to market only through AOL's pipes. And if this platform does emerge, it looks like the regulators will require the company to let others stand on it as well.*

*So as AOL and Time Warner finally start living together, it looks more and more that Time Warner got taken in by the Internet hype that persuaded so many others.*[31]

Reprinted by permission of FORBES.com © Forbes Inc.

certain events take place, and even then the amortization charged against earnings will only be a portion of the total goodwill involved in the deal. (See the National Venture Capital Association website—*www.nvca.com*—for a more detailed description.) This new ruling is especially significant for online companies, which typically have a large number of intangible assets, which in turn increases the goodwill paid by potential acquirers.

# FUTURE OF CAPITAL MARKETS

The new-economy boom from 1994 through mid-2000 coincided with the enormous capital-market boom that sustained it. In 2001, after the steady decline of the Nasdaq and questions around whether the economy may be faced with recession, market conditions are significantly different than a year ago. While we cannot claim to read the writing on the wall in terms of where exactly the capital markets are headed, we do have some notion of trends we may see in the post-new-economy boom era.

## Return to Classic Venture Capitalism

The new-economy boom saw many anomalies to the traditionally careful and calculated investments of venture-capital firms. Green entrepreneurs with big ideas, but without proven track records, were given chunks of cash to stake out ground in the Internet land grab. Speed to market was seen as a priority and careful due diligence fell by the wayside. Although VC investments were traditionally technology oriented—the more surefire way of guaranteeing an investment with sustainable competitive advantage—investment dollars poured into business-to-consumer businesses. Businesses without complete management teams or even business strategies were funded, and sometimes even launched into the public markets. In addition, as a way of trying to explain the high valuations in the public and private markets, some venture capitalists (indeed, the public market itself) started to value companies on revenue multiples, rather than the traditional earnings multiple. While some of these investment anomalies paid off, many venture-capital firms were burned, and with that, we will see a return to more classic venture capitalism. "VCs are going back to old ways: Instead of giving unproven executives a chance, venture capitalists prefer to rely on entrepreneurs with a track record of dazzling successes, or at least a few dazzling failures."[32]

What does this mean? For one, far more carefully selected and monitored investments. Entrepreneurs will need to prove that they truly have a sustainable competitive advantage with a promise for profits in the future. Operationally experienced management teams will become a must. Firms will be more careful about setting operational milestones for startups before each additional cash outlay. The timeline to liquidity, especially initial public offering, will be longer as investors become increasingly careful about making sure that startups are more fully developed before "release" into the public markets.[33] Venture-capital firms will evaluate each potential investment on its own merits, rather than following investment fads. And for those new companies that do make the cut, venture capitalists will demand a higher equity stake than we saw in the preceding year. Another key element will be portfolio diversification across multiple industries—the classic "don't put all of your eggs in one basket."

Does this mean venture-capital dollars will dry up for entrepreneurs? In the near term, the answer is no. Eighteen VC firms raised billion-dollar funds in 2000, even as the Nasdaq spiraled downward.[34] Charles River Ventures closed a $1.2 billion fund in January 2001.[35] In January 2001 alone, venture-capital firms spent $700 million in early-stage financing for information technology startups.[36] To that end, there are venture-capital dollars available, but investors will be very choosy about their investments. The allocation of venture-capital funds to Internet-related ventures is likely to continue to decline, as depicted in Exhibit 13-10.

However, if the market downturn continues, it is unlikely that these mega-funds will continue to be raised as institutional investors and other sources of funding for venture-capital firms become increasingly tightfisted. Some venture-capital firms have even turned down money. A case in point is Crosspoint Venture Partners. After investors had committed to a $1 billion fund, a decision was made to hold the fund at $852 million, given market conditions and a decision to focus on improving current portfolio companies.[37] Overall, we will see a return to classic, more conservative venture capitalism.

## A Shakeout—Both for Funding Sources and Startups

The rapid decline of the Nasdaq has coincided with the rapid demise not only of Internet startups, but also sources of funding. In the past year, 97 Internet-related companies filed for bankruptcy or closed down their operations.[38] The shakeout will continue in 2001 at multiple levels in the capital markets.

Venture-capital firms, corporate-venture funds, and holding companies will reevaluate their portfolios and determine which startups are worth saving and which they will simply abandon. This reevaluation will take place in the public markets as well, as those Internet startups without the promise of profits in the near future will find themselves strapped for cash as the public markets dump

**Exhibit 13-10** ALLOCATION OF VC INVESTMENT TO INTERNET-RELATED VENTURES

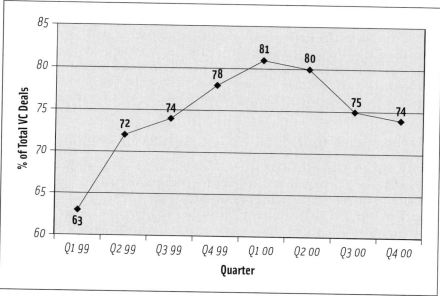

Source: PricewaterhouseCoopers Moneytree Survey 2000

increasingly devalued stocks. We have already seen the results of this: massive dot-com lay-offs and bankruptcy of those companies that were not wise enough to conserve cash.

Some sources of funding will experience a shakeout as well. Many of the smaller venture-capital funds that put all their eggs in the Internet basket will disappear, unable to recoup losses from their investments and unable to raise additional funds from investors based on their track record. Incubators as stand-alone entities have all but disappeared, few having required actual cash fees from their portfolio companies in hopes that equity stakes would pay off. Angel investing will most likely be curtailed as well, as the private wealth of these investors is likely to have shrunk with the markets. Corporate venturing, on the other hand, is likely to increase in prominence as these funds are strategic, rather than financial, in nature—often a necessity for acquiring new technologies or ideas. Darwinian theory prevails—only the fittest will survive.

## A Rougher, Tougher Breed of Entrepreneur

Challenging financial markets will bring us a rougher, tougher breed of entrepreneur. As investors become more conservative and choosy in picking their investments, entrepreneurs that choose to stay in the game will have to be more driven and prepared. In essence, the balance of power in the venture-capital community is shifting back to investors. Just one year ago, entrepreneurs were the ones who had the upper hand, and they were able to get investment dollars without having to prove themselves. Now, the burden of proof will be higher to obtain funding. The entrepreneur will need to spend more time putting together a solid, winning business idea and an operationally experienced management team. Twenty-somethings with a bright idea and no experience are unlikely to get several million dollars. This most likely means finding alternative sources of funding in the early stages of development, and going through the pains of bootstrapping.

Startup valuations will be lower (read: more realistic). Timelines to liquidity will lengthen. Investors will carefully monitor cash expenditures and set up milestones for additional cash outlays. The entrepreneur who dives in under these conditions must truly believe in his business idea and have the determination and patience to operate even in less favorable capital markets. In essence, we are likely to see self-selection of individuals who are willing to take on the entrepreneurial challenge under more difficult conditions. In addition, we will see entrepreneurs who are more interested in actually building a company that will last into the foreseeable future, rather than working towards a high valuation in hopes of quickly cashing out.

## Entrepreneurs Will Seek Other Sources of Liquidity

The IPO market all but died in the fourth quarter of 2000. According to VentureOne, only 16 venture-backed companies completed public offerings, raising $1.4 billion. This sounds like a lot of money, yet it is the lowest total since the fourth quarter of 1998. For further comparison, in the third quarter of 2000, 70 companies raised $6.6 billion. Even more frightening, in the fourth quarter of 2000, not one Internet-related venture-backed company completed an IPO, and, according to IPO.com, 43 companies have withdrawn their public offerings (totaling more than $3 billion) since Dec. 1, 2000.

So what does this mean for the entrepreneur? Quite simply, it means that raising money from the public markets can no longer be considered a sure thing. One source of liquidity that many entrepreneurs snubbed in the past few years is being acquired by or merging with another company. Merger and acquisition activity traditionally rises and falls in reverse to the ebbs and flows of the U.S. stock market, with the noted exception of the Internet boom. During this time, the market boom coincided with an M&A activity rise, as companies raced to snap up competitors and consolidate market share or use acquisition as a quick way to get into a market.[39] With the market downturn in 2000, it would seem logical that M&A activity would increase as startups look for other ways to capitalize value. However, as the data from Exhibit 13-11 indicates, M&A activity actually decreased overall throughout 2000. The reason? One hypothesis is that startups hoped they could ride out the Nasdaq downturn back to high market capitalizations, and scorned the idea of being acquired by larger companies.

As confidence erodes and capital-market conditions remain harsh, startups will become humbler. The Madison, Wisconsin-based company Guild.com, a premium arts and crafts company, spurned the overtures of Ashford in the summer of 2000 when the company was valued at $80 million.[40] Under market pressures, it eventually accepted Ashford's offer in January 2001, for a mere $4.1 million in stock. Many startups will find themselves in similar positions, and acquisition will become an increasingly desirable alternative for many startups. But these acquisitions will be of a very different flavor from those of the Internet boom. Acquisition will often be the only alternative for startups that would otherwise have to close their doors, and increased desperation leads to lower valuations. The average Internet M&A deal in the first quarter of 2000 was valued at $209 million. In the fourth quarter of 2000, the average value was $5 million.[41] So while we are likely to see increased willingness on the part of startups to be acquired, the value of these acquisitions will similarly decline as willing buyers become more difficult to find.

**Exhibit 13-11** DECLINE OF MERGERS IN 2000

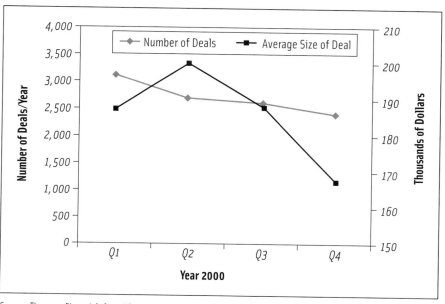

Source: Thomson Financial, from "Garage Startup to Garage Sale." *The Industry Standard.* February 19, 2001.

# Where Will the Investment Dollars Go in 2001?

While the current climate is less than hospitable to startups, there are still investment dollars looking for good ideas. But in this climate, what is a good idea? Lark Park, a writer at the *Industry Standard*, points out that "the great ideas are ones that find a problem and propose a solution. Are people still griping about slow Internet speeds? Give them faster networks. Under pressure to cut costs? Bring out software to run more efficiently online. There are new nuts to crack as well: How will companies move information through a mobile wireless network? How do you make money off the plumbing that's already been built?"[42] Venture capitalists look to the future to find the industries that will be hot a few years from now, not necessarily what is hot this minute. There are some industries to which investment dollars are still flowing, but these dollars are only going to the companies that have a good track record and an excellent management team.

According to *The Industry Standard*, examples of industries to watch are networking and communications and enterprise software. Venture capitalists are looking to the future, when they believe that the demand for bandwidth will grow. Consequently, they are investing in companies that try to solve the bandwidth problem. Take the example of Seneca Networks, which received $25 million in January 2001 from the Sprout Group. According to the CEO of Seneca, his company had no problem raising money, even in this chilly climate. Another example is enterprise software, which, according to VentureWire, received $173 million in investments in January. Many venture-capital firms are investing in these industries.[43] Exhibit 13-12 shows a breakdown of recent seed financing by industry.

## Exhibit 13-12 RECENT SEED FINANCING BY INDUSTRY

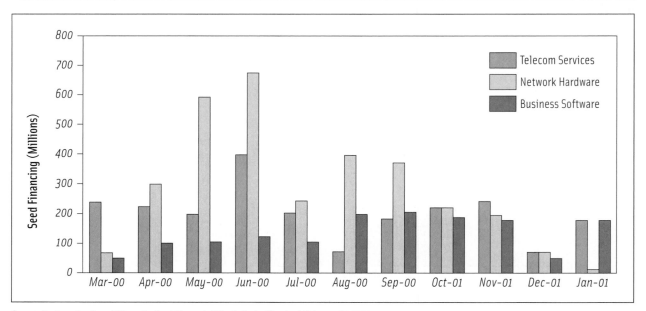

Source: Venturewire, from "Where the Seed Money Is." *The Industry Standard*. February 19, 2001

The bottom line? Venture capitalists are looking for companies that are creative problem solvers. These companies will continue to receive investments, regardless of the climate.

In conclusion, while the exact future of the capital markets going forward is unknown, the general climate will be far more conservative than the "irrational exuberance" of the Internet boom. Investors and entrepreneurs alike will return to more traditional business sensibilities and be more cautious about where they choose to spend their time and dollars. However, even in light of renewed conservatism, the capital markets will continue to exist and continue to seek investments, and quality business ideas with experienced personnel will continue to receive funding.

## SUMMARY

### 1. What are the major sources of equity financing, and how do these sources differ from one another?

The major sources of equity financing are bootstrapping, angels, and venture capital. Bootstrapping is the process of using personal resources to get a company financed. This could include taking out a personal loan, taking cash advances from credit cards, and borrowing from friends and family. Angels are wealthy individuals who invest their own money in a startup, while venture capitalists invest large amounts of money into companies they believe will give them a high return on investment. While bootstrappers are able to keep all the equity in the company for themselves, they often cannot grow very fast because they are working with limited resources. Also, bootstrappers do not benefit from the personal networks that come with angels and VC investors.

### 2. How is the value of a startup determined?

The major methods of determining valuation for a startup are the comparables method, the financial performance method, and the venture-capital method. The comparables method requires a startup to find companies that are comparable to it; and use them as the basis from which to extrapolate its own value. The financial performance method uses a company's earnings to project future cash flows and then applies a discount rate to determine the present value. The venture-capital method values a company by determining the terminal value (usually by looking at comparables) and then applying a larger discounted rate to the terminal value than the free cash-flow method.

### 3. What are the factors involved in negotiating with investors?

When negotiations begin, the startup's management team and the investors must agree upon the terms. Agreement must occur on the amount being invested, the valuation of the company, the type of security they will use in the transaction, the rights and privileges the investors will have, and what antidilution provisions there will be for the investors. The basic types of securities include zero coupon bonds, convertible debentures, preferred stock, and common stock. The rights of the investors include right of first refusal, preemptive right, redemption right, registration right, covenants, and antidilution provisions (which include full-ratchet antidilution and weighted-average antidilution).

4. **What is an initial public offering? What process must an entrepreneur undertake to complete an IPO successfully?**

An IPO is the sale of shares to public investors of a company that has never been traded on a public stock exchange. To complete an IPO, the company must choose underwriters, prepare the registration statement for the SEC, distribute the preliminary prospectus, prepare for and complete the road show, incorporate the comments from the SEC into the registration statement, agree on a final share price and number of shares for the offering, and close the offering and distribute the final prospectus.

## KEY TERMS

| | |
|---|---|
| valuation | common stock |
| comparables method | right of first refusal |
| financial performance method | preemptive right |
| present value | redemption rights |
| proforma income statement | registration rights |
| free cash flow | covenants |
| terminal value | antidilution provisions |
| discount rate | dilution |
| venture-capital method | full-ratchet antidilution |
| retention ratio | weighted-average antidilution |
| asset valuation method | pre-money valuation |
| term sheet | post-money valuation |
| zero coupon bond | initial public offering |
| convertible debentures | red herring |
| preferred stock | |

## Endnotes

[1]Long, Mark. *Financing the New Venture* (Massachusetts: Adams Media Corporation, 2000).

[2]"Frequently Asked Questions" Garage.com
*http://www.garage.com/forums/commercialBanking/qandaArchive.shtml#Q7*

[3]Red Herring.com

[4]Bhide, Amar. "Bootstrapping Finance: The Art of Start-up," *The Entrepreneurial Venture* (Boston: Harvard Business School Press, 1999).

[5]Bhide, Amar. *The Entrepreneurial Venture* (Boston: Harvard Business School Press, 1999).

[6]Gates, Stephanie. "Angels are, increasingly, among us," *Red Herring* 17 June, 1999.

[7]Aragon, Lawrence. "Bankrolled by an angel," *Red Herring* 15 December, 1999.
*http://www.redherring.com/insider/1999/1215/vc-vcps.html.*

[8]Aragon, Lawrence. "Bankrolled by an angel: part 2," *Red Herring* 18 December, 1999.
*http://www.redherring.com/insider/1999/1218/vc-vcps.html.*

[9]Aragon, Lawrence. "Bankrolled by an angel: part 2," *Red Herring* 18 December, 1999.
*http://www.redherring.com/insider/1999/1218/vc-vcps.html.*

[10]Aragon, Lawrence. "Bankrolled by an angel: part 3," *Red Herring* 22 December 1999. *http://www.redherring.com/insider/1999/1222/vc-vcps.html.*

[11]Aragon, Lawrence. "Bankrolled by an angel: part 3," *Red Herring* 22 December 1999. *http://www.redherring.com/insider/1999/1222/vc-vcps.html.*

[12]"Venture-capital investments achieve record levels in 2000, torrid pace relaxed in the fourth quarter." News Release, National Venture Capital Association, January 29, 2001.

[13]PricewaterhouseCoopers and VentureOne. "Aggregate National Data," PWC Moneytree Survey, 2000. *http://www.pwcmoneytree.com/aggregatemenu.asp.*

[14]Taylor, John. "Established venture capital funds continue fundraising success." News Release, National Venture Capital Association, 28 November, 2000.

[15]Red Herring.com Footnote from the slides.

[16]Richtel, Matt. "Less venture capital," *The New York Times* on the Web 30 January, 2001.

[17]Roberti, Mark. "A new business cycle," *The Industry Standard* 5 February, 2001. *http://www.thestandard.com/article/display/0,1151,21913,00.html?nl=int*

[18]Pratt, S. *Valuing a Business: The Analysis and Appraisal of Closely Held Companies* (Illinois: Dow Jones-Irwin, 1996).

[19]Neidorf, Shawn. "Ready for the startup game? Try these tough questions," *Mercury News* 5 July, 2000. *www.siliconvalley.com/columns/termsheet/.*

[20]White and Lee. "White paper on business valuation techniques and negotiations," White and Lee *http://www.whiteandlee.com/papers_transactions_bvtn.html.*

[21]For more information on options analysis, please refer to Copeland, Tom and Vladamir Antidarov. *Real Options: A Practitioner's Guide* (New York: Texere LLC, 2001).

[22]Nuechterlein, Jeffrey D. *International Venture Capital: The Role of Startup Financing in the United States, Europe and Asia,* Council on Foreign Relations and Westview Press, West View Press, 2000, p. 2.

[23]Bartlett, Joseph W. *The Fundamentals of Venture Capital* (New York: Madison Books, 1999).

[24]Bartlett, Joseph W. *The Fundamentals of Venture Capital* (New York: Madison Books, 1999).

[25]Bagley, Constance, and Craig Dauchy. "Going Public" in *The Entrepreneurial Venture* (Boston: Harvard Business School Press, 1999).

[26]Zemel, Tamar. "Venture-backed IPOs scarce in 4Q'00," VentureOne online, *www.ventureone.com.*

[27]Mowrey, Mark. "Net IPO pipeline floods," *The Industry Standard,* 18 September, 2000.

[28]We are deeply indebted to the outline provided in *The Entrepreneurial Venture* (Boston: Harvard Business School Press, 1999), on the process of going public. Please refer to this work for a more comprehensive overview of the IPO process.

[29]+C4 Venture-Backed IPOs Scarce in 4Q'00", VentureOne press release, *http://www.ventureone.com/press/4Q00Liquidity.pdf.*

[30]VentureOne.com, *www.ventureone.com.*

[31]Ackman, Dan. "Top of the news: AOL Time Warner's tragic marriage," *Forbes.com* 12 January, 2001. *http://www.forbes.com/2001/01/12/0112topaol.html;$sessionid$KY3BFLAAAASA3QFIAGVSFFQ.*

[32]Park, Lark. "Where the seed money is," *The Industry Standard,* 19 February, 2001.

[33]Pallatto, John. "Internet World annual VC roundtable," *Internet World,* 2001.

[34]Kumar, Vishesh. "Venture buzz: time to ignore the stock market," *The Industry Standard,* 16 February, 2001.

[35]Kumar, Vishesh. "Venture buzz: count your billion-dollar blessings," *The Industry Standard,* 22 December, 2000.

[36]Park, Lark. "Where the seed money is," *The Industry Standard,* 19 February, 2001.

[37]Kumar, Vishesh. "Venture buzz: the week in venture capital," *The Industry Standard,* 17 December, 2000.

[38]Schiffrin, Anya. "From garage startup to garage sale," *The Industry Standard,* 19 February, 2001.

[39]Nesheim, John L. *High Tech Start Up* (New York: The Free Press, 2000).

[40]Schiffrin, Anya. "From garage startup to garage sale," *The Industry Standard,* 19 February, 2001.

[41]Schiffrin, Anya. "From garage startup to garage sale," *The Industry Standard,* 19 February, 2001.

[42]Park, Lark. "Where the seed money is," *The Industry Standard,* 19 February, 2001.

[43]Park, Lark. "Where the seed money is," *The Industry Standard,* 19 February, 2001.

# Media Transformation

The purpose of this chapter is to provide an understanding of media convergence. Media convergence—and its expected synergistic benefits—has been a key driver behind several recent megamergers of media companies, including the marriages of AOL and Time Warner, Viacom and CBS, and The Walt Disney Company and Capital Cities/ABC. Increasing fragmentation of media usage in American households, recent shifts in federal telecommunications laws, and advances in digital technologies (especially broadband) suggest that media convergence will usher in a future of widespread, convenient access to new and innovative media services.

## QUESTIONS

*Please consider the following questions as you read this chapter:*

1. What is media convergence?

2. What conditions make media convergence possible?

3. How do new-media companies leverage traditional media channels?

4. What are reasons for media megamergers?

This chapter was coauthored by Bernie Jaworski, Jeffrey Rayport, Dickson Louie, and Michael Yip.

# INTRODUCTION

In Chapters 2 and 3, we reviewed the market infrastructure, which showed how the Internet is evolving as the digital platform of the networked economy. We explained how the Internet has grown and how businesses now use the Web as a single, digital media base to create an electronic architecture for commercial applications. As discussed, the infrastructure convergence from analog to digital technology involves the conversion of all data streams into bits of zeros and ones—the binary language of computers.

The **media infrastructure** includes all of the various communications companies and the channels of communication—such as radio, television, newspapers, and magazines—they use in mass communication with the general public. Whereas network infrastructure refers to the hardware and software used in communication, media infrastructure refers to the content of the communication. Media companies produce the content for print media distribution chains or for programs that are broadcast over a chain or network of radio or television broadcast stations.

# WHAT IS MEDIA CONVERGENCE?

**Media convergence** is the process by which different types of media content—news, information, and entertainment—found across various types of media platforms—text, images, audio, and video—are evolving into a single media platform through the Internet. Media convergence can be defined as the evolution and migration of the many types of content from traditional, analog media platforms to a digital platform, or cross-platform, where all content will be accessible through various digital devices—wireless telephones, personal computers, PalmPilots, and interactive television set-tops, for example. Media convergence, and its expected synergistic benefits, has been a key driver behind several recent megamergers of media companies, including the mergers of America Online (AOL) and Time Warner, Viacom and CBS, The Walt Disney Company and Capital Cities/ABC, Tribune Company and the Times Mirror Company, and MCA and Vivendi.

In this chapter, we review the current and potential future impact of media convergence across an array of old- and new-economy media, and examine areas of public policy that will need to be addressed. We review the proliferation of media and the fragmentation of media usage for news, information, and entertainment over the past three decades. We explore how Internet companies are beginning to leverage the media of the old economy to build brand awareness and usage for their products and services in the new economy. We examine how the possibility of media convergence has become a driving force behind several of the megamergers between media companies that have taken place in the last few years. And we review the potential impact of media convergence on various media platforms and their current revenue models. Finally, we look at the public policy issues governing media convergence.

# WHAT CONDITIONS MAKE MEDIA CONVERGENCE POSSIBLE?

Through the use of a coder-decoder (codec), analog signals can be converted to digital equivalents through an analog-to-digital (A-to-D) process, and digital bit streams can be converted into analog signals through a digital-to-analog (D-to-A) process. These routine processes bring all types of analog signals into the digital domain as a series of "bits," represented by 0s and 1s. These bits make fast, inexpensive, precise, and accurate computer-based processing, as well as mixing with other digital signals, possible. Ultimately, they are returned to the analog physical world for our consumption.

## Continued Advances and Decreasing Cost of Digital Technology

Advances in computers, and the decreased cost of PCs and all their related digital technology, have led to the creation of a cost-effective common platform for placing all types of media content into binary form. Most media content now begins in digital form. And once text, audio, video, and graphics are in the digital domain, the digital forms of content are easily manipulated, combined, stored, and transmitted across the Internet and onto digital devices such as PCs, digital television sets, or any other type of Internet-enabled device.

## Low-Cost Digital Network Infrastructure

The development of a nonproprietary Internet Protocol (IP), Hypertext Transfer Protocol (HTTP), and HyperText Markup Language (HTML) allowed Internet hardware and software development to occur in a relatively unencumbered environment. The standardization of HTTP and HTML led to the development of a universal graphical user interface for the Internet browser, which reduced navigation to a click of the mouse. With the lifting of commercial-use restrictions, the Internet fast became the backbone of digital communications—and the low-cost digital network infrastructure of the World Wide Web began its explosive growth.

## Media Proliferation

At the start of the twentieth century, daily printed newspapers were the only form of mass media. In the 1920s, radio and magazines emerged as additional sources for news, information, and entertainment. After World War II, in the late 1940s and throughout the 1950s, broadcast television emerged, and TV sets became the primary media source in many American households.

In the 1960s, most Americans had just three network channels to choose from; by the 1970s, cable television had emerged, with channels such as HBO and Turner Broadcasting's TBS Superstation picking up viewer traffic. Cable television expanded further in the 1980s. That decade saw the birth of CNN, ESPN, and MTV, as well as the emergence of the VCR. In the 1990s, direct broadcast satellite services found their way into American homes, and the number of cable television channels continued to grow.

## Media-Usage Fragmentation in American Households

In the spring of 2000, the Pew Research Center in Washington, D.C., conducted a survey on the increasing fragmentation of media usage. The results showed that while broadcast television news, both network and local, remained the primary media source for those surveyed (newspapers were second), its total audience penetration continued to decline. The decline was most obvious in regular viewership of broadcast television network news programs—morning shows, nightly news, or news magazines—which dropped from 74 percent in 1996 to 51 percent in 2000.[1]

The Pew Research study noted that the declining size of the audience for television news was apparent in all demographic groups, but particularly evident among younger people. The audience penetration of network, local, and cable news channels (CNN, MSNBC, and Fox) was lowest among people under 30 years of age, and second lowest among people 30 to 49 years of age. Regular viewing of all three types of news programming was highest among people 50 years of age and older.[2]

Despite the decline in the viewership of network news programs, the Pew Research study showed that the percentage of Americans who regularly turned to online news sites for news and information grew from 20 percent in April 1998 to 33 percent in April 2000. Younger audiences were particularly likely to access news and information directly from the Internet. Forty-six percent of those 30 years of age or younger accessed the Internet once a week for news; people between the ages of 30 and 49, and those over age 50, did so 37 percent and 20 percent, respectively.[3]

As with television news, the television entertainment-show audience has also declined, largely due to the increased penetration of cable television. For example, during the 1985-86 television season, approximately 93 percent of the primetime viewing audience in the United States tuned in to a network affiliate, an independent television station, or public television; only 7 percent had watched a primetime show on cable television. During the 1998-99 season, however, the percentage of households watching a show on a network affiliate, an independent television station, or public television had declined to about 59 percent, while those watching a show on cable television increased to 41 percent.[4] Over the same 13-year period, the number of subscribers to basic cable had increased from 39.8 million (or 46.2 percent of all households) in 1985 to 68.5 million (or 68 percent of all households) in 1999.[5] The number of cable systems increased from 6,600 to 10,466 over the same period.[6] Table 14-1 shows how cable television has slowly lured away primetime viewers from the broadcast networks.

Although the amount of time that members of all age groups spend watching network television has steadily declined over the past two decades, the percentage of households with alternative forms of media entertainment and information has dramatically increased—thus contributing to the further fragmentation of media usage. For example, as 2000 came to an end, 98 percent of all U.S. households had at least one color television set and at least one radio. Ninety-one percent of households had a VCR; 54 percent had a personal computer; 44 percent had a video-game unit; 51 percent had a cellular telephone[7]; and 12 percent had a DVD player.[8] Approximately 31 percent of all households had access to the Internet, and 68 percent were wired to cable television.[9] Ten years earlier, by comparison, only 68 percent of all U.S. households had access to a VCR; 23 percent, a personal computer; 15 percent, a video-game unit; and 59 percent, cable television.[10] Very few households had access to the Internet or owned a cellular phone.

With such a range of media devices available in the typical American household, it is no surprise that children spend a large percentage of their time immersed in multimedia. A November 1999 study by the Kaiser Family Foundation showed that American children spent, on average, 5.5 hours per day—or just over 38 hours per week—using media. Television viewing accounted for almost half of that usage, followed by music listening, reading, video viewing, and using a computer. The study found that the typical American household had three television sets, three radios, two VCRs, two CD players, and a video-game player.[11]

## Table 14-1 PRIME-TIME VIEWING SHARES OF FREE AND CABLE TELEVISION NETWORKS (1985–1998)

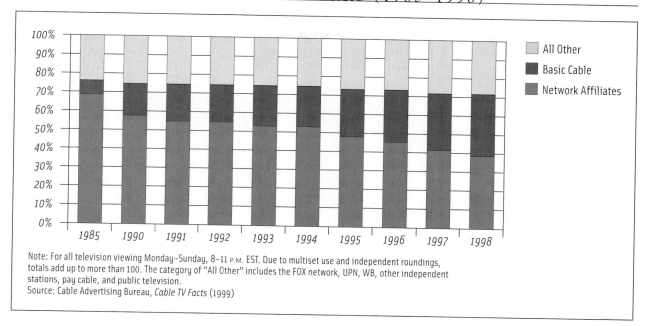

Note: For all television viewing Monday–Sunday, 8–11 P.M. EST. Due to multiset use and independent roundings, totals add up to more than 100. The category of "All Other" includes the FOX network, UPN, WB, other independent stations, pay cable, and public television.
Source: Cable Advertising Bureau, *Cable TV Facts* (1999)

## Forecasted Continued Media Proliferation and Media Usage Fragmentation

The continued proliferation of television channels and services, as well as other media outlets, has led to a considerable increase in audience fragmentation. Furthermore, experts predict that over the next 10 years, consumers will be presented with an even more diverse range of media choices. Advances in wireless technology, digital compression, two-way networks, and high-definition television—not to mention continued advances in the technology that powers the Internet—certainly support this prediction (see Table 14-3).[12]

Table 14-3 provides a breakdown of the number of hours per year that consumers were exposed to media, tracked from 1990 to 2002. Television viewing accounts for almost one-half of the typical consumer's annual media usage, with the average American watching an estimated 1,571 hours of television in 2000 (an increasing percentage of those hours are spent watching cable). In addition, the time spent listening to music, watching videos, playing video games, and surfing the Internet has also increased significantly since 1990.[13]

## HOW DO NEW-MEDIA COMPANIES LEVERAGE TRADITIONAL MEDIA CHANNELS?

While much has been written recently about the Internet as an increasingly important source for news, information and commerce, the new economy has actually been quite dependent on the traditional news outlets of the old economy. Online

## Table 14-2 PENETRATION OF MEDIA TECHNOLOGIES INTO U.S. HOUSEHOLDS (2000)

| Penetration of Service/Device in U.S. Households | | | |
|---|---|---|---|
| | **1990** | **2000** | **Difference** |
| Satellite Dish | 3% | 13% | +10 |
| Video Game Console | 5% | 44% | +39 |
| Online Services | 0% | 31% | +31 |
| Camcorder | 10% | 33% | +23 |
| PC | 23% | 53% | +30 |
| PDA | 0% | 20% | +20 |
| CD Player (Audio) | 19% | 55% | +36 |
| VCR | 68% | 91% | +23 |
| DVD Player | 0% | 22% | +22 |
| Home Fax Machine/Modem | 19% | 51% | +32 |
| Answering Machine | 31% | 74% | +43 |
| Cellular Phone | 0% | 51% | +51 |
| Cordless Phone | 25% | 78% | +53 |
| Corded Phone | 98% | 96% | −2 |
| Telephone Service | 48% | 98% | +50 |
| Radio | 99% | 98% | −1 |
| Basic Cable Television | 21% | 68% | +47 |
| B & W TV | 50% | 47% | −3 |
| Color TV | 96% | 98% | +2 |
| All Television | 99% | 99% | 0 |

Source: National Cable Television Association, Nielson Media Research, Electronic Industries Association, Consumer Electronics Manufacturers Association, U.S. Department of Commerce

media companies are using traditional media channels to build an audience for new media. Dot-coms are using newspapers, magazines, and broadcast television to attract "early adopters" as well as mainstream users.[14] In 2000, an estimated 32 percent of all American households were online—approximately a threefold increase from the 9 percent of 1996.[15]

To build brand awareness for a rapidly growing mainstream audience of Internet users, dot-com companies were predicted to spend an estimated $5 billion to $6 billion in advertising in 2000,[16] with approximately 90 percent of those dollars being spent on ads placed in traditional media outlets, such as network television, national newspapers, and network radio.[17] Among the top dot-com advertisers in local and national newspapers in 2000 were E*Trade, Dow Jones, Cheap Tickets, Priceline.com, and Charles Schwab's online trading site.[18]

Table 14-3
# HOURS SPENT PER YEAR PER CONSUMER PER MEDIA (1990–2000)

| Number of Hours Per Person Per Year Using Consumer Media | | | |
|---|---|---|---|
| | **1992** | **1997** | **2002** |
| Total television (broadcast and cable) | 1510 | 1561 | 1575 |
| Radio | 1150 | 1082 | 1040 |
| Recorded music | 233 | 265 | 289 |
| Daily newspapers | 172 | 159 | 152 |
| Consumer books | 100 | 92 | 97 |
| Consumer magazines | 85 | 82 | 79 |
| Home video | 42 | 50 | 58 |
| Movies in theatres | 11 | 13 | 13 |
| Video games | 19 | 36 | 46 |
| Consumer online | 2 | 28 | 49 |
| **Total Hours Per Person:** | **3324** | **3368** | **3398** |

Sources: Veronis, Suhler & Associates, Wilkofsky Gruen Associates, Nielsen Media Research, Simmons Market Research, Interactive Digital Software Association Paul Kagan Associates, Motion Picture Association of America, Book Industry Study Group, Magazine Publishers of America, Software Publishers Association.

Online companies' decision to try to build brand awareness primarily through traditional media ads (versus online banners or button advertisements) is not unexpected. Approximately 32 percent of all Internet users say that they use articles in magazines or newspapers to discover URLs; 28 percent say that they learn about URLs through word-of-mouth; 27 percent find them on products; 26 percent, through print advertisements; 24 percent, through ads on television; 22 percent, in product literature; and 15 percent, on radio advertising.[19]

Most online-news users say that they still read newspapers and listen to radio news at about the same or at a higher rate since going online. Although this is not surprising, given that most Internet users are more interested in current events than non-Internet users, it is interesting to note that the Internet is emerging as a mechanism for supplementing, not replacing, traditional media sources.[20] Furthermore, 75 percent of all online-news users use traditional news outlets *more* often to get their news and information. Sixty-three percent say they use offline sources about the same amount as they did before going online, and 11 percent say that being online has decreased the time they spend perusing offline sources.

## Case Example: *The New York Times* on the Web

Launched in January 1996, NYTimes.com has emerged as the leading newspaper site on the Web—by year-end 2000, it had 14 million registered users and was getting 178 million page views. The site gives users free access to two weeks' worth of content, but forces them to register in order to access the archives or other site services. During registration, users enter an e-mail address, along with basic demographic information such as age and income. Like its print counterpart *The*

Exhibit
14-1     MEDIA FRAGMENTATION (1960s–2010s)

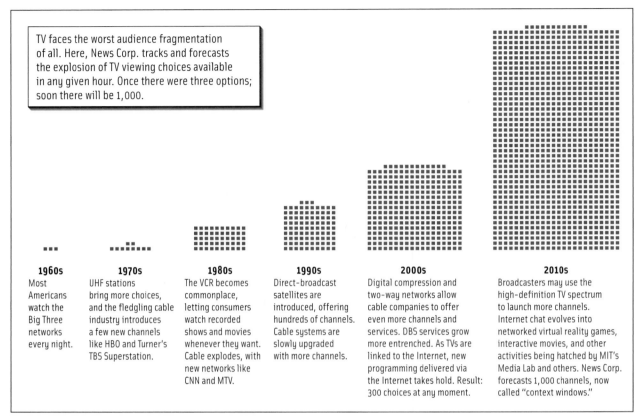

TV faces the worst audience fragmentation of all. Here, News Corp. tracks and forecasts the explosion of TV viewing choices available in any given hour. Once there were three options; soon there will be 1,000.

**1960s**
Most Americans watch the Big Three networks every night.

**1970s**
UHF stations bring more choices, and the fledgling cable industry introduces a few new channels like HBO and Turner's TBS Superstation.

**1980s**
The VCR becomes commonplace, letting consumers watch recorded shows and movies whenever they want. Cable explodes, with new networks like CNN and MTV.

**1990s**
Direct-broadcast satellites are introduced, offering hundreds of channels. Cable systems are slowly upgraded with more channels.

**2000s**
Digital compression and two-way networks allow cable companies to offer even more channels and services. DBS services grow more entrenched. As TVs are linked to the Internet, new programming delivered via the Internet takes hold. Result: 300 choices at any moment.

**2010s**
Broadcasters may use the high-definition TV spectrum to launch more channels. Internet chat evolves into networked virtual reality games, interactive movies, and other activities being hatched by MIT's Media Lab and others. News Corp. forecasts 1,000 channels, now called "context windows."

Source: *Business Week*, February 16, 1998

*New York Times*, NYTimes.com sought to deliver a targeted, upscale audience to advertisers. This differed markedly from the approach of leading portal sites such as Yahoo and AOL, which continue to provide advertisers with a wide and massive audience.

Martin Nisenholtz, president and CEO of the New York Times Digital Company (which oversees NYTimes.com, as well as Boston.com, NYToday.com, and wine.com), says that there are four key reasons why the company's "bricks-and-clicks" strategy (integration of online and offline operations) has been more successful than the Internet "pure-play" strategy of many of its competitors: having access to editorial content from *The New York Times*; leveraging the brand of *The New York Times*; building upon the advertising sales infrastructure of *The New York Times*; and taking advantage of offline promotion capabilities on the pages of its print counterpart.[21]

## Case Example: RealNetworks

Founded in 1994 by Rob Glaser, a Yale-trained computer scientist and economist and former Microsoft executive, Seattle-based RealNetworks has emerged as the leading maker of streaming-media software products, which deliver audio, video, and other multimedia services to PCs and digital devices. RealNetworks's first product was RealPlayer, which allowed Internet users to listen to live audio broadcasts over the Internet for the first time. Currently, RealPlayer products (which also include RealVideo, RealJukebox, and GoldPass) are used by 170 million people. Alliances with several major media content-makers—such as CNN, ABCNews.com, Oxygen, ESPN Sports, and Bloomberg, as well as over 2,500 local radio stations, have not only enabled users of RealNetworks' products to play video or audio on the Web, but have also helped make RealNetworks the leading brand in delivering streaming media (ahead of Apple's QuickTime and Microsoft's Windows Media Player). Excluding acquisition charges, the company earned an operating profit of $30.9 million on net revenue of $241.5 million in fiscal year 2000.[22]

Although RealNetworks initially built its brand through alliances with many traditional media companies, Glaser leaves open the possibility that the company will someday create its own content, and therefore become a media company in its own right. As Glaser told *The Industry Standard* in 1999:

> *Most networks, even ESPN, started with lesser programs like ping-pong tournaments or repurposed content, in the case of MTV. We're in that first wave. The second wave is when you create your own content. Who's going to be in that wave? Either us or our content partners.*[23]

**Exhibit 14-2**

## NYTIMES.COM HOMEPAGE

**Exhibit 14-3** REALNETWORKS' REALPLAYER

## Case Example: MSNBC

Launched in July 1996, the cable and online news channel MSNBC is jointly owned by Microsoft and General Electric, the parent company of NBC. By providing 24-hour news coverage on both cable television and on the Web, MSNBC is an example of how news and information content from multiple media platforms—broadcast television, cable television, and print—can be utilized on the Web. For example, the visitors to MSNBC.com's homepage can view segments from the various NBC news shows broadcast on network television, participate in an audience jury vote regarding a *Dateline* court case, or watch the MSNBC cable news channel live on the site. Traffic to MSNBC.com is driven by promotions across multiple media platforms, including the NBC news shows, the MSNBC and CNBC news channels, and the MSN site. In addition, a strategic alliance with The Washington Post Company allows MSNBC.com to also post print stories from *The Washington Post* and *Newsweek* on its site. According to a November 2000 Media Metrix report, MSNBC.com is the leading news site on the Web, with 12.3 million unique visitors.[24]

In a 1998 speech at the University of Southern California, Merrill Brown, editor in chief of MSNBC.com, made the following observation about media convergence:

> We are all moving, all of us, to a world that will deliver television and Internet material over the same platform, whether it's the PC or the TV ... we'll be delivering the news in a convergence environment, bringing people a newscast and

**Exhibit 14-4**

MSNBC.COM HOMEPAGE

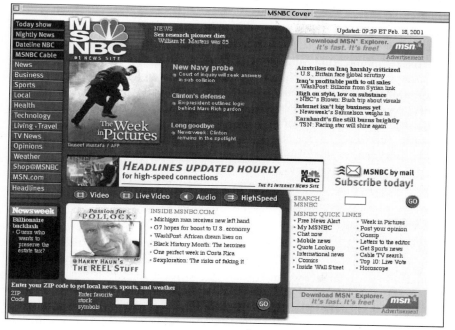

Screen shot of MSNBC used by permission of MSNBC.

*video as well as Internet-like content. Whether the platform is the PC or the TV, via Windows 98, an Internet device attached to the TV, a satellite-delivered service, it is clear we'll be getting Internet and television content through the same appliance before long. This development too will change news delivery and news cycles, issues we all must devote attention to.[25]*

# WHAT ARE THE REASONS FOR MEDIA MEGAMERGERS?

The increased fragmentation of media usage, as well as the promise of "broadband" technology, which gives media users quick access to a variety of media forms over the Internet, have together sent many media companies searching for new ways to capture wide audiences. One strategy has been to develop vertical integration for content and distribution across all three core media types—print, video, and audio. This has been achieved largely through mergers. During the last three years, the pace for media mergers has increased dramatically. Recent media megamergers include the following:

- Time Warner and Turner Broadcasting (1995)
- The Walt Disney Company and Capital Cities/ABC (1995)
- Westinghouse and CBS (1995)
- Viacom and CBS (1999)
- AOL and Time Warner (2000)
- Tribune Company and Times Mirror (2000)

There were several reasons behind each of these mergers. In the following section, we examine five reasons that are common to all: changes in telecommunications laws; vertical integration of both content and distribution channels; pursuit of multiple revenue streams; advances in new digital technologies; and entry into global markets.

# Telecommunications Act of 1996

The **Telecommunications Act of 1996**, signed into law by President Bill Clinton on February 8, 1996, was the first major overhaul of federal laws regulating the communications industry since 1934. The act increased competition by fostering a shift from a regulation-based telecommunications industry to one that was market-based. The act also allowed for increased ownership of television stations by a single entity (up to 25 percent of the total U.S. market), and, more importantly, for media convergence. Telephone service providers, cable television companies, and utility companies could now directly compete with one another to provide telephone, cable, and utility services to American homes.

# Vertical Integration

While the Telecommunications Act of 1996 allowed for increased competition of regulated media distribution channels into the typical U.S. household, media companies were often at the center of the media megamergers as part of an overall strategy, which called for **vertical integration** of media content with media distribution. For example, the Disney-Capital Cities/ABC and Viacom-CBS mergers saw traditional providers of movie and television content linking up with a television network as a way to distribute content into the households through broadcast television.

The most common reason given for such media mergers was "synergy." As Michael Eisner, chairman and CEO of The Walt Disney Company, explained to a gathering of Chicago executives in 1996:

> It is the justification most executives use when grilled on why the merger of two companies make sense. It is the dreaded "S" word—"synergy." At Disney, it is our conviction that synergy can be the single most important contributor to profit and growth in a creativity-driven company.
>
> It is simply this. When you embrace a new idea, a new business, a new product, a new film or TV show, whatever, you have to make sure that everyone throughout the company knows about it early enough so that every segment of the business can promote or exploit its potential in every other possible market, product or context.
>
> [For example, if a film] does well in its initial domestic run, it almost ensures later success in international distribution, domestic and international home video, network, and foreign television, pay-per-view TV and cable. At Disney, a well-received film will also provide profitable opportunities in our theme parks—new rides, new characters, new parades, new attractions, and in consumer products for Disney stores, for Sears, and for others.[26]

# Pursuit of Multiple Revenue Streams

Consolidation of media companies—and also of advertising agencies—provides an opportunity to seek increased advertising revenue through increased cross-selling, niche media buys, and advertising sales packages. In the recent merger of AOL and

Time Warner, advertising executives promised to seek increased cross-selling opportunities among the advertisers of Time (print), CNN (cable television), and AOL (online) as a way to deliver upon the additional $1 billion in pretax earnings promised by management.[27] As a result, AOL Time Warner has created an internal advertising council made up of executives throughout the organization, representing various media divisions, to promote cross–media advertising sales. The company hopes to generate a 12 percent to 15 percent increase in revenue, and executives note the current lack of client duplication among Time, CNN, and AOL, for the upside potential.[28]

## Advances in New Digital Technologies

With rapid advances in new digital technologies, media companies are presented with the opportunity to put their content online in various forms, ranging from the current streaming technology to playing short audio and video clips over a narrowband feed to the future promise of playing movies on demand through broadband delivery.

An example of media convergence on the Internet is ABCNews.com (see Exhibit 14-5), which The Walt Disney Company owns through the ABC Television and Radio Network. On the ABCNews.com site, visitors can read, listen, or view ABC News content from both its television and radio news programs. For example, digitalized technology allows for selected video clips from the television network's branded news shows—*Good Morning America, 20/20,* and *World News Tonight*—to appear both on television through any one of its 215 affiliates and over the Internet on the ABCNews.com site. Hourly audio clips of news and sports reports from ABC Radio are also available on the ABCNews.com site through audio streaming.

## Entry into Global Markets

With no geographic barriers to the distribution of digitized content on the Internet, many media companies have sought to create global markets for their content through mergers. Expansion of brand names into overseas markets included CNN International, MTV Overseas, ESPN, and The Disney Channel.

With increased digitization of content and the promise of broadband delivery in the near future, the PC will not be the only receiver of Internet content. Other Internet receivers include digital telephones, handheld computers, and video-game consoles. In fact, many predict that by mid-2001, the Sony PlayStation 2 (see Exhibit 14-6), with its ability to become a DVD player, a CD player, and an Internet connection (in addition to being a video-game player), has the potential to become the primary household appliance for converging media applications. Howard Stringer, CEO of Sony Corporation of America, observed, "Synergy was forced in the analog world, but in the digital world, people can't get out of the way of each other."[29]

## Media Economics

As stated previously, media companies have been merging over the last five years as a way to develop vertical integration for content and distribution across all types of media. For today's media company, the strategy is to collect and, through media convergence and digital convergence, create a synergistic combination of what were once disparate media that produces a direct bottom-line benefit. Each form of media has its own economics and, therefore, a different business model. The types of media most

**Exhibit 14-5**   ABCNEWS.COM HOMEPAGE

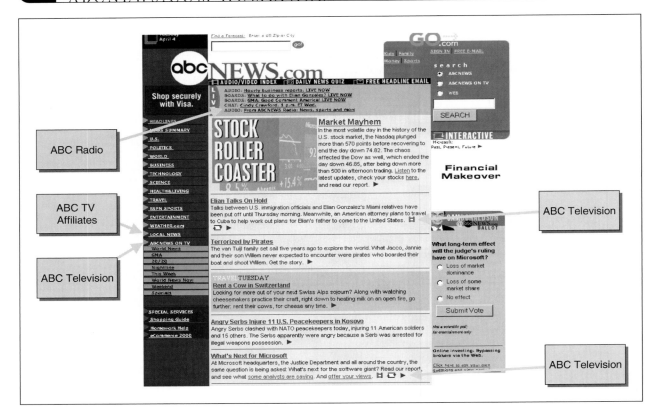

commonly discussed in connection to convergence include newspapers, magazines, books, broadcast television, cable television, radio, film, videos, DVDs, CDs, and MP3.

**Newspapers.** At the end of 1999, there were 1,483 daily newspapers in the United States, with a cumulative total daily circulation (the number of copies sold) of approximately 56 million, and a total Sunday circulation of 59.9 million. Although only one-half of the daily newspapers were published in the morning, those morning publications accounted for 82 percent of the total circulation—or about 46 million.[30] The top four newspapers in the United States were *USA Today, The Wall Street Journal, The New York Times*, and *The Los Angeles Times*, all of which had a daily circulation of 1 million or more.[31]

After reaching a peak of 62.8 million in 1987, total daily newspaper circulation began to decline. There were several reasons for this drop-off, including the closing of several evening daily newspapers, the increase in the number of alternative weekly newspapers, and the emergence of other electronic news sources. In 1987, the number of evening newspapers being published was 1,166; in 2000, that number had slipped to 760. Over that same time period, however, the number of weekly newspapers increased from 7,600 to 8,138, with total weekly circulation growing from 47.5 million to 74.4 million.[32]

Paralleling the overall decline in daily newspaper circulation was a continued decline in the percentage of adults reading daily newspapers. In 1970, 78 percent of

**Exhibit 14-6**

SONY PLAYSTATION 2

Games: Runs PS1 titles, but new PS2 will make the old ones look like Pong.

DVD Player: Can play digital movies right out of the box. Not a bad deal just for that.

Music CD s: PS2 spins them, too. Pressed for space? Give the old player away.

Download: Beginning in 2001; store and replay digital music and video from the Web.

Internet: In 2001, Sony says, you can add Net connectivity. Browse and buy.

## DRILL-DOWN

# How Is Media Content Delivered Over the Internet?

When text, photos, graphics, audio, and video are transmitted across the Internet in digitized form, they are first broken into bits, then reassembled at the end-user's computer. For example, graphics files can be transmitted in various formats, the two most common being Graphics Interchange Format (GIF) and Joint Photographic Experts Group (JPEG). Both **GIF** and **JPEG** files contain binary data that will display an image when viewed with proper software and hardware. A computer graphics card takes the image data and displays it on a computer monitor. The Web browser reads and displays these graphic files without needing any additional software.

Binary multimedia files for audio and video are transmitted the same way, though they take much longer over current narrowband transmission speeds of less than 128 kilobits per second. Windows sound files, which end in a WAV extension, and Macintosh sound files are among the most common types of files that users can download to their computers and play through a sound card.[33]

## What Is Meant by Streaming Media?

Certain sound files, such as those created by RealAudio software, allow a computer user to listen while the file is still downloading instead of waiting until the file is completely downloaded. This process is called **streaming audio**.

With a video player such as RealPlayer or Windows Media Player, a computer user can watch a video file as it is downloading. This process is called **streaming video**. Apple's QuickTime and MPEG files are common streaming video formats.

Currently, streaming audio and video content is possible over a narrowband transmission by using media-player software in conjunction with a personal computer.[34]

At the end of November 1999, 16.9 million Internet users (or 22.7 percent of all users) had access to a media player. RealPlayer controlled 53 percent of the market; Macintosh QuickTime, 32.5 percent; and Windows Media Player, 15 percent.[35]

## How Do Digital Cameras Work?

Digital cameras do not use film. The quality of a digital picture is based on resolution, just like traditional photography. But in the digital world, resolution is based on the number of tiny electronic picture elements, or "pixels." The more pixels there are, the better and higher the resolution of the picture. When examining the "megapixel" (million square pixel) technical specification of a digital still camera, be aware of the horizontal resolution as well as the vertical resolution, and that the stated resolution numbers are not equal to that of a display monitor.

The colors that we see in an image are the varying red, green, and blue (RGB) amounts of light reflected from illuminated objects that our eyes can detect. Similarly, reflected light is focused on the sensor elements of a charged coupled device (CCD) internal to the digital camera. Each element is designed to detect red, green, or blue light within the image before the lens. Because of this, the actual display resolution is the stated horizontal pixels divided by three and the stated vertical pixels divided by three. For example, a 2.3 megapixel digital camera with 1800x1200 has an approximate display resolution of 600x400.

**Expose.** As with a traditional film camera, a digital camera's shutter admits light when you take a picture. (A scanner uses its own light source to illuminate the film or print it is scanning.) The subject is reflected onto light-sensitive material composed of the millions of tiny electronic elements of the CCD.

**Develop.** Even while you are setting up your next shot, the camera is instantly adjusting the light detected by the cells and correcting it for color, temperature, and balance. The press of the button triggers the digitizing process, which creates a set of digital data to represent the image.

**Record.** This data is stored as a picture file in the camera, on a floppy disk, or in a removable memory card. Once your pictures are transferred to a computer, they can be modified or combined with other images—the possibilities are endless.[36]

**Table 14-4**

## SUMMARY OF MEDIA ECONOMICS

| Media Economics | Industry Sales | Average $ Per Consumer | Revenue Streams | Time Spent With | Leading Franchises |
|---|---|---|---|---|---|
| Newspapers | $69.7 billion | $53.75 per year | Advertising and circulation | 3.0 hours per week | The New York Times, USA Today |
| Magazines | $20.8 billion | $40.61 per year | Advertising and circulation | 1.5 hours per week | Time, Sports Illustrated, People |
| Consumer books | $17.9 billion | $87.84 per year | Book sales | 1.9 hours per week | McGraw Hill, Little Brown, etc. |
| Broadcast television | $42.7 billion | Free | Advertising | 15.5 hours per week | CBX, NBC, ABC, Fox WB |
| Cable television | $54.3 billion | $205.75 per month | Advertising and subscription fees | 14.7 hours per week | HBO, Turner Networks, ESPN, etc. |
| Radio | $18.2 billion | Free | Advertising | 20.3 hours per week | Infinity Radio Westwood One |
| Film | $7.7 billion | $31.67 per movie | Ticket sales | 0.25 hours per week | Universal, Paramount, Disney |
| Home videos | $19 billion | $89.93 per year | Video sales | 1.1 hours per week | Universal, Paramount, Disney |
| DVDs | — | — | DVD sales | 0.2 hours per week | Universal, Paramount, Disney |
| Video games | $4 billion | 18.71 per year | Console sales, video games | 0.8 hours per week | Sony, Nintendo, Sega |
| Music CDs | $12 billion | $61.64 per year | CD sales | 5.17 hours | BMP, Sony, Disney |

all adults in the United States said that they read a newspaper daily. By 1999, this percentage had shrunk to 56.9 percent. The dropoff in Sunday readership was less dramatic, declining only from 72 percent in 1970 to 66.9 percent in 1999.[37]

The average newspaper reader is older, well-educated, and earns a relatively high income. Over 66 percent of all daily-newspaper readers have college degrees, and two-thirds have household incomes of $50,000 or more (the median household income in the United States is approximately $37,000).[38]

Interestingly, newspaper sales only account for a portion of a daily newspaper's revenue—approximately 75 percent comes from advertisers, who covet access to the well-educated, high-income audience that newspapers target. In 1999, advertising in newspapers accounted for $46.6 billion (or 21.7 percent) of all advertising expenditures in the United States.[39] The bulk of this advertising was retail and classified advertising, which, respectively, accounted for an estimated 45 percent (or $21.5 billion) and 40 percent (or $19.4 billion) of the total advertising in newspapers in 2000. The balance of the newspaper advertising comes from national advertising, which represented national accounts such as financial services, airlines, and hotels.[40]

## Will Newspapers Survive?

Doomsayers say that the increasing popularity of the Internet as a primary news source and the loss of classified advertising revenue to online career sites such as Monster.com spell the potential death of newspapers. Supporters of newspapers point out that local newspaper web-sites—such as Boston.com, operated by *The Boston Globe*—often bring in higher usage rates locally than national news sites, such as CNN or MSNBC.[41] They also point out that television was supposedly going to kill the newspaper industry in the 1950s, the same way people are predicting that the Internet will do today. John Morton, a newspaper industry analyst, observed, "We've heard it all before. A newspaper is cheap, easy to use, portable, and a great way to get information out to the masses without straining eyes or a budget."[42]

*(continued on page 539)*

In January 2001, AOL reported that it had more than 29 million subscribers—more than the circulation of the top 26 daily newspapers in the United States combined.[43] With the increasing usage of the Internet, newspapers have rushed to create a presence on the Web in an effort to win a share of this audience. At year-end 2000, over 1,000 newspapers in North America had online products of some kind, ranging from classified ads to complete reproductions of the entire newspaper.[44]

**Magazines.** At the end of 1998, there were over 500 consumer magazines and 2,700 trade publications published in the United States. The top 100 consumer magazines had a combined total circulation of approximately 248 million. Among the top magazines were *Modern Maturity*, *Reader's Digest*, *AARP Bulletin*, and *TV Guide*—each with a circulation base greater than 11 million.[45]

Unlike newspapers, consumer magazines range from the very specialized, such as *Cooking Light* or *Runner's World*, to those of general interest, such as *Newsweek* or *People Weekly*. Approximately 82 percent of all consumer magazines are sold through subscriptions; the remaining 18 percent are sold through retail outlets, such as supermarkets and newsstands. Trade publications are magazines with a nar-row focus in a particular area of business, such as restaurants and computers, and most are sold by subscription or distributed free.

Like newspapers, almost all magazines make money through a combination of circulation and advertising revenue. Magazines usually guarantee their advertisers a base circulation of readers. The top six magazines by advertising revenue in 1999 were *People Weekly* ($714 million), *Time* ($658 million), *Sports Illustrated* ($614 million), *Parade* ($533 million), *TV Guide* ($499 million), and *Better Homes and Gardens* ($444 million).[46]

Although magazines are not as directly threatened by the growth of the Internet as newspapers are, many magazines have launched companion websites as a way to enhance subscriber benefits and to build home-delivery circulation. For example, beginning in 1999, several Time Warner magazines sought to strengthen their pres-ence on the Web by offering exclusive services to their subscribers, such as free archival searches and chats with editors and writers.

**Books.** According to the Book Industry Study Group, which tracks the reading habits of American households, sales of books in the United States increased in 1999 for the ninth straight year. Unit sales of hardcover books grew by 3 percent, while paperback unit sales increased by 4 percent.[47] Approximately 100,000 book titles were published in the United States in 1999—more than twice the number published in 1990. The most popular subject areas are sociology, fiction, juvenile, and technology.[48] Part of the reason for the growing popularity of books is the continued increase in educational attainment among Americans over the past two decades. In 1998, 83 percent of the U.S. adult population had completed high school, compared to 68 percent in 1990. Twenty-four percent had attained a college degree, compared to only 17 percent in 1980.[49] In the year 2000, the average American consumer spent an estimated $87.94 on books.[50]

With the increased usage of the Internet, book publishers are increasingly looking into the possibility of going from a "print and distribute" model to a "distribute and print" model. An example of this is the distribution of Stephen King's 66-page online book, *Riding the Bullet*, in March 2000; the book was available for downloading from Amazon.com, BarnesandNoble.com, and PalmPilot sites.[51] By early 2000, computer-hardware companies such as Hewlett-Packard were exploring the possibility of publishing houses using these new technologies to exploit this business model.[52]

Another possibility for book distribution in the future is the concept of electronic books, or "e-books." With a pocket-size electronic book device, consumers can download the digital content of popular books over the Internet or a dedicated phone line, often at reduced prices and months ahead of a book's print publication date. For example, the e-book version of Scott Turow's novel *Personal Injuries* might cost $21.60 in hardback from a bookstore—but only $10 if downloaded from a book retailer's site.[53] Consulting firm Accenture predicts that e-books will be a $2.3 billion business by 2005, which represents one-tenth of the $23 billion consumer book market.[54] Microsoft and Amazon.com are already teaming up against Adobe, Barnes & Noble.com, and Gemstar to see which alliance will dominate this emerging submarket.[55]

While many doomsayers predicted that increased PC usage would spell the demise of book reading, ironically it has been one of the key reasons for the increase in book production since 1990. Computers reduce publishers' production costs and enable the publication of many more titles. The computer has also made possible book "superstores," such as Borders and Barnes & Noble, where computer indexes, rather than humans, keep track of titles and local consumer buying patterns.[56]

**Broadcast Television.** Unlike most businesses that produce or sell tangible products and services, TV network broadcasting is essentially a programming service. The three major U.S. networks—ABC, CBS, and NBC—each have approximately 200 local television affiliates, and generate revenues by creating and delivering audiences to advertisers. On average, each network airs 90 hours of programming a week. The amount of money that a network or a station charges advertisers for commercial spots within a show depends on the size and composition of the program audience. Because advertising is sold on a cost per thousand (CPM) basis, the larger the audience for a particular show, the higher the advertising rates. CPM rates do, however, vary considerably depending on a particular audience's demographics. In contrast with other media, such as newspapers, magazines, cable television, and a few websites, broadcast television is fully supported by advertising revenue rather than fees.[57]

**SOUND BYTE**

*(continued from page 538)*
What we do know is that it works two ways. It's a symmetrical medium. And so it's still a part of the discovery process is where we are today, and the honest answer is we don't have all the answers. But what we do know is that as we go back and look at things that worked before, we may reorder the priority.

In the old world of mass marketing, the priority was television—it's big, bold, expensive, but it does its job. In the new world that may not be true, and it may actually be things like public relations with word-of-mouth. It may be getting people involved in communities and chat rooms and talking about something and generating interest. In fact, the users are creating as much of the content in this new medium as the so-called professional content creators.

*Get the full interview at www.marketspaceu.com*

# A Paper Goes Paperless

by Peter Meyers, staff writer for tnbt.com

 *The Wall Street Journal* figures you may not want to read its newspaper. So they've decided to let you listen to it. Or slip it into your pocket.

While the jury's still out on whether newspaper readers will widely adopt new technologies for absorbing news, no one is working harder to profit from the nascent wireless revolution than *The Wall Street Journal*. The daily paper has gone decidedly paperless, already publishing news to a host of portable devices, including handheld organizers, e-books, even audio players.

The Journal, which has offered its Web-based "Interactive Edition" since 1996, began its efforts to deliver handheld daily editions in early 1999 when it teamed up with a company called AvantGo to prepare its articles for the handheld organizers known as personal digital assistants, or PDAs. AvantGo's system operates via a free "mini-browser," which users install on their PDAs to read articles provided by publishers and downloaded from AvantGo's servers.

The Journal had a leg up in the process, having already stored its content in XML, the data markup language used by many publishers to format content across a variety of platforms. (The Journal had been using XML to code its articles for distribution to its various paper editions.) All it had to do was filter its already XML-coded content through several templates and scripts, and presto: The Journal was ready to AvantGo.

The conversion to handhelds was made easier still by another long-time Journal practice: boiling all of its key articles down to a concise, two-sentence summary for publication in the print edition's front-page "What's News" section. It is those bite-size summaries and accompanying headlines that users see when reading the AvantGo-enabled Journal on their handhelds—an ideal format, given the devices' tiny screens.

Some publishers, by contrast, have chosen to display not a summary but an article's first sentence, thus allowing readers to click through if they want to read the full text. But a PalmPilot may not be the ideal medium on which to read a 700-word article. "People are going to go blind trying to read the damn things," offers Jack Gold, an analyst for the Stamford, Connecticut-based market research firm Meta Group.

That said, the Journal does have a program for users of the Palm VII (Palm's top-of-the-line, Internet-connected handheld) that presents some articles in their full-text glory. But since users pay according to how much data they download, the Journal offers the content incrementally: Readers are given a choice of viewing either summaries or the more costly full text.

Today, Journal junkies can get their daily fix on more than a dozen different handheld devices, including the PalmPilot, Handspring's Visor, the Rocket eBook, and handhelds from Compaq and Hewlett-Packard. And who knows, sometime in the not-too-distant future, the Journal may have more "listeners" than "readers": Among the paper's post-desktop forays is an early stab at audio publishing via Audible.com, one of the Web's leading providers of downloadable spoken text. Together, the Journal and Audible prepare spoken-word digest summaries of articles that users can download and play back on their PCs, or on handheld devices such as Compaq's Aero 1500 and the Diamond Rio 500 MP3 player.

So far, most subscribers to the "Journal on Audible" service listen at their PCs, but, according to Audible.com, a growing number are commuters who listen to the "paper" on their way to or from work. To do so, however, they must download the audio file to a PC, transfer it to a handheld device, then hook the device up for playback through their car audio system—not exactly a recipe for mass-market acceptance.

One day, however—and it may not be far off—the Journal may be automatically downloaded overnight to your Internet-enabled car radio. And you'll be off to work with your commuter mug and your morning paper, the memory of needing a desktop computer to enjoy the Web's myriad glories receding like the scenery in your rearview mirror.

*Read more articles about* The Next Big Thing *at* www.tnbt.com

Cable has changed the television broadcasting landscape, drawing up to 40 percent of the total television viewing audience. With the many available television channels and the increasingly fractured nature of today's television audience, no single broadcast television program will ever reach the kind of viewership numbers achieved during the 1960s and 1970s, when viewers were limited to three or four choices. For example, the final episode of *Seinfeld* in May 1998 drew fewer viewers than the regular episodes of *The Beverly Hillbillies* during the 1960s.[58]

The introduction of digital television (DTV) will increase the number of network channels and, therefore, increase the number of programs offered in the future. Digital compression techniques will permit the transmission of several DTV channels over the same bandwidth currently required for a single analog standard-definition television (SDTV) channel, but the transmission of a single digital high-definition television (HDTV) will require even more bandwidth than is used currently for conventional television. Broadcasters and policymakers will need to determine what is in the public interest.

Digital television, which offers a lifelike picture and CD-quality sound, is considered by some to be the biggest broadcast innovation since color television was introduced in the 1950s. All commercial stations will be required to broadcast a digital signal by the summer of 2003, and all analog broadcasts will stop by the spring of 2006. Each of the three networks currently broadcasts select programs, such as *ER* or *Judging Amy*, using high-definition digital technology.[59]

**Cable Television.** Cable television was originally introduced as a way to improve television reception in outlying rural areas. In the 1960s, cable operators realized that viewers were willing to pay for commercial-free programming, but their efforts to do so were hampered by Federal Communications Commission restrictions.[60] The industry began to boom when RCA launched its first communication satellite into orbit in 1975.[61] Under the name Home Box Office (HBO)—which was later sold to Time Warner—RCA began to transmit programming to independent cable operators around the country, who then relayed the programming to subscribers at minimum cost. With the 1977 federal court dismissal of most of the FCC's regulations governing cable television, the door opened for what has become a $50 billion industry.[62] The number of cable television subscribers has grown from 469,000 in 1975 to 48.4 million in 2000,[63] and the number of available television channels in the average American household has grown from 7.1 in 1970 to 46.6 in 1998.[64]

The number of cable subscribers is currently increasing by about half a million per year. Despite deregulation and increased competition from direct-satellite service providers, the average cable bill has risen from $7.69 in 1980 to $28.92 in 1999.[65] The cable channels make their revenue through a combination of advertising and subscription fees. By the end of 1999, the top six cable channels in the United States were the TBS Superstation, The Discovery Channel, USA Network, ESPN, C-SPAN, and CNN—all available to 75 million or more cable subscribers.[66] The top five pay cable services were The Disney Channel, HBO, Encore, Showtime, and Spice.[67]

In 1997, the nation's largest cable operators were the AT&T-owned Tele-Communications Inc. (TCI), with over 14 million basic subscribers; Time Warner, with 12.3 million subscribers; and U.S. Media Group, with 4.9 million subscribers. With the changes brought forth by the Telecommunications Act of 1996, cable companies are now able to compete directly with telephone and utility companies to providing cable, telephone, and electrical services to the home. Because of the increased competition allowed by the act and the anticipation of broadband delivery and media convergence, several megamergers involving cable television systems and the regional telephone companies have taken place, including AT&T's acquisition of TCI in 1998 and US West's acquisition of MediaOne in 1999.

**Radio.** In 1999, there were a total of 576.5 million radios in the United States, with 98 percent of households owning at least one. They were distributed as follows: 367.4 million (or 63 percent) were in homes; 142.8 (or 24.7 percent) million in cars; 43.7 million (or 7.5 percent) in trucks, vans, and RVs; and the remaining 22.6 million (or 6.1 percent) in the workplace.[68] Ninety-five percent of listeners over the age of 12 listened to the radio for an average of three hours and 20 minutes each workday.

Similar to broadcast television, radio generates nearly all of its revenue from advertising by delivering a select audience to advertisers. Unlike broadcast television, however, radio channels are more highly specific in their targeting of audiences. In 1999, the three most popular radio formats were country, adult contemporary, and news/talk.[69] At the end of 1999, there were 12,641 radio stations on the air, approximately 81 percent of which were commercial stations.[70]

Radio and audio programs are now offered on the Internet; however, they do not fall under the authority of the Federal Communications Commissions. Anyone, from relative unknowns such as Dan Schulz and Scott Wirkus to celebrities such as Robin Williams (on Audible.com), can host their own radio program from their home basement and make it available to the public through the Internet.[71]

**Film.** The motion-picture industry earned an estimated $7.7 billion in 2000,[72] with the various studios releasing an average of 400 films per year.[73] The cost of making movies has escalated dramatically in recent years. In 1988, the average pricetag of a motion picture was $18.1 million, according to the Motion Picture Association of America. By 1998, the average cost of making a movie had nearly tripled to $52.7 million, largely due to rising actor salaries, increased demand for special effects, and other spiraling costs. On average, studios spent $25.3 million on publicity and advertising—or almost half of total production costs per film—in 1998.[74]

**Videos.** In the decades since its introduction to the market in the late 1970s, the videocassette recorder (VCR) has become a common household appliance—91 percent of American households own at least one. Despite studio companies' initial resistance to the concept of home VCRs, video releases of movies are now the largest part of a motion picture's revenue stream. In 1995, a film's domestic and foreign theatrical releases accounted for almost 30 percent of its total revenue; cash intake from video releases accounted for over 40 percent.[75]

With high-quality digital technology now available to many people at relatively low cost, aspiring directors can more easily make films without the assistance of the major film studios (although distribution of those films is another matter). "It's too late for the studios to panic. They've already lost," says director Francis Ford Coppola, whose Zoetrope.com allows filmmakers to read scripts, get feedback, hire directors, and show their work. "The minute artists don't need studios, they'll abandon them."[76]

**DVDs.** Digital video discs (**DVD**s) have become a popular format for viewing movies since their introduction in the mid-1990s. In 1999, approximately 3.9 million DVD players and 45 million DVDs were sold in the United States, which accounts for approximately 15 percent of all video sales.[77] According to the Consumer Electronics Association, as of December 2000, the total number of DVD players sold in the United States since their introduction in March 1997 was 13.1 million units, reflecting a 12 percent household penetration.[78]

The DVD storage capacity is 4.7 gigabytes (a CD's is 680 megabytes), which allows DVD producers not only to provide a much higher resolution video image than with VHS tape (up to 720 horizontal line resolution using MPEG-2 compression versus less than 400 horizontal line resolution with VHS), but also to offer many more features—called "bonus material"—in special edition DVDs in addition to the traditional movie video. For example, viewers of *The Sound of Music* special edition DVD can choose to watch the movie in either normal or wide-screen television format; view original trailers promoting the movie; or see behind-the-scenes interviews with the film's stars.

In February 2001, there were an estimated 11,000 movie titles available on DVD.[79] The average cost of a DVD movie ranges from $15 to $20, with special edition DVDs priced a bit higher.[80] A number of DVD variants that exist include DVD-Audio, an additional prerecorded application format for consumer players introduced in mid-year 2000; DVD-ROM, a prerecorded data format; and DVD-R, a recordable data format (Apple Computer recently made this a standard available option in the Power Mac G4).

**Music CDs.** Since its introduction to the market in 1982, the digital audio compact disc, developed jointly by Sony and Philips Electronics, has become the most popular music format among consumers.[81] Fewer than 100,000 CDs were sold in 1983—the first full year they were available—but CDs quickly overtook LPs by 1988, and topped cassette sales in 1992.[82] In 1999, CDs accounted for almost 85 percent of all music sold, followed by cassettes (8 percent) and singles (5 percent).[83] While CDs cost no more than albums or cassettes to produce, consumers are still willing to pay a premium for the digital format, largely due to its superior sound quality and compact format.[84]

The total U.S. dollar value of all music sold was $13.7 billion in 1998 (the top four genres: rock, country, R&B, and pop). About one-third of all consumers of musical devices were 24 years old or younger.[85]

**Video-Game Consoles.** As one of the fastest growing forms of home entertainment, the $5.5 billion video-game console market is dominated by three companies: Sony, Nintendo, and Sega. The first home video games were introduced in 1966 by Magnavox, which had developed a game that could be played on a color television set.[86] In 1972, Atari entered the competition, followed by Nintendo, with its 8-bit console, in 1986.

In 1990, Sega launched a 16-bit console called Genesis; Nintendo quickly matched it in 1991 with Super Nintendo—and established an industry standard of rapid one-upmanship. In 1994, Sony introduced PlayStation. Nintendo countered with its Nintendo 64, and then Sega released its Saturn in 1996. Sony pulled ahead as market leader in the selling of video-game consoles with the 2000 launch of PlayStation 2.[87] Given that, plus the expected launch of Microsoft's Xbox in 2001, Sega decided to withdraw from the manufacturing of video-game console hardware in January 2000, and began to focus entirely on the production of video-game software. As video games become increasingly more lifelike and sophisticated, the average time that American consumers spend playing them increases. In 1992, the average consumer spent 19 hours per year playing video games; by 2000, that number had risen to 43.[88]

**MP3.** The music industry has been thrown into turmoil recently by the emergence and mainstreaming of digital music technologies. At the center of the current firestorm is MP3.com, one of the most visited music sites on the Internet. MP3 technology offers musicians and listeners a community and experience that is revolutionizing the way that music is consumed. Members of MP3.com gain online access to over 45,000 CDs on the MP3.com site, where they can copy music-file recordings free of charge to their computer hard drives, and then listen to those recordings whenever they like. Since digital music does not vary with subsequent copying, a 50th-generation copy is the same as a 2nd-generation copy.[89] MP3.com's activities have attracted the attention—and ire—of many in the traditional music industry. Along with a consortium of major record labels, the Recording Industry Association of America (RIAA) has filed suit against MP3.com. Michael Robertson, the man who launched MP3.com in 1997, believes that consumers have the right to do what they want with music after it has been purchased, and that current copyright laws will not prevent further piracy in the future.

Adding more fire to the MP3 controversy is the use of Napster software, which allows an individual to easily search and swap MP3 musical files with other individuals. Napster has become so popular among college students that several universities have banned the use of the software altogether because it can cause such high computer-network traffic during the simultaneous transfer of many MP3 files that networks become effectively useless. As with MP3.com, the RIAA has also filed a lawsuit against Napster, charging that it "is operating a haven for music piracy on an unprecedented scale."[90] In October 2000, Napster reached an agreement with recording giant BMG, a division of Bertelsmann, whereby Napster would start charging users and pay royalties to the recording companies. However, at press time, a number of other lawsuits are still

---

## What Is MP3?

**MP3** is the most popular format for audio compression on the Internet. The acronym stands for MPEG Layer-3, and MPEG itself is an acronym for Moving Picture Experts Group, though MPEG is most often used in reference to the set of digital video compression standards developed by the group. The two most important MPEG standards are **MPEG-1** and MPEG-2; the first produces VCR-quality video resolution; the second is used by DVD-ROMs and produces CD-quality audio. MPEG is not to be confused with JPEG (Joint Photographic Experts Group), which is a computer file format and compression specification for photographs, not video/audio. MP3 is one in a series of audio encoding standards developed under MPEG and formalized by the International Organization for Standardization (ISO).

For "hi-fi" quality sound reproduction, the frequency response to human hearing ranges from 20Hz to 20kHz; in other words, humans can typically hear sounds with frequencies between 20 cycles per second through 20,000 cycles per second. Nyquist's Theorem states that to accurately capture an analog signal digitally, one must use a sample rate of at least twice the highest frequency desired. Therefore, to capture 20kHz sounds as well as a few harmonics above, standard CD-quality digital audio is typically created by taking 16-bit samples of the analog sound signal at 44.1kHz. This means that CD-quality stereo sound requires two channels × 16 bits × 44,100 times per second—some 180k bytes of data for one second of stereo audio.

MP3 includes a compression algorithm that reduces the "noise" around sounds that listeners cannot perceive. MP3 allows the compression of any sound sequence into a small file (typically a 10:1 compression ratio) while mostly preserving the original sound quality. MP3 files are usually downloaded and played through free MP3 player software.

pending.[91] Although Napster has offered $1 billion to settle the case out of court, many experts believe that Napster may eventually transform itself into a subscriber-based service for its 50 million members and transfer a portion of its revenue to the recording industry.[92]

# SUMMARY

## 1. What is media convergence?

Broadly defined, media convergence is the process by which content across various media platforms—print, audio, and video—will ultimately become available through a single Internet platform. With the emergence of broadband, not only will traditional graphics, streaming video, and streaming audio become available on one platform, but so will video on demand, software distribution, books on demand, and multi-player games.

## 2. What conditions make media convergence possible?

The following conditions have contributed to the coming together of various forms of media: continued advances in digital technology; the existence of a low-cost digital network infrastructure; growing media-usage fragmentation in American households; and the forecasted continued proliferation of new media types. Together, these conditions encourage digital convergence, and make the media environment attractive for consolidation and vertical integration.

## 3. How do new-media companies leverage traditional media channels?

While the Internet is an increasingly important source for news, information, and commerce, the new economy has been quite dependent on traditional old-economy news outlets. For example, online media outlets have attempted to build their audiences through traditional media channels. Dot-coms spread their word through newspapers, magazines, and broadcast television during the first stage of attracting early adopters and into a secondary stage of attracting mainstream users.

To build brand awareness for a rapidly growing mainstream audience of Internet users, dot-com companies spent an estimated $3 billion to $4 billion in advertising in 1999; some 90 percent of those dollars were spent in traditional media outlets, such as network television, national newspapers, and network radio.

## 4. What are reasons for media megamergers?

The Telecommunications Act of 1996 allowed both for increased ownership of television stations by a single entity and for the convergence of media through the direct competition among telephone companies, cable television companies, and utility companies. Mergers became part of the overall strategy of media companies to vertically integrate media content with media distribution. With no geographic barriers to the distribution of digitized content on the Internet, many media companies seek to create global markets for their content through mergers. With increased digitization of content and the promise of broadband delivery in the near future, the personal computer will not be the only receiver of information over the Internet. For today's media company, the strategy is to collect and, through media convergence and digital convergence, create a synergistic combination of what were once disparate media to produce a direct bottom-line benefit.

## KEY TERMS

media infrastructure

media convergence

Telecommunications Act of 1996

vertical integration

GIF

JPEG

streaming audio

streaming video

DVD

MP3

MPEG-1

## Endnotes

[1]Pew Research Center, 2000. "Internet sapping broadcast news audience," Spring 2000 and Pew Research Center, 1996. "TV news viewership declines." Press release, 13 May.

[2]*Pew Research Center. "2000*, Internet sapping broadcast news audience," Spring 2000.

[3]*Pew Research Center. "2000*, Internet sapping broadcast news audience," Spring 2000.

[4]*The New York Times 2001 Almanac.* "Primetime viewing shares of free and cable TV networks," 1988–1999. Citing from National Cable Television Association, Cable TV Developments, Nielsen Media Research.

[5]*The New York Times 2001 Almanac*, s.v. "Basic and pay cable TV systems and subscribers, 1952 to 2000." Citing from National Cable Television Association, Cable TV Developments, Nielsen Media Research.

[6]*The New York Times 2001 Almanac*, s.v. "Basic and pay cable TV systems and subscribers, 1952 to 2000." Citing from National Cable Television Association, Cable TV Developments, Nielsen Media Research.

[7]*The New York Times 2001 Almanac*, "Sales penetration of telecommunications products in U.S. homes," 2001.

[8]Statalla, Michelle. "Get movie popcorn, then check the mail," *The New York Times*, 22 February, 2001.

[9]*The New York Times 2001 Almanac*, s.v. "U.S. online households and Internet users 1996–2002." Citing U.S. Department of Commerce.

[10]*The New York Times 2000 Almanac*, s.v. "Basic and pay cable TV systems and subscribers, 1992–99." Citing from Television Association, *Cable TV Developments* (Spring 1999), Nielsen Media Research; *The New York Times 2000 Almanac*, s.v. "Sales penetration of telecommunications products in U.S. homes," p. 811. Citing from 1999 Electronics Industries Association.

[11]Haddock, Vicki. "How media saturates American kids' lives," *San Francisco Examiner*, 17 November, 1999.

[12]Stevens, Elizabeth Lesly. "The entertainment glut," *Business Week*, 16 February, 1998.

[13]Veronis, Suhler & Associates. "Veronis, Suhler & Associates Communications Industry Forecast," October 1998.

[14]Modahl, Mary. *Now or Never: How Companies Must Change to Win the Battle for the Internet Consumer* (New York: Harper Business, 2000).

[15]*The New York Times 2000 Almanac*, s.v. "U.S. online households and internet users, 1996–2002." Cited from the U.S. Dept. of Commerce, eStats.

[16]Marsh, James, Brian Shipman, and William Lerner. "Media monthly," Prudential Securities, June 2000.

[17]Drewry, William. 1999. *Newspapers.com*. Newsletter, 8 November, p. 6. Citing the *Advertising Age Interactive Special Report* (1 November, 1999); Lake, David, and Stacy Lawrence. 2000. "Two years of change," *Industry Standard*, 1 May, pp. 296–7.

[18]Drewry, William. 1999. *Newspapers.com*. Newsletter, 8 November. Citing the *Advertising Age Interactive*

*Special Report* (1 November, 1999).

[19]Reents, Scott. "Expert insight: Leveraging TV-Net synergies," *Industry Standard*, 28 October, 1998.

[20]*Pew Research Study*. 1998. "The Internet news audience goes ordinary," 15 December.

[21]Nisenholtz, Martin. "Presentation at U.S.B. Warburg Conference," The New York Times Company 6 December, 2000. *http://www.nytco.com/financial/man.prs.U.S.B.html*.

[22]Press Release, "Real networks reports fourth quarter results," 31 January, 2001.

[23]Anderson, Lessley. "Guess what? Real is a media company," *Industry Standard*, 5 November, 1999.

[24]Barringer, Felicity. "News site race is just as clear as election," *The New York Times*, 25 December, 2000. For the same month, Nielsen Net Ratings placed CNN.com ahead of MSNBC.com.

[25]Brown, Merrill. "Is technology changing everything?," speech at University of Southern California, 7 April, 1998.

[26]Eisner, Michael. 1996. Speech to Chicago Executives Club, 19 April. Used by permission from Disney Enterprises, Inc.

[27]Orenstein, Susan. "Carving out an empire," *The Industry Standard*, 5 February, 2001.

[28]Fine, Jon. "AOL Time Warner still faces hurdles," *Advertising Age*, 15 January, 2001.

[29]Levy, Steve. "Here comes Playstation 2," *Newsweek*, 6 March, 2000, 57.

[30]*The New York Times Almanac 2001*, "Daily newspapers, number and circulation, 1900–99," p. 384. Citing Newspaper Association of America, *Facts about Newspapers*, 2000.

[31]*Newspaper Assoc. of America's Facts about Newspapers*, s.v. "Top 20 daily newspapers by circulation." Citing *Editor and Publisher*. URL: *http://www.naa.org/info/facts99/14.html*.

[32]*Newspaper Assoc. of America's Facts about Newspapers*, s.v. "Number of U.S. daily newspapers." Citing *Editor and Publisher Yearbook 1999*. URL: *http://www.naa.org/info/facts99/11.html*.

[33]Gralla, Preston. *How the Internet Works* (Indiana: QUE books, 1998).

[34]Gralla, Preston. *How the Internet Works* (Indiana: QUE books, 1998).

[35]Richtel, Matt. "Microsoft aims at real network in MediaPlayer software duel," *The New York Times*, 10 January, 2000.

[36]*Capturing digital*. 1999. From *www.kodak.com*.

[37]*Newspaper Assoc. of America's Facts about Newspapers*, s.v. "U.S. daily and Sunday/weekend newspaper reading audience." Citing NAA; W.R. Simmons & Associates Research, Inc. 1970-1977; Simmons Market Research Bureau Inc. 1980-1994; Scarborough Research—Top 50 DMA Market Report, 1995-1998. URL: *http://www.naa.org/info/facts99/02.html*.

[38]*The New York Times 2000 Almanac*, s.v. "General median income of households with selected characteristics, 1997," p. 333. Citing Bureau of the Census, *Current Population Reports: Money Income in the U.S.*; *Newspaper Assoc. of America's Facts about Newspapers*, s.v. "U.S. daily and Sunday newspaper readership demographics." Citing Scarborough Research—Top 50 DMA Market Report, 1998 (Release 1).

[39]*The New York Times Almanac 2001*, "Total U.S. advertising volume by medium, 1998–99," p. 349. Citing *Advertising Age*, 22 May, 2000.

[40]Marsh, James M., Brian Shipman, and William Lerner. "Media monthly," Prudential Securities, June 2000.

[41]Drewry, William. "*Advertising Age Interactive Special Report*," *Newspapers.com* Newsletter 19 August, 1999.

[42]Anderson, James A. "Newspaper investors may have the last laugh," *Business Week* 17 April, 2000, 212. URL: *http://www.businessweek.com/2000/00_16/b3677133.htm?scriptFramed*.

[43]*The New York Times 2000 Almanac*, s.v. "The print media," p. 401.

[44]*Newspaper Association of America's Facts about Newspapers*, s.v. "Newspaper voice and online services." Citing NAA. URL: *http://www.naa.org/info/facts99/18.html*.

[45]*The New York Times 2000 Almanac*, s.v. "Top 100 U.S. magazines by circulation, 1998," p. 402. Citing Magazine Publishers of America.

[46]*The New York Times Almanac 2001*, "Top 50 magazines by advertising revenue," p.387. Citing Magazine Publishers of America, *Publisher's Information Bureau Publications Ranked by Revenue, 1999*.

[47]*The New York Times Almanac 2001*, "Number and value of U.S. books sold, 1990–99 (in Millions)." Citing Book Industry Study Group, Inc. *Book Industry Trends, annual (2000)*.

[48]R.R. Bowker Co. 2000. *The Bowker Annual: Library and Book Trade Almanac*. Cited in *The New York Times 2001 Almanac*, s.v. "New books and editions published, by subject, 1980–99," p. 390.

[49]*The New York Times Almanac 2001*, "The print media—books," p. 387.

[50]Veronis, Suhler & Associates, "Veronis, Suhler & Associates Communications Industry Forecast," October 1998.

[51]Ratnesar, Romesh, and Joel Stein. "Everyone's a star.com," *Time* 27 March 2000. URL: *http://www.time.com/time/everyone/magazine/main.html*.

[52]Hardy, Quinten. "Balancing the need for speed with a respect for HP's past," *Forbes* 13 December 1999, 141.

[53]"A new book look," *Los Angeles Times,* 9 September, 2000.

[54]Andersen Consulting. "The new digital content consumer: large and in charge," 25 October, 2000.

[55]"A new book look," *Los Angeles Times*, 9 September, 2000.

[56]*The New York Times 2000 Almanac,* s.v. "Books," p. 403.

[57]Louie, Dickson. 1999. *CBS Evening News.* Case no. 9-898-086. Rev. 11 March (Boston: Harvard Business School Publishing).

[58]*The New York Times 2000 Almanac,* s.v. "Cable television," p. 408.

[59]Best Buy Co. 1999. *Change the way you look at TV.* Brochure.

[60]*The New York Times 2001 Almanac,* s.v. "Cable television," p. 392.

[61]*The New York Times 2001 Almanac,* s.v. "Cable television," p. 392.

[62]*The New York Times 2001 Almanac,* s.v. "Cable television," p. 393.

[63]*The New York Times 2001 Almanac,* s.v. "Cable television," p. 393.

[64]Marsh, James M., Brian Shipman, and William Lerner. "Media monthly," Prudential Securities, June 2000.

[65]*The New York Times 2001 Almanac,* s.v. "Cable television," pp. 409–10.

[66]*The New York Times 2001 Almanac,* "Top 15 cable television networks, 1999," p. 392. Citing National Cable Television Association, Cable TV Developments (2000).

[67]*The New York Times 2001 Almanac,* "Top 5 pay-TV services, 1999," p. 393. Citing National Cable Television Association, Cable TV Developments (2000).

[68]*The New York Times 2001 Almanac,* s.v. "Radio," p. 394.

[69]*The New York Times 2001 Almanac,* "Radio stations by primary format, 1990–99," p. 394. Citing M.Street Corporation, 1999.

[70]*The New York Times 2001 Almanac,* "U.S. radio stations and radio sales, 1946–99," p. 394. Citing M.Street Corporation, 2000.

[71]Winters, Rebecca. "Live from your basement," *Time* 27 March, 2000. URL: *http://www.time.com/time/everyone/magazine/sidebar_dj.html.*

[72]Associated Press, "Movie revenues post another record year," *San Francisco Chronicle*, 1 January, 2001.

[73]*The New York Times 2001 Almanac,* s.v. "Film," p. 396.

[74]*The New York Times 2001 Almanac,* s.v. "Film/movie budgets," p. 398.

[75]Vogel, Harold. *Entertainment Industry Economics* (England; New York: Cambridge University Press. 4th ed., 1998).

[76]Ratnesar, Romesh, and Joel Stein. "Everyone's a star.com," *Time,* 27 March, 2000.

[77]*The New York Times 2001 Almanac,* s.v. "The recording industry," p. 396.

[78]"CEA DVD Player Sales," The Digital Bits, Inc. 2000. URL: *http://www.thedigitalbits.com/articles/cemadvdsales.html.*

[79]Statalla, Michelle. "Get movie popcorn, then check the mail," *The New York Times*, 22 February, 2001.

[80]*The New York Times 2001 Almanac,* s.v. "The recording industry," p. 396.

[81]*The New York Times 2001 Almanac,* s.v. "The recording industry," p. 394.

[82]*The New York Times 2001 Almanac,* s.v. "The recording industry," p. 394.

[83]*The New York Times 2001 Almanac,* "Recorded music sales by genre, format and age group, 1987–99," p. 395. Citing Recording Industry Association of America, 1999 Consumer Profile.

[84]*The New York Times 2001 Almanac,* s.v. "The recording industry," p. 394.

[85]*The New York Times 2001 Almanac,* "Recorded music sales by genre, format and age group, 1987–99." p. 395. Citing Recording Industry Association of America, 1999 Consumer Profile.

[86]Brandenburger, Adam. "Interactive games: Sega versus Nintendo," Harvard Business School Publishing, 3 February, 1994 (9-794-074).

[87]Storm, Stephanie. "Why PlayStation 2 isn't children's play", *The New York Times*, 10 October, 2000.

[88]Veronis, Suhler & Associates, "Veronis, Suhler & Associates Communications Industry Forecast," October 1998.

[89]Tucker, Chris. "Online pirates beware," *Southwest Spirit Magazine,* April 2000.

[90]Greenfield, Karl Taro. "The free juke box," *Time,* 27 March, 2000.

[91]"An attempt at harmony," *The New York Times*, 18 December, 2000.

[92]Cohen, Adam. "In search of Napster II," *Time,* 26 February, 2001.

# The Future of Media Usage

This chapter provides an overview of the future of consumer media usage. While we cannot predict this future with certainty, we can make some key assumptions. Media content—video, audio, and text—will continue to be transformed onto multiple digital platforms, and fragmentation of media usage will continue to rise as consumers choose from increasing numbers of outlets that deliver news, information, and entertainment.

This chapter is divided into three key parts. First, we look at the home of the future, which will impact consumers' media usage, trying to understand what is meant by the "digital lifestyle." In the second part, we seek to understand how emerging technologies such as wireless communications, video-on-demand, and personalized media content will further fragment media usage. Finally, we will discuss media giants of the future that will make the digital lifestyle possible.

## QUESTIONS

*Please consider the following questions as you read this chapter:*

1. What is meant by the digital lifestyle?

2. How will broadband technology impact Internet usage?

3. What are the differences among the following Internet-delivery mechanisms: digital subscriber lines (DSL), cable lines, and satellite?

This chapter was coauthored by Bernie Jaworski, Jeffrey Rayport, Dickson Louie, and Michael Yip.

4. Which household device will serve as the gateway to the Internet?

5. How will increased wireless communications, video-on-demand, and personalized media content further fragment media usage?

6. How will the increased size of media companies allow them to capture efficiencies of scale among diverse audiences?

## INTRODUCTION

In Chapter 14, we examined the underlying issues behind media convergence, showing how the shift from analog to digital platforms was fragmenting media usage among consumers with new technologies—such as the Internet, CDs, and DVDs—and why major media companies—such as Disney and Capital Cities, Viacom and CBS, and America Online and Time Warner—are merging to build larger consumer audiences across multiple media platforms.

Underlying the shift in consumer media usage is the market infrastructure, or the general industry environment, which is outside the boundaries and largely beyond the control of the specific business. This environment, with both opportunities and constraints, can be subclassified into two broad categories: network infrastructure and media infrastructure. Two forms of convergence have already been occurring between network and media (see Exhibit 15-1). Both of these infrastructures are converging due to the digitization of information. As noted in Chapter 14, we have digital convergence with the network infrastructure, which refers to a basic, underlying group of electronic devices (such as telephone, broadcast radio and television, computers, etc.), and connecting circuitry designed as a system to share and transport information. This has led to massive cross-industry competition for the same customers. We also noted that a second type of convergence, what we term *media convergence*, is unfolding. It is marked by the recent mergers of several major players—including radio, television, magazine, film, newspaper, and online companies—that deliver media content to these same target segments.

 **Exhibit 15-1** NETWORK AND MEDIA CONVERGENCE

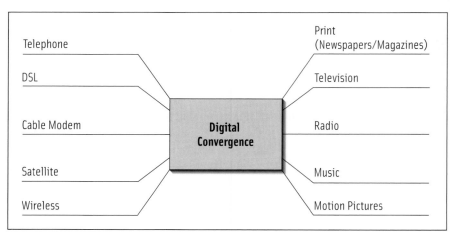

In this chapter we build upon these concepts and look at the issues that will impact media infrastructure. First, we examine the meaning of the term "digital lifestyle", which has been used often by high-profile CEOs to describe a fully digitized future society. Second, we explore how digital news, information, and entertainment will flow into homes via broadband technology—instead of today's low-cost, narrowband technologies—and whether that will happen with cable lines, telephone lines, or satellite transmission. Third, we debate what household device will become the command center of digital technology in the home. Will it be the personal computer, the video-game console, or the interactive television set-top box? Fourth, we examine how emerging digital devices and technologies, such as interactive television and mobile wireless devices, will further fragment media usage. And finally, we see how the mergers of media companies will allow for economies of scale and make it possible to reach broad and diverse segments of media users.

# WHAT IS MEANT BY "DIGITAL LIFESTYLE"?

## The Digital Home of the Future

What will media consumption be like in the digital home of the future? Experts predict that as media-based household appliances—from the television set to the camera to the video-game player—become digitally based and interconnected, they will fulfill a vision foreseen almost 20 years ago by Nicholas Negroponte, the cofounder of the Media Lab at the Massachusetts Institute of Technology. Negroponte observed that as bits become "the DNA of information"—replacing atoms as the basic commodity of human interaction—"commingled bits and bits-about-bits" will "change the media landscape so thoroughly that concepts like video-on-demand and shipping electronic games down your local cable are just trivial applications—the tip of a much more profound iceberg."[1]

As more household appliances convert from analog to digital platforms, it becomes easier to imagine the digital lifestyle that Negroponte wrote about 20 years ago, one in which we can access the media with the mere touch of a button. For example, through basic interactive television services such as Microsoft's UltimateTV and AOL Time Warner's AOLTV, today's consumers can access e-mail, chat with others, surf the Web, and watch their favorite sit-coms, all on the same television set, by using a set-top box and telephone modem hookup. With increased adoption of broadband technology (usually defined as having a connectivity speed exceeding 128 kilobits per second, significantly faster than the narrowband speeds of 40 to 53 kilobits per second achieved over regular telephone lines) they will also have access to a wider range of media services over the Web, from downloading books to videoconferencing to exchanging video clips with family members.

## The Digital Lifestyle

Several CEOs have already envisioned this digital lifestyle (see Exhibit 15-2 for a comparison of life in 2000 and 2010). For example, Bill Gates, the chairman, cofounder, and chief software architect of Microsoft Corp., believes that the personal computer, the set-top box for interactive television, and the video-game console will all be important household devices. In a recent speech, Gates observed:

*The PC is going to be the place where you store the information, and really the center of control, the place where you can edit the information, where you can communicate it out to your friends. But it won't just be the PC, it will be all these things connected up to the PC, both in wired and wireless fashion. The PC itself, by having a microphone, by having a digital camera built in, will provide new forms of communications.*

*. . . Another key piece of hardware in the home, of course, is the set-top box. It really defines the TV viewing experience. Well, the set-top boxes that connect up to the satellite world, they're changing and changing very rapidly. That's where the cutting edge is right now. But it won't stay that way; it won't just be satellites. It will also be the entire cable infrastructure, and this year we'll see the first significant rollout of digital set-top boxes, where the software in those devices allows people to work between their video and between the Internet to have rich access to what they're interested in.*

*. . . Last, but not least, there's a revolution about to take place in game consoles. People want something that's rich. They want something where game developers have no limits on their creativity. . . . As it comes together, all these things happening at once are about a digital lifestyle.[2]*

As a result of these trends, at the end of 2000 Microsoft chose to invest in developing a wide range of digital platforms that can serve as home Internet portals. In addition to improving the interface of its Windows platform for personal computers, Microsoft is developing several products: a Pocket PC version of the Windows CE platform in wireless handheld devices, which competes directly with the Palm platform; the Windows Reader for electronic books, which will compete with Adobe's Acrobat Reader; the Xbox, a video-game console with Internet access that should launch in late 2001 and will compete directly with Sony and Nintendo consoles; and the UltimateTV set-top box, which will connect to cable and satellite television and will compete with AOLTV and direct-recording services such as TiVo and ReplayTV.[3]

While Microsoft has invested broadly in a wide range of Internet platforms, several CEOs believe that the PC will remain the home's command center. Craig Barrett, CEO of Intel Corp., talks about an "extended PC era," with consumers adopting PC accessories such as the digital camera, personal digital assistants (PDAs), and digital sound morphers. In a recent speech, Barrett said:

*The world is digitizing, whether it is communication or information or the Internet. We are getting more and more digital information. It is a big digital universe. And if you look at the center of that digital universe, the central focal point for the big bang, it really is the core of the PC. . . . The PC is really at the center of the Internet, the main client. But what we are seeing today is more and more devices attached around the PC, extending the PC's influence.*

*Whether it is audio or video or still images or animation . . . more and more of these devices are going digital, and more and more of them are getting connected to the PC. . . . If you add up all of these devices, you are seeing the center of each one of these activities is the PC. That's where the processing power is. That is where the action is. But these other devices extend the range, extend the user interface.*

*Metcalfe's Law, which was really proven out with the Internet, is that the value of a network equals the square of the number of nodes on the network. I think increasingly the value of the PC is really associated with the number of these consumer interface devices that we have attached to the PC.[4]*

**Exhibit 15-2** THE DIGITAL LIFESTYLE—2000 VS. 2010

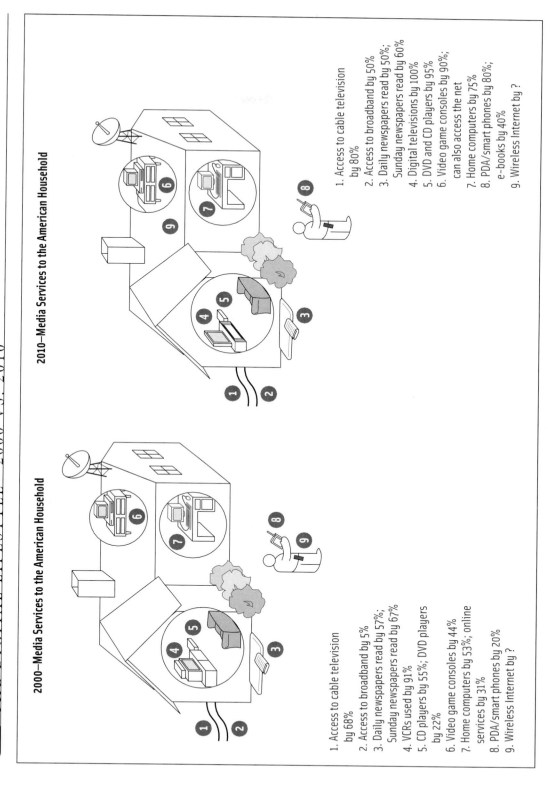

**2000—Media Services to the American Household**

**2010—Media Services to the American Household**

1. Access to cable television by 68%
2. Access to broadband by 5%
3. Daily newspapers read by 57%; Sunday newspapers read by 67%
4. VCRs used by 91%
5. CD players by 55%; DVD players by 22%
6. Video game consoles by 44%
7. Home computers by 53%; online services by 31%
8. PDA/smart phones by 20%
9. Wireless Internet by ?

1. Access to cable television by 80%
2. Access to broadband by 50%
3. Daily newspapers read by 50%; Sunday newspapers read by 60%
4. Digital televisions by 100%
5. DVD and CD players by 95%
6. Video game consoles by 90%; can also access the net
7. Home computers by 75%
8. PDA/smart phones by 80%; e-books by 40%
9. Wireless Internet by ?

Steve Jobs, founder and chairman of Apple Computer Inc., shared Barrett's sentiment about the personal computer as command center. In addition to seeing the PC as the home's Internet portal, Jobs envisioned it as the digital hub, where consumers could edit their own movies or create customized CDs with easy-to-use interfaces. In fact, 320 million writable CDs were sold in the United States in 2000, indicating a trend toward customized digitized media.[5] In a recent *New York Times* article, Jobs observed:

> We believe that the PC or Mac can become the digital hub of our new digital lifestyle. . . . The Internet is a wonderful thing, and for a while it was such a blinding bright light that it obscured other bright lights. It's a wonderful thing. It's a magical thing. Music is a wonderful thing, movies are wonderful things.[6]

Other CEOs, including Nobuyuki Idei, chairman and CEO of Sony Corp., take a countering view, believing that personal electronic devices—such as the PlayStation 2 video-game console, which could serve as a portal to services including online banking, online gaming, and music and video downloading—will be the future digital command centers for the home. Noting that personal computers are difficult to navigate and that digital audio and video content will be easy to use through a number of home devices, Idei said, "The world is moving toward a broadband and networked environment and new digital hardware [other than the personal computer] will enable customers to manipulate it for their own personal enjoyment."[7]

Howard Stringer, chairman and chief executive officer of Sony Corp. of America, the U.S. subsidiary of Sony, echoed Idei's thoughts:

> Video-on-demand is around the corner. Digital channels will put interactivity at your fingertips. Furthermore, delivery systems are multiplying. Soon wireless-electronic delivery of customized content to home networks may bypass traditional gatekeepers. . . . You've read about PlayStation 2, which is a super PC or an advanced set-top box with a 128-bit processor more powerful than the Pentium III. It's another independent delivery system, a Trojan horse into the home for all kinds of digital content. After all, there are more than 50 million PlayStation 1's out there, and PlayStation 2 is backward compatible.[8]

While opinions differ on whether the personal computer, the interactive television set-top, or the video-game console will be the home's digital hub, Michael Dell, chairman, founder, and CEO of Dell Computer Corp.—the largest computer manufacturer in the United States at the end 2000—noted that four key trends will continue to drive the personal-computing market over the next few years: increased consumer migration to high-speed connections through broadband, increased demand for data storage through servers, an expanding number of new computer-powered devices, and a continued shift to mobile computing. Dell explained:

> The shift from electrons to photons and the huge investments in fiber connections—DSL and cable—are creating massive increases in bandwidth. And when people get high-speed connections, they find that they want more computing power.
>
> Another trend we're seeing is the growth of the Internet as companies come online. This is driving strong demand for cost-effective, powerful servers, and storage that can scale to meet ever-increasing traffic. . . . A third trend is the huge variety of new devices that are emerging—from Internet in your car to handhelds to MP3 players, to data-enabled phones and pagers.

*. . . Finally, as always, the PC is changing. Wireless technologies and the capability for massive data storage and throughput are unleashing the Internet and driving a shift from fixed to mobile computing.[9]*

With an increasing number of digital platforms being introduced by both hardware and software makers, media content providers such as AOL Time Warner, The News Corporation United, and The Walt Disney Company will seek to have their content and services available on as many platforms as possible. Steve Case, chairman of AOL Time Warner, reflected on how new technologies in the household will impact content-based media companies and their consumers:

*. . . If the last five years have been about leveraging the PC and modem, the next five years will be about cellphones and wireless devices across a range of platforms designed to bring all the benefits of the Internet to consumers in a seamless, easy way that really improves their lives.*

*Consumers are driving these trends, but they shouldn't have to be systems integrators to figure them out. So the companies that will lead in this new world will be those that listen to consumers and connect the dots for them.*

*They will be the companies that are able to make sense of this world of dizzying complexity both by building on trusted brands that people can count on and by creating new services to collect and package products and services.*

*They will be the companies that utilize multiple delivery platforms, giving consumers multiple access options for a wide range of content and services through cable, DSL, and wireless providers, and using interfaces that give consumers the simplicity, functionality, and personalized services they desire.*

*And they will be the companies that have a breadth of perspective large enough to balance the convenience, control, and variety consumers are increasingly demanding with the real needs of businesses to preserve the value of their products and the rights of their artists.[12]*

# HOW WILL BROADBAND TECHNOLOGY IMPACT INTERNET USAGE?

## Applications of Broadband

The increased use of **broadband** technology will allow for more applications—such as video-on-demand, multiplayer games, streaming of audio and video, and software distribution—to be offered over the Internet (see Exhibit 15-3). Motion-picture companies, video-game makers, streaming-media companies (such as RealNetworks), and software companies will all benefit.

At the beginning of 2000, Nielsen//NetRatings estimated that only 5.1 million American households had access to broadband technology.[13] By the end of 2005, the Yankee Group projects, more than 30 million Americans will have access to broadband, with 15 million American households accessing it through a cable modem, 10 million through DSL, and 5 million through satellite.[14] Adoption of broadband technology will happen faster in the workplace, with Jupiter Communications projecting that the number of workers with access to broadband will increase from 24.4 million, or 22 percent of the workforce, in 2000 to 54.6 million, or 47 percent of the total workforce, in 2005. Consequently, the number of individuals who access the Internet through dial-up service will decrease from 18.5 million in 2000 to 8.1 million in 2005.[15]

## Internet Service Providers

At the end of 2000, many in the United States still accessed the Internet primarily by dialing a telephone number provided by Internet service providers (ISPs). These ISPs ranged from well-known services (America Online, EarthLink, and the Microsoft Network) to regional telecoms (BellSouth, NYNEX, and Pacific Bell) to local firms (Access Internet Communications in Cupertino, California, and Montana Communications Network in Bozeman, Montana). By the middle of July

## Exhibit 15-3 CERTAIN APPLICATIONS ARE MORE DEPENDENT ON BROADBAND

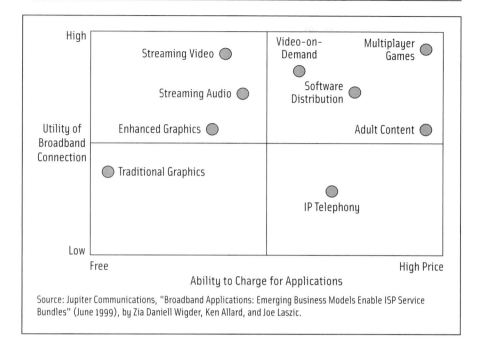

Source: Jupiter Communications, "Broadband Applications: Emerging Business Models Enable ISP Service Bundles" (June 1999), by Zia Daniell Wigder, Ken Allard, and Joe Laszic.

1999, there were an estimated 6,000 ISPs in North America.[16] In December 2000, AOL was the largest ISP in the United States with more than 29 million members, followed by EarthLink/MindSpring, the Microsoft Network, AT&T, and NetZero.

Prior to the increase in Internet usage during the mid-1990s, online commercial services such as AOL, CompuServe, and Prodigy were often closed-end, proprietary systems. Registered members usually paid an hourly fee to access each of a service's proprietary features, such as sending e-mail, reading online content, or participating in chat rooms. With the increase in Web popularity—made possible by the development of Web browsers—many Internet users began seeking direct access to the Internet through independent ISPs. By 1997, almost all commercial online services offered a direct connection to the Internet as part of their online services packages in an effort to retain members. Delphi was the first national commercial online service to offer Internet access, including e-mail, to its subscribers in 1992.[17]

In 1999, 86 percent of the estimated 81 million home Internet users worldwide accessed the Web from a PC through a telephone line, via an analog modem.[18] At the time of this writing, analog modems have a theoretical maximum speed of 56 kilobits per second (for illustrative purposes, one page of text is roughly 2.7 kilobytes and one webpage is 30 kilobytes), although most run at top speeds of up to 40 to 53 kilobits per second, depending on line quality and the distance from the telephone company's central office.[19] Bits of data are transmitted from a PC through a modem, which converts (or modulates) the digital bits into analog signals and sends them over the phone lines. When the modem receives analog signals, it converts (or demodulates) the analog signals into digital form before transferring them into the receiving computer. The term *modem* (MOdulate/DEModulate) comes from this behavior.

**Exhibit 15-4**

BROADBAND USAGE PROJECTIONS (2000–2005)

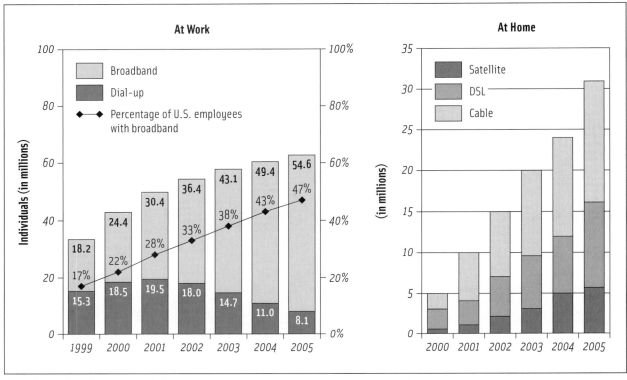

Source: Projected Broadband Usage at Work, Jupiter Communications

---

## DRILL-DOWN

# Baud Rates

What does the term "baud rate" refer to? Named after J.M. Emile Baudot, baud rate initially referred to a unit of telegraph signaling speed, where one baud was equal to one Morse code dot per second. In recent terminology, one baud is equal to one bit per second. The slow early modems were measured on baud rate instead of kilobits per second.[20] Common rates for PCs when they were introduced in the early 1980s were 300-baud (300 bits per second) or 1,200-baud (1,200 bits per second). Baud rate equaled the number of voltage or frequency changes in a second. But with today's advanced data compression and advanced modulation techniques in data communications, baud rate is no longer equated with the bit rate of data transmitted.[21]

As noted in Chapter 14, the passage of the Telecommunications Act of 1996 allowed regional telephone companies and cable companies to compete with each other for the first time. Telephone companies can offer cable TV services to their customers, and cable companies can offer telephone services to their customers. With the growing demand for broadband Internet service, the competition between telephone and cable companies has never been more fierce. Each wants to become the primary provider of home broadband service. The primary types of broadband services are digital subscriber lines (DSL), cable modems, and satellite transmission. A discussion of each type of broadband connection to the Internet follows.

# DIGITAL SUBSCRIBER LINES (DSL), CABLE LINES, AND SATELLITE TRANSMISSION

## Digital Subscriber Line

Also known as **DSL**, a digital subscriber line allows for high-speed connections over existing copper telephone wires. The service requires DSL modems on each end of the connection, in the user's home and at the telephone company's central office. DSL modems are different from traditional modems in that DSL modems send and receive all data as digital data—no translation to analog signal ever takes place—allowing for faster data transmission.

One advantage of DSL is that it enables people to talk on the telephone and use the Internet simultaneously—all over a single phone line. DSL divides the phone lines into three channels: one for receiving data, one for sending data, and one for talking on the telephone. To work properly, a DSL modem must be within a certain distance—usually 18,000 feet, or about three miles—from the phone company's answering DSL modem. The exact distance varies according to the DSL service, the speed being offered, and even the gauge of the copper telephone wire. DSL speeds range from 128 kilobits per second to over 1 megabit per second.

There are several variations of DSL, but the most common versions are the data rate digital subscriber line (HDSL or T1) and the asymmetric digital subscriber line (ASDL). HDSL uses four transceivers: two at the subscriber's end and two at the telephone company's central office. Data, both download and upload, can be transmitted across an HSDL at a speed of 1.5 megabits per second. ASDL is more common than HDSL because it is less expensive. ADSL uses only two transceivers and is capable of uploading and downloading at different maximum prescribed speeds. Downloading speed through an ADSL is usually between 1 and 12 megabits per second, while uploading is typically between 160 kilobits and 1.5 megabits per second. Users generally upload only a few characters to select and control the download of webpages with large graphic files. The uneven speeds for uploading and downloading are why ASDL is labeled asymmetric.

Another form of DSL is the **ISDN** (integrated services digital network) line. It can dial the Internet at higher speeds than regular non-digital phone lines, usually between 64,000 and 128,000 bits per second. Special ISDN modems must be used at both a subscriber's location and the telephone company's central office. ISDN lines cost more than normal phone lines, so user telephone rates are usually higher. ISDN requires the installation of a second line because it cannot run over the same line as regular telephone lines and, like DSL, must be within 18,000 feet of a central office.

## Cable Modem

With the use of a special modem, the Internet can be accessed over some cable TV systems through the existing coaxial cable that carries TV signals. Starting around 1996, most cable companies began upgrading their plants by installing fiber-optic transmission technology. By replacing the coaxial copper with fiber-optic lines, cable operators could improve signal reliability and reception quality, increase channel capacity, and support the introduction of two-way interactive services.[22] To date, cable operations in the United States have spent $10 billion to transform their aging phone lines from coaxial to fiber optic. Another $20 billion is projected to be spent over the next few years.[23] **Cable modems** send and receive data at speeds of 2 to 3 megabits per second, or 35 to 52 times faster than conventional analog modems of 56 kilobits per second.

## Satellite Transmission

Three types of **satellite systems**—geostationary, medium earth orbit (MEO), and low earth orbit (LEO)—have been proposed for Internet access. Geostationary satellites would orbit 22,000 miles above the equator at the same speed as the earth's rotation, appearing stationary from the ground. They would communicate with fixed-orientation dish antennas attached to customer homes and use advanced-signal processing to compensate for transmissional delays caused by the great distances their signals must travel. MEO and LEO satellites, on the other hand, would circle the globe once every two hours at altitudes of between 500 and 10,000 miles, reducing the time needed to beam signals to and from the earth's surface. Both MEO and LEO satellite methods, however, would require sophisticated subscriber antennas that can track and communicate with fast-moving MEO and LEO satellites.

The advantages of satellite transmission include ubiquity, economics, and performance.[24] Disadvantages are that dozens of satellites are required to service a single downlink station with continuous transmission, and handoffs from one satellite to the next could often be technically complex.[25] Direct PC from Hughes Electronics currently offers satellite-based Internet access and data delivery downstream at 400 kilobits per second. Upstream access is available only by modem or other landline connections through ISPs.[26] By 2003, after the launch of the three-satellite, $1.4 billion Spaceway system, Hughes Electronics hopes to offer Internet service to consumers via satellite at a speed of 1 megabit per second.[27]

## Relative Speed of Various Internet Connections

As shown in Exhibit 15-4, cable modems offer consumers access speeds of 3 to 4 megabits per second, followed by DSL at an average of 1.5 megabits per second, ISDN at 1 megabit per second, and traditional phone lines at 56 kilobits per second. A 2-megabyte file—approximately the size of this chapter—would take roughly eight seconds to download on a cable system. By comparison, it would take just over 10 seconds on a DSL or ISDN line, and 6 minutes on a standard phone line running at a maximum speed of 45 kilobits per second.

## Advocating an "Open System"

Freestanding ISPs such as EarthLink or NetZero do not believe that cable MSOs (multiple system operators) or telecoms will automatically become the leading ISPs of the future because of their dominance of the channels for broadband

**Exhibit 15-5** RELATIVE SPEED OF VARIOUS TYPES OF INTERNET CONNECTIONS

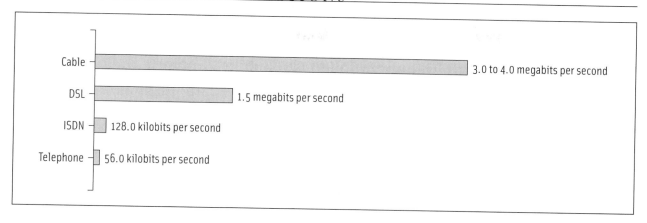

- Cable — 3.0 to 4.0 megabits per second
- DSL — 1.5 megabits per second
- ISDN — 128.0 kilobits per second
- Telephone — 56.0 kilobits per second

technology. These independent ISPs advocate an "open system" in which telephone or cable subscribers still choose an ISP. These ISPs believe that they can differentiate themselves through price or superior customer service. As one of the conditions for the $105 billion merger of AOL and Time Warner, completed in January 2001, the Federal Communications Commission mandated that AOL Time Warner keep Time Warner's cable systems open (or available for lease) to freestanding ISPs.

## POINT-COUNTERPOINT

### Which Is Better—Cable or DSL?

The battle for "the last mile" of transmitting broadband into the home has largely been between the telecoms that provide DSL-type services and cable companies that provide the same services through cable-ready modems. While the monthly costs of $30 to $40 are comparable, cable-modem access has lower installation costs and can download data from the Internet at much faster speeds than DSL.

With the expected increase in services for video-on-demand and multiplayer games, which are services that require downloading speeds of at least 3 megabits per second, advocates of cable modems say DSL may become outdated. Supporters of DSL, however, say it is more reliable and secure than cable modems because the additional subscribers in a neighborhood hub dilute the quality of cable-modem service. Also, there is less risk of an outsider hacking into an individual's personal computer system when using DSL. Some observers, such as the Yankee Group, see potential for Internet access via satellite transmission because an estimated one-fourth of U.S. homes will still not have access to DSL or cable modems by 2004.[28]

# WHICH HOUSEHOLD DEVICE WILL SERVE AS THE GATEWAY TO THE INTERNET?

Just as it is unknown whether DSL, cable, or satellite transmission will become the ultimate pipeline for broadband technology, a parallel debate ensues at the receiving end. The question is whether the personal computer, video-game console, or interactive TV set-top box will dominate as the household command center.

At the end of 2000, approximately 55 million U.S. households, or 53 percent, had personal computers.[29] Of these households, 35.3 million, or 34.2 percent of all households in the United States, had Internet access, for a total of 62 million individual users.[30] In 2000, 16.8 million computers were sold, at an average price of $1,000.[31] At the end of 1999, there were an estimated 200 million personal computers in use,[32] with most using the Windows/MS-DOS operating system.

Despite the fact that the PC is the primary gateway for most Americans to access the Internet, many consumers say they would prefer to have an easier Web interface at home. According to a survey conducted by AOL and the research firm Roper Starch Worldwide in September 2000, almost half of all American adults who are currently online said they would be interested in checking their e-mail on a television, and two-thirds said they would be interested in checking a website directly on a television without leaving it to log on through a PC.[33] Sixty percent said they believed that in 10 years, every room in the house would be Internet-ready, and 54 percent said they would be interested in using a small device to access the Internet from any room in their house.[34]

As a result of this, many experts believe that the video-game console—such as Sony's PlayStation 2, Microsoft's Xbox, or Nintendo's GameCube—or the interactive television set-top box could emerge as the preferred "gateway entry," over the personal computer, for accessing the Web at home.

## Digital Household Applications of the Future

**Video-Game Consoles.** Launched in the United States on October 26, 2000, PlayStation 2 is the sequel to the original PlayStation system, which launched in December 1994 and was considered the first video-game console with the potential to access a wide range of broadband services on the Internet.[35] Like its predecessor, PlayStation 2 is a **video-game console**, but a more powerful version that can generate 66 million polygons per second—220 times faster than the 300,000 polygons-per-second speed of the original. The increased polygon usage allows for more realistic—almost lifelike—three-dimensional images. To develop 3-D images for video games, the polygons are the basic building blocks. Graphic artists then take thousands of these polygons and cover them with textures to represent a single color or multiple colors to create objects, shadows, and characters.[36]

In addition to being a video-game player, PlayStation 2—with 32 megabytes of random access memory and powered by a 128-bit central processor—could function as a CD and DVD player. In 2001, Sony plans to add to the console a hard-drive device that will allow broadband Internet access. With their PlayStations 2s, users could bank, shop, and e-mail through a television set,[37] as well as download, store, and replay digital music and video from the Web.[38] In January 2001, Sony announced it planned to create an Internet bank in a joint venture with Sakura Bank and J.P. Morgan as the first step in providing Web-based services.[39] In addition to a hard drive, the PlayStation 2 has built-in "firewall" ports, which will allow it to transfer data seamlessly from camcorders, digital cameras, and other PC peripheral devices in the future.[40] Jeremy Schwartz, a senior analyst at Forrester Research, commented on the impact of using game consoles to access the Web:

> Certainly the arrival of these new game consoles coming online represents a significant shift from what we have had in the past, being tied to a living room and crowding around a television set playing to friends and family across town and country.[41]

The PlayStation 2 system, which is sold at a near-cost-of-production price of $299, with profits coming largely from video games,[42] is considered one of the cornerstones of Sony's strategy to create digital-based products for the entire household. It is based upon Nobuyuki Idei's "Digital Dream Kids" philosophy.[43]

However, Sony's two key competitors—Nintendo and Microsoft—are not standing still. They hope to take advantage of Sony's recent production woes that left it unable to meet demand for the PlayStation 2. Nintendo plans to introduce its GameCube console in October 2001, which features a 405-megahertz chip that will make it 33 percent faster than the PlayStation 2, although the video-game console will not be able to play CDs or DVDs. Microsoft plans to introduce its Xbox in fall 2001. The Xbox will also be able to access the Internet and will have a chip twice as fast as the PlayStation 2's. Unlike Nintendo's GameCube, however, the Xbox will be able to play CDs and DVDs.[44]

**Interactive Television.** Another potential Internet gateway is the set-top box for **interactive television**. Currently AOL and Microsoft offer basic interactive TV services—through AOLTV and UltimateTV, respectively—that allow users to access e-mail, chat, and surf the Internet with a set-top box and dial-up modem while watching TV. Additional features that cable companies may someday offer as premium services include a choice of camera angles for sporting events, local entertainment guides during the airing of local news shows, and online purchases (such as CDs from an artist giving a televised concert).[45] Forrester Research projects that by 2005, 40 million households will have access to digital set-top boxes, almost an eightfold increase from the 4.9 million households that had access to set-top boxes at the end of 1999.[46] Michael Willner, president of Insight Communications, the nation's ninth-largest cable company, observed, "I think the implications of being able to do things between television shows without having to get off your sofa, without turning on the computer, are enormous."[47]

Interactive television was tried before the widespread usage of the Internet, most notably with Warner Cable's Qube System in the late 1970s in Columbus, Ohio, and Time Warner's Full Service Network in the mid-1990s in Orlando, Florida.[48] Both experiments failed due to the high cost to the consumer and inadequate technology.[49] Experts believe that interactive television is no longer as cost-prohibitive as it was almost a decade ago because of recent improvements to its delivery infrastructure by cable companies, which will finally make interactive features a possibility.[50] The recent testing of Enhanced TV—which lets television viewers log on to their computers for interactive features while watching TV—by ABC-TV during *Who Wants to Be a Millionaire* and *Monday Night Football* indicates that there is widespread interest in interactive TV. Although TV viewers log on to a separate computer while using Enhanced TV, ABC says that an estimated 20,000 of the 20 million viewers of *Millionaire* play along on the Web, while between 50,000 and 100,000 of the 18 million viewers of *Monday Night Football* log on for additional player statistics. Once the demand for interactive set-top boxes increases, ABC plans to move Enhanced TV from the Web to interactive television systems,[51] where the network thinks the interactive audience would be larger.[52]

In addition to interactivity, another service that will become more widely available through interactive television is the use of video-on-demand, whereby consumers can choose to watch any movie or television show at any time and can even pause in the middle of it. This service would be similar to the digital video-recording services currently offered by TiVo and ReplayTV—potential competitors to the interactive services offered by cable companies—which allow consumers to record television shows and then pause or fast-forward when viewing.[53] According to a survey conducted by Jupiter Communications, the six features online viewers want most in interative television are (1) the ability to pause live television shows, (2) television program reminders, (3) more program information, (4) a program feature, (5) e-mail, and (6) the capability to view websites.[54]

**In-House Wireless Technology.** One near-term application is the use of Bluetooth, an **in-house wireless technology** named after the Scandinavian monarch Harold Bluetooth, who sought to unite the countries of Norway and Denmark during the tenth century. Bluetooth would allow ubiquitous Web access throughout the home without the need for a modem or any other accessories. It is being developed by a consortium of companies, including Ericsson, IBM, Intel, Nokia, and Toshiba.[55] With Bluetooth-enabled devices—which use short-range radio frequency to transmit data—users can connect their PCs, personal digital assistants, digital cameras, and other devices to the Web and to each other within 30 feet, without the use of connecting cables.[56] Merrill Lynch estimates that the number of Bluetooth chipsets now being used in select IBM and Toshiba laptops, as well as by Nokia phones in Europe and Asia, will grow from 9.2 million in 2000 to 2.1 billion in 2005. Over the same period, the average price of a Bluetooth chipset is expected to fall from $15 to $2.02.[57] Beginning in 2001, Palm will build Bluetooth transmitters into most of its Palmtops.[58] "The thing about Bluetooth," says Martin Reynolds, an analyst with Gartner Group's Dataquest, "is that it really will ship in the billions of units once it gains momentum. It's really a multibillion-dollar market."[59]

An alternative wireless technology is a networking system called 802.11, which is already being used by Apple Computer in its AirPort wireless system. 802.11 differs from Bluetooth because it functions more like a wireless Ethernet system that would allow two or more computers to interact with one another, instead of merely connecting devices with a personal computer. 802.11 can operate computers within a distance of 100 feet and at speeds equivalent to the low end of today's Ethernet systems.[61]

A third home wireless technology being developed by a consortium comprised of Microsoft, Intel, Motorola, Hewlett-Packard, and Compaq is Home RF. Like Bluetooth, Home RF operates on a similar 2.4 GHz frequency band and is also intended to create a wireless network for the home market.[62]

# HOW WILL INCREASED WIRELESS COMMUNICATIONS, VIDEO-ON-DEMAND, AND PERSONALIZED MEDIA CONTENT FURTHER FRAGMENT MEDIA USAGE?

Forecasters see **mobile wireless technology** as one of the fastest-growing alternatives to PCs for accessing the Web, especially when it is used as an "electronic wallet" or to check on stock quotes, which requires relatively low bandwidth. Projections estimate that the number of installed wireless Web devices—whether they be Qualcomm's PDQs (a combination of a Palm organizer and a cellular phone), National SemiConductor Web Pads, or Nokia WAP phones—will grow almost 20-fold, from 3.4 million to 67.4 million, between 1999 and 2004.[63]

Palm-size computers are now enabled to receive wireless data through the Internet as well. These computers do everything from serving as electronic appointment calendars to acting as MP3 players to doubling as digital cameras. The market is dominated by Palm, which has a 76 percent market share in the United States.[64] Palm-size computers using Windows CE (short for Windows Compact Edition) are second, with 10 percent of the market. Sales of palm-size computers, TV set-top devices, and gaming devices are projected to increase from 5.6 million in 1999 to 20.8 million by 2002.[65] In the future, the mantra will be to "give [users]

## POINT-COUNTERPOINT

## How Should Operating Standards Be Set in the Future?

Consumers have already had to choose between Betamax and VHS for the home videocassette recorder. Then they had to choose between the Macintosh or Windows platform for the home PC. Tomorrow there will be more choices—such as deciding whether to use WAP, G3, or DoCoMo protocol for the wireless phone, or choosing among the Bluetooth, I.E.E.E. 802.11b, or Home RF protocol for mobile digital devices. As the number of digital media devices multiplies, so will the choices of operating platforms. For example, users of mobile wireless technology may need to carry cards of two or three protocol standards in their digital devices to be able to communicate when they travel.[66] Proponents of establishing a single, nationwide operating standard for each emerging technology note that increased market efficiencies would reduce the acquisition cost for new customers[67] and allow consumers easy, seamless access through a single standard, similar to the widespread use of WAP protocol for mobile phones in Scandinavian countries. Opponents argue it would stifle free-market competition, which brings innovation and price reductions to the consumers over the long run.

what they want when they need it," observed Alan Kessler, general manager of Palm's platform solutions group. "That's a lot different than the PC era, when everyone said, 'Give me more memory. Give me more power. Give me more complex software.'"[68]

Another popular wireless device is the BlackBerry, which allows users to receive and send e-mail from their regular accounts. It features a miniature, built-in QWERTY keyboard. As of September 2000, there were 200,000 BlackBerrys in use, compared to 4 million Palm devices.[69] Users of the BlackBerry, which is manufactured by the Canadian firm Research in Motion, pay about $500 for the device and a monthly service fee of $30. The server software to connect the BlackBerry to a company's e-mail system costs roughly $3,000.[70] The device itself weighs about five ounces, is powered by a 32-bit Intel 386 chip, and can run up to three weeks on a AA battery.[71] Unlike the multitask Palm devices, the BlackBerry is devoted to e-mail. "We don't want to become the center of your life," said Mike Lazaridis, founder and co-CEO of RIM.[72]

One technology that enables other wireless communications is WAP, an open system (originally advocated by Finnish mobile-phone manufacturer Nokia) that allows Internet users to access information from the Web on their cellphones. The key to WAP is a language called eXstensible Markup Language (XML), another open standard. This language tags all the data being distributed wirelessly and makes sure that it is displayed in a comprehensible way to the user's device.[73]

Another emerging wireless communications service is i-mode, which was introduced in Japan in February 1999 by the mobile-phone company NTT DoCoMo.[74] In less than two years, i-mode has added more than 17 million subscribers in Japan who access the Internet through their digital phones at an average cost of $20 per month, making NTT DoCoMo the fastest growing ISP in the world and the corporation with the third-highest market capitalization, behind Microsoft and General Electric.[75] Subscribers to i-mode—which offers 24-hour Internet access, unlike WAP-based phones, which require dialing an ISP—can send e-mail, watch cartoons, search the Web, or check stock quotes. In addition, i-mode provides Web services through third-party agreements and adds the costs to subscribers' monthly phone bills. Long-term plans call for NTT DoCoMo to launch the next generation of broadband wireless Internet services, which "can be 100 times faster than existing speeds and make the mobile phone the all-purpose communication, entertainment and information device, where users can also read e-books, play MP3 music, and watch television shows."[76] DoCoMo has already purchased minority stakes in wireless carriers in Asia, South America, Europe, and most recently, AT&T Wireless in the United States.[77] Kei-Ichi Enoki, managing director of i-mode, said this about the future of wireless phones:

> We will all eventually have our own wireless phone. The PDA and PCs will be secondary. We humans, it does not matter whether we're Americans or Japanese, we are all lazy in nature. It's just too much to carry two devices around.[78]

Just around the corner is the introduction of 3G—short for third generation—networks, which will allow for increased broadband wireless usage on telephones. Currently, wireless phone connections, such as those for i-mode, operate at a top speed of between 9.6 and 19.2 kilobits per second.[79] With 3G, information can be sent across the wireless network at a speed of 64 kilobits per second, which would be a bit faster than existing dial-up modems for personal computers.[80] 3G technology will also enable increased, online mobile multitasking—allowing users to send e-mail, utilize video-conferencing, surf the Web, take digital photos, and listen to MP3 music—all on a single wireless cellphone.[81] While the operating speed for 3G is seemingly slower than that of broadband speed to the house, fewer bits are needed to fill up the tiny screens on a cellphone compared to that of a PC screen.[82] DoCoMo planned to introduce the use of 3G technology in Japan in spring 2001—in addition to i-mode usage—before rolling it out in Europe and the United States later in the year.[83]

Even so, some experts believe that wireless Web technology will be less likely to take off in the United States, where 55 percent of the population accesses the Internet through desktop computers, compared to 25 percent in Japan.[84] As a result of a more established telecommunications infrastructure, only 32 percent of all Americans have cellphones, compared to 45 percent in Japan, 59 percent in Sweden, and 65 percent in Finland.[85] Amanda McCarthy, an analyst with Forrester Research, said this about the importance of the interface of these small wireless devices:

> Nothing is going to happen through these devices if it isn't relatively simple, involving a small sum of money, and suited to real-time transactions. . . . You're not going to have a relationship with a handset that you aren't first going to have with a PC screen.[86]

# HOW WILL INCREASINGLY LARGE MEDIA COMPANIES CAPTURE EFFICIENCIES OF SCALE AMONG DIVERSE AUDIENCES OF MEDIA USAGE?

## Media Content of the Future

With the continued fragmentation of media usage, mergers of content-based media companies will continue as a way to reach different segments of consumers. For example, the $105 billion merger of AOL and Time Warner will allow the company to reach an estimated 60 percent of all American households through its magazines, cable television, movies, books, or online service. AOL Time Warner reaches 29 million households through its online service and 14 million through its cable systems, owns 40 magazines through Time Inc., has 37 million subscribers to its HBO channel, and reaches 12 percent of all moviegoers through Warner Bros. Studios.[87] With

### POINT-COUNTERPOINT

## E-Wallets of the Future

Will personalized electronic wallets (**e-wallets**) become the preferred method of payment in the United States? In the Scandinavian countries of Finland and Sweden, where approximately 60 percent of the population has cellphones, consumers are already using wireless mobile devices to pay for everyday purchases like sodas, magazines, movie tickets, and groceries. Proponents of electronic wallets say that the economy would be much more efficient with electronic-payment

capabilities embedded into mobile wireless devices (or what Bill Gates labeled as "frictionless economy" in his book, *The Road Ahead*), and it would help society move away from paper dollars and coins. Opponents of electronic wallets say that the lack of protocol standards between wireless carriers and security concerns by consumers make this form of electronic payment very unlikely in the near future.

**Exhibit 15-6** AOL TIME WARNER SYNERGIES

**Legend**

- 🖥 Broadband
- ⊘ Digital Music
- ✕ Cross Promotion
- 📖 E-Books
- 📱 Wireless

| The AOL–Time Warner Empire | Estimated 2001 Revenues | Synergies |
|---|---|---|
| America Online, Inc. –29 million subscribers, AOL is the leading online service in the United States. The company is not migrating AOL service beyond personal computers to pagers, cell phones and other mobile devices | $10.3 Billion | 📱 ✕ 🖥 |
| Time Warner Cable–The second largest U.S. cable operator, AOL–TW is pushing digital services and broadband access to its customers. Plan to offer interactive shopping and entertainment | $6.9 Billion | 🖥 ✕ |
| Time Inc.–Publisher of 40 magazines, including four with the largest circulation: Time, Sports Illustrated, People, and Fortune. With the merger it is promoting magazine subscriptions heavily | $5 Billion | 📖 ✕ |
| Home Box Office–Largest premium cable network with 37 million subscribers | $2.4 Billion | ✕ |
| Turner Broadcasting System Inc.–Includes some of cable television's top networks including CNN, TBS, and TNT. CNN is already promoted on the Netscape website and AOL | $5.1 Billion | 📱 ✕ 🖥 |
| WB Television Network–The "Fifth" network after the big three and FOX. Targets young viewers with hits such as Felicity and Buffy, the Vampire Slayer. | $495 Billion | ✕ |
| Warner Brothers–Third largest movie studio with 12% market share. Ultimately, movies will be delivered on demand through cable television and over the web | $7.1 Billion | 🖥 ✕ |
| NewLine Cinema–Ninth largest movie studio | $1.6 Billion | 🖥 |
| Warner Music Group–With artists such as Faith Hill, AOL dela will allow digital distribution of music over the web | $4.4 Billion | ⊘ ✕ |
| Warner Trade Publishing–Parent company of Warner Books and Little, Brown, company has launched iBooks, an online publisher dedicated to e-books | $300 Billion | 📖 ✕ |

Source: Business Week, January 15, 2001, Internal analysis

multiple media channels, increased digitalization will allow AOL Time Warner to feed its content across different platforms, such as delivering Warner Bros. motion pictures on demand over its cable channel and on the Web, or distributing music from its Warner Music Group over the Internet[88] (see Exhibit 15-5). Observed Robert Pittman, vice chairman of AOL Time Warner:

> With all its copyrights, Time Warner is in a marvelous position to take advantage of the Net and not be frightened by it. AOL's mind-set, assets, and expertise help them in that path.[89]

Renetta McCann, chief executive of Starcom North America, a Chicago-based media services agency, added this about the merger of AOL and Time Warner and its benefit for advertisers, the main source of revenue for many media companies:

> In this world of fragmentation, what this does is re-aggregate some of the media vehicles, so you can get an Internet presence, a TV presence, a cable presence packaged for a particular demographic.[90]

Even as media companies continue to merge so they can distribute content across multiple media channels, Nobuyuki Idei, chairman and chief executive officer of Sony, foresees a day when the companies that create the network infrastructure will also dominate the media infrsastructure. Sony itself began to do this with its acquisition of CBS Records—originally established as a joint venture between CBS and Sony—and Columbia Studios in the late 1980s. Microsoft also began doing this in the late 1990s with its development of the MSN Network and the online newsmagazine Slate.com, and its joint ownership of the MSNBC News Channel with General Electric (see Exhibit 15-6). Some observers note that Sony's interest in CBS/Sony Records helped the company set the standard for compact discs in 1982, whereas its failure to own a major Hollywood studio or movie library allowed JVC's Video Home System (VHS) to be selected over Betamax as the operating standard for videocassette recorders in the late 1970s.[91] Idei noted in 1998 that:

**Exhibit 15-7**

MICROSOFT STRATEGY: TODAY AND TOMORROW

| Microsoft-Strategy Today | Microsoft-Strategy Future |
|---|---|
| Operating Systems | Operating Systems |
| Applications | Applications |
| MSNBC Joint Venture | MSNBC Joint Venture |
| MSN Network | MSN Network |
| Web TV | Web TV |
| Servers | Servers |
| Windows CE for palmtops | Windows CE for palmtops |
| Windows Media Player | Windows Media Player |
| | Microsoft Reader- eBooks |

*In the Age of Networks [hardware will be deprived of its stand-alone value]. It won't matter whether TV screens are bright and have beautiful resolutions. What matters will be the content: who creates it and who controls the networks that distribute it.*[92]

# SUMMARY

### 1. What is meant by the digital lifestyle?

High-tech CEOs such as Michael Dell, Bill Gates, and Steve Jobs envision the home of the future evolving around electronic appliances with digital-based platforms. As more analog-based appliances—such as the television set, the video recorder, and the audio player—evolve to digital-based technology, it will be easier for consumers to access, transfer, and manipulate information and data (broken down in bits and bytes) across various media platforms. The outstanding question is which household device will be at the hub of this digital lifestyle: the personal computer, the interactive television set-top box, or the video-game console?

### 2. How will broadband technology impact Internet usage?

Broadband technology involves connectivity speeds exceeding 128 kilobits per second, faster than the usual 40 to 53 kilobits per second over regular telephone lines. It will give consumers greater access to a range of media choices over the Web, from video-on-demand to real-time gaming to online software purchasing. At the beginning of 2000, Nielsen//NetRatings estimated that only 5 percent of all U.S. households had broadband access. By 2005, the Yankee Group projects, 30 percent of U.S. households will have broadband access.

### 3. What are the differences among the following Internet-delivery mechanisms: digital subscriber lines (DSL), cable lines, or satellite?

Speed, security, and accessibility are the three key differences in the types of broadband transmission. Broadband transmission over cable lines is the fastest, at 2 to 3 megabits per second, followed by DSL at 1.5 megabits per second, and satellite at 400 kilobits per second (although this is expected to increase to 1 megabit per second by 2003 with the launch of additional satellites). DSL is the most secure because it uses the same dedicated phone lines that already run into a particular house. With cable lines, which are shared among neighborhood homes, there is the risk that someone could hack into another person's computer system without the installation of a firewire. While DSL and cable lines are the most popular types of transmission, they are much more accessible in major metropolitan areas than in rural areas, where experts believe that satellite transmission has the most growth potential.

### 4. Which household device will serve as the gateway to the Internet?

The PC, video-game console, and interactive television set-top box are each in the running to become the hub of the digital lifestyle in the home. Today, the PC is the command center for digital activity in the home, acting as a hub for digital cameras, MP3 players, and compact-disc writers. That may change with consumers' adoption of video-game consoles and interactive set-top boxes. A study conducted by AOL and Roper Starch Worldwide in September 2000 indicated that consumers were reluctant to leave the couch, go to the PC, and boot up the computer to search for a Web address seen on TV. This demonstrates the need for interactive television, which would be the convergence of TV and the PC. Even so, the concept of video-on-demand, which has been labeled the next "killer application" for the past several years, has so far failed to materialize.

**5. How will increased wireless communications, video-on-demand, and personalized media content further fragment media usage?**

The increased number of media outlets for news, information, and entertainment for consumers will further fragment media usage, especially traditional mass media such as newspapers, magazines, and television. As consumers use other media, less time will be spent on traditional media outlets.

**6. How will the increased size of media companies allow them to capture efficiencies of scale among diverse audiences?**

With the continued fragmentation of media usage, mergers of media companies will continue as a way to reach fragmented segments of consumers. For example, the $105 billion merger of America Online and Time Warner will allow the media company to reach an estimated 60 percent of all American households through its magazines, cable television, movies, books, or online services.

# KEY TERMS

| | |
|---|---|
| analog | satellite systems |
| digital | video-game consoles |
| broadband | interactive television |
| DSL | in-house wireless technology |
| ISDN | mobile wireless technology |
| cable modems | e-wallets |

# Endnotes

[1] Negroponte, Nicholas. *Being digital*, New York: Knopf, 1995.

[2] Gates, Bill. Speech at Consumer Electronics Show, 6 January, 2001. Remarks by Bill Gates, CES 2001. Portions reprinted with permission from Microsoft Corporation. URL: *www.microsoft.com/billgates/speeches/2001/01-06ces.asp.*

[3] Markoff, John. "For Microsoft, a shift toward new vistas," *The New York Times*, 18 December, 2000, C-25.

[4] Barrett, Craig. Kickoff Keynote Speech at Consumer Electronics Show, 5 January, 2001. Intel Corporation. URL: *www.intel.com/pressroom/archive/speeches/crb200010105ces.htm.*

[5] Markoff, John. "Thinking revolution, talking evolution at Apple," *The New York Times*, 21 January, 2001, Money and Business, p. 4.

[6] Markoff, John. "Thinking revolution, talking evolution at Apple," *The New York Times*, 21 January, 2001, Money and Business, p. 4.

[7]Sony CEO outlines vision for networked world," 15 November, 1999. URL: *www.sony.com.au/media_room.asp?room=6&ID=1066.*

[8]Stringer, Howard. "Digital or die: Broadcasting in the 21st century," speech before the National Association of Broadcasters, 19 April, 1999. URL: *www.hollywoodreporter.com/inwords/speeches/HowardSt.asp.*

[9]Dell, Michael. "PC goes wireless," speech at Comdex 2000, 13 November, 2000. URL: *www.dell.com/us/en/gen/corporate/speech/speech_2000-11-13-lv-000.htm.*

[10]*The New York Times 2000 Almanac*, s.v. "Glossary of Computer Terms," p. 808.

[11]Rayport, Jeffrey, George C. Lodge, and Thomas Gerace. 1997. *National Information Structure(A): The United States in Perspective*, 20 March. Boston: Harvard Business School Publishing, p. 4.

[12]Case, Steve. Goldman Sachs Communicopeia Conference, 28 September, 2000. URL: *http://corp.aol.com/press/speeches/092800communicopeia.html.*

[13]Nielsen//NetRatings, Internet Media Strategies, Spring 2000.

[14]Schiesel, Seth. "Rules for AOL Time Warner may have only a narrow impact," *The New York Times*, 18 December, 2000.

[15]Press Release. "Almost 50 percent of U.S. employees to have broadband access by 2005," Jupiter Communications. URL: *www.jsp.com.*

[16]Richel, Matt. "Small Internet service providers survive among the giants," *The New York Times*, 16 August, 1999.

[17]"Timeline of the Internet," *The Sunday Contra Costa Times*, 19 December, 1999.

[18]PriceWaterhouseCoopers. e-Business Technology Forecast. 1999. Menlo Park, CA; PriceWaterhouseCoopers Technology Centre, p. 216, Citing International Data Corporation (1999).

[19]Light, Jay O., Lynda M. Applegate, and Dan J. Green. *The Last Mile of Broadband Access*, Case no. 9-800-976, 25 January, 2000. Boston: Harvard Business School Publishing.

[20]*The New York Times 2000 Almanac*, s.v. "Glossary of Computer Terms," p. 807.

[21]Siegel, Allan M., and William G. Connolly. 1999. *The New York Times Manual of Style* (New York, NY: Times Books, p. 43.

[22]Eisenmann, Thomas R. *Telecommunications Inc.: Accelerating Digital Deployment*, Case no. N9-899-141. 3 December, 1998. Boston: Harvard Business School Publishing, p. 2.

[23]Wallack, Todd. "The need for speed," *The San Francisco Chronicle*, 28 March, 2000.

[24]Norcross, Richard T. "Satellites: The strategic high ground," *Scientific American*, October 1999.

[25]Light, Jay O., et al. *The Last Mile of Broadband Access: Technical Note*, Case no. 9-800-076, 25 January, 2000. Boston: Harvard Business School Publishing, p. 15.

[26]PriceWaterhouseCoopers, e-Business Technology Forecast. 1999. Menlo Park, CA, PriceWaterhouseCoopers Technology Centre, p. 217.

[27]Pollack, Andrew. "Coming soon, downloads from up and above," *The New York Times*, 27 February, 2000.

[28]Pollack, Andrew. "Coming soon, downloads from up above," *The New York Times*, 27 February, 2000.

[29]*The New York Times Almanac 2001*, "Personal computer households," citing U.S. Department of Commerce and Media Metrix, p. 796.

[30]*The New York Times Almanac 2001*, "U.S. online households and internet users, 1996–2001," citing U.S. Department of Commerce, p. 806.

[31]*The New York Times Almanac 2001*, "Personal computer sales, 1984–2000," citing Consumer Electronics Manufacturers Association, p. 796.

[32]Markoff, John. "A strange brew's buzz lingers in silicon valley," *The New York Times*, 26 March, 2000.

[33]America Online/Roper Starch, "Worldwide annual adult 2000 cyberstudy," September 2000.

[34]America Online/Roper Starch, "Worldwide annual adult 2000 cyberstudy," September 2000.

[35]The Sega Dreamcast, launched in September 1999, had the capability for dial-up Internet access, but not broadband Internet access.

[36]Kent, Steven L. "PlayStation 2: The wait is over," *Sony Style*, Holiday 2000.

[37]Kent, Steven L. "PlayStation 2: The wait is over," *Sony Style*, Holiday 2000.

[38]Rayport, Jeffrey, and Bernard Jaworski. *e-Commerce*, New York: McGraw-Hill, 2000, p. 377.

[39]Clifford, Bill. "Sony applies for Net banking license," CBS MarketWatch.com, 31 January, 2001.

[40]*Official U.S. PlayStation 2 Magazine*, November 2000.

[41]Marriott, Michel. "PlayStation 2: Game console as Trojan horse," *The New York Times*, 26 October, 2000.

[42]Storm, Stephanie. "Why PlayStation 2 isn't child's play," *The New York Times*, 10 October, 2000.

[43] Asakura, Reiji. *Revolutionaries at Sony: The Making of Sony Playstation and the Visionaries Who Conquered the World of Video Games*, New York: McGraw-Hill, 2000.

[44] Marriott, Michel. "PlayStation2: Game console as Trojan horse," *The New York Times*, 26 October, 2000.

[45] Syken, Bill. "Do touch that dial," *Time Digital*, September 2000.

[46] Syken, Bill. "Do touch that dial," *Time Digital*, September 2000.

[47] Syken, Bill. "Do touch that dial," *Time Digital*, September 2000.

[48] Syken, Bill. "Do touch that dial," *Time Digital*, September 2000.

[49] Syken, Bill. "Do touch that dial," *Time Digital*, September 2000. For an excellent article on the launch of the Full Service Network, also read Ken Auletta's "The magic box," in the April 11, 1994 issue of the *New Yorker*.

[50] Syken, Bill. "Do touch that dial," *Time Digital*, September 2000.

[51] Hansell, Saul. "Clicking outside the box," *The New York Times*, 20 September, 2000.

[52] Syken, Bill. "Do touch that dial," *Time Digital*, September 2000.

[53] Hansell, Saul. "Clicking outside the box," *The New York Times*, 20 September, 2000.

[54] Syken, Bill. "Do touch that dial," *Time Digital*, September 2000.

[55] McLaughlin, Kevin. "Bluetooth Reality Check," *Business 2.0*, URL: *www.business2.com/content/channels/technology/2000/12/20/23949*.

[56] "Emerging technology: Bluetooth," *www.techpilgrim.com*.

[57] McLaughlin, Kevin. "Bluetooth reality check," *Business 2.0*, URL: *www.business2.com/content/channels/technology/2000/12/20/23949*.

[58] Pogue, David. "New Palms will use Bluetooth to cast a much wider net," *The New York Times*, 15 February, 2001.

[59] McLaughlin, Kevin. "Bluetooth reality check," *Business 2.0*, URL: *www.business2.com/content/channels/technology/2000/12/20/23949*.

[60] Sony Corporation, AIBO sales brochure, November 2000.

[61] Gomes, Lee. "The wireless world—in English," e-Commerce, *The Wall Street Journal*, 11 December, 2000.

[62] "A primer on Bluetooth technology," 15 December, 2000. URL: *123jump.com*.

[63] Lake, David. "Worldwide information appliance installed forecast," *Industry Standard* (online version only), 3 April, 2000. URL: *http://www.thestandard.com/research/metrics/display/0,27799,13508.00.html*. Citing IDC.

[64] "The News at Hand," *The New York Times*, 10 April, 2000. p.C-21.

[65] Ervin, Keith. "Bsquare riding high on success of Windows CE," *Seattle Times*, 8 April, 1999.

[66] Fleishman, Glen. "The Web, without wires, wherever," *The New York Times*, 22 February, 2001.

[67] Fleishman, Glen. "The Web, without wires, wherever," *The New York Times*, 22 February, 2001.

[68] Holstein, William J. "Moving beyond the PC," *U.S. News and World Report*, 12 December, 1999.

[69] Newman, Michael. "BlackBerry preserve", *e-Company*, September 2000.

[70] Newman, Michael. "BlackBerry preserve", *e-Company*, September 2000.

[71] Newman, Michael. "BlackBerry preserve", *e-Company*, September 2000.

[72] Newman, Michael. "BlackBerry preserve", *e-Company*, September 2000.

[73] Holstein, William J. "Moving beyond the PC," *U.S. News and World Report*, 12 December, 1999.

[74] Nickell, Joe Ashbrrok, and Michele Yamada. "Exporting Japan's revolution," *The Industry Standard*, 5 February, 2001.

[75] Nickell, Joe Ashbrrok, and Michele Yamada. "Exporting Japan's revolution," *The Industry Standard*, 5 February, 2001.

[76] Nickell, Joe Ashbrrok, and Michele Yamada. "Exporting Japan's revolution," *The Industry Standard*, 5 February, 2001.

[77] Nickell, Joe Ashbrrok, and Michele Yamada. "Exporting Japan's revolution," *The Industry Standard*, 5 February, 2001.

[78] Nickell, Joe Ashbrrok, and Michele Yamada. "Exporting Japan's revolution," *The Industry Standard*, 5 February, 2001.

[79] Larimer, Tim. "Internet a la i-Mode," *Time Magazine*, 5 March, 2001.

[80] Gomes, Lee. "The wireless world- in English," *The Wall Street Journal*, 11 December, 2000.

[81] Larimer, Tim. "Internet a la i-Mode," *Time Magazine*, 5 March, 2001.

[82] Gomes, Lee. "The wireless world- in English," *The Wall Street Journal*, 11 December, 2000.

[83]Larimer, Tim. "Internet a la i-Mode," *Time Magazine*, 5 March, 2001.

[84]Romeo, Simon. "Weak reception," *The New York Times*, 29 January, 2001.

[85]Romeo, Simon. "Weak reception," *The New York Times*, 29 January, 2001, citing International Telecommunications Union.

[86]Hamilton, David. "Going Places". *The Wall Street Journal*, 11 December, 2000.

[87]Yang, Catherine, Ronald Glover, and Ann Therese Palmer. "AOL Time Warner: Showtime!" *Business Week*, 15 January, 2001, pgs 57–64.

[88]Yang, Catherine, Ronald Glover, and Ann Therese Palmer. "AOL Time Warner: Showtime!" *Business Week*, 15 January, 2001, pgs 57–64.

[89]Yang, Catherine, Ronald Glover, and Ann Therese Palmer. "AOL Time Warner: Showtime!" *Business Week*, 15 January, 2001, p. 57.

[90]Elliott, Stuart. "Ready or not, the future is big and bundled," *The New York Times*, 13 November, 2000.

[91]Nathan, John. *Sony: The Private Life,* Boston: Houghton Mifflin, 1999, pg. 106, 144 and 183.

[92]Nathan, John. *Sony: The Private Life,* Boston: Houghton Mifflin, 1999, p. 321.

# Public Policy: Regulation

Government regulation has encountered new challenges with the emergence of the Internet. This chapter will discuss the impact the Internet has on both current and future legislation. We will look at how the new technology and lack of physical boundaries have forced governments to examine their current laws at both the local and federal level.

Public policy can have a very serious impact on businesses. By either outlawing certain activities, or imposing regulations that can cost a company hundreds of thousands of dollars for compliance, the government can either help a company grow or cripple it. Because of this impact, this chapter looks at the current legislation not only as a governmental issue, but as a very real issue for businesses as well.

## QUESTIONS

*Please consider the following questions as you read this chapter:*

1. How is the Internet currently regulated?

2. What are the challenges the Internet has brought to regulation?

3. What are the main regulation issues on the Internet today?

4. How are the United States and Europe working together to regulate the Internet?

---

This chapter was coauthored by Bernie Jaworski, Jeffrey Rayport, and JoAnn Kienzle.

# INTRODUCTION

While public policy is the last issue we will cover in this book, it should in no way be an afterthought when starting an e-commerce business. Napster and MP3.com have lost millions of dollars because of rulings against them in the courts, many content sites could have their sole revenue source—personalized advertising— threatened if strict privacy laws are passed in Congress, and many commerce sites could lose valuable customers if the Internet Tax Freedom Act is not renewed and states decide customers must pay sales tax on their online purchases.

The Internet presents many challenges to government regulation. Throughout the world, countries must decide not only how to regulate, but how much to regulate. Plus, they must decide who should regulate the Internet within their own boundaries and how to regulate the Internet with other countries as well. In this chapter, we will focus mostly on regulation within the United States. While there are different laws in other countries, the main issue is basically the same—governments are trying to figure out how to regulate the Internet without hurting their economies, but also without infringing on the rights of the citizens and businesses that exist within their borders.

In this chapter, we will also focus on regulation issues that affect e-commerce companies, rather than ISP providers or software developers.

# HOW IS THE INTERNET CURRENTLY REGULATED?

So far, there have been few laws passed in the United States intended to regulate the Internet (Table 16-1 provides a brief overview of Internet regulation). The following list cites some of the reasons:

- The Internet was born without regulation, it has thrived without regulation, and regulation would only stifle its growth.
- The Internet has stimulated the U.S. economy, and regulation could hurt the Internet businesses responsible for that growth.

**Table 16-1** LAWS REGULATING THE INTERNET

| Issue | Year | Law |
|---|---|---|
| Privacy | 1998 | Children's Online Privacy Protection Act (COPPA) |
| Intellectual Property - Copyright | 1998 | Digital Millennium Copyright Act |
| Intellectual Property - Trademark | 1999 | Anti Cyber-Squatting Consumer Protection Act |
| Taxation | 1998 | Internet Tax Freedom Act |
| Gambling | | |
| Free Speech | | |

- The Internet has no physical borders, making it extremely difficult to regulate—if a site set up in Australia breaks the U.S.'s rules, what right does the U.S. have to shut it down?
- Because the Internet changes so rapidly and new technology is constantly being developed, it would be impossible for the government to stay on top of all of the issues; by the time the president signed a law regulating a certain technology, it would be obsolete.

While the first two reasons certainly have their supporters, the last two present the biggest challenges for those who want to regulate the Internet.

Adding to the complexity is that there is no single governing body that oversees the Internet. There are as many different departments and commissions as there are issues. So far, the Federal Trade Commission (FTC) has been handling the privacy issues, the U.S. Copyright Office enforces copyright laws, and free speech (First Amendment) issues have been fought out in the courts. To make things even more confusing, issues such as sales tax and gambling are decided by each state, so there can be as many as 50 laws for each issue. This means that in order to create new laws or change any existing federal or state laws, an incredible amount of debate occurs for each public policy issue: Opinions can come from the department currently handling the issue, the legislature, judicators, president, society, and businesses.

Interestingly enough, many Internet businesses welcome this gridlock. They believe that government regulations would only restrict them by making them comply with laws. While the government debates the privacy issue, e-commerce businesses are selling customer information. While states debate the sales-tax issue, e-tailers have an advantage over their offline counterparts.

# WHAT ARE THE CHALLENGES THE INTERNET HAS BROUGHT TO REGULATION?

## Overview

The new technology and lack of physical borders associated with the Internet are changing the way we are looking at existing laws. While new technology allows businesses and consumers new freedoms, it also poses problems to regulation. While being able to easily download digital-quality music files off the Internet is a great capability for consumers to have, it poses a challenge to existing copyright laws, which were written when materials were harder to copy and, especially for sound files, the copy was often of inferior quality. The Internet's lack of physical borders raises the question of whose laws should be applied to certain transactions. If a consumer is sitting at a computer in California, connected to a server in Massachusetts, buying something from a business in Iowa, where does the transaction take place? Whose sales tax should that person pay? If an American goes to a French website, which country's free-speech laws should she follow?

In this section we will discuss the five biggest issues affecting Internet regulation today: privacy, intellectual property, taxation, gambling, and free speech. While privacy and intellectual property are affected by the issue of new technology, taxation and gambling are affected more by the lack of physical borders. Free speech, one of the United States' most protected freedoms, is affected by both.

We will discuss each issue in four parts. First, we will give an overview of the issue; next we will discuss the current status of Internet regulation. Then we will discuss legislation on the subject still in the pipeline. We will end by discussing the impact that this issue will have on the future of e-commerce companies, consumers, and the government.

# Privacy

**Overview.** In *Database Nation: The Death of Privacy in the 21ˢᵗ Century*,[1] Simson Garfinkel points out that 30 years ago, the Nixon administration created a commission to study the impact of computers on privacy. They drafted the **Code of Fair Information Practices**, a set of rules that stated: (1) there should be no secret data banks of personal information; (2) if your name or personal information is in a data bank, you should have the right to see it; (3) if your records contain errors, you should have the right to correct them; (4) information collected for one purpose should not be used for other purposes without the consent of the person who is the subject of the information; and (5) organizations should protect information in their possession (for example, organizations should limit access to authorized individuals and ensure that false information is not intentionally added).

Due to the Watergate scandal and changing presidents, no law was ever enacted that supported those guidelines. Perhaps if it had, many of the battles being fought today over privacy on the Internet would be moot, since many of those battles are based on the very principles in the Code of Fair Information Practices. Instead, we are at a crossroads. The government originally expected the industry to regulate itself, with privacy policies and seals of approval from companies such as TRUSTe (see Drill-Down, "Online Privacy Seals"). But as more and more dot-coms are struggling to make a profit, they are finding that their customer database is one of their biggest assets, and many companies are doing less and less self-regulating. Therefore, consumers are becoming more and more concerned about the privacy of their information.

**Current Status.** So far, there has been only one law passed that specifically protects privacy on the Internet, and it pertains only to children. The 1998 Children's Online Privacy Protection Act (COPPA) requires websites to get permission from children's parents before using the child's information if the child is under the age of 13 (see Drill-Down, "Children's Privacy"). Current laws may eventually have an effect on privacy and the Internet. For instance, financial services legislation gives states the latitude to enact tough financial privacy laws and limit how financial companies use their customers' data. While this legislation was intended for offline companies, it will also have an effect on how online financial companies use customer data.

In August 2000, the Federal Trade Commission (FTC) submitted to Congress its report on online profiling by e-commerce firms. The report accepted the proposal of the Network Advertising Initiative (NAI), which stated that its members would not use "personally identifiable information about sensitive medical or financial data, information of a sexual nature, or Social Security numbers for marketing purposes." The proposal also stated that privacy policies must be "clear and conspicuous" and advertisers had to give "robust" notice before they combined a user's click-track data with any of their personal information. Furthermore, if the user protested, the advertiser had to give the user the option to "opt-out."[2]

The state governments have been more active in taking action against what they view as privacy violations. In June 2000, the Michigan attorney general formally notified several U.S. websites that the state may file lawsuits against them unless the sites' privacy policies explained how they share visitors' information with advertising services such as AdForce, DoubleClick, MatchLogic, and Netscape Communications.[3] Also, in September 2000, Missouri filed suit against More.com, claiming the health and nutrition retailer shared customer information with third parties in direct conflict with its stated privacy policy.

As we will discuss later in this chapter, the United States' approach to privacy on the Internet is very different than Europe's approach. In Europe, where there are stricter laws protecting privacy in general, most governments require marketing programs to be **opt-in**, which allow the customers to choose to have their information shared with others in exchange for more personalized sites, marketing, and special offers. In the United States, almost all websites have **opt-out** options, which force customers to actively find out how to exit a company's marketing program, if there are any options at all (see Point-Counterpoint, "Opt-In vs. Opt-Out").

***Public Opinion.*** Perhaps the most difficult part of the privacy debate is gauging public opinion. Many surveys suggest that people are overwhelmingly concerned about privacy on the Internet. According to a Fox News/Opinion Dynamics Poll, 91 percent of Web users believe their personal information on the Internet is not secure; according to a 1999 Jupiter Communications report, nearly two-thirds of consumers distrust online privacy policies. A survey by Yankelovich Partners found that 90 percent of respondents considered privacy protection the most important issue of the Internet, and 46 percent thought the government needs to regulate privacy more carefully.

However, a survey done by The Pew Internet & American Life Project found that, although 54 percent of online users believe that a website's tracking of users is harmful because it invades their privacy, over half of those online do not know how that information is tracked, and only 5 percent of users have used "anonymizing" software, which hides their computer identity from websites they visit. While most consumers are at least somewhat concerned about their privacy on the Internet, many have not even taken the time to learn how to protect it.

Also, despite their fears, many users seek very personal information and conduct personal transactions on the Internet. And each year the number of these users increases. Table 16-2 shows how the range of personal activities that users do on the Internet has increased, despite the threat to their privacy. In an America Online/Roper Starch study,[4] 94 percent of Internet users said that privacy was "very important" (only 3 percent responded that it was only somewhat important). If 94 percent say privacy is very important, but 19 percent of users still keep their personal calendars online, there is obviously some sort of conflict.

It remains to be seen if the conflict comes from people becoming more concerned as they see Internet companies viewing their personal information as an asset, or if consumers are concerned about privacy, but not enough to give up the advantages the Internet has brought to their lives.

One thing is certain: Privacy advocates are in no way satisfied with the current governmental attitude toward regulation. Even when the FTC recommended its guidelines to Congress, many privacy advocates believed the guidelines were not enough. The Electronic Privacy Information Center responded: "We do not see why Internet advertisers, who could create far more detailed profiles of the personal lives of Americans than any of the sectors currently subject to legislation, should be able to escape the fundamental obligations that would otherwise be established by law."

Orson Swindle, the commissioner of the FTC, spoke out against the FTC's recommendation of the guidelines, calling the decision "embarrassingly flawed."[5]

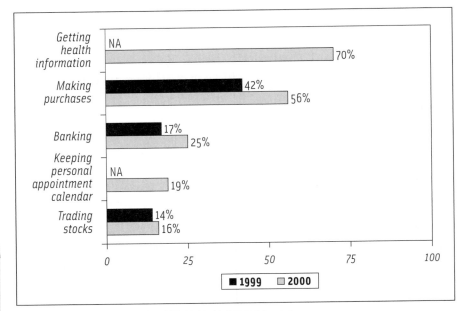

| Table 16-2 | PRIVATE ACTIVITIES AMERICANS DO ONLINE |
|---|---|

Getting health information — NA / 70%

Making purchases — 42% / 56%

Banking — 17% / 25%

Keeping personal appointment calendar — NA / 19%

Trading stocks — 14% / 16%

■ 1999    □ 2000

Source: The America Online/Roper Starch Worldwide Adult 2000 Cyberstudy

Many Internet executives believe that if the privacy advocates get their way and strict regulations on data gathering are enforced, it could mean the end of the Internet. "You wouldn't have the Internet without advertising," says Kevin Ryan, president of DoubleClick. He and others fear that regulation would result in a world where every website requires visitors to sign in—and then bills them for access.

Others believe that the public's fear of what companies are doing with their information comes from a lack of information. "This is the future. We're going to get more targeted, and data drives advertising," says Bruce Carlisle, CEO of SF Interactive marketing agency. "But there's a backlash right now, and the industry needs to educate the public and policy makers." And that is just what DoubleClick has done by announcing a privacy-education campaign and setting up a website that informs people of their rights and allows them to opt-out of DoubleClick's monitoring.[6]

***How Businesses Are Dealing with the Privacy Issue.*** Businesses have responded in very different ways to the lack of government regulation and growing public concern over privacy. Some have tightened their privacy policies to assuage consumers' concerns, while others have loosened their privacy policies to afford them more room to leverage customer data.

In September 2000, Internet travel site Expedia.com expanded its privacy policy to give consumers more control over their personal information. Under the revised policy, the company will not sell or rent customer information, and customers have the ability to add, change, or remove any personal identifiers from the site. Expedia also hired accounting firm PricewaterhouseCoopers to verify whether the company was following its written privacy policy, and it passed the audit.

At the other end of the spectrum, Amazon.com, in August 2000, changed its privacy policy, revealing that the company "might sell or buy stores or assets. In such

## Children's Privacy

In 1998, the FTC implemented the Children's Online Privacy Protection Act (COPPA), which stipulates two separate methods of obtaining parental consent: more reliable and less reliable. The more reliable ways include getting consent through postal mail, fax, use of a credit card, a phone call, or a digital signature. Less reliable methods are only necessary for sites that intend to sell or post user data. The less reliable methods will no longer be available in April 2002, at which point companies can only gain consent through more reliable ways.[7]

Businesses claim that the cost of complying with the COPPA is too high. Some websites, such as Zeek.com, have spent over $100,000 to change their site in accordance with the law, only to see a 20 percent decline in traffic.[8] Furthermore, Zeek.com estimates that it will cost $200,000 a year to comply with the law. Just hiring a lawyer to evaluate a company's privacy practices can cost between $10,000–$20,000, and that is before actually taking any action.

Some sites have decided to simply change their objectives to avoid the cost—about one quarter of websites have stopped collecting information on children altogether, while some websites have changed to only allow children 13 and over on their site, so they are no longer affected by the law. The marketplace is also changing. A new company called WiredKids has started, which acts as a central repository allowing parents to fill out one permission slip to be used at various sites, making it easier for both the parents and the companies to conform to the law.

But what happens when parents are the ones who want to know what their children are doing on the Internet? In New Hampshire in November 2000, James Knight won a suit against his school district when he asked to see the logs that listed the sites the users in the school system were visiting. He originally asked for the logs when he received notice from his children's school that the school system would not be monitoring which sites the students accessed—their policy was to trust the children to do what was appropriate. When the school system refused to show the logs to Knight, citing privacy concerns, he took them to court, saying he had a right to see the logs under the "Right-to-Know" act.[9]

And then there are the parents who use the technology to keep track of their children. From keeping in touch with pagers and cellphones, to giving their children credit cards that send an e-mail to the parent every time the credit card is being used, to using devices within their Internet browsers to track their children's movements on the Internet, parents are finding that the very devices that give their children freedoms they never had as children, also give the parents information their parents never had when they were young.[10]

---

transactions, customer information generally is one of the transferred business assets. Also, in the unlikely event that Amazon.com Inc., or substantially all of its assets are acquired, customer information will of course be one of the transferred assets."[11] Amazon also indicated that it buys information about customers from unnamed sources. Amazon's contention is that customer information is its intellectual property, which can be sold or shared as the company changes through mergers, acquisitions, or other routes. Many believe Amazon's revision of its privacy policy was done in case, under pressure to show a profit, it decided to sell its customer data.

When Toysmart filed for bankruptcy in June 2000, it listed its customer database as one of its assets, even though its privacy policy had ensured its customers that it would never disclose their information to any third party. Though the FTC approved a settlement that would allow Toysmart to sell its customer list, a federal judge denied the motion because of the conflict with its privacy policy. CraftShop.com also came under fire when it, too, contradicted its privacy policy, which stated that it would never share its customer database with a third party, and tried to list its customer list as an asset. CraftShop.com believes that it can use the database if it is acquired, since the new company would be a parent company, not a third party.

Even the federal government came under fire when it was found that not only did its own websites not conform to the privacy policy standards endorsed by the FTC, but those websites aimed at kids did not follow COPPA's restrictions and were compiling information on children under 13. The government countered that it was not required to adhere to the FTC's standards and did adhere to the privacy policy set by the Office of Management Budget of the Clinton administration. Nevertheless, the criticized government sites have started to modify their data-gathering policies.

**Proposed Legislation.** It has been estimated that over a hundred bills regarding privacy on the Internet are currently in Congress. Most—such as Boucher's Internet Growth and Development Act in the House of Representatives and a bill sponsored by Senators John McCain and John Kerry—generally follow the FTC's guidelines, proposing that websites be required to have clear privacy policies. These bills advocate that websites let customers know what data the company is collecting, inform them about what the company intends to do with that data, and give customers a chance to opt-out of having the company share that data with third parties.

A bill sponsored by Senator Ernest F. Hollings has won the support of many consumer advocates because it would require sites to obtain permission from visitors (opt-in) before collecting any personal data that could be used to identify them in the future and allows anonymous information to be used for marketing purposes only if the user consents. Another bill, sponsored by Senators Conrad Burns and Ron Wyden, falls between Hollings' and McCain's bills because it gives consumers the chance to view and modify their data and provides stiffer penalties for violators.

**Impact.** While many Internet companies are afraid of government regulation, which they believe could curb their revenue by limiting the amount of information they can collect or preventing them from selling their customer databases, they might actually suffer more if the government does not get involved and consumers' fears of having their privacy invaded keep them off the Internet. Forrester Research estimates that consumer fears about privacy resulted in almost $3 billion in lost online retail sales in 1999, approximately 10 percent of what shoppers spent last year. A Cognitiative survey found that of 250 people who do not shop on the Internet, 65 percent said they do not because of concerns about privacy. Some companies have even reacted by creating a new position: chief privacy officer (see Drill-Down, "Chief Privacy Officers").

No matter what the government does in the next few years, some things are certain: Some will like it, others will not, and it will have an impact on how Internet companies are run and, perhaps more importantly, how revenue on the Internet is generated.

# Intellectual Property

**Overview.** The most notable area in which intellectual property has been changed by the Internet is through copyright. While **trademarks** and **patents** have also been affected (see the "Trademarks" and "Patents" Drill-Downs), copyright law has proved to be the biggest and most immediate challenge for Internet businesses and consumers today.

## Opt-Out Vs. Opt-In

Opt-in is the standard European policy that requires consumers to ask to be involved in data collection and marketing, while opt-out companies automatically include customers in data collection practices unless a customer specifically asks to not be included. Proponents of opt-in contend that users should be able to choose whether or not they want to participate before any data is collected. Opt-in forces companies to be more up-front about what information they are collecting and how they will use it since they have to get the consumer's approval first. Furthermore, companies that are opt-out rarely make their data-gathering processes obvious; if consumers do not realize that they can opt-out or if they are unaware that any data is being gathered, then the option to opt-out does not help them. Since it is in a company's best interest to make it difficult for consumers to opt-out (that way they have more consumer information to sell) they cannot be trusted to give consumers the proper amount of information.

Proponents of opt-out point out that, even when consumers know how to opt-out, few of them do. They believe that, since selling data to advertisers and marketers is often the only source of revenue many online companies have, forcing an opt-in policy on all websites would cause the closure of many content sites and, therefore, would hurt the growth of the Internet.

## Online Privacy Seals

By Matt Villano, contributor to tnbt.com

Think a consumer's personal information stays private on every website she visits? Think again. Website visitors typically have no assurance of privacy—that is, unless they visit sites that boast tiny icons known as privacy seals. The question is: Do the seals comfort customers enough to make them happy to shop and surf?

Like badges of courage, privacy seals indicate that a third party has deemed a site safe. Only two organizations distribute the seals—BBBOnLine, a Better Business Bureau subsidiary, and TRUSTe, an independent, non-profit based in San Jose, California—but more than 2,500 companies display them, and that number rises steadily each year. Privacy on the Internet is nothing new, but for the first time in their brief history, the organizations that distribute seals are beginning to gain respect among companies within the Web community. Finally, it seems, the seals once assailed by critics as "meaningless" are carrying some weight.

"What would you rather have—a site that guarantees your information is safe or a site that doesn't?" asks Gary Laden, director of the BBB's Online Privacy Program, based in Washington, D.C. "The reasons for emphasizing privacy are numerous and straightforward." As Laden suggests, the idea behind these programs is simple: Companies sign up for regulatory nods by submitting their privacy policies for scrutiny and approval. In return for an annual fee, seal organizations evaluate the policies one by one, matching them up against a predetermined set of rigorous specifications. If a company's policy meets these

(continued on page 584)

*(continued from page 583)*

specifications, it gets a seal. If a policy fails to meet the requirements, the organization informs that company's officials what they need to do to be better.

Logistically, the BBBOnLine and TRUSTe programs are almost identical. While BBBOnLine, founded in March 1999, promotes the BBB's famous standards for openness and honesty, TRUSTe, founded in June 1997, rewards sites that give users the ability to correct inaccuracies in their information and to choose whether they want their data shared. (TRUSTe's membership is roughly 2,000; BBBOnLine's membership is 600.) Both sites stress security, both conduct periodic impromptu privacy checks of member organizations and both charge annual fees for membership (ranging from $75 to $4,999 a year, depending on a company's revenues). Perhaps most importantly, both programs allow users to file complaints if they feel their privacy has been violated or abused.

"We believe the company is doing what they say they're doing," says TRUSTe spokesman David Steer. "We offer a dispute resolution service if you believe they're not."

These services are not, however, without controversy. Marc Rotenberg, director of the Washington, D.C.-based Electronic Privacy Information Center, criticizes the redress aspect of the programs from the beginning, emphasizing the fact that neither hands out serious penalties to sites that violate consumers' privacy. Sure, Rotenberg says, these programs let users file complaints, but if a complaint is found to be accurate, the only penalty is dismissal from the program as a whole. What's more, Rotenberg insists that companies tend to focus simply on having privacy policies—not on developing policies that work well.

Still, executives at companies that have latched on to privacy-seal programs say that among consumers, having a seal makes a big difference. Excite's chief privacy officer Chris Kelley says the seal program has been "terrific," and admits he receives numerous e-mails from customers who say the seal on Excite's site makes them more comfortable. At New York-based teen portal Bolt.com, company spokesperson Elvin Can says parents can "rest easy" that the information their children submit never leaves the server room.

With this kind of support from participating businesses, Steer says he doesn't pay much attention to critics. Instead, both he and Laden say they plan to continue to grow their programs, adding more members on a regular basis until the end of the year. In the wake of the European Union's recent privacy directive, which requires advance consent from a consumer before information can be collected, Laden says the next big issue will be global privacy—and seals that protect and ensure it.

"The Internet is borderless," he says. "Now that we've developed a program to reward privacy policies here in the U.S., it's time to turn our gaze elsewhere."

*Read more articles about The Next Big Thing at www.tnbt.com*

---

**Copyright** is not intended to give the creator of a work blanket ownership and control of his or her work. Rather, it is meant to strike a balance between protecting a creator's work and letting the public use it so that both can prosper. Justice Sandra Day O'Connor noted:

> The primary objective of copyright is not to reward the labor of authors, but "[t]o promote the Progress of Science and useful Arts." To this end, copyright assures authors the right to their original expressions, but encourages others to build freely upon the ideas and information conveyed by a work. This result is neither unfair nor unfortunate. It is the means by which copyright advances the progress of science and art.[12]

While it can be debated whether or not pirating a copy of the latest pop single is infringing on "useful arts," there is no doubt that, without copyright laws, many businesses and industries would not be able to survive. So far, it is mostly the music industry that has grappled with the copyright issues raised by new technology. However, all companies that create intellectual property—whether it be film, books, software, or sewing patterns—will sooner or later confront the copyright issue.

## Current Status.

There are three main aspects to copyright laws that affect the Internet: the Copyright Act of 1976, Fair Use Doctrine (part of the Copyright Act of 1976), and the Digital Millennium Copyright Act (DMCA). The Copyright Act of 1976 protects literary, musical, dramatic, motion picture, and architectural works, as well as sound recordings. It gives the owner of the copyright the ability to, among other things, reproduce the work, create derivative works based on that work, distribute copies of the work, and perform the work publicly.[13]

The Copyright Act, though, also gives the public the right to **fair use** of the work. Under fair use, people can use the work for educational, critical, commentary, reporting, or parody purposes. A person can also use the work if he or she creates a new work of value, only uses a small amount so that it does not constitute most of the work, or does not have an impact on the market for the original.

The **Digital Millennium Copyright Act** was signed into law in 1998 by President Clinton. While the law is complicated and has many provisions, there are two main parts of interest for most businesses. The first is the implementation of provisions in the World Intellectual Property Organization (WIPO) treaties that prohibit the circumvention of copyright protection systems. This part makes it a crime for someone to go around a "technological protection measure" that was created by the copyright owner to keep people from stealing the work. The second part states that a copyright owner cannot hold an online service provider liable if one of its subscribers infringes on the owner's copyright. In order to be protected, though, the online service provider must agree to remove the infringing material and/or terminate the subscriber as soon as it becomes aware of the infringement.[14]

As discussed in Chapter 14, MP3 files are digital sound files that are smaller than conventional sound files, and therefore easier to download. These files have caused problems for the record industry. With the advent of Napster's music-sharing application (See Drill-Down, "Napster"), it has become easier not only for users to download music, but to find files from strangers and download them. While before it would have taken time for someone to make a copy of a CD on a cassette tape (where there would also be a loss of sound quality), digital music, MP3 files, and file-swapping applications all converged to make it easy for millions of Internet users to swap pirated music with one another. With MP3 and Napster, one copy had the potential to become millions of copies at digital or near-digital quality.

This threat has caused the recording industry to go on the offensive, filing suits against My.MP3.com and Napster. It has also created alliances between record companies and Internet companies, as the offline music industry tries to evaluate the optimal way to access the millions of music lovers on the Internet. Another outcome from this battle has been the emergence of new digital rights management technology, which is expected to be able to stamp each file with an identifying number and watermark, ensure that the file goes through approved channels, and track where the file goes. Record companies hope this technology will enable them to offer their products online, without having to risk unauthorized copying.

## Proposed Legislation.

So far, the courts have leaned toward the copyright holders, so, as a balance, much of the proposed legislation protects Internet users. Laws that would allow users to make digital recordings of CDs they have purchased and store them on the Internet have been suggested, and bills allowing companies to do the

# Chief Privacy Officers

By Joseph Daniel McCool, contributor to tnbt.com

Increasing numbers of American consumers are becoming point-and-click purchasers. But their conversion to e-commerce may be fleeting unless companies can assure them that their privacy will be protected—in other words, that their personal data will not be sold, shared, or in any way used without their knowledge and permission.

Enter a new breed of corporate executive: the CPO, as in chief (or corporate) privacy officer.

Computer-privacy experts have already assumed CPO roles at companies such as American Express, Go.com, Delta Airlines, and Dun & Bradstreet. Many are being hired from universities, or promoted from government-affairs, corporate-counsel, and consumer-policy positions within the firms themselves.

"In this environment, every consumer-oriented company should seriously consider appointing a corporate privacy officer to help guide the company in developing and implementing fair information practices," says David Medine, associate director of the Federal Trade Commission's financial practices division.

The CPO helps a company set its consumer privacy policies and monitor their enforcement. He or she scrutinizes potential business deals for potential violations of those policies and educates employees about their practical application.

CPOs have been gaining corporate influence as more consumers realize that technology can track their every move on the Internet—and more companies realize that breaching customers' confidence can have legal repercussions. (Perhaps the highest-profile privacy suit pending is that brought by the FTC against now-defunct Toysmart.com, which tried to sell its customer database—along with other assets—despite previous promises to shield its customers' privacy.)

"Privacy is now a top-tier issue with consumers online and offline," says Alan F. Westin, a consumer-privacy expert and author who has founded a training course and trade group for CPOs. "Within a short time, every sensible company will have a CPO on its management team." Earlier this year, Microsoft raised both the profile and scope of its consumer-privacy protection initiative by elevating Richard Purcell from data-protection manager to director of corporate privacy, a role that now has him reporting directly to the company's chief operating officer. Purcell had worked in his lower-level privacy-control position for three years before his promotion. Now, he has the power to set company policy and reject any deal that might conceivably expose Microsoft customers' personal information—and/or create legal or public-relations problems for the company.

Purcell says his appointment represents "a transition to an active corporate stance on privacy."

"It is no longer a case of defensive risk management," he notes, "but recognition that privacy is a product that establishes our organization's credibility and trust with consumers and society."

*Read more articles about The Next Big Thing at www.tnbt.com*

---

same thing have been drafted. Senator Orrin Hatch, a songwriter himself, has been a vocal legislative proponent of both users and copyright holders, supporting Napster only because he feared that users would go to decentralized systems like Gnutella and FreeNet. The biggest question is whether the courts will continue to find in favor of the companies suing for copyright infringement, or if they will start leaning the other way, trying to maintain the balance between copyright holder and consumer.

**Impact.** The impact of copyright law on the Internet has yet to be fully felt. Since the courts have mostly sided with the copyright owners, the websites that have infringed on copyrights have been the most affected. In its court battles, Napster insisted its existence was not detrimental to the record industry by showing evidence that CD sales went up by $500 million in 2000, when Napster was going

# Patents

In 1998, a federal appellate court ruling upheld "the right of inventors to patent methods of doing business if those ideas were new and not obvious."[15] This ability given to companies to patent business models has changed the patent landscape. The year of that ruling, patent applications rose from 925 from the year before to 1,300, and then rose steadily, reaching around 7,500 in 2000.[16]

This ability to patent business models has worried many critics. When Amazon was awarded two patents for its "1-Click" technology (which allowed returning customers to purchase items without having to reenter their information) critics complained that the patent was unnecessary and hurt other businesses. Even Jeff Bezos agreed that the patent system needed to be updated for the Internet age—he issued a letter saying that, while he was certainly going to keep his patents, he did think that patents for software and business methods should be cut down from 17 to 3 to

5 years. Bezos, however, still sued Barnes & Noble.com for patent infringement.

In October 2000, Representatives Rich Boucher and Howard Berman introduced the Business Method Patent Improvement Act of 2000, which would "create the presumption that the computer-assisted implementation of an analog-world business method is obvious and thus not patentable." The bill would also include an "opposition procedure" that would give the public a chance to challenge the award of a business-method patent.[17] While the outcome of this particular bill remains to be seen, it seems certain that Congress and the courts are beginning to question the validity of business-method patents. On February 14, 2001, the U.S. Court of Appeals for the Federal Circuit told Barnes & Noble.com that it could continue to use its single-step ordering process, citing that "Barnes & Noble has mounted a serious legal challenge to the validity of Amazon's patent."[18]

# Trademarks

As the Internet grew more popular in the late 1990s, a new type of "entrepreneur" emerged—the cybersquatter. Cybersquatters registered domain names of famous corporations and people with the hope that the party would pay large amounts of money for the privilege of using the URL. And, during the initial Internet frenzy, companies were willing to pay: Bank of America bought Loans.com for $3 million and eCompanies bought Business.com for $7.5 million.

In December 1999, President Clinton signed a law that banned cybersquatters from intentionally registering names that are already trademarked. But trademark suits continue, mostly now among small and medium-size companies that cannot easily claim

license to the domain name. To win a suit, the offended person or company must either prove that consumers will be confused by the site or—when the trademark is famous enough—that the site will dilute the distinctive quality of the trademark. In October 2000, singer Madonna was able to win the right to use Madonna.com, a site that had been an adult-entertainment portal site. The Internet Corporation for Assigned Names and Numbers (ICANN)—one of the regulating bodies for domain names—agreed with Madonna.[19]

With proposed new top-level domain names such as .biz, .info, .name being added, trademark suits are sure to rage on, and ICANN will have to decide if Madonna also has the right to Madonna.biz and Madonna.name.

strong. The Recording Industry Association of America, however, contends that the purchase of singles went down by 38 percent in 2000 because so many people were swapping pirated singles from Napster.[20] A Forrester report confirms the idea that the record companies would be hurt, rather than helped, by file-swapping sites. It concluded that the recording industry stands to lose $3.1 billion by 2005.

## DRILL-DOWN

# Napster

 We have discussed Napster in every section of this book. This Internet phenomenon embodies everything unique and exciting about the Internet—the rise of a company started by an 18-year-old who, frustrated that he could not find good MP3 files on the Internet, wrote his own program and revolutionized an industry; the questions surrounding how a company that has 51 million users and no revenue stream can survive; and the fall of a company that believed it could beat a copyright infringement case filed by the record industry.

Napster is, by far, the most publicized test of copyright law on the Internet. As described in Chapter 14, Napster is a music-sharing application that allows users to search other users' hardrives for MP3 files, and then download the files directly from the other users' computers instead of through the Internet—a faster and more efficient way (see Exhibit 16-1). Napster Inc. was founded in May 1999, and a copyright-infringement suit led by the Recording Industry Association of America (RIAA) was filed in December of that same year.

The RIAA claimed that Napster was infringing on copyright by knowingly allowing its users to find other users' MP3 files over its servers and giving the users the technology needed to easily download them onto their own computers. Napster countered, saying that because of the way its system was set up, with no copyrighted material on its server, Napster itself was not guilty of copyright infringement. Furthermore, its users were covered by the fair use doctrine and by the 1992 Audio Home Recording Act that allows for non-commercial copying of music (since Napster's not making any money off of it). Napster also claimed that they were protected under the DMCA.

The next 14 months brought varying degrees of legal success to the RIAA. In March 2001, as this book goes to print, a federal judge prohibited Napster from engaging in or facilitating the trading of copyrighted songs. The record labels must provide Napster with artist name, song title, file names, and proof of copyright ownerships.[21]

While the RIAA has won the first major battle in the copyright wars, other file-sharing software has popped up since it filed suit against Napster, including Gnutella, FreeNet, and Scour. While Napster had a central server that users went through to find the files, Gnutella and FreeNet do not, and are, therefore, much more difficult to control. What is becoming increasingly apparent is that the record companies are better off embracing the new technology and benefiting from it than from fighting its use. It is clear that users will find a way to get what they want, whether or not the record companies step up to the plate and help consumers access digital music. While most of the major record labels announced in 2000 that they were launching initiatives to distribute music on the Web, as of March 2001, those offerings have yet to be seen.

Chances are, even with all the publicized court cases, Napster will not change copyright law. Instead, it will be an example of a company that should have tried to work more with the copyright holders instead of simply trying to beat them in court. Ultimately, the biggest impact that Napster will have is how it has changed the way the music industry views its consumers. In an interview with *Time* magazine, Hillary Rosen, RIAA's CEO, admitted that, even if they won against Napster, the landscape is changing:

> In the pre-Internet era, Rosen observes, the electronics industry would select a new format for music—albums, cassettes, eight-tracks, or CDs. The record labels would record to that format, and consumers would buy the end product. "In the future, the cycle will be working backward," she says. "Consumers will be dictating the business models, and we'll be adopting them."[22]

Exhibit
16-1

## HOW NAPSTER WORKS

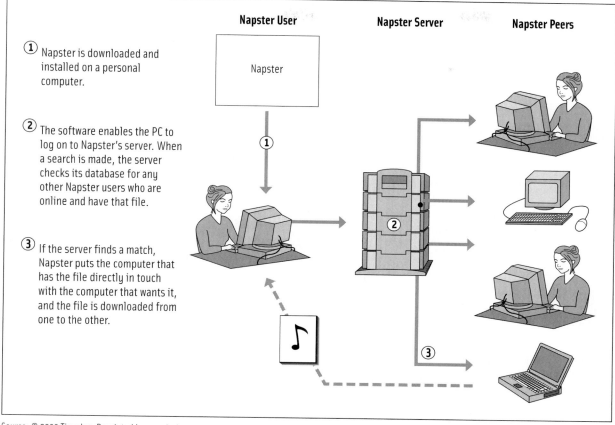

**Napster User**   **Napster Server**   **Napster Peers**

① Napster is downloaded and installed on a personal computer.

② The software enables the PC to log on to Napster's server. When a search is made, the server checks its database for any other Napster users who are online and have that file.

③ If the server finds a match, Napster puts the computer that has the file directly in touch with the computer that wants it, and the file is downloaded from one to the other.

Napster

Source: © 2000 Time Inc. Reprinted by permission

# Taxation

**Overview.** Even without the complexity of the virtual world, sales and use tax laws are not simple. There are currently over 36,000 state and local taxing jurisdictions in the United States, with approximately 7,000 of these jurisdictions imposing sales and use taxes. To add to the confusion, these taxes change from year to year. The current taxing structure requires the company to understand sales tax, nexus, use tax, and tax exemptions (which include knowledge of tax holidays, certain tax-exempt merchandise, or buyers who are tax-exempt through government or non-profit affiliation). Once the Internet is added into the equation, there can be up to 15 possible locations where tax may or may not be required: Variables include the location of the business, the location of the consumer, the location of the consumer's ISP, and the location of the company's server.[23]

While e-commerce companies benefit from being able to attract consumers who do not want to pay taxes, they also benefit from not having to pay the high costs associated with collecting sales tax in this current complicated system. In an attempt to simplify the current tax system and make it more Internet friendly, a coalition of states have begun work on the Streamline Sales Tax Project (see Drill-Down).

**Current Status.** In October 1998, the Internet Tax Freedom Act was enacted. Despite its name, this law does not free Internet companies from taxes. Rather, it restricts changes to current laws and limits new taxes from being imposed on e-commerce purchases and Net access. For now, Internet companies must impose the current sales taxes that apply to remote sales—laws that catalog companies have been adhering to for years. The law is currently up for renewal in Congress. If they do vote to renew it, the tax moratorium will be extended until 2006.

While purchasers enjoy being able to buy online without having to pay the same sales tax they would have to pay at their local store, offline stores have begun to protest. One of the biggest issues is that many bricks-and-mortar stores have started separate online companies, so their online counterparts do not have to charge sales tax in the same states that they—and their offline competitors—have stores. A bill that went before California Governor Gray Davis would have required that businesses that had both bricks-and-mortar stores in California and Internet counterparts charge sales tax for online purchases sent to residents in California. One of the lobbyists for the bill was the Northern California Bookseller's Association, protesting companies such as Borders.com and Barnes & Noble.com. The bill was vetoed by Governor Davis.[24]

While almost all online corporations support the tax moratorium, state and local governments are mostly against extending the moratorium because of the lost revenue. State governments are, however, wary of enacting laws that would push online companies out of their states and, therefore, take money away from the local economy.

**Proposed Legislation.** The Internet Tax Freedom Act is up for renewal. While the House Committee studying the problem recommended it be extended until 2005, whether or not that occurs remains to be seen. While the chances that the Streamline Sales Tax Project (SSTP) will be adopted are quite slim, proponents are hopeful that it will at least open up a dialogue for simplifying the tax system.

**Impact.** As far as consumption is concerned, the effect that an Internet sales tax would have remains to be seen. Preliminary evidence suggests it would be minimal. Table 16-3 shows the effect sales tax would have on users' online purchases. Basically, the higher the item's price tag, the more likely the user is to decide not to purchase the item online.

The biggest impact from the Internet tax issue would be felt by the states, who stand to lose considerable money if a sales tax law is not passed. As much as $12 billion may go uncollected if taxes on Internet transactions continue to be suspended. It is estimated that, by 2003, states such as California, New York, and Texas may each lose $1 billion in e-commerce sales tax each year (see Table 16-4).

## Gambling

**Overview.** Gambling laws rely on physical borders. Forty-seven states currently allow some form of gambling (Utah, Tennessee, and Hawaii being the hold-outs) whether it be physical casinos, state-run lotteries, or gambling nights for charity. The Internet poses a new challenge to gambling regulation because of the lack of borders. Unlike taxation, gambling poses ethical issues as well. While no one has ever had to seek treatment for an obsessive need to pay taxes, many believe gambling addiction is a problem that causes both psychological and financial hardship to addicts and their loved ones.

Though most people are able to gamble without becoming addicted, the National Gambling Impact Study Commission cited Internet gambling as problematic for potential addicts because of its ease and anonymity. The study reported that:

## Streamlined Sales Tax Project

**The Streamlined Sales Tax Project**, started in March 2000, is an attempt by tax administrators from 27 participating states and 12 observing states to simplify the tax system and make it easier for states to collect taxes. Its purpose is to "simplify and modernize sales and use tax administration" in the participating states. The SSTP has proposed many ways to simplify and unify the sales-tax laws. Some of their proposals include the following:

*Simplify state and local tax rates*, so that, after December 31, 2005, all local and state taxes are identical, unless prohibited by Federal law.

*Provide uniform sourcing rules* for all taxable transactions, so that the tax rate for the purchase of goods is based on the shipping address, and the tax rate for services is based on the billing address.

*Provide uniform definitions*, so that items such as "clothes," "delivery charges," and "food" are the same from state to state.

*Provide uniform tax returns* for businesses selling goods and services.[25]

Whether or not the SSTP will actually be adopted by the participating states—and whether or not a streamlined sales tax that only affects half the states can be effective—remains to be seen. Even simple points like agreeing on a uniform definition of candy can cause an argument among states. Because the states have had the power to decide on their taxes for so long, it will be difficult to get them to agree on anything. Still, the SSTP represents the first concerted effort among the states to simplify sales tax in order to make it easier to collect it. It still has a long way to go—the SSTP will have to first educate the states on how the tax system needs to be reformed, and then persuade them to do it.[26]

*Gambling on the Internet is especially enticing to youth, pathological gamblers, and criminals. There are currently no mechanisms in place to prevent youths— who make up the largest percentage of Internet users—from using their parents' credit card numbers to register and set up accounts. For pathological gamblers, the Internet's anonymity provides a shield from public scrutiny . . .[27]*

**Table 16-3**

IMPACT OF SALES TAX ON CONSUMERS

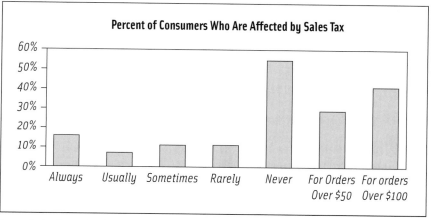

Source: Jupiter Communications, as cited in *The Industry Standard*, "Execs Say No Net Taxes," July 3, 2001.

Table
16-4
SALES TAX LOSS FORECAST—
TOP 10 STATES

| | 2000 | | 2003 | |
|---|---|---|---|---|
| | **All Remote Sales** | **Internet Sales** | **All Remote Sales** | **Internet Sales** |
| California | $298–$1,446 | $23–$533 | $686–$3,650 | $86–$1,720 |
| New York | $196–$889 | $22–$357 | $521–$2,339 | $81–$1,155 |
| Texas | $252–$992 | $26–$342 | $655–$2,446 | $96–$1,125 |
| Illinois | $117–$545 | $13–$212 | $298–$1,389 | $44–$671 |
| Florida | $120–$503 | $13–$179 | $321–$1,279 | $48–$595 |
| Pennsylvania | $102–$381 | $12–$156 | $281–$1,012 | $45–$505 |
| Ohio | $108–$357 | $11–$141 | $286–$955 | $43–$454 |
| New Jersey | $101–$346 | $10–$130 | $256–$879 | $37–$419 |
| Michigan | $109–$346 | $10–$125 | $276–$882 | $39–$415 |
| Washington | $82–$284 | $8–$98 | $213–$712 | $30–$326 |
| Total for all U.S. States | $6,100–$9,100 | $2,500–$3,800 | $13,600–$20,400 | $7,800–$12,400 |

Source: General Accounting Office Estimates, as cited in *The Industry Standard*, "The State of Net Tax Loss," August 14, 2000.

Despite these problems, the Commission went on to state that, since the parameters of Internet gambling have yet to be defined, and regulation of the industry would be costly, current efforts undertaken to regulate it could be "premature and unwarranted."

Another strike against Internet gambling: While casinos stimulate the local economy by enticing tourists and providing jobs, most gambling sites are not located in the United States and, therefore, only take money away from the U.S. Although 80 percent of Internet gamblers are American, many gambling sites have set up their offices outside of the United States in an effort to circumvent existing and potential legislation against online gambling. In Costa Rica alone, there are at least 80 offices for Internet gambling sites.[28]

**Current Status.** One of the most confusing aspects of the gambling issue is that it is difficult to collect information on it. There have been estimates of anywhere from 350 to 21,000 gambling sites (because often many gambling sites are housed on one server, the real number is probably around 700). In its report, the National Gambling Impact Study Commission cited studies finding that, from 1997 to 1998, the amount of online gambling revenues jumped from $300 million to $651 million. Other estimates state that Internet casino revenues were $1.1 billion in 1999, $2.2 billion in 2000, and will reach $6.3 billion in 2003.[29] Another study found that 2 percent of Internet users gamble online at least once a day, and 4.5 million have gambled online at least once.[30]

One thing is for sure: The number of sites and gamblers, and the amount of both time and money spent on online gambling, is increasing at a great rate. State governments, Indian reservations, and entrepreneurs are all trying to acquire a share of the estimated $6 billion that will go into online gambling in 2002. In 1999, Rolling Good Times Online estimates that in 1999, there were over 250 online casinos, 64 lottery websites, 20 bingo websites, and 139 sites for online sports betting.

Since Americans spent $54 billion on both offline and online gambling in 1998 (as estimated by CCA), the potential for the market could easily go even higher than the predicted $6 billion, as more and more users become comfortable with making transactions over the Internet. Also, as people who would never have bothered to go to Las Vegas or Atlantic City find the convenience of online gambling sites, those numbers could rise even further.

This is worrisome to many. The National Association of Attorneys General, the National Coalition Against Legalized Gambling, some members of Congress, and Gamblers Anonymous are all concerned about the toll this potential for easy gambling could take on society, especially on children. While there are currently no specific laws banning gambling on the Internet, many cite the 1968 Wire Communications Act, which makes sports betting over the phone illegal, as a law that should apply to Internet gambling.

Jay Cohen, the co-owner of World Sports, an online gambling site in Antigua, was sentenced by a federal court in New York to 21 months in prison and fined $5,000 for illegally accepting bets from Americans over the Internet.[31] While he returned to the U.S. to stand trial, the two co-owners of the site did not, and continue to live in Antigua. All three owners insist that their site is legal since gambling is legal in Antigua, and they even have a permit from the Antigua government allowing them to run a gambling site. Jay Cohen says that one of the reasons he was found guilty was because the judge refused to let the jurors consider whether the U.S. has jurisdiction over a foreign company, even if the company's sites can be accessed by U.S. citizens.

Not everyone is against online gambling, though. The Nevada Gaming Board has approved websites operated by Coast Resorts (owner of four casinos in Nevada). These websites would only be open to residents living in Nevada and would use "eBorder" control technology from Virtgame.com to keep people outside Nevada from placing bets.[32] These sites will be watched by both proponents and opponents of online gambling. If the technology works, proponents can claim that the U.S. has no right to outlaw online gambling in states or countries where it is legal. If the technology does not work, opponents will have an easier time proving that, since online gambling cannot be controlled, it should be outlawed all together.

**Proposed Legislation.** The Internet Gambling Prohibition Act, which would have made it a crime to operate a website that accepts wagers from Americans, proposed sending offenders to prison for up to four years and fining them $20,000 or more. While this bill was defeated in the House in July 2000, chances are there will be more bills like this to follow, as this one was backed by the FBI, the Christian Coalition, the National Council of Churches, and the National Association of Attorneys General.

**Impact.** Given that gambling is currently the fourth largest offline leisure activity, with spending amounting to over $54 billion, the stakes are high. Legislation over the next few years could determine how much of that $54 billion migrates online, or how much of the estimated $2.2 billion currently spent online moves to other sites.

An interesting opponent to online gambling is physical casinos. Since they already have large revenues, casinos would not want to risk putting their own websites on the Internet in case the government decides to prosecute. If government continues to be noncommittal about whether or not online gambling is really allowed, the casinos will most likely stand on the sidelines, watching the foreign-run gambling sites' revenues double each year while their own revenues do not.

## Free Speech

**Overview.** The right to free speech is one of America's most protected rights. While Americans are allowed to speak their minds, they must also face the consequences of how their opinions are received by others. On the Internet today, Americans are enjoying their right to free speech as never before—entering chat rooms, putting up postings on bulletin boards, and offering their opinions on everything from books to sex. The Internet has brought an interesting twist to the free-speech issue—while most Americans believe in the right to free speech, do they also believe in the right to anonymous free speech?

Free speech on the Internet combines the complications of a new technology—the ability to anonymously communicate with others—with a lack of borders that obfuscates whose free speech rules to use. While an American's right to free speech is highly open (unless someone intentionally slanders another person), many European countries have stricter laws about what can and cannot be said. This difference in regulation has often put Europe in a position where it insists that the U.S. sites censor their users, while the U.S. sites defend themselves with the First Amendment.

**Current Status.** The Internet has created an easy way for people with similar interests from all over the world to meet. When the subject area is cooking or baseball, there is very little controversy. When that interest is neo-Nazism, however, it becomes an issue. So far, the courts have been handling the Internet free-speech issue with the same test that they use in offline free speech issues: Is the speech a direct, credible threat against a specific target, or a direct incitement to imminent illegal action?

On the Internet, though, there is an added step. If people feel they have been slandered, they often must first sue the ISP for the identities of the offenders before they can actually sue the offenders themselves. ISPs often refuse to release the identities of their customers. The courts ruled that America Online and Yahoo had to reveal information about the identities of eight people who anonymously posted defamatory comments in a Yahoo financial chat room that suggested Eric Hvide, CEO of Hvide Marine, was guilty of securities violations. Hvide resigned from the company, saying that the allegations ruined his career. Also, Fischer Imaging Corp. filed a complaint in December 2000 against Yahoo, asking for the identities of users who disclosed trade secrets about the company and made slanderous remarks about the management. Yahoo still insists that it does not have to reveal the identities of its users.[33]

Hatewatch, a group that tracks hate sites, believes there are 500 hate sites on the Internet. While U.S. companies will make small concessions for their sites meant for citizens of other countries—Amazon's agreement to stop selling copies of Mein Kampf to German readers and Yahoo's filtering of Nazi paraphernalia from its French site—they are not willing to abandon the right to free speech on behalf of citizens of other countries. While Yahoo France did filter the Nazi objects from French citizens, it refused to block those citizens from access to the auctions through its other sites. Even though Yahoo says that it forbids "hateful or racially, ethically or otherwise objectionable materials," it still hosts many online chat clubs devoted to neo-Nazism and other such causes.[34]

The Internet has also given teenagers, often bound by rules of parents and schools, a new sounding board. The ACLU has fought on behalf of students in Missouri, California, and Washington state who have been suspended for putting up websites that criticized their schools and the students there.[35] While the schools claim that they are concerned because of websites like the one operated by the students responsible for the killings at Columbine High School, free speech advocates believe that students, often unable to speak their minds in their high school newspapers, should be allowed to speak their minds on the Internet.

While protecting the opinions of teenagers, the right to free speech has struck down laws and practices designed to protect children. The Children's Online Protection Act, which prohibited sites from knowingly exposing children to pornographic images, has been deemed unconstitutional because it violates the websites' free-speech rights. Also, Web filters that have been installed on school computers to keep students from visiting inappropriate sites have come under fire from free speech advocates.

**Proposed Legislation.** While the First Amendment solidly protects free speech, the courts will determine not only who can sue whom for slanderous remarks, but also when ISPs have to disclose the names of their users.

**Impact.** The impact of free-speech rights remains to be seen in business. One of the most promising features of the Internet was the idea of community—people from all over the world with similar interests coming together to chat. If people felt that they could be taken to court for what they say on the Internet, that legislation would have a chilling effect on those who state opinions online. Also, if the courts say that the government has the right to force ISPs to reveal the identity of users who say hateful things, then the ISPs would risk losing customers who decide that the threat of being sued is greater than the benefit of using the chat room.

If people are never held responsible for what they say, though, that could have a detrimental effect on the perceived veracity of the Internet. While newspaper journalists have strict standards they must adhere to before they report something as true (having to get confirmation of a story from a second source), Internet journalists often publish stories on their websites without even trying to get confirmation. In a study done by the UCLA Center for Communication Policy, when asked if they thought information on the Internet is reliable and accurate, 52 percent of users said most of it was, and only 29.4 percent of Internet nonusers said it was. The amount dropped down to less than 3 percent for both groups when asked if all the information was accurate and reliable.

# THE UNITED STATES AND EUROPE

As the Internet grows around the world and more and more countries stand to profit from it, some sort of understanding between countries must be reached so there can be as easy an exchange of ideas and information as possible. The first steps toward this understanding have come as the United States and Europe try to work together on the issues of privacy and cybercrime.

Europe's privacy policies are much more strict than the U.S.'s—European websites all have opt-in policies along with specific rules about what a website can and cannot do with personal information. The European Union wants U.S. sites to adopt those privacy policies in order to do business with European citizens. But, when a "safe harbor" agreement was reached between the United States and the E.U. that required companies that signed up to promise to adhere to Europe's privacy standards, less than 15 companies actually signed up. (The companies that did sign up were mostly companies like Hewlett-Packard that do not rely on selling customer information for revenue.) American companies complain that Europe should not have the right to regulate their business practices—while they may be selling to European residents, they are still based in the United States and should only have to adhere to U.S. standards. How this debate will be resolved remains unclear. Given the potential revenue streams on both ends, it is in the best interest of both American and European companies to find a common ground.

Every issue on the Internet causes debate. Even **cybercrime** (often referred to as hacking), which refers to crimes that are committed over the Internet, raises controversy. Both governments and businesses agree that the costs incurred by companies and governments due to cybercriminals are detrimental to their economies. It is difficult to estimate exactly how much cybercrime costs businesses, because many businesses do not want to admit that hackers were able to access their computers. One survey estimates that cybercrime costs companies $2 million a year each.[36]

As Europe and the United States have started efforts to fight cybercrime, though, privacy advocates are watching them very carefully. They fear that the government's desire to catch criminals infringes on the rights of citizens, giving them a right to intercept e-mail and monitor online behavior. This monitoring of private citizens will not only affect the guilty, but the innocent as well. Still, the E.U. and U.S. governments have been trying to come to an understanding, especially since cybercriminals in Europe can have a devastating effect on U.S. companies, and vice versa.

So far, the E.U.'s attempts to develop a cybercrime treaty have suffered more criticism than praise. Since May 1997, it has been working on a treaty that would establish laws against hacking, fraud, computer viruses, child pornography, and other Internet crimes, and also set practices of securing digital evidence to trace and prosecute criminals. This treaty has come under attack by the technology industry, which insists that companies would break the treaty simply by testing their own security programs. Privacy and human rights advocates, both in Europe and the U.S., have also criticized the treaty, saying that it would give government too much leeway.[37]

# SUMMARY

## 1. How is the Internet currently regulated?

So far, few laws regulating the Internet have been passed, as the government has mostly favored self-regulation over government regulation. There are various reasons for this stance, including the idea that the Internet will be stifled if the government starts imposing regulations. Also, the sheer complexity of getting local, state, and federal governments to agree on one law, when they are used to creating their own laws, has government gridlocked on most issues.

## 2. What are the challenges the Internet has brought to regulation?

The two major challenges the Internet has brought to regulation are new technology and lack of physical borders. New technology affects issues like privacy and intellectual property, the lack of borders affects taxation and gambling. Free speech is affected by both issues.

## 3. What are the main regulation issues on the Internet today?

The five main issues are privacy, intellectual property, taxation, gambling, and free speech. Privacy is an issue because Internet companies have new technology that can track a user's every movement. Intellectual property has become an issue because new technology makes it easy to copy high-quality music files and trade them over the Internet. Taxation is an issue because e-commerce companies do not have to collect sales tax on their customers' purchases. While this is an advantage to customers, it costs the states billions of dollars a year. Gambling is an issue because the Internet makes it difficult to decide exactly where the transaction takes place, and, therefore, which region's laws should regulate that transaction. Free speech has become an issue because the Internet now allows millions of people to speak their minds anonymously, something that has never happened before.

## 4. How are the United States and Europe working together to regulate the Internet?

So far, the United States and Europe have been trying to work together on both privacy and cybercrime issues. While Europe has stricter laws regulating privacy than the United States, U.S. e-commerce companies are reluctant to adopt them since the regulations would limit their ability to do personalized advertising. Europe wants to ban American companies from doing business with its citizens until European privacy standards are implemented. The European Union and the United States are also working together to create laws prohibiting cybercrime. These laws have come under attack from privacy advocates who are concerned with giving governments the right to monitor online behavior.

# KEY TERMS

| | |
|---|---|
| Code of Fair Information Practices | copyright |
| opt-in | fair use |
| opt-out | Digital Millennium Copyright Act (DMCA) |
| patent | Streamlined Sales Tax Project |
| trademark | cybercrime |

# Endnotes

[1]Garfinkel, Simson. *Database Nation: The Death of Privacy in the 21st Century* (Sebastopol: O'Reilley & Associates, Inc., 2000).

[2]Clark, Paul Coe III. "FTC in middle of privacy fray," *Communications Today* via COMTEX, 1 August, 2000. URL: *http://www.tnbt.com/jsp/PrinterFriendly.jsp?a=9609&type=8.*

[3]Livingston, Brian. "Do privacy policies really protect you?," CNET News.com, 30 June, 2000.

[4]The America Online/Roper Starch Worldwide Adult 2000 Cyberstudy. October 2000.

[5]Oaks, Chris. "FTC commish: regulate thyself," *Wired News,* 11 October, 2000. URL: *http://www.wired.com/news/politics/0,1283,39344,00.html.*

[6]Anderson, Diane, and Keith Parine. "Marketing the double click way," *The Standard,* 6 March, 2000. URL: *http://www.thestandard.com/article/display/0,1151,12400,00.html.*

[7]Gouthro, Liane. "Protecting kids privacy online: Lifeguarding junior surfers," *The Next Best Thing* TNBT.com, 20 September, 2000.

[8]Marsan, Carolyn Duffy. "Net privacy law costs a bundle," CNN.com, 16 May, 2000. URL: *http://www.cnn.com/200/tech/computing/05/16/privacy.bill.idg/index.html.*

[9]Walsh, Mark. "Schools must reveal Internet logs, judge says," washingtonpost.com, 20 November, 2000.

[10]Petersen, Andrea. "Its not big brother invading kids' privacy, it's mom and dad," WSJ.com, 6 November, 2000.

[11]"Amazon.com move worries privacy pros," Tech Web—CMP via COMTEX, 3 September, 2000.

[12]Justice Sandra Day O'Connor (Feist Publications, Inc.) Rural Telephone Service Co., 499 US 340, 349 (1991), from arl.org site. URL: *http://www.arl.org/info/frn/copy/fairuse.html.*

[13]U.S. Copyright Office, "The Basics of U.S. Copyright Law." URL: *http://www.gigalaw.com/articles/loc-2000-03-p2.html.*

[14]For a more detailed explanation of the DMCA, see the paper written by Jonathan Band, *The Digital Millennium Copyright Act.* URL: *http://www.arl.org/info/frn/copy/band.html.*

[15]Pressman, Aaron. "The great patent giveaway," *The Industry Standard*, 4 December, 2000. URL: *www.thestandard.com/article/display/0,1151,20543,00.html.*

[16]Pressman, Aaron. "The great patent giveaway," *The Industry Standard*, 4 December, 2000. URL: *www.thestandard.com/article/display/0,1151,20543,00.html.*

[17]Ellis, Kathleen. "Net patent bill introduced," *Wired News*, 3 October, 2000. URL: *http://www.wired.com/news/politics/politics/0,1283,3928,00.html.*

[18]Glasner, Joanna. "Amazon loses patent suit round," 14 February, 2001. URL: *http://www.wired.com/news/print/0,1294,41824,00.html.*

[19]Sinrod, Eric J. "Upside counsel: Madonna.com: No longer a legal virgin," *Upside Today*, 24 October, 2000.

[20]Leeds, Jeff. "Record industry says napster hurt sales," latimes.com, 24 February, 2001. URL: *http://www.latimes.com/business/columns/innovation/20010224/+000016601.html.*

[21]Welte, Jim. "Napster injunction issued," *Business 2.0*, 6 March, 2001.

[22]Adam Cohen. "A crisis of content," *Time Magazine*, October 2000, p. 73.

[23]Yancey, William F., Gregory W. Mitchell, and Dana E. Lipp. "Electronic commerce snares sellers in multistate tax web," Ryan & Company, 7 December, 1999.

[24]Olsen, Stefanie. "California governor vetoes Internet tax bill," CNET News.com, 25 September, 2000. URL: *http://news.cnet.com/news/0-1007-200-2861946.html.*

[25]Yancey, "Electronic Commerce Snares Sellers in Multistate Tax Web."

[26]Sharrad, Jeremy. "Making Net sales tax pay," The Forrester Report, November 2000.

[27]National Gambling Impact Study Commission, June 18, 1999. For the full report, go to *http://www.ngisc.gov/reports/finrpt.html.*

[28]"Costa Rica a new paradise for online gambling companies," *AP Worldstream*, 24 October, 2000.

[29]Sinrod, Eric. "Upside counsel: Cracking down on Internet gambling," *Upside Today*, 10 October, 2000. URL: *http://www.upside.com/texis/mvm/print-it?id=39e1f680&t=texis/mvm/upside_counsel.*

[30]Pew Internet & American Life Project Survey, April 2000.

[31]Brunker, Mike. "Net betting operator isn't wavering," MSNBC, 10 August, 2000. URL: *http://www.msnbc.com/NEWS/369978.asp.*

[32]Enos, Lori. "Nevada oks web gambling sites," *E-Commerce Times*, 16 October, 2000. URL: *http://www.ecommercetimes.com/news/articles2000/001016-1.shtml.*

[33]"Companies increasingly suing their online critics." *The Denver Post* via COMTEX, 15 January, 2001.

[34]Perine, Keith. "The trouble with regulating hate," *The Industry Standard*, 24 July, 2000. URL: *http://www.thestandard.com/article/display/0,1151,16967,00.html.*

[35]Anderson, Lessley. "High school confidential—Not!," *The Industry Standard*, 30 October, 2000. URL: *http://www.thestandard.com/article/display/0,1151,19709,00.html.*

[36]Oreskovic, Alexei. "FBI Warns of Growing Digital-Crime Wave." *The Industry Standard*, 12 March 2001.

[37]Oreskovic, Alexei. "FBI Warns of Growing Digital-Crime Wave." *The Industry Standard*, 12 March 2001.

# Internet and Society

In this chapter, we explore how the Internet is changing society and how society is changing the Internet. With issues such as community, the digital divide, education, and e-government, the Internet is changing how people communicate, seek information, and shop, and even how they interact with the various local, state, and federal government agencies. These changes have implications for society, but also for the e-commerce businesses working within this new society.

## QUESTIONS

*Please consider the following questions as you read this chapter:*

1. Who is on the Internet, and what are they doing?

2. What is the digital divide?

3. How is the Internet changing education?

4. How is government using the Internet?

This chapter was coauthored by Bernie Jaworski, Jeffrey Rayport, and JoAnn Kienzle.

# INTRODUCTION

In Chapter 1, we discussed the revolution businesses have undergone with the advent of the Internet. In this last chapter, we look to see how the Internet has affected society and whether or not society has undergone a revolution as well.

With all the fanfare about the Internet, its incredible growth in the mid to late 1990s and its reality check in 2000, the question still remains, who is on the Internet and what are they doing there? While there have been many small, category-specific studies of the Internet, there have been few comprehensive ones addressing whether the Internet has really significantly changed society, or if it has simply given a small part of the population a new way to buy CDs or get their news.

However, there are definitely some constants across the surveys. The number of online users is growing rapidly across almost all income and education levels, and more and more are making purchases on the Web. Exhibit 17-1 shows the top six online activities current users already do or want to do on the Internet. Notice the top three involve community activities, two involve government activities, and one involves educational activities. In this chapter, we will look closer at all of these activities.

## WHO IS ON THE INTERNET AND WHAT ARE THEY DOING?

Over the past few years, the Internet has grown at an incredible rate. Online users increased from 45 million in 1998, to 63 million in 1999, to 76 million in 2000.[1] For a while it seemed that Internet businesses could not fail, as venture-capital dollars

**Exhibit 17-1** WHAT USERS WANT TO DO ON THE INTERNET

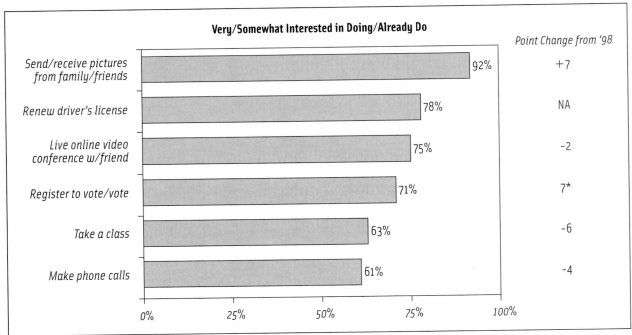

Source: The America Online/Roper Starch Worldwide "Adult 2000 Cyberstudy," October 2000.

backed startups at record numbers and being first on the Internet seemed to guarantee success. Now, after the Nasdaq has crashed and many companies with poor business strategies have gone out of business, companies are reevaluating their strategies. Part of this reevaluation must include knowledge of who is on the Internet and the kinds of activities in which they are, and are not, participating.

Table 17-1 shows who is currently online. While people with lower incomes and lower education levels are increasingly on the Internet, 62 percent of the online population makes over $35,000, with 23 percent (more than one in five) making over $75,000. Since many companies (and therefore advertisers) target people with disposable income, this is good news for online companies that rely on advertising revenue.

As people become more familiar with the Web, they spend more time on it doing more activities. Exhibit 17-2 shows how the number of hours online increases as a user's expertise increases. Users also do different activities depending on their experience level. While an average of 56 percent of users now make purchases online, 66 percent of users who have been on the Internet for more than three years make purchases online (balanced by only 42 percent of new users).[2] Also, people who have been online for more than three years are much more likely to use the Internet to do research, book travel reservations, and communicate with business associates. What are tenured Internet users *less* likely to do? Online instant messaging, playing games, and chatting.[3] For most activities, though, online users, no matter what their experience level, do the same two types of activities: gather information and communicate.

The top five activities on the Internet are researching, communicating with friends and family, getting information about products to buy, getting news, and finding health information. Making purchases comes in sixth (up 14 percentage points, from 42 percent in 1999 to 56 percent in 2000). Depending on the survey, e-mail is always either the first or second most common activity. One survey says that 93 percent of Internet users use e-mail and 49 percent check it every day.[4]

**Table 17-1**

WHO'S ONLINE

| | | General Population % | Internet Users % |
|---|---|---|---|
| Gender | Men | 48 | 51 |
| | Women | 52 | 49 |
| Education | HS or less | 51 | 24 |
| | Some college | 27 | 34 |
| | College graduate or more | 23 | 40 |
| Income | <$35,000 | 34 | 13 |
| | $35,000–$74,999 | 28 | 36 |
| | $75,000 or more | 10 | 23 |

Source: The America Online/Roper Starch Worldwide "Adult 2000 Cyberstudy," October 2000.

**Exhibit 17-2**

TIME ON THE INTERNET

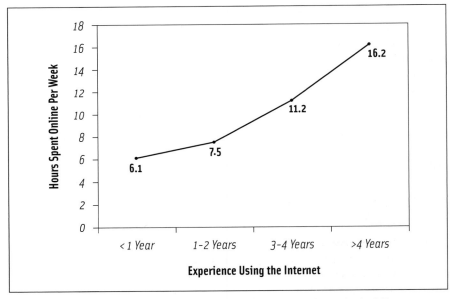

Source: The UCLA Internet Report: "Surveying the Digital Future," UCLA Center for Communication Policy

What does this mean? Although a lot of attention has been paid to traditional e-tailing sites, with the right revenue model, communication and content sites could make a lot of money. Even though the effectiveness of online advertising is coming into question, and content sites are currently struggling to find a revenue model, content sites are by far the most popular sites on the Web. There is huge potential for companies to capture the incredible consumer attention that these sites are able to attain and turn it into dollars. The Internet is definitely changing how people communicate and search for information, but how businesses can benefit from this change remains to be seen.

## Community

Much has been made about online community and how the Internet helps bring together people from all over the world with similar interests. The Internet is also thought to encourage people to form unreal relationships with strangers who may or may not be who they claim. At least in its infancy, online community is turning out to be more about facilitating relationships that already exist than forming new ones. Communicating with friends and family is the second most common activity among Internet users, and the first among people who have only been on the Net for a year or less.

Another study found that 55 percent of Internet users say e-mail has improved their connections with significant family members, and 66 percent say the same thing about communicating with significant friends. Also, 40 percent who e-mail family members communicate with them through e-mail more often than by phone. Siblings who have an e-mail relationship send e-mail much more often than they phone each other: 69 percent of these siblings e-mail each other once a week or more.

During the 2000 holiday season, every business publication had predictions and reports about how much Americans would spend on purchases on the Internet. While the amount of online purchases did go up and more Americans did purchase gifts over the Internet, other holiday activities were mostly ignored in the press. While 24 percent of users purchased gifts on the Internet, 53 percent used it to send e-mails to discuss holiday plans, and 32 percent used it to send e-greeting cards. Purchasing tied for third with another popular holiday activity on the Internet—getting information on holiday crafts and recipes online.[5]

As far as people who do use the Internet to meet people with similar interests, while 26 percent, or about 25 million Americans, have used a chat room, only 4 percent visit one daily. And, though 36 percent have visited an online support group, only 3 percent do it on a daily basis. When asked if "it's easier to meet people online than in person," on a scale of 1 (strongly disagree) to 5 (strongly agree) the response was 2.5, and when asked if "you share intimate details of your life on the Internet that you would not reveal in person," the response was 1.6.[6]

This is not to say the predictions of people becoming friends with strangers online were completely wrong. More than one in four users (26.2 percent—the same number that visit chat rooms) create online friendships with users whom they have never met in person, and, for these users, the average number of online friends is about 12.[7] So, for those who do want to meet people online, the Internet seems to have fulfilled its promise.

What do these numbers mean for businesses? That, while Internet transactions are on the rise and the online environment has certainly fostered a community specific to the Internet, the Web often acts as more of a community-facilitator for people who already have friends and family in place and are looking for ways to keep in touch with them. While it is tempting for businesses to want to tap into the global community established by the Internet, there is also a physical community with needs. Businesses such as Evite Inc., a company that helps users send and manage online invitations to parties, and myteam.com, which helps parents organize their local little league teams, use this market effectively.

## Global Internet Use

While the United States is certainly one of the biggest users of the Internet, other countries are starting to get wired at fast rates (see Table 17-2). Canada and Sweden already have slightly higher percentages of their population online than the United States. Others, such as Brazil and France, do not even hit 10 percent. Estimates for the year 2005 say that the North American portion of users will diminish (43.2 percent to 30.2 percent) with Asia and Eastern Europe gaining.[8] In fact, Asia is expected to grow from 116.2 million users in 2000 to 304.7 million users in just three years. The Middle East and Africa, while also expecting an increase in users (13 million in 2000 to 36.1 million in 2003), will have a relatively small wired population.

The amount of e-commerce dollars generated per country presents an even more striking picture. The United States will have $409 billion in e-commerce revenues (over half of the world revenues), far outshining Germany with $62.8 billion and the United Kingdom with $47.6 billion.[9] This is contrasted, however, by per capita usage, where the U.S. is, by far, not the highest. Per capita, the U.S. is surpassed by Canada (491 users per thousand), Sweden (490), and Iceland (489). The U.S. ranked sixth with 478.

Table
17-2

## INTERNET USERS IN OTHER COUNTRIES

| Internet Users in Top 15 Countries | | | |
|---|---|---|---|
| | Online Population in Millions, 1999 | Total Population in Millions, 1999 | Percentage of Total Population Online |
| United States | 110.8 | 273 | 40.6% |
| Japan | 18.2 | 126 | 14.4% |
| United Kingdom | 13.9 | 59 | 23.6% |
| Canada | 13.3 | 31 | 42.9% |
| Germany | 12.3 | 82 | 15.0% |
| Australia | 6.8 | 19 | 35.8% |
| Brazil | 6.8 | 172 | 4.0% |
| China | 6.3 | 1,247 | 0.5% |
| France | 5.7 | 59 | 9.7% |
| South Korea | 5.7 | 47 | 12.1% |
| Taiwan | 4.8 | 22 | 21.8% |
| Italy | 4.7 | 57 | 8.4% |
| Sweden | 3.9 | 9 | 43.3% |
| Netherlands | 2.9 | 16 | 18.1% |
| Spain | 2.9 | 39 | 7.4% |

Note: Total population data are July 1999 estimates
Source: Computer Industry Almanac, Central Intelligence Agency

## Digital Divide

Now that we have discussed who is on the Internet, we should discuss who is not. The term **digital divide** has been used in many different ways, but mostly it refers to the gap between people who have computers (and, therefore, computer skills) and people who do not. Most research on the digital divide is done on race, income, and education variables. Some research examines age. According to a recent Commerce Department study, 43.6 million households, or 41.5 percent of the U.S. population, have Internet access. As time goes on, the Internet is starting to look more and more like the general population (see Table 17-1). While women have traditionally been underrepresented, they are now gaining presence on the Internet. Table 17-3 shows the gain of users over a six-month period of time as a percentage of the population. While minorities, people with lower incomes, and people with lower educational levels are all rising at great rates, they are still underrepresented in the Internet population. One group not represented in Table 17-3 is households with an income under $15,000. Just 19.2 percent of those households have computers, and only 12.7 percent have Internet access. Even more alarming is that, while other groups are averaging a 10 percent gain every six months, this group only gained 5 percent more access from 1998 to 2000.

**Table 17-3** INTERNET POPULATION GROWTH

| Where the Internet Population Grew The percentage of each group online: | | |
|---|---|---|
| | **May–June** | **November–December** |
| **All Adults** | **47%** | **56%** |
| Men | 50% | 58% |
| Women | 45% | 54% |
| Whites | 49% | 57% |
| Blacks | 35% | 43% |
| Hispanics | 40% | 47% |
| Parents of children under 18 | 55% | 66% |
| Non-parents | 43% | 50% |
| **Age Cohorts** | | |
| 18–29 | 61% | 75% |
| 30–49 | 57% | 65% |
| 50–64 | 41% | 51% |
| 65+ | 12% | 15% |
| **Income Brackets** | | |
| Under $30,000 | 28% | 38% |
| $30,000–$50,000 | 50% | 64% |
| $50,000–$70,000 | 67% | 72% |
| $75,000+ | 79% | 82% |
| **Educational Attainment** | | |
| High school or less | 28% | 37% |
| Some college | 62% | 71% |
| College degree or more | 76% | 82% |

Source: Pew Internet & American Life Project surveys, May–June and November–December, 2000.
Note: Margin of error is ±3%

One of the most overlooked groups trapped in the digital divide are senior citizens. According to the Pew Internet Project, only 15 percent of people 65 and over are Internet users, and they are one of the slowest growing segments of the online population—only an additional 3 percent went online from June to December 2000. (The next smallest group is people with incomes under $30,000, with a 38 percent use rate.) Perhaps what is more alarming is that 56 percent of non-users over 60 say they will never go online.

Part of the reason could be that many of the potential users in that group have disabilities (over half has a disability of some kind), which makes it difficult for them to use the Internet, especially if they have vision problems (11.4 percent) or difficulty using their hands.[10] One survey found that while 17 percent of people 65 and over had home Internet access, only 9.3 percent of people 65 and over with a disability had Internet access. What is frustrating about these numbers is that this very segment of the population is often the least mobile (17.7 percent have difficulty walking), but could benefit the most from Internet features such as purchasing and getting health information online.[11]

Even though many seniors insist that they will not go online, this is bound to change. As the current population grows older, and people who are comfortable with computers move into their sixties, more older Americans will be online. Not only is half of the population of users aged 50 to 64 online, but their population segment gained 10 points between June and December 2000. Perhaps as more of the 50-plus group go online and Internet companies start catering to older people (see Drill-Down, "Senior Web Surfers"), the sixty-plus group will start to see the value of the Internet.

While the digital divide continues to shrink as far as ethnic and education levels are concerned, the difference between those who are and are not wired will become more pronounced. The gap between the haves and have-nots will grow larger as the federal, state, and local governments move features to the Web, schools require more Internet research, and, most importantly, more jobs require computer skills.

There have been many initiatives, both in government and the private sector, to ease the digital divide among underprivileged youths (see Drill-Down, "Training Urban Kids for IT Jobs"). The government has provided computers to schools and libraries, and private companies—especially in the technology sector—have donated goods and services. Providing computers, though, will not be enough; people will need to be trained on the computers and have time to develop their skills if they are going to benefit from provided computers.

---

### DRILL-DOWN

# Senior Web Surfers
#### By Lisa Ferri, tbnt.com staff writer

A funny thing is happening down in Jonesboro, Arkansas, population 50,000. In this sleepy little town, Melissa Prater can't keep up with the demand for the "Computer Science 101" classes she conducts. With enough space for just 70 students each semester, she receives between three and five calls daily inquiring whether, by some stroke of luck, a seat has opened up. Prater doesn't advertise the classes in catalogs or coffee-houses; the buzz is purely driven by word of mouth, and still the waiting list tops 350.

It's not the coeds from nearby Arkansas State University who are banging down Prater's door. It's their grandparents.

Ann Wrixson, president and CEO of SeniorNet, a nonprofit organization of computer-using seniors, points out that the situation in Jonesboro is not so strange. At learning centers like the one where Prater teaches, waiting lists for senior computer classes regularly reach 200 names. Seniors.com Inc. estimates there are between 3 million and 5 million seniors online and expects that number to balloon to 20 million by 2006. It looks like, more than ever before, senior citizens are getting wired.

Given the tough times in the e-commerce climate, it would seem that this fresh audience is emerging just in the nick of time. Yet e-tailers have been slow to court these new shoppers, making some wonder

*(continued on p. 607)*

*(continued from page 606)*

whether ignoring the senior-citizen niche may turn out to be the biggest lost opportunity of the new economy. As Wrixson puts it, "This is the single largest untapped market right now—they should be salivating over them!"

Henry Harteveldt, a Forrester Research analyst, is troubled that seniors haven't been aggressively pursued as an Internet audience. "Don't write them off," he warns. "They have money."

According to census data, Americans over the age of 50 own 80 percent of the assets in all U.S. savings and loans institutions and $66 of every $100 in the stock market. Of this group, 64- to 75-year-olds are the richest subsegment. Wrixson points out that this makes seniors doubly desirable: They are both the richest and the longest-living demographic in the history of the world.

Nonetheless, the breathless enthusiasm so often displayed by netcos appears to be reserved for baby boomers and Generation Y members. Some, like Senior.com's CEO Craig Schub, find the phenomenon baffling because seniors are, in some ways, better online customers than their children and grandchildren. He notes that Gen Y'ers usually don't have credit cards and baby boomers grapple with mortgage payments and tuition bills. Seniors, on the other hand, have a lifetime of savings, often with no significant bills. So why aren't e-tailers wooing them? "Quite frankly, [companies] aren't used to having this huge older population with lots of money," says Schub. "They're used to aiming everything from advertising to product offerings at 18- to 34-year-olds." Grandma may want to go online and buy a "senior booze cruise," but until e-tailers have a chance to get used to the idea, she'll have to settle for a Rio MP3 player.

According to Harteveldt, new-economy companies balk at selling to online grandmas, believing that mature audiences have not embraced technology en masse so far and never will. "The problem with that thinking is, in the blink of an eye, today's technologically savvy 45- and 50-year-olds will be senior citizens," he says. "Seniors may seem to be a minor, emerging market now, but when the baby boomers grow old, things are going to change."

Susan Hayward, research director of Greenfield Online, an online market-research firm, concurs. "When the baby boomers hit the senior market, they're going to expect every company to be able to serve them digitally," she says. "And it's not just going to be a 'wave' of baby boomers turning into senior citizens. It's going to be a tsunami."

Rather than waiting until the storm hits, Harteveldt suggests using older Web surfers as guinea pigs. "If they're smart, companies will use today's seniors as a learning laboratory—an organic investment in the future," he says.

That's where Jonesboro comes in. SeniorNet, in a joint venture with eBay, has committed to making at least 1 million seniors computer-literate by 2005. In classrooms like the one in Arkansas, teachers are noting just what works for seniors—and what doesn't. For example, mice present problems for arthritic hands. Also, Wrixson has found that many seniors are the "victims of well-meaning children" who pass along hand-me-down computers that make a senior's first online experience daunting.

While SeniorNet trains the nation's grandparents in basic computer skills, Harteveldt hopes to see Dell, Gateway, Microsoft and others do their part by developing "senior-specific" hardware and software, such as larger screens, fonts, and mice. If they start now, he says, they have an outside chance of being ready to go to market when the tsunami hits.

*Read more articles about The Next Big Thing at www.tnbt.com*

# EDUCATION

One of the most promising uses for the Internet is education. Given the Web's networking abilities, multimedia applications, and low cost (at least compared to the room and board required to go to college), the Internet education market has huge potential. Still, there is a long way to go before we see how significant the impact is.

# Training Urban Kids for IT Jobs

By Elizabeth Millard, tnbt.com

 A few years ago, the only thing Romke de Haan looked forward to was the click-clack of a ball bearing in a spray paint can. Having dropped out of high school, de Haan spent his nights cruising around Milwaukee with friends, producing "urban art." During the days, however, he was getting strong suggestions from his pastor about joining a new program, called Homeboyz Interactive, geared toward training gangbangers and other at-risk youth in Web design, software development, and other IT skills.

After two years of cajoling, de Haan passed the program's office while driving around aimlessly with a friend one day and decided to go in just to make the pastor happy. He hasn't picked up a spray paint can since.

Homeboyz Interactive was founded in 1996 by Jim Holub, a Jesuit priest on a mission to help Milwaukee's disadvantaged youth. Holub saw that Web jobs were plentiful, but computer training was not. So on an old PC in the basement of a convent on the city's south side, Holub taught himself HTML and began to tutor kids in the basics. The program took off as private and public sector groups donated software and hardware, and eager students began to employ snazzier tactics for site design, like cascading style sheets and JavaScript. After Homeboyz's initial client, Amoco, praised the young people's work and asked for more interns, other companies came calling, from LeMond Bicycles to necktie company Ralph Marlin.

"Technology is going to be destroying occupations as fast as it creates them," says Danny Goldberg, local director for Homeboyz. "The world of work is changing, and we need to have strategies for training people in the new economy—especially people who don't have access to resources. That's why this program is important."

Since its inception, the program has launched 125 students into good-paying high-tech jobs ranging from Web design to hard-core programming. Many, like de Haan, didn't realize how tech-minded they could be until they booted up for the first time. "I became addicted to the programming," he says. "It was my niche. I used to stay in the training office until midnight. They'd give me a programming book to read; I'd read it in a night and ask for another one."

After graduating from the four-month training, de Haan did an internship at a marketing company, where he says the final transition from street kid to responsible adult kicked in. "I saw that people who were setting goals for where they wanted to be were enjoying life," he says. "They weren't doing extreme things like I had been doing; they weren't just living for today. I wanted to be like them." He got his chance when Homeboyz hired him as creative director after the internship concluded.

Homeboyz is one of a growing number of programs aimed at getting kids off the streets and into the computer lab. San Francisco-based OpNet offers low-income youth training and internships to prepare for Internet careers; similar programs are cropping up in other parts of the country. Homeboyz plans to expand in the next few years into other cities like Chicago, Los Angeles, New York, and even Dublin, Ireland.

The idea of training at-risk youth for internships and eventual employment is nothing new, says Michael Boyd, a human-resource strategies analyst at research firm IDC. What's different about programs like Homeboyz, he notes, is the IT spin. And if they can't by themselves alleviate the yawning IT labor crunch, Boyd says, such initiatives can produce enormous benefits at the small-business and community levels.

"I think the people who go through programs like Homeboyz will make a remarkable contribution," he asserts. "Mainly because they'll be an example for other gang members who feel hopeless and don't see any way out of their situation.

"It's not a new idea," he adds. "But it's a really good old idea that works very well."

*Read more articles about The Next Big Thing at www.tnbt.com*

While many classrooms and students are getting wired, schools have been slow to truly integrate computers and the Internet into day-to-day learning. Generally, there are four categories of online education: K–12, higher, corporate, and leisure (or casual).

# K-12

Currently, 96 percent of U.S. schools are connected to the Internet, and 63 percent of public school classrooms are wired. In 1999, $1.3 billion went into K–12 online education, with this number estimated to jump to $6.9 billion by 2003.[12] While this market is large (total U.S. spending is $340 billion for K–12),[13] businesses have had a difficult time figuring out how to position themselves in it. Though elementary and secondary schools are anxious to become connected to the Internet, this is the education segment most reluctant to substantially change its curricula to include the Internet in students' learning in any significant way. Still, many companies are hoping to break in.

Established companies such as Scholastic have started Web initiatives that allow them to distribute their products and to also offer information to parents and teachers. The Scholastic website (*www.scholastic.com*) offers lesson plans and web-page builders for teachers.[14] New Internet companies such as bigchalk.com serve as educational portals, linking parents, teachers, and students with information and services, while Schoolpop helps schools with fundraising efforts.

It is difficult to find surveys that discuss how much students actually use the Internet for education. In one study by the National Center for Education Statistics, about half of all teachers in the public schools said they used computers and the Internet for instruction. Even teachers with Internet access, though, reported problems. The biggest barriers included not having enough computers, lack of free time for teachers to learn how to use the technology, and also a lack of time in the class schedule. Of the teachers that did use computers and the Internet for educational purposes, some assigned their students drills and word processing and spreadsheets as tasks, while others assigned their students research and problem-solving tasks.

Children in Canada and Sweden often spend more time using the Internet at school than American children do. Still, 90 percent of students in the United States, Canada, and Sweden do class-related research online.

# Higher Education

While most people in the U.S. live relatively close to a K–12 school, many potential students either live overseas or simply cannot afford the room and board necessary to live near a college. Therefore, the online distance-learning market, because of convenience and necessity, is expected to grow. In 1999, 72 percent of two- and four-year colleges offered "distance-learning" courses, and by 2002 it is expected that 15 percent of all students will have the option of online classes.[15] Like the K–12 market, the market for online college education was estimated at $1.2 billion in 1999 and expected to rise to $7 billion by 2003.[16] Though the market may be as big as K–12, online higher education is probably easier to tap into, as young adults are more likely to try new approaches to education than school systems.

Columbia University, which has had a correspondence program since 1986, has started an online presence, Columbia Video Network (CVN). It expects to enroll 600 students in 2000, with a profit of $1.5 million, hoping to earn $6 million in the near future. The UCLA Extension school has started OnlineLearning.net, which has offered over 1,400 online courses to more than 17,000 students. Its courses range from general business studies to English as a foreign language to computer certification classes. While CVN has degree programs, most established universities (including UCLA) do not. Though online education offered by established universities is certain to grow in the future, the number of those universities that will actually offer online degree programs is uncertain.

What is occurring even more, though, is that established colleges and universities are teaming up with online companies to offer courses (and online degrees) through them. Table 17-4 shows four of the strongest online universities. Cardean University is associated with Stanford University, Carnegie Mellon University, and Columbia, among others. Fathom.com (not on the list) is a cooperative effort by Columbia, the University of Washington, and other colleges to sell high-caliber

### Table 17-4  ONLINE UNIVERSITIES

| | University of Phoenix Online | Jones International University | Cardean University |
|---|---|---|---|
| URL | www.uoponline.com | www.jonesinternational.edu | www.cardean.edu |
| Year Founded | 1989 | 1993 | 2000 |
| Enrollment as of 1/01 | 18,500 | 4,000 | 2,000 |
| Graduates | 8,000 | 25 | NA |
| Cost of B.A. / Time | $24,000 /2–3 Years | $17,000 / 2 Years | NA |
| Cost of M.A. / Time | $24,000 < 2 Years | $9,500 / 2 Years | NA |
| Cost of M.B.A. / Time | N/A | $11,500 / 2 Years | $30,000 /3–5 Years |

Source: The schools, from "Off Campus," *The Wall Street Journal,* March 12, 2001.

courses. Jones International University has professors from schools such as the London School of Economics teach their courses.

Critics argue that distance learning is not equivalent to sitting in a classroom. Since interaction with students and teachers is an important part of college life, they believe that distance learners are only receiving part of an education. While being able to sit in a classroom and debate issues directly with students and teachers may be ideal, many students are choosing online programs for practical reasons.

## Corporate Learning

While many people expect education to stop once they have gotten a job, this is often not the case. Many corporations, especially in the technology sector, not only offer training but require it. Because of this, **corporate learning** is the biggest education category of them all, and it is expected to grow to $11.4 billion by 2003.[17] With corporations willing to pay money to keep their work force trained in the most up-to-date technology, many companies have started to appeal to this market. While the biggest demand for corporate learning is in the field of IT training, companies such as Cognitive Arts, SkillSoft, and SMGnet offer training in such areas as management, customer service, human resources, and performance improvement.

As with the higher-education companies, how effective online corporate learning is remains to be seen. As with all online education, preliminary reports show that workers appreciate the convenience, but many miss the interactions. Presently, corporations are willing to pay money in the hope that online learning will be cheaper and more efficient. If, as the corporations see the effects of their courses, they find them ineffective, that money could easily dry up.

## Leisure Education

Now that every once-unique website has a competitor and there is little opportunity to be a first mover, websites are trying to distinguish themselves in other ways. To this end, many websites have decided to offer classes to encourage traffic and customer retention on their website. These **leisure education** courses do not give the students any credit and are usually taken simply for fun (the equivalent to night classes at a local community college or adult center). Barnes & Noble.com offers courses in everything from literature to life improvement, while Jobs.com offers courses in computer or writing skills. Powered Inc. (formerly notHarvard) is one company that is using the Web for "educommerce." It says it is at the intersection of online education and customer management.[18] While most of these classes are free, the quality is often inconsistent.

## GOVERNMENT AND THE INTERNET

Most government agencies and municipalities have been slow to develop an online presence and use it to its potential. The quality and complexity of government sites varies greatly. While some government websites offer functions such as the ability to pay a parking ticket or apply for a permit, others act only as directories for the agency. In this section, we will discuss where these websites are headed.

# E-Government

**E-government** is defined as "federal, state, and local government applications that elicit payment or documentation submission over the Net."[19]

Currently, there are two laws that are pushing the federal government online: the Paperwork Elimination Act and the Clinger-Cohen Act. These two acts require that federal government departments move services online and focus on realizing results from their IT investments. Citizens are also anxious for the government to go online. Exhibit 17-3 shows citizens' interest level in online government activities.

Another study shows what users want to do most on government websites is obtain medical information from the National Institutes of Health and other agencies, view candidates' voting records, access Social Security benefit information, register their motor vehicles, and apply for student loans.[20]

Almost all federal and state government agencies have websites, although many do not have good websites. Many of the sites have static webpages that offer only a description of the department and a phone directory. A survey done by the Taubman Center for Public Policy at Brown University found that only a third offered frequently asked questions, and only 22 percent offered any online service. (Even the websites that offer online services are often not well-known, since governments have not marketed their websites and are dependent on press coverage and word of mouth.) The same study found that few government websites offer a security policy (7 percent) or a privacy policy (5 percent); therefore, the fact that most government websites do not offer the ability to do transactions may be for the best, especially since governments often deal with very sensitive data that could compromise the privacy of the user.

**Exhibit 17-3**  NET USERS' INTEREST IN E-GOVERNMENT

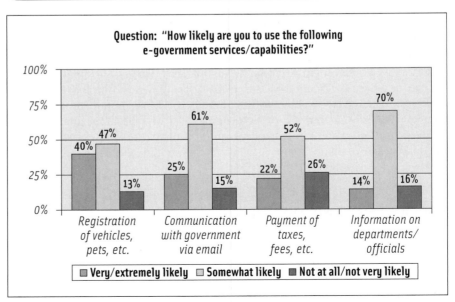

Question: "How likely are you to use the following e-government services/capabilities?"

Source: Forrester Research.

The ability of governments to conduct transactions online is no minor issue. Currently, the United States' 80,000 local governments collect $4 trillion a year from their 273 million constituents, and collections from the federal government market will grow from $679 million in 1998 to nearly $3 billion in 2003.[21] If the government made it easier to pay online it would not only be more convenient for Internet users, but would save both financial and human resources. Also, one of the great benefits of the Internet—the ability to conduct transactions at any time of the day, any day of the week—would encourage people to pay the taxes, tickets, and permit fees required, and the government would seem more responsive.

While the government is aware of the amount of money it could save, there are still major hurdles that it must overcome in order to truly be a working e-government. One hurdle is security. Governments deal with the most sensitive personal information—salaries, social security numbers, arrest records. It is imperative that the websites be more secure than regular e-commerce websites. In this regard, another barrier for e-government is the need to recruit and hire IT personnel. Creating a website that offers all of what citizens are looking for requires a huge upfront cost that many smaller departments and states cannot afford. Also, trying to lure the talent needed away from the private sector could be difficult.

Another problem is that there is no single person or department in charge of supervising the government's online efforts. As such, each department decides how much money to allocate, what content to carry, and which interactive functions, if any, should be included. The amount of money spent on a website also varies greatly. Exhibit 17-4 shows the websites for two large states—California and Texas. While both states' websites offer mostly the same functions, they have a very different appearance, and users who use one of these websites would not be able to easily use the other. Also, smaller states and departments that have much smaller budgets often cannot afford websites with a lot of functionality, which would probably make the website for Texas much different from Rhode Island's website. It is no coincidence that states with big budgets boast the top state websites, while states like Rhode Island, with much smaller budgets, are at the bottom. Also, those that stand to save money or time in transactions, like the IRS, or those, like congressmen, who want to seem in touch with their constituents, are much more motivated to offer a fully functional site than those, like Supreme Court judges, who interact with citizens infrequently and need little public support.

While the current state of government websites is a mixed bag, it will not stay that way, as many government agencies are expected to continue adding features (see Exhibit 17-5). In 2000, it is estimated that governments planned to spend $1.5 billion to go online. It is also estimated that federal, state, and local governments will combine to collect $602 billion online in 2006. Income tax and employer payment collections from small businesses at the federal level will constitute the bulk of e-government collections.[22]

**Criticism of E-Government.** While no one questions the appropriateness of the White House having its own website, some question the government's reach, since some of its departments seem to be competing with private companies. The Computer and Communications Industry Association (CCIA) has criticized the Labor Department's website, which hosts America's Job Bank (ABJ), an online job posting service. ABJ is the largest online job database, with nearly 1.5 million positions listed and nearly 2.5 million registered job seekers. The CCIA concedes, though, that while this is a direct competitor of sites such as Monster.com and Jobs.com, it does provide its own unique service in that it lists jobs for lower-skilled workers, a market that is usually overlooked by online career companies.

**Exhibit 17-4**

COMPARISON OF STATE WEBSITES

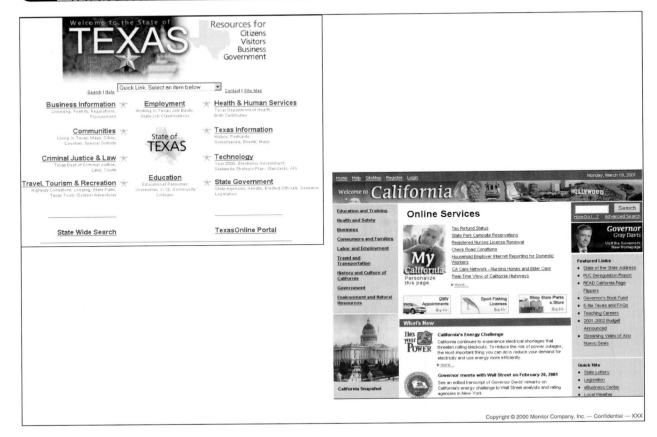

The CCIA, though, has come out strongly against the U.S. Postal Service's eBillpay program, which provides online legal information, online tax preparation software, and a fee-based search engine operated by the National Technical Information service. The CCIA believes that this program is a direct competitor to private companies that offer the ability to pay bills electronically. The USPS disagrees, citing that it has two private-sector partners—Checkfree and Youraccounts.com.[23]

# Election 2000

Like e-government, election coverage on the Internet shows a lot of promise, but has so far underperformed. Given the spirit of the Internet, it seems to be an obvious place for election coverage—up-to-the minute news, in-depth reports, chat rooms to discuss views and issues, and sites to help people come together to support a candidate or cause. In reality, the 2000 election online interaction was mixed. Only 18 percent of the public (33 percent of online users) got election news online. Of those that used the Internet to get election news, though, 43 percent said it affected their vote.

What worked on the Internet? Fundraising, for one. While candidates raised about 95 percent of their money offline, and 40 percent of campaign websites did

**Exhibit 17-5**

GOVERNMENT EXPANSION ON THE INTERNET

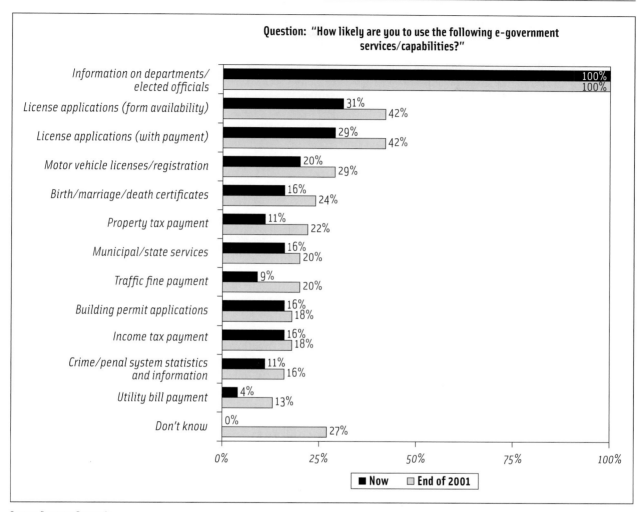

Question: "How likely are you to use the following e-government services/capabilities?"

| | Now | End of 2001 |
|---|---|---|
| Information on departments/elected officials | 100% | 100% |
| License applications (form availability) | 31% | 42% |
| License applications (with payment) | 29% | 42% |
| Motor vehicle licenses/registration | 20% | 29% |
| Birth/marriage/death certificates | 16% | 24% |
| Property tax payment | 11% | 22% |
| Municipal/state services | 16% | 20% |
| Traffic fine payment | 9% | 20% |
| Building permit applications | 16% | 18% |
| Income tax payment | 16% | 18% |
| Crime/penal system statistics and information | 11% | 16% |
| Utility bill payment | 4% | 13% |
| Don't know | 0% | 27% |

Source: Forrester Research.

not even have a mechanism to accept contributions, there was one success story—John McCain collected more than $1 million online less than two days after his victory at the New Hampshire primary. Also successful were the high-speed delivery of election returns and the spread of election-related humor: One study found that 54 percent of Net users trafficked in e-mail jokes about the election.[24]

What did not work? Interactivity: Websites such as Web, White, and Blue, which was supposed to host a cyberdebate over the course of the election in which the candidates answered voter questions, ended up just posting spiffed-up press releases. For-profit portals such as Grassroots.com, SpeakOut.com, and voter.com also did not live up to their promise.[25] Also, only 56 percent of congressional campaigns even had websites in 2000, and only 35 percent of people received political news from the Internet.

## E-Government Companies

Citizens will not be the only ones benefiting from the government's initiatives to set up interactive websites. Gartner estimates that spending on information technology products and related services will increase over the next five years to about $6.2 million by 2005. Companies such as Ezgov.com, govWorks Inc., and NetClerk are poised to capture some of this market by providing software, hardware, and Internet services specifically for government websites.[26]

Ezgov.com offers application packages as well as hosting services to government agencies for their websites. It claims to have more than 60 state and local government agencies and is growing all the time. GovWorks has two offerings. To citizens they offer a portal that links them to public-sector jobs and government websites, as well as the ability to pay permits and taxes online. They offer government agencies transaction services so they can set up their websites to collect licenses and taxes online. NetClerk has a more specific offering: GovCentral, an online permit submission and response application, which allows local building departments to provide and manage online permitting for contractors and citizens.

Another player in this space is Pay.gov. Pay.gov is not a private company, but is a product of the U.S. Treasury, designed to offer agencies the ability to process payments. They are hoping that this will help streamline the payment process and provide a standard for agencies collecting money.

As time goes on, politicians are bound to learn from their mistakes and become more Web-savvy. Already, political parties are starting to use software to collect data to target voters. Republicans in Iowa have begun to use a software program called GeoVoter, which can link up to 5,000 categories of information to each user. A GOP campaign worker can use it to target voters based on their age, ethnicity, religion, marital and socioeconomic status, the value of their homes, or even, if the information is available, their stand on issues like abortion, and whether they have a bank card or own a gun.[27]

## Vote-Swapping Sites

During the 2000 presidential election, a new breed of website appeared: the **vote-swapping** site. Sites such as VoteExchange.com, Nader-Trader.org, and Voteswap2000.com matched Gore voters from states where it seemed Gore would definitely win with Nader voters in states where Gore's position was shaky. In theory, these websites let the two users swap votes so that the Nader voters could try to get the 5 percent vote they wanted to receive federal funding, and the Gore voters would not lose a vote where Gore's hold was shaky.

Legislators were not as excited by the idea, though. California Secretary of State Bill Jones said the Los Angeles-based Voteswap2000 was guilty of conspiracy and corruption of the election process. Authorities in Minnesota, Oregon, and Wisconsin also threatened other vote-swapping sites. The ACLU in turn filed suit against Jones claiming that he was infringing on free speech.

# E-Voting

The fifty-fourth presidential election was held on November 7, 2000. By November 14, the public outcry for **e-voting** (voting electronically) had begun. After days of watching both parties worry about whether a ballot had a pregnant chad, dimpled chad, or two punched-out chads, people started wondering if there was a better way. There were public outcries to implement online voting, and many software and hardware companies joined those cries, claiming that electronic voting would have never resulted in such a botched election.

Maybe, maybe not. As anyone who has ever had their credit card stolen from a site or received someone else's online order in the mail can tell you, technology is far from perfect. Given that the presidency of the United States is at stake, few citizens would probably want to risk a hacker breaking into the election server and changing the vote. What is much more possible are electronic voting booths set up the way manual voting booths are now. Instead of punching a chad, voters would vote on some type of electronic device, and privacy and security would be no more an issue than with paper ballots. However, an electronic election is a long way away, as most politicians are uneasy about changing things. With no paper ballots there could never be a recount. To many citizens, though, that would be a blessing.

# SUMMARY

## 1. Who is on the Internet, and what are they doing?

Internet users tend to be well-educated, higher-income individuals who engage primarily in online activities that involve communication and gathering information. The top five activities on the Internet are researching, communicating with friends and family, getting information about products to buy, getting news, and finding health information. Making purchases came in sixth. Generally, users with more tenure do more activities than new users.

## 2. What is the digital divide?

The digital divide refers to the gap between the people who are on the Internet and the people who are not on the Internet. While the digital divide is closing across education levels, income levels, and race, it remains significant among people with low-income levels ($15,000 and under) and individuals over 65 years of age. The digital divide could become more significant in years to come as the Internet plays a more prominent role in people's lives and those without Internet access or computer skills are not able to get the same information or the same jobs as those with Internet access and computer skills.

## 3. How is the Internet changing education?

While much attention has been paid to getting primary and secondary schools wired and getting students on the Internet, the effects of the Web on K–12 education remain to be seen. More and more colleges and universities are offering online courses, which appeal to those who do not have the time or cannot live close to a school in order to get a degree. While many colleges and universities offer online courses, most do not offer online degrees. Corporate education is also changing, as workers have more access to training classes.

## 4. How is government using the Internet?

While almost all federal, state, and local agencies are creating websites, they all have varying degrees of functionality. The most simple sites offer only a directory, while the more complex ones offer citizens the ability to register for permits online, pay parking tickets, or pay taxes. There are many hurdles preventing the government from using the Internet to its full potential, including each municipality and agency designing its website to meet its own specific criteria and budget problems with smaller agencies and municipalities.

## KEY TERMS

| | |
|---|---|
| digital divide | e-government |
| corporate learning | vote-swapping |
| leisure education | e-voting |

## Endnotes

[1] The America Online/Roper Starch Worldwide Adult 2000 Cyberstudy, October 2000.

[2] The America Online/Roper Starch Worldwide Adult 2000 Cyberstudy, October 2000.

[3] The America Online/Roper Starch Worldwide Adult 2000 Cyberstudy, October 2000.

[4] Pew Internet & American Life Project Survey, November–December 2000.

[5] Horrigan, John. "The holidays online: Emails and e-greeting outpace e-commerce," Pew Internet & American Life Project.

[6] The America Online/Roper Starch Worldwide, "Adult 2000 Cyberstudy," October, 2000.

[7] Cole, Jeffrey I. "Surveying the Digital Future," The UCLA Internet Report, November, 2000.

[8] Source: Computer Industry Almanac, as shown in "The Net world in numbers." *The Industry Standard*, 7 February, 2000. URL: *http://www.thestandard.com/research/metrics/display/0,2799,10121,00.html*.

[9] Source: International Data Corp, in "The Net World in Numbers." *The Industry Standard*, 7 February, 2000.

[10] U.S. Department of Commerce, "Falling Through the Net: Toward Digital Inclusion." October 2000.

[11] U.S. Department of Commerce, "Falling Through the Net: Toward Digital Inclusion." October 2000.

[12] Grimes, Ann. "The hope . . . and the reality," *The Wall Street Journal*, 12 March, 2001, R6.

[13] Rendon, Jim. "Learning potential," *The Industry Standard*, 12 September, 2000.

[14] Schuchman, Lisa. "Lesson plans," *The Industry Standard*, 29 January, 2001. URL: *http://www.thestandard.com/article/display/0,1151,21647,00.html*.

[15] Carr, Lisa. "College off-campus," *The Industry Standard*, 13 September, 2000.

[16] Source: Merrill Lynch

[17] Grimes, Ann. "The hope . . . and the reality," *The Wall Street Journal*, 12 March, 2001, R6.

[18] Park, Andrew. "School's out," *Business 2.0*, 28 June, 2000.

[19] Sharrard, Jeremy. "Sizing U.S. eGovernment," Forrester Reports, August 2000.

[20] Enos, Lori. "Study: Americans back e-government," *E-Commerce Times*. URL: *http://www.ecommercetimes.com/news/articles2000/000929-4.shtml*.

[21] Richardson, Vanessa. "GovWorks receives VC vote," *Red Herring*, 8 November, 1999.

[22] Sharrad, Jeremy. "Sizing U.S. eGovernment," The Forrester Report, August 2000.

[23] Enos, Lori. Report: "E-Gov choking E-Commerce," *E-Commerce Times*.

[24] Derfner, Jeremy-Slate. "So, was it really a Net election?" TheStandard.com, 30 January, 2001. URL: *http://www.thestandard.com/article/display/0,1151,21793,00.html*.

[25]Derfner, Jeremy-Slate. "So, was it really a Net election?" TheStandard.com, 30 January, 2001. URL: *http://www.thestandard/com/article/display/0,1151,21793,00.html.*

[26]Saia, Rick. "Gartner sees 'e-government explosion'," *Computerworld* 12 April, 2000.

[27]Stepanek, Marcia. "How the data-miners want to influence your vote," BusinessweekOnline, 26 October, 2000. URL: *http://www.businessweek.com/bwdaily/dnflash/oct2000/nf20001026_969.htm.*

APPENDICES
GLOSSARY
INDEX

# Widget Wonders

## EXECUTIVE SUMMARY
## CONFIDENTIAL, MARCH 1, YEAR 1

**Widget Wonders**
**777 Widget Way**
**Widgetville, OH 12345-1234**
**Phone: (123) 123-1234**
**Fax: (123) 123-1234**
***www.widgetwonder.com***

Created by Ellie Kyung.

NOTE: This business plan, while based on some real industry data, is entirely fabricated in concept and content, including all company names and individuals. It is meant to illustrate an example of format and useful data that can be included in a business plan and should not be construed as a model for financials or ideal market opportunity.

**EXECUTIVE SUMMARY**

Table of Contents

# A. WIDGET WONDERS LEADERSHIP TEAM

## Management Team

### Dr. JoAnn Jenkins, President and CEO

Prior to founding Widget Wonders with Mr. Alcott, Ms. Jenkins served as the COO of U.S. Wireless. She was responsible for much of U.S. Wireless's success, including overseeing the merger with American Wireless, creating the largest wireless service provider in the United States. During her 15-year tenure with American Wireless, Ms. Jenkins also served as the head of research and development in the wireless division—specifically working on the issue of bandwidth maximization—and as VP of Eastern Region Operations.

**Education:** Ph.D., Scientific University; MBA, Hubbard Business School; BS, Knowledge College

### Dr. Andrew Alcott, VP Engineering and Product Development

Before founding Widget Wonders, Mr. Alcott was a professor of computer science at Scientific University specializing in the development of wireless technologies. His renowned Wireless Wizzy™ device—an earring that also serves as a wireless phone—won numerous scientific prizes and awards, including Scientific Device of the Year in 2000. He has been a consultant to nearly every Fortune 100 company involved in the telecommunications industry, including U.S. Wireless, Magnificent Mobile Phones, Crystal Clear Cellular, Fantastic Phones, and Shifty Software.

**Education:** Ph.D., MS, Scientific University; BS, Knowledge College

### Eleanor Elkin, VP Business Development

Ms. Elkin comes to Widget Wonders after 10 years with U.S. Wireless, where she was also the head of business development. There, she was responsible for the development of partnerships and identification of possible acquisition targets—including the partnerships with Top-Notch Mobile, Biggie ISP, and Commercial Cable. She was also instrumental in engineering the landmark U.S. Wireless/American Wireless merger.

**Education:** MBA, Standard Business School; BS, Hi-Tech University

### Chris Cullins, VP Sales and Marketing

Prior to joining Widget Wonders, Mr. Cullins was the head of MacMillan Consulting's market-research practice for five years, developing and implementing marketing strategies for Fortune 100 companies. For the past 10 years, Mr. Cullins has been working with MacMillan, specializing in the telecommunications and high-tech industries, and is responsible for such phenomenal marketing successes as the Handy Dandy PDA.

**Education:** BA, Marketing College of America

### Dorsey Davis, VP Strategic Planning

In her 15-year career, Ms. Davis has successfully launched four businesses. All four were in high-tech telecommunications-related industries, including an ISP, an ASP, and a MSP. Her most recent business—Unlimited Bandwidth—was recently acquired by Crystal Clear for $200 million. After the acquisition, Ms. Davis served as the head of e-business strategy development for Crystal Clear, and was responsible for its recent 20 percent increase in market share, driven primarily by online sales.

**Education:** MBA, Hubbard Business School; BS, Hi-Tech University

## Advisory Board

| | |
|---|---|
| **Fred Franco** | Director, United States Communications Board |
| **Jayne Johnson** | President, E-Business Solutions, Crystal Clear Cellular |
| **Max Miller** | CEO, U.S. Wireless |
| **Robert Rollins** | VP of Sales, Fantastic Phones |
| **Eunice Edwards** | Computer Science Department Chairman, Scientific University |

## B. PROFILE

An estimated 38 percent of Americans carried wireless phones in 2000, and that number is expected to reach 62 percent by 2005. However, a mere 6 percent of Americans own browser-enabled wireless phones.[1] Consumer demand for wireless service remains low, constrained by device limitations, service pricing, and slow access speeds—currently limited to 14.4 Kpbs.

Widget Wonders has the potential to change the wireless landscape in the United States. Our patent-pending Widget Wonder™ is a stamp-size adhesive device that can turn any normal wireless phone into a browser-enabled phone, allowing data transfer at the rate of 1.5 Mbps—the equivalent of a T1 connection. The Widget Wonder™ is compatible with any wireless phone, regardless of make or manufacturer, and can even be used with browser-enabled phones to increase data access speeds. It also overrides any existing network shortcomings regarding bandwidth. There is currently no device like the Widget Wonder™ available on the market, and we estimate that top competitors are still two years behind in development.

Widget Wonders is currently finalizing agreements with leading phone manufacturers and wireless service providers for a national rollout. An infusion of capital will allow Widget Wonders to increase production to a nationally available product, providing every wireless phone user in the United States the potential for cost-effective, high-speed wireless Internet access.

[1]Yankee Group, October 2000

| Industry | Wireless Internet access |
|---|---|
| Approach | Enabling standard wireless phones to serve as browser-enabled phones through a stamp-sized adhesive device and increasing the access speed of current browser-enabled phones |
| Target Market | Current and future U.S. wireless phone owners |
| Market Opportunity | 38% of Americans own wireless phones (2000)<br>An estimated 51% of Americans will own browser-enabled phones by 2004 |
| Market Growth in Five Years | 253% growth of mobile e-commerce revenues (CAGR 2000–2004)<br>270% growth of wireless Internet users (CAGR 2000–2004) |

**Financial Forecast (Year 3)**

| Revenue | $409 MM |
|---|---|
| Users | 8.6 MM |
| Gross Margin | 70% |

**Capital Requirements**

| Series A | $1 MM | Secured through private investors, enabled beta testing |
|---|---|---|
| Series B | $10 MM | Full-scale national launch |

| Current Development Stage | Beta version developed and tested locally, patent pending |
|---|---|

# Key Advantages

**Technology**
- Patent-pending Widget Wonder™ technology
- Quickly scalable, low-cost production process

**Team**
- 100 years combined experience in the telecommunications industry
- Former top-level executives from U.S. Wireless and Crystal Clear
- 15 years of designing wireless applications
- Top technologists in the wireless industry

**Partnerships**
- Letters of intent with leading wireless phone manufacturers Magnificent Mobile and Fantastic Phones for joint product distribution and marketing
- In negotiations with top two U.S. service providers, U.S. Wireless and Crystal Clear, for bundled services
- Definitive agreements with top content and commerce sites buyalot.com, Yipee!, tradealot.com, bankhere.com, and others.

# C. INTRODUCTION

Although 40 percent of Americans own wireless phones, less than 1 percent use their phones to tap the resources available on the Internet. This is due primarily to the following limitations:

- Slow access speed
- Cost of access (service agreements)
- Limited availability of content
- Cost of Web-enabled wireless phones versus non-Web-enabled wireless phones

Through a combination of the proprietary Widget Wonder™ technology and pricing agreements with wireless providers, Widget Wonders is uniquely positioned to significantly grow the market for wireless Internet use in the United States through

- Offering significantly faster 1.5 Mbps data transfer
- The relatively low price and simplicity of the Widget Wonder™ device
- Arranging special lower-priced access through major wireless providers

Widget Wonders is also in talks with a number of the top content providers to provide promotion for the Widget Wonder™, as well as offer an increased amount of content that can be accessed through wireless phones. Low price and ease of use make it possible for the Widget Wonder™ to have a high adoption rate, which can in turn increase the number of content providers willing to format information in an easily accessible format for phone users.

Regional beta testing with current partners experienced great success with consumers, resulting in the letters of intent and negotiations with U.S. Wireless, Magnificent Mobile, Crystal Cellular, and Fantastic Phones. Widget Wonders is also currently developing a version of Widget Wonder™ for PDA devices.

# D. MARKET OPPORTUNITY

## U.S. Wireless Phone Usage

- The number of wireless phone owners in the United States is steadily growing, increasing from 38 percent in 2000 to 62 percent in 2005.[2]
- Ownership of browser-enabled wireless phones is expected to grow over the next five years (CAGR 58 percent from 2000–2005)—growth that can be jumpstarted and supplemented with the Widget Wonder™.

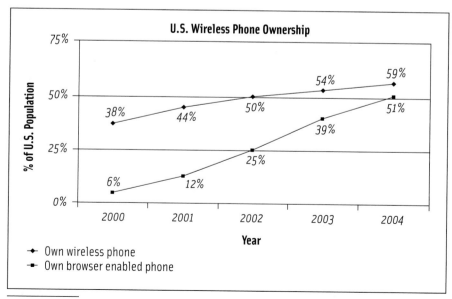

---
[2]Yankee Group, October 2000

# Growth of Wireless Internet Usage

Even with current technological limitations,

- 60 percent of Internet users have some degree of interest in wireless access[3]
- Growth of wireless Internet users is estimated at 170 percent (CAGR 2000–2004)
- Growth of mobile e-commerce buyers is estimated at 103 percent (CAGR 2000–2004)[4]

# E. FINANCIAL SUMMARY

## Revenues

Revenues are generated through

**(1)** Sale of the Widget Wonders™ directly to the consumer and to wireless phone manufacturers ($50 per device)

**(2)** Monthly residuals from partner service providers ($1 per month per user)

Widget Wonders will generate revenues in excess of $19 MM in Year 1.

## Projections

**Financial projections (Year 3).**

- $409 MM annual revenue
- 8.6 MM users
- 70% gross margin
- Widget Wonders becomes EBITDA positive in Q3 Year 2

## Series B Funding

**Widget Wonders seeking $10 MM for the following:**

- Full scale production facilities—to enable national product roll-out
- Customer acquisition—to support activities with partners
- Working capital requirements—to expand management team and employee base
- Marketing expenses—to promote brand awareness and enable public relations activities

---

[3]Strategis Group
[4]Ovum

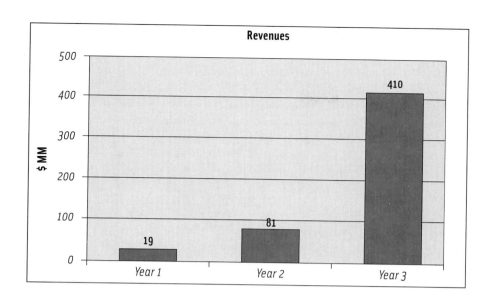

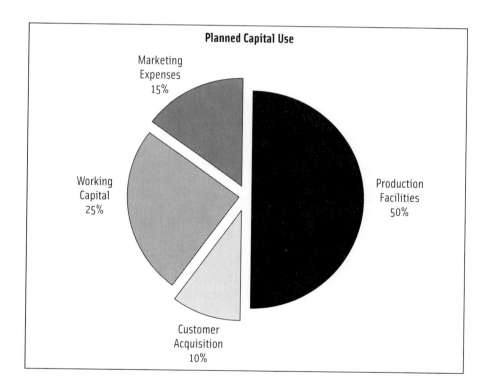

# F. BUSINESS STRATEGY

Widget Wonder's value proposition is designed to be attractive to any current wireless phone user with an interest in wireless Internet access. The combination of the Widget Wonder™ technology with a sophisticated network of partnerships provides customers with low-cost, high-speed wireless Internet access and specialized content.

# Revolutionary Proprietary Technology

Widget Wonder™ (patent pending):

- Unique proprietary technology developed by award-winning technologists
- Simple components and manufacturing process lead to low per-unit cost
- High-speed (1.5 Mbps) access makes wireless Internet access far more attractive to the customer
- Small, stamp-size adhesive format makes installation and use simple with existing wireless phones, including allowing high-speed access for phones that are already browser-enabled
- Technology is easily compatible with any website

# Strategic Partnerships

Manufacturing partnerships:

- Partnership agreements currently being refined with Magnificent Mobile and Fantastic Phones would bundle the Widget Wonder™ with wireless phones when sold through certain wireless providers
- Partnerships with other phone manufacturers currently pending

Service-provider partnerships:

- Pending partnerships with U.S. Wireless and Crystal Clear would provide users of the Widget Wonder™ with unlimited wireless Internet access for $10.00 per month

Content partnerships:

- Definitive agreements with current partners (buyalot.com, shop24.com, Yipee!, tradealot.com, bankhere.com, ultimateauction.com) provide content specifically for the increased speed of the Widget Wonder™
- Current brand-name partnerships will provide leverage in the development of future partnerships

# Broad Product Appeal

The Widget Wonder™ advantage lies in its compatibility and potential use across a number of customer groups:

- New wireless phone purchases (to allow access)
- Current wireless phone owners (to allow access)
- Current browser-enabled phone owners (to improve speed of access)
- (Within 6-8 months) PDA owners (to allow access or improve speed of access)

# G. MARKETING STRATEGY

Widget Wonders will provide brand recognition not only through its own marketing efforts, but also through the support of partners, which will significantly reduce the cost of a national-scale marketing campaign.

# Leveraging Strategic Partnerships

Content-site partners:

- Provide specialized content for the Widget Wonder™ with onsite purchase link

Manufacturers:

- Joint television and print advertising campaigns
- Joint in-store displays

Service providers:

- Joint television and print advertising campaigns
- Special promotional offers
- Provide printed advertisements and offers in current customer bills

# Raising Public Recognition

In conjunction with working with strategic partners, Widget Wonders will engage in the following standard brand-building activities:

- Participation in conferences, tradeshows, and other industry-related meetings
- Press releases and other media-driven public relations
- Carefully placed banner advertisements on sponsor sites
- Targeted print and radio advertising
- Direct mailings to current wireless phone users

# Sales Channels

The Widget Wonder will be sold

- To current wireless phone users through electronic and wireless phone stores
- To new wireless phone buyers as an add-on bundle of services with new phone purchase (subsidized by the wireless service provider)
- Through online electronics stores and retailers
- Directly on the *www.widgetwonder.com* site

# H. COMPETITIVE LANDSCAPE

While there are wireless phones that provide Web-enabled access, few customers actually use their browser-enabled phones, primarily due to limitations in bandwidth and content. Widget Wonders believes that it is uniquely positioned in the market to provide impetus to grow the wireless-Internet user base, in turn leading to a greater number of content providers providing wireless-accessible information. Customer feedback from beta testing with partner sites has confirmed that speed was a significant barrier to wireless Internet use. Below is a comparison of the Widget Wonder™ versus several types of competitors:

- Web-enabled phones
- Wireless PDA devices
- Active Attachment (large pack-of-cards-size attachment that allows standard wireless phones access to the Internet)

While PDAs do offer the advantage of a larger screen interface, slow speed significantly limits the capabilities of these devices. With the expected launch of its PDA product expected in the next six to eight months, the Widget Wonder™ will ultimately be a complimentary product to the wireless PDA device. Similarly, the Widget Wonder™ also complements the technology of Web-enabled phones, allowing much faster access speeds.

# I. PRELIMINARY FINANCIAL PROJECTIONS

The projected quarterly income statement for the first three years of operations is included below. Detailed financials and analysis of assumptions are available upon request. The projections during the three-year period are based on the following key assumptions:

- Cost of producing each Widget Wonder™ is quite low, with economies-of-scale, costing only $15 per unit when production hits 1 MM units per year
- Each unit will be sold for $50
- Commission from service agreements of $1 per user per month
- Very conservative customer acquisition assumptions of 100,000 the first quarter, growing at 50 percent per quarter (even at Year 3, this would constitute a market share of only 5 percent of wireless phone owners)

| Primary Features | Widget Wonder™ | Web-Enabled Phones | Wireless PDA Devices | Active Attachment |
|---|---|---|---|---|
| Partnerships with key wireless service providers | √ | √ | √ | |
| Partnerships with content providers for specialized content | √ | √ | √ | |
| Partnerships with key phone manufacturers | √ | √ | | |
| Proprietary technology | √ | | | |
| Compatibility with any mobile phone device | √ | N/A | N/A | |
| Access speed | **1.5 Mbps** | 14.4 Kpbs | 14.4 Kpbs | 9.6 Kpbs |
| Cost of device | **$50** | $299 | $400 | $200 |
| Cost of monthly service agreement (unlimited access) | **$10** | N/A* | $45 | $45 |

*Typically included as use of wireless phone plan minutes, with each additional minute as 10 cents, or 39 cents per minute without a plan

# Projected Quarterly Income Statement (Years 1-3)

| | Year 1 | | | | |
| --- | --- | --- | --- | --- | --- |
| | Q1 | Q2 | Q3 | Q4 | Year 1 |
| Revenues | $5,300,000 | $2,950,000 | $4,425,000 | $6,637,500 | $19,312,500 |
| Cost of Sales | 3,180,000 | 1,622,500 | 2,212,500 | 2,986,875 | 10,001,875 |
| Gross Profit | 2,120,000 | 1,327,500 | 2,212,500 | 3,650,625 | 9,310,625 |
| Gross Margin | 40% | 45% | 50% | 55% | 48% |
| General & Administrative | 2,000,000 | 2,400,000 | 2,880,000 | 3,456,000 | 10,736,000 |
| Sales & Marketing | 1,000,000 | 1,400,000 | 1,960,000 | 2,744,000 | 7,104,000 |
| EBITDA | (880,000) | (2,472,500) | (2,627,500) | (2,549,375) | (8,529,375) |
| EBITDA Margin | -17% | -84% | -59% | -38% | -44% |
| | Year 2 | | | | |
| | Q1 | Q2 | Q3 | Q4 | Year 2 |
| Revenues | $9,956,250 | $14,934,375 | $22,401,563 | $33,602,344 | $80,894,531 |
| Cost of Sales | 3,982,500 | 5,227,031 | 6,720,469 | 10,080,703 | 26,010,703 |
| Gross Profit | 5,973,750 | 9,707,344 | 15,681,094 | 23,521,641 | 54,883,828 |
| Gross Margin | 60% | 65% | 70% | 70% | 68% |
| General & Administrative | 4,147,200 | 4,976,640 | 5,971,968 | 7,166,362 | 22,262,170 |
| Sales & Marketing | 3,841,600 | 5,378,240 | 7,529,536 | 10,541,350 | 27,290,726 |
| EBITDA | (2,015,050) | (647,536) | 2,179,590 | 5,813,929 | 5,330,932 |
| EBITDA Margin | -20% | -4% | 10% | 17% | 7% |
| | Year 3 | | | | |
| | Q1 | Q2 | Q3 | Q4 | Year 3 |
| Revenues | $50,403,516 | $75,605,273 | $113,407,910 | $170,111,865 | $409,528,564 |
| Cost of Sales | 15,121,055 | 22,681,582 | 34,022,373 | 51,033,560 | 122,858,569 |
| Gross Profit | 35,282,461 | 52,923,691 | 79,385,537 | 119,078,306 | 286,669,995 |
| Gross Margin | 70% | 70% | 70% | 70% | 70% |
| General & Administrative | 8,599,634 | 10,319,561 | 12,383,473 | 14,860,167 | 46,162,835 |
| Sales & Marketing | 14,757,891 | 20,661,047 | 28,925,465 | 40,495,652 | 104,840,055 |
| EBITDA | 11,924,936 | 21,943,084 | 38,076,599 | 63,722,487 | 135,667,106 |
| EBITDA Margin | 24% | 29% | 34% | 37% | 33% |

# APPENDIX B
## Contributing Authors
## (in alphabetical order)

**Jennifer Barron** joined Monitor Company in 1985 as a strategy consultant. Ms. Barron has a broad range of experience in helping clients solve business problems, with a particular focus on competitive positioning and marketing strategies. She has worked with executives across many industries, including financial services, technology, and consumer packaged goods.

Ms. Barron is a principal and founder of Monitor Company's Strategic Marketing and Research (SMR) division. She has been instrumental in driving the growth of the group and oversees product development and new business development initiatives. Ms. Barron is currently actively involved in helping clients with their brand design and delivery issues.

Ms. Barron graduated from Dartmouth College with an honors degree in economics. She received her master's in business administration from Harvard Business School.

**Yannis Dosios** is a Marketspace consultant in Los Angeles. He received a bachelor's in mathematics from Harvard University. Since he joined Monitor in August 1997, Mr. Dosios has worked in a number of industries, including e-business, telecommunications, entertainment, high-tech, consumer products, and the nonprofit sector. His work has primarily focused on market analysis, corporate strategy, streamlining of activities, processes and systems, and identification and development of new business concepts. Outside of work, Mr. Dosois enjoys traveling, playing tennis, and watching international movies.

**Colin Gounden** brings a combination of technology and business experience to his position as head of advisory services in North America for Marketspace. In 1996, Mr. Gounden founded the technology services arm of Conduit Communications in London, a company that provided consulting on the use and implementation of Internet technology to support organizational change. As a senior partner with Conduit, Mr. Gounden became the trusted advisor on technology and digital economy issues to executives at firms such as Royal Dutch/Shell, Barclays Capital Group, and Harvard Business School Publishing.

Mr. Gounden rose to the position of CEO of Conduit's United States operations before selling his 150-person firm to digital business consultancy Razorfish in 1999. As a director of strategy at Razorfish, Mr. Gounden led many of the company's largest digital strategy engagements in the United States before joining Marketspace in 2000.

Prior to joining Conduit, Mr. Gounden designed and developed business software for large organizations with IBM, focusing on both global implementation engagements and rapid, proof-of-concept projects. His client roster included La Lyonnaise des Eaux (the world's second largest water company) and Telefonos de Mexico (the largest telecoms operator in Latin America).

Mr. Gounden earned a bachelor's in biochemistry and molecular biology from Harvard College, and his research in the field of auditory systems of bats won him the Ford Undergraduate Research Scholarship for three consecutive years.

**Leo Griffin** is a leader of Marketspace's Los Angeles office. Leo received a bachelor's in industrial economics at the London School of Economics and received his MBA with distinction from Kellogg. During his career he has worked in the United States, the United Kingdom, Spain, Italy, Canada, and Russia. Prior to joining Monitor, Mr. Griffin worked for an Internet startup. When not at work he enjoys biking in the nearby Santa Monica mountains.

**Joseph Hartzell** is a consultant with Monitor's Los Angeles office. He received his bachelor's in business administration from the University of California at Berkeley. Since joining Monitor in 1999, Mr. Hartzell has worked in biotechnology, health insurance, and manufacturing. Prior to working in management consulting, Mr. Hartzell cofounded an Internet startup and spent several years in marketing management at network equipment manufacturers. Outside of work, Mr. Hartzell enjoys surfing, sailing, and scuba diving off of the California coast.

**Ellie Kyung** is a consultant with Marketspace's New York office. Since joining Monitor in 1998, she has focused primarily on the development of marketing and branding strategy, working closely with Monitor's Market2Customer group. Ms. Kyung's client work has been focused in the health care and e-commerce industries. Her research work has focused on branding, new business development, and the digitalization of information. She graduated cum laude from Yale University with a dual bachelor's in economics and international studies.

**Dickson Louie** is principal of Louie & Associates, a San Francisco Bay Area consultancy that provides business development, marketing research, and competitive analysis to media companies. Clients of Louie & Associates include *The San Francisco Chronicle*, Monitor Company, and the Maynard Institute.

Prior to establishing his own consulting practice in February 1999, Mr. Louie spent 13 years in the newspaper industry. From 1984 to 1995, he was a member of the management team of *The Los Angeles Times* and its parent company, Times Mirror. As a member of the circulation department's senior management, Mr. Louie was responsible for management reporting, subscriber retention analysis, and department operational reviews. In November 1989, Mr. Louie drafted the initial business plan that helped make *The Los Angeles Times* the largest metropolitan daily newspaper in the United States. More recently, Mr. Louie served as business development and planning manager for *The San Jose Mercury News*. He was responsible for the development of several new product and revenue initiatives, including the launch of *Viet Mercury*, a Vietnamese-language newspaper that serves the growing Vietnamese-American community in Silicon Valley. In 1996, Mr. Louie was appointed as a research associate at Harvard Business School, where he has authored over 20 case studies for the Marketspace course, including those on Amazon.com, CBS Evening News, New York Times Electronic Media Company, QVC, and Monster.com.

Mr. Louie is a graduate of California State University, Hayward, where he received his bachelor's degree in business administration with a minor in journalism in 1980, and of the University of Chicago, where he received his master's in business administration in 1984.

**Andy Macaleer** is a Managing Director at Breakaway Solutions, responsible for managing its practice focused on implementing net marketplaces and exchanges. Mr. Macaleer has been in systems integration for 14 years, 11 of which were spent with Andersen Consulting in the process manufacturing industry focusing on business process re-engineering and implementation of systems for ERP, manufacturing, supply chain management and e-business. At Breakaway, Mr. Macaleer manages a practice that has experience implementing over 25 net marketplaces and exchanges across almost as many vertical industries. Mr. Macaleer holds a bachelor's in engineering and management systems from Princeton University.

**Vijay Manwani** has 15 years of consulting experience in delivering information technology solutions to a variety of industries. He was most recently the CTO at Breakaway Solutions, where he was responsible for technology strategy and for developing a strong technology culture within Breakaway. Prior to that, he was the CTO and cofounder of Eggrock Partners, an e-business consulting firm that was acquired by Breakaway in early 2000. Before founding Eggrock, Mr. Manwani worked in senior technology and operations roles at Cambridge Technology Partners and Teknekron Communication Systems. Mr. Manwani serves on several technical advisory boards and has a patent for his work in the travel industry. He is currently an EIR (entreprenuer-in-residence) at Battery Ventures, as he explores opportunities to start his next company.

**Dorsey McGlone** is a consultant for Marketspace in Cambridge, Massachusetts. She received her bachelor's in English language and literature from the University of Virginia in 1991 and her MBA from Harvard Business School in 2000. Prior to business school, Ms. McGlone worked at a high-tech startup that built and sold speech-activated, wearable computers; this company went public in 1996. Since joining Marketspace in September of 2000, Ms. McGlone has worked on a variety of projects with both startups and old-economy companies, as well as internal projects profiling venture-capital investments and the venture-capital community.

**Nancy Michels** has been a consultant with Monitor Company since 1992. Over the course of her career at Monitor, she has worked in health care, technology, financial services, and industrial manufacturing. Her work in these areas has focused primarily on marketing strategy, including customer segmentation, market assessment, competitive analysis, and brand positioning. She also has experience in distribution analysis, new product development, process design, and organizational change management. As part of Marketspace, Ms. Michels has concentrated on online branding. She is currently working with the marketing department of a large biotechnology company on a new product launch.

Internally, Ms. Michels has been a faculty member in Monitor's marketing training program for new consultants and is a professional development advisor for other consultants. She received her MBA from Harvard Business School and graduated magna cum laude from Brigham Young University with a bachelor's in economics. Ms. Michels currently resides in San Francisco with her husband, David, and daughter, Elise.

**Rafi Mohammed** has been a consultant with Monitor Company since 1998. He has worked in areas of the new economy, broadband, and online service marketing and development strategy. Prior to joining Monitor, Dr. Mohammed had his own media strategy consulting practice in Los Angeles and worked on deregulatory issues at the Federal Communications Commission in Washington, D.C.

Dr. Mohammed has a Ph.D. in economics from Cornell University and holds economics degrees from the London School of Economics and Boston University. His academic research has focused on media and business strategy topics.

**Mark W. Pocharski** is an officer and global account manager in Monitor Company's marketing strategy group. Mr. Pocharski works with B2B and B2C clients in a variety of industries, including consumer packaged goods, consumer financial services, pharmaceuticals, beverages, business telecommunications, health insurance, and natural gas. He has managed client relationships in North America, Europe, and Asia.

Mr. Pocharski's recent projects include developing an integrated online/bricks-and-mortar new-business offering for a major U.S. consumer products company; turning around the growth trend for a leading consumer financial services company with online and bricks-and-mortar marketing initiatives; devising a growth of strategy for a major beverage brand; refreshing the brand personality for a leader in skin-care products; creating a set of innovative product offerings for and introducing a new product-development process to a major U.S. telecommunications player; designing and implementing a segment-based marketing strategy for a major U.S. health insurance company; creating an account-management program for a national energy company; and redesigning the roles and service offerings of market research groups for global leaders in consumer packaged goods and pharmaceuticals.

In addition to client project work, Mr. Pocharski designed and teaches a strategic marketing course for clients.

Mr. Pocharski received his MBA from Harvard Business School. He was graduated, cum laude, from Dartmouth College with a degree in economics and government.

**Marco Smit** is a senior project manager in Monitor Company's Cambridge, Massachusetts, office. He has more than five years of consulting experience in Europe, Asia, and the United States. Since he joined Monitor in 1998, he has worked in a variety of industries, including biotechnology, high technology, consumer products, financial services, and the nonprofit sector. Within these industries, he has worked on market segmentation, organizational design, competitive strategy, new business development, private/public partnerships, and mergers and acquisitions. Recently, Mr. Smit's work has focused on biotechnology and e-business strategy, including business-plan development, partnership strategy, implementation, organizational strategies, and growth-path development.

Mr. Smit holds a Master's in economics from the Erasmus University in Rotterdam (Netherlands), where he studied economic integration with a specialization in financial derivatives. He also studied strategy at the post-graduate school of management of ESSEC in Paris (France). He is a fluent French, German, Dutch, and Bahasa-Indonesia speaker.

**Tobias H. A. Thomas** is an officer and global account manager in Monitor Company's marketing strategy group. Mr. Thomas is a cofounder and leader of M2C's Web-based marketing services group. In addition, Mr. Thomas is the head of M2C's GrowthPath® Application Group, which enables Monitor's clients to systematically identify and capture new growth opportunities.

Mr. Thomas is one of the primary developers of the GrowthPath®, Customer Portrait® and Action Segmentation™ frameworks, as well as many of the other core technologies used in M2C's Web-based marketing services group and Monitor client engagements today. Mr. Thomas has advised clients on their e-commerce strategies as well as starting up M2C's own Web-based business.

In addition, Mr. Thomas has developed impactful marketing, business-unit, and corporate strategies for clients in a variety of B2B and B2C contexts including consumer packaged goods, financial services, telecommunications, chemicals, metals, travel, and beverages industries, often doubling their historical rate of growth. Mr. Thomas' most recent client work includes developing detailed local and national consumer, brand, and channel strategies and frameworks for a global beverage company; creating targeted offers channel strategies for a telecommunications client; and building the internal marketing capabilities of a leading investment bank.

Mr. Thomas received a MBA from Harvard Business School, where he was an honors student, and a bachelor's in chemical engineering, with honors, from Queen's University in Canada.

**Michael Yip** joined Marketspace in 2000 as a member of the R&D team and served as project manager and writer for the development of the textbook *e-Commerce* and its companion textbook, *Cases in e-Commerce*.

From 1992 to 1999, Mr. Yip worked in international treasury and finance at Sony Pictures Entertainment, where he developed foreign-exchange hedge strategies and managed all company-wide foreign-exchange transactions, cross-border funds transfers, and international lines of credit and letters of credit.

Mr. Yip has also worked in film and television production. He has been a studio engineer, a production manager of national television commercials, and a producer for Jim Henson, where he developed interactive video- and game-controller devices. He was also a faculty head and taught graduate and undergraduate courses in television production and new technologies at New York University's Tisch School of the Arts.

Mr. Yip is a graduate of the University of California at Berkeley, where he received his bachelor's degree in psychology, and New York University, Tisch School of the Arts, Institute of Film and Television, where he received a bachelor's in fine arts.

**Eugene Wang** is a consultant with Monitor Group's Los Angeles office. Prior to joining Monitor, Eugene worked with several Web-based companies in a variety of roles, including finance and business development. In addition, he has also spent significant time working as an administrator of an elementary after-school program. Mr. Wang graduated with a bachelor's in business administration from University of California, Berkeley's Haas School of Business.

# GLOSSARY

**10-step branding process**  Branding framework that includes ten steps: clearly identify the brand audience, understand the customer, identify key leverage points in customer experience, continually monitor competitors, design compelling and complete brand intent, execute with integrity, be consistent over time, establish feedback systems, be opportunistic, and invest and be patient.

**Acquiring bank**  A financial institution that a merchant works with to process credit cards. The acquiring bank typically processes credit card transactions through the credit card networks and then deposits the funds into the merchant's bank account.

**Acquisition of customer**  Second stage of the life cycle of a company. The goal is to build market share as quickly as possible by aggressively spending on partnerships and promotion.

**Actionable segmentation**  Segmentation that is easy to recognize, readily reached, and can be described in terms of its growth, size, profile, and attractiveness, but does not provide much insight into customer motivations.

**Affiliate program**  Directs users to affiliated websites through links or links embedded in site banners or other advertising materials.

**Analog modem**  A technology that uses slow (up to 64 kbps) analog signals over existing copper phone lines for communication between computers.

**Analog**  Processes and transmits electronic information using a continuous varied amplitude, frequency, or phase of an electronic signal and/or carrier. Analog technology is also used for transmitting voice data over telephone wires and broadcasting AM and FM radio and TV.

**Analyst reports**  Data sources that are a blend of primary market data on a particular topic and an analyst's view of the market.

**Angel**  Wealthy individual who invests personal capital in startups in exchange for equity.

**Antidilution provisions**  Protects the investor from dilution in ownership that might occur in future rounds of financing.

**Asset valuation method**  A baseline for negotiations to determine valuation of the company.

**Auction pricing**  Buyers bid against each other and the highest bidder wins supplier products or services.

**Authentication**  The process of ensuring the identity of another entity on the Internet (e.g., a website).

**B2B sell-side solution**  B2B sell-side solutions can include capabilities such as online searchable catalogs, orders populated with shopping-cart functions, online fulfillment information with expected ship date, delivery date, and shipping status.

**Backbone network**  The major wide area network to which other networks attach to form the Internet.

**Backbone sites**  Computers that are directly connected to the backbone network.

**Balanced Scorecard**  Introduced by Kaplan and Norton in response to their perception that managers overwhelmingly focus on short-term financial performance. To address this concern, they argued that firms must "balance" their financial perspective when analyzing other domains of the business that include internal business processes and customer responses.

**Bandwidth**  The amount of data that can be transferred by or through a device in a given amount of time (often measured in kilobytes per second or megabytes per second).

**Banner ads**  Websites display these boxlike advertisements to entice viewers to click the ad, which links to the advertiser's website.

**Bit**  A unit of information stored as either a one or a zero.

**Bootstrapping**  The process of using personal resources to finance the early stages of a startup.

**Brand equity**  Combination of assets that can be viewed from both the firm's and the customer's perspective.

**Branding and implementation metrics**  Measurements of supply-chain performance, organizational dynamics, and marketing communication effectiveness (including branding).

**Branding**  Concerns the consumer's perception of the offering—how it performs, how it looks, how it makes one feel, and what messages it sends to others.

**Broadband**  A type of data transmission with connectivity speeds exceeding 128 kilobits per second.

**Broadcast**  First stage of B2B capabilities evolution, in which businesses are able to create simple, static webpages that provide information in one direction from a business to its trading partners.

**Business-model metrics**  Measurements that capture the subcomponents of the business model: the value proposition, Egg Diagram, resource system, and financial metrics.

**Business model**  A new-economy business model requires four choices on the part of senior management. These include (1) the specification of a value proposition or "value cluster" for targeted customers; (2) a marketspace offering, which could be a product, a service, and/or information; (3) a unique, defendable resource system; and (4) a financial model.

**Business plan**  A document that provides a framework for testing the business from conception through early development to capitalize on strengths, compensate for weaknesses, and serve as a resume for potential investors.

**Business planning process**  A framework or theory to define the product or service, identify customers, attract customer acquisition, manufacture and design the product, make money, hire the team, and envision the future of the company.

**Business-to-business (B2B)**  The full spectrum of e-commerce that can occur between two organizations, including purchasing and procurement, supplier management, inventory management, channel management, sales activities, payment management, and service and support.

**Business-to-consumer (B2C)**  E-commerce sites that sell from businesses to consumers (e.g., Amazon.com, Yahoo.com, and Schwab.com).

**Byte**  Eight bits of information, typically representing one character of text.

**Cable modem**  A type of modem that gives users high-speed access (2 to 3 megbits per second) to the Internet through the coaxial cable used for cable television signals.

**Caching**  Temporary storage of frequently accessed information for the purpose of making the information available to users more quickly and reducing network bandwidth demands.

**Capital infrastructure**  The financial and management communities that enable the creation of new business.

**Card-not-present transactions**  A credit card transaction executed without the credit card physically being present during the purchase. These types of transactions are common on the Web and carry implications for the assumption of chargeback liability.

**Cash businesses**  A business that only accepts cash as a form of payment.

**Catalog management**  Catalog management provides basic capabilities of taxonomy, populate and load, and search. The catalog management system allows the organization to load and manage a Web-based product or service catalog. Catalog management for sell-side organizations creates and manages a catalog of their own products, while buy-side organizations must include those of their suppliers and other trading partners.

**Catalog pricing**  The price of goods and services is preset by the seller. Users select items from displayed catalogs and pay the associated prices.

**Catalog taxonomy**  An internal set of rules used by an organization to classify and manage its products. When this taxonomy coincides with the product organization that is naturally and logically used by customers to find and purchase products, the internal taxonomy becomes the catalog taxonomy and is transferred to the online catalog. In some industries, and for some types of products, standard categorizations exist, such as the UNSPC specification. The maintenance of the catalog taxonomy must be ongoing for new products and services sold.

**Changing the basis of competition**  Innovations that create a new competitive position or niche in a market.

**Chargeback**  A refund given back to a credit card holder resulting from a disputed charge.

**Circuit-switched networks**  Networks in which only one data transfer can occur at a given time.

**Click stream**  Series of links that a user goes through when using the Web.

**Click-through rate**  The number of times a link is "clicked."

**Client**  A computer that is connected to the host computer or server on a network.

**Co-opetition**  Companies that are both competitors and collaborators at the same time.

**Code of Fair Information Practices**  Created by the Nixon administration to study the impact of computers on privacy. The code is comprised of five rules set forth by the commission that are designed to protect personal information by restricting what companies can do.

**Collaborate**  The fourth and final step in the evolution of B2B capabilities, in which businesses utilize Web-based capability to allow the buyer, seller, and other trading partners to collaborate for all aspects of business.

**Collaboration pyramid**  Collaboration is a process that is executed with different levels of effectiveness and can be illustrated with the Collaboration pyramid. In a typical organization, collaboration evolves from a single extended enterprise to formal exchange of information, to exchange of qualitative information, to consultative decision-making.

**Collaborative communities**  Allows community participants to provide the "human glue" to discover and trust each other, and thus transact.

**Collaborative forecasting, planning, and replenishment (CPFR)**  Strategic initiative to synchronize supply-chain planning across multiple plants and to support extended supply-chain efforts.

**Collaborative service chains**  Refers to collaboration up and down the service chain that service companies use to manage communication with their distribution channels and subscriber base. Collaborative service-chain functions include document management and workflow, collaborative proposal management, contract management, project management and extended enterprise personnel management, and subscriber base management.

**Collaborative supply chains** Collaborative supply chains are intracompany and intercompany collaborations that span all core functions of manufacturing organizations. Some of these collaborative supply-chain functions include collaborative design, collaborative planning, inventory management, and bundling of multivendor products and services.

**Co-located server hosting** Hosting of a website from a dedicated server that is owned by the Web host's customer.

**Commerce Nets** Existing consortia or vertical e-hubs (another term for commerce nets) are focused on MRO—not direct materials. Private exchanges have focused on direct materials that are managed by large organizations at the hub. The goal is to create a network of buyers and sellers that are connected to each other via a commerce net and operators of the commerce net to broker a customer order for direct materials to the constituent suppliers in the commerce net and, then, coordinate the fulfillment of the order.

**Commerce** The sale of goods, products, or services.

**Commercial bank loan** An installment loan in which the business borrows a certain amount of money, for a specified length of time, with a fixed or variable interest rate.

**Common stock** Stock that does not provide investors protections such as a fixed return on investments, special voting rights or privileges, or liquidation preference.

**Communication** The dialogue that unfolds between the site and its users.

**Community** The interaction that occurs between site users.

**Comparables method** Placing a value on a company by comparing it to other companies that are similar.

**Connection** The extent of formal linkages between the site and other sites.

**Consumer-to-business (C2B)** Business transactions that occur when consumers band together to form and present themselves as a buyer group to businesses. These groups may be economically motivated, as with the demand aggregator Mercata.com, or socially oriented, as with the cause-related advocacy groups at voxcap.com.

**Consumer-to-consumer (C2C)** Exchanges that involve transactions between and among consumers. These exchanges may or may not include third-party involvement, as in the case of the auction-exchange eBay.

**Content management** An application used to create, transfer, and administer a wide variety of company information, such as marketing brochures, product and service information, and help content, which is converted into an electronic format and posted to the company's public website for customer access.

**Content** All digital subject matter on the site.

**Context** The aesthetic and functional look-and-feel of a website (e.g., graphics, colors, design features).

**Convertible debenture** A loan that is convertible into equity.

**Copyright** The legal right of writers, publishers, and other creators to the exclusive ownership of their works.

**Corporate venture** Large corporations that set up venture funds as a subsidiary to make investments on behalf of the parent company.

**Corporate learning** Training offered by corporations to further education in the most up-to-date technology.

**Covenants** A contract ensuring that the money provided by the investor is used in a manner that is consistent with the agreement between the entrepreneur and investor.

**Customer decision process** The process a customer goes through in deciding how to purchase and dispose of goods.

**Customer metrics** Measurements intended to assess the management of customer relationships by the firm.

**Customer support/handling processes** Process that handles customer questions, either when the customer is on the website or once the customer has completed a transaction.

**Customization** The personalization of communications between users and a website.

**Cybercrime** Crime that is committed over the Internet.

**Data storage capacity** The amount of data (in bytes) that can be stored on a device (e.g., a hard disk drive).

**Debt financing** The type of financing in which a business borrows a certain amount of money for a specified time period and repays the principal with interest in regular payments.

**Dedicated server hosting** Hosting of a website from a dedicated server that is owned by the Web host.

**Delivery system** The most detailed and concrete expression of the company's value proposition. The delivery system translates the resource system from a conceptual structure into a concrete configuration of resources, processes, and supply chains.

**Demand aggregations pricing** Pricing buyer demand for specific products is aggregated in order to achieve economies of scale.

**Demand chain** The demand chain is focused on the activities related to an organization's customers, channels, and markets, as well as other external factors.

**Destination site** Provides almost exclusively site-generated content with very few links to other sites.

**Developer-driven development** Type of innovation that occurs when a firm develops a new way of meeting an existing consumer need.

**Development server** A Web server used primarily for the design and development of a website and Web applications. This server is not available to customers.

**Digital certificate** A piece of software provided by a trusted third-party certification authority that contains a person's or company's public encryption key and verification of that person's or company's identity.

**Digital divide**  The gap between people who have computers (computer skills) and people who do not.

**Digital Millennium Copyright Act (DMCA)**  Signed into law in 1998 to implement the provisions of the WIPO treaties, which prohibit the circumvention of copyright protection systems, and to state that a copyright owner cannot hold an online service provider liable if one of its subscribers infringes on the owner's copyright.

**Digital signature**  A piece of software that identifies an entity on the Internet (e.g., a website).

**Digital subsciber line (DSL)**  A set of digital telecommunications protocols designed to allow high-speed data communication over the existing copper telephone lines between users and telephone companies.

**Digital video discs (DVD)**  A high-density CD with a greater storage capacity (4.7 gigabytes), allowing it to display a much higher-resolution video image and better quality sound.

**Digital**  A binary language of computers that allows for easy generation, processing, and transmission of signals with the assistance of microprocessors. The binary language is a series of discrete bits represented by zero or one.

**Dilution**  A decrease in the equity position of an investor's stake due to the issuance of new company shares.

**Direct communications**  Can take many forms, including the use of the classic business-to-business sales representative calling on accounts, retail sales clerks, and telephone customer sales representatives, as well as the use of direct marketing and telemarketing.

**Direct competitors**  Companies offering similar or competing products.

**Direct marketing**  Marketing that involves directly contacting customers (typically by phone or mail) with the intent of making an immediate sale.

**Direct offline communications**  Examples include monthly statement inserts and special targeted mailings, or telephone calls made to investors who could be having difficulty (e.g., investors who have been inactive for long periods of time).

**Discount rate**  Discounts future earnings to determine an appropriate present value for those earnings.

**Discovery packet**  A request sent by the user's computer for an IP address along with other connection information from a DHCP server.

**Disruptive technologies**  Innovations that create an entirely new market through the introduction of a new kind of service or product.

**Distributed innovation model**  A step away from the classical funnel process, this process model puts continuously maintaining a fit between the organization and the evolution of the online domain at the very heart of the innovation process.

**Domain name**  The name-based address of a website or other server that is mapped to the server's IP address (e.g., *www.yahoo.com*).

**Dorothy Leonard innovation framework**  Framework that categorizes five types of innovations: user-driven enhancement, new application or combination of technologies, developer-driven development, user-context development, and technology/market co-evolution.

**Drop shipping**  Requires e-commerce companies to depend on its manufacturers or distributors to pack and ship its retail Web orders.

**DVD**  See digital video discs.

**Dynamic host configuration protocol (DHCP) server**  A server that assigns computers on a private network IP addresses for use on the Internet for one session only.

**Dynamic inventory repleshment**  An inventory model that allows the market demand signal to flow directly through to the contract manufacturers without any distortion or delay.

**E-commerce service providers (ESP)**  Fulfillment houses that serve multiple e-commerce companies for the purpose of leveraging economies-of-scale advantages in picking, packing, and shipping, as well as reducing seasonality and cyclical risk among e-commerce players.

**E-commerce**  Technology-mediated exchanges between parties (individuals or organizations), as well as the electronically-based intra- or inter-organizational activities that facilitate such exchanges.

**Egg diagram**  Maps the products and services of a particular company (or website) onto the consumer decision process.

**E-government**  Federal, state, and local government applications that elicit payment or documentation submission over the Net.

**Electronic Data Interchange (EDI)**  EDI is an ANSI x12 standard format for exchanging business data developed by the Data Interchange Standards Association. Standard formats exist for most of the industry-standard business documents exchanged by two organizations to facilitate commerce, which include purchase orders, invoices, advanced shipping notices (ASN), and material receipt.

**E-mail**  Messages sent and received electronically via telecommunication links, as between microcomputers or terminals.

**Encryption**  Technology that uses complex mathematical formulas to encode and decode information.

**Enterprise application integration (EAI)**  Enterprise Application Integration focuses on applications integration within a single organization and involves the coordination and integration of systems and applications supporting the continuous back and forth flow of data from business processes across an organization.

**Enterprise resource planning (ERP)**  Allows an entity to establish a digital nervous system within its company whereby data is shared electronically—using a company intranet—among corporate managers by unifying key business processes.

**Entrepreneur**  The person with the "big idea" that puts the startup in motion.

**Equity financing** The type of financing in which a business exchanges a portion of ownership for cash, and the investor expects financial return in the future as the value of the business goes up.

**E-voting** Voting electronically online.

**E-wallets** Electronic wallet that uses wireless mobile devices to pay for everyday purchases.

**Extensible Markup Language (XML)** A language written in SGML, XML is a flexible way to create common data or information formats and to share both the format and the data with other applications or trading partners. XML provides an organization and its trading partners with a consistent method for sharing information. XML differs from traditional data format mechanisms in that it provides not only the data, but also a tag or description of each piece of data.

**Fair use** Allows any property that has a copyright to be used for educational, critical, commentary, reporting, or parody purposes.

**FAQs** Frequently asked questions typically listed on a website to help users find the answers to common questions about the site.

**Financial metrics** Financial metrics capture the revenues, costs, profits, and balance-sheet metrics of the firm.

**Financial performance method** The valuation of a company based on earnings or potential earnings, which applies a discount rate to determine the present value of the cash flow.

**Firewall** A computer (or specialized appliance) that sits between the Internet and anything a company wants to protect on its internal network (such as a Web server).

**Fit and reinforcement** Fit refers to the extent to which each of the 7Cs individually support the business model. Reinforcement refers to complementarity—or synergy—between each of the Cs.

**Flexible development process** A model of product development created by Iansite and MacCormack that emphasizes the integration of technology with customer preferences.

**Form vs. function** The argument that there is a clear trade-off between form and function, and it is impossible to design a site that is high in both.

**Free cash flow** The amount of cash a company has at its disposal after normal operations.

**Fulfillment intermediaries** The people or companies that take care of all back-office operations for e-commerce companies. They process orders, direct orders to suppliers, keep customers updated on their order progress, handle order cancellations, and process product returns.

**Full-rachet antidilution** A provision that increases the number of shares owned by the original investors to the number of shares the investor would have received if he had invested at the lower price per share.

**Functional hubs** Provide common business functions or automate the same business processes horizontally across different industries. They possess business-process expertise, but tend to lack deep industry-specific knowledge.

**Gateway** See proxy server.

**Gigabytes** 1,024 megabytes.

**Graphics Interchange Format (GIF)** A graphic file format that contains binary data that will display an image when viewed with the proper software and hardware.

**Growth model** A firm's revenue growth strategy.

**Guerilla marketing** Marketing a product or service using relatively inexpensive, grassroots, nontraditional means.

**Haggle pricing** Pricing model in which users and the site can negotiate over price. Users select products and exchange offers and counter-offers with the site until a deal is reached or refused.

**Holding company** Large corporations that exchange cash for equity in a startup company and often are the majority stakeholder for an extended period of time.

**Host** A computer containing data or programs that another computer can access through a network.

**Hub site** Site that provides a combination of site-generated content and links selective to sites of related interests.

**Human capital** The business team made up of the entrepreneur, management team, strategic advisors and partners, and logistical advisors and partners.

**Human-resource management processes** Processes by which a company upgrades its human-resource capabilities in a manner that is in line with the value proposition.

**Incubator** A company that offers services to new companies in exchange for an equity stake. Some common services include coaching, information technology, public relations, recruiting, office space, and legal and accounting services.

**Indirect competitors** Companies offering a product that attracts the same customer or develops a technology, platform, or offering that might compete with your offering.

**Indirect e-procurement** Automated business functions for the purchase of nonstrategic products and services—also referred to as indirect materials or maintenance, repair, and operations (MRO) materials for manufacturing companies. These are a mirror image of the sell-side capabilities, but from the buyer's point of view, which includes catalog management, transaction processing, and fulfillment status capabilities.

**In-house hosting** Hosting of a website off of a server physically located on the company's premises.

**In-house wireless technology** Allows ubiquitous Web access throughout the home without being near a modem or wiring computer accessories to a PC. Users can connect their PCs, personal digital assistants, digital cameras, and other devices to the Web and to each other within 30 feet, without the use of connecting cables.

**Initial public offering (IPO)** The sale of shares to public investors of a company that has never been traded on a public stock exchange.

**Innovation by design**   Occurs when the manager and a subset of his staff cull ideas from the brainstorming session for those ideas that are cost effective and show promise in consumer acceptance. As a team, they reduce the initial set of ideas into a smaller commercially viable idea set, then into a final set of marketing concepts to fully implement in the market.

**Innovation by direction**   Occurs when, working from the commercially viable set of ideas, the staff undertakes market research, test runs, and further test implementation viability. After reviewing the results of these tests, the staff further narrows the commercially viable idea set into a final set of marketing concepts to fully implement into the market.

**Innovation by doodling**   Occurs when a manager knows that his staff has a great deal of experience, knowledge, and interesting ideas. He gathers them into a conference room and announces that he wants to create a free form brainstorming session where "no idea is dumb." At the end of the session, they have several pages of innovative marketing ideas.

**Innovation funnel process**   Process in which the offline world innovates using three distinct and successive phases: innovation by doodling, innovation by design, and innovation by direction.

**Innovation**   The ways in which online and offline companies change themselves and, consequently, their industries.

**Integrated services digital network (ISDN)**   Another form of DSL that can dial the Internet at a higher speed. The rate of dialing is between 64,000 and 128,000 bits per second.

**Interact**   Second stage of B2B capabilites evolution, in which information exchange becomes bidirectional, and businesses utilized e-mail and simple interactive webpages to gather data from trading partners.

**Interactive television**   A service that allows users to e-mail, chat, and surf the Internet with a set-top box and dialup modem while watching TV.

**Interactivity**   The user's (or firm's) ability to conduct two-way communication between the user and the site.

**Intermediaries**   Well-connected individuals in the investment community who match a startup with the right investors and, in some instances, acquisition targets.

**Internal business process metrics**   Focus on operations inside the company. In particular, this set of metrics focuses on the critical value-adding activities that lead to customer satisfaction and enhanced shareholder value.

**Internet Protocol (IP)**   A set of rules for packet routing over the Internet and many private networks.

**Joint Photographic Experts Group (JPEG)**   A graphic file format that contains binary data that will display an image when viewed with proper software and hardware.

**Keys**   Pieces of software that let users of encryption software ensure that only intended recipients of information are able to view it.

**Kilobyte**   1,024 bytes, often rounded to 1,000 bytes.

**Learning and growth metrics**   Learning and growth metrics broadly capture the employee, information systems, and motivation.

**Legacy systems**   Older computer systems that a company has that need to be integrated with newer systems.

**Leisure education**   Courses taken that do not offer any kind of credit and are taken for fun.

**Life cycle of a company**   Includes four stages of development: startup, acquisition of customers, monetization, and maturity.

**Line extensions**   One of three types of innovation, line extensions are innovations that are incremental advances to an existing product.

**Links**   Objects on webpages that allow users to connect to other webpages by clicking on them.

**Local area networks (LAN)**   A group of connected computers that spans a few square kilometers or less.

**Log in**   The process of entering a site using an account that consists of a user name and password.

**Logistical advisors and partners**   Paid outsourced parties that can fill missing skill sets on an as-needed basis.

**Make-to-order (MTO)**   The custom design and manufacture of products based on order specifications—usually from key business customers.

**Management team**   Group that orchestrates the strategic direction and operations of the startup.

**Manufacturing and distribution processes**   Also known as supply chains; how a company manufactures and distributes its goods.

**Market communications**   All the points of contact that the firm has with its customers. This includes the obvious offline communications such as television advertising, promotions, and sales calls, as well as the emergent advertising approaches on the Internet.

**Market opportunity analysis**   An organizing framework to look systematically for unmet or underserved needs. Occurs in six stages: seed opportunity in existing or new value system; uncover opportunity nucleus; identify target segments; declare company's resource-based opportunity for advantage; assess competitive, technical, and financial attractiveness; and make go/no-go assessment.

**Market research**   Online market research firms collect primary customer data through online surveys or customer submissions. These firms tend to put a strong emphasis on site usability, customer satisfaction, and traffic level. Offline market research includes surveys, experiments, and focus groups.

**Market opportunity metrics**   Market opportunity metrics assess the degree to which the firm can accurately gauge the market opportunity. Generic indicators would include the ability of the firm to target the most attractive segments, the ability of the firm to understand and map competitor's strategy evolution, and the ability of the firm to track the evolution of target segment needs.

**Marketspace**   The digital equivalent of a physical-world marketplace.

**Maturity**   Last stage in the life cycle of a company. Goal is to control costs and optimize marketing expenditures to achieve profitable growth.

**Meaningful segmentation**   Segmentation that generates real insight on customers but is difficult to address.

**Media convergence**   The evolution and migration of the various media content (news, information, and entertainment) from traditional analog media platforms (print, audio, and video) to a digital platform or cross-platform where all content will be accessible through various digital devices.

**Media infrastructure**   The various communications companies and their channels of communication, such as radio, television, newspapers and magazines, used in mass communication with the general public.

**Megabyte**   1,024 kilobytes or 1,048,576 bytes, often rounded to 1,000,000 bytes.

**Meta tags**   HTML tags that most search engines read when indexing the Web. Keyword tags provide keywords for search engines to associate with websites, and description tags allow the website developer to substitute his or her own description for the website in place of the description that the search engine would normally generate.

**Meta-software**   Utility and plug-in software applications created to assist users in narrowly defined tasks. These applications may reside as stand alone on the user's desktop or as plug-ins to the Internet browser.

**Metcalfe's Law**   States that the value of a network to each of its members is proportional to the number of other users (which can be expressed as (n2-n)/2).

**Metrics**   Measurements by which companies can assess the progress and health of their online businesses. Metrics include benchmarks such as sales, margins, profit, and market share, as well as metrics that reflect the entire strategy of the company.

**Mobile wireless technology**   Allows users to access the Web and receive e-mail via handheld devices that use relatively low bandwidth.

**Monetization**   Third stage in the life cycle of a company. Goal is to increase revenues and customer lock-in by developing new revenue streams.

**MP3**   The acronym for the standards specifications to the MPEG-1 Audio Layer-3.

**MPEG-1**   A computer file format and compression specification for motion video with audio.

**Net marketplaces and Net exchanges**   Provide Web-based capabilities to facilitate the interaction and exchange of commerce transactions among buyers, sellers, and other trading partners.

**Network-to-network integration**   A many-to-many systems integration between networks that is integrated across networks of multiple trading partners. Participants in these markets must work to resolve business issues related to network-to-network integration, such as cross-network recognition of buyers by sellers and sellers by buyers and the information that must be exchanged to facilitate a commerce transaction.

**New application or combination of technologies**   Part of the Dorothy Leonard innovation framework. Innovation occurs when an established technology is applied to a new industry.

**New industries**   A category of offline innovation. These are innovations that can create a new industry.

**New product introductions (NPI)**   The new product introduction process includes strategy and planning, execution, and deployment phases. The strategy and planning phase may study feasibility, manufacturability, product cost, and market demand. The execution phase may involve several iterations of prototype and pilot builds to be ready for deployment.

**New-to-the-world value**   New offerings that create value for customers. Examples include customizing offerings, radically extending reach and access, building community, enabling collaboration among multiple people across locations and time, and introducing new-to-the-world functionality or experience.

**Normalization**   Normalization facilitates comparison of products sold across suppliers along with associated price—allowing the buyer to select a product category and to drill-down through subcategories to the actual desired product. A denormalized catalog would not be organized by logical product categories and subcategories—the buyer might first see a list of suppliers, then drill-down to products sold by the selected supplier. Normalization necessitates the creation of a catalog taxonomy and the mapping of contents from individual supplier catalogs to that taxonomy.

**Offering**   The specific product or service a company offers to its customers.

**Online implementation process**   The online implementation process can be divided into two phases. First, the firm is concerned with the delivery of the offering. In the second phase, the firm is concerned with the extent to which the offerings and infrastructures are modified to "fit" the evolution of the market.

**Opportunity nucleus**   A set of unmet or underserved need(s).

**Opt-in marketing**   Programs where the customers have to choose to have their information shared with others, in trade for more personalized sites, marketing, and special offers.

**Opt-out marketing**   Option for users to actively find out how to not be included in a company's marketing program.

**Outsource warehousing**   Generally involves the use of logistics specialists, such as Federal Express or UPS, to stockpile and ship Web orders.

**Outsourced content**   Content that has been generated by third parties. Third-party suppliers can often create content of higher quality, greater appeal, or at a lower cost than the website operation.

**Packet switching**   A method of data transmission in which small blocks of data are transmitted rapidly over a channel dedicated to the connection only for the duration of the packet's transmission. Not all packets, even for the same file or message, necessarily follow the same route.

**Packets**   A short block of data (often a piece of a larger file) transmitted in a packet-switching network.

**Patent**   Gives the owner the sole right to make, use, and sell his invention.

**Payment gateway**   Provides merchants with real-time authorizations for credit cards.

**Performance Dashboard**   Standards that reflect the health of a business, comprised of five categories of metrics: opportunity, business model, customer interface and outcomes, branding and implementation, and financial.

**Permission marketing**   When customers agree to share personal information in exchange for receiving targeted market communications. Permission marketing presumes successful marketing campaigns can be created by establishing a mutually beneficial and trusting relationship between the firm and its customers.

**Personalization by user**   This form of customization enables the user to modify site content and context based on consciously articulated and acted-upon preferences. The user can make layout selections and content source selections.

**Pitch**   A presentation or campaign that summarizes the key aspects of the new business in order to get investors interested.

**Plug-in**   A software program that extends the capabilities of a Web browser or other application. Also known as an add-in.

**Point-to-network integration**   A one-to-many systems integration between a firm and a network that is integrated with multiple trading partners. Net marketplaces provide individual organizations a point-to-network integration capability that eliminates recurring costs of point-to-point integration.

**Point-to-point integration**   A one-to-one systems integration between a firm and one of its trading partners.

**Portal site**   A website that consists almost exclusively of absolute links to a large number of other sites.

**Post-money valuation**   The value of the company immediately after an investment.

**Preemptive right**   The right of the investor to maintain her percentage of ownership by investing additional funds in the next round of financing.

**Preferred stock**   Affords the VC preference over common stock while providing an upside to the investor; the three most common forms are convertible preferred, redeemable preferred, and participating convertible preferred.

**Pre-money valuation**   The value that the investor puts on the company before his investment.

**Present value**   The value of an investment at a specific moment. Often used to determine the worth of investment by comparing the value of cash put into the investment today versus its value when the investment period is over.

**Private key**   The key typically used to decrypt information that has been encrypted with the corresponding public key.

**Processing power**   The amount of data that can be processed at a given time.

**Production server**   The production server mirrors the finalized content on the staging server. This server is available to customers.

**Professional services automation (PSA)**   Professional services automation software is designed to support independent IT consultants and professional services organizations; it provides automation for managing human resources and information capturing, storing, and sharing among service professionals, their managers, and customers. Solutions may include functions such as opportunity and proposal management, resource allocation and scheduling, project management, time and expense management, and knowledge management.

**Proforma income statement**   A company's future income statement.

**Proxy server**   A computer that forwards packets from a company's internal network of PCs to the Internet. Many proxy servers also cache information to improve performance on the network.

**Public key**   A key used to encrypt information before it is sent to the holder of the corresponding private key.

**Public policy infrastructure**   The laws and regulations that influence strategies, technology, capital, and media in business.

**Red herring**   A preliminary prospectus that is sent to the SEC for review.

**Redemption rights**   Gives the investor the right to achieve liquidity if the company has not been sold or undergone a public offering within a predetermined time period.

**Redundancy**   Having backup systems in case of failure of primary systems (e.g., Web servers, power supplies).

**Registration rights**   Allow shares to be freely traded on the market.

**Resource allocation process**   Formalization of the trade-offs and prioritization that the company uses when making choices about which opportunities to pursue.

**Resource system**   A unique combination of resources (within and outside) and a firm that delivers promised benefits.

**Retention ratio**   Determines a new, higher percent ownership required for the current investment.

**Revenue models**   How a company plans to generate revenue.

**Reverse-auction pricing**   Where sellers bid against each other and the lowest bid wins the buyer's business.

**Right of first refusal** Safeguarding investors by locking in the opportunity to invest in future rounds.

**Ripping software** Software that allows users to convert their CDs into highly compressed files (such as MP3 and RealAudio files).

**Router** A computer or appliance in a network that handles data transfer between computers.

**Salesforce efficiency** Extent to which the salesforce operates in the most time-effective manner; it has increased on the Internet because fewer transactions need to be routed through the salesforce. Also, salesforce personnel that handle calls originating from the Internet have a higher "close" rate.

**Satellite system** Enables wireless technology by using satellites that orbit the earth. Three proposed systems for Internet access include geostationary, medium earth orbit (MEO) and low earth orbit (LEO).

**Secure electronic transaction (SET)** A protocol that facilitates the secure authentication of credit card transactions on the Web as well as other payment processing issues, such as debit card transactions and credits back to credit cards.

**Secure Sockets Layer (SSL)** An encrypted "tunnel" automatically set up between a user's browser and a Web server that ensures secure communication between them.

**Segmentation** The process of dividing the diverse population of target customers into homogenous segments, any of which may be selected as the one to be reached with a distinct marketing mix.

**Sense and respond** An approach to strategic development that focuses on quick responses to market developments.

**Servers** Computers that store and transmit information to the browers to be displayed.

**Service chain** While the term supply chain is reserved for manufacturing industries, the service chain is applicable to service industries such as professional services, insurance, and finance. Because there is no physical movement of goods involved, service chains are focused on the delivery of information value.

**Service efficiency** Extent to which service operations operate in the most time-effective manner; this has been increased on the Internet because many inquiries can be handled by an automated system instead of by person-to-person contact.

**7Cs Framework** Framework for customer interface. The seven Cs are context, content, community, customization, communication, connection, commerce.

**Shared server hosting** Hosting of a website off of a server that other companies are using as well.

**Shareholder value models** How a company plans to generate cash flow or shareholder value.

**Shrink inventory** Theft from a company by its own employees.

**Simple rules** A point of view that strategy is about simple decision rules (e.g., only acquire firms with less than 75 employees).

**Sniffing software** Software that allows users to view other users' data as it moves across a network.

**Spam** Unsolicited marketing messages sent by e-mail or posted on newsgroups.

**Staging server** The server that prepares the content on the development server for the Web. This server is typically not available to customers.

**Standards** Rules that companies agree to adhere to so that their products can interact.

**Startup** Beginning stage in life cycle of a company. The goal is to develop a platform for rapid growth by building a strong team and creating a flexible site.

**Stateful inspection** The internal inspection of packets to determine whether or not they are harmful.

**Stock-it-yourself** Generally involves an automated warehouse that can directly fulfill online orders.

**Stock-keeping unit (SKU)** A unique type of product or part in a company's inventory; a company that has only one SKU sells only one type of product but may keep many units of that SKU in inventory.

**Strategic advisors and partners** A group comprised of the advisory board, board of directors, and strategic alliance companies that provide strategic direction and advice through their own experience and help attract potential investors.

**Streaming audio** Sound files that allow a computer user to listen to a file while it is still downloading, rather than waiting until the file is completely downloaded to listen to it.

**Streaming video** Audio files that allow a computer user to watch a file while it is still downloading, rather than waiting until the file is completely downloaded to watch it.

**Streamlined Sales Tax Project** A project launched in March 2000 to simplify the tax system and make it easier for states to collect taxes.

**Strength of association** The intensity with which the target consumer links a particular word, phrase, or meaning to a particular brand.

**Supply-chain models** Supply-chain models in the new economy focus on rapidly changing structures in B2C, B2B, C2B, and C2C markets. These new supply-chain options have significantly changed the manner that customers and suppliers interact with manufacturers.

**Supply chain** The suppliers, contract manufacturers, and distributors that a company utilizes as sources of materials and services to manufacture a product. The supply chain is focused on the activities (plan, execute, control) related to meeting needs based on a combination of an organization's capacity and its suppliers' capacity.

**Supply Web** The term supply chain implies a series of serial steps that make up a chain. While both information and physical goods tend to flow along the supply chain, the Internet allows for control and flow of information to manage the flow of goods that comprise more of a "supply Web" than a chain.

**Switching cost**   The cost—both financial and personal—of switching from one business or product to another.

**Tailoring by site**   Form of customization that enables the site to reconfigure itself based on past behavior by the user or by other users with similar profiles. These sites can make recommendations based on past purchases, filter marketing messages based on user interests, and adjust prices and products based on user profiles.

**Targeting**   Marketing a product or service only to customers that are most likely to buy the product.

**Technology infrastructure**   The foundations of the Internet system that enable the running of the e-commerce enterprises. One half of the technology equation is the hardware backbone such as the routers, servers, fiber optics, cables, and modems. The other half includes software and communication standards that run on top of the hardware.

**Technology/market coevolution**   Occurs when the customer base is not clearly known and the technology is not well-established. These products sometimes appear to have a more or less "accidental" growth path but can be the beginning of entire new markets.

**Telecommunications Act of 1996**   Signed into law in 1996, this represented the first major overhaul of federal laws regulating the communications industry since 1934. With the passing of this act, emphasis was changed from a regulation-based industry to a market-based industry to allow for increased competition.

**Telemarketing**   Marketing by a salesforce over the telephone.

**Terabytes**   1,024 gigabytes.

**Term sheet**   A nonbinding description of the proposed deal between the financier and the entrepreneur.

**Terminal value**   The expected value of a company at the end of a projected period.

**Top-level domain**   The far-right portion of the domain name or URL that refers to the nature of the organization that uses the particular address (e.g., .com or .edu).

**Total supply chain profits and costs**   Profits and costs that affect all trading partners across a supply chain in total. These include costs of design/production, costs of poor quality, as well as costs of longer cycle times and costs of poor trading partner relationship management.

**Trade credit**   Credit extended to a business by its suppliers.

**Trademark**   A name or symbol that identifies a project and is officially registered, limiting the use of that name or symbol to the owner of the trademark.

**Traditional mass media**   Consists of television (network, cable and local), print media (including high circulation newspapers and magazines), and national and local radio.

**Transact**   Third step of B2B capabilities evolution, in which businesses use the Internet to facilitate commerce transactions.

**Transmission Control Protocol (TCP)**   Software that ensures the safe and reliable transfer of data.

**Transparent**   A system that functions in a manner not evident to the user (such as links on a webpage).

**Trapped value**   Can be unlocked by creating more efficient markets, creating more efficient value systems, enabling easier access, or disrupting current pricing power.

**Uniqueness**   The degree to which a brand is distinct, relative to other brands.

**URL (Uniform Resource Locator)**   An address used for sites on the Web to make them easier to remember than the underlying numerical IP address to which they are mapped (e.g., *http://www.microsoft.com* is a URL).

**User interface (UI)**   The display of images and controls on a device that allows the user to interact with the device.

**User context development**   Occurs when firms develop products to meet a previously unexpressed need. In many cases, careful market research revealed these needs and firms built products to meet these needs.

**User-driven enhancement**   No-risk improvements to a product. Common types of user-driven enhancements include lowering product price; low-cost, high-value feature enhancements; and cost-efficient quality improvements.

**Valence**   The degree to which the association with a product is positive or negative.

**Valuation**   Determination of a company's worth.

**Value chain**   According to Michael Porter, a value chain represents the collection of activities that are performed to design, produce, market, deliver, and support a product. A firm's value chain and the way it performs individual activities are a reflection of its history, strategy, and approach to implementing its strategy, and the underlying economics of the activities themselves.

**Value cluster**   Form of value proposition that is no longer singular but composed of three parts: (1) the choice of target customer segments, (2) a particular focal combination of customer-driven benefits that are offered, and (3) the rationale for why this firm and its partners can deliver the value cluster significantly better than competitors.

**Value proposition**   Construction of a value proposition requires management to specify three items: (1) choice of target segment, (2) choice of focal customer benefits, and (3) rationale for why the firm can deliver the benefit package significantly better than its competitors in the same space.

**Value system**   An interconnection of processes and activities within and among firms that create benefits for intermediaries and end consumers.

**Venture-capital firm**   Private partnerships or closely held corporations that raise money from a group of private investors and invest in companies in exchange for an equity stake.

**Venture-capital method**   Values a company by determining a terminal value for a potential investment by using either a "multiple" or terminal value technique, but with a much larger discount rate.

**Vertical hubs**   Serve either vertical markets or a specific, narrow industry focus.

**Vertical integration**   Occurs when a company deepens its position in a particular market by acquiring complementary firms in a value system (e.g., Amazon acquiring/building warehouses to distribute books).

**Video-game console**   Video-game system with the potential to access a wide range of broadband services on the Internet.

**Viral marketing**   Company-developed products, services, or information that are passed from user to user. It is analogous to how a viral infection is passed between two people.

**Vote-swapping**   Occurs when two citizens in different regions swap votes for two different candidates to maximize the vote.

**Waterfall concept of new product innovation**   Also known as the innovation funnel process, the purpose is to make internal choices about innovations that the company should pursue and to launch only the innovations with the highest chance of succeeding.

**Web address**   See URL.

**Web host**   A company that rents the use of its high-bandwidth Internet access and Web servers to other companies.

**Web server**   A computer that processes requests from browsers for documents over the Web.

**Webpage**   A document on the World Wide Web usually consisting of an HTML file and files linked to it, such as images or scripts often linked to other webpages.

**Website**   Series of linked webpages that are maintained or owned by the same orgainization. A website typically consists of a homepage that allows navigation to the remainder of the webpages (e.g., *www.NYtimes.com/business*) that comprise the website.

**Weighted-average antidilution**   A provision that adjusts the number of new shares the investor receives proportionally when many shares are sold at a lower price.

**Wide area network (WAN)**   Technology that allowed engineers to build networks to connect computers and LANs separated by large geographical distances.

**Wireless Markup Language (WML)**   Language that allows the display of content on cellular telephones, personal digital assitants (PDAs), and other wireless browsers via wireless access. WML is a part of the wireless application protocol (WAP), a standard communication protocol for the display of wireless content.

**Zero coupon bond**   Debt securities with warrants attached that protect the investor's original investment by giving interest on the investment, and providing the option to buy stock.

# INDEX

## G

Gambling, regulatory issues, 590, 592–594
Garage.com, 451
Gartner, user interface, 72
Gear.com, content dimensions, 196–197
General Motors, B2B e-commerce, 296
General online communications, 241, 242–250
    affiliate programs, 245
    banner ads, 242–243, 247
    brand and, 247–248
    coupons, 248
    direct communications, 253
    e-mail, 243–244, 248
    information, providing, 249
    innovation in customer acquisitions, 249
    interstitials, 247
    leveraging of customer base, 249–250
    loyalty programs, 248
    MarketWatch.com, 275
    partnerships, 248–249
    pay-per-advertising-view, 248
    personalized online communications, 250–252
    sponsorship and exclusive partner agreement, 245
    sponsorships, 247–248
    traditional mass media communications, 252
    viral marketing, 244–245, 246
GIF (Graphics Interchange Format), 42–43, 535
Gillette Women's Cancer Connection/gillette-cancerconnect.org, 208, 209
Global Internet users
    demographics, 603–604
    regulatory issues, 582, 595–596
Global markets, media companies and, 533
Goal implementation, 307
Go/no-go assessment, 129
Government
    legislation. *See* Legislation online; Government online
Government online, 611
    e-government, 612–614, 615, 616
    election 2000, 614–616
    e-voting, 617
Granger, B2B sell-side solutions, 362–363
Graphics Interchange Format (GIF), 42–43, 535
Greenfield Online/greenfieldonline.com, 339–340
Growth, customer dynamics and, 127
Growth models
    financial, 167
    MarketWatch.com, 178–179
Guerrilla marketing, 69–70
    BAMs and, 67

## H

Haggle pricing, 231
Higher education, online presence, 609
Holding company, 466–467
Homeboyz Interactive, 608

Home robotics, 564
Home site background, 222
Hoover's Online/hoovers.com., 338, 340, 341
Horizontal *versus* vertical marketplaces, 375
Host computer, 49, 50. *See also* Web host
Hotjobs, branding, 271, 272, 273
Hotmail, 100
HTML (HyperText Markup Language), 40–41, 523
    conversion to webpage, 44
HTTP (HyperText Transfer Protocol), 48, 523
Hub sites, 223, 224
Human capital. *See also* Human resources
    and companies, 434
    components, 433–434. *See also specific component*
    entrepreneur, 433, 438–444
    financial capital and, 431
    involvement in, 434
    logistical advisors and partners, 450–452
    management team, 433, 444–447
    strategic advisors and partners, 447–450
Human-resource management process, 291
Human resources
    business planning and, 437
    as capital. *See* Human capital
    delivery and, 290, 291
    MarketWatch.com, 314–315
Hybrid communication, 217
Hybrid funding sources, 467
HyperText documents *versus* paper, 39
HyperText Markup Language (HTML). *See* HTML
HyperText Transfer Protocol (HTTP), 48, 523

## I

Idea *versus* management team, 448
Identification
    of customer decision process, 148–149
    Internet, 33–34
    of target customers, 97
IFilm.com, 209–210
Image
    BAMs and, 58
    e-commerce stores and, 59
Images
    capture, 43
    as Web content, 41
Implementation
    branding and implementation metrics, 333
    business planning and, 436
    credit card transactions and, 79
    location and, 62–66
    MarketWatch.com, 349–350, 352
    strategic. *See* Online implementation process
Incubators, 452
Indicators, metrics and, 337
    MarketWatch.com, 352–353, 354

Indirect competitors, 124
Indirect e-procurement, 360, 361
    challenges, 370–373
    *versus* direct procurement, 367
    early movers, 369
    product *versus* services, 368
    technology components, 369–370
Industries, new, 302, 303
Industry boundaries, competition and, 98
IndustryCentral, 223
Information. *See also* Metrics
    general online communications and, 249
Information-dominant content archetypes, 200–201
Information flow, Computer Corporation of America, 408–410
Information technology (IT) training for children, 608
In-house wireless technology, 564–565
Initial public offering (IPO), 504–505
    process, 506–508
    pros and cons, 509, 510
    timing, 505–506
Innovation
    in customer acquisitions, 249
    failure and, 289
    MarketWatch.com, 315–318
    modes, 303–304
    offline, 302–304
Innovation by design, 303, 304
Innovation by direction, 303, 304
Innovation by doodling, 303, 304
Innovation funnel process, 303
Instant messaging, 387
Integrated context archetype, 194, 196
Integrated services digital network (ISDN) line, 559
Integration
    B2B sell-side solutions and, 366–367
    indirect e-procurement and, 372–373
    of market communications and branding, 240
Integration metrics, 343–345
Integrity, branding and, 262
Intel Capital, 467
Intellectual property, regulatory issues, 582
    copyright law, 584–586, 588
    Napster and, 588–589
    patents, 587, 590
    trademarks, 587
Interact, 358, 359
Interactive communication, 217
    community and, 206
Interactive Custom Clothes Company, customization, 213
Interactive television, 563–564
Interactivity
    community focus *versus* community interactivity, 211
    consumer behavior and, 10

Intermediaries
fulfillment, 293–294
startup, 451
Internal anchors, 41
Internal business process metrics, 328–329
Internationalization, Net marketplaces and exchanges and, 392
Internet
connection speed, 558, 560
growth factors, 51–53
nature of, 31–33
operation(s), 33–39
television on, 538–539
*versus* Web, 40
Internet digital divide, 604–606
Internet operation(s), 33
addressing, 34
domain name system, 34
identification, 33–34
packet switching, 34–36
reliability and TCP, 36–37
routing, 36, 37
standardization, 38–39
Internet Protocol (IP), 32–33, 523
address sharing, 49
Internet service providers (ISPs), 556–559, 560–561
third party, 388–390
Internet users. *See also* Customer interface
backward-integrated, 171
characteristics, 601, 605
community and, 602–603
e-government and, 612
global demographics, 603–604
growth in, 605
nonresponding, 217, 218
online activities, 600–602
personalization by, 214, 216
responding, 217–218, 219, 220
sales tax impact on, 590, 591
senior Web surfers, 606–607
time online, 601–602
Interstitials, 247
Intranet, Sun Microsystems, 288–289
Inventory
B2B, 295
dynamic inventory replenishment, 416
virtual, sell-side collaboration and, 419
Investment(s). *See also* Financial capital; specific means of investment
branding and, 262
costs, online innovation and, 305
future directions, 516–517
investor and, 499–502
metrics and, 327
stages, 502–503
startup businesses, 429
Investor rights and privileges, 499–502
IP. *See* Internet Protocol (IP)
IPO. *See* Initial public offering (IPO)
ISDN (integrated services digital network) line, 559

ISPs. *See* Internet service providers
IT (information technology) training for children, 608

J

Jones International University, 610
JPEG (Joint Photographic Experts Group) files, 43, 535

K

Keys, 82
Kmart, online *versus* offline branding, 266
KMGI/Kmgi.com, 194, 195
Kodak (Eastman Kodak), competitor profiling, 125–126
K-12 schools, online presence, 609

L

LAN (local area networks), 31–32
Lands' End, site performance, 187–188
Latecomers, 100–101
Learning and growth metrics, 329
Legislation
Code of Fair Information Practices and, 578
copyright laws, 585
Digital Millennium Copyright Act, 585
e-government, 612
free speech, 595
privacy, 578, 581
proposed
copyright law, 585–586
free speech, 595
gambling, 593
privacy, 582
sales and use tax, 590
tax laws, 590
Leisure education, 611
Leonard innovation framework, 308–310
Leveraging
of customer base, 249–250
customer experience and, 260–261
Life cycle of a company, 333
Line executive, 18
Line extensions, 302–303
Links/linkages, 39
implementation and, 286
linking metrics to indicators, 337
MarketWatch.com, 352–353, 354
to pages, 41
to sites, 222
Liquidity
IPOs and, 504–509
mergers/acquisitions and, 509–512
Net marketplaces and exchanges and, 394
paths to, 504–512
Listening in a new manner to customers, 8

Live interaction
one-to-many, 218, 219
one-to-one, 220–221
LivePerson.com, communication archetype, 220–221
L.L. Bean, chat rooms, 74
Local area networks (LAN), 31–32
Location
BAMs and, 58–59
implementation and, 62–66
organizational, 18
Logistical advisors and partners
as human capital, 434
startup businesses and, 450–452
Loss *versus* lossless compression, 45
Lowest prices model, 164, 166
Loyalty programs, 248

M

Magazines, 538
Mail to, as Web content, 41
Make-to-order (MTO) products, 406
Management team, 444–447
as human capital, 433
*versus* idea, 448
Manufacturing
Computer Corporation of America, 407
and distribution, delivery and, 291
outsourced, 410–411
Mapping
competitor maps, 126, 127
of Internet research onto Performance Dashboard, 340, 343
market mapping, 118–119
MarketWatch.com, 134–135
Market coevolution, 310, 311
Market communications. *See also* Branding
advertising network managers, 255
branding and, 239–277
categories, 241–253
customer decision process and, 241–242
defined, 240
MarketWatch.com, 271, 273, 275
Market-dominant content archetypes, 201–202, 203
Market environment, implementation and, 286
Marketing
business basics
BAMs and, 67–68
e-commerce, 68–75
Computer Corporation of America, 407
Market mapping
MarketWatch.com, 134–135
target customers and, 118–119
Market opportunity
business planning and, 436
MarketWatch.com, 130–135, 347
Market-opportunity analysis, 95–135
framework, 96–98
generic value types, 101–107